Millennial
ECUADOR

Millennial
ECUADOR

Critical Essays on Cultural Transformations

and Social Dynamics

EDITED BY NORMAN E. WHITTEN, JR.

University of Iowa Press Iowa City

University of Iowa Press, Iowa City 52242

Printed in the United States of America
Design by Richard Hendel
http://www.uiowa.edu/uiowapress

The publication of this book was generously supported by the
University of Iowa Foundation and the University of Illinois at Urbana-Champaign.

Printed on acid-free paper

Library of Congress Cataloging-in-Publication Data
Millennial Ecuador: critical essays on cultural transformations and
social dynamics / edited by Norman E. Whitten, Jr.
p.   cm.
Includes bibliographical references and index.
ISBN 0-87745-863-4 (cloth), ISBN 0-87745-864-2 (pbk)
1. Ecuador—Social conditions.   2. Indians of South America—Ecuador—
Social conditions.   3. Indians of South America—Ecuador—Government relations.
4. Indians of South America—Ecuador—Politics and government.   5. Indigenous
peoples—Ecuador—Social conditions.   6. Indigenous peoples—Ecuador—
Government relations.   7. Indigenous peoples—Ecuador—Politics and
government.   8. Ecuador—Social policy.   9. Ecuador—Race relations.
10. Ecuador—Politics and government.   I. Whitten, Norman E.
F3721.3.S65M55 2003
305.898'0866—dc21   2003050741

03   04   05   06   07   C   5   4   3   2   1
03   04   05   06   07   P   5   4   3   2   1

CONTENTS

Norman E. Whitten, Jr.

Michelle Wibbelsman

NOTES ON ORTHOGRAPHY, PRONUNCIATION, AND ACRONYMS

Spanish orthography is standard in the Americas. Unless diacritics are added, emphasis is always placed on the penultimate syllable, including proper names and place-names.

Quichua orthography is close to that of Spanish, with some exceptions: [w] is used instead of [gu] or [hu] as in *wasi* (house) except when the word is widely recognized by its Spanish spelling, as in *ayahuasca* (soul vine). This is to facilitate correct pronunciation by English readers and speakers. Unless diacritics are added, emphasis is always placed on the penultimate syllable, including proper names and place-names.

An alternative orthography for Quichua is based on English spelling. It has witnessed a strong movement in Ecuador in recent years. Particularly prominent are the use of [w], as used in this work, and [k] instead of [c] and [j] and even [g]. Examples include Kichwa instead of Quichua, and *yachak* instead of *yachaj* or *yachac* (shaman), and the plural suffix *kuna* instead of *cuna* or *guna*. In this work, [j], [c], and [g] are often retained because they correspond to most (but not all) Quichua-Spanish dictionaries. This use also allows us to more accurately represent dialect differences and variants.

All place-names and proper names are rendered in their most common spelling, as in Tungurahua and Zumbagua (both endings are pronounced "wa"), and Guatatuca (pronounced "Watatuca").

All names of political parties or social movements are rendered in their common spelling, so Pachakutik is the social movement but *pachacutic* is used otherwise as an episteme of transformation from one space-time system to another.

Words in other languages are rendered in the most accessible manner for English speakers by use of variants of the International Phonetic Alphabet.

For simplicity's sake, all acronyms are fully identified in the glossary.

PREFACE AND ACKNOWLEDGMENTS

Millennial Ecuador became visible worldwide on January 21, 2000, when thousands of indigenous and nonindigenous peoples from all over the republic "took" the Legislative Palace in Quito, the country's capital. There, in the democratic heart, soul, and cerebrum of the nation, portals of power were opened to them by the Heroes of Cenepa, the soldiers — of all races and ethnic identities — who fought bravely in the war with Peru in 1995. The subsequent ramifications of the conjuncture of military might and expanding indigenous social and political space received global scrutiny, and publications within Ecuador documented, and continue to document, ways by which indigenous people came to epitomize *el pueblo*, the people themselves.

In 1981 the University of Illinois Press published the 811-page edited book *Cultural Transformations and Ethnicity in Modern Ecuador*. It marked, for me, twenty years of experience in Ecuador and on Ecuadorian subjects, including especially the dynamics of Afro–Latin American culture of Esmeraldas Province of the northwest coast, Canelos Quichua and Achuar Jivaroan cultures of Pastaza Province in the Amazonian region, and peoples and their cultural systems in Tungurahua, Cotopaxi, Pichincha, and Imbabura Provinces in the Sierra. Twenty-two more years have passed, *Cultural Transformations* is out of print, and our attention again turns to the subjects that I have pursued since first visiting northern Andean and coastal Ecuador in the summer of 1961.

In some ways, *Millennial Ecuador* is a sequel to *Cultural Transformations*. The first work stressed modernity and surgent ethnicity and sought comprehensive coverage of available contemporary ethnography. The emergence in nationalist consciousness of indigenous peoples of the Amazonian region and the cultural systems of contemporary indigenous peoples in this and other areas were stressed as examples of national modernity. The comprehensive coverage was an endeavor to represent as many of the cultural facets of modern Ecuador as possible, given the experiences and talents of the ethnographers whose expertise emerged in the context of sustained field research.

Modernity referred to the complex of features that surfaced in the Americas soon after the European conquest as the colonial empires of Spain and Portugal culminated in a system of economic prosperity and class mobility for some, the oppression of indigenous and Afro-Latin American peoples, and a false resolution of this oppression through the ideology of *mestizaje*. By combining modernity and ethnicity and heightening the representation of peoples of the Amazonian region, *Cultural Transformations* sought to move current scholarship to a new level of understanding of resurgent cultural forces within structures of domination and hegemony.

Some criticized *Cultural Transformations* for its emphasis on the underlying system of power of the Amazonian peoples in the context of nationalist modernization. Time has proven our focus quite appropriate, if not prescient. Only nine years after publication of the tome, the first indigenous uprising occurred. Two years after that, the *Caminata de Pastaza a Quito*, later called the March for Land and Life, from Amazonian Puyo to the capital of Quito embodied some of the very imagery suggested in *Cultural Transformations* and elaborated in my final, reflective chapter in the book edited by Jonathan D. Hill, *Rethinking History and Myth*: "It is as though the collective body of forest natives is growing toward the Quito head, itself transformed by conquest to something alien yet attainable." In March 1992, this reflection was mirrored not only in the indigenous march to Quito but also in the internal symbolism and dramatic metaphors that unfolded as the *caminata* proceeded. In 1994, the millennial social movement Pachakutik formed in Amazonian and Andean Ecuador and joined with the Nuevo País movement radiating out of Quito. The indigenous peoples of Amazonia have been central in the recent ousters of two presidents of the republic, and their presence is now felt, if not always recognized, in every sector where power is exercised.

In *Millennial Ecuador*, we turn our attention to the dual system of globalizing modernity and millennial movements and the multiple postmodernities of their conjunctures that have come to characterize this nation-state. Following Peter Worsley, who wrote of these matters more than forty-five years ago, by *millennium* and *millenarianism* I mean a situation in which people express serious dissatisfaction with existing social relations and yearn for a happier life. A happier life is imagined in a setting that transforms people's current social situations — by their own volition — but uses global resources for localized dynamics. In millennial situations, strong antiauthoritarian sentiments are expressed, symbolic inversions abound, and movements of self-determination emerge.

I do not refer to the classic definition of *millennial* as the change of the millennium or the second coming of Christ. Rather, these medieval ideas are transformed into the Quichua concept of *pachacutic*, the return of space-time (chronotope) of a healthy past to that of a healthy future. In English, as in Spanish, Quichua, and other languages, we can say that humans live in an inchoate present poised between a remembered past and an imagined future. Oppression is remembered, and movements toward collective self-determination are enacted. In any language, imagination is crucial to memory. It is to remembrance that social action is directed; remembrance and destiny are culturally intertwined. By such a rendition we come to millennial Ecuador, a future-oriented imaginary filled in the present with the plans, dreams, and actions of peoples who imbue perceived reality with transformative hope.

Millennial here subsumes what Clifford Geertz long ago defined as *epochalism* and *essentialism*. The former is the position of a nation in its global time and place, its political-economic chronotope; in the latter, cultural attributes are self-ascribed and represented by diverse peoples in epochal space-time, its symbolic and metaphoric chronotope. But unlike Geertz's pioneering analysis of "new nations" four decades ago, our focus is on emerging and enduring nationalities with millennial agendas within a framework of a globalizing and localizing country — Ecuador — which, from time to time, has forced others in the Americas, in the American diasporas, and beyond to take a careful look at alternatives to the modernities of Euro-American developmentalism and neoliberalism.

By explicating and interpreting facets of the generative founts of cultural features that constitute a dynamic twenty-first-century South American republic, we contribute to a growing understanding of heretofore unknown or unexplored systems. We hope that readers will pause and reexamine cherished paradigms of Latin Americanist thought and come to reflect on dynamics that, we submit, presage the future of serious research agendas.

All the authors in this work began to understand the dynamics of cultural systems through extensive field research in particular places and spaces of Ecuador. This is as true of the Ecuadorian authors (indigenous and non-indigenous) as it is of the others. In our research, we were drawn constantly to great transformations racking the country as they ramified through a vast but compressed system of coastal, Andean, and Amazonian regions, each with multiple ecological, social, and cultural particularities. We were also drawn to the remarkable continuities in the diverse sectors that constitute our research. Ecuador and some of its diverse peoples have been the productive sources of our creativity and the empirical bases for our analyses. When we turn to disciplinary paradigms, mostly anthropological, but also historical and sociological, we confront canonical thought systems of the academy and its critics with Ecuadorian realities, memories, and imaginaries observed and experienced.

Ecuador is a real place that exists in a present time with multiple envisioned destinies fortified by a rich and varied history. It is a sovereign nation-state with territoriality intact if threatened. It is now in its twenty-third year of democracy; never before in its republican history has it gone so long without a military coup. In 1995, it successfully concluded a war with Peru in the

Cenepa Valley of the southern Amazonian region, thereby altering the map by such a small fraction — one square kilometer at Tiwintza — that two years passed before a way to incorporate the alteration on paper could be found. Citizens identify themselves as *ecuatorianos(as)* and as *gente* (people). Collectively, they constitute *el pueblo* (the people). As a force (*fuerza del pueblo*), the people often confront *el gobierno* (the government) — the paternalist, powerful, but corrupt father figure. Collective identity of the people is with *el país* (the country or fatherland) and even more strongly with *la patria* (the motherland or reverential country). The nation may be in chaos, but *la patria* endures.

Diversity is a key feature in the sovereignty of Ecuador and in the oneness of the motherland's people. With a topography as diverse as any in the world, its ethnic and cultural makeup constitutes a mosaic of local and regional traditions that respond variously to the forces of globalization, modernization, and neoliberalism. One needs only to sit for a couple of hours in the Ecuadorian consulate in Chicago to glimpse Ecuador in its regional variants. There, a bilingual Quichua- and Spanish-speaking Otavalan may help a coastal person from Manabí fill out a form to give power of attorney in Jipijapa to his sister, or a poor Quiteña may be assisted in completing her marriage certificate by a Guayaquileño trader.

The same happens within the republic. When stepping out of the Hotel Amazónico in Amazonian Puyo, one encounters a monolingual Quichua speaker from the *páramo* region of Zumbagua-Tigua selling two wolf hides; three hefty Quiteños wearing dark business suits, white shirts, and somber ties emerge from the Hotel Los Cofanes to head for a meeting at the Banco del Austro, but they are stopped by two trilingual Achuar-Quichua-Spanish speakers who want to know about their pending bank loan. Up the street, a money exchange employee greets people in English and Spanish as they return from the United States and Spain with new currencies, while an Afro-Esmeraldeño pedals by with four huge baskets of freshly baked bread.

Knowledge acquired by people from one system about people of another is a second key feature of millennial Ecuador. A Salasacan weaver in New York City learns about the roadway system extending from coast to coast in the United States, just as he learned not long ago about the subtle colorations and behaviors of diverse iguanids in a Guayaquil zoo. The knowledge of the road systems of the United States helps him get contract work from Otavalan traders who need drivers in the United States, and the iguanid information helps him to better instruct his balsa carvers and painters in Otavalo to meet tourist and ethnic market demands in Quito, Guayaquil, the Galápagos Islands, Miami, and San Francisco. We are far from the economic dynamics envisioned by Ecuadorian presidents and their economic advisors, and far from the realm of constraints and rewards imposed by the International Monetary Fund and the World Bank, but we are deeply into the *ecuatorianidad* of adaptive livelihood.

There are deeper knowledge systems — indigenous and Afro-Ecuadorian gnosis — at work, too. For example, an Amazonian shaman may interpret the images of mystic forces represented by artists of the *páramo* of the Andes and of urban Quito; Afro-Ecuadorians perceived the cosmos of saints, spirits, devils, conjurors, and humans as divided into the domains of the divine and the human (hell being much closer to, and an integral part of, the latter) in much the same way as do some people of the high Andes.

Through physical travel — as when people from Saraguro take a bus to Quito and converse during a long, cold night — and spiritual travel, as when sick people from Salasaca seek the help of an Amazonian shaman, information about everything from the mysteries of the cosmos to the realities of political takeovers are imparted. Reflexive-laden networks of information are thereby strengthened across cultural and ethnic diversity in a multiplicity of regions. Such horizontal organization binds people, promotes interculturality, and enhances human oneness in diversity.

El pueblo unido, people together or united, is a theme that helps mobilize Ecuador's diverse peoples. "*El pueblo, unido, jamás será vencido*" is chanted at such occasions as a national transportation strike, a takeover of the national congress, or the ouster of a president of the republic. Individuals and collectivities in a particular location may act cooperatively at one time and divisively at another time, only to return to centralizing power when millennial social action prevails.

Cultural Transformations focused on the theme of modernity and, within it, the emergent consciousness of the collective power of diversity that foreshadowed millennial events. Ecuador has been dollarized since 2000. The Yankee greenback is the only legal tender of this South American country. The United States now has a military base in Manta that exceeds in scope and surveillance capacity that of the former Panama Canal Zone. From this base come the international forces of Plan Colombia, the U.S. program to eliminate or reduce the flow of cocaine into its drug-starved country. From Colombia and into Ecuador and other countries flow the forces of the leftist guerrillas and rightist paramilitaries as well as the cocaine dealers and professional "delinquents" who kill, kidnap, rape, and intimidate people along the entire Colombian-Ecuadorian border of Coast, Sierra, and Oriente. According to Henry A. Kissinger, these forces, and the military, police, and civilian actions to curtail them, carry northern South America into an epochal political climate analogous to that of Southeast Asia in the 1960s.

Since 1990, Ecuador has been racked by indigenous uprisings and marches, some with collaboration of people in other social sectors, some without such assistance. In terms of power, the space of indigenousness has expanded exponentially as diverse peoples, many bilingual or trilingual — Andean Quichua, Amazonian Quichua, Jivaroan, those who identify as Záparo in many languages, Waorani, Cofán, Tucanoan, Barbacoan, Afro–Latin American, and other Spanish-speaking peoples far from the centers of globalization — seek formal and informal control of local, regional, and national resources within and against globalizing governmental and economic strategies.

The authors of this book seek cultural insights into salient themes of the new millennium in Ecuador. We reach into the country's diversity for insights into its oneness. We offer insights into the similarities and differences among real peoples and cultures within the framework of a sovereign republic of South America. By publishing simultaneously in paperback and hardcover, we hope to communicate with those interested not only in Ecuador, per se, and neighboring countries but also with those anthropologists, sociologists, political scientists, and area specialists who seek to learn something about cultural dynamics in the vortex of globalized power.

Acknowledgments

Debts to those who contributed to the processes of thought and reflection that led me to organize this work are enormous. I here thank only those whose insights have guided me through special phases of my quests for understanding that led to this book. First and foremost, I thank my wife, research collaborator, and constant companion, Sibby, for being the critical part of our joint endeavors in Ecuador, which began in 1964. The use of the first-person plural brings her into the acknowledgments with me, since most of our debts are inseparable.

In the port town of San Lorenzo in 1961, Aurelio Fuentes Contreras began to instruct me on Ecuadorian lifeways as he watched me learn the Afro-Ecuadorian variants and contradictions to such ways. Later, in Puyo in 1968, Sibby and I struck up an acquaintance with the late Joe Brenner, whose friendship we cherish. In Salasaca, Quito, and Urbana, Illinois, Rudi Masaquiza contributed to our understanding of facets of Andean indigenous and nonindigenous cultural systems.

In Pastaza Province, Marcelo Santi Simbaña and Faviola Vargas Aranda have worked constantly and reflexively to establish a mutual understanding, one that now spans thirty-two years and includes numerous adventures throughout Pastaza and beyond. Also in the greater Puyo region, we are indebted to Clara Santi Simbaña and Abraham Chango for their insights,

Clara's often expressed through song. In Unión Base in the late 1960s and early 1970s, the late Pastora Guatatuca and the late Venancio Vargas took pains to help us understand indigenous history and imagery. To Alfonso Chango and Luzmila Salazar, both collaborators in multiple research projects, our gratitude is great.

In Salasaca, in Otavalo, and in Urbana and other parts of the United States, Julio Chicaiza has studied us, offered us counsel, and sought our counsel; it is sometimes difficult to know where his insights into Ecuador leave off and ours begin. And back in Puyo, it is to Estela Dagua to whom we turn frequently, as we have since the 1980s, for inspiration about the essence and substance of cultural life. She is clearly a *muscuyuj warmi*.

In Quito in the 1980s, María del Carmen Molestina facilitated the work of many of the contributors to this volume and to the 1981 tome; she also pulled me from the brink of political jeopardy and moved me into the orbit of the Universidad San Francisco de Quito, the institution that has supported our research since 1990, the year of the first Levantamiento Indígena. Thanks also to Santiago Gangotena, the chancellor of the university, for his timely support. Also in Quito, we offer very special thanks to Diego Quiroga for his sustained assistance, collegiality, and friendship. We first met Diego in 1983 and we continue to collaborate twenty years later. His help with infrastructural matters in Quito, together with the enduring assistance of his mother, Amparo Ferri de Quiroga, has proved of inestimable value.

Other contributors to this work have also been pivotal in shaping our understanding and deepening our perceptions of Ecuadorian humanity while generating and explicating rich lodes of data necessary to maintain the ethnographic particularities that form the core of a critical anthropology. Bill and Gigi Vickers have communicated with us since the 1970s about our mutual interests in Amazonia, always offering insight and hospitality. The work of Kris Lane and Jean Rahier in Esmeraldas and Quito (and elsewhere) has turned up information of vital importance in understanding the subjects of our endeavor. Jean's comparative Afro-Americanist studies in Esmeraldas, Imbabura-Carchi, and Quito take that special area to a new level of scholarship, while Kris's historical-ethnographic studies of greater Ecuador (including southwestern Colombia) shed new light on the forces that constrain and impel the present.

Rachel Corr, Jim and Linda Belote, Rudi Colloredo-Mansfeld, and Mary Weismantel plumb the intricacies of Andean life in Salasaca, Saraguro-Quito, Tigua-Quito-Otavalo, and Cuenca-Latacunga-Zumbagua, respectively, to offer fresh and critical perspectives drawn from the enduring and transforming lifeways of the people of these regions. Together these scholars represent a formidable fount of ethnographic excellence and display this against a solid background of comparative ethnology and interpretive history. Although I do not know Luis Macas well, I have followed his work with care since the mid 1980s and have learned greatly from it. In Amazonia, Mike Uzendoski skillfully unites the global economy and Evangelical Protestant movement with the locality of Runa life, offering new insights into a transforming but enduring Oriente people.

In the United States, since 1986, Dee Robbins, assistant to the director of the Spurlock Museum of World Cultures of the University of Illinois at Urbana-Champaign, has coordinated our efforts to undertake research in Ecuador while maintaining at least minimal continuity with our academic responsibilities. We are very appreciative not only of her competence but also of her continued creativity and good sense in making key decisions. Without the prompting of Liz Dulany of the University of Illinois Press, the impetus to initiate this collaborative endeavor might have been delayed. Colleagues in the University of Illinois at Urbana-Champaign Department of Anthropology have strongly influenced my orientation to cultural anthropology and Latin American and Caribbean studies; they include especially Angelina Cotler, Michelle Wibbelsman, Andy Orta, and Arlene Torres. Through their publications, manuscripts, conference papers, and proposals, I have been particularly informed, enlightened, and influenced by the work of Steve Gudeman, David Guss, Jon Hill, Sally Price, Richard Price, Mick Taussig, and Terry Turner. Beyond the confines of Latin American and Caribbean studies, I owe a continuing debt to the scholarship of Clifford Geertz, Marshall Sahlins, the late Victor Turner, and the late Peter Worsley.

Beginning in late December 2001, Michelle Wibbelsman joined this project as my research assistant, funded by the Research Board of the University of Illinois at Urbana-Champaign. It is thanks to Michelle's indefatigable work on multiple copies of multiple manuscripts, all coming and going electronically between Urbana and authors from many locations (including Ecuador and England), that this work could be submitted on time to the University of Iowa Press. Her intellectuality, love of Ecuador, and dedication to scholarship combined to create a pleasant and productive work environment, for which I am most grateful.

Funds allocated to my research through the University of Illinois at Urbana-Champaign over the last decade came from the Research Board, the College of Liberal Arts and Sciences, and the Graduate College. Other funds in support of our field research that were pivotal in developing the basis for *Millennial Ecuador* include the Wenner-Gren Foundation for Anthropological Research in 1990 and a National Endowment for the Humanities Summer Fellowship in 1992.

The editor and authors gratefully acknowledge subsidies from the Research Board and the College of Liberal Arts and Sciences of the University of Illinois at Urbana-Champaign that facilitated publication and pricing of this book. We are indebted to the director of the University of Iowa Press, Holly Carver, for overseeing every phase of its development and for maintaining cheery correspondence throughout the process.

Postscript, August 25, 2003

On August 6, 2003, President Lucio Gutiérrez broke all ties with the Pachakutik social movement that propelled his "Patriotic Society 21st of January" to power. Thus ended the millennial processes within the executive power structure of Ecuador. Gutiérrez continues to replace pre-election supporters he originally appointed to his cabinet with frequently overlapping close family, military, and political allies, as he forges strong ties with his once rival Social Christian Party overseen by León Febres Cordero and Jaime Nebot. Gone from the central administration are Nina Pacari and Luis Macas along with about four hundred other appointees affiliated with Pachakutik. Ex-President Gustavo Noboa, who succeeded Jamil Mahuad as president after the coup of January 21, is in exile in the Dominican Republic in the wake of accusations by Febres Cordero of misuse of World Bank funds diverted to failed banks that did not recover. Ex-President Rodrigo Borja of the Democratic Left Party urges Ecuadorian officials and legislators to explore constitutional means of deposing Gutiérrez. Analysts of Ecuadorian history and destiny lament the loss of sociopolitical reform and stress the apparent inability of the republic to alter its course of governance. Antonio Vargas has moved his base of millennial operations to the coast, where he hopes to mobilize huge numbers of disgruntled peasant, proletariat, indigenous, Afro-Ecuadorian, and other ("*montuvio*") ethnic peoples under a rubric of ethnic and grassroots resurgence and the emergence of new contrapowers. Pachakutik has organized a "parallel government" to challenge the oligarchy and its political class, and Vargas himself speaks of an "alternative government" to do the same. The processes sketched in this book continue but are once again outside the dynamics of structural power.

Millennial
ECUADOR

CHAPTER 1

Introduction

NORMAN E. WHITTEN, JR.

The world over, millenarian and revivalistic movements . . . originate in
periods when societies are in liminal transition between major orderings of social
structural relations.
—Victor Turner, *Dramas, Fields, and Metaphors*

Power is an instrument to complement what we are creating:
democracy and a new Ecuador.
—Antonio Vargas, "Nos Faltó Estrategia"

The coup of January 21, and the symbolism of respect for diversity that it condensed, epitomizes the drama that marks millennial Ecuador. At 10:00 A.M.
Friday morning, January 21, 2000, on a signal from the national police, the
armed forces guarding the empty Legislative Palace in Quito pulled back
from the doorways and allowed a throng of thousands of indigenous and
nonindigenous peoples to enter. As they waved the national flag and shouted
"*E-cua-dór! E-cua-dór! E-cua-dór!*" people again parted to allow three emis-
saries of the new national power figures to enter and take center stage. One
of these was Carlos Antonio Vargas Guatatuca, a Canelos Quichua indigenous man from the hamlet of Unión Base, just southeast of Puyo in the Amazonian region. Another was Colonel Lucio Edwin Gutiérrez Borbúa, a Quiteño originally from Tena, one of the heroes of the Cenepa Valley conflict in
Amazonia from which Ecuador emerged victorious in 1995 in its sporadic
armed conflict with neighboring Peru. The third, dressed in a well-appointed
suit and tie, was the former supreme court judge Carlos Solórzano Constan-
tini, a resident of Guayaquil.

Vargas voiced, loudly and clearly, words that were heard live on national
television and ramified worldwide. "*El pueblo está en poder*" (The people are
empowered). The three of them formed the Junta of National Salvation,
joined hands with one another and with other indigenous and nonindigenous peoples, and led the assembled throng in the national anthem. Later,
they joined hands again and recited the Lord's Prayer.

The coup itself came as no surprise. During the first year of his presidency,
Jamil Mahuad Witt placed supreme confidence in the activities of prominent

<u>bankers, a group of distinguished gringos known</u> as the Harvard Boys, and especially the officers and advisers of the International Monetary Fund. Mahuad brought the dignity of a master of arts degree in business administration from Harvard University and his experience as mayor of Quito to bear on the worsening economic situation of the republic. He championed the ideology of a neoliberal political economy, which, essentially, affirms that "the market" should dictate global economic activities within the sovereign state, as though any market could exist outside of a social and cultural context (e.g., Gudeman 1992, 2001:94–109). Mahuad relied heavily on the ideological trappings of modernity and neoliberal capital enterprise, and he gave those in charge of state and private banks free reign to wheel and deal with millions of dollars of entrusted capital. In the strong and hyperbolic words of Jean Comaroff and John Comaroff, one might say that Mahuad's image of the state turned to dimensions of "intensified magicalities and fetishes in order to heal fissures and breaches in the fabric of the polity" (Comaroff and Comaroff 2001b:36; also Palmié 2002).

The fetishes and magicalities that undergird and surround the reified image of a self-regulating "market" are embodied in the International Monetary Fund, the World Bank, the Group of Paris, the Harvard Boys, and the national banking elite. The result of policies and practices during Mahuad's presidency exacerbated a currency crisis in which the sucre was devalued radically from a few thousand sucres per dollar to more than twenty-five thousand sucres per dollar. According to *Vistazo* magazine (2000:66) devaluation between January 1999 and January 2000 was 249 percent. Mahuad and his banking crews froze all bank accounts in order to dollarize the economy at twenty five thousand sucres per dollar. Within one year, people with capital lost 75 percent or more of their purchasing power.

Lest these comments and information lead readers to think that I write to condemn Ecuadorian banking and governmental officials as isolated pirates of the modern global economy, or to fix specific blame on one modern president, Mahuad, quite the opposite is the case. Ecuador at the end of the 1990s and into the 2000s may be seen as a globalized vortex of economic and political modernity (e.g., Hernández, Rodríguez, and Bejarano 2000). Its elected president in 2000 epitomized this global political-economic system. As such, Ecuador stands at one and the same time as a unique national system of the modern Americas and also as microcosm of cognate systems worldwide. It is essential, then, to look at Ecuador in its multifaceted particularities and to set its historical and emergent cultural systems in global dimensions.[1]

Andrés Oppenheimer (2001), a distinguished Latin Americanist journalist for the *Miami Herald*, has written a devastating critique of U.S. banking, business, and governmental procedures that create a modern economic field sown with growing money for some and peppered with political-economic land mines for most others. To appreciate the degrees to which modern banking, financial, and business institutions may injure thousands of citizens to the enrichment of the very few, one need only glimpse the process of "Enronitis" (now a Spanish word) in the United States in 2002 and the activities of prominent banks (and bankers), some financial institutions, and some accounting practices vis-à-vis massive short-term profit. As Scott Burns, a syndicated business columnist for the *Dallas Morning News*, wrote on May 5, 2002, "In 10 fast years, the raw greed of American executives has transformed us [the United States] from the most highly respected, well-regulated and robust market in the world into a New Economy banana republic."[2] Mahuad and those he trusted fell victim to the New Economy and neoliberal ideology, and he paid the price of ouster and exile.

Steve Forbes visited Ecuador during the summer of 2001 and commented that "countries like Ecuador [that follow the policies and directives of the IMF] are like a hemophiliac turning to Dracula in search of aid" (*Hoy*, July 13, 2001). In his pithy, conservative manner, Forbes identifies the International Monetary Fund as the epitome of what Andean people call the *pishtaco* or *ñakak*, or *carasiri*, the foreign, white bogey man who renders and sells "indian fat" and sucks the blood of indigenous people. When confronted with certain realities, western capitalist metaphors resonate remarkably closely with those of indigenous South American people (see, e.g., Taussig 1986; Wachtel 1994; Orta in press; Whitten 2001; Uzendoski and Quiroga this volume; and especially Weismantel 2001).

In the spring of 1999, public figures suggested that Mahuad leave office (e.g., Mendoza Poveda 2001:49, 58), and by December 1999, elites and members of what is called the "political class" were calling for Mahuad to resign (e.g., Hernández, Rodriguez, and Bejarano 2000; Lucas 2000a, 2000b; Ponce 2000; Dieterich 2000; Mendoza Poveda 2001; Selmeski 2000; CONAIE 2000). Expresident Osvaldo Hurtado Larrea, the founder and leader of the Popular Democratic Party of which Mahuad was a prominent member, wrote a formal letter to him asking him to step out of office (see, e.g., Mendoza Poveda 2001:150).[3] Word was rampant in Ecuador that a junta would be established to include one or two prominent military generals and a few of those prominent in the *clase política*. It was widely speculated that Hurtado would be a participating member of such a junta. All this reorganizing and speculating was based on the modern premise that the "ruling class" would, with the support of the military high brass, run the country for a while and sort out the carnage seemingly caused by what appeared to be extreme greed and corruption within the powerful and influential banking fraternity.

The surprise — a jarring one for many — was caused by the chiliastic forces unleashed primarily by indigenous people, but supported and perhaps abated well in advance by the military colonels and captains. Generals of the armed forces were in on agreements to overthrow Mahuad's government and, at first, seemed to be in collusion with the colonels, some of whom were in serious conversation with indigenous leaders. Ecuadorian social structure had changed radically. No longer could the republic be seen in terms of the stability suggested in *Cultural Transformations*, wherein the pendulum of power swung between elected governments and military coups and where the United States supported both (e.g., Agee 1975; Whitten 1981a; Kissinger 2001). Ecuador emerged in 2000 poised between radically different systems of governance; the military might support either system; and it might even support both. The United States, however, would no longer support a military coup with a grassroots uprising as its social and cultural base.[4]

Millennial Ecuador and Persistent Modernity
A Review of the Fin de Siècle

In 1979, after nine long years of military rule, the people of Ecuador overwhelmingly elected Jaime Roldós Aguilera as president and Osvaldo Hurtado Larrea as vice president, resoundingly defeating the military's own candidate, Sixto Durán Ballén (Whitten 1981c:776). Roldós believed that "only the clash of ideas can ignite the light of truth."[5] In his inaugural speech in the Legislative Palace, following the presidential elections overseen by the military, the newly elected President Roldós addressed the nation in Quichua. Recently enfranchised Quichua speakers of the Sierra had bloc-voted for him and they now heard him address them, as citizens, in *runa shimi* (human speech): "*Kunan punchaka, mana pushaita japinchik*" (Today we are no longer entrapped [as in the year past]), he began (Whitten 1981c:776–78, 795; *El Comercio*, August 11, 1979). Rudimentary though this speech was, in the opinion of many "experts" on the language, Roldós effectively communicated with perhaps one-third of the people of Ecuador in a way they never before had experienced. On August 10, the historical day of the shout for independence, they heard in their own language about new freedoms and ethnic liberation from the pinnacle of presidential power, the head and embodiment of *el gobierno*. A new civil society with millennial overtones was in the making.

One of the new president's first acts was to formally expel the personnel of the Summer Institute of Linguistics/Wycliffe Bible Translators. By so doing he complied with requests of Amazonian indigenous people and placed the onus of clear communications from Amazonia to governing Quito in the hands of Ecuadorian agencies, including nascent indigenous organizations. As Roldós continued to construct an administrative policy based on a plank of cultural diversity and awareness of oneness in diversity, his vice president began to speak publicly of a unified and central "cultural policy," reminiscent of that proclaimed earlier by the deposed nationalist military dictator, General Gonzalo Rodríguez Lara (Whitten 1976; Stutzman 1981; Whitten 1981c). The policy of blending or hybridization focused on what Hurtado called *in-domestizaje*, an ideology of racialized and cultural mixing and ontology that stressed the rediscovery of "authentic" cultural roots and the "whitening" powers of Euro-American value and administrative orientations. Contemporary people classed as *indio* (Indian) and all people of black or dark complexion were excluded from the ideology of cultural mixing to enlighten. Immediately after the tragic death of Roldós on May 21, 1981, Hurtado became president.

Bit by escalating bit the people who spoke indigenous languages as first languages and those who identified with them by parentage or other persuasion increased their ranks and worked toward informal and formal modes of communication across lines that were often hostile and dangerous under the rules of racialized modernity. In 1989, Rodrigo Borja Cevallos of the Democratic Left Party became president and immediately put his first cousin (their mothers are sisters), Alfonso Calderón Cevallos, into Carondelet (the presidential palace, Ecuador's White House) as assessor of indigenous affairs. One of the first things that Calderón did was revise his book, now in its fifth edition, entitled *Reflexión en las culturas orales* (1987). This was a blueprint for indigenous resurgence to claim lands lost during the European conquest and colonial and republican rule.

In 1990 the first nationwide Levantamiento Indígena occurred (see, e.g., Almeida et al. 1992; Whitten 1996). In the aftermath of negotiation, a delegation of indigenous people from the Amazonian region met with President Borja in the special room at Carondelet reserved for meetings with diplomats. There, the people presented Borja with their document, which stated their needs and made some demands. The hubris of the document was taken entirely and exactly (the necessary changes having been made for specific localities) from *Reflexión en las culturas orales*.

Calderón and indigenous people had worked together on the document in the offices of CONFENIAE, which is just southeast of Puyo, abutting the small Canelos Quichua hamlet of Unión Base. Glaring at Antonio Vargas, who is from Unión Base, Borja asked, "¿Ima shuti tiangui?" (What's your name? Who are you?). Vargas answered in Quichua, since the president asked the question in his language, and began to state the positions of indigenous people of Amazonia. Borja abruptly cut him off and, on the national television network, went ballistic. With his long index finger raised and gesticulating, and his classical Spaniard countenance beamed at the entire nation, he lectured the people present and their families nationwide about the inappropriateness of their position. Borja's position on indigenous rights, on the one hand, and his regal but controlled fury at those who sought the promise of indigenous self-determination, on the other hand, call for critical interpretation. Mine goes like this: it is one thing for his cousin to take a "pro-Indian" stance in writing, but quite another for real indigenous people to ask for the same national concessions that the book recommends. The first position is literate, philosophically socialist-liberal, and redemptive; the second is indigenous, pragmatically socialist, and, consequently, dangerous and subversive to national sovereignty. The text or discourse of liberation, in other words, is interpreted according to its position in class-ethnic hierarchies as these reflect conflictive arenas, contrasting cultural paradigms, and enduring polarizations (e.g., Turner 1974).

When ideological polarizations such as *blanco/indio* exist, the text on one side of the contrast takes on the opposite meaning of that which it represents on the other. Following Victor Turner (1974), we could say that the text itself in its symbolic dimensions oscillates between the official (institutional) pole and the dynamic, agentive (orectic) pole of human discourse and social action. With this speech and its polarized (indigenous/nonindigenous, upper middle class/lower class) reception nationwide, the modern (institutional) and millennial (agentive) dynamics that continue to play out became publicly established.

In 1992, the March for Land and Life from Amazonia to Quito took place. Antonio Vargas was one of the leaders, and Borja was still president. Various officials including César Verduga Vélez, the minister of government (who fled to Mexico in 1997 after purloining the national reserve funds and is now director of the Latin American Association of Human Rights), took the necessary steps to eliminate the possibility of serious violence. The police and the military protected the marchers all the way from Puyo to Quito (Whitten, Whitten, and Chango, this volume). There, indigenous organizations of Amazonia received 1,115,574 hectares, with rights to be divided according to contemporary occupation of land, ancestral occupation of land, identity with *nacionalidades*, and allegiance to or membership in specific indigenous organizations.

In 1995, under the presidency of Durán Ballén, who was defeated in 1979 by Roldós, Ecuador engaged in a war with Peru and emerged victorious. During that war, crack Ecuadorian military troops became dependent on the skills and knowledge of indigenous Shuar people resident in the area, on an elite indigenous military organization named IWIAS, after the mythic Shuar cannibal *iwianch* (palpable and corporeal image, translatable as "monster"), and on the organization known as ARUTAM, which is composed of retired and active Shuar soldiers trained in guerrilla warfare. *Arutam*, in Jivaroan cosmology, is the almost overwhelmingly powerful vision that a male youth encounters on a special quest to a site of rushing water (e.g., Harner 1972; Descola 1994). After the vision quest, the youth "knows" who his true ancestors are, and he must control with care a strong urge to kill. In the valley of the upper Cenepa River, according to many testimonies of military colonels (e.g., Dieterich 2000), knowledge and respect for indigenous people by those self-identifying as *blanco* (white) reached a new and positive level. The ideology of diversity and the positive imagery of interculturality thus emerged in the middle and upper ranks of the military hierarchy during a time of war, turbulence, and high nationalist spirit.

The testimony of Colonel Jorge Luis Brito Albuja is most telling. Brito is a veritable Audie Murphy of Ecuador, the most decorated war hero in the nation, honored repeatedly for his valor not only in the Alto Cenepa armed conflict, but also for previous valor in 1985 in the Battle of Paquisha, where Peru triumphed. On January 21, 2000, he was in line for promotion to general in the armed forces of the Republic of Ecuador.

Brito comes from a prominent upper-middle-class family from Ambato and was reared to think of himself as *blanco*, in a society of class-ethnic differentiation with *indios* (Indians) and *negros* (Blacks) making up the lower portion. "My parents had haciendas and I can say that the *indios* were truly slaves, they were [regarded as] inferior people" (Brito 2000:117). Brito explains in this testimony that from 1980 the most intelligent people in the military knew that they must identify with the people, and that key dynamic elements of *el pueblo* were the indigenous people. He learned over the last two decades that the indigenous people were in every way his equal, that the country could not survive without them, and that their social movements were for national liberation (Brito 2000).

Brito was called to the legislative palace on January 21 by General Carlos Mendoza Poveda. He was not part of a conspiracy and he was not a participant in the takeover. After *el golpe del 21 de enero* (the coup of January 21), those who had "taken" the building turned to General Mendoza and put the fate of the nation in his hands as junta leader (e.g., Vargas 2000; Brito 2000; Gutiérrez 2000). Mendoza accepted his role, but two hours later he succumbed to pleadings of his family and the unrelenting demands of the United States, which were expressed and broadcast live on Quito radio by the former ambassador to Ecuador, Peter Romero, and U.S. State Department representative Thomas Pickering. Mendoza left the junta and created a huge power vacuum in the movement. The next day, Mendoza, in the name of the military, turned the government over to Vice President Gustavo Noboa Bejarano who, soon after, publicly decorated him. Contradictory though it seems, Mendoza then had Brito and the other military participants arrested and eventually forced them into retirement even though the national legislators voted overwhelmingly to pardon them. President Noboa, for his part, continued the processes of dollarization begun by the ex-president (and now Harvard professor) Mahuad. In the year 2000, millennial forces tripped over modernity as structural power (Wolf 1999:5) on a global scale was wielded by the U.S. State Department within the sovereign nation of Ecuador.

Brito asserted that Antonio Vargas and the other indigenous people, and the military personnel who took part in the coup, were veritable heroes and that the generals were the real traitors (Brito 2000). And the indigenous people made it clear that their uprisings, takeovers, and strikes were for all the Ecuadorian people. *Nada solo para los indios* (Not only for the Indians) became a key figure of speech in 2000 (e.g., Acosta et al. 2001). In 2001, some members of the coup formed a political party, the Society of January 21st, but most of the military officers who were forced to resign joined the social movement Pachakutik that serves, at times, as the political arm of the national indigenous organization (see, e.g., Whitten, Whitten, and Chango, this volume; Macas, Belote, and Belote, this volume; Macas 2001).

The relationships that obtain among the human forces that constitute the people and "politico-economic classes" of Ecuador are complex and intricately interrelated. Modernity and millenarianism are inextricably intertwined. They constitute a mutualist dynamic that propels Ecuadorian cultural systems from one historical event to another. The conjuncture that they form is impelling and synergistic; it cannot be unbundled or its elements dissected. Unpacking facets of the conjuncture of millennial Ecuador as they are manifest by real people in real Ecuadorian places is a purpose of this book. No dichotomy or dialectic can help us understand the transformative dialogues, dramatic events, and charged political and cultural fields and paradigms that punctuate recent and distant history. Only an understanding of the changing significations and resignifications of diversity can lead us to an illumination of real people at local levels, the national affects of conjoined localities in motion, and the all-encompassing contradictory and complementary globalizations that constrain and release these affects (see, e.g., Abercrombie 1998; Guss 2000; Appadurai 2001; Comaroff and Comaroff 1993, 2001a; Gaonkar 2001). We seek to put human faces in the modern-millennial picture and to understand that real lives move into and through the conjunctures.

Epochalism *El País* and *El Estado-Nación*

Ecuador is a nation the size of the State of Oregon in the United States. Second smallest of the Spanish-speaking republics, Ecuador is the western-most country of South America. Flying due south from Miami, a plane would pass over its west coast. The topography of Ecuador is as rugged and varied as any place on Earth. The coastal region ranges from tropical rain forest in the north through dry-monsoon forests in the center and south. A rugged western cordillera rises to six thousand feet just in from the sea in many areas. Over half of the population lives in this region, whose major urban center — the largest in Ecuador, with a population of more than three million — is Guayaquil, on the turgid Guayas River.

In the Sierra, with a population slightly less than that of the coast, permanently snowcapped volcanic mountains, some active, rise higher than 20,000 feet. Interspersed in this Himalayan-like environment are innumerable microenvironments ranging from deep valleys at 3,000 to 6,000 feet, to wet and rugged páramos at more than 13,000 feet. The famous "corridor of the volcanoes" undulates between the western and eastern cordilleras and connects major Ecuadorian cities to the capital, Quito, the national administrative center, with a population now approaching two million. Quito itself spreads from north to south in an Andean valley, at 9,000 to 9,500 feet altitude. West of the active volcano Pichincha lies Esmeraldas, a province within which Afro–Latin American freedom emerged in the 1540s (Cabello Balboa 1945 [1582]; Lane 2002); and to the east, over the high wet *páramo* and cloud forest, lies the Amazonian piedmont region, which experienced the first indigenous revolt, that of the shamans, or *pendes*, in 1579 (Oberem 1971; Lane 2002, this volume).

Quito and Guayaquil clash systemically. The former is staid, conservative, cerebral, and hierarchical in its idealized and essentialized cultural system, but it is also highly commercial, with a substantial banking establishment. Petroleum, controlled by governmental agencies in Quito, is refined just west of Esmeraldas and is exported from coastal ports. Guayacos place stress on commerce, banking, shipping, and commercial agriculture as their raison d'être. People speak different Spanish dialects in the two cities, and in their respective regions, and mutual oppositional stereotypes abound.

Caudillos, men and occasionally women, who are able to bring together opposing parties in times of crisis, characterize the major and minor power moves in both Quito and Guayaquil (e.g., Blanksten 1951; Linke 1960; Whitten 1981a). It behooves the *caudillo* to precipitate a crisis and to be ready to take advantage of one. Writing of the *caudillos* of these two cities in the new millennium, journalists (e.g., Jijón 2001) sometimes refer to their collective power as *el Parque Jurásico* (Jurassic Park). The focal political megasaurians include León Febres Cordero, Jaime Nebot Saadi, and Abdalá Bucaram Ortíz (the latter exiled in Panama since February 5, 1997) in Guayaquil and Hurtado, Borja, and Durán Ballén in Quito.

In the southern Andean sector of the Sierra, known as El Austro, Cuenca is the primary city. Now named to the UNESCO international Heritage of Humanity roster, Cuenca shares many social and cultural features with Quito (which is also a Heritage of Humanity global treasure) but often allies with the power moves of prominent coastal leaders. Another Heritage of Humanity site is the Galápagos Islands, six hundred miles off Ecuador's coast in the Pacific Ocean. El Austro, and especially the region around Cuenca, is the locus of massive, predominantly male migration to the United States and Spain (e.g., Weismantel, this volume; Macas, Belote, and Belote, this volume) and the inflow of remittances that serve to transform the livelihoods of the poor. In this sense, the greater Cuenca region is Ecuador's emigration system writ large.

To the east of the Andes lies the Oriente, officially the Amazonian region. This part of Ecuador constitutes more than half its territory and is shrouded not only by sporadic cloud cover moving across the tropical rain forest and twisting rivers, but also by urban myths and the historical narratives of conquest that affirm that "neither God nor Law" exist there (see, e.g., Lane, this volume; Whitten 1976, 1981a, 1985; Whitten and Whitten 1988, 1993). Long ignored by national planners and developers, except for sporadic schemes to unite the Coast, Andes, and Amazonian regions with a modern transportation system giving the nation access to both coasts — its own coast and the Brazilian Amazon as well as the Atlantic, thousands of miles away — the Oriente emerged as a national resource in the mid 1960s when a Texaco-Gulf consortium rediscovered oil in large quantities under the surface of its rich and diverse tropical rain forests and rivers. The nation then entered a mode of intensified modernity and established the cultural infrastructure for millennial ideology and cosmology (Whitten 1981a, 1981b, 1981c).

The nationally shrouded land of the Oriente is home to many people who speak many languages. Shuar, Achuar and Shiwiar speak Jivaroan, the Amazonian Quichua speak three discernible dialects, the Siona and Secoya speak Western Tucanoan, and the Cofán and Waorani speak languages unrelated to any other South American languages (and unrelated to one another). Bilingualism is fairly common, and Shiwiar speakers may converse in Shuar, Achuar, Shiwiar, Quichua, and perhaps Zaparoan. Záparo people mainly speak Quichua, and many Waorani are trilingual in Spanish, Quichua, and their own Wao language. Often erroneously portrayed as the Amazon Basin, the Ecuadorian Oriente is two thousand miles from the Amazon proper.

La región amazónica ranges from the Amazonian *montaña* and upland forest (piedmont) to the Upper Amazonian regions. Only in a few places does a true Amazonian biotope exist; but again, the Amazon itself and the true basin so beloved of writers is far away. Indeed, the Sierra de Cutucú has forested areas that range to nine thousand feet, the very height of Andean Quito.

Epochal Ecuador refers to a nation-state in its global social, political, and economic matrices. Epochalism, as Geertz (1973 [1963, 1971]) long ago explained, refers to the mode of interpretation of such a geopolitical positioning. The two polarized positions of those who would direct Ecuador's nationalist course into the future are those of neoliberal economic and political reform, on the one side, and the quest for partial autonomy, or self-determination, for sectors of Ecuador's people, on the other side. In some ways, both challenge the sovereignty of the state, *el estado*, and question the veritable existence of the nation, *la nación*. Both stress the need for a national political-economic transformation within a context of a repositioning of the networks that extend between nations and powerful corporations, on the one side, and those that link real people and their livelihoods within and beyond a given nation, on the other side. Epochalism has both modern and millennial dimensions, and both dimensions adhere to the two polarized positions of neoliberalism and the quest for partial autonomy and self-determination. All this ramifies through coastal, sierran, and Amazonian diversities, each with its own diversity linked to dozens of others and all of these connections ramify into multiple international arenas.

Out of the international arenas comes debt, severe debt, debilitating debt. Governments, banks, development agencies, small and large businesses, and people from all walks of life borrow money and accrue compounding interest that can amount to 100 percent or more per annum. National and regional debt was acquired in massive amounts in 1999, when it was known that a severe El Niño season was coming and local and regional government agencies requested advance funds to prepare and later to repair. By the time the coastal infrastructure was indeed destroyed, the money for rehabilitation had been spent elsewhere, or invested elsewhere, or just deposited elsewhere. Nothing remained in Mahuad's regime but to borrow more money to resuscitate the entire coastal system of infrastructural modernity.

Sometimes in Ecuador, it seems as though people are reluctant to spend money on the plan or project for which the money was allocated or loaned. Reasoning may be that if international agencies allocate (more often loan) money once for a project, they will continue such a policy of financially crippling loans after the original money runs out. It is perhaps safer, or preferable, then, to use the money for something else (including personal gain) for which no funds are available. In the face of such observations, the U.S. ambassador to Ecuador, Leslie Alexander, raised the issue publicly in an interview with *Vistazo* magazine: "¿Dónde está la plata?" (Where is the money?) he asked in 1999. He was referring to 160 million dollars recently loaned to the government of Ecuador for its coastal resuscitation. The rhetorical trope was featured on the cover of the magazine and became a rallying cry for dissenting voices nationwide; where, indeed, is the money that was loaned to Ecuador? Where does it go, and to whom? How does it relate to the (decontextualized) market so revered by the followers of modern and millennial neoliberalism? As money for projects finds its way elsewhere, the debt derived from the original and subsequent loans continues to compound.

Essentialism *El Pueblo* and *La Patria*

The people of Ecuador reflect the diversity of the national topology in their contrasts, languages, ecologies, and cultural and social systems. Two paradigms compete for salience in the politics and poetics of identity and representation (e.g., Herzfeld 1997) within the republic. One is that of *el mestizaje* (the blending) (e.g., Espinosa Apolo 1997) and the other is that of *multinacionalidad* (multinationalism, multinationality), subsuming multiculturalism. The first emanates from the elite; the second swells up from *el pueblo*. Both compete today in millennial Ecuador (Stutzman 1981; Whitten 2003; Rahier, this volume; Weismantel, this volume), and either one may serve as an ideological basis for the collectivity known as *la patria* (the motherland).

Mestizaje ideology carries a strong subtext of *blanqueamiento*, which means whitening in both racializing and cultural senses (see Rahier, this volume; Weismantel, this volume; Torres and Whitten 1998). *Multinacionalidad* carries the explicit text of respect for cultural diversity and the powers of unity across diversity. Both constitute multivocalic metatropes that may serve as polarizing symbols or as condensing symbols (e.g., Turner 1973, 1974; Whitten 2003). Who is to be identified as *el pueblo* at any given event, in any given context, in any specific arena, during any particular crisis, depends, in part, on the ways by which the macrotropes of *el mestizaje* and *multinacionalidad* play out on the stages of millennial transformation now ongoing in the Republic of Ecuador.

The postmodernist critiques of anthropology, which began in the 1980s and continue, chastise us to learn not to "essentialize" people by attributing to them special, inner, cultural, "essences." In his article "Goodbye to Tristes Tropes," Marshall Sahlins (1994) argues convincingly that many, perhaps most, people themselves insist on their very essentialist being (see also Guss 2000). I agree that we must not "essentialize others," but in the process of not doing this, I suggest that we learn with great care to understand the processes of self-essentializing. As Rachel Corr (2001, personal communication) recently pointed out, "essentializing is at the heart of self-empowerment, pride, and alternative modernity."

One cannot understand Ecuador today, its history, or the statements about the destinies of its peoples, in the absence of a hermeneutics of essentialism writ large and the clashing essentialisms of its many and diverse peoples. Using Sahlins's (1994:389) terms, Ecuador is, and has long been, a significant "Culture of cultures," a national system of differences. *La patria* (Culture) represents the collectivity of Ecuadorians. It is to the essences of *la patria* that people give their loyalty, often in opposition to *el gobierno*, the paternalist and presumed-to-be-corrupt entity constituted especially by the presidency, the congress, and the judiciary.

El pueblo, the dynamic collective of "the people," is the essence of the motherland. Guayaquileños sometimes burn the Quito flag and threaten to secede from the nation, but the red, yellow, and blue national flag, with its central coat of arms, is sacrosanct. Indigenous peoples, Afro-Ecuadorian people, and many other people initiate political meetings where strikes or other activities against the government are planned by singing the national anthem. The macrospace for diverse peoples is *El Ecuador*. The *nacionalidades* (the cultures) constitute the essentialist manifestations of the particular people.

Roldós recognized all or much of this in 1979, when he named diverse peoples of Ecuador, "I speak for all the people who live in this country . . . those of the Oriente, from whence the sun rises — Shuar, Waorani, Secoya, Siona, Cofán — to where it sets, the Occidente," naming here the Tsháchila and Chachi in the colloquial vernacular as "Colorado" and "Cayapa," who, along with Awá, are Barbacoan speakers of the northern rain-forest region; they share their territory with Afro-Ecuadorians. By speaking in Quichua, he had already acknowledged the Quichua speakers of the Sierra and Oriente, and he did not know of the Achuar, Shiwiar, or Záparo, such peoples being still relegated to "folklore" and "ethnography." But Roldós was well aware of diverse peoples, including black people, as humans and as Ecuadorians, a position that was to emerge in an arena of contestation in the next two decades with increasingly chiliastic force.

A generation later, when indigenous and other people "took" the national legislature in the coup of January 21, spokesmen for the government and the military under the presidency of Mahuad gave the order to use *la mano dura* (armed force) to put down the insurrection. Those with the arms of state and government, the military and police consortium, or task force, refused to fire on fellow citizens. They gave as their reason: "these people are Ecuadorians." They opened the portals of contrastructural powers to the people and signaled an emergence of a millennial civil society to the entire world.

Ecuador in Global Perspective

Ecuador is clearly an Andean country, but not so according to many "Andeanists" who regard the "Central Andes," heartland of the imperial Inca, as the "authentic zone" of Andeanist concern. The Inca conquered Sierra and part of the southern coast of Ecuador in the mid fifteenth century, and Quito became the northern capital of the Inca by about 1480, a scant fifty years before the Spanish conquest smashed into a conflict-ridden system where Atahualpa of Quito was waging civil war against his half-brother Huascar, in what is now Peru. The Spanish truncated the divided Inca empire, planted their own colonial system on its monumental ruins, and confronted almost immediately indigenous and black resistance in the Andes and the east, and African and free black Spanish resistance to the west (Oberem 1971; Phelan 1967; Lane 2002, this volume; Rueda Novoa 2001).

Colonial Ecuador was born in extraordinary conflict, controlled by the rich and powerful, locked in Spanish rule for three hundred years and peopled by diverse souls who were forced to maintain multiple subsistence systems while bent to the will of the rich and greedy (e.g., Salomon and Schwartz 1999; Lane 2002). After the wars of liberation led by Simón Bolívar in the north and José de San Martín in the south, Ecuador eventually emerged as a national cultural system of diversity undergirded by systems of knowledge of diversity. Cultural resiliency has endured, manifest within a system of extraordinary differential power, prestige, and wealth.

Some writers place Ecuador and some Ecuadorians in a millennial political movement derived from the colonial wars of liberation, especially that led by Simón Bolívar. This is the activist-Marxist position of "Bolivarianism" that equates the Ecuadorian indigenous movement, the forty-year-old guerrilla movement in Colombia, and the nationalist politics of President Hugo Chávez in Venezuela (e.g., Dieterich 2000) with a special kind of social revolutionary force (sometimes Castro's Cuba, the Zapatistas of Mexico and the *cocaleros* [coca growers] of Bolivia are thrown into this mix). The concept of Bolivarian stresses the history of liberation led by Simón Bolívar juxtaposed with the powerful attempts made by the United States to control South American resources and with a shared history of imperial colonial power and self-liberating rebellion.

In 2002, the ideological symbolism and imagery generated by this position are dangerous for real people in an Anglo-dominated, xenophobic world. According to Kinnto Lucas (2000b:76, 79), Bolivarianism as an ideological doctrine emerged as the *movimiento bolivariano por la nueva colombia* (Bolivarian movement for a new Colombia) on April 29, 2000, in San Vicente del Caguán, so named by FARC guerrilla Comandante Manuel Marulando Vélez, whose nickname is Tirofijo (Sureshot). Marulando, born Pedro Antonio Marín, took the name of a prominent labor organizer of Medellín after the Intelligence Service of Colombia allegedly assassinated this leader in 1930. In 1998, President Andrés S. Pastrana Arango ceded forty-two thousand square kilometers radiating from San Vicente del Caguán, in the Amazonian province of Caquetá, to the FARC to provide them with a safe-haven "demilitarized" reserve. This territory is the size of Switzerland, or twice the size of El Salvador, with a population of one hundred thousand and an estimated ten thousand hectares planted in coca for the express purpose of creating the paste that forms the basis for commercial cocaine.

Out of this protected safe haven, members of this movement continued to attack villages, police stations, and military outposts; to hijack planes; to kidnap Colombians and foreigners (including Ecuadorians); to extort whatever they could from whomever they could; to assassinate political, judicial, and other leaders; and to take a significant profit by taxing the escalating cocaine production for export to the United States and Europe. On January 10, 2002, the president rescinded his promise to provide the FARC with this vast demilitarized zone and ordered them out within forty eight hours or he would send thirteen thousand elite military troops into the region.

Negotiations between the FARC and the government of Colombia continued, broke down again, and the Colombian army bombed and then invaded the territory on February 20 (e.g., *New York Times*, February 22, 2002). Subsequently, Pastrana declared the FARC to be international terrorists comparable to those in the al-Qaeda network (Isacson 2002:10–13). In summer 2002, the European Union also declared the FARC and the ELN to be terrorist organizations, and, by the end of June, FARC leaders threatened to assassinate or kidnap 1,098 town and city mayors (including those of the largest cities of Bogotá, Medellín, and Cali) and issued the same threat to all the municipal councillors, which amounted to four thousand in twenty-two departments (e.g., *El Comercio*, June 27, 2002). In the face of this threat, Pastrana put a two-million-dollar bounty on Tirofijo and one million on the other FARC leaders, while a new special military group initiated a search similar to that being conducted in Pakistan for Osama bin Laden. On August 7, during the inauguration of the new president, Álvaro Uribe Vélez in Bogotá, FARC guerrillas managed to fire mortar shells at and into the national legislative palace, killing many citizens and wounding many more. Nothing in the Colombian experience with leftist guerrillas and rightist paramilitaries resembles the dynamics of the Ecuadorian indigenous movement or other contemporary Ecuadorian social movements.

Adding to the geopolitical complexity of this region is Tres Esquinas, just south of the FARC safe-haven zone near the borders of Ecuador and Peru, also in Caquetá. The U.S. military maintains a highly sophisticated surveillance unit here, which it established in 1998, coordinated with its military base in Manta, Ecuador (for a synopsis of the U.S. military bases in Colombia, see http://www.ciponline.org/coipro02.htm). Once a secondary site for rubber collection and Catholic missionizing, the sector of Tres Esquinas was, at the turn of the twentieth century, a focus of the worse-known atrocities of the Amazon rubber boom (Casement 1912; Taussig 1986). This is the very region from which Taussig (1986 : 3–126) developed his concepts of "the culture of terror and the space of death."

Imageries of peoples and events can quickly become global phenomena. When structural power is challenged, there is a tendency to condense master symbols into representations that conjoin by association vastly different activities. By associating — as do Dieterich (2000) and Salgado Tamayo (2002), among others — indigenous people engaged in millennial activities to change the democratic structure of Ecuador (and who have been instrumental recently in ousting two presidents without bloodshed) with the longest-standing guerrilla movement in the world (the FARC), the metonymic associations of Bolivarian, communist, terrorist, and indigenous can easily emerge. Bolivarian by such syntagmatic structural or functional set of associations could easily be juxtaposed to al-Qaeda in the Middle East and elsewhere.

Indeed, right after September 11, 2001, Ecuador was named by a U.S. agency as one of two South American nations that might have an al-Qaeda cell, and FBI agents were sent there immediately to investigate (Garrastazu and Haar 2001). An important reason for such naming, apparently, was the existence of a significant indigenous movement in the country.[6] On February 29, 2002, and subsequently, President Pastrana specifically used the analogy of FARC and al-Qaeda to influence the United States to provide increased military aid to fight the guerrillas to whom he had previously granted safe haven. As Pastrana made the analogy, military in the northern Ecuadorian Amazonian province of Orellana and Sucumbíos fired on people who had occupied sites of petroleum exploitation, killing four and wounding many.

In the early 2000s, Ecuadorian leaders in the political classes and people working for a newly constructed nation made strong cases that the guerrillas and paramilitaries of Colombia should be looked on as revolutionaries, not as terrorists. But in pressing their case, the syntagmatic chain that runs from

Marxist guerrilla to indigenous social movements is again strengthened in its negative imagery. It is against such negative and harmful stereotypes that the multiple social movements of Ecuador struggle. By mid 2002, however, the word *terrorism* gained ascendancy in public discourse about guerrillas and paramilitaries.

To be black in modern Ecuador can also be dangerous. After the assassination of black *esmeraldeño* congressman Jaime Hurtado González (no relation to Osvaldo Hurtado) and his two bodyguards in 1998 in front of the Legislative Palace, and the subsequent accusations of his alleged linkages with the Colombian FARC, the Ecuadorian military occupied the black areas of the interior of Esmeraldas Province, especially the Ónzole River region. This is a region where Afro-Ecuadorians had recently been granted legal rights to land they had worked since the mid sixteenth century (de la Torre Espinoza 2002; Lane 2002). In this occupation, an association was made between an unconfirmed accusation of a congressman's involvement with radical Colombian politics and an Ecuadorian region known for its "blackness" and its "remoteness." In the face of this military action, publicly espoused blackness, as ideological negritude, retreated into local and regional discussion groups (e.g., Whitten 2003).

The United States has long had a powerful role in internal Ecuadorian affairs (see, e.g., Agee 1975). It backed Peru in "the War of 41" when, at the outset of World War II, Peru invaded Ecuador, appropriated half of the Oriente, and retained that land in the Treaty of Río de Janeiro in 1942. After the 1995 conflict, Ecuador regained one square kilometer of territory at Tiwintza. To understand the role of the United States in Ecuador, we must take a view of more of South America. Ecuador is abutted by Colombia to the north and Peru to the east and south. As peace held between Ecuador and Peru in 1998, President Mahuad made a strong move to decrease the power of the Ecuadorian military and to boost the power of the United States through its program (initiated during World War II and during the Eisenhower administration) of "civic action" and by stepped-up loans for development. The United States also regularly trains troops in Ecuador and favors multiple sites in the Oriente for exercises and to give special forces trainees firsthand experiences in "jungle warfare."

Within this historical and contemporary framework, the Clinton administration of the United States launched Plan Colombia in July 2000 and moved its southern command from Panama to Manta, on the central coast of Ecuador. From there, it coordinated with Tres Esquinas deep in the rain forest of Amazonian Colombia. Reflecting on current United States policy in Latin America in global perspective, and on the United States and its policies and actions, Henry A. Kissinger (2001:91) writes:

Plan Colombia bears within it the same fateful momentum which drove America's engagement in Vietnam first to stalemate and then to frustration. . . . But once the effort goes beyond a certain point, the United States, to avoid the collapse of the local forces in which it has invested such prestige and treasure, will be driven to take the field itself. Panama, Ecuador, Peru, Venezuela, and Brazil are in the active borderlands of the internal war of Colombia.

The Ecuadorian border segments with Colombia are held by the FARC, the ELN, and the United Self-Defense System of Colombia (AUC). Each has its own defined sector; there is no mixing. All three are linked to the cocaine and heroin drug trade within Colombia and between Colombia and other nations, especially the United States. In spite of cutbacks by the Mahuad regime and the internal frictions and disputes culminating in the coup of January 21, the Ecuadorian military has broadened and strengthened its activities all along its northern border, in the entire province of Esmeraldas, and in every province of the Oriente. There is no permanent Colombian military installment in the Ecuadorian border region in Colombia; the entire area is controlled by FARC, ELN, or AUC, each in its own sector.

In many sites, fighters from these revolutionary and paramilitary groups enter Ecuador for rest and relaxation (see Vickers, this volume). In September 2001, U.S. State Department spokesperson Walter Taylor issued a statement that declared all three of these organizations to be "terrorist" and thereby subject to U.S. sanctions. Not mentioned was the allegation in Colombia, Ecuador, and elsewhere that the AUC have been assisted by the U.S. CIA and that they operate with the consent of the Colombian military, and hence in apparent collaboration with the U.S. military, as part of Plan Colombia (e.g., Youngers 2000; Ricanchi 2002a, 2000b: 20).

A prominent feature of Plan Colombia is the systematic spraying of Ultra Glyphosate (Glyphosate, N-[phosphonomethyl] glycine) onto coca and subsistence crops such as bananas, manioc, maize, and beans. This is Monsanto's RoundUp or RoundUp Pro mixed with Cosmoflux, an herbicide manufactured in Colombia that has never been approved for use in the United States (El Comercio, October 8, 2002). On January 13, 2002, the U.S. television program "60 Minutes" described the abundance of coca in this area by analogy to "soybeans in Indiana" and went on to say that such spraying kills fish and cattle, destroys what canopy of the rain forest still exists, and perhaps causes severe body and facial sores and rashes, especially in children. Such spraying near the Ecuadorian border has resulted in large-scale forest, garden, and river pollution, illness, and the death of many Ecuadorians, including indigenous women and children. Sixty thousand acres of coca are so targeted, the result being that other plants subsequently will not grow, but the coca, like the *cocaleros* of the region, grow stronger and adapt. In 2002, the cocaine trade to the United States from Colombia appears stronger and more profitable than ever.

The cocaine export trade is now officially acknowledged as existing in Ecuador, and some of Ecuador's banks are internationally considered to be important money launderers. The FARE-DP (Fuerzas Revolucionarias Armadas del Ecuador — Defensa del Pueblo; Revolutionary Armed Forces of Ecuador — Defense of the People) emerged in the northern Oriente after the coup of January 21. In 2001, another group, Comandante Amazónico Revolucionario (CAR), emerged. Allegedly, CAR is (or was) composed of military dissidents, political figures, and some indigenous leaders. Some people of the Oriente allege that the military organizations called ARUTAM and IWIAS (named after Jivaroan power images) are divided and that some support CAR. Its motto is *fuera yanquis del Ecuador* (Yankees out of Ecuador).

Kidnappings and rural terror have increased in all of the areas bordering Colombia, from the coast through the Sierra and across the entire Oriente, dipping southward to the central west Amazonian region into Canelos Quichua and Shuar territory. In 2000, indigenous ideology coming from a few spokespersons in the Organización Indígena de los Pueblos de Pastaza (OPIP) called for an eastern Oriente indigenous zone that would be closed to nonindigenous Ecuadorians, but open to Colombians. By the end of December 2001, it was announced that the police-military joint task force would operate in all six provinces of Amazonia.

The U.S. military base at Manta has expanded to an intelligence gathering and surveillance system of the southern command that is now larger and more sophisticated than its predecessor in the Panama Canal Zone. The base at Manta together with the Plan Colombia initiative are contested dimensions of Ecuadorian and Colombian (and Panamanian, Venezuelan, Brazilian, and Peruvian) international geopolitics. In 2001 and 2002, the United States provided $1.3 billion to Colombia, which makes Colombia third only to Israel and Egypt in the amount of money received in military foreign aid ($899 million in 2000, *USA Today*, December 4, 2001). The U.S. Senate also approved a package of $567 million to the Andean region for counterdrug activities, cutting $164 million from the Bush administration's request.

Colombian and Ecuadorian indigenous people are caught up in all of the processes entailed in these international politics, inflows of capital, border militarizations, poisonous sprayings, consequent escalating and compounding debts, and ubiquitous promise of wealth. In Colombia, the indigenous groups affected by guerrilla, paramilitary, and drug activities number in the eighties (e.g., Oyuela-Caycedo 2001), while in Ecuador, Cofán, Siona, Secoya,

Napo Runa, Shuar, Chachi, Awá, and Afro-Ecuadorian people are directly affected, and all other people of north coast, Sierra, and Amazonia are, in one way or another, involved in the ramifications of the conflict and the promises of economic opportunities that it ironically offers to some.

As an Andean nation, Ecuadorians share much with Peruvians and Bolivians. They also share a heritage and cultural orientation in their coastal region with people in the Spanish Main countries of Colombia and Venezuela, which extend into Central America and the Caribbean. Their Amazonian systems of ecology, knowledge, and cosmology (e.g., Sullivan 1988) range through Colombia, Venezuela, the Guianas, eastern Peru and Bolivia, and Amazonian and eastern Brazil. Ecuador is a microcosm of South American conflict and contradiction in its modernity, and a model of transformation without bloodshed in its millenarianism. Its Culture of cultures is unique, highly diversified, yet unquestionably connected to other peoples in adjacent and diaspora places (see especially Weismantel, this volume).

Ecuador National Infrastructure

With its wonderful scenery, topographical mosaics, gracious and friendly people, vibrant festivals and arts, and interesting places, Ecuador should have a thriving tourist industry, and indeed tourism provides significant income to the gross national product. From the coast of Ecuador, more bananas are exported than from any other nation in the world, with a history very different from the United Fruit–dominated Central American nations (Striffler 2002). Shrimp farming on the coast, now in remission from the scourge of viral infections, not only provides a valuable export but is also responsible for ecosavagery on the mangrove and tropical rain-forest systems (e.g. Quiroga, this volume). Hundreds of thousands of livelihoods by various Ecuadorian peoples, including indigenous Ecuadorians and Afro-Ecuadorians, are threatened by this modern industry. From the valleys of the Andes comes an escalating export business in roses, carnations, and other cut flowers. And then there is oil, the flow of which brought the economy out of bucolic modernity and into global modernism in the 1960s. Cocaine also contributed: it helped to build banks, many of which crashed under the weight of corruption and millennial capitalism — and it made some people from many nations very wealthy.

In a modern world where international agencies measure the health of the people of a nation in terms of wealth and poverty, the political-economic body of Ecuador is clearly ill. Of a population estimated at thirteen million, 70 percent live in poverty or subpoverty, and 7 to 10 percent live abroad (Weismantel, this volume). Probably 70 percent of the diaspora population

Map of Ecuador drawn by Stephen Holland.

is in another country illegally. In the words of one talented Andean indigenous artist who witnessed firsthand the air assault on the World Trade Center (where thirteen Ecuadorians died) from a vantage point on the Brooklyn Bridge, "Dollarization was fatal to my country; I love the mountains and scenery, but I have to live." Soon after he was selling American flags and T-shirts with American flags near the site of the terrorist attack. Then he sold lapel pins with the American flag for a dollar each and others with an apple showing the twin towers for two dollars each. He earned enough money to buy an expensive T-shirt stenciling machine to take back to Otavalo.

Others reflect differently on dollarization and say that, for the first time in their lives, they know the actual value of their bills and coins and consequently of their labor and products. Remittances from Ecuadorian emigrants now account for a percentage of national income in Ecuador second only to that from petroleum. Money from the Ecuadorian diaspora, in other words, exceeds that from banana, shrimp, tuna, and flower exports. Export of Ecuador's poor is obviously profitable (Weismantel, this volume), and banks spring up rapidly in the regional centers of remittance flows. Profit has its human costs, and Ecuadorians in their diaspora have established an organization called *llactacaru* (distant territory) to press for their rights as human beings and as Ecuadorians. In the new millennium, *llactacaru*, with its own international newsletter and web site (http://www.llacta.org/organize/llactacaru/) and e-mail address (llactacaru@llacta.org), stretches from the United States to Spain (where Ecuadorians constitute the second-largest immigrant group after Moroccans; *New York Times*, April 19, 2002) and includes smaller aggregates in Italy, France, Germany, and Holland.

National economic change may be in the wind, because Ecuador closed 2001 with an inflation rate of 22.5 percent, which, while extraordinarily high, is down from its astronomical 91 percent for 2000. In 2002 the rate had fallen to 13.5 percent. And as joblessness throughout Latin America climbs to about 8.5 percent, in Ecuador joblessness is projected to decline, because foreign investment in Ecuador went up to $184.7 million in 2001 (it was only $26.6 million in 2000). What all this may mean for the essentialist and epochalist features of *el pueblo* and for the essentialist and epochalist features of *la ecuatorianidad* remains to be seen.

The national resources of this country should make it wealthy, healthy, and wise. Ecuador is first in exports in the world in bananas and hearts of palm, second in shrimp and flowers, and the oil wealth of Amazonia is well known. The condition of poverty or subpoverty, however, characteristic of perhaps 70 percent of the population is compounded by the radical decrease in subsistence agriculture, animal husbandry, and other such activities and by the severe pollution of rivers. All agencies of the media document striking examples of embezzlement, theft, blackmail, kickbacks, and many other forms of corruption by prominent people in the top of the class structure. Scores of people take significant amounts of money and leave the country. Those with money in banks that expire are compensated by bonds in the defunct bank or told to wait until the bank transfers funds to another bank at some point in the indeterminable future.

In many parts of Latin America, it is thought that dwellings and properties can become ill through acts of sorcery and witchcraft. Sometimes a shaman or other healer is called upon to diagnose the affliction and cure the entity. In Ecuador, the discourse of social movements of nationalities — indigenous, Afro–Latin American, and others — stresses the idiom of curing the totalized dwelling of *la nación*. Two primary afflictions of this body usually so identified are racism and corruption. There are too few people with too much power and wealth who run the country or compete actively with current people in the "political class" and too many people stigmatized by racialized ideology and praxis. As such, spokespeople for a new democracy in Ecuador argue that the nation lacks dignity and that this lack constitutes illness.

People in the very small upper class divide loosely into two parts, one of which includes those who self-identify as *gente bien* or *gente de bien* (good, proper, righteous people) and as *la sociedad* (the society; the definite article is crucial here). This elite sector constitutes part of the pinnacle of economic control, political power, and social esteem. Parallel to the elite in a sector that is designated by criteria of wealth and power is another oligarchy — sometimes known as *gente de bienes* (people of money; *nouveaux riches* — those whose categorical position is a direct result of accumulated economic and political capital. They are very wealthy people, people of substantial means. Taken together, this small elite sector, divided into old wealth, prestige, and power (the *gente de bien*) and new wealth and political position (the *gente de bienes*), stands apart from other aspiring sectors. All members of these oligarchies self-identify as — and until recently were usually identified by others as — *blancos*.

Like many countries of Latin America, Ecuador's social structure also includes a system of intellectual interaction among men and women of varied economic means. In this system, professors, publicists, journalists, administrators, and artists share and create a tradition of sociopolitical and economic analysis of the nation and the place of its people in the world. Many participants in this system move in and out of politics, present position papers in public forums, publish books, write for prominent newspapers, and even found universities. Prominent examples mentioned in this introduction and elsewhere in this book include Rodrigo Borja, Osvaldo Hurtado, Jamil Mahuad, and Luis Macas.

The concept of *el mestizaje*, the blending body of *la ecuatorianidad*, emanates from the oligarchic positions. *El mestizaje* is a projection of mixture downward from those who stand atop the class and ethnic pyramid. To move upward in wealth, power, or prestige is to engage in *blanqueamiento*, sometimes designated by the more vulgar or pejorative label of *cholificación* (which is also used in Peru and Bolivia). People who are recognized as successful in the sector of economic mobility are sometimes known as *gente de categoría* (prominent people). To compress all of this, and more, scholars writing in English often speak of *blanco-mestizo* society or *blanco-mestizo* people. People in various walks of life struggle to restore national dignity from the structure constituted of ethnic names and racial slurs (e.g., Whitten and Quiroga 1998; Whitten 2003). The various struggles that range from

Afro–Latin American to indigenous, from "popular" classes to intellectual debate, generate social movements of human value. Here emerges the internationalist movement to affirm the *nacionalidades* as veritable Ecuadorian people, and it is here that new powers are manifest and a new democracy is envisioned (e.g., Van Cott 1995). As stated in the opening paragraph to this introduction, the coup of January 21 epitomizes the drama that marks millennial Ecuador.

The bloodless rebellion initiated by indigenous people in 2000, in collaboration with many others, including upwardly mobile and prominent members of the modern military, moved rapidly from crisis through millennial liminality to reaggregation in a modern world where global power exercised especially by U.S. representatives threatened to declare the nation-state of Ecuador, and its people, the "Cuba of the Andes" and to apply all the sanctions necessary to isolate it from contemporary geopolitics and to shut down its international economy.

In chapter 2, William T. Vickers offers a microhistory of a small but significant group, the indigenous Tucanoan-speaking Secoya (sometimes referred to as the Siona-Secoya). Here we can grasp something of the regional-specific contours of a north Oriente chronotope (a sector of space-time; see Bakhtin [1937] 1981) of transformation of approximately 750 people who not only maintain their livelihood in Amazonian ways, but live in the modern and millennial world of two nations. When Vickers first went to Ecuador, some forty years ago, as a member of the U.S. Peace Corps, no one of academic or political authority knew who the Secoya were. Indeed, in his otherwise remarkably accurate "Ethnic Map of Ecuador," Edwin N. Ferdon, Jr., marks their contemporary and ancestral territory as "uninhabited" (Ferdon 1950: fold-out map). By explicating the forces involved in the political transformation of Secoya people, Vickers underscores the cultural and social resilience of indigenous people when they are able to acquire international coping mechanisms. In a couple of generations the Secoya have changed from a position of national and international invisibility to actors in a New York federal court against the mighty Texaco pan-national corporation.

Legacies, Histories, and Memories
Medieval Fragments of Postmodernity

One of the favorite modern labels of those whom Marshall Sahlins (1999: 404–5) says follow the invented traditions of "afterology" is that of "post-colonial society" (e.g., Hansen and Stepputat 2001). The label, which many use to characterize Ecuador and all other Latin American republics, suggests strongly that this modern and millennial sovereign nation-state carries the burdens and manifests the legacies of three hundred years of overseas rule by the Spanish Crown. Such rule was closely articulated to the sacred crucible of the Roman Catholic Inquisition (e.g., Lea 1908) and aimed witchhunts at indigenous people and at African and Afro–Latin American people (e.g., Schwartz and Salomon 1999; Taussig 1986; Whitten and Torres 1998; Quiroga, this volume).

Kris Lane in chapter 3 uses the metaphor "haunt" to discuss colonial and other historical legacies. This is a notion taken from the realm of the spiritual, where "ghosts of the past" either return to or stay with people in the present. Whether people revere what they take as their significant past, disguise it to outsiders (Herzfeld 1997), or "silence" it (Trouillot 1995), that past always has two dimensions: something that happened and the myriad stories told about the event. Historicity and the consequent cultural chronotope lie in the intersection of the event and the narration or imagery (Trouillot 1995:1–30; see also Comaroff and Comaroff 1992). To help understand relationships among features of colonial legacy and republican history and to connect them to modern and millennial Ecuadorian places, Lane offers insights through an explication of five themes: frontiers and borders, mineral extraction, political corruption, and concentration of wealth, racial division, and religion. If we substitute "petroleum" for "mineral," the very same themes are found in Vickers's chapter. Lane points out, among other things, that it is the indigenous people of Ecuador, rather than those in the political-economic classes, who are changing the shape of contemporary and future Ecuadorian democracy (see also Collins 2000; de la Torre Espinosa 2002: 148–49).

With these two exemplars of ethnographic and historic significance, we move deeply into the realm of the sacred, the spiritual, and the downright scary. In chapters 4, 5, and 6, by Rachel Corr, Michael Uzendoski, and Diego Quiroga, respectively, the realms of the spiritual vis-à-vis contemporary life are explored at local and regional levels for the Salasaca people of central Andean Ecuador, the Napo Runa people of Upper Amazonian Ecuador and the Afro-Esmeraldian people of north coastal and riverine Ecuador. Although highly specific and syncretic in their systems of meaning and evocation, the symbol systems presented ethnographically, and with appropriate historical underpinnings, may, under some conditions, take on dimensions of contrastructural powers in the hegemonic totality when people seek to break from national and even global totalizing situations.

Corr writes about Roman Catholic religiosity in Salasaca, a parish of indigenous Andean people often thought to be among the most "traditional" of Ecuador. Their religiosity is infused with medieval European symbols and imagery drawn from Roman Catholicism, including ideas about how to get around purgatory, how to get around dangerous crossroads where demons lurk and where cauldrons of boiling oil are hidden, and how to achieve insights into life through near-death experiences. Salasacans relive and consequently reconstruct historical experiences that stem from the Inca conquest and the Spanish conquest, the former of which may have displaced them from what is now Bolivia, and the latter of which initiated the Spanish Inquisition that sought to bend the bodies of indigenous peoples such that their souls could get stuck in purgatory.

The medieval Roman Catholic symbolism of purgatory is central to contemporary evangelical Napo Runa people of Upper Amazonia, as described and discussed by Michael Uzendoski. His chapter addresses salient issues that, to the best of my knowledge, have been addressed by no one else, and they are critical to an understanding of contemporary Quichua-speaking people. The issues include evangelical Protestantism among indigenous peoples and the cultural mechanism of conversion and transformation involved therein. This takes Uzendoski to the systemic relationships among Amazonian (and, by implication, Andean) people and to Western religion and indigenous lives. As the explication unfolds, we learn about debt peonage, capitalism, ethnicity, indigenous protest, masculinity, femininity, and the living and the dead and their enduring relationships. As the argument based on serious ethnography develops further, the power structure of oppression that unites purgatory in the afterlife and debt peonage for the living is revealed.

Purgatory is also important to the Afro-Ecuadorian population of Esmeraldas (Whitten 1994 [1974] : 127–45) where debt-peonage is a fundamental part of oppressive modernity. In his chapter on Afro-Esmeraldians of Muisne, in the conjuncture of influences from Afro-Esmeraldas and coastal Manabí, Quiroga demonstrates that beliefs infrequently associated with the Christian devil a quarter century ago are, in the late 1990s and twenty-first century, synergistic of critical thought and reflection on economic development. These social reflections and cultural imaginations configure around the devil, as part of the domain of *lo humano* (the human realm), which is the region of the cosmos where we all must live and where we are buried when we die. But the devil and many demons are here, too, and indeed for some we are now ourselves the devils incarnate due to developmental processes. Far from the human realm is that of *lo divino* (the divine sector of the cosmos). A sharp male/female dichotomy enters here, for only women can initiate the opening of the divine to the moral community of men, women, and children. And paradoxically, it is women who people may blame for opening the doors to sin and hell and who are accused of, or referred to, as bloodsucking witches, *las brujas*.

These systems of symbols-in-action constitute rich, enduring, and transforming conjunctures of cosmology and quotidian life that resonate strongly across the topography of Coast, Sierra, and Oriente (see D. Whitten, this volume). Acrylic, oil, and enamel paintings on sheepskin by Tigua people living in areas as diverse yet connected as the páramos of Cotopaxi, urban Quito, Cuenca, and Otavalo yield imagery that, in some cases, is strikingly similar to that described by Quiroga (D. Whitten, this volume). In greater Otavalo, too, *lo humano* and *lo divino* emerge in indigenous imagery as highly salient, just as with the Afro-Esmeraldians and inhabitants of the province of Manabí (Wibbelsman, personal communication, 2002).

We must not take the imagery and symbolism embodied differently but congruently across very different cultural systems as "relics" or "vestiges of tradition." Quite the contrary; these ideas, some with roots in medieval Europe, began to enter Africa by the 1450s (e.g., Russell-Wood 1995) and were part and parcel of the European conquest, Roman Catholic Inquisition, and colonial systems (Wynter 1994; Moreno 1997, 1999; Palmié 2002). For centuries, they were appropriated by and incorporated into the varied and diverse cultural systems of indigenous people and Afro–Latin American people — the very people to whom Spanish conquerors and Creole colonists attributed diabolical powers. They were appropriated as systems of power to resist and transform the very processes that generated them (Quiroga, this volume; Corr, this volume; Uzendoski, this volume; Taussig 1987; Whitten and Torres 1998; Kohn 2002).

Brief Reflections on Anthropological Perspectives on Symbolism and Modernity

To understand the dynamics and endurance of symbolic systems in Ecuadorian modernity, we need to dip briefly into the history of anthropological thought and transformation. During and after World War II, when anthropology began to engage globality and history while preserving its possession of — and passion for — local-level phenomena, exotic places, dark people, and distant lands, schemes to understand transformations from "rural" to "urban" became popular (e.g., Linton 1949). One well known to Americanists was Robert Redfield (1941) in his construction of a "folk-urban continuum." Another less known in the United States but often cited among British social anthropologists was that of Godfrey Wilson and Monica Wilson (1945), who wrote about "the analysis of social scale" in Africa.

Following the framework established by Émile Durkheim, both Redfield and the Wilsons lined up socioeconomic and political variables and then tried to make religiosity and magicality conform to a rural-to-urban transformation to increasingly secular, impersonal, and stratified sets of relationships. This is where they failed, and this is where the undergirding symbolic and fetishist qualities of modernity became suppressed. The cultural imaginaries of people undergoing modernization processes simply do not follow the canon of socioeconomic rationalization. Once again, I want to point out that Peter Worsley (1957) brought millennial movements and chiliastic symbolism into the picture of wrenching, global social transformations some forty-five years ago.

Using only *The Folk Culture of Yucatán* (Redfield 1941) and *The Analysis of Social Change* (Wilson and Wilson 1945) as illustrations, both groundbreaking books found that what one could call "magic," "religion," "folk culture," "primitive culture," "folk healing," "witchcraft," "sorcery," and "divination" (the list is not inclusive) increased under the impress of urbanization and urbanism. They are thoroughly modern phenomena (see also Comaroff and Comaroff 1993), and they represent the symbolic stuff of alternative modernities and contribute to millennial movements (Whitten, Whitten, and Chango, this volume).

These modern imageric phenomena may constitute empowering systems for people living in less-than-satisfactory situations. As Worsley (1957) demonstrated, they could be drawn together in times of collective crisis and stress to help people organize and constitute millennial movements. Modernity emerged out of medieval systems to stress the following components as globalizing ideology: profit seeking; science for economic gain; phenotypic color coding (racializing) of labor; concepts of humans as vestiges or relics of an antipodal past; the "growth" of wealth; fetishism of commodities; commodification of land, labor, and humans; ethnic cleansing; the hypostasis of racial fixity; and the power of print languages. These imageric features as guiding ideological forces for Western colonial and republican political-economic powers transformed the West and wrecked their savagery on the rest.

Millenarianism in its multiple manifestations confronts these forces of modern globalizing ideology as people endeavor to restore human dignity to its inevitable diversity and to forge interculturality on the anvil of this very human difference. Capitalism and millenarianism are both intricately linked to Western democracy. The transformation of modern democracy to a system of equitable social relationships and reasonable life chances for all citizens in a civil society has long permeated the struggles now ongoing in Ecuador. Once again, we come to see Ecuador as a very significant microcosm of localized globality (e.g., Van Cott 1995).

Victor Turner (1974), in his article "Passages, Margins, and Poverty: Religious Symbols of Communitas," bridged the early *puzzle*-ment (*be-wil-der*-ment) of all those who discussed the commonsensical contradictory findings of Redfield and Wilson and Wilson. The contradiction is that as social processes became increasingly "rationalized," and "routinized" in Max Weber's terms, cultural reflexivity and imagery became increasingly "magical" and "supernatural" in Frazer's or Malinowski's terms. These processes are found throughout the class structure and in all systems of prestige and power (e.g., Thomas and Humphrey 1994; Comaroff and Comaroff 2001a; Gaonkar 2001). Where Antonio Vargas might consult shamans before recommending collective action to achieve a democratic goal, Jamil Mahuad turned uncritically to the magicalities and fetishes of the reified and decontextualized "market" to absolve Ecuador's persistent poverty and escalating debt.

Between the promise of wealth and the reality of poverty lie dynamic symbol systems to enhance critical insight and to sustain movements into and out of liminality and into new dimensions of social relationships. Corr (2001) links such concepts as Richard N. Adams's "alternative power," Victor Turner's "power of the weak," and Michael Taussig's "power of the primitive" to the modern possessions of the globalizing state. People within such systems of state power, or "structural power" as the late Eric R. Wolf calls it, come themselves to intensify the strengths projected onto them and to appropriate conceptions embedded and embodied in structural power. With such appropriation, however, comes sustained symbolic counterhegemony as people create what Turner might have referred to as antistructural power, and which I refer to as "contrastructural powers."

Two features of contrastructural powers are the sense of the journey and the processes of symbolic inversion (Babcock 1978; Campbell 1988). In chapter 7, Dorothea Whitten and I, working with Alfonso Chango, directly address these two features that carry special meaning for the Canelos Quichua peoples of Pastaza Province, Upper Amazonia, in terms of such contrastructural powers or antistructural system of power relations. Turner (1974:273) defined "anti-structure" as the "positive, generative center" of social relations. It becomes apparent when collective action takes place and when people evoke the dynamic dimensions of symbols that may, in quotidian life, lie dormant or passive in their institutional manifestations.

In March of 1992, Achuar, Shiwiar, and Canelos Quichua people started off on a collective, pragmatic, millennial journey to Quito to demand usufruct of their Amazonian territories. Soon after, antistructural powers came into play and motivated still further the resolve of diverse people — including Salasacans and Tiguans, among others — from different sectors of Ecuador to march together toward a common liberation from oppressive institutional controls. The myriad local-level symbols discussed throughout this book serve as condensing mechanisms for commonality within diversity.

Ecuadorian Symbolism and Pragmatic Action Issues of Power

We return now to the first epigraph of *Millennial Ecuador:* "The world over, millenarian and revivalistic movements . . . originate in periods when societies are in liminal transition between major orderings of social structural relations" (Turner 1974:53). It resonates with the second epigraph, "Power is an instrument to complement what we are creating: democracy and a new Ecuador" (Vargas 2000:48). The latter is by an indigenous leader who, with many others, turned not only to material forces within the modern nation-state of Ecuador, but also to Andean and Amazonian shamans for symbolic, religious, and mystical support. The fact that social movements and ritual enactment become transformed into a dynamic synergy is summed up by Thomas Abercrombie (1998:421), who writes: "Ritual action is capable of transforming the relationship between context and human subjectivity and, consequently, of transforming the ways in which messages can be interpreted and by whom."

Contrastructural powers may shape and transform a nation, but structural power, the very force held by the rich and influential people and institutions through which they govern, seems never to go away. Unlike vulgar Marxism's prediction attendant on the Russian Revolution, the state does not wither away. It may crumble from time to time, but the reality of nation-states and their systems of governance, taxation, and positioning in a global system seem to endure and grow strong. Most important to state systems are their sovereignty and their territoriality. Boundaries are their instruments and their revered normative symbols of collective identity. When, as is usually the case worldwide, diversity of ethnicity and race exists within a nation, the issue of boundaries arises (see Geertz 1973).

With this in mind, I turn to nationalism and its relationships to racism. Benedict Anderson (1991:149), in his second edition of *Imagined Communities*, writes, "Nationalism thinks in terms of historical destinies, while racism dreams of eternal contaminations transmitted from the origins of time through an endless sequence of loathsome copulations: outside history." According to Michael Herzfeld (1997:21), whose cultural reifications may be instructive when combined with those of Anderson,

The nation-state is ideologically committed to ontological self-perpetuation for all eternity. While it may seek to embrace technological or even social change . . . it maintains to the semiotic illusion of cultural fixity and may well try to impose a static morality on others. . . . The technology for the construction of this timelessness pragmatically connects a mythological notion of pure origins with respect for perfect social and cultural form; innovations are coopted by being treated as the realization of an eternal essence.

In *Cultural Intimacy*, Herzfeld's ultimate hypostasis with regard to what he calls "social poetics" is that "Cultures have national boundaries." To this I would add (Whitten 1999; Rahier, this volume; see also Anderson 1991) that in Ecuador, and elsewhere in the Americas, cultures have socially constructed racialized boundaries. When nationalism in its essentialist and epochalist dimensions (see Geertz 1973; see also Herzfeld 1997) is challenged by the modern and millennial forces of the global economy, as is the case of Ecuador today, then the national boundaries and the racialist boundaries clash and contradict one another (e.g., Rahier, this volume; Weismantel, this volume).

When he was a very young man, Saraguran Luis Macas experienced firsthand the oppression of racism in Ecuador. Through his hard work and extraordinary creativity, he moved upward through the educational and political system to a position in the nation-state as one of the best-known indigenous people not only in that country, but in the world. In the early 1960s, he began to interact with Peace Corps volunteers Linda and Jim Belote. In chapter 8, Macas joins the Belotes to tell a moving story of the formation of indigenous movements — as intercultural movements — in Ecuador and their articulation to Native American movements in the United States. Macas was the vice president of CONAIE when the first Levantamiento Indígena began in 1990, and he subsequently became its president. He gave the initial speech launching the *caminata* from Puyo to Quito in 1992 and has been painted into history by Tigua artists in many dramatic renditions of Ecuadorian millennial movements (D. Whitten, this volume).

While undertaking field research with Canelos Quichua women artists of the Amazonian region, Dorothea Scott Whitten became fascinated with paintings produced by men (and later women) from Andean Tigua. She has followed the development of these paintings from their emergence in the ethnic-arts market in the mid to late 1970s to their contemporary national and international recognition. The painters' ability to communicate significant messages through artistic expression parallels that of the women ceramists of Pastaza Province. In chapter 9, Whitten demonstrates something of the multiple connectivities that led to and lead to a crisscrossing of knowledge, information, symbols, and power formations across very different cultural systems of Amazonia and the Andes. Indeed, the dynamics sketched in this introduction and in many of the book's chapters can be seen in the aesthetic renditions of the Tigua artists and Canelos Quichua potters, as presented in her chapter. She writes that "[t]he Amazonian and Andean artists are actors in the political world and their actions are seen in their arts."

Such a transformative movement in aesthetic systems has an undergirding in modern economics and in the forces of urbanization and urbanism. These modernizing systems take their toll on social and cultural organizations and on the very structure of creativity. In chapter 10, Rudi Colloredo-Mansfeld focuses on Tigua out migrations, mobility systems, the urban ambience of Quito, and the struggle for social recognition as these powerful factors impinge on the lives and livelihoods of bilingual Quichua- and Spanish-speaking artists and their families, whose depictions of Ecuadorian life are so sought after by North Americans and Europeans. Among other things, he offers grassroots insights into the legal system of Ecuador and into the awful effects of midrange corruption on endeavors of indigenous people to find satisfactory life situations as they participate in the increasingly dangerous sectors of urban existence.

Jean Rahier, in chapter 11, zooms down on Quito itself to reveal much of the exoticism and eroticism of racist thought through a depiction of four Afro-Ecuadorian women, all of whom are from Quito, but each of whom is often seen by others as to be from a distant, exotic place, either the province of Esmeraldas, or the Chota–Mira River Valley of Imbabura and Carchi. Rahier takes up the interrelated subjects of race, racism, femininity, embodiment, sexuality, and urbanity as these features are revealed in the excerpts of discussions with four black Quiteñas, each of whom has a very different life style, and each of whom resists dominant national ideology while succumbing in one dimension or another to facets of its racist hegemony. We again encounter the concept of "power" through this explication. Rahier quotes a phrase from Judith Butler's book *The Psychic Life of Power* (1997) to clarify the commonalities in Afro-feminine diversity, and, in so doing, underscores an observation remarkably congruent with indigenous male voices, such as the second epigraph of this introduction: "Power is not simply what we oppose but also, in a strong sense, what we depend on for our existence and what we harbor and preserve in the beings that we are."

Reference to "beings" takes Mary Weismantel, in chapter 12, from "real" market women, called *cholas* in Ecuadorian vernacular, to the male imagery of the romantic, "folkloric," and idealized "brown woman" of the white city of Cuenca, in Ecuador's Austro region. After explicating the contradictions inherent in symbolic renditions and realities of the Chola Cuencana she turns to an even more powerful, and seemingly incongruous symbol of cultural diversity, the Mama Negra (black mother) celebration in the nonblack city of Latacunga, the capital of Cotopaxi Province, where Tigua is located. In the process she provides vivid glimpses of the Ecuadorian diaspora, especially as it exists in the U.S. eastern seaboard focused on New York City and Newark, New Jersey.

Both Rahier and Weismantel point to a transformation now taking place in Ecuador, which is the very strong feminine emergence of contrastructural powers, prestige, and economic standing in virtually every sector of Ecuadorian life. This is a highly significant emergent cultural feature of the transforming mosaic of Ecuador's human topology. It is countered by the hegemonic forces of modernized masculinized whiteness, projected downward from the elite through the "white-mestizo" middle sector in an endeavor to exclude indigenous and Afro-Ecuadorian people, especially women, from participatory democracy, a decent economic situation, and participatory civic society.

An illustration of the struggle that informs these two penultimate works is that of the run for the presidency by Abdalá Bucaram. He and his party chose Cuencana Rosalía Artiaga as his vice-presidential running mate, and they won. But the corruption in this government was noticed in every sector of Ecuador, and on February 5, 1997, Bucaram was deposed by a combination of indigenous uprising, nationwide grassroots protest movements, and a congressional act that decreed him "mentally incompetent." He fled to Panama, where he resides as leader of his Roldosist Party. This event led immediately to the issue raised by some of the appropriateness of a woman president of Ecuador. Artiaga assumed the presidency and held it as a contested office for three days, as seemed to be her right as vice president. A significant number of deputies of the national legislature would not have this situation, however, and they elected Fabián Alarcón, then president of the legislature, as president of the republic, leaving Artiaga entirely out of office and out of power. She was, nonetheless, the first Ecuadorian woman president in the nation's history, even if for a brief time.

In 2002, as the inchoate and liminal presidential race heats up for preliminary elections on October 20, 2002, candidates and precandidates strive for the symbolism of feminine and indigenous contra powers. Osvaldo Hurtado has chosen as his running mate Gloria Gallardo, from Guayaquil; Rodrigo Borja is running with another Guayaquileña, Eva García Fabre; León Roldós (brother of the late Jaime Roldós) is united with Quiteña Dolores Padilla; Lucio Gutiérrez spoke of his need for a *costeña* but chose a male businessman; and Ivonne Baki, Ecuadorian ambassador to the United States, has returned to her native Guayaquil to run as an independent. Antonio Vargas launched his campaign through his party, Amauta Jatari. As of October 2002, the desirable combination of indigenousness and feminism has yet to gel in any systemic manner, and only one indigenous person is in the presidential race. But the symbolic infrastructure has become transformed; a new paradigm is emerging. What was once seemingly unthinkable — feminism and indigenousness in nationalist party politics and in grassroots social movements with political affect — now constitutes a highly salient emergent cultural paradigm. If the two forces of feminine power and indigenous power fuse in practical and political ways and expand paradigmatically, then another truly millennial transformation may take place.

We turn now to the chapters themselves to understand the exquisitely detailed and specific facets of multiculturality that are moving toward an intercultural Ecuador as a microcosm of modern and millennial globality.

ACKNOWLEDGMENTS

In 1990, the Wenner-Gren Foundation for Anthropological Research (grant 5232) sponsored our project in Ecuador and allowed us the flexibility to completely change our focus when the first Levantamiento Indígena took place a few days after our arrival. In 1992, the second truly millennial movement occurred with the indigenous March for Land and Life from Amazonia to Quito. Funds from the National Endowment for the Humanities on the chiliastic symbolism "1492–1992" launched a series of projects that year that led to this edited book. Continuing research over the last decade has been possible thanks to funding from the Graduate College, the Research Board, and the College of Liberal Arts and Sciences of the University of Illinois at Urbana-Champaign. For critical and highly productive comments on drafts of this introduction, I thank, in particular, Dorothea Scott Whitten and Michelle Wibbelsman and, in alphabetical order, Rachel Corr, Kris Lane, Arlene Torres, Michael Uzendoski, and William T. Vickers. For technical assistance, I am indebted to Jennifer Jacobs and Gloria Ribble of the Center for Latin American and Caribbean Studies.

NOTES

1. *Cultural Transformations and Ethnicity in Modern Ecuador* was submitted to the University of Illinois Press in the spring of 1980 and published in the fall of 1981. Because of the death of Roldós on May 24, 1981, the afterword carried a brief notice of his last words spoken in Quito as he boarded the presidential twin-engine Cessna for his fatal trip to Loja: "Ecuador amazónico desde siempre y hasta siempre — ¡Viva la Patria!" (Amazonian Ecuador forever and ever — long live the motherland!). If possible, the reader is asked to consult *Cultural Transformations* for a firsthand view of national and nationalist transformations that characterize Ecuador's intertwined modern and millennial systems. A handful of people like to talk about how "out of date" *Cultural Transformations* is. I submit that it represents a careful presentation by a number of ethnographers who inscribed Ecuador in its modernity at the very point in time when the activities leading to millennial movements were incipient. Chilias-

tic forces were unleashed on the national scene in 1990. For the observant, their underpinnings were apparent if inchoate in innumerable localities in the mid 1970s, and President Roldós signaled attention to them to the entire nation in 1979. In that sense, the data and interpretations in *Cultural Transformations* were well positioned; the focus of its authors, especially on the Oriente's peoples, was appropriate; and the metaphors deployed to express the changes of modernity in many regions were later borne out by dramatic events. As anthropologists, we should not "put the past behind" as in a criticism of "dated books." Systems of cultural transformation require the documentation that sustained ethnography offers, and that is just what *Cultural Transformations* gave to its readership.

2. The scandals occurring in the United States and Europe are reported repeatedly and accurately in the Ecuadorian media. Information appears in Ecuadorian media simultaneously with publications in the United States, Europe, or elsewhere. There is no time lag. Scandals are often front-page news in the nation's most prominent newspapers. They are also grist for endless cartoons. For example, in the Friday section of *El Comercio* there is a section called "Babosadas," by Sajac Najul, which is dedicated to lampooning prominent people by repeating a quotation and then following that with a cartoon. In the July 19, 2002, edition of *El Comercio*, there was a cartoon of the acting U.S. ambassador to Ecuador, Larry Palmer, quoted as saying, "In Ecuador our [the United States's] priority is to reduce corruption and make sure that the guilty are punished." Under the accurate quotation is a cartoon wherein a rat says: "Enron, Worldcom, Global Crossing, Kmart, Merck, Qwest . . . it is said that they are coming to make an assessment [of Ecuadorian corruption]." In July 2002, the word *corruptocracia* appeared in letters to the editor and elsewhere.

3. Mahuad ran as the candidate of the Popular Democratic Party (DP). Populist parties in Ecuador form a tripartite structure of conflict and alliance with the central left and the conservative parties. As they have done in the past, the DP and Mahuad swung right to capture a tentative alliance with the dominant conservative power in the congress, the Social Christian Party (PSC), long the primary bastion of conservative wealth and politics of Ecuador, its primary spokesmen being León Febres Cordero and Jaime Nebot.

4. In April 2002, however, the United States did seem to back, or at least support, a military coup against President Hugo Chávez in Venezuela when the social and cultural base was located in elite businessmen (e.g., Rosen 2002; Ellner and Rosen 2002). Subsequently, rumors of U.S. involvement in the ousting of Chávez persisted. The United States stood alone, however, as the presidents of the republics of Latin America rallied behind the concept of democracy in government; even those powerful figures in executive and legislative branches opposed to Chávez stood behind the Venezuelan electoral process. For history, it might be recalled that September 11, 1973, was the date of the U.S.-sponsored coup against the elected socialist president of

Chile, Salvador Allende. A prominent figure in this coup, in which more than three thousand Chilean civilians were killed, was Henry A. Kissinger, then national security advisor to President Richard Nixon (Volk 2002).

5. *El Comercio*, January 27, 1979. See Whitten 1981c:776–81, 795. In late February 2003, U.S. Secretary of State Colin Powell acknowledged that the U.S. support of this coup was "an error" (*New York Times*, February 25, 2003).

6. There was brief mention in *El Comercio* and *Hoy* of an alleged al-Qaeda member extradited from Colombia to Ecuador (from Bogotá to Quito), who then mysteriously disappeared (Garrastazu and Haar 2001:1–4).

REFERENCES AND CORE BIBLIOGRAPHY

Abercrombie, Thomas A.

1998   *Pathways of Memory and Power: Ethnography and History Among an Andean People*. Madison: University of Wisconsin Press.

Acosta, Alberto, et al.

2001   *Nada solo para los indios: El Levantamiento Indígena del 2001*. Quito: Abya-Yala.

Agee, Philip

1975   *Inside the Company: CIA Diary*. Harmondsworth, Eng.: Penguin Books.

Almeida, Ileana, et al.

1992   *Indios: Una reflexión sobre el Levantamiento Indígena de 1990*. Quito: Abya-Yala.

Anderson, Benedict

1991   *Imagined Communities: Reflections on the Origin and Spread of Nationalisms*. 2nd revised edition. New York: Verso.

Appadurai, Arjun

2001   (editor) *Globalization*. Durham: Duke University Press.

Babcock, Barbara

1978   (editor) *The Reversible World: Symbolic Inversion in Art and Society*. Ithaca: Cornell University Press.

Bakhtin, Mikhail

1981   *The Dialogical Imagination: Four Essays by Mikhail Bakhtin*. [1937] Michael Holquist, ed., Caryl Emerson and Michael Holquist, trans. Austin: University of Texas Press.

Blanksten, George I.

1951   *Ecuador: Constitutions and Caudillos*. Berkeley: University of California Press.

Brito Albuja, Jorge Luis

2000   Es necesario tomar el poder. In *La cuarta vía al poder: El 21 de enero desde una perspectiva latinoamericana*. Heinz Dieterich, comp. Pp. 72–114. Quito: Abya-Yala.

Cabello Balboa, Miguel

    1945   [1582] *Obras*, vol. I. Quito: Editorial Ecuatoriana.

Calderón Cevallos, Alfonso

    1987   *Reflexión en las culturas orales*. 4th edition. Quito: Abya-Yala.

Campbell, Mary

    1988   *The Witness and the Other World: Exotic European Travel Writing,*
           400–1600. Ithaca: Cornell University Press.

Casement, Roger

    1912   *Correspondence Respecting the Subjects and Native Indians Employed*
           in the Collection of Rubber in the Putumayo Districts. House of Commons
           Sessional Papers 68 (14 February 1912–March 1913).

Chancoso, Blanca

    2000   Degradarnos como algo sin identidad. In *La cuarta vía al poder: El 21 de*
           enero desde una perspectiva latinoamericana. Heinz Dieterich, comp.
           Pp. 31–41. Quito: Abya-Yala.

Cobo, Fausto

    2000   *¡No utilicen las armas!* In *La cuarta vía al poder: El 21 de enero desde una*
           perspectiva latinoamericana. Heinz Dieterich, comp. Pp. 115–32. Quito:
           Abya-Yala.

Collins, Jennifer

    2000   *A Sense of Possibility: Ecuador's Indigenous Movement Takes Center Stage.*
           NACLA 33 (5): 40–46, 48, 50.

Colloredo-Mansfeld, Rudi

    1999   *The Native Leisure Class: Consumption and Cultural Creativity in the Andes*.
           Chicago: University of Chicago Press.

Comaroff, Jean, and John L. Comaroff

    1993   *Modernity and Its Malcontents*. Chicago: University of Chicago Press.

    2001a (editors) *Millennial Capitalism and the Culture of Neoliberalism*. Durham:
           Duke University Press.

    2001b Millennial Capitalism: First Thoughts on a Second Coming. In *Millennial*
           Capitalism and the Culture of Neoliberalism. Jean Comaroff and John L.
           Comaroff, eds. Pp. 1–56. Durham: Duke University Press.

Comaroff, John L., and Jean Comaroff

    1992   *Ethnography and the Historical Imagination*. Boulder, Colo.: Westview
           Press.

CONAIE

    2000   *La dignidad de los pueblos: Levantamiento del 21 de eñero 2000*. Video.
           Quito: CONAIE.

Cornejo, Justino

    1974   *Los que tenemos de mandinga*. Portoviejo, Ecuador: Editorial Gregorio de
           Portoviejo.

Corr, Rachel

2001   Modern Landscapes, Ancient Knowledge: Moral Topography, Ethnicity,
        and Shamanic Power in Ecuador. Paper presented at the 100th Annual
        Meeting of the American Anthropological Association.

Dávalos, Pablo

2001   (editor) *Yuyarinakuy: Una minga de ideas*. Quito: Instituto Científico de
        Culturas Indígenas (ICCI) and Abya-Yala.

de Brito, Miriam

2000   La patria antes que la familia. In *La cuarta vía al poder: El 21 de enero desde
        una perspectiva latinoamericana*. Heinz Dieterich, comp. Pp. 133–42.
        Quito: Abya-Yala.

de la Torre Espinosa, Carlos

2000   *Afroquiteños: Ciudanía y racismo*. Quito: Centro Andino de Acción
        Popular.

Descola, Phillipe

1994   [1986] *In the Society of Nature: A Native Ecology in Amazonia*. Cambridge:
        Cambridge University Press.

Dieterich, Heinz, comp.

2000   *La cuarta vía al Poder: El 21 de enero desde una perspectiva
        latinoamericana*. Quito: Abya-Yala.

Donoso Pareja, Miguel

1998   *Ecuador: Identidad o esquizofrenia*. Quito: Eskeletra Editorial.

Ellner, Steve and Fred Rosen

2002   Chavismo at the Crossroads. *NACLA* 35(6):8–12, 50.

Espinosa Apolo, Manuel

1997   *Los mestizos ecuatorianos y las señas de identidad cultural*. 2nd edition.
        Quito: Editorial Tramasocial.

Ferdon, Edwin N., Jr.

1950   *Studies in Ecuadorian Geography*. Monographs of the School of American
        Research 15. Santa Fe: School of American Research and the University of
        Southern California.

Gaonkar, Dilip Parameshwar

2001   (editor) *Alternative Modernities*. Durham: Duke University Press.

Garrastazu, Antonio, and Jerry Haar

2001   International Terrorism: The Western Hemisphere Connection. *North-
        South Center Update*, October 10 Newsletter.

Geertz, Clifford

1973   [1963] The Integrative Revolution: Primordial Sentiments and Civil
        Politics in the New States. In *The Interpretation of Cultures: Selected
        Essays*. Pp. 255–310. New York: Basic Books.

1973   [1971] After the Revolution: The Fate of Nationalism in the New States. In *The Interpretation of Cultures: Selected Essays*. Pp. 234–54. New York: Basic Books.

1973   *The Interpretation of Cultures: Selected Essays*. New York: Basic Books.

Gudeman, Stephen

1992   Markets, Models, and Morality. In *Contesting Markets*. Roy Dilley, ed. Pp. 279–94. Edinburgh: Edinburgh University Press.

2001   *The Anthropology of Economy: Community, Market, and Culture*. Oxford: Blackwell Publishers.

Guss, David M.

2000   *The Festive State: Race, Ethnicity, and Nationalism As Cultural Performance*. Berkeley: University of California Press.

Hansen, Thomas Blom, and Finn Stepputat

2001   *States of Imagination: Ethnographic Explorations of the Postcolonial State*. Durham: Duke University Press.

Harner, Michael J.

1972   *The Jívaro: People of the Sacred Waterfalls*. New York: Natural History Press.

Hernández, Marco Aráuz, Byron Rodríguez V., and Leonel Bejarano

2000   *21 de enero: La vorágine que acabó con Mahuad*. Quito: El Comercio.

Herzfeld, Michael

1997   *Cultural Intimacy: Social Poetics in the Nation-State*. New York: Routledge.

Hill, Jonathan D.

1988   *Rethinking History and Myth: Indigenous South American Perspectives on the Past*. Urbana: University of Illinois Press.

1996   (editor) *History, Power, and Identity: Ethnogenesis in the Americas, 1492–1993*. Iowa City: University of Iowa Press.

Isacson, Adam

2002   Colombia Peace in Tatters. *NACLA* 35(5):10–13, 52.

Jijón, Carlos

2001   *Parque jurásico*. Vistazo, July 19:29–31.

Kissinger, Henry A.

2001   *Does America Need a Foreign Policy? Toward a Diplomacy for the 21st Century*. New York: Simon & Schuster.

Kohn, Eduardo

2002   Infidels, Virgins, and the Black-Robed Priest: A Backwoods History of Ecuador's Montaña Region. *Ethnohistory* 49(3):545–82.

Lane, Kris

2002   *Quito 1599: City and Colony in Transition*. Albuquerque: University of New Mexico Press.

Lea, Henry Charles

    1908   *A History of the Inquisition of the Middle Ages*. 3 vols. New York: Macmillan.

Linke, Lilo

    1960   *Ecuador: Country of Contrasts*. 3rd edition. London: Oxford University Press.

Linton, Ralph

    1949   (editor) *Most of the World*. New York: Columbia University Press.

Lucas, Kintto

    2000a *La rebelión de los indios*. Quito: Abya-Yala.

    2000b *Plan Colombia: La paz armada*. Quito: Editorial Planeta.

Macas, Luis

    2001   Diez años del levantamiento del Inti Raymi de junio de 1990: Un balance provisional. In *Yuyarinakuy: Una Minga de Ideas*. Pablo Dávalos, ed. Pp. 171–178. Quito: Instituto Científico de Culturas Indígenas (ICCI) and Abya-Yala.

Mendoza, Carlos Poveda

    2001   *¿Quién derrocó a Mahuad?* Quito: Ediecuatorial.

Moreno, Isidoro

    1997   *La antigua hermanidad de los negros de Sevilla: Etnicidad, poder y sociedad en 600 años de historia*. Seville: Universidad de Sevilla y la Consejería de Cultura de la Junta de Andalucía.

    1999   Festive Rituals, Religious Associations, and Ethnic Reaffirmation of Black Andalusians: Antecedents of the Black Confraternities and Cabildos in the Americas. *In Representations of Blackness and the Performance of Identities*. Jean Muteba Rahier, ed. Pp. 3–17. Westport Conn.: Bergin & Garvey.

Nordstrom, Carolyn, and JoAnn Martin

    1992   *The Paths to Domination, Resistance, and Terror*. Berkeley: University of California Press.

Oberem, Udo

    1971   *Los Quijos: Historia de la transculturación de un grupo indígena en el oriente ecuatoriano, 1538–1956*. 2 vols. Madrid: Memorias del Departamento de Antropología y Etnología de América.

Oppenheimer, Andrés

    2001   *Ojos vendados: Estados Unidos y el negocio de la corrupción en América Latina*. Buenos Aires: Editorial Sudamericana.

Orta, Andrew

    in press *Catechizing Culture: Missionaries, Aymara and the "New Evangelization."* New York: Columbia University Press.

Oyuela-Caycedo, Augusto

2001   What Can the AAA Do for Indigenous People in Colombia? *Anthropology News* 42(7):7.

Palmié, Stephan

2002   *Wizards and Scientists: Exploration in Afro-Cuban Modernity and Tradition*. Durham: Duke University Press.

Phelan, John Leddy

1967   *The Kingdom of Quito in the Seventeenth Century: Bureaucratic Politics in the Spanish Empire*. Madison: University of Wisconsin Press.

1970   *The Millennial Kingdom of the Franciscans in the New World*. 2nd revised edition. Berkeley: University of California Press.

Ponce, Javier

2000   *Y la madruga los sorprendió en el poder*. Quito: Editorial Planeta.

Quintero, Luis, and Erika Silva

1991   *Ecuador: Una nación en ciernes*. Quito: FLACSO.

Quishpe, Salvador

2000   Una democracia demasiado leve. In *La cuarta vía al poder: El 21 de enero desde una perspectiva latinoamericana*. Heinz Dieterich, comp. Pp. 126–32. Quito: Abya-Yala.

Radcliffe, Sarah A.

2001   Imagining the State As a Space: Territoriality and the Formation of the State in Ecuador. In *States of Imagination: Ethnographic Explorations of the Postcolonial State*. Thomas Blom and Finn Stepputat, eds. Pp. 123–45. Durham: Duke University Press.

Radcliffe, Sarah A., and Sallie Westwood

1996   *Re-Making the Nation: Place, Politics, and Identity in Latin America*. London: Routledge.

Redfield, Robert

1941   *The Folk Culture of Yucatán*. Chicago: University of Chicago Press.

Ricanchi, Nazih

2000a   *Systems of Violence: The Political Economy of War and Peace in Colombia*. Albany: State University of New York Press.

2002b   Colombia at the Crossroads: The Future of the Peace Accords. *NACLA* 35(4):17–20, 44.

Rosen, Fred

2002   Venezuela: Washington Suffers a Setback. *NACLA* 35(6):7.

Russell-Wood, A. J. R.

1995   Before Columbus: Portugal's African Prelude to the Middle Passage and Contribution to Discourse on Race and Slavery. In *Discourse, and the Origin of the Americas*. V. Lawrence Hyatt and R. Nettleford,

eds. Pp. 134–68. Washington, D.C.: Smithsonian Institution
Press.

Rueda Novoa, Rocío

2001   *Zambaje y autonomía: Historia de la gente negra de la provincia de
esmeraldas, siglos XVI–XVII.* Esmeraldas: Municipalidad de Esmeraldas,
Taller de Estudios Históricos (TEHIS).

Sahlins, Marshall

1976   *Culture and Practical Reason.* Chicago: University of Chicago Press.

1994   Goodbye to Tristes Tropes: Ethnography in the Context of the Modern
World. In *Assessing Cultural Anthropology.* Robert Borofsky, ed.
Pp. 377–95. New York: McGraw Hill.

1999   Two or Three Things I Know about Culture. *Journal of the Royal
Anthropological Institute* 5(3):399–421.

Salgado Tamayo, Manuel María

2002   *Drogas, terrorismo e insurgencia: Del Plan Colombia a la cruzada libertad
duradera.* Quito: La Tierra.

Salomon, Frank, and Stuart B. Schwartz

1999   (editors) *The Cambridge History of the Native Peoples of the Americas:
South America,* vol. 3, parts 1 and 2. Cambridge: Cambridge University
Press.

Schwartz, Stuart B., and Frank Salomon

1999   New Peoples and New Kinds of People: Adaptation, Readjustment, and
Ethnogenesis in South American Indigenous Societies (Colonial Era).
In *The Cambridge History of the Native Peoples of the Americas: South
America,* vol. 3, part 2. Frank Salomon and Stuart B. Schwartz, eds.
Pp. 443–501. Cambridge: Cambridge University Press.

Selmeski, Brian

2000   *Imágenes impresiantes.* Video. Quito: Fulbright Commission.

Striffler, Steve

2002   *In the Shadows of State and Capital: The United Fruit Company, Popular
Struggle, and Agrarian Restructuring in Ecuador, 1900–1995.* Durham:
Duke University Press.

Stutzman, Ronald

1981   *El Mestizaje:* An All-Inclusive Ideology. In *Cultural Transformations and
Ethnicity in Modern Ecuador.* Norman E. Whitten, Jr., ed. Pp. 45–94.
Urbana: University of Illinois Press.

Sullivan, Lawrence

1988   *Icanchu's Drum.* New York: Macmillan.

Taussig, Michael

1987   *Shamanism, Colonialism, and the Wild Man: A Study in Terror and Healing.*
Chicago: University of Chicago Press.

Thomas, Nicholas, and Caroline Humphrey

    1994   (editors) *Shamanism, History, and the State*. Ann Arbor: University of Michigan Press.

Torres, Arlene, and Norman E. Whitten, Jr.

    1998   (editors) *Blackness in Latin America and the Caribbean: Social Dynamics and Cultural Transformations*, vol. 2. Bloomington: Indiana University Press.

Trouillot, Michel-Rolph

    1995   *Silencing the Past: Power and the Production of History*. Boston: Beacon Press.

Turner, Victor W.

    1973   Symbols in African Ritual. *Science* 179(16 March):1100–05.

    1974   *Dramas, Fields, and Metaphors: Symbolic Action in Human Societies*. Ithaca: Cornell University Press.

    1985   *On the Edge of the Bush: Anthropology As Experience*. Tucson: University of Arizona Press.

Van Cott, Donna Lee

    1995   *Indigenous Peoples and Democracy in Latin America*. New York: St. Martin's Press in association with the Inter-American Dialogue.

Vargas Guatatuca, Carlos Antonio

    2000   Nos faltó estrategia. In *La cuarta vía al poder: El 21 de enero desde una perspectiva latinoamericana*. Heinz Dieterich, comp. Pp. 42–48. Quito: Abya-Yala.

Vistazo

    2000   Revista de Colección: 45 Años. *Vistazo* 835(6).

Volk, Steven

    2002   *Judgement Day in Chile. NACLA* 36(1):5–6, 43–44.

Wachtel, Nathan

    1994   [1992] *Gods and Vampires: Return to Chipaya*. Carol Volk, trans. Chicago: University of Chicago Press.

Weismantel, Mary J.

    2001   *Cholas and Pishtacos: Stories of Race and Sex in the Andes*. Chicago: University of Chicago Press.

Whitten, Dorothea S., and Norman E. Whitten, Jr.

    1988   *From Myth to Creation: Art from Amazonian Ecuador*. Urbana: University of Illinois Press.

    1993   (editors) *Imagery and Creativity: Ethnoaesthetics and Art Worlds in the Americas*. Tucson: University of Arizona Press.

Whitten, Norman E., Jr.

    1976   *Sacha Runa: Ethnicity and Adaptation of Ecuadorian Jungle Quichua*. Urbana: University of Illinois Press.

1981a (editor) *Cultural Transformations and Ethnicity in Modern Ecuador*.
       Urbana: University of Illinois Press.

1981b Introduction. In *Cultural Transformations and Ethnicity in Modern
       Ecuador*. Norman J. Whitten Jr., ed. Pp. 1–41. Urbana: University of
       Illinois Press.

1981c Afterword. In *Cultural Transformations and Ethnicity in Modern Ecuador*.
       Norman J. Whitten, ed. Pp. 776–97. Urbana: University of Illinois Press.

1985   *Sicuanga Runa: The Other Side of Development in Amazonian Ecuador*.
       Urbana: University of Illinois Press.

1988   Historical and Mythic Evocations of Chthonic Power in South America.
       In *Rethinking History and Myth: Indigenous South American Perspectives
       on the Past*. Jonathan Hill, ed. Pp. 282–306. Urbana: University of Illinois
       Press.

1994   *Black Frontiersmen: Afro-Hispanic Culture of Ecuador and Colombia*.
       Prospect Heights, Ill.: Waveland Press.

1996   The Ecuadorian Levantamiento of 1990 and the Epitomizing Symbol of
       1992: Reflections on Nationalism, Ethnic-Bloc Formation, and Racialist
       Ideologies. In *Culture, Power and History: Ethnogenesis in the Americas,
       1492–1992*. Jonathan Hill, ed. Pp. 193–217. Iowa City: University of Iowa
       Press.

1999   Los paradigmas mentales de la conquista y el nacionalismo: La formación
       de los conceptos de las "razas" y las transformaciones del racismo. In
       Ecuador racista: Imágenes e identidades. Emma Cervone and Fredy Rivera,
       eds. Pp. 45–73. Quito: FLACSO.

2001   Sociocultural Overviews: South America. *International Encyclopedia
       of the Social and Behavioral Sciences*. Neil J. Smelser and Paul B. Baltes,
       eds. Ulf Hannerz, volume ed. Pp. 14607–12. Oxford: Elsevier Science;
       Pergamon.

2003   Symbolic Inversion, the Topology of "el mestizaje" and the Spaces of "las
       razas" in Ecuador. *Journal of Latin American Anthropology*. 8(1):14–47.

Whitten, Norman E., Jr., and Rachel Corr

1999   Imagery of "Blackness" in Indigenous Myth, Discourse, and Ritual. In
       Representations of Blackness and the Performance of Identities. Jean
       Matebu Rahier, ed. Pp. 213–34. Westport Conn.: Bergin & Garvey.

2001   Contesting the Images of Oppression: Indigenous Views of Blackness
       in the Americas. In The Social Origins of Race: Race and Racism in the
       Americas. Special issue, part I. *NACLA* 34(6):24–28, 45–46.

Whitten, Norman E., Jr., and Nina S. de Friedemann

1974   La Cultura Negra del Litoral Ecuatoriano y Colombiano: Un Model de
       Adaptación Étnica. *Revista colombiana de antropología* 17(2): 75–115.

Whitten, Norman E., Jr., and Diego Quiroga

1998   "To Rescue National Dignity": Blackness as a Quality of Nationalist Creativity in Ecuador. In *Blackness in Latin America and the Caribbean: Social Dynamics and Cultural Transformations*, vol. I. Norman Whitten and Arlene Torres eds. Pp. 75–99. Bloomington: Indiana University Press.

Whitten, Norman E., Jr., and Arlene Torres

1992   Blackness in the Americas. *NACLA:* Report 4 on the Américas 25:16–22, 45–46.

1998   (editors) *Blackness in Latin America and the Caribbean: Social Dynamics and Cultural Transformations*, vol. I. Bloomington: Indiana University Press.

Whitten, Norman E., Jr., Dorothea S. Whitten, and Diego Quiroga

2001   Ecuador. *Countries and Their Cultures*. Pp. 659–72. New York: Macmillan Reference USA.

Williams, Jeremy M., and Robert E. Lewis

1993   (editors) *Early Images of the Americas*. Tucson: University of Arizona Press.

Williams, Raymond

1977   *Marxism and Literature*. Oxford: Oxford University Press.

Wilson, Godfrey and Monica Wilson

1945   *The Analysis of Social Change: Based on Observations in Central Africa*. Cambridge: Cambridge University Press.

Wolf, Eric R.

1999   *Envisioning Power: Ideologies of Dominance and Crisis*. Berkeley: University of California Press.

Worsley, Peter

1957   *The Trumpet Shall Sound: A Study of "Cargo" Cults in Melanesia*. London: Macgibbon & Kee.

Wynter, John

1994   1492: A New World View. In *Race, Discourse, and the Origin of the Américas*. V. Lawrence Hyatt and R. Nettleford, eds. Pp. 169–98. Washington, DC: Smithsonian Press.

Youngers, Coletta

2000   Cocaine Madness: Counternarcotics and Militarization in the Andes. *NACLA* 34(3): 16–23, 55.

CHAPTER 2

The Modern Political Transformation of the Secoya

WILLIAM T. VICKERS

Since the 1970s, the small Secoya population of northeastern Ecuador has been transformed from an invisible minority into a recognized political entity on the provincial, national, and international scenes. This transformation has seen the Secoya move from scattered and autonomous settlements to a centralized political system that displays increasing sophistication and effectiveness in dealing with the outside world. The rise of the Organización Indígena Secoya del Ecuador (OISE) parallels and is part of the growth of indigenous political power in Ecuador during the late twentieth and early twenty-first centuries.

This chapter describes and analyzes the factors leading to the political transformation of the Secoya, including such influences as missionaries, bilingual education, government agencies (including IERAC, INCRAE, and INEFAN), regional and national indigenous organizations (CONFENIAE and CONAIE), nongovernment organizations (NGOs), and the national and international news media. Secoya leaders now have an enhanced sense of their ability to respond to the many external threats posed by Ecuador's rapidly developing Amazon frontier, and they have become active lobbyists seeking to promote the welfare of their people. Examples of this growing political activism include a recent lawsuit against Texaco for environmental damage and ongoing negotiations with Occidental Petroleum concerning drilling rights on Secoya lands.

This chapter also considers the 1995 Peru-Ecuador war and the resulting Acta de Brasilia of 1998, a treaty that has allowed the Secoya to reconnect with their Peruvian kin. The Secoya see this as vital to their cultural survival. The impacts of the current Colombian civil war and the U.S.-funded Plan Colombia on Sucumbíos Province are also evaluated. The new organization and awareness of the Secoya reflects larger processes within Ecuador and the world. The many ramifications of ethnic awareness, international politics, globalization, and the information age have shaped the new Secoya reality.

The People

The Secoya are Amazonian natives whose ancestors traditionally inhabited lands from the north bank of the Napo River to the south bank of the Putumayo River near the present border between Ecuador and Peru. Today Secoya settlements are found in both Peru and Ecuador, and all are situated on tributaries that flow into the Napo and Putumayo. Secoya villages in Ecuador are located along the Middle Aguarico River, a northern tributary of the Napo.

The Secoya language belongs to the western branch of the Tucanoan language family. From the late 1500s through the 1700s, the Europeans who entered these regions referred to the Secoya and related Western Tucanoan communities (including the Siona of Ecuador) as Encabellado because of their custom of wearing unusually long hair (Chantre y Herrera 1901). For these explorers and missionaries, the numerous Encabellado communities represented a distinctive cultural and linguistic group. The anthropologist Julian H. Steward (1949) estimated that the Encabellado population numbered about sixteen thousand at the time of European contact.

In the nineteenth century, use of the Encabellado designation waned and outsiders began to use the term Piojé to refer to these communities (Simson 1879, 1886; Tessmann 1930). Other ethnonyms were also used, such as Santa Marías to refer to the natives of the Santa María River and Aguaricos to refer to those of the Aguarico River. However, the proper ethnonym in the Secoya dialect of Western Tucanoan is *pai* (or *bai*), which means "people."

Today the Western Tucanoan speakers of Ecuador are commonly referred to as Secoya and Siona. Indeed, these names have been adopted by the native communities who use them on the official stationery of their communal organizations. The term Secoya is a corruption of Si'ekoya (river of stripes), which is the name of a small tributary of the Santa María River in Peru. This name is actually a reference to the people of Si'ekoya, who painted their faces with stripes. Many Secoya families now living in Ecuador trace their ancestral roots to communities that were located on this stream. They use the term Si'ekoya pai (people of the river of stripes) to refer to themselves. During the twentieth century, missionaries and other outsiders simplified this to Secoya and this form has caught on.

The Siona of Ecuador are the descendants of the traditional Western Tucanoan speakers of the Aguarico River basin who, like the ancestors of the modern Secoya, were once called Encabellado. The principal distinction between the Siona and the Secoya is that the Siona consider the Aguarico and its tributaries to be their homeland (there are other Siona of the Putumayo and San Miguel Rivers in Colombia). The Ecuadorian Siona see the Secoya as more recent arrivals in their ancestral territory. In reality, the Siona and Secoya have always been close neighbors. They speak mutually intelligible dialects of the same language, intermarry frequently, and essentially share the same culture. Many people who today proclaim their Secoya or Siona identity actually have ancestors from both communities.

European contact exacted a terrible toll on the Encabellado population, primarily through the introduction of infectious diseases such as smallpox, measles, and the common cold. The demographic decline probably reached its nadir in the early twentieth century, when many communities suffered epidemics of measles. Although there are no precise data on the population at that time, it is clear that the descendants of the Encabellado were reduced to a few small communities in Ecuador, Peru, and Colombia. On the basis of my community censuses in Ecuador since 1973, it now appears that the Secoya and Siona populations are now growing at a rate of about 2.5 percent per year. This turnaround is probably due to the increased availability of modern medicines and vaccination programs carried out by missionaries and government agencies since the 1950s. Still, the combined Secoya and Siona population in Ecuador remains very small at approximately 750 individuals.

Traditional Culture and Social Organization

Like many native Amazonian societies, the Secoya have a subsistence economy based on shifting cultivation, hunting, fishing, and the collecting of forest foods and products. Their settlements are located along rivers and streams. These sometimes consist of a single dwelling housing an extended family. Other settlements have small clusters of houses for several families. The largest settlements are called *dadipï* (village) and may have fifteen to twenty families in residence. These settlements tend to be widely dispersed and are impermanent because the people periodically relocate to new sites.

In the seventeenth and eighteenth centuries, each Encabellado community was associated with a particular tributary or section of land along the larger Napo and Aguarico Rivers (Vickers 1983, 1989a). These local territories averaged 1,150 square kilometers in size. When people relocated their settlements, they typically did so within their own territories. This pattern is still prevalent among the modern Secoya and Siona, though external pressures have produced a few long-range migrations, such as those in 1941 and 1974 when some Secoya families moved from Peru to Ecuador. The 1941 migration was motivated by the desire of some Secoya to escape the clutches of a *patrón* (white plantation owner) who had ensnared them in a debt-peonage labor system. The 1974 migration was stimulated by the visit of an

American missionary to the Secoya of the Santa María River in the late 1960s. He promised their lives would improve if they joined his mission among the Secoya in Ecuador.

When Jesuit missionaries began working among the Encabellado in the seventeenth century, they quickly realized that each scattered community was completely autonomous. This made the Jesuit effort to unite various communities in large *reducciones* (mission villages) extremely difficult and it eventually failed. Encabellado and Secoya social organization is largely based in household structure and kinship. The kinship system is patrilineal and patrilocal residence is prevalent (although some variation exists). Traditional dwellings were oval long houses inhabited by extended families based on the male line (i.e., the sons remained at home and took wives from outside their patrilineages). The eldest male typically served as the head of the extended family household.

Often, a settlement consisted of a single long house located kilometers from any other household. Other settlements consisted of multiple long houses with their extended families. Some of these were large enough to be considered *dadipï*. The most salient characteristic about Encabellado and Secoya settlement patterns is that they were and are dynamic and shifting in response to social, political, and environmental considerations. Decisions of when and where to relocate were made by the leaders of individual households and they could easily leave an established village to move elsewhere. Such decisions might be motivated by tensions with neighbors, a death in the family, fear of disease, local resource depletion, or other factors. Hence, both Encabellado and Secoya settlements were and are marked by a high degree of flexibility and fluidity, and even established villages have changing compositions over time.

Beyond the individual heads of households, there was another form of leadership based on shamanism. One Secoya term for *shaman* is *yahé unkukï* (drinker of *yahé*). *Yahé* is a hallucinogenic potion made from the woody vine *Banisteriopsis caapi* of the Malpighiaceae family. Its drinkers experience hallucinations similar to those induced by LSD. To become a shaman, a Secoya male must undergo a lengthy apprenticeship that involves fasting, sexual abstinence, and frequent drinking of *yahé* and other psychotropic potions made from plants such as *Brugmansia* x *insignis* and *Brunfelsia grandiflora* (both of the Solanaceae family). This taking of hallucinogens is essentially a vision quest in which the apprentice comes to know the supernatural realms of existence and the many spirits and demons that inhabit them. The shaman is the medium through which the Secoya maintain their relationships with the spirit world, which they believe are vitally important to their health and welfare. Shamans are seen as the supernatural protectors of Secoya communities. They diagnose and cure illnesses, punish evil sorcerers, provide abundant game, and influence the weather via their *yahé* rituals.

In the past, many Secoya youths aspired to become shamans, but only a few had the dedication and tenacity to endure the lengthy apprenticeship. And it took additional years of ritual performance and healing for a novice shaman to gain the confidence and respect of his community. The successful shaman was seen as someone who endured great hardships and sacrifices to benefit his community. Such shamans were community leaders, but they led by example and influence rather than by authority. They could advise, but not command.

The highest status in traditional Secoya society was that of the headman-shaman, the *intipa'ikï* (literally "this one who lives," meaning that the person has lived a nearly perfect life according to the ideals of Secoya culture). These were shamans who led such exemplary lives that their communities reached a consensus that they were the best and most knowledgeable protectors of the people. While Secoya villages might have several shamans, they could have but one *intipa'ikï*. Despite the honor of this recognition, an *intipa'ikï* still led by influence rather than authority. In other publications I have referred to the position of the *intipa'ikï* as that of a "headman-shaman" (Vickers 1981, 1989b). The anthropological literature is replete with accounts of headmen in foraging and village-level social systems whose leadership was ephemeral because it was based on influence alone and lacked any enforcement mechanisms whereby a headman could impose his will on his followers. This description fits the *intipa'ikï* quite well. Indeed, the concept of authority is quite alien to the Secoya ethos and cognitive orientations, which emphasize egalitarian values and freedom of action.

Perhaps the only true authority in traditional Secoya culture was the authority of parents over their children. Indeed, the principal locus of decision making resided in the family and household, which was the nucleus of the social organization. Within this sphere, the male heads of households made the most important decisions, including where to live and when to relocate. The healing reputation of a successful shaman might attract additional families to his village, but he could not detain them should they decide to leave.

Traditional Secoya social and political organization was highly atomistic; there were no tribal chiefs or village leaders who were vested with the power to command. Indeed, the Secoya disparage anyone who "tries to stick out his chest" (i.e., who attempts to assume authority). The prestige of the *intipa'ikï* is based on the gradual development of a consensus that a particular shaman is more knowledgeable and wise than other men and has the best interests of the community at heart. Therefore his views and suggestions are respected. People listen to his advice, but are free to ignore it.

Another important aspect of traditional Encabellado and Secoya culture is that relations among the scattered communities were often marked by suspicion and mistrust. The principal reason for this was sorcery accusations. The Secoya believe that illness and death are inflicted on them by sorcerers. In diagnosing an illness, a local shaman typically projects the blame on another shaman of a different settlement, who is believed to have sent the illness through the air with the aid of an enlisted spirit. Similar theories of disease etiology are very common in native Amazonian societies. And the Secoya, like many other lowland South American peoples, sometimes retaliated by launching raids to kill offending shamans.

This is not to say that all of the relations among the various Secoya communities were bellicose. Intercommunity visitation, feasting, trade, and intermarriage did occur. But as with the Yanomamö of southern Venezuela (Chagnon 1968), such interactions were often tinged with apprehension and the fear that things could go terribly wrong.

Political Transformations

Foreign influences began to intrude on the Encabellado in the fifteenth and sixteenth centuries in a series of early contacts by European explorers and missionaries. In the seventeenth and eighteenth centuries, almost twenty Jesuit missions were established along the Napo and Aguarico Rivers, but these tended to be unstable because the Encabellado resisted the Jesuit effort to combine different communities in larger mission villages. A major reason was that the various Encabellado groups distrusted one another because of their fears of sorcery. The mission settlements also suffered epidemics of introduced diseases and the Encabellado fled those outbreaks. The declining Encabellado missions were terminated in 1767 when King Charles IV of Spain expelled the Jesuits from South America.

Less is known about the Encabellado and Secoya during the nineteenth century. The only references for this period are the sketchy accounts of a few explorers who spent little time among the natives (Osculati 1854; Simson 1879, 1886; Villaviciencio 1858). In the early nineteenth century, the Encabellado were feared and avoided by travelers who canoed by their territories as quickly as possible. The hostility of the natives was based on the fact that their children were sometimes abducted by white slave raiders.

By the second half of the nineteenth century, the term Piojé replaced Encabellado as the general term of reference for the Western Tucanoan speakers of the Napo and Aguarico Rivers. In the latter part of the century, the Piojé had sporadic interactions with river traders, with whom they exchanged hammocks and forest products for tools and other manufactured items. Some communities also fell under the influence of *patrones* along the Napo River. These white and mestizo men used indigenous labor to collect tree resins and other forest products, to clear fields, and to cultivate crops. The labor system was a form of debt-peonage in which advances of shotguns, ammunition, fish hooks, cloth, pots, sewing needles, and other sundry goods were "paid for" by work. Abuses abounded because the *patrones* managed the books so that indigenous debts continually mounted, resulting in a condition akin to slavery. The Piojé living along the Aguarico and its tributaries seem to have been less drawn into this labor than those residing on the Santa María River in Peru, a northern tributary of the Napo.

The 1941 migration of some Secoya families from the Santa María to the Cuyabeno River in Ecuador was motivated by the desire to escape the domination of Mauricio Levi, a *patrón* and plantation owner on the Napo. Here the Secoya established residences within a preexisting Siona community, some of whose members had kinship ties with the Secoya. The mistreatment of the *patrones* affected Secoya families in many ways, but it did not alter the traditional leadership patterns based on local shamans and *intipa'ikï*. When the *patrón* Mauricio Levi died in 1949 (Casanova Velasquez 1980: 82) the Secoya attributed his demise to the sorcery of one of their shamans.

The modern political transformation of the Ecuadorian Secoya began with the arrival of an American missionary family in the Cuyabeno community in 1955. Orville and Mary Johnson were members of the Summer Institute of Linguistics (SIL), a nondenominational Protestant missionary organization that is dedicated to the translation of the Bible into native languages. The SIL worked in Ecuador under a contract with the ministry of education that charged them to develop programs of "practical, patriotic, and moral services" in the "tribes" they worked with (Summer Institute of Linguistics 1969:3). To fulfill these obligations, SIL missionaries typically established bilingual schools and health clinics in native villages. They also promoted small-scale agricultural and livestock projects by introducing cattle and pigs, and new cultivars such as rice, beans, and onions. However, the Johnsons, like other SIL missionaries, were also very keen on converting the indigenous people to their fundamentalist evangelical version of Christianity.

The Johnsons lost no time in trying to wean the Secoya and Siona away from the influences of their shamans and *intipa'ikï*, for they saw the devil's work in the traditional religion and healing practices. The Secoya *intipa'ikï* at Cuyabeno was Fernando Payaguaje, one of the migrants from the Santa María River in Peru. Mary Johnson admonished one Secoya woman not to seek Fernando's cures in the following terms:

"I know Fernando is great among you," said Mary, "but I must tell you that the greatest above Fernando and above the moon and all demons and evil spirits — and Satan himself — is Jesus Christ. He alone is God's Son, and He alone has the power to overcome Satan."

"Fernando works his power from himself and for selfish gain, to hold people in fear. But Jesus is stronger because He comes to us in love. And you and all the Secoyas can have this power and freedom from fear just by taking Jesus into your mind and heart. It is Jesus alone who has conquered death, and He alone can deliver us from fear." (Steven 1988:131)

Over time, the Secoyas increasingly turned to the Johnsons for medical assistance. And some of their earliest and most faithful converts were members of Fernando's family. Yet despite the Johnsons' teachings, none of the Secoya truly abandoned their beliefs in their spirits and shamanism. Often the people consulted both the Johnsons and their shamans when seeking treatment for illnesses, as if Jesus Christ and Western medicines had merely been accepted as recent additions to an already complex and multifaceted worldview that involved hundreds of spirits and supernatural forces.

One of the strategies employed by the SIL was to train a new generation of native leaders who would be divorced from traditional spiritual and religious practices. The new bilingual schools needed native teachers, and these teachers were prepared in annual courses held at Limoncocha, the SIL base camp in Amazonian Ecuador, in the Napo River region. Candidates for this teacher training were carefully selected and groomed by the missionaries, who were quite explicit in proclaiming their desire to establish a new leadership system in the native communities. Unlike the shamans, these new teachers would be fully bilingual and able to represent their communities before government agencies and other outside entities. They would also be evangelical Christians and serve as Christian role models and the leaders of their communities (although they could not bring religious instruction into their classrooms due to the Ministry of Education's curricular policies).

The first Secoya youth selected for teacher training was Celestino Piaguaje (sometimes spelled Piyahuaje), a nephew of the *intipa'iki* Fernando Payaguaje. Much as the Johnsons had envisioned, Celestino became an important leader within the Secoya community. Celestino acknowledged that as a boy he had aspired to become a shaman's apprentice under the tutelage of his uncle Fernando, but that the missionaries had opened a new path for him. He was an extremely intelligent young man and took advantage of this opportunity.

By the 1970s, Celestino was the de facto leader of the Secoya community in many respects. He was the director of the village school and had other native teachers under his supervision. And he led the Sunday services for the Protestant congregation. Finally, he was the Secoya person who most frequently represented his community in dealings with outside authorities.

By this time, Fernando was in semiretirement as the headman-shaman and had even stopped performing *yahé* ceremonies at the urging of his Christian family members. Regardless, he confided that he could still cure people, even without *yahé*. He said his vast knowledge and experience gave him those powers. Some other shamans in the vicinity continued their *yahé* ceremonies, but none of them were fluent in Spanish and none represented the native community in meetings with government officials and agencies. Such encounters were typically arranged by the SIL, which sometimes organized tours of native villages for ministry of education inspectors and military staff officers. On other occasions, native delegates were sent to educational conferences in Limoncocha and Quito. In almost all such cases, Celestino was presented as the teacher and leader of the entire Secoya community.

Although Celestino was energetic, bright, and competent, some people within his community expressed negative feelings about his status and behavior. Unlike most Secoya, he had a salary and could afford goods that were beyond the reach of others. And he did not feel compelled to share his "wealth" with everyone in the community (in the subsistence economy, sharing is a prime value). Celestino himself observed that the Secoya were not accustomed to having someone give them "orders." Since this was not part of their traditional culture, he said the best he could do was to "offer suggestions" to the community.

Celestino was very much identified as a member of a particular extended family. As discussed previously, the family is the basic building block of Western Tucanoan society (both for the ancestral Encabellado and for their modern Secoya and Siona descendants). Family identity and loyalty come before all else, and there are often suspicions and frictions among different families. Celestino's extended family was a prominent one, with close ties to the SIL missionaries, an *intipa'ikï* (Fernado Payaguaje), and a coveted teaching position (Celestino), but it also had rival families whose members were not enthralled at the prospect of being led by someone of another clan.

Things fell apart for Celestino in the 1980s. The proximate cause was that he had an affair with the wife of a fellow teacher and subsequently ran off with her. In the process, he abandoned his own wife and children. After a period of self-exile in Colombia, he returned to Ecuador, but never regained his former status as the preeminent leader of the Secoya community.

Celestino subsequently published an autobiography (Piaguaje 1990) that describes his odyssey from boyhood through his development as a teacher and leader, his painful fall from grace, and his continuing desire to help his people. He currently lives in the frontier town of Lago Agrio, where he works for the ministry of education and prepares bilingual texts for Secoya schools. Despite his past problems, he is now viewed as a Secoya elder and is respected for his great knowledge of Secoya traditions. I consider him one of the greatest living Secoya intellectuals, for he has the knowledge and ability to make sophisticated analyses of Secoya culture and how it contrasts with Western ideas and behavior.

After Celestino's denouement, his younger brother, Elias, assumed the role of community leader. Unlike Celestino, he was not a teacher. But like his older brother he was bright, energetic, and articulate, and he had close ties to the SIL mission. Both Celestino and Elias spoke excellent Spanish, and both had worked closely with Orville and Mary Johnson in the translation of the Bible into the Secoya language. Elias had all of the skills necessary to represent the Secoya before the wider world that was increasingly impinging on them in the 1980s.

The election of leaders was a foreign concept in traditional Secoya society. Shamanic leaders and *intipa'ikï* became recognized via the gradual building of a consensus concerning their abilities and good intentions. Such reputations took many years to develop. Nor was Celestino elected during his 1970s stint as the principal leader of the Secoya. In effect, he had been selected and prepared for the role by the SIL missionaries. Things were bound to change. The presence of the Ecuadorian state in the northern Oriente developed very late due to the region's isolation. There simply was no adequate infrastructure for transportation between the Sierra and Oriente until the middle decades of the twentieth century. Roads did not enter the Aguarico River Basin before the late 1960s. The discovery of a large oil field near Lago Agrio in 1968 changed all that. The construction of a pipeline and roads of penetration soon followed, and the Aguarico region was opened to development and colonization. The new oil fields, pioneer settlements, logging operations, and agribusiness enterprises of the late 1960s and 1970s invaded traditional territories of the indigenous Cofán, Tetete, Siona, and Secoya peoples. Within the political context of the expanding nation-state, native communities needed to develop some form of communal aggregate or "tribal" organization to represent their interests and defend their lands.

As early as 1979, Enrique Vela, an anthropologist with the Instituto Nacional de Colonización de la Región Amazónica Ecuatoriana (INCRAE), was urging the Secoya to establish a formal "tribal" organization to represent the native community in dealings with state agencies. Indeed, Ecuadorian law stipulated that for indigenous communities to be officially recognized they must organize as native *comunas* (communes) and must have elected officers. The government considered such *comunas* necessary to provide a basic administrative structure for articulation with government ministries. And the pioneering Shuar Federation of the southern Oriente (established in 1964 with the assistance of Salesian missionaries) had demonstrated the value of having formally constituted indigenous organizations (Salazar 1981).

In 1983 the Secoya formed the communal organization OISE, which immediately became active in the struggle to increase the expanse of communal territory that was legally recognized by the Ecuadorian state. In 1978, the Siona and Secoya of the Aguarico River had received titles to 7,043 hectares from IERAC, but this was only a tiny fragment of their traditional territory. In 1987, the Secoya held a joint assembly with their closely related Siona neighbors and together they decided to establish the integrated Organización Indígena Secoya-Siona del Ecuador (OISSE). These organizations functioned as communal governments and became the vehicles through which native leaders made representations to the Ecuadorian government on behalf of their people. The native leaders also forged friendships and alliances with a number of influential Ecuadorian citizens, government officials, NGOs, and the regional and national indigenous federations known as CONFENIAE and CONAIE. OISSE continued to lobby for the expansion of the legal land holdings of the Secoya and Siona.

After a long and difficult demarcation process, the Siona and Secoya residing along the Aguarico River received title to four additional plots of land totaling 32,414 hectares in 1989. The resulting communal reserve of 39,457 hectares (395 square kilometers) was substantial by the Ecuadorian standards of the day. Regardless, this area constitutes only one-third of the land the Secoya and Siona communities used before the oil boom.

In 1993, the Siona withdrew from OISSE and established the separate Organización de la Nacionalidad Indígena Siona del Ecuador (ONISE). The Secoya then reverted to the name OISE for their organization. This rupture was precipitated by a disagreement over the handling of Solstice Foundation funds (from Denmark) that had been granted for the demarcation of native lands within the Cuyabeno Wildlife Reserve. Long standing rivalries between certain Siona and Secoya families contributed to the dispute.

As a result of this organizational split, some villages came to be represented by OISE and others by ONISE. It must be noted that OISE villages, while designated Secoya, contain some Siona families. Similarly, some Secoyas reside in the nominally Siona ONISE settlements. While many outsiders find these ethnic complexities confusing, they are completely understandable if one comprehends the degree of intermarriage among the people who are now referred to as Siona and Secoya. As discussed earlier, all are considered *pai* or *bai* (people) in the native dialects, and their historical roots are closely intertwined. The division of OISSE into two separate organizations is understandable if one grasps the fact that Western Tucanoan communities have always been characterized by the processes of fission and fusion in response to changing social, political, and environmental conditions. The interfamily frictions that contributed to the breakup of OISSE have many parallels in the long history of the Secoya and Siona and their Encabellado ancestors.

The internal structure of indigenous organizations such as OISE and ONISE are largely patterned on those of preexisting Ecuadorian institutions and bureaucracies. They follow a Western model of organization that is hierarchical and contains both elected and appointed positions. Within OISE, there are both an overarching set of elected officers (president, vice president, secretary, treasurer) and a board of directors (*dirigentes*), as well as local officers and directors for three settlements (San Pablo, Si'ekoya, and Eno). The central organization also has appointed secretaries of health, agriculture, education, tourism, and women's affairs. Ernesto Salazar made a prescient observation in his study of the Shuar Federation (1981:611) that could be applied to the development of subsequent indigenous organizations in Ecuador:

> It appears that acculturation among the Shuar . . . has been extensive enough to favor the adoption of administrative structures characteristic of western institutions. Indeed, with the establishment of the frontier system, the Shuar became continuously involved in the framework of Ecuadorian institutions.

Although I agree with Salazar's finding that Western administrative structures characterize Ecuador's indigenous organizations, I am not so certain that the Secoya and Siona cases were determined by their degrees of "acculturation." Rather, they had reached a critical period in their history occasioned by the opening of the Aguarico Basin to the competing interests of development and colonization. Something had to be done to protect their land, resources, and civil rights, and it had to be done posthaste. I believe the Secoya and Siona embraced the only administrative model that was suggested to them or available to them. In a sense, this was useful because this model replicated the standard pattern in Ecuadorian institutions, and therefore met the expectations of government officials and others who would deal with the native organizations. But the new organizational structures are alien to the traditional leadership patterns and decision-making processes of the Secoya and Siona people (see Whitten 1985 for similar findings among the Amazonian Quichua).

Secoya village life is now punctuated by frequent community meetings and an annual congress in May to discuss and make policies on the prevailing issues of the day. These are usually held in the village schoolhouses. Like meetings elsewhere, there are agendas, reports, the taking of minutes, discussions, and votes. Many meetings go on for hours, and the Secoya display extraordinary patience for sitting on the hard wooden benches. People often wander in and out or step outside to comfort crying children or carry on side conversations. But the meetings go on and community business is attended to. When meetings come too frequently, some people complain about their interfering with work activities such as gardening, caring for animals, and hunting. Still, the ability of the Secoya to adapt to this new form of governance is remarkable.

Since its inception in 1983, OISE has had several different presidents and many people have served on its board of directors and in other official capacities. Some individuals, such as Elias Piaguaje, stand out because they have served multiple terms in multiple capacities and always seem to be near the center of political influence. Elias, in particular, has served several terms as the president of OISE and currently holds that position. However, not all of his terms have been contiguous, and he has facilitated transitions to new administrations when his time in office was over.

When I first went to Ecuador in the 1960s, the Secoya were, for all practical purposes, invisible. In two years of Peace Corps service, I never heard them mentioned, nor did I see their name on a map. Most of the people of the highlands where I worked had only a rudimentary knowledge of the native peoples of the Oriente. One heard vague references to *aucas*, Jívaros, and Quichuas, but nothing else.

The dramatic rise of the indigenous federations and their political activism since that time have changed things irrevocably. CONAIE, the national indigenous federation, and its political arm, the Pachakutik Party, are now recognized as major forces in Ecuadorian politics. CONAIE's smaller member organizations such as those of the Secoya, Cofán, and Siona are increasingly visible in the national political discourse. Over time, OISE's leaders have become more experienced and sophisticated. They have established networks and alliances that reach into almost every sector of Ecuadorian society and government, and across South America and the wider world beyond. A number of Secoya have traveled to international events, conferences, and training programs. They are regularly represented at meetings within Ecuador and are often interviewed by newspaper and television reporters.

Some Important Issues Confronted by OISE

OISE deals with a plethora of both small and large issues that affect the Secoya community, from cutting the grass on village soccer fields to maintaining relationships with government ministries, regional and national indigenous federations (CONFENIAE and CONAIE), and NGOs. OISE meetings also serve as a forum for the discussion and resolution of internal community problems. One of the principal concerns of the organization is to protect native land, resources, and civil rights. Another is to seek funding from government agencies and NGOs for community projects that are often related to education, health, agriculture, economic development, community infrastructure, and cultural preservation. OISE has also developed policies concerning academic research within its jurisdiction, and reserves the right to refuse projects that do not meet its criteria for benefitting the community.

Space limitations do not allow a description of everything OISE does, nor a discussion of its entire political history. Needless to say, the organization has had its share of internal conflicts and some of its administrations have accomplished more than others. And some of its leaders have been accused of nepotism and malfeasance (such charges are also common in other indigenous organizations and within most Ecuadorian institutions, including the national government). However, there have been a number of critical issues that OISE has faced that deserve mention here. In briefly outlining these cases, I hope to illustrate the importance of the organization and the problems with which it deals.

As described earlier, OISE has played an important role in the process of demarcating Secoya lands and obtaining land titles from the Ecuadorian government. It continues to defend these legalized holdings from encroachment by colonists, illegal logging operations, and poachers. In addition, OISE is currently attempting to acquire additional land use rights in areas that were part of the traditional Encabellado territory, but are not currently deeded to the Secoya.

One of these areas is Lagarto Cocha, a northern tributary of the Aguarico River, which is within the Cuyabeno Wildlife Reserve. OISE has been negotiating with INEFAN (the government ministry in charge of national parks and reserves) for access rights to Lagarto Cocha. Lagarto Cocha is located along the Ecuador-Peru border, and the Secoya would like to use it as a meeting place at which they can reestablish links with their kin in Peru. Given the small and vulnerable populations of Secoya in both nations, such interactions could do much to strengthen Secoya culture via visitation, the sharing of oral history and traditions, reciprocal feasting, and potential marriage arrangements. The 1998 peace treaty between Ecuador and Peru opened the door for such binational contacts between formerly divided indigenous peoples.

One of the most publicized battles of the Secoya has been their participation in a class action lawsuit against Texaco. Texaco played a central role in the development of the Oriente's Lago Agrio and Shushufindi oil fields in the late 1960s and 1970s, and in the construction of the Trans-Ecuadorian Pipeline that carries oil over the Andes to the Pacific port of Balao, just west of Esmeraldas. Since production began in 1971, there have been about thirty major oil spills from the Trans-Ecuadorian Pipeline, with most occurring on the Amazon side of the Andes (Kimerling et al. 1991:60). It is important to note that these spills are not cleaned up and that they eventually enter the region's streams and rivers.

Exploratory drilling and normal production also contribute to environmental contamination by releasing pollutants (Kimerling et al. 1991:65). These include toxic brine (a mixture of oil and underground formation water with toxic levels of salts and drilling chemicals), sulfates, bicarbonates, hydrogen sulfide, cyanide, and heavy metals such as arsenic, cadmium, chromium, lead, mercury, vanadium, and zinc. Many of the rivers in the northern Oriente now carry toxic levels of pollutants (Center for Economic and Social Rights 1994), causing the Secoya and other residents to avoid drinking their water and bathing in their rivers, streams, and lagoons.

Because of these problems, the Secoya, Siona, and Cofán joined other indigenous groups and nonindigenous settlers in a class-action lawsuit against Texaco seeking compensation for $1.5 billion in damages and restoration of their contaminated lands and waters. This suit was filed in New York's U.S. District Court on November 3, 1993 (Salpukas 1993:C3). This venue was chosen because Texaco's home office is in White Plains, New York. The indigenous and colonist plaintiffs were represented by attorney Cristobal Bonifaz of Amherst, Massachusetts, and the Philadelphia law firm of Kohn, Nast, and Graf, which took the case on a contingency basis.

Texaco countered by arguing that New York was an improper jurisdiction and by offering a settlement to the Ecuadorian government in the form of a $10 million cleanup fund. Initially the Ecuadorian government, under the conservative President Sixto Durán Ballén supported Texaco's proposal. Plaintiff attorney Bonifaz commented that this sum was ridiculously low and that the proposed resolution was like "two thieves agreeing to settle with each other while ignoring their victims" (1994). He also argued that the federal court in New York was the proper jurisdiction because Texaco managed its Ecuadorian operations from its White Plains headquarters.

After a long process of discovery and many delays, U.S. federal judge Jed

Rakoff dismissed the class-action suit against Texaco in November 1996, ruling that it should be tried in Ecuador. But in October 1998, the U.S. Court of Appeals for the Second Circuit remanded the case to Judge Rakoff to reconsider his decision. On May 30, 2001, Rakoff again dismissed the case, saying that Ecuadorian courts were the appropriate forum for the litigation. On August 16, 2002, the U.S. Second Court of Appeals let this decision stand. It remains to be seen how the case will fare under the Ecuadorian legal system. Regardless, the active participation of the Secoya and other indigenous peoples in this lawsuit has been a well-publicized and resounding warning to multinational corporations that would threaten native lands and environmental quality in third world countries.

Another important example is OISE's negotiations with the Occidental Exploration and Production Company (OEPC), which has the oil concession known as Block 15. OEPC is a subsidiary of the Occidental Petroleum Corporation of Bakersfield, California (also known as OXY), an oil, gas, and chemical concern that has ongoing production in nine countries and active exploration projects in fifteen countries. OXY employs about 12,400 people worldwide, and its 1997 net sales and operating revenues totaled $8 billion (Occidental Petroleum Corporation 1997).

OXY operates in Ecuador's Amazon region under a contract with Petroecuador that was signed in January 1985. Block 15 is located between the Napo and Aguarico Rivers east of the frontier town of Coca. It covers about 950 square kilometers and is superimposed on a number of indigenous and colonist communities, including the Amazonian Quichua along the Napo and the Secoya of the Aguarico. OXY began its field operations in Block 15 in 1992 and since then has developed five oil fields around Limoncocha in the western part of its concession. In December 1995, OXY reached an agreement with Petroecuador to explore the rest of Block 15, including the portions that encroach on lands titled to the Secoya.

Perhaps learning from Texaco's mistakes, Occidental presents itself to the public as a responsible corporate citizen that is safeguarding the environment and assisting indigenous communities (Williams 1997a, 1997b). Among its stated operational policies are cluster drilling from central drill pads (to minimize scattered wells and concomitant deforestation), reinjection of all produced water, burial of flow lines and pipelines (to reduce risk of ruptures), use of "invisible and smokeless" gas flares, and reforestation with native plant species (Williams 1997a:45). OXY also says it aims to "respect indigenous cultures; encourage government agencies to provide basic services that are available to other Ecuadorians; live in harmony with local communities; [and] help native villages pursue sustainable, self-reliant forms of economic development" (Williams 1997a:47).

By early 1996, the Secoya learned that Occidental Petroleum planned to extend its explorations into the portion of Block 15 that overlapped their communal lands. OISE initially disapproved of OXY's entrance. The Secoya had observed the results of oil "development" and colonization in the Oriente and did not want to see their communities invaded and further polluted. A number of environmental groups and NGOs, including Acción Ecológica and the Coalition for Amazonian Peoples and Their Environment, offered advice and moral support for the Secoya stand against oil.

According to Secoya leaders, threats were made that they might forfeit their communal land titles if they resisted OXY's operations. The Secoya were reminded that subsurface oil and gas rights are state patrimony and that landowners have no legal grounds for blocking state-approved development of oil and mineral reserves. Hence, the OISE's opposition to OXY's plan rested on the principle that small and vulnerable native communities should not be subjected to unwanted disruption (often called "development") that might threaten their cultural survival.

From mid 1996 through 1999, OISE and OXY conducted a series of very complex and rocky negotiations concerning the various phases of the intended oil operations. A complete history of these negotiations would fill several volumes. Agreements were signed, sometimes nullified, and then renegotiated. Incredible pressures were applied to the Secoya community by both state agencies and Occidental Petroleum, and at times OISE broke off negotiations when it believed it was being taken advantage of. In April 1999, OISE demanded that the negotiations cease unless all parties were bound by a code of conduct. OXY initially resisted this proposal, but subsequently agreed to negotiate such a code. These deliberations took many months. Finally, on October 31, 1999, the code of conduct was formally agreed to and negotiations resumed.

After additional months of negotiations, OISE and OXY signed a contract in March 2000 to allow the drilling of four test wells on Secoya lands. The Secoya community was to receive a compensation package of $750,000 for this work. These funds were divided into various allocations, including small cash payments to each native family and funds for a variety of community development projects. The first two test wells drilled by OXY were not promising, and it remains to be seen whether a definitive oil strike will be made in Secoya territory. Should sufficient oil be found to allow production, OISE and OXY will enter a new round of negotiations concerning expanded drilling and compensation for the Secoya.

OISE's negotiations with OXY have been criticized by some Ecuadorian environmentalists and by the Siona organization ONISE, which, to date, has refused to negotiate with oil companies. The Secoya community itself was often divided over the negotiations, and several ballots on specific phases of OXY's operations went against the company. However, OISE was continually reminded by both the Ecuadorian state and OXY personnel that it faced expropriation of some of its lands under the legal doctrine of eminent domain should it continue to resist oil activities. This pressure was probably the decisive factor in leading OISE to negotiate.

On the positive side, OISE accomplished a great deal with its successful demand for a code of conduct to guide the negotiations. This code remains in force and will apply to any future dealings with OXY. Its provisions give the Secoya independent legal assistance, access to technical advisers, and the right to have an independent monitoring team to check for company compliance with environmental regulations. All of these provisions are paid for by OXY. Many observers see the code of conduct as an important precedent that will serve as a model for other indigenous communities to emulate as they deal with multinational corporations.

Crisis in the Northern Oriente

It is not sufficient to analyze the modern political transformation of the Ecuadorian Secoya without some reference to the dramatic and unfortunate events presently occurring in the northern Oriente. Many of these recent happenings relate to the civil war in Colombia and its effects on adjacent areas of Ecuador. While the Secoya have not experienced the worst of these effects, the deteriorating situation may yet engulf them. The Cofán, another small indigenous minority of the region, have suffered more direct consequences of the Colombian situation at this writing.

The Ecuadorian Secoya live in Sucumbíos Province, the northern-most province of the nation's Amazonian region. Sucumbíos is a new province whose lands were administratively separated from Napo Province in 1991. The Aguarico Basin's rapid development and population growth following the 1968 discovery of oil provided the rationale for this subdivision. The principal city of Sucumbíos Province is Lago Agrio (also known as Nueva Loja), a booming oil town located only 16 kilometers south of the Colombian border. Despite its importance as the provincial capital, Lago Agrio is a rough frontier town with many bars, numerous houses of prostitution, and a high crime rate. Several military bases are located in the vicinity of Lago Agrio, including an air force installation and various army posts. These were initially established to guarantee the security of the oil fields that are Ecuador's greatest economic resource and that provide approximately half of the government's revenues.

Before 1995, Ecuador's military forces paid more attention to Ecuador's southern border with Peru than to its border with Colombia. For more than 150 years, Ecuadorian-Peruvian relations were shaped by a territorial dispute and periodic skirmishes along the contested borders of the two nations. In 1828–1829, 1904, 1941, 1981, and 1995 the fighting was of sufficient scope and intensity to be called "war," though neither nation made formal declarations of war against the other. However, in October 1998, Peru and Ecuador signed the Acta de Brasilia peace accord, which has allowed both nations to begin to normalize their relations, promote bilateral trade, and reduce their military forces along their common border.

Lago Agrio and Sucumbíos Province have, by contrast, become more dangerous since 1995. In large measure, this is due to the ongoing civil war in Colombia and its spreading effects. Colombia's department of Putumayo shares a common border with Sucumbíos Province and it produces half of Colombia's coca crop. Large areas of the department of Putumayo are controlled by the guerrillas of the Revolutionary Armed Forces of Colombia (FARC). While the FARC operates with relative impunity in the Putumayo region, its units have been known to take refuge on the Ecuadorian side of the border when pressed by the Colombian army or conservative paramilitary forces. This fact is highly discomforting to the Ecuadorian government, which strongly desires to protect Ecuador's territorial sovereignty.

As early as December 1993, there was an encounter between the FARC and an Ecuadorian patrol (*New York Times* 1993). Several canoes transporting an Ecuadorian antidrug force on the San Miguel River were ambushed by guerrillas armed with machine guns and rockets. After inflicting fourteen casualties, the guerrillas escaped into the forest. Following this attack, Ecuadorian forces conducted sweeps of colonist communities along the San Miguel River and detained a number of people who were suspected of being guerrillas or guerrilla sympathizers. These men and women denied participation or complicity in the attack and claimed to be nothing more than poor farmers who were being subjected to military abuse and torture. This case provoked a human rights controversy and a Quito judge eventually ordered the release of most of the prisoners.

The worsening political situation in Colombia has caused rising concerns among U.S. politicians and calls for greater assistance to the administration of Colombian President Andrés Pastrana. In 2000, Pastrana proposed a $7.5 billion program called Plan Colombia, of which $4 billion would be contributed by the Colombian government and $3.5 billion by the "international community" (U.S. Department of State 2000). Since 2000, the United States has been the primary foreign supporter of Plan Colombia, with allocations of nearly $1.5 billion. While Plan Colombia is a multifaceted program, about

80 percent of its budget is focused on military and police assistance in the fight against guerrilla organizations and narcotics traffickers.

According to Colombia's minister of defense, Gustavo Bell, one of the principal goals of Plan Colombia is to reestablish the presence of the Colombian state in areas now controlled by guerrilla groups and illegal drug cartels (*El Comercio* 2001a). Ecuador's concerns are that increased military action in Colombia will have spillover effects, such as the displacement of refugees and coca cultivation to Ecuador, the use of Ecuadorian territory as a base of operations by Colombian guerrilla groups, and the possible disruption of Ecuadorian civil and economic life due to the spread of the conflict. These fears are well grounded; some of these problems have already begun to manifest themselves.

Both leftist Colombian guerrillas and right-wing paramilitaries frequently travel to Lago Agrio to purchase supplies and to engage in "rest and relaxation" from their fighting. While such visitors wear civilian clothes, they are often able to identify their enemies and not infrequently attack them. In Lago Agrio, it has become common to refer to such killings as *ajustes de cuentas* (settlings of accounts). From January through September 19, 2001, the police in Lago Agrio recorded fifty-four murders (*El Comercio* 2001b). If this is converted to a standard murder rate (the number of murders per 100,000 population per year), Lago Agrio's rate approaches an astounding five hundred per year (the U.S. murder rate averages about eight per year). While some of these killings are criminal acts unrelated to guerrillas and paramilitaries, most people in Lago Agrio attribute their *ola de violencia* (wave of violence) to Colombians and the Colombian conflict. One of the consequences of this violence is that the formerly thriving ecotourism business in Sucumbíos Province is practically dead. The marketing of agricultural products has also been severely affected as buyers are discouraged from entering the region.

Kidnappings have also been on the rise in Sucumbíos Province and most of these are attributed to Colombians. The most notorious case began on September 11, 1999, when twelve people were abducted near kilometer sixty-eight of the Lago Agrio–Tarapoa road (*El Comercio* 1999a). Eight of these (including seven Canadians and one American) were employees of United Pipeline, a subsidiary of City Investing Company that operates an oil field at Tarapoa. The remaining victims were three Spaniards and a Belgian who were on an excursion to the Cuyabeno Wildlife Reserve in Siona territory. The kidnappers were well armed and organized. According to an Ecuadorian woman who was first seized and then released, there were about twelve men and three women dressed in camouflage uniforms and carrying assault weapons, submachine guns, and a radio for communications (*El Comercio* 1999b, 1999c). This witness also reported a clear chain of command within the band and that most members spoke with Colombian accents, while some sounded like Ecuadorians.

The Ecuadorian army quickly mobilized and conducted searches in the rain forest, but it could not locate the kidnappers and their victims. Because the kidnappings took place near the Ecuador-Colombia border many people theorized that the abductors were members of the FARC guerrilla organization. Others suggested the band might be a Colombian paramilitary group or just common criminals. After an initial release of the Spaniards and the Belgian, the eight United Pipeline workers were released on December 19, 1999. Press reports said a ransom of $3.5 million was paid for the oil workers (Carlos Antonio 1999a, 1999b).

Ecuador initially anticipated a large influx of Colombian refugees when Plan Colombia began to be implemented in July 2000. While some have arrived, their numbers, to date, have not been as high as expected. The northern highland province of Carchi is reported to have eleven thousand to thirteen thousand refugees, and neighboring Imbabura 1,322 (*El Comercio* 2001c), although officials say many additional refugees in these two provinces may be undocumented. It is known that 304 are in Sucumbíos Province, where they receive assistance from the Iglesia de Sucumbíos and the United Nations High Commission for Refugees (*El Comercio* 2002a).

One aspect of Plan Colombia that has gained worldwide attention is its fumigation activities. The strategy is to spray coca and opium poppy plantations with herbicides to discourage growers and deny income to drug dealers and guerrilla organizations. This fumigation is being carried out by both terrestrial and aerial spraying with a chemical mixture composed of the herbicide glyphosate and a surfactant named CosmoFlux (CBS "60 Minutes" 2002). While both the Colombian and the United States governments claim this is a safe preparation, many people affected by the spraying complain of serious health effects, including skin rashes, fevers, diarrhea, and untimely deaths. Furthermore, the herbicides are indiscriminate in that they kill food crops and medicinal herbs as well as coca and opium plants. Farmers on the Ecuadorian side of the border, where coca cultivation is rare, have also reported crop losses and health problems, which they attribute to the spraying. In August 2001, the Ecuadorian government made a proposal to Colombia that no fumigation be done within ten kilometers of the border to prevent such problems. The Colombian response was negative.

Small communities of Cofán indigenous people living along the Colombian-Ecuadorian border have experienced some of the worst effects of the spraying program and have been terrorized by paramilitary bands and guerrillas. On December 26, 2000, a Cofán leader of the Yarinal community in Colombia, Henry Pascual, was assassinated by an armed band, presumed to be a paramilitary group. Pascual's wife, Lidia Queta, was also killed. She was four months pregnant at the time. Another assassination on January 3, 2001, took the life of Pablo Diaz Queta, a vice president of the Cofán Traditional Authority of the Valle de Guamez and San Miguel (Abya-Yala 2001). Paramilitaries are also suspected in this case. As a consequence of these attacks, as well as devastating aerial sprayings of gardens in several Cofán villages, about eighty Cofán families have fled Colombia and sought refuge among their Ecuadorian kin residing along the Aguarico River.

Nathan Horowitz, a frequent visitor to the Secoya, reports that residents of the village of Si'ekoya were confronted by FARC guerrillas in September 1999 (Horowitz, personal communication 2002). According to the villagers Horowitz talked to, the guerrillas told the Secoya they would appropriate foodstuffs from native gardens, but the Secoya must not report this to Ecuadorian authorities. The FARC members said they would kill any informers. Horowitz also says the Secoya have not had any recent encounters with Colombian guerrillas. Si'ekoya is located eighty kilometers south of the Colombian border, which is a considerable distance for a guerrilla intrusion into Ecuadorian territory.

As a result of the increasing insecurity in the northern Oriente, Ecuador's armed forces have developed the Plan de Defensa Interna (Plan of Internal Defense). The military presence in the region is being beefed up. Currently there are eleven battalions in the Oriente with ten thousand troops (*El Comercio* 2001d), and new bases are being established. The Plan de Defensa Interna has six objectives: to protect the civil population and its rights and liberties, to achieve the effective control of Ecuador's Amazonian territory, to defend the infrastructure of the national patrimony, to strengthen vigilance and respect for the law, to support the operations of the national police, and to assist activities related to national development and disaster relief.

However, in late February 2002, some elected officials of Sucumbíos and Orellana provinces organized a citizens' protest to complain about the deteriorating conditions in the northern Oriente and the central government's neglect of the region. This *paro amazónico* (Amazon shutdown) began on February 23 as citizens erected barricades on the major roads of the region and stopped all vehicular traffic. Most businesses and shops in the towns of Lago Agrio and Coca shuttered their doors. Demonstrations in Lago Agrio on Sunday, February 24, resulted in the death of one man, Marcelo Zambrano, who was killed in a "confusing incident" between citizens and the police (*El Comercio* 2002b).

The government quickly declared martial law in the two provinces and imposed a curfew. During the morning of February 27, an "enraged mob" burned the building of the electrical utility Empresa Eléctrica de Sucumbíos in Coca, the capital of Orellana Province (*El Comercio* 2002c). Around noon, the police attempted to regain control of Coca by deploying police at street corners and other strategic points, while helicopters dropped tear gas on groups of protestors. A twenty-six-year-old man, Luis Guerra Pachacama, was killed by a soldier's bullet as he watched the demonstrations from the doorstep of his house (*El Comercio* 2002b). The army dispatched units to protect oil wells and other petroleum installations. Catholic church leaders in the region called on the central government to declare a "state of emergency" and to establish a dialogue with the protest leaders (*El Comercio* 2002c).

On February 28, 2002, a legislative commission was hastily formed to mediate the dispute between the two Amazon provinces and the central government (*El Comercio* 2002d). Negotiations between the central government and the Asamblea Biprovincial de Orellana y Sucumbíos began on March 2 at a United Nations building north of Quito (*El Comercio* 2002e). The demands of the Amazonian delegates included renovation of the inadequate and unreliable electric service in the Orellana and Sucumbíos provinces, assistance for the region's farmers, road improvements, and the release of approximately forty individuals who had been detained by the police during the demonstrations. The lifting of the "state of emergency" restrictions was also requested, along with a call to relieve army General Jorge Miño of his command in the Oriente (he was accused of using excessive force in putting down the protests). On March 5, the government and the Asamblea Biprovincial reached a six-point agreement that ended the Amazon strike. This agreement addressed most of the concerns of the delegates from the Sucumbíos and Orellana provinces, save the reassignment of General Miño.

The Amazon strike opened a breach between the military and the civil population of the northern Oriente that may take some time to heal. Many Ecuadorians wondered whether the events in Sucumbíos and Orellana were linked to the Colombian conflict and leftist subversion, but there was no clear evidence for such connections. Rather, the Comité de Paro, which organized the Amazon shutdown, was composed of some of the leading politicians and citizens of the northern Oriente. Still, an editorialist in Quito opined:

> From Quito or Guayaquil, we tend to view the poverty of our nothern Oriente compatriots as something distant, [they are] without light in the middle of violence, unable to transport their products to market, [and] producing goods whose prices fall abruptly. Hopefully, we won't wait for

the violence to reach our cities before we act, as is the custom in myopic nations. (Herrera 2002)

It remains to be seen whether Ecuador's government will follow through on its promises of assistance to farmers and infrastructural improvements in the Sucumbíos and Orellana provinces. Likewise, it is unclear whether a political settlement can be reached between the Colombian government and the guerrillas of the FARC and other rebel groups. Negotiations over the past few years have yielded few results. Given the severe social, economic, and political problems faced by the northern Oriente, the future of the region looks very uncertain.

Conclusion

Over the past two decades, the Secoya have been participants in a nation-wide process of indigenous political enfranchisement. The momentum of the native movement is growing and is resulting in a new political reality for Ecuador. This reality was reflected in Article 1 of the new Ecuadorian constitution of 1998, which declares that Ecuador is a "pluricultural and multiethnic state," and Article 3.1, which says, "It is the primordial duty of the State to strengthen national unity in diversity" (Republic of Ecuador 1998). The old rhetoric of *mestizaje* (ethnic and racial "mixing") has been rejected by Ecuador's indigenous peoples, though it is still advocated by some middle- and upper-class Ecuadorians (for discussions of the *mestizaje* concept, see Stutzman 1981 and Whitten 1981).

The adoption of the 1998 Constitution was an important symbolic act that signifies greater respect for the ancient traditions and contemporary presence and diversity of Ecuador's indigenous peoples and the important contributions they make to modern national life. Conservative fears that the "multiethnic" clause would weaken the state were belied by the 1995 war with Peru, when the vast majority of Ecuadorians rallied behind their nation's cause regardless of their ethnic or regional differences.

The new organization and increasing political sophistication of the Secoya has many roots, including the establishment of schools within their communities, increasing access to information via radio and other media, and opportunities to interact with representatives of other indigenous peoples whose own organizations have served as models to emulate. Relationships with missionaries, government officials, tourists, anthropologists, and NGO workers have also helped shape their understanding of the wider world and, in many cases, reenforced their ethnic awareness and pride in their uniqueness as a people.

At the same time, some prominent Secoya leaders of today are critical of traditional shamanism and the use of *yahé* as a medium through which one may experience the supernatural realms. They see *yahé* as a dangerous aspect of traditional culture that may be documented in books, but not ingested. Secoya leader Elias Piaguaje justifies this position by explaining that the use of *yahé* leads to sorcery accusations, which, in turn, leads to violence and revenge killings. These negative attitudes toward *yahé* can be traced to the influence of the SIL missionaries who worked with the Secoya and branded shamanism as "the work of Satan." However, they have also been reinforced by interactions with uneducated Ecuadorians in the Oriente, who have ridiculed the native religion as "savage" and "irrational." Paradoxically, such people have been known to threaten and beat native shamans because they fear their efficacy and power. A recent study by Luisa Elvira Belaunde (2001:225–29) reports similar attitudes are developing among the Secoya (Airo Pai) of Peru due to their increasing exposure to evangelical religion.

A few Secoya shamans still practice *yahé* ceremonies despite the disapproval of some of their younger and more "modern" community leaders. Some of these ceremonies are traditional in nature while others are arranged by tourist guides for their New Age customers who are seeking self-exploration and mind expansion. The best known tourist shaman is Cesario Piaguaje, a dramatic and delightful man who has been featured in various magazine articles (e.g., Pinchbeck 2001) and programs on the Travel Channel. Catering to such tourists provides much needed income for a few Secoya families. Still, the future prospects for Secoya shamanism seem clouded, since few of today's youths choose to enter shamanic apprenticeships.

The newer forms of indigenous leadership based in the communal organization OISE have achieved many practical benefits for the Secoya of Ecuador, and this bureaucratic structure is likely to evolve and endure. Indeed, OISE's current president, Elias Piaguaje, has announced his intention to help organize the Secoya communities of Peru along similar lines. His ultimate ambition is to institutionalize periodic binational congresses of the Secoya communal organizations. This is an admirable goal, and I believe it would strengthen the Secoya, who, after all, nearly joined the lengthy list of extinct Amazonian cultures.

The Secoya's political space within Ecuador's powerful indigenous movements seems to have been well established within the past two decades. These movements now benefit from national and international alliances and networks, and the growing political awareness and activism of all of Ecuador's native communities. Such progress is long overdue and offers real hope for a better and more just Ecuador of the future.

ACKNOWLEDGMENTS

I would like to thank Norman E. Whitten, Jr., for inviting me to contribute to this volume. I first became aware of his scholarly research on Ecuador in 1970, when I was a beginning graduate student in anthropology at the University of Florida. Although at the University of Illinois, he was generous in responding to my questions and has always given me much useful advice for my research in Amazonian Ecuador. Norm and his wife, Dorothea ("Sibby"), have been trusted friends and colleagues through the years.

I have studied and lived among the Secoya and Siona peoples of Ecuador for various periods since 1972. This research has been supported by a number of funding sources, including an NDEA Title IV Fellowship (1972), the Henry L. and Grace Doherty Charitable Foundation (1973–74), the National Institute of Mental Health (1975–76), the Florida International University Foundation (1979, 1984), Cultural Survival (1980), the National Endowment for the Humanities (1985–86), the School of American Research (1985–86), the Fulbright Scholar program (1994), the Institute for Science and Interdisciplinary Studies (1997, 1998), and the Latin American and Caribbean Center and College of Arts and Sciences of Florida International University (1980, 1984). My affiliations with Ecuadorian institutions have been with the Instituto Nacional de Antropología e Historia, the Instituto Nacional de Colonización de la Región Amazónica Ecuatoriana, the Facultad Latinoamericana de Ciencias Sociales, and the Pontificia Universidad Católica of Quito. I greatly appreciate this support and the many friendships formed with the colleagues and staff of these foundations and institutions.

Needless to say, I am most indebted to the Secoya and Siona people who have been my gracious hosts and research collaborators. Their good humor, friendship, and intellectual stimulation have always made my fieldwork enjoyable and unforgettable. I owe them a great deal.

REFERENCES

Abya-Yala
  2001   Denunciation of the Assassination of Indigenous Cofán Leader of
         Putumayo. Electronic document. http://abyayala.nativeweb.org/
         ecuador/cofan/cofan1.php.
Belaunde, Luisa Elvira
  2001   *Viviendo bien: Género y fertilidad entre los Airo-Pa de la Amazonía Peruana.*
         Lima: Centro Amazónico de Antropología y Aplicación Práctica y el Banco
         Central de Reserva del Perú.
Carlos Antonio, Soria
  1999a Liberados ocho rehenes tras 79 dias de cautiverio. *Hoy* Web site,
         December 1.

1999b Plagio deja incógnitas. *Hoy* Web site, December 21.

Casanova Velasquez, Jorge

1980 Migraciones Aido Pai (Secoya, Pioje). *Amazonía Peruana* 3(5):75–102.

CBS "60 Minutes"

2002 Herbicide Problems. CBS "60 Minutes." January 14, 2002. New York: Columbia Broadcasting System.

Center for Economic and Social Rights

1994 *Rights Violations in the Ecuadorian Amazon: The Human Consequences of Oil Development.* New York: Center for Economic and Social Rights.

Chagnon, Napoleon A.

1968 *Yanomamö: The Fierce People.* New York: Holt, Rinehart, and Winston.

Chantre y Herrera, José

1901 *Historia de las misiones de la Compañía de Jesús en el Marañón Español, 1639–1767.* Madrid: Imprenta de A. Avrial.

El Comercio, Quito, Ecuador

1999a Operativo en la frontera con Colombia. *El Comercio* Web site, September 12.

1999b 3 comunicados oficiales. *El Comercio* Web site, September 12.

1999c El secuestro de 12 extranjeros en la Amazonía. *El Comercio* Web site, September 13.

2001a Las operaciones deben ser conjuntas. *El Comercio* Web site, September 9.

2001b 54 asesinados en manos de sicarios. *El Comercio* Web site, September 21.

2001c Centenares de colombianos solicitan refugio en Ibarra. *El Comercio* Web site, October 24.

2001d Los militares aplican 3 planes en la Amazonía. *El Comercio* Web site, December 10.

2002a Los albergues en Sucumbíos y Napo, listos para los asilados. *El Comercio* Web site, January 14.

2002b Mediación gana terreno en paro Amazónico. *El Comercio* Web site, March 1.

2002c El paro Amazónico se torna violento en Coca. *El Comercio* Web site, February 28.

2002d El enredo Amazónico. *El Comercio* Web site, March 1.

2002e Paro Amazónico: diálogo va por buen camino. *El Comercio* Web site, March 3.

Herrera, Washington

2002 Las penurias del nororiente. *El Comercio* March 5.

Kimerling, J., et al.

1991 *Amazon Crude.* Washington, D.C.: Natural Resources Defense Council.

New York Times

   1993   Colombian Rebels Suspected in Ecuador Ambush. *New York Times*
           December 19: 11.

Occidental Petroleum Corporation

   1997   *Annual Report.* Bakersfield, Calif.: Occidental Petroleum Corporation.

Osculati, Gaetano

   1854   *Esplorazione delle regioni equatoriali lungo il Napo ed il fiume delle*
           Amazzoni. 2nd ed. Milano: Fratelli Centenari e comp.

Piaguaje, Celestino

   1990   *Ecorasa: Autobiografía de un secoya.* Shushufindi, Ecuador: Ediciones
           CICAME.

Pinchbeck, Daniel

   2001   What I Did on My Shamanic Vacation. *Men's Journal* March: 93–98.

Republic of Ecuador

   1998   Constitución Política de la República de Ecuador. Quito: República de
           Ecuador.

Salazar, Ernesto

   1981   The Federación Shuar and the Colonization Frontier. In *Cultural*
           Transformations and Ethnicity in Modern Ecuador. Norman E. Whitten, Jr.,
           ed. Pp. 589–613. Urbana: University of Illinois Press.

Salpukas, A.

   1993   Ecuadorean Indians Suing Texaco. *New York Times*, national edition,
           November 4: C3.

Simson, Alfred

   1879   Notes on the Piojes of the Putumayo. *Journal of the Anthropological*
           Institute of Great Britain and Ireland 7: 210–22.

   1886   *Travels in the Wilds of Ecuador and the Exploration of the Putumayo River.*
           London: Sampson Low, Marston, Searle, and Livingston.

Steven, Hugh

   1988   *Never Touch a Tiger.* Nashville: Thomas Nelson Publishers.

Steward, Julian H.

   1949   The Native Population of South America. In *Handbook of South*
           American Indians, vol. 5. The Comparative Ethnology of South
           American Indians. Julian H. Steward, ed. Pp. 655–88. Bureau of
           American Ethnology, Bulletin 143. Washington, D.C.: U.S. Government
           Printing Office.

Stutzman, Ronald

   1981   El Mestizaje: An All-Inclusive Ideology of Exclusion. In *Cultural*
           Transformations and Ethnicity in Modern Ecuador. Norman E. Whitten, Jr.,
           ed. Pp. 45–94. Urbana: University of Illinois Press.

Summer Institute of Linguistics

1969   *La obra civilizadora del Instituto Lingüístico de Verano entre los aucas*.
Quito: Summer Institute of Linguistics.

Tessman, Günter

1930   *Die Indianer Nordost-Perus: Grundlegende Forschungen für eine
Systematische Kulturkunde*. Hamburg: Friederichsen, De Gruyter & Co.,
G.M.B.H.

U.S. Department of State

2000   United States Support for Colombia (fact sheet). March 28, 2000.
Washington, D.C.: Bureau of Western Hemisphere Affairs, United States
Department of State.

Vickers, William T.

1981   Ideation As Adaptation: Traditional Belief and Modern Intervention in
Siona-Secoya Religion. In *Cultural Transformations and Ethnicity in
Modern Ecuador*. Norman E. Whitten, Jr., ed. Pp. 705–30. Urbana:
University of Illinois Press.

1983   The Territorial Dimensions of Siona-Secoya and Encabellado Adaptation.
In *Adaptive Responses of Native Amazonians*. Raymond B. Hames and
William T. Vickers, eds. Pp. 451–78. New York: Academic Press.

1989a *Los sionas y secoyas: Su adaptación al ambiente Amazónico*. Quito and
Rome: Ediciones Abya-Yala and MLAL.

1989b Traditional Concepts of Power among the Siona-Secoya and the Advent of
the Nation-State. *The Latin American Anthropology Review* 1(2):55–60.

Villavicencio, Manuel

1858   *Geografía de la república del Ecuador*. New York: Imprenta de Robert
Craighead.

Whitten, Norman E., Jr.

1981   Afterword. In *Cultural Transformations and Ethnicity in Modern Ecuador*,
Norman E. Whitten, Jr., ed. Pp. 776–97. Urbana: University of Illinois
Press.

1985   *Sicuanga Runa: The Other Side of Development in Amazonian Ecuador*.
Urbana: University of Illinois Press.

Williams, Bob

1997a OXY's Strategy on Environment, Community Issues Key to Success of
Project in Ecuador's Rain Forest. *Oil and Gas Journal* April 21:44–48.

1997b Foreign Petroleum Companies Developing New Paradigm for Operating
in Rain Forest Region. *Oil and Gas Journal* April 21:37–42.

CHAPTER 3

Haunting the Present
Five Colonial Legacies for the New Millennium

KRIS LANE

The colonial past is an unclosed chapter in Latin America. Its history seems to bequeath to its postcolonial successor an unresolved inheritance. This living inheritance, often politically charged, unsettles unilinear notions of the march of historical time.
— Steve Stern, "The Tricks of Time: Colonial Legacies and
Historical Sensibilities in Latin America"

The Republic of Ecuador has been politically independent for approximately 170 years. By contrast, the Kingdom of Quito, its colonial antecedent, was subject to Spanish rule for much longer, almost three centuries. Thus, Ecuador has been a nation-state for roughly half as long as it was a colony. Given this fact, one might expect to encounter not only substantial colonial buildings and artwork in Ecuador but also numerous, less tangible colonial survivals — perhaps sociocultural, economic, or political patterns that have persisted since before 1830. Beyond this, one might expect to find more and perhaps deeper colonial imprints on the present in Ecuador than, for example, in the United States (an older American nation-state with a shorter colonial past). Even casual observers have tended to affirm these expectations, but does the weight of time alone explain why Ecuador's colonial past seems so persistent in haunting the present?

A concerted project of colonial ghostbusting might serve Ecuador's national psyche someday, but this essay has a more modest aim: to lend historical shape to several of the nation's most troublesome — indeed, seemingly intractable — specters. Given Ecuador's multiple and perennial modern crises, editorializing on what appear to be colonial bugbears has become something of a cottage industry, particularly in Quito dailies such as *El Comercio* and *Hoy*. From the perspective of Guayaquil, the greater coast, much of the south, and even the Oriente the word Quito alone serves to conjure a grand, isolated, and haunted colonial house. The problem with such reflexive reactions is that, like clichés, they resist explanation. However true it may sound, what does it mean to say, "the colonial past is an unclosed chapter"?

Can colonial influences be measured with precision? In what regions or sectors of society are they most manifest? Are there false as well as genuine colonial legacies? Are some specters reconstituted, composite ghosts slapped together to meet particular ends? Is awareness of the colonial past potentially more burdensome than ignorance of it? This essay approaches these and other questions from a historical perspective, with emphasis on the following five themes: frontiers and borders, mineral extraction, political corruption and concentration of wealth, racial division, and religion. In historicizing these themes, some of Ecuador's presumed colonial legacies appear more firmly rooted in the nineteenth and early twentieth centuries; others seem more linked to older, global processes. Only a few may represent genuine continuities, and even these might be more accurately regarded as historically contingent, or altered, recurrences. All have been manipulated by elites at the expense of the common folk.

Frontiers and Borders

It could be argued that the study of history in modern Ecuador grew out of a very particular kind of border studies. Much of the early documentation for the colonial period, particularly with regard to Amazonia, was collected by state-commissioned individuals such as Enrique Vacas Galindo, a turn-of-the-century priest and scholar of Jivaroan languages (Vacas Galindo 1905, 1909). The mission of border historians like Vacas Galindo was not to describe colonial life "on the frontier," but to establish legal precedence, specifically colonial-era documentary support for the modern notion of Ecuador as *un país amazónico*.

Ecuador's long-standing border dispute with Peru, which with luck may at last be resolved, certainly had colonial roots. There have been others. Given the Peruvian invasion of 1941 and subsequent events, most Ecuadorians today tend to think of border issues solely in terms of shame and loss. (An exception may be the apparent Ecuadorian victory in the 1995 War of the Upper Cenepa [Marcella and Downes 1999], but — with all due respect to the "heroes of Tiwintza" — this counted for little in terms of territory regained.) Few remember that Ecuador was at one time the aggressor, a precocious, young, expansionist state quite willing to prey on a weak neighbor embroiled in internal conflict.

On two occasions in the nineteenth century, under Conservative presidents Juan José Flores (1830–34, 1839–45) and Gabriel García Moreno (1861–65, 1869–75), Ecuador sought to annex large portions of southern Colombia. Ecuadorian designs were not simply on patches of rain forest or de facto indigenous territories, but rather included substantial cities such as

Pasto, Popayán, and Cali. Only the tenacity of Colombia's war-hardened political faction leaders prevented Ecuadorian victory on both occasions.

In the same way that Lima repeatedly claimed sovereignty over Ecuador — as a district of the original viceroyalty of Peru — Quito could claim the old governorship of Popayán, a very large subdistrict within its colonial *audiencia* jurisdiction. The problem with these attempts to cobble the modern nation-state from colonial entities was that Lima had never exercised full control over Quito (city or colony), nor Quito over Popayán. Church jurisdictions, furthermore, did not match political ones.

To complicate matters further, the Bourbons entirely redrew viceregal limits in the northern Andes after 1739. Quito consequently pertained to New Granada, with its capital of Bogotá. A century later, at independence, this late-colonial redistricting would render Ecuador but a small province of Bolívar's Gran Colombia (a macrostate that Ecuador's pan-Americanist president Eloy Alfaro would try to revive in 1898).

In short, colonial borders, early and late, were neither firm nor natural. Far more salient were numerous and substantial geographical barriers; entrenched regional elite interests; competing power centers in Lima, Bogotá, and Madrid; lowland disease regimes; and vehemently independent indigenous groups on all sides. These and other factors prevented the formation of neat boundaries before 1830. It was imperial design, not effective possession or local ethnic division, that determined the cartographic shape of the colony. But as in Africa, map was not territory. To assume so was, and unfortunately continues to be, quite deadly (Mamdani 2001).

The old northern Inca border at Rumichaca ultimately stuck, but the other great *frontera* (border) problem, dominion in the Oriente, would not fade so readily. At one time, the Audiencia of Quito boasted jurisdiction over the entire Amazonian Basin region — Andes to Atlantic. This claim was based entirely on the very lucky but ultimately inconsequential 1541 voyage of Francisco de Orellana, which just happened to set out from Quito. During the remaining three centuries of the colonial period, only tiny plots along the Putumayo, Napo, Pastaza, Marañón, and select other rivers were in fact occupied by Spanish speakers. In all cases, Spanish presence, strictly speaking, was thin and discontinuous.

Indigenous resistance, not physical geography or disease, was the principal reason for this state of affairs. Just east of Quito, the Quijos uprising of 1579, though violently put down, effectively squelched Spanish colonization of the Upper Napo. Meanwhile, the southeastern lowlands, which drew hordes of gold seekers after 1549, were entirely abandoned by outsiders after a series of devastating Jivaroan raids between 1570 and 1620 (Taylor

1999, 215–19). Similar resistance negated Pastuzo attempts to colonize Mocoa, on the Upper Caquetá.

Only in 1803 was the jurisdiction of Mainas, a relatively tiny (in Amazonian terms) Jesuit-built enclave on the Marañón, formally recognized as a Quito subdistrict, following the Jesuits' expulsion in 1767 (Porras B. 1987). Because Hispanic colonists from what later became Colombia and Peru were neither more nor less intrepid than proto-Ecuadorians in colonial-era Amazonia, *post hoc propter hoc* claims of sovereignty by these nations must be regarded as equally spurious. In short, the Oriente pertained to neither Quito, Lima, nor Bogotá in colonial times; it was thoroughly indigenous territory.

Unfortunately, in many areas that hard-won respect did not survive independence. Since the days of Bolívar and Sucre, Ecuador, Peru, and Colombia have consistently rejected both autonomous-indigenous and one another's claims to Amazonia. Rather, following the Mosquera-Pedemonte Treaty of 1830, emphasis was placed on expansion of extractive enterprises into what these, like most Western nations, have traditionally regarded as unsettled territory and virgin forest; in short, the "wild frontier."

Cinchona bark, gold, live birds, and other exotic products attracted outside interest following independence, but it was industrial demand for latex in the late nineteenth century that opened the floodgate for atrocities in Amazonia. At worst, they were hauntingly reminiscent of those described by Bartolomé de las Casas in the context of the sixteenth-century Spanish Caribbean. The great Amazon rubber boom, decried for its inhumanity by only a few Western journalists, was certainly as cruel and probably grander in scale than any colonial-era enterprise of pillage (Hardenburg 1912; Casement 1997; Taussig 1986).

Whether colonial revival or something else, in terms of frontiers, the rubber boom drove home this unsettling fact: Quito was virtually impotent in Amazonia. Angry that the nation lacked the necessary capital to penetrate, much less ruthlessly exploit, its own claimed territory, Ecuador's Liberal politicians blocked implementation of the 1890 Herrera-García border treaty with Peru. It did not help that the agreement had been the brainchild of Antonio Flores Jijón, Ecuador's first Progressive president (1888–92) and son of the nation's dictator-founder. Thus, as Colombian, Brazilian, Peruvian, and other foreign capitalists bled the forests of Amazonia dry, killing and maiming as they went, Ecuador could neither brake nor gain much from this neocolonial project. In summary, it was arguably party factionalism in the national period more than colonial machinations or delusions that kept the border with Peru an open wound for another century.

Frontera, of course, also means frontier in the "wild" North American sense, and in the relatively recent promotion of lowland homesteading Ecuador has followed, if somewhat belatedly, a predictably disastrous course. Although more recently imagined — à la the romantic internal colonialism schemes of 1980s Brazil and Peru — as a rancher's or farmer's paradise (Whitten 1985), the Ecuadorian Oriente has long promised other treasures for the entrepreneurial adventurer, large or small. Gold mining is the subject of the next section, but other patterns suggesting colonial persistence, or at least revivalism, are evident.

The experience of modern *colonos* (homesteaders) in Ecuador, like that of the earlier rubber tappers, seems eerily to repeat the colonial past. For displaced Serranos and Costeños alike, living conditions in the Oriente are alternately primitive and urbane, depending on one's distance from roads or resource caches (e.g., petroleum camps). The "civilizing" process, thus defined, is thought to derive from a blend of individual vision and tenacity. Corporations similarly paint themselves unabashedly as heroes, and, as in the idealized North American West, the colonizing folk also pride themselves on personal character traits such as perseverance and resourcefulness.

With such assumptions about the hardness of frontier life in mind, the search for readily extractable wealth is predictably desperate and largely based on legend or misinformation. Environmental degradation, particularly from deforestation and cattle running, is astonishingly quick and universally evident. Worst of all, as in every other Amazonian nation, relations with long-independent indigenous peoples in eastern Ecuador have ranged from strained to murderous. In a seeming paradox, both colonist and corporation ruefully acknowledge these effects, yet neither will discuss causal agency.

Is frontier life, or rather the essentially unmitigated disaster of internal colonialism, a ghost from the *audiencia* days come back to haunt the present? Certainly for historians, a sinking déjà vu feeling is palpable. But, as with border problems proper, it may be misleading to single out Ecuador's colonial past as the prime culprit, or ghost.

This is partly because one could just as easily argue that what is seen here (and throughout Amazonia) is an extention of Western imperialism in the broadest sense. This global process is not just one of capitalist corporations and bourgeois-dominated nation-states competing for resources, but also, as suggested previously, of numerous families and individuals desperately searching to improve on ways of life that they have come to regard as normative (Limerick 1987, 2000). What is novel, at least in some parts of Ecuador, is that all three are seeking, competing for, and rapidly exploiting natural resources in a very old-fashioned (i.e., "measured by the ton") way, but in a radically new and surprisingly fragile ecological context.

This seemingly unstoppable combination of corporate, state, and folk forces of expansion could be said to have defined much of the history of the Western Hemisphere, and indeed the world, since 1492. But, it should also be kept in mind that other, and perhaps equally significant, human colonizations of Amazonia clearly predated the arrival of Europeans. Indeed, desire to transform landscapes is, for better or worse, an almost universal human legacy. This particular ghost, perhaps the only one with the potential to bring about total ruin of the human species, haunts much more than Ecuador (Fernández-Armesto 2001).

In summary, recent battles over Ecuador's borders, particularly in the Amazonian region, have had little to do with colonial realities, but much to do with colonial mentalities of sovereignty. When one considers, especially, the fact of long-standing indigenous independence in Amazonia and notes Ecuador's early claims on southern Colombia, the issue of borders emerges as a prime example of the reconstituted colonial legacy. In order to manipulate public opinion on this matter in recent times, the nation's genealogy has been subjected to numerous and very selective cuts and grafts. In truth, Ecuador's map has never been an accurate representation of its territory (Radcliffe 2001).

This suggestion of state manipulation leads to another problem: if the bloodshed and loss resulting from the Peruvian aggression of 1941 was born of spurious claims, why did it hurt so much? No doubt because, as in nearly all postcolonial nations, the phenomenon of nationalism, however frequently manipulated for nefarious purposes, is genuine. It is not simply a cynical creation but also a sentiment, like Catholicism, that ultimately belongs to the people. Nationalism is not so much rooted in the reconstituted or fabricated glories of the past, but in the pains of the present. For Ecuadorians of all classes, colors, and ethnicities, faced as they have been since independence with seemingly incessant challenges and humiliations, national pride is one salve that keeps despair at bay. This die-hard, underdog nationalism is why one cheers the heroes of Tiwintza and also the national soccer team.

Ghosts of El Dorado

Like its Andean neighbors, Ecuador has long been regarded as one of South America's fabled treasure houses, and not without reason. Since colonial times, gold hoards pertaining to the Inca and their predecessors have been rumored to be hidden in this or that cave, mound, lake, or mountain range. From conquest times to the present, significant caches have in fact been discovered, excavated, and looted. Others have been elaborately faked (Von Däniken 1973).

As noted by the earliest historians of Spanish colonization of the Andes, when searching out a supposedly secreted portion of Atahualpa's ransom in the 1530s, gold-hungry conquistadors, such as Quito's Sebastián de Benalcázar, put many indigenous feet to fire (Cieza de León 1998:216, 325). The Jesuit Juan de Velasco, arguably Ecuador's first nationalist historian, revived several of these tales for moralizing purposes in his classic *Historia Moderna del Reino de Quito* (Velasco 1790:43–46).

Since Velasco's day, references to lost treasure have filled numerous pages in foreigners' memoirs, sometimes accompanied by enigmatic "colonial" maps (Hassaurek 1868; Spruce 1908). The spirit of this bygone era has not disappeared. In the most extreme case, the Llanganatis Andean wilderness east of Ambato continues to lure the intrepid, avaricious, and stupid (Lourie 1991, Andrade Marin 1970).

Even early colonial prospectors knew that the existence of numerous and intersecting cordilleras meant that there was more to be had in the equatorial Andes than pre-Columbian grave goods. In colonial times the region claimed by Quito, as historians are now realizing, produced substantial quantities of raw mineral wealth (Lane 1996, 2002). The fabled emeralds of Esmeraldas and mercury of Azogues proved elusive in the end, and only a little silver was found in the hinterlands of Cuenca and Latacunga. What colonial Quito had, and in quantity, was gold.

Ecuadorians may be duly proud to know that their early colonial predecessors were not as dependent on Potosí silver (i.e., "Peru") as was once assumed (Estupiñán Viteri 1997, Vargas 1980). Unfortunately, as with most colonial topics, there is a dark side. In this case, it was twofold. First, when gold production dwindled rapidly after 1600, the regional economy reoriented sharply toward textile production for Peruvian markets, only to falter in the 1690s (Andrien 1995). Second, mineral exploitation, like textile production after it, exacted an enormous human and environmental cost.

In excavating gold for the benefit of domestic and foreign elites, untold thousands of Native Americans, Africans, and their descendants were violently displaced, enslaved, beaten, and worked to death (Lane 1996). Depopulation of prime agricultural lands, malnutrition, and disease were accompanied by deforestation (for mine timbers and fuel) and widespread mercury contamination (from refining). The disturbance of El Dorado, like the opening of Tutankhamen's grave, seemed to release an immediate and irrevocable curse. Despite the initial promise of prosperity, Quito — city and colony — was much the poorer for its gold boom. This was the object lesson drawn by Velasco, the Jesuit historian.

Jump to the present, or rather, very recent past. It is July 2000: Ecuador's economy is a disaster and national politics are in total disarray. Humiliatingly, the U.S. dollar has just been adopted as the official currency. Meanwhile, Nambija, a rough-and-tumble gold camp high in the hills of Zamora-Chinchipe Province, not far from the Peruvian border, is going bust. In the eye of the storm is a Canadian firm with the appropriately absurd name Canuc Resources (known locally as Andos).

This company, aided repeatedly by Ecuador's Department of Mines and Energy and directly by army intervention in 1999, is bankrupt but will not admit it. In Canada, the Ontario Securities Commission recently (2001) ordered the company to cease trading stock for failure to file a standard financial report. To blame for Canuc's dissolution are a consistently low price of gold, a missed buyout opportunity from a huge multinational, and the continuing exploitation of company holdings by freelance miners whom the company and government call "invaders."

These latter, among Ecuador's hardiest and most resourceful, albeit most environmentally destructive, citizens, are poised to reconquer Nambija completely as soon as Canuc/Andos pulls out. Unlike the foreigners, the freelance miners do not regard mining as a modern capitalist enterprise, a series of hype-and-hope-driven investments aimed at unlimited profit for suburban shareholders in northern latitudes. Rather, they are so poor that "illegally" grubbing for gold amid human waste and in constant danger from cave-ins and rockfall is a subsistence activity. There are numerous women and children living and working in the squalor that is Nambija, but among the young men, the universal dream is to discover just enough gold to buy a plane ticket to Madrid. The Ecuadorian government forcibly removed these miners at the margins from Canuc's claims in 1999.

Such stories of corporate conflict with folk miners are of course a modern commonplace in the Andes and the Amazon (Godoy 1990; Cleary 1990). But Nambija is still somewhat special. In what must be regarded as one of the more unusual twists of Ecuadorian history, in 1979, a North American prospector is said to have located these same mines of Nambija. He conjoined descriptions collected from transcribed colonial documents with hired local guides. It seems that following a series of Jivaroan raids dating to the early colonial period, Nambija, a place-name repeatedly mentioned in the first records, had been lost to "official" history (e.g., Garcés 1957). Thanks to indigenous resistance, it had reverted to the status of hunting ground for almost four centuries.

Suddenly, Nambija, like a good colonial specter, became once again Ecuador's archetypal Oriente boomtown, its great hope and its great shame. There were treacherous footpaths leading to the remote mines, frequent landslides, drownings, murders, rampant prostitution, gambling, armed theft — everything one could imagine in an early-1980s cross between "green hell" and Sin

City; there was even a clapboard disco called Studio 54. There was decadent high life, but also huge and tragic mine collapses, floods, and disease epidemics. Survivors mostly blanch at talk of those days.

In terms of environmental impact, streams and rivers around Nambija quickly became choked with geologically significant quantities of refuse, and, as in colonial times, thoroughly tainted with mercury and human feces. Vast tracts of forest disappeared overnight. Of course, there were also many acts of cooperation and occasional heroism (as predicted by the intrepid *colono* ideal), but, on the whole, Nambija was a national disgrace, a disaster. The only thing that stemmed the tide of destruction was an abrupt drop in gold prices in the mid 1980s. Meanwhile, the nation, as old Padre Velasco might have predicted, gained virtually nothing and lost much.

By the early 1990s, Andean neoliberalism, or "the other path," became the breathless mantra of Quito technocrats. Pressure from foreign lenders was on the rise and oil revenues were stagnant. Gold prices also remained low, but new technologies were available and local labor was, as usual, exceedingly cheap. Ecuadorian legislators were encouraged to reconsider mining laws that had limited exploitation by foreign corporations. With virtually no resistance, the laws were quickly relaxed during the presidency of Sixto Durán Ballén (*Engineering and Mining Journal* 1995).

It was in this new, relaxed environment that companies such as Canuc accepted the government's invitation to dig without restriction, only to fail to produce a profit after fouling more local streams and deeply upsetting Nambija's already desperate community of artisanal miners. It should be kept in mind that Canuc's aim was not to mine Nambija's gold itself (hence its clunky, 1920s-style operation), but rather to bait a huge multinational corporation capable of operating profitably in a cheap-gold world. Engineers from Placer Dome, as of this writing (spring 2002), the world's fifth-largest gold-mining corporation, came to have a look around in 1998, but ultimately declined to acquire the mine. Foreigners, in any case, were allowed to gamble freely with Ecuadorian chips and to do so with armed Ecuadorian protection. Canuc lost, but many such speculations continue. A quick Internet search pulls up dozens of foreign mining corporations that have fared rather well in post-1991 Ecuador.

A few salient examples: Across Ecuador's southern mountains to the west, practically the entire town of Zaruma, the Americas' longest, continuously running gold camp, is being courted by another Canadian firm. Major test drilling was near completion in July 2000. This company bears the inconspicuous name of "I Am Gold" (known locally as "Yangol") and, unlike tiny Canuc, it controls major stakes in a number of gold properties in developing countries, most in West Africa. East of Quito, the alluvial gold of the Upper Napo, which has been only marginally exploited since colonial times, is claimed by yet another Canadian firm, Ascendant Exploration.

There are many other similar examples from Esmeraldas to El Oro, and mineral deposits such as copper and silver are also being examined closely. Some of the deposits are said to be very large, perhaps large enough to re-direct Ecuadorian history. One is tempted to call this trend "neocolonial," but "neoliberal," in the literal, historical sense of the term, might be more appropriate.

Ecuador's recent shift in mining policy is less a return to colonial times than it is a revival of policies dating to the late nineteenth and early twenti-eth centuries. It was in this period, after all, beginning in the 1870s, that truly foreign (i.e., not Spanish colonial) capital first made a move to mine in Ec-uador. The focus during the Gilded Age was almost entirely on the proven gold reserves of Zaruma. From the perspective of foreign investors, Ecua-dor's gold was especially attractive for two reasons: it was conveniently dis-tant from the capital city of Quito and it was close to the Pacific Ocean. A rail link to the coast was immediately planned. It was oddly similar, by the way, to the one described in Joseph Conrad's *Nostromo*.

First came the British, establishing in 1880 the Great Zaruma Gold Mining Company. After difficulties with the rail link, they sold out to the North Amer-icans who, in the midst of Eloy Alfaro's Liberal Revolution in the 1890s, formed the South American Development Company in 1896. The latter, still remembered by old timers today as la SADCO, operated substantial mines in the Zaruma-Portovelo district until 1950. The reasons for the pullout in-cluded flooding of the deepest mine works, but the deciding factor was labor struggles. These latter combined, in the end, with a growing recognition on the part of the Ecuadorian government that the nation was being bled, and cheaply, of its riches.

Like many Andean nations in this not-so-distant period (most of which claimed vastly greater mineral wealth, e.g., Bolivia, Peru, and Chile), Ecua-dor responded to "underdevelopment" by restricting foreign investment and bolstering labor laws (Cueva 1982). The nation, momentarily invigorated by the exposure of foreign dependency, set out to manage its own resources. As in colonial times, however, domestic capital and domestic technical sup-port — not to mention political resolve — were lacking.

Although the old environmental impacts were perhaps dampened by declining gold output after la SADCO's departure, Ecuadorian mining essen-tially went from science to art. In short, mining reverted, in a very real sense, to colonial forms (technique, capital structure, labor arrangements). Al-though this artisanal form of mining is of interest to social scientists, unfortunately for the local folk "colonial" devolution has brought neither prosperity nor security, nor for that matter, good health. Migration, as one result, so essential to survival, became a permanent feature of the mining districts. Given the failure of the state to improve living conditions, it is little wonder that many residents of Zaruma and Portovelo today wish "Yangol" success.

In summary, the story of gold mining, as with the much better known story of oil, reads like a cautionary tale. With all these riches, why can't Ecuador be rich? Why do mineral resources always end up benefiting outsiders? Why must their exploitation ruin the environment? And why does the path of exploitation, foreign or domestic, seem to lead, as if inevitably, to deeper debt?

The conundrum, or curse, certainly has colonial echoes. One recognizes immediately the urge to quick riches, the violent disregard for ecosystems and native rights, the careless exploitation of labor. But viewed closer up, the processes and patterns of the last decade are more reminiscent of nineteenth-century Liberalism, when Ecuador was a weak and needy nation-state seeking aid from abroad. Perhaps the current, millennial revival of un-challenged global capitalism (Comaroff and Comaroff 2001) is but another "trick of time."

Corruption and Latifundismo

In the 1630s, Quito's *audiencia* president, Dr. Antonio de Morga, was charged with graft on a grand scale. Apparently, the kingdom's highest-ranking public servant was not a servant at all, but a colonial wanna-be prince. Whereas modern Ecuadorian presidents charged with corruption have routinely fled to Panama with ill-gotten millions, Morga arrived in Quito from Panama with his wealth in 1615. His considerable baggage included hundreds of bales of contraband Chinese silks that had somehow followed him from his previous post in Manila (Phelan 1967:296–307).

Still more reminiscent of a modern politician, perhaps, Morga was unrepentant despite proven guilt. As far as the president was concerned, he had done nothing wrong. He died in the midst of a multiyear investigation believing thus. The president's story might be dismissed as ephemeral except for one fact: in Ecuador, the idea that public office is something akin to winning a lottery has persisted. Denial of wrongdoing in the face of incontrovertible proof remains standard practice. Even worse, the notion of sincerely sacrificing one's own interests for the public good is regarded, as in baroque times, as appropriate only for religious figures. (The bizarrely ascetic twentieth-century populist José María Velasco Ibarra may be the exception that proves the rule.)

The same period as Morga's administration, the early seventeenth century, witnessed the maturation of mercantile capitalism in Quito and its hinterland. Forced indigenous and African labor was harnessed to mines, haciendas, ranches, tanneries, artisanal shops, and protoindustrial textile mills. Cloth and leather goods, along with some agricultural products, were then shipped by Quito's wholesalers via Guayaquil to the viceregal capital of Lima, and to the silver city of Potosí. A food subsidy was sent to ships in the Pacific (most of them built by African slaves in Guayaquil) and to Panama. Imports, meanwhile, consisted largely of European and East Asian luxury goods to be consumed by men such as Morga and their cronies. Thus were personal loyalties, the true coin of the realm, maintained.

A mixed Creole-peninsular elite emerged quickly in colonial Ecuador, blending mercantile savvy with traditional *latifundismo (latifundium)*. The attraction was natural: compared with most of Peru, Quito was flat, wet, and green. Beginning in the 1590s, the Habsburg crown inadvertently encouraged elite land consolidation by the process of *composición* (titling), always at the expense of indigenous communities. This process, intended solely to raise cash, would eventually result in the formation of haciendas whose names survive today.

By the early seventeenth century, the Catholic church also emerged as a major beneficiary of colonial economic expansion, and religious corporate groups such as the Franciscans and the Jesuits (Cushner 1982) made the most of the temporary bonanza. Within a century of European conquest, then, a handful of Hispanic elite clans and church organizations controlled the vast majority of Andean Quito's arable lands and pastures.

Clearly, *latifundismo* and what is today regarded as political corruption, existed and flourished throughout colonial times. Both appear so familiar that it is tempting to argue, as do the *dependentistas* (advocates of dependency theory) and world-systems theorists, that they represent simple, unbroken continuities, all-too-familiar colonial ghosts. Perhaps this is so, but as with frontiers, mineral extraction, and other specters, one must consider other possibilities.

Alternatives that might make these two categories seem less peculiarly colonial would include the following: patterns of corruption and concentration of land-wealth may have changed considerably after independence, and both tendencies, like the push to "civilize" frontiers, might be nearly universal. Both are, perhaps, inherent features of Western political economy, if not world history.

As for the first option, it should be remembered that the Spanish crown was, as a general rule, despotic toward both colonists and native Americans. Some policies were remarkably pronative, and to the extent that they were enforced, they sharply countered the interests of established elites. Perhaps most important of all, from the beginning to the end of the colonial period, the crown was chronically short of money due to wars in Europe, massive palace construction, and properly ostentatious "maintenance" of king and court. Crown officers were constantly charged with finding new means of extracting revenue, whether through tribute, customs duties, sales taxes, or forced loans, or donations. In return, the king offered a modicum of mercy, justice, protection, prestige, and religious charisma. Even if the exchange seemed unfair, as was often the case, one had to comply. A cranky outburst against a 1592 royal sales tax (regarded by some as a very early cry for independence) left Quito unable to choose its own aldermen for one hundred years. When the money stopped flowing, heads literally rolled.

In such a paradoxical and capricious environment, colonial power relations became skewed. The crown's proclivities evident, Creole elites came to regard "Indians," in particular, as natural enemies, and poorly paid incoming officials as readily corruptible targets of opportunity. State caprice and insatiability in fiscal matters led to tax evasion on a massive scale. Meanwhile, the constant cash drain on the colonies encouraged elite consolidation of landed wealth. This was done not so much to increase production, which required more developed markets, lower taxes, and better infrastructure anyway, as to secure credit from church lenders. A substantial portion of these church-administered *censos* (mortgages) went toward maintenance of ostentatious, even quasi-regal households. Eighteenth-century "reforms" mostly included new taxes (which led, in turn, to new rebellions, as in 1765).

Did these patterns change after 1830? In the main, no, or at least not very quickly. "Indians" were still the enemy — and still the primary source of state revenue until 1857 (Guerrero 1997; Spindler 1987:48). Church institutions were still enormously powerful, both politically and economically. The Jesuits, who had been stripped of their schools, rental properties, haciendas, slaves, and sugar plantations in 1767, were invited back to Ecuador in 1851 by pious citizens. The difference, of course, was that oligarchs now had to deal with a president, not a king, and a host of minor officials who, for the most part, were locally born.

Ecuador's first president, the Venezuela-born Juan José Flores, chose to ease the transition to freedom by playing the role of capricious king off-and-on until 1845 (Van Aken 1989). Meanwhile, lesser characters such as the *tenientes políticos* (appointed officials who oversee parishes) peddled influence and abused power after the manner of Habsburg *corregidores*. "Au plus cela change," sighed rare critics like the Liberal firebrand Juan Montalvo.

As a number of scholars have shown, it was only with the Liberal Revolution of 1895 that Ecuador's political and economic culture was substantially altered (Ayala Mora 1994; Clark 1998). Under Eloy Alfaro Delgado and his successors, major rail links were begun, state finances made public, suffrage expanded, the death penalty eliminated, church influence curbed, and so on down the yellow brick road of modernization.

The entwined phenomena of corruption and *latifundismo*, however, particularly in the very populous and still isolated Sierra, were by no means eliminated. Despite strong support, including military aid, from indigenous groups, the Liberals failed to ease either rural oppression or urban poverty. Among the middle class, such as it was, intimidation and violence by Alfaro's gangs of *garroteros* (thugs) did little to change public perceptions of power as something to be abused. Friends of the Old Warrior got the jobs.

The Liberal Revolution was not in the end socially revolutionary; it was a reform movement aimed at making Ecuador a modern Latin American nation, a safe investment for laissez-faire capitalists such as la SADCO. Furthermore, it was a movement financed and dominated by a coastal cacao oligarchy that, however bourgeois its tastes and pronouncements, was itself latifundist at heart. The Liberal ban on debt-peonage, passed in 1918, allowed oppressed workers this freedom: to leap from the frying pan of the "colonial" Andean hacienda and into the fire of the "modern" coastal plantation.

Land reform would only come much later, during the military dictatorship of the early 1960s. The 1964 redistribution decree, though driven by powerful new influences from abroad as well as boiling pressure from below, nevertheless failed to ease rural poverty or delegitimize the *hacendado* (hacienda owner) once and for all. This failure, along with much other contemporary and historical evidence, suggests that wealth concentration in the form of *latifundismo* is in Ecuador a genuine (rather than a fake or "reconstituted") colonial legacy. It is also possible that this urge could be a universal feature of Western culture dating back at least to the Romans.

Meanwhile, corruption in Ecuador has reached the reductio ad absurdum point of self-fulfilling prophecy, denounced almost before it occurs. Indeed, it is assumed that becoming a successful politician in the current carnival (unless one is independently wealthy) requires being corrupt. Why else would one risk the humiliation? The scripted cycle proceeds rapidly from seduction of the electorate to conquest, followed by scandal, then denunciation, ouster, and bittersweet (financially padded) exile. As the preferred destination for the "poor," humiliated exile, Panama has suddenly lost cachet to North American cities and most recently a university campus. As if by magic, there always seems to be a post for technocrat alumni.

Certainly a similar, if slower, trajectory was traced by colonial-era bureaucrats such as Antonio de Morga, but is the corruption one sees today a bona fide colonial legacy? In today's moneygrubbing free-for-all, civic virtue appears to have become conflated with the ability to accumulate wealth, particularly in the United States and in Europe. The scene is such that "corruption," a nineteenth-century term of political denunciation, seems quaintly antique in a world where yesterday's sins are today's virtues. In poor "banana republics" such as Ecuador, the violent pushes and pulls of millennial neoliberalism simply strip the fur and glitter off what may everywhere amount to a base struggle for global power and wealth. In such an environment, political selflessness (Chico Mendes comes immediately to mind) is little more than an invitation to martyrdom.

Racial Division

Perhaps the most haunting and daunting of Ecuador's colonial specters is persistent racial division. At the turn of the millennium, hints of colonial-era apartheid are everywhere: in the urban workplace (whether home, office, shop, or factory); in neighborhoods; by province and region (north, south, Coast, Sierra); in village and countryside; in churches and affiliated organizations; in business, top to bottom; and, most glaringly, in politics. At the equator, where melanin ought to be worth its weight in gold, why is it bad to be brown? Or is color all there is to "race" in Ecuador?

The Ecuadorian premium on whiteness may remain a mystery for some time to come, but the answer to the second question is an unequivocal "no." As most observers quickly discover, and as numerous scholars have demonstrated in detailed studies (Whitten 1981; Muratorio 1994; Rahier, this volume; Weismantel, this volume), there is much more to race than color in Ecuador. As in most of Latin America, other factors contributing to or mitigating discrimination and exclusion include ethnicity, language, religion, class, age, appearance, gender, education, and political affiliation. Ecuador, in short, is probably more socially complex today than it was in colonial times.

Colonial rule was unequivocally racist. Incoming Europeans immediately set about reducing indigenous peoples of myriad ethnicities and extraordinarily disparate lifeways to a single, legally binding and inferior category: *indios*. Groups deemed rebellious for their continued autonomy, such as the Shuar or Awá were actually hunted from time to time, and lived subject to temporary enslavement virtually throughout the colonial era. Equally innocent people of African descent, meanwhile, were enslaved en masse and put to work in field, mine, ship, and shop, with no apologies or explanations. As early as 1600, if not before, "black" meant "slave" in the Kingdom of Quito (Lane 2000).

For the majority of indigenous groups subjected to Spanish domination after 1532, the system — rather like a penal colony — was structured so as to efficiently extract surplus produce (tribute) and labor (*mita*) from adult males between the ages of eighteen and fifty. Women, children, and the elderly were not exempt: they subsidized these constant and forcible extractions (including, frequently, the death, disability, or permanent disappearance of adult males) by augmenting labor inputs at home, in the field, in elite households, and even in mines and textile mills. In short, everyone paid tribute, everyone was subject to the *mita*, everyone was reminded what it meant to be *indio*. People of mixed heritage might be free, but all but the most privileged worked with their hands.

It is immediately evident that across the nearly three centuries of Spanish rule the colony was literally built by — and on the backs of — indigenous, mixed, and Black Ecuadorians. In this, more than any other way, colonial Ecuador, as with most of Latin America, differed from British North America. While the North Americans engaged in their share of slavery and *métissage*, in the Andes proper, British tactics such as mass exile, ethnocide, and genocide were only occasionally employed against the indigenous majority. In Quito, as elsewhere in Spanish America, the plan favored by pope and crown was instead subjugation in situ. *Indios* were regarded as the colonies' greatest and most valuable natural resource. When unavailable, Africans would substitute.

Meanwhile, waves of epidemic disease swept periodically through the Andes, decimating already beleaguered indigenous villages just as they began to recover (Alchon 1991; Newson 1995). Under these circumstances, mere survival, much less maintenance of cultural vibrancy, was no mean feat. For conquering elites, tribute and *mita* labor were but another kind of gold, to be extracted at any cost.

On the face of it, then, slavery and indigenous subjugation, and by extension, "blackness" and "Indianness," were stand-ins for class. But there was more to it, even then: enslavement, tribute payment, segregation, exclusion (from priesthood and convents), and forced, rotational service were also symbolic punishments, ritualized humiliations intentionally heaped upon "the conquered" to remind them of their inferiority. To be "white," entailed becoming a spectator-participant in this cruel sport, no matter what one's specific origins (Creole, Extremaduran, Basque, Andalusian, Old Castilian, Portuguese). Among nonwhites, color became only one of a dizzying array of traits used to define salient difference (Minchom 1994).

Because slavery remained relatively marginal in Ecuador, white, or rather *español/a* (and eventually *criollo/a*), identity in large part came to be defined as the opposite of *indio/a*. Among other things, a self-proclaimed *blanco/a*, certainly by the early eighteenth century, had to be a Spanish speaker who did not pay tribute (Juan and Ulloa 1964 [1748]). As the anthropologist John Hawkins has shown for modern Guatemala, this tendency toward "inverse images," with numerous markers of difference and color losing significance with time, became standard in many former Spanish colonies with large indigenous populations (Hawkins 1984). Although difficult for outsiders to fathom, it seems that in almost inverse relationship with the shrillness of the rhetoric, the incidental alchemy of human attraction had a way of making "white" people brown, and vice versa. In a seeming paradox, *mestizaje* could exacerbate, rather than eliminate (as predicted by some optimists), racial division. Like its northern neighbor, Jim Crow (i.e., "one drop" legal blackness), *mestizaje* in Ecuador, as in much of Latin America, has had a strange career.

It should be remembered that resistance to the hateful, apartheidlike structuring of colonial society was manifold and frequently successful. As with the history of slavery throughout the world, there is ample evidence from colonial Ecuador of violent rebellion, flight, selfless harboring of fugitives, work stoppages, racial dissimulation, sabotage, and even genuine love and marriage across racial lines. Some individuals and communities meanwhile learned to exploit the evolving intricacies of the new racialized system with stubborn ingenuity.

One would perhaps expect things to have changed rather dramatically at independence (given the example of Eugenio Espejo, and Bolívar's ardent liberalism and promise to Haiti), but such was not the case. Ecuador's first president turned out to be not only a military man but a conservative monarchist. When he did propose modest social reforms toward the end of his presidency, he was unceremoniously exiled. Thus, primarily as a result of elite conservatism, colonial-style abuse of indigenous and African-descended peoples continued apace, and perhaps even accelerated following freedom from Spain (and Gran Colombia). Slavery was maintained until 1851, to be followed not by genuine freedom, but rather *concertaje* (a combination of debt peonage and *mita*-type requirements) and other forms of racialized persecution and exploitation (Guerrero 1997).

For indigenous Ecuadorians, particularly, national independence had drawbacks. The colonial system had, in fact, offered mediation, some brakes on abuse. Now there were no indigenous courts, no "royal ear" that might listen to grievances and check the power of local oligarchs. The abolition of tribute in 1857, as with the end of slavery, did little to improve the situation, particularly in the countryside. Indeed, the *huasipungaje* (serfdom) of Jorge Icaza's (1934) day may well have been more abusive than its colonial antecedent. Freedom in the city, meanwhile, was mitigated by García Moreno's showcase panopticon prison, one of the first of its kind in Latin America.

Racial division in Ecuador has deep colonial roots, most only touched upon lightly here. It may, in fact, be the archetypal example of the "unresolved inheritance." Its resolution is, of course, the core goal of today's pan-indigenous and Afro-Ecuadorian political movements. Nevertheless, as in the cases of mineral extraction and land concentration, one must distinguish between global and strictly Ecuadorian processes. The tendency for human groups to tyrannize their fellows (and rebel against tyranny) under pretexts of differences in skin color, ethnicity, language, and religion, certainly predates the colonization of the Americas. European expansion after 1492 simply globalized and formalized such tendencies. The core postcolonial—and now millennial—predicament, for both ex-colonizer and ex-colonized, is determining how to exorcise this extraordinarily tenacious and multifaceted ghost (Nandy 1983). One can only hope that Ecuadorians will prevail in this project of reconciliation without reviving the violence of colonial times.

Religion

Regardless of one's personal views or preferences, Ecuador's churches and vast colonial artistic corpus still serve as an astonishing reminder of the power of religion in everyday life. For some, the omnipresent retables, portals, canvases, and convents are just so many priceless cultural treasures. For others, they are hollow symbols, silent but incontrovertible testimony of centuries of physical and psychological oppression. In both cases, they bring to mind another of Ecuador's most durable colonial specters.

Although the heading is "Religion," the ghost in question is rather obviously the Roman Catholic church. The power of the church, by way of both formal institutions and popular belief, can hardly be underestimated in Ecuador, past and present. Indeed, Ecuador is still regarded by many scholars as the most religiously conservative nation in the Andean region, perhaps in all of Latin America. This may be true, but to what extent is church influence on modern life a colonial legacy? Also, is the sudden rise of non-Catholic religious influence in Ecuador's recent past to be regarded as a disjuncture or a continuity?

Apropos of the times, perhaps, Spain's colonization of the Americas was from beginning to end a religious as much as an economic and political enterprise. American treasure, though a constant obsession, was to be used not only for secular gain or royal aggrandizement, but also for funding the Catholic crusade against Islam, Judaism, and Protestantism. Native souls constituted yet another prize, a kind of heavenly booty. The most optimistic of Spanish missionaries, like those who renamed Quito in honor of Saint Francis (San Francisco) in 1534, even believed that preaching the gospel to native

Americans would bring about the millennium, the final, thousand-year reign of Christ on Earth (Phelan 1956).

That this did not occur was a disappointment, but in the end was not cause for undue concern. Christianity, like many durable religions, could accommodate both manic optimism and crippling self-doubt. Priests first blamed native peoples for their obstinacy, then colonists for their greed, and then, of course, themselves for excessive pride. In short, Spain's clergy, backed by a string of pious Habsburg kings, decided that beating the devil in the Americas was going to take some time. The church consequently settled in for a long stay, and a plethora of institutions charged with the twin duties of conversion to and conservation of the faith emerged. They ranged from the Jesuit order to the Inquisition to exclusive convents and popular sodalities. Sin and apostasy were by no means checked, but within a century of conquest, the spiritual transformation of the Kingdom of Quito, like much of Spanish America, was deep and wide.

Religion has been called the opiate of the people, and the new faith probably served to dissuade direct action and solidarity on several key occasions in colonial Ecuador. Roman Catholicism, preached constantly in Spanish or broken Quichua, appealed to notions of human equality and thus to the universal desire for justice. Church organizations and religious personages, including Quito's bishops, served occasionally to push for reform, particularly of indigenous labor assignments. The church also took over colonial education, such as it was. Charity, furthermore, was integral to baroque Catholicism, prompting the formation of institutions to care for the sick, poor, and orphaned. As has been seen, the early colonial church was such an effective fundraiser that, by the mid-seventeenth century, it controlled the lion's share of the Kingdom of Quito's liquid and landed wealth.

However tempting it might be, it would be fallacious to say that nothing has changed since then. In the eighteenth and nineteenth centuries, particularly, the church's good deeds did not go unpunished. Unlike their Habsburg predecessors, the Bourbons were rather suspicious of church power, both in Spain and abroad, and even cast a jaundiced eye on the priesthood itself. Scandalous reports from colonies such as Quito only confirmed their fears (Juan and Ulloa 1978). The growing anticlerical mood led eventually to dramatic acts such as the expulsion of the Jesuits in 1767 (the Creole Padre Juan de Velasco among them) and the *consolidación de vales*, or calling in of all church loans, in 1804. Spanish American bishops from Mexico City to Santiago were outraged, and some priests urged civil disobedience. Heeding the call, conservative Creoles banded together to fight for independence on behalf of their beloved "old" church. This was not Bolívar's or Espejo's dream, of course, but it certainly was that of their successors.

In independent Ecuador, President Flores set the tone for things to come by reestablishing the primacy of the church in state affairs immediately after secession from Gran Colombia. Roman Catholicism was declared the nation's only tolerated religion. It would remain so until 1904. As in colonial times, the state would enforce collection of tithes. Facing a powerful mix of deadly force, economic intimidation, and apparently widespread popular resistance, liberal attempts to separate the Ecuadorian church from state failed throughout the nineteenth century.

By the second presidency of García Moreno (1869–75), Ecuador was essentially a theocracy. Despite being the Andes' poorest, the nation was taxing its citizens to subsidize the embattled Pope Pius IX. The national motto was Religión y Patria. An Inquisition-style index of prohibited books was established in 1871, and, in 1873, the president himself played Good Friday penitent, bearing a cross through the streets of Quito. More telling still, the nation was officially dedicated to the Sacred Heart of Jesus in 1873. This dedication was renewed by President Caamaño in 1885, along with a decree to begin construction of the national basilica, the site of future, church-sponsored presidential accessions. President Flores Jijón followed in 1888 by expanding state support of Jesuit, Franciscan, Dominican, and Salesian missions in Amazonia (Spindler 1987).

As these trends indicate, the Catholic church was considerably more powerful in Ecuador in the 1880s than it was in the 1780s. In fact, it was probably more powerful than it had been in the extraordinarily pious 1680s. Was this a reconstitution of a legacy or straightforward colonial persistence? Church retrenchment in the nineteenth century certainly mirrored colonial patterns and aspirations, but one should bear in mind that the context was different. Ecuador was now an independent, albeit weak and vulnerable, nation. The feeble state had essentially become an instrument of the church. How, some asked, was this neomedieval "cloister of the Andes" to compete in the modern world?

The Liberal Revolution of 1895 was initially heralded as the death knell of pietism, but Alfaro and his followers moved slowly to restrict church power. It was not until Plaza Gutiérrez's 1904 Law of Religions that things really changed. Thanks to nineteenth-century conservatism, in Ecuador religious freedom, divorce, and public education are still less than a century old. The dismantling of Roman Catholic church power in the formal sense continued to be a major liberal cause throughout the twentieth century, but there was another side to the "ghost" of religion.

From the moment of its introduction to the Americas, Roman Catholicism was embraced by millions of people of many classes, ethnicities, and colors. Much to the consternation of church fathers, however, local and female interpretations of doctrine escaped control. Consequently, folk religion in its myriad, hybrid forms continues to thrive in Ecuador, as in much of Latin America. Evangelicals, Mormons, Seventh-Day Adventists, and other sects have eroded Catholic hegemony in recent years, but popular choice still reigns. If history is a guide, assimilation of Protestant doctrines is likely to follow a similarly twisted, or rather forked, path in millennial Ecuador; there will be fundamentalists and relaxed quasi-agnostics, and a whole range of believers in between — none quite doing as they are told. Although some regard the embrace of folk religion and evangelism as a retrograde choice unlikely to improve standards of living, there is no doubt that many Ecuadorians will continue to find solace in this arguably genuine colonial legacy.

Conclusion

This essay is in no way intended as an indictment of the Ecuadorian people. When compared with their similarly beleaguered Andean neighbors in recent years, the people, if not the national government, of Ecuador have demonstrated extraordinary patience, flexibility, cooperativeness, creativity, and fortitude, all combined with an admirable distaste for violence. To my knowledge, the colonial, and even precolonial, record does not predict Ecuadorian exceptionalism of this kind. But what of persistence, or at least recurrence?

To some extent, continuity in Ecuador — of colonial-style patterns of governance, landholding, resource extraction, religious belief, and race and labor relations — should come as no surprise. After all, Ecuador, unlike France, Haiti, the United States, Mexico, Russia, China, Cuba, or Nicaragua, has never experienced a genuine social revolution. One may argue about the nature or durability of these other modern transformations, but major breaks with the past they undoubtedly were. Ecuador's independence, by contrast, was patently unrevolutionary, and the so-called Liberal Revolution of 1895 was far less transformative than it might have been. Twentieth-century politics certainly veered across the ideological spectrum, but no regime managed to overturn old patterns of lopsided wealth distribution, race and gender inequality, or environmental destruction.

If this lack of Western-style progress is what one means by the "hauntedness" of Ecuador's present, then the long colonial past would seem an obvious nursery for its ghosts. In the vast colonial record, one indeed finds myriad forms of oppression in field, mine, and household, yet there is also ample evidence of sustained resistance and clever adaptation. People under stress ran away, collaborated, or shifted identities according to their needs, and authorities appear to have been hard pressed to stop them. Colonial territories, furthermore, were large and barely known to their usurpers. Indeed,

throughout the colonial period, the bulk of Quito's claimed territory remained in the hands of autonomous indigenous peoples. Cities, by contrast,
were, by modern standards, very small. Guayaquil was but a village. If this is
a taste of colonial reality, how might colonial ghosts be classified?

Some of the specters examined above appear to be genuinely Spanish
colonial legacies, others less specifically so (i.e., they seem more global),
and still others false or reconstituted. In examining Ecuadorian history "up
close and skeptical" one sees few perfect continuities and many complex and
contingent sets of relationships linking the early colonial, late colonial, nineteenth-century, and twentieth-century periods. For example, despite some
clearly colonial demons such as racism and *latifundismo*, it may be that Ecuador in the twentieth century was struggling mostly to overcome the ghosts
of nineteenth-century conservatism (for contemporary U.S. and European
examples, cf. Trouillot 1995:149–53). New ghosts, such as massive foreign
debt, also have traceable nineteenth-century roots, but they only became
truly haunting in the twentieth century. But besides the business of incon-
gruent details, are there other problems with overgeneralizing about Spanish colonialism as the root of all evil?

If the aim is truth and reconciliation, then perhaps the impulse to project
the Ecuadorian present back onto the colonial past must itself be thoroughly
interrogated. In Padre Velasco's day, a highly selective, even fictive study
of the early colony provided moral edification for an enlightened, mostly
European few. Later, nationalist histories of the colonial period entailed little
more than a genealogical search for heroes, visionaries, and villains. More
recently, radical history has served to celebrate the colonial oppressed. The
colonial period was certainly long and complex enough to accommodate a
variety of interpretations, but it may be time to acknowledge presentist assumptions. Perhaps the colonial past should be allowed to surprise us, rather
than simply affirm our suspicions.

As in most modern nations, in Ecuador, history has been used for many
purposes. In public discourse, it has often been manipulated cynically by
those in power. With politics shifting abruptly, the challenge today may be to
know just what to do with a colonial (or nineteenth-century, or twentieth-
century) ghost when one finds one. This is no laughing matter, in fact, as the
mishandling of colonial-era specters continues to yield a steady stream of ca-
davers from Africa to Micronesia (e.g., Cole 2001). In light of such tragedy,
one may be tempted to think that knowledge of the colonial past is more burdensome than ignorance of it, that so-called third-world countries are con-
demned to repeat past "mistakes" no matter what. Certainly Ecuador's credit
history does not bode well for the immediate future, but not every hope is
bound by such neocolonial, much less real colonial, shackles. The desire for

peacefully effected change is at an all-time high. The fact that it is indigenous Ecuadorians who are most vigorously and creatively challenging the inherited, nineteenth-century model of the nation-state is compelling evidence of life — of vitality and originality rather than ham-strung hauntedness — after colonialism.

ACKNOWLEDGMENTS

Many thanks to Norman E. Whitten, Jr., for his insightful comments and suggestions on various drafts of this chapter, from inception to finish. Thanks also to Judith Ewell, for curbing unnecessary asides and excessive sarcasm. Remaining errors and excesses are to be blamed entirely on me.

REFERENCES

Adelman, Jeremy

    1999   (editor) *Colonial Legacies: The Problem of Persistence in Latin American History*. New York: Routledge.

Alchon, Suzanne A.

    1991   *Native Society and Disease in Colonial Ecuador*. Cambridge: Cambridge University Press.

Andrade Marin, Luciano

    1970 [1937] *Llanganatis: Expedición Italo-ecuatoriana Boschetti-Andrade Marin, 1933–34*. Quito: Editorial Santo Domingo.

Andrien, Kenneth J.

    1995   *The Kingdom of Quito, 1690–1830: The State and Regional Development*. Cambridge: Cambridge University Press.

Ayala Mora, Enrique

    1983–1995 (editor) *Nueva Historia del Ecuador*. 15 vols. Quito: Corporación Editora Nacional.

    1994   *Historia de la revolución liberal ecuatoriana*. Quito: Corporación Editora Nacional.

Casement, Roger

    1997   *Roger Casement's Diaries. 1910: The Black and the White*. Roger Sawyer, ed. London: Pimlico Press.

Cieza de León, Pedro de

    1998 [1554] *The Discovery and Conquest of Peru*. Alexandra Parma Cook and Noble David Cook, trans. and eds. Durham: Duke University Press.

Clark, A. Kim

    1998   *The Redemptive Work: Railway and Nation in Ecuador, 1895–1930*. Wilmington, Del.: SR Books.

Cleary, David

    1990   *Anatomy of the Amazon Gold Rush*. Iowa City: University of Iowa Press.

Cole, Jennifer

    2001   *Forget Colonialism? Sacrifice and the Art of Memory in Madagascar.* Berkeley: University of California Press.

Comaroff, Jean, and John L. Comaroff

    2001   (editor) *Millennial Capitalism and the Culture of Neoliberalism.* Durham: Duke University Press.

Cueva, Agustín

    1982   *The Process of Political Domination in Ecuador.* Danielle Salti, trans. New Brunswick, N.J.: Transaction Books.

Cushner, Nicholas P.

    1982   *Farm and Factory: The Jesuits and the Development of Agrarian Capitalism in Colonial Quito, 1600–1767.* Albany: SUNY Press.

Engineering and Mining Journal

    1995 (January) Ecuador Wants to Energize its Mining Sector. Electronic document. http://e-mj.com/ar/mining_ecuador_winter_energize/index.htm.

Estupiñán Viteri, Tamara

    1997   *El mercado interno en la Audiencia de Quito.* Quito: Banco Central del Ecuador.

Fernández-Armesto, Felipe

    2001   *Civilizations: Culture, Ambition, and the Transformation of Nature.* New York: Free Press.

Garcés G., Jorge

    1957   (editor) *Las minas de Zamora: Cuentas de la Real Hacienda, 1561–1565.* Quito: Archivo Municipal.

Godoy, Ricardo

    1990   *Mining and Agriculture in Highland Bolivia: Ecology, History, and Commerce among the Jukumanis.* Tucson: University of Arizona Press.

Guerrero, Andrés

    1997   The Construction of a Ventriloquist's Image: Liberal Discourse and the Miserable Indian Race in Late-nineteenth-century Ecuador. *Journal of Latin American Studies* 29(3):555–90.

Hardenburg, Walter

    1912   *The Putumayo, the Devil's Paradise; Travels in the Peruvian Amazon Region and an Account of the Atrocities Committed upon the Indians Therein.* London: T.F. Unwin.

Hassaurek, Friedrich

    1868   *Four Years among Spanish Americans.* New York: Hurd & Houghton.

Hawkins, John

    1984   *Inverse Images: The Meaning of Culture, Ethnicity, and Family in Postcolonial Guatemala.* Albuquerque: University of New Mexico Press.

Icaza, Jorge

    1934   *Huasipungo*. Quito: Imprenta Nacional.

Juan, Jorge, and Antonio Ulloa

    1964 [1748] *A Voyage to South America*. Irving Leonard, ed. New York:
        Alfred A. Knopf.

    1978 [1749] *Discourse and Political Reflections on the Kingdoms of Peru*.
        J. J. TePaske, ed. Norman: University of Oklahoma Press.

Lane, Kris

    1996   Mining the Margins: Precious Metals Extraction and Forced Labor
        Regimes in the Audiencia of Quito, 1534–1821. Ph.D. dissertation.
        University of Minnesota.

    2000   Captivity and Redemption: Aspects of Slave Life in Early Colonial Quito
        and Popayán. *The Americas* 57 : 225–46.

    2002   *Quito, 1599: City and Colony in Transition*. Albuquerque: University of
        New Mexico Press.

Limerick, Patricia

    1987   *The Legacy of Conquest: The Unbroken Past of the American West*.
        New York: Norton.

    2000   *Something in the Soil: Legacies and Reckonings in the New West*. New York:
        Norton.

Lourie, Peter

    1991   *Sweat of the Sun, Tears of the Moon*. Lincoln: University of Nebraska
        Press.

Mamdani, Mahmood

    2001   Beyond Settler and Native as Political Identities: Overcoming the Political
        Legacy of Colonialism. *Comparative Studies in Society and History* 43 : 4
        (October) : 651–64.

Marcella, Gabriel, and Richard Downes

    1999   (editors) *Security and Cooperation in the Western Hemisphere: Resolving
        the Ecuador-Peru Conflict*. Miami: North-South Center Press.

Minchom, Martin

    1994   *The People of Quito, 1690–1810: Change and Unrest in the Underclass*.
        Boulder, Colo.: Westview Press.

Muratorio, Blanca

    1994   (editor) *Imágenes e Imageneros: Representaciones de los indígenas
        ecuatorianos, siglos XIX y XX*. Quito: FLACSO.

Murillo, Rodrigo

    2000   *Zaruma: Historia minera; identidad en Portovelo*. Quito: Abya-Yala.

Nandy, Ashis

    1983   *The Intimate Enemy: Loss and Recovery of Self under Colonialism*. Delhi:
        Oxford University Press.

Newson, Linda

    1995   *Life and Death in Early Colonial Ecuador*. Norman: University of Oklahoma
            Press.

Phelan, John L.

    1956   *The Millennial Kingdom of the Franciscans in the New World: A Study of*
            the Writings of Gerónimo de Mendieta, 1525–1604. Berkeley: University of
            California Press.

    1967   *The Kingdom of Quito in the Seventeenth Century*. Madison: University of
            Wisconsin Press.

Porras B., María Elena

    1987   *La gobernación y el obispado de Mainas, siglos XVII y XVIII*. Quito:
            TEHIS/Abya-Yala.

Radcliffe, Sarah A.

    2001   Imagining the State As a Space: Territoriality and the Formation of the
            State in Ecuador. In *States of Imagination: Ethnographic Explorations of*
            the Postcolonial State. Thomas Blom and Finn Stepputat, eds. Pp. 123–45.
            Durham: Duke University Press.

Spindler, Frank M.

    1987   *Nineteenth-century Ecuador: An Historical Introduction*. Fairfax, Va.:
            George Mason University.

Spruce, Richard

    1908   *Notes of a Botanist on the Amazon and Andes*. London: Macmillan.

Taussig, Michael

    1986   *Colonialism, Shamanism, and the Wild Man: A Study in Terror and Healing*.
            Chicago: University of Chicago Press.

Taylor, Anne-Christine

    1999   The Western Margins of Amazonia from the Early Sixteenth to the Early
            Nineteenth Century. In *The Cambridge History of the Native Peoples of the*
            Americas, Part III: South America. Frank Salomon and Stuart Schwartz,
            eds. Pp. 188–256. Cambridge: Cambridge University Press, part 2.

Trouillot, Michel-Rolph

    1995   *Silencing the Past: Power and the Production of History*. Boston: Beacon
            Press.

Vacas Galindo, Enrique

    1905   *La integridad territorial de la República del Ecuador*. Quito: Tipografía
            encuadernación Salesiano.

    1909   *Resumen de la cuestión de límites del Ecuador con el Perú*. Madrid: Impreso
            del Asilo de Huérfanos del S.C. de Jesús.

Van Aken, Mark J.

    1989   *King of the Night: Juan José Flores and Ecuador, 1824–1864*. Berkeley:
            University of California Press.

Vargas, José María

    1980 [1957] *La economía política del Ecuador durante la colonia*. 2nd edition, with introduction by Carlos Marchán R. Quito: Banco Central del Ecuador.

Velasco, Juan de

    1941 [1790] *Historia moderna del reino de Quito*. Quito: Caja de Seguro.

Von Däniken, Erich

    1973   *The Gold of the Gods*. New York: Putnam.

Whitten, Norman E., Jr.

    1981   (editor) *Cultural Transformations and Ethnicity in Modern Ecuador*. Urbana: University of Illinois Press.

    1985   *Sicuanga Runa: The Other Side of Development in Amazonian Ecuador*. Urbana: University of Illinois Press.

CHAPTER 4

The Catholic Church, Ritual, and Power in Salasaca

RACHEL CORR

Many years ago there was a drought in the province of Tungurahua. The people of Salasaca gathered together, bringing maize beer, *mote* (hominy), drums (*bombos*) and flutes (*quenas*), and ceramic vessels full of water to pour onto the sacred mountain Quinchi Urcu. It was like a *minga* (collective work force) in which each person had to contribute some water for the mountain offering. The people went to cry (*wacangabuj*), and to beg (*rogangabuj*) so that the drought would end. This event is etched in the collective memory of the people of Salasaca, reproduced through narrative, and cited today as evidence of the power of the mountain. Marta, a woman in her late fifties, told me her memories of the event in a 1998 interview:

> I remember it like this. There in Quinchi Urcu, when it hadn't rained for a while, they held a fiesta. The people went carrying water in *puños* and in *pondos* [types of ceramic vessels] to pour it there, so that it would rain. We poured it in the *achupalla* plants on Quinchi Urcu. There had just been sun, day after day. The old ones said, "Let's go! It hasn't rained. Let's all go to pour water in the *achupalla*. It's just been sunny everyday." Everyone went, saying "Let's go" and carried water. [They went] to pour the water. . . . They poured the water there, and one or two days later it just rained. Upon putting the water there it rained. Nowadays, we don't do this anymore. When it doesn't rain, we just let it go.

Since shamans and others who leave offerings on the mountain pray to Dius (God), and the Mother Mountain (Mama Quinchi), I asked Marta exactly who caused it to rain. According to Marta, God made it rain on seeing the water placed in the mountain:

> The people placed the water there saying "Please make it rain; it hasn't rained at all. We can't sow any crops. There is nothing." In this way, asking God, we put the water and it just rained. . . . Since long ago the old ones would perform fiestas there so that it would rain and it would just rain. When water is put there it rains; that's what the old ones would say. Hav-

ing heard that, we also said "Let's go put water there" when it didn't rain, we went too.

Nearly two centuries earlier, during a drought in the province of Imbabura, the people gathered on Imbabura mountain "with the object of committing idolatry" in the form of mountain worship (ANH/Q 1792 cited in Moreno Yánez 1991:535). A local priest learned of the procession, which involved over 100 Otavalans gathered together on the mountain. The priest, Father Michilena, ordered one woman to be publicly punished for her alleged participation. The husband of the woman testified to the brutality of the punishment; he stated

> that the Sunday of Casimodo, finding all the people gathered in the cemetery . . . at the time of the public *doctrina*, it happened that this parish priest, without having investigated whether it was a true fact, executed that violent punishment, making them tie my wife to a walnut tree [and] making two *indios* take the clothes off her back he ordered them to discharge 100 lashes . . . and I was hurt to see my wife in such a miserable state. . . . I went to her and covered her with my mantle . . . and just for this act the Priest ordered two *indios* to hold me and he made them give me 52 lashes. (Cited in Moreno Yánez 1991:535–36)[1]

It is significant that the punishment took place during *la doctrina*, the Catholic religious teachings (indoctrinations) that indigenous peoples were required to attend. The husband, Juan Paulino Carlosama, petitioned the *protector de naturales* (protector of natives), insisting that his wife had only gone to gather firewood, and went to see the people out of curiosity when she heard so many voices praying and singing "Christian songs." The *protector de naturales* ruled that the punishment was just. The priest who gave the order was acting on a suggestion made one hundred years earlier by Bishop Alonso de la Peña Montenegro in his *Itinerario para párrocos de indios*, in which he recommends public flogging to combat "idolatry." Furthermore, the eighteenth-century ruling established the authority of priests by claiming that Father Michilena was acting "not as a man but as a judge of God" (Moreno Yánez 1991:536). This case presents one example of how colonial rulers defined religion and established the authority of priests.

Given such a history, we can view the modern-day religious practices of begging, collective prayer, rites on a sacred mountain, memories embedded in narratives of such an event, and the use of such narratives to proclaim that the mountain is powerful, as evidence of the persistence of religious beliefs deeply rooted in experience and narrative. The continuing practice of mountain offerings in indigenous communities underscores the resilience of indigenous religion through historical periods of conquest and colonialism, the extirpation of idolatries, attempts at assimilation, catechism, globalization, and modernity. The description of one hundred indigenous people gathered on a sacred mountain during a drought in 1792 sounds much like the description of the Salasacans one generation ago. In our focus on modernity and globalization, to ignore the persistence and resilience of local-level practices is to "write out" or "silence" (Trouillot 1995) an important aspect of indigenous culture and identity. I am not, however, suggesting that indigenous practices have remained unchanged, or that modern-day indigenous peoples are "baptized but not evangelized" (Abercrombie 1998:109). Rather, in this chapter, I focus on how indigenous people resisted, accommodated, and read their own meanings into Roman Catholicism.

Several writers have noted the Western tendency to introduce a false dichotomy when discussing indigenous peoples, especially with regard to religion. This dichotomy opposes Western, modern, and urban lifeways to indigenous, pre-Columbian, traditional, or rural systems (Starn 1991). Indigenous peoples can be rural and/or urban, Catholic or Evangelist. In studies of indigenous religion, there is a polar tendency to portray indigenous peoples either as passive victims whose culture has been destroyed by colonialism or as resistant bearers of their ancient heritage under a thin cover of Christianity (Abercrombie 1998; Griffiths 1999). Both views are flawed. Certainly the story of the rainmaking rite on the sacred mountain shows resistance to the violent attempts to end such "idolatries," and scholars must recognize this resistance to do justice to indigenous peoples as active agents in Latin American history. Yet we cannot deny the historical forces of colonial powers and, of equal importance, the fact that many indigenous peoples identify with Christianity and fully accept many of its teachings. Studies of modern-day, local-level narratives and rituals can increase our knowledge of the multifarious ways by which indigenous peoples in Ecuador (and elsewhere) accepted, contested, and accommodated the hegemony of the Roman Catholic Church.

In this chapter, I analyze the beliefs and rituals of the people of Salasaca as a response to the historical forces of Catholic indoctrination.[2] An analysis of Salasacan narratives and rituals illustrates the power of church hegemony and how power and hegemony infuse religious experience. But the subtle persistence of rituals not officially sanctioned by the church also attests to the limits of that hegemony. In this regard, Salasacan religious expressions are interesting because the Salasacans have long been independent of debt peonage. Unlike many other indigenous peoples, they were not subject to indoctrination through the hacienda. Documented historical references to the Salasacan people are scarce; therefore, to place modern narratives and ritual practices in historical context, I rely on information about the general history of church teachings in Ecuador (for a history of *la doctrina* in Ecuador, see Albuja Mateus 1998; for a study of catechism during the colonial period, see Hartmann 2001).

I begin with a brief description of how the church established colonial control of Catholic ritual-transformative powers by specifically defining the food substances and symbols to be used for the sacrificial offering and by excluding indigenous peoples from the priesthood, so that the sacraments that led to eternal salvation were controlled by European, *criollo*, and sometimes mestizo priests. I then discuss Andean resistance movements to European church hegemony through subaltern definitions of priestly power over the sacraments of the Eucharist and confession. Finally, I turn to modern Salasacan Catholicism to look at narratives of near-death experiences in which European Catholic imagery is fused with local indigenous constructions of the sacred landscape, the ritual burial of a bread baby that mimics the Catholic sacraments of baptism and transubstantiation, and a funerary ritual called the *mondongo miza* in which clerical authority is mocked while priestly powers are appropriated. The narratives and rituals in Salasaca show that indigenous peoples responded to the homogenizing efforts of indoctrination in local, creative ways. They incorporated images of purgatory, appropriated priestly powers, and challenged priestly authority through rituals that produce locality. Salasacans are well aware of the uniqueness of their rituals, and they are quite conscious that, through rituals, they maintain individual and collective identity while they simultaneously remember their cultural past and create an alternative modernity in the present.

Race, Religion, and Sacraments in Historical Perspective
Symbols Defined, Sacramental Powers Controlled

The colonization of the Americas created new problems for the sixteenth-century Roman Catholic church. Europeans "defined" new racial categories, based on their ethnocentric constructions of classes of beings. Priests had to administer sacraments to indigenous peoples in remote areas, where they did not always have access to christening oils, holy water, or the "fruit of the vine and work of human hands," which would become the Blood of Christ. Questions raised included the following: Can *negros* (or *indios*, mestizos, or *mulatos*) be ordained without dispensation? Can maize flour be used for the Eucharistic bread if wheat is not available? Can the "wine" of the maguey (*cabuya de Méjico*) be consecrated when wine from grapevines is not available? Such questions indicate the problems faced by religious specialists in a new situation, with new "races" of people. They reveal that the clergy considered the sacraments a life and death matter, as shown by the concern on the part of priests for administering confession, penance, baptism, and communion to *indios* in remote areas. The responses of the archbishop Alonso de la Peña Montenegro provide a window to the multiple views of Catholicism in indigenous parishes in colonial times.

The archbishop, in his *Itinerario para párrocos de indios* taught, for example, that "the sacrament is that which, under the species of bread and wine, contains the Body and Blood of Christ to conserve the spiritual life received at baptism" (Penã Montenegro 1668:174). In remote indigenous parishes, bread made from maize and wine made from maguey plants were not acceptable materials for the sacraments, even though the archbishop acknowledged that in some parts, bread made from maize was the only bread the indigenous people knew. As for the ordination of indigenous peoples, blacks, and mestizos, the archbishop sent a contradictory message. First, he stated that the "Church of God regularly admits to its service and holy ministries all who are apt, suitable, and willing." *Indios* could be ordained provided they were the children of a legitimate marriage. In practice, however, the indigenous peoples were excluded from the priesthood. As Phelan (1967: 55) explains:

> The objection to an Indian clergy by all branches of the Spanish clergy stemmed from a selfish desire to preserve their lucrative Indian parishes as well as from genuine convictions. Although the Spanish-born and American-born clergymen engaged in bitter quarrels over who would dominate their particular ecclesiastical corporations, both groups closed ranks in their resolve to prevent the growth of an Indian clergy. An occasional mestizo and even a mulatto did manage to secure holy orders, but they were always a small minority. And they seldom received the more lucrative ecclesiastical benefices.

According to the *Itinerario*, mestizos could be ordained provided they were legitimate and "had no vice other than that of their mixed blood." The archbishop stated that here the category mestizo included the offspring of unions of *indias* and Spaniards as well as mulattos. However, because the *mancha* (stain) of the *mulato* was "uglier and more extraordinary, as is the generation of the mule (from which came the name)," it was preferable to ordain the mestizos who were the offspring of Spaniards and *indias* to teach and preach to the indigenous peoples (Peña Montenegro 1995:223). Perhaps the most paradoxical of these responses was the question of whether black slaves could be ordained in those places where there were many *negros* and *esclavos* (slaves).

The answer was that no slave could be ordained into major or minor orders,[3] the reason being that "slavery has within it a great indecency, which consists of being a minister of divine things he who is busied with mundane things, without having the liberty or free will to excuse himself from them" (Peña Montenegro 1995:223). If a slave were to be ordained as a priest, then he would have to be free. If the bishop had been aware of the man's slave status at the time of ordination, the bishop would have to pay twice his value to the master. Such were the contradictions of a church colonizing the new classes of beings created by European conquest and colonization.[4]

Definitions Subverted, Control Appropriated

Throughout South American history, indigenous peoples responded to domination by creating new religious movements and reworking old symbols. Messianic movements in the sixteenth and the nineteenth centuries challenged church hierarchical authority while simultaneously appropriating Christian symbols. For example, South American leaders of the Taqui Onquoy religion in Peru rejected many symbols of Spanish culture and identity. Native messiahs challenged the authority of Catholic priests while using the transformative powers of Catholic ritual:

> They questioned the efficacy of sacraments administered by corrupt priests, asserting instead the sacred power of Andean priests and shamans. . . . Confession was valid only when made before Andean priests. Similarly, food offered in sacrifice to the gods and the dead, like human food, had to consist of Andean products. (MacCormack 1991:185)

Some native Andeans resisted Spanish Catholic domination by becoming saints and messiahs. These individuals embodied and subverted Catholic sacred powers. As Saignes (1999:127) states, "By internalizing in their bodies the power of the sacred, in the form of a sainthood that also subsumed pre-Christian sacra, Indian protagonists revealed the profound transformation of their religiosity. . . . Native messiahs were eminently subversive figures."

One of these messiahs, Miguel Acarapi/Chiri, performed his own version of the Catholic Eucharistic ritual of transubstantiation and encouraged his followers to drink maize beer as the Blood of Christ and to eat the hallucinogenic San Pedro cactus (Abercrombie 1998; Saignes 1999). Maize beer (called *chicha* in Spanish and *asua* in Quichua) was and continues to be an important component of South American indigenous ceremonies. During Andean insurrections in the sixteenth century, the "sacramental beverage par excellence, *chicha*, became the indians' communion wine used in their own versions of the mass" (Abercrombie 1998:364).

Although the Taqui Onqoy movement did not take place in Ecuador, it gives historical meaning to the Catholic sacraments as contested symbols and a means by which to challenge European clergy as the only authority figures and ritual specialists. The indigenous appropriation of church powers was part of the process of negotiation of power systems in South American colonial history. The link between sacred and political power was manipulated by both Catholic clergy and indigenous shamans. A system of shamanic ritual power existed and continues to exist alongside church ritual powers, and shamans have historically appropriated some of the latter into their arsenal of supernatural resources. Trial records from 1786 tell of a shaman from the Ecuadorian coastal town of Punta Santa Elena who would hide his ritual objects under the church altar during mass in order for them to absorb some of the religious power (Salomon 1983:420). The shaman wanted the objects to be under the sacraments on the altar while the priest performed the ritual-transformation over them.

Amazonian peoples formed other religious movements. These movements enacted transformations in which indigenous shamans became prophets, and certain Christian symbols came to stand for themes of indigenous cosmology as expressed in myth, ritual, and shamanic discourse (Brown and Fernández 1991; Wright 1998). In Oyacachi, Ecuador, oral narratives link the geography of this unique *montaña* region with the history of conversion and with symbols of the Catholic Eucharist (Kohn 2002). These studies and others shed light on the ways by which indigenous peoples encode the history of conversion in the landscape, in narrative, and in rituals, and how they read into the meanings of Catholic sacraments. Throughout South American history church power has at times represented alterity, and at other times a source of religious power. When shamans challenged priests, when indigenous people rebelled against church obligations, and when native messiahs encouraged followers to reject Christianity, the church represented alterity, the colonial Other. Nevertheless, indigenous people appropriated symbols from Christianity and used them to empower themselves.

Salasacans did not participate in millennial or messianic movements; they did, however, incorporate Catholic symbols into local rituals. Certain aspects of Catholic imagery and ideology are an integral part of Salasacan traditions. The very landscape on which Salasacans depend for their livelihood holds historical and religious meanings. For instance, an old pathway that leads from Salasaca to Pelileo is called Soltera Ñan (*soltera*, young single woman; *ñan*, trail), because in the past young women who were engaged to be married were kept in the convent in Pelileo while they received religious instruction. Every day, grooms-to-be had to bring their wives-to-be "natural" foods from Salasaca, and they took this pathway. Thus the toponym Soltera

Ñan recalls the passage of young couples secretly going for indoctrination in the town of Pelileo before marriage.

Other aspects of religious experience include images found in sixteenth-century European Catholic worldviews. Indoctrination relied on the use of images of hell and purgatory in order to convert the "infidels" to Christianity. Descriptions of punishments administered by devils in the afterlife were incorporated into Salasacan cosmology, although this is only one aspect, among many, of indigenous views of the afterlife. As with stories about the rainmaking ritual on Quinchi Urcu, personal narratives play a major role in shaping people's views of the local landscape. In Salasaca, such narratives include stories of people who have had near-death experiences. These people are referred to as *wañush vueltacuna* (temporarily died and returned) or *wañusha causaricuna* (temporarily died and lived again) because they are said to have died, traveled the path to the afterlife, and come back. Although the individual experiences vary, there are several reports that describe a lake or a lake of fire and a large four-handled cauldron at the most sacred crossroads in Salasaca, Cruz Pamba. In the next section, I analyze the narratives of near-death experiences as evidence of the incorporation of Catholic indoctrination into indigenous experience.

At the Crossroads of Purgatory Narratives of Near-Death Experiences

Cruz Pamba is located on the eastern border of the parish. At Cruz Pamba, four roads merge into two roads, which then merge into one road. There is a hole in the ground in the space between the two roads before they merge. For generations, people have left offerings in the hole. In 1994, the *alcaldes* (festival sponsors) dedicated a large stone cross to the community. The cross is built over the hole, so that people can continue to leave offerings. Sometimes people come to Cruz Pamba to leave the used medicinal plants from cleansing a sick child. Sometimes people bring the sick child to Cruz Pamba and have the child roll in the sacred dirt there. People leave coins, pieces of broken plates, and candles as offerings to pray for petitions such as healing and animal fertility. In the past, some women would go there to pray that they not have more children. The same place is used for witchcraft. For most festivals, the participants must go to Cruz Pamba to dance and share food and maize beer.

Thresholds, including crossroads, symbolize different kinds of entrances, the crossing over into a new status (Douglas 1966:115). Cruz Pamba serves as a threshold for many ritual contexts in this life. Some people refer to it as the middle world, *chaupi mundo*, because it marks the location of purgatory in the afterlife. Not everyone refers to Cruz Pamba as purgatory, but time and again, as I asked people about the properties of this sacred place, people told me of the *paila de cuatro orejas*, the four-handled cauldron, that is there, but that we cannot see in this life. The following account, which I recorded in 1996, provides one depiction of the crossroads in the afterlife:

> My grandmother was Josefina Curichumbi.[5] She spoke of this, and she told my father, and my father told me. When she was a child, about ten years old, she died. She was dead for three days. All the family members were feeding the *accompaña genteguna*, the attendants at the funeral. They had slaughtered a cow or sheep. She had been dead more than two days, she was already in the coffin, and they had already held a wake. By the third day, they went to bury her. All the family members were crying. They went to bury her, and upwards there is the Cruz Pamba road, one road goes to Quinchi Urcu, another goes to Cruz Pamba, and there they part and there is a crossroads. . . . In Cruz Pamba there is a *paila* of flames that the old ones knew about. Right in that crossroads, upon arriving at that crossroads, my grandmother saw black dogs, *black dogs* [his emphasis], and nobody could pass there. There are black dogs in that *cruzero*, she said, devils. Right upon arriving at that *cruzero* she came to life [*causari*]. She knocked on the coffin. Everyone got scared. In that *cruzero* she said there are lots of devils, the black dogs are waiting there, the fire cauldron is there, with many *brujocuna* [witches-sorcerers] stirring it up, those who practiced witchcraft enter inside the *paila*, and among themselves they move it, in the *infierno* [hell]. My grandmother saw that, and there she woke up. People got scared, because she had been dead for three days. They went home, saying "she died and returned to life" [*wañushcash causari nisha*]. Those who had been crying were happy. . . . There is a *nina paila*, where the cemetery is today. Here there is a *nina cocha* [fire lake] and *nina paila* [fire-frying pan]. Since long ago [*sarun*], I remember when I was a child, where the cemetery is now, people never went straight [when carrying the coffin], they went around it . . . the *almas* couldn't cross it.

The narrative is a thirdhand account: the narrator's grandmother told it to her son, who then told the narrator. This is one among several narratives of people who have seen the devil's cauldron during near death experiences. The narratives describe different parts of the soul's journey along the landscape, to the volcano Tungurahua, where a mountain mistress spins wool. The first part of this journey, at Cruz Pamba, is near the border of the parish. The roads here merge into one road that leads out of Salasacan indigenous space and into the town of Pelileo, the historical center of church and state authority for Salasacans. Until recently, people would walk this road to go to Pelileo to get certification and official ritualization of births, baptisms, marriages, and deaths. In this life, people walk to or from Pelileo for festivals. In the afterlife, it is a threshold across which the souls must pass, and in which sinners, such as those who practiced witchcraft, get trapped.

South American Christianities emerged from the persistence of certain indigenous ideologies under church hegemony. The near-death experience described here includes several elements of Andean Christianity: witches (*brujocuna*), devils (*diablocuna* or *demoniocuna*), and black dogs. Black dogs were part of Incan beliefs about the afterlife as reported by the chronicler José de Arriaga (Marzal 1993:95). According to Arriaga's report, some descriptions of the afterlife tell that the deceased had to pass by black dogs to get to the other world. Dogs are also associated with haciendas. Mary Crain (1991:86) reports that black dogs were "the ominous gatekeepers without whom a traditional hacienda would not be complete."

In another case, a woman who saw the *paila* in the afterlife had a revelation that she would become a healer. In 1998, I interviewed Teresa, a woman in her mid thirties, about how she became a healer. Teresa went into premature labor after a serious argument with her husband. She "died" while giving birth, and God revealed himself to her. God came down from the mountain called Palama Cruz to Cruz Pamba, and he showed her two roads. There God said, "Look, there is the *paila* of hell. Think well. Do you want to go to the *paila* or do you want to be saved? Those who believe in me will be saved." He then showed her all the medicinal plants in the world that were good for healing and told her to pray to him at noon and midnight. God told her that after four years she would be called upon to heal. But God warned her not to charge a lot of money to her clients. Four years later, a neighbor was in bed dying, and Teresa's call to healing began. Now when she heals, she uses medicinal plants from the mountain Teligote, places stones taken from twelve different springs in boiling water, and gives that water to the patients. She leaves offerings on the mountain Palama Cruz so that her clients will heal.

The image of a four-handled cauldron with the souls of sinners boiling inside appears in sixteenth- and seventeenth-century European and Latin American representations of hell. One of these is an anonymous painting from sixteenth-century Portugal called *Inferno*. In the painting, a devil sits above a four-handled cauldron in which souls are being boiled. Another painting of hell is found in the Jesuit Church of La Companía in Quito. This painting depicts a range of punishments for different sins, among them a large cauldron in which, again, the souls are being boiled. The painting in the church in Quito is an 1879 copy of the original, painted in 1620 (Parsons 1945:87). Franciscan missionaries brought a similar painting to the church in Baños, located in the same province as Salasaca. It is likely that indigenous people visited the church and saw such images, or that Catholic missionaries communicated the imagery of hell. In 1570, at the first church council of Quito, it was declared that the Dominican friars would make the *indios*

> understand the great errors of their infidelity, and the penalty and punishment that God gives to the infidels in Hell, and the great favor he has granted them by making himself known to them, because they will enjoy the glory of heaven if they were good Christians and did good works. (El Sígnodo, cited in Moreno Yánez 1991:534)

As Catholic missionaries taught their beliefs about the afterlife, they also used those beliefs to control indigenous peoples and enforce obedience to the clergy, who were connected politically to colonial authorities. Indigenous people were aware of the relationship between the colonial church and the colonial state, and they frequently rebelled against the clergy (Moreno Yánez 1991:543) even as they incorporated aspects of Catholicism into their worldview and religious rituals.

The mapping of particular aspects of Catholic cosmology onto the local sacred landscape is part of the "history of imageries" anchored in "the power-charged social relations that constitute their human creators" (Silverblatt 1988:175). Imagery is a powerful and effective tool for communicating (Gillespie 1993; Whitten and Whitten 1993:12–14) and was used by missionaries to convert native South Americans. The Capuchin missionaries used imagery in their indoctrination of the Huitoto in the Colombian Putumayo region. Taussig describes their use of oil paintings to teach about sin, heaven, and hell:

> It had been Father Gaspar's explicit intention to use paintings to ensure that the souls of the savages would be penetrated not merely by the evangelical word but by visual imagery. Yet for that imagery to take hold of the savages' souls and become part of their imagining, the savages had to put that imagery into words, their own words, through the medium of communal ritual and narcotic stimulation. (Taussig 1987:386)

In Salasaca, people mapped this visual imagery onto a local landscape that mediates religious experiences, including a brush with death and travel to the other world.

Purgatory Catholic Imagery and Colonial History

Purgatory, as a "third place" between heaven and hell, became part of official Church teaching in the twelfth century (Le Goff 1984:3). Purgatory was a place where souls underwent a trial, a place where they were purged of their sins before they entered heaven. The depictions of the trials of purgatory and torments of hell draw on many traditions, including pre-Christian Greek, Roman, Egyptian, and Persian cosmologies. Symbols of the trial in the afterlife include the bridge and the ladder (Hughes 1968). Fire is a theme in descriptions of the afterlife, and was a polysemous symbol in Medieval Europe. Fire is both punishing and purifying. Fire, argues Jacques Le Goff (1984), is "part of a rite of passage, quite appropriate to this place of transition."

As a place of transition, it makes sense that, in the Andes, purgatory would be located geographically at the crossroads, on a part of the landscape that symbolizes a threshold. Gary Urton (1980) provides linguistic evidence for the relationship between crossroads and thresholds. In the southern Andes, the union or bifurcation of roads is called *chaca*. In various dialects of Quechua, the words *chaca* and *chacana* refer to crosses, the Christian crucifix, crossroads, thresholds, bridges, lintels, and ladders. The ladder and the bridge, which are symbols of a trial in the afterlife in medieval European cosmology, are linguistically linked to crossroads in southern Quechua dialects in the Andes, further corroborating the association of crossroads with a threshold.

The spatialization of purgatory in Andean Ecuador occurred through historical, ideological processes of power and authority in which popular folk beliefs, sacred geography, and symbols from various old-world traditions were appropriated by the Catholic church, made into official church teaching, and again incorporated into the symbol system, sacred geography, and folklore of Andean indigenous peoples. Although the church today maintains that purgatory is a state of being and not a place (Le Goff 1984:13), older discourse located the entrances to hell and purgatory geographically.

In Salasaca, part of the colonial imagery of hell was grafted onto an indigenous sacred landscape and incorporated into representations of the afterlife. The punishments at the *paila* of the sacred crossroads are for sins that express Salasacan moral teachings. The *paila*, witchcraft, devils, and sacred geography are part of the indigenous world, shaped by powerful images and historical experience. Narratives of near-death experiences not only provide information about the sacred landscape, but also may enforce moral values. By connecting landscape features such as crossroads, depressions, and the volcano Tungurahua with stages of the journey to the afterlife, people reconstruct the landscape to serve as a mnemonic device, a reminder of the otherworld.

Although the descriptions vary somewhat in individual details, the route and the locations remain the same, and, when discussing the sacred place of Cruz Pamba, people often remember and discuss what they have heard about this from the *wañusha causaricuna*. The following account is from a woman in her thirties who cures by cleansing, that is, sweeping bundles of medicinal plants over the body, thereby ridding it of any negative substances. In a 1998 interview, she reported:

> I help people to have luck [*suerte*]. For instance, a friend wanted me to cleanse his pickup truck so that he would have luck with it. I cleansed it with medicinal plants and threw them right in the middle of the cross-roads [at Cruz Pamba]. Also, the owner rolled around in the dirt there. . . . The *paila* is not there, but a little below there are two *pailas* side by side, that's what the *wañusha causaricuna* people have said. They say that's "the road that goes to God's land." People who yelled at their parents, or people who were sexually promiscuous during life can't pass that cauldron, they go to another road. There are dogs and the people get punished with *cuchinilla* or *tunis* [prickly pear cactus] thorns. God has a book with a list of names of sinners. The sinners [*juchayujcuna*] work in that land, in the dirt, like us. God has a nice house, like a church. God looks like a mirror, very bright [a bright shadow], only white. Like sheets. With his book he says wait, your time hasn't come yet. It's a sad *pacha* [time-space] there. That's why they say, "don't live a life of sin, don't yell at your own mother who gave birth to you, don't leave your husband."

Among the sins people have seen punished in the afterlife are disrespect for parents, lying, promiscuity, leaving one's husband, wife beating, and witchcraft. In the reports that I recorded, witchcraft was emphasized as the main reason souls would "fall in" to the cauldron. The experience of soul travel along the landscape, then, has meaning for people in a world in which sorcery is a reality and a threat to life. Strange and sudden illnesses and deaths are suspicious. One way to harm someone is to take the dirt from their footprint to the *yumbos*, the powerful sorcerers of Pastaza Province. In highland constructions of human geography, the *yumbos* of the Amazonian region are the most powerful shamans and sorcerers. But the imagery of the *paila* attests to an infernal punishment awaiting those who would harm others through witchcraft.

Another image common in near-death experiences relates to indigenous understandings of blanco-mestizo literacy (see Wogan 1997). An old narrative about ancient times tells that the Incas were the past inhabitants of Salasacan lands. In the story, the Incas chose to bury themselves in the earth rather than allow the Spanish to baptize them. The two factors expressed about the Incas, after confirming their human qualities, were "they weren't baptized, nor did they have writing" (Athens et al. 1975). This statement refers to two forms of domination: the Catholic church controlled the sacrament of baptism and the use of documents. Furthermore, God has a book with a list of birth and death dates for every individual, and near-death experience narratives confirm this for Salasacans (Wogan 1997).

Peter Wogan (1997) has analyzed Salasacan views of "textual domination" by examining forms of "literacy magic." This includes the use of literacy, books, and lists for witchcraft and for appeasing the souls of ancestors. These views of literacy, clearly a result of historical, colonial and postcolonial experiences with state and church control, also impinge on Salasacan religious experience in the form of the private symbolism of dreams. According to some interpretations of dream symbolism, if one is waiting for *papeles*, any type of official document that they need, they must dream of white clothing, such as the Salasacan *runa sumiro* (white hat). In dreams, white clothing symbolizes documents. White sheep, as the source of Salasacan clothing, also symbolize documents. This dream symbolism reflects historical experience: the elders used to say that in the past everything was written on sheepskin.

Indigenous views of literacy reflect the colonial experiences with state and church officials. The dream symbolism of writing in Salasaca can be compared to that of the indigenous peoples of the Sibundoy. Among the Sibundoy of Andean Colombia, to dream of papers means the dreamer will encounter a white person and fall into some misfortune, such as a legal suit (Taussig 1987:263). Writing and paper constitute part of the cosmos for the Siona people of lowland Colombia, who imagine a cosmic layer of the universe above God. In that layer are doves writing on paper. For the Paez of Colombia, their land titles were born of supernatural origins in a sacred stream (Rappaport 1985). Thus, views of literacy and writing in both the personal symbolism of dreams and the collective consciousness of historical narratives, myths, and descriptions of the cosmos, reflect what Wogan (1997:244–46) calls a "multiplicity of responses" to "textual domination" by the church and state. The narrative "The Incas Bury Themselves" refers to the Incas' lack of literacy and baptism. In the story, the Incas prefer to bury themselves within the earth than allow the Spaniards to baptize them. This discourse reflects past views of literacy, although today indigenous leaders use writing and historical documents to their advantage.

To summarize, near-death experiences occur under varying circumstances, including accidents, illness, and fainting spells. Although individual reports vary, people often refer to stories told by the *wañusha causaricuna* when describing the sacred landscape and the afterlife. The narratives of near-death experiences constitute a collective representation embedded in individual consciousness. As cultural expressions, narratives play a key role in the cultural representations of a community. Cultural expressions are "constitutive and shaping" (Bruner 1986:7) and stories "produce the world they describe" (Taylor 1995:244). Narratives also reveal native interpretations of historical experiences (Hill 1988).

In the narrative "The Incas Bury Themselves" indigenous people express their views of European domination through writing as well as the church's ritual control of indigenous peoples. Wogan's work on textual domination reveals that literacy became symbolic of the power of white state and church domination. The telling of personal memories reproduces the sacred landscape of Salasaca. Stories of the rainmaking ritual confirm the power of a local sacred mountain, while anecdotes of near-death experiences incorporate colonial teachings of purgatory into indigenous constructions of sacred crossroads. The most common image described in such narratives is that of a giant cauldron, such as the one depicted in colonial paintings of hell. Narratives of near-death experiences illustrate indigenous interpretations of Roman Catholic imagery.

In this section, I have analyzed how Catholic indoctrination shaped individual experiences with death. Narrative is the vehicle by which the imagery and symbolism of personal experiences become part of the collective body of discourse that reproduces the imagery and symbolism. People also enact themes from Catholicism in ritual. I now turn to symbolic expressions in ritual events. It is through collective rituals that people create and maintain their identities and their places in modern Ecuador.

The Burial of the Bread Baby

One institution of colonial Catholicism that now constitutes the basis of indigenous social and ritual life is the festival sponsorship system. Festivals, usually held in honor of a patron saint or to celebrate feast days of the Roman Catholic calendar, became a part of the rhythm of life in the Andes. The festival of Caporales ("leaders," "sponsors"), celebrated in February in Salasaca, honors the baby Jesus and the patron Saint Buenaventura. Men volunteer to sponsor the festival, paying for food, drink, and music. A man who volunteers to sponsor the festival is called "Taita (father) Caporal" and his wife is called "Mama Caporala."

The Caporal asks several men to be his *negros* (black soldiers)[6] and other young men or boys to perform as *doñas*. The *doñas*, who dress as women, dance with the men portraying black soldiers during the three days of the festival. The Taita Caporal and his wife, Mama Caporala, refer to the dancers as their "children." One *doña*, called the *ñuñu*, dances with Taita Caporal. The other *doñas* carry food on their backs while the *ñuñu* carries bread baked in the form of a baby.

There are really two babies wrapped together, one male and one female, but people speak of it as one baby, and I shall refer to it this way throughout the discussion. The *ñuñu* keeps this bread baby, called *tanda wawa*, for one year after the celebration. After a year, the former festival participants reunite to hold a funeral for the "baby."

The transformation of the physical body through death and the regeneration of the social body are enacted in this burial. The events of the bread baby funeral are as follows. The day before the burial, a man makes a coffin for the baby, and later that night the participants gather at the home of the *ñuñu* to hold a wake. Just before the wake, a *rezachic* (indigenous man who knows Catholic prayers) "baptizes" the bread baby and gives it a name (the term *shutichina* means both to name and to baptize), and prays the blessing of the Father, Son, and Holy Spirit, the Our Father, and the Hail Mary. The babies are named Manuel and Manuela, because, according to one *rezachic* "Our Lord was born in Bethlehem [as] niño Manuel (Jesús Manuel)."

The participants then go to the home of the Caporal to hold a wake. They wrap the bread baby in Salasacan home-woven textiles. It is swaddled tightly the way Salasacan babies are, and a member of the group nestles it in the little coffin. At the wake, the participants pray, eat, and drink together. They sit around the coffin, which is surrounded by candles in the patio. The next day, the men acting as pallbearers take the coffin to the Catholic church for mass. The little coffin, with the bread child inside, enters the sacred space of the church during the Catholic mass, then the public space of the central plaza where musicians play the traditional music of children's funeral wakes, and other attendants distribute maize beer. The pallbearers (who are former *negros* of the festival), carry the coffin to the home of the Caporal, where they dig a hole and bury it in the patio.

Aside from the naming ceremony–baptism, two other transformations of Catholic theology are evoked by this event. The first is the transcendence of death through sacrifice and resurrection. In 1998, when I attended the mass, the (blanco-mestizo) priest related the mass for the "child" to the celebration of the Eucharist and the child's ascension among the angels. He also took the opportunity to speak about Protestant denominations that have gained a small number of converts in the region, mentioning that while many accept Christ's resurrection, the Jehovah's Witnesses do not. The homily, therefore, emphasized the centrality of this concept of resurrection to Christianity, since the priest acknowledged that Protestants also accept the resurrection.

The second transformation evoked during the event is that of transubstantiation. After the mass, in the patio at the home of the Caporal, the *rezachic* led the prayers over the child and stated: "This is not just divine bread. There is flesh in here (*aicha sirigunmi*). Our flesh, our blood, our bone, our pus (ñu-

cuchij aicha, ñucuchij yahuar, ñuchuchij tullu, ñucuchij quía)." The prayers, which are the same prayers said at the burial of a human, emphasize that flesh dies, but the soul goes to heaven. Aside from giving the blessing of the Father, Son, and Holy Spirit, the *rezachic* also mentioned the collective contribution, eating, and drinking of those who came together. He emphasized the hard work of the people, the sweat that goes into producing food, and the thanks they give for the food. He spoke of the past memories of the tradition, and the future memories they would have together. With that, the bread child was buried, with the understanding that it decomposes (*se pudre*) and transforms to earth (*allpa tucun*).

The emphasis on collective eating and drinking, the bodily fluid (sweat) exuded to produce food, and the linking of people into one social body represented by a bread baby that embodies flesh, bone, blood, and pus enact themes similar to those of the Catholic sacraments. These include incarnation, birth, and death expressed in the Catholic sacraments of communion, baptism, and transubstantiation. This indigenous Andean expression of the bodily experiences of life and death includes both a male and female sacrificed child. In accordance with Andean concepts of duality and gender complementarity, the sacrifice in the patio has both male and female aspects that return to earth. Despite centuries of domination by a patriarchal church hierarchy, indigenous rituals in the Andes express the significance of gender complementarity (Belote and Belote 1988). In fact, in my recording of the burial, the wife of the Caporal cried for her *ushushi* (daughter) and the *rezachic* prayed for the collective "sister" (*ñucuchij pani*). When I asked an elder why the male bread baby was left out of the orations, he responded "because for us the little female is always more meaningful." While Christianity celebrates the birth of the Christ child, named Immanuel ("God is with us"), Salasacans recognize a sister-child, "Manuela," in this ritual.

The ritual expression of the body, death, resurrection, and the afterlife is also enacted at the time of death in mortuary rituals for humans. By taking on the role of Catholic priests, lay persons enact their own transformations above and beyond that which the priest has done. In the ritual of the *mondongo miza*, friends of the deceased play act a church-ritual performance and enable the soul to transcend death, move out of earthly space, and move on to God's land.

The *Mondongo Miza* Subversion and Appropriation of Church Power

When a person dies, family and friends hold an all-night wake, a mass, and a burial. Despite the Catholic mass and the priest's prayers for the soul, two other rituals must be performed by Salasacans to ensure that the soul of the deceased leaves local space. One of these is the *ucu pichina* (house-cleansing ritual). Two days after the burial, the pallbearers return to the home of the deceased with medicinal plants and a *cuy* (guinea pig) to cleanse the home of the deceased in a manner similar to the way the body is cleansed during curing rituals. The other ritual is the *mondongo miza*,[7] which is performed the day after the burial. *Mondongo* usually means "tripe" in Ecuador, but in Salasaca people use it to mean "head." Since time immemorial, the ancestors of modern Salasacans refer to this funerary ritual as the *mondongo miza*. The pallbearers and friends gather at the home of the deceased and receive food and drink from immediate family members. Two men dress as *curas* (priests), use typical Salasacan home-woven mantles for their regalia and a notebook or upside-down Bible for their scriptures (Wogan 1997:185).

One priest, located at the part of the patio near the door of the house, is the "upper head" priest. The other, located at the adjacent side of the patio, is the "lower foot" priest. Explanations for this ritual are that the people are "making fun" of the priests, yet through this burlesque role-playing the men perform the ritual transformation of sending the soul of the deceased from earthly space to God's land or the upper world. The priests sprinkle maize beer, which they call holy water, onto the attendants and hand out raw potato slices, which they call the Body of Christ. The crisp, white slices of the raw potato bear some physical resemblance to the communion host of the Catholic mass. In Catholic ritual, the bread of the Eucharist becomes the sacrificed Body of Christ, who transcends death through resurrection. The Andean potato, as a metaphor for the Eucharist, is employed in this ritual of death to send the soul off to its new life. The use of raw potato slices as host may serve as a reminder of this transformation from food to life-giving body.

Maize and potatoes are staple foods for Andean indigenous people. They are also key elements in ceremonial foods. Almost all social events involve the *miza*, or table. The *miza* appears to mimic the Catholic altar, but it has been a part of indigenous Ecuadorian feasts since pre-Columbian times (Salomon 1986). The *miza* is covered with red and purple mantles, and it contains a wooden tray full of *mote* (hominy), a bottle of *trago* (cane alcohol), and a bucket of maize beer. An indigenous *rezachic* blesses these ceremonial foods before consumption. During the *mondongo miza*, in addition to the ceremonial use of maize and potatoes, these foods come to represent symbols of the Catholic mass.

Mimesis and Alterity in the *Mondongo Miza*

The mock priest does not just make fun of the clergy; by mimicking Catholic priests, the Salasacan men enact a transformation and become mediums for sending prayers to God. The mimicry actually does something; it effects a religious transformation, one in which people have the power to send the dangerously powerful soul of the deceased out of the space of the living and on to God's world. Within the space of the church, and in the cemetery on the Day of the Dead, Catholic priests control the powers of transubstantiation and the other sacraments. They also serve as mediators, asking for God's blessing of deceased loved ones and sending prayers to God for those people. During the ritual performance of this mediator role, indigenous men take over the religious power that is controlled by priests in church settings. They walk to an area behind the house of the deceased and choose a spot from which to send the soul to God's land. This ritual evokes the memory of other kin who have passed on to the other world, and family and friends ask the men mimicking the priest to pray for those souls. This ritual in domestic space is a necessary supplement to the Catholic mass in which the priest prays for the soul of the deceased. By mimicking the Catholic priests, by producing an upper (head) and lower (foot) duality, and by symbolically inverting the ritual paraphernalia (robes, texts, and ceremonial foods) of the priest, indigenous men become the mediums for sending prayers and souls to the Christian God.

During this funerary ritual, the "priests" make use of what Taussig (1993: xii) calls the mimetic faculty: "The wonder of mimesis lies in the copy drawing on the character and power of the original, to the point whereby the representation may even assume that character and that power." Taussig emphasizes that this mimesis is produced through historical processes. He cites cross-cultural studies that show how the mimetic faculty operates in colonized societies: colonized peoples mimic the colonial Other, and thereby use that power for magic, curing, and ritual.

The power of mimetic magic enables Panamanian Kuna sacred objects, which depict the white man, to cure. Members of the Hauka movement of Niger practice what Stoller (1995) calls the embodiment of colonial memories as they mimic colonial officers during possession ceremonies. Like the indigenous priest who substitutes local indigenous objects for the priest's sacred symbols, the Hauka choose local materials to imitate symbols of colonial authority. A termite's nest is painted to represent the governor's palace, an egg cracked over a statue of the governor represents the white and yellow plumage of the colonial hat, and "there is something immensely powerful released at this moment, begging for interpretation" (Taussig 1993:242). French authorities found this native representation of themselves so offensive that members of the Hauka movement were jailed. And, like the near-death experiences of Salasacans, the embodiment of colonial memories was also an intense religious experience, involving altered states of consciousness. Taussig argues that mimesis allows people to assume the identity of the European and at the same time to stand apart from it. The Salasacan use of Catholic symbols suggests an indigenous appropriation of powers and an indigenous interpretation of ritual.

The rituals of both the bread-baby funeral and the *mondongo miza* create a sacred space for alternative powers. The bread baby in the casket moves from the Salasacan home to the Catholic church during mass, where it stands in front of the altar. During mass, the bread and wine on the altar become body and blood of Christ. Afterward, an indigenous *rezachic* prays while the pallbearers bury the "baby" in the patio of the home of the festival sponsor. The *mondongo miza* is a necessary ritual in addition to the one carried out for the deceased in the Catholic church. Here, the patio is divided into upper-head and lower-foot space, and the two mock priests appropriate clerical powers in this domestic space.

Duality plays a role in both rituals. The bread baby expresses indigenous values of gender duality, while the *mondongo miza* enacts a transformation within a dualistic division of domestic space at the home of the deceased. Both rituals produce Salasacan locality. They are intimate performances involving collective eating, drinking, laughing, and crying among friends, neighbors, and kin. They are ritual complements to the public, official, church-sanctioned rituals performed in the public space of the church and plaza. It is through such local-level rituals that Salasacans carve out an identity for themselves in the pluricultural nation-state of Ecuador.

Conclusion

I have focused here on one aspect of historical experience — Catholic indoctrination — and the way by which it is encoded and expressed in narrative and ritual. Responses to indoctrination into a world religion reveal the changes, transformations, and continuities of local cultural expressions and cosmologies. Religion, as a set of beliefs and practices that take shape through historical processes, is embodied in personal experiences and reproduced through collective rituals and narratives; it continues to be an important part of indigenous life and it plays a role in identity politics.

As indigenous peoples move into the new millennium, they are increasingly reflexive of their histories and identities as indigenous peoples and as bearers of a proud heritage. The influence of pan-Ecuadorian indigenous movements, the political culture of Ecuador, and this increased reflexivity have also produced various responses to institutionalized religion and indigenous cosmology. Some indigenous peoples in other parts of Ecuador now consider beliefs in purgatory and hell as part of the colonial legacy, and they embrace other forms of Christianity such as liberation theology (Lyons 1998) and Evangelical Protestantism (Uzendoski, this volume). In Salasaca, there is an Evangelical church with a small number of followers, and their beliefs are respected by other Salasacans. For example, at social events, men tend to pressure one another to share drinks as a form of sociality, but those who are known to be Evangelicals are never pressured to drink alcoholic beverages.

Many Salasacans self-identify as Catholics, and there is one indigenous priest. A few politically active indigenous people embrace what they consider the authentic forms of Andean indigenous religion, emphasizing traditional medicine, ritual pathways, and the Earth Mother. Given the respect that indigenous leaders have for their elders, it would be difficult to completely challenge the influence of Catholicism, because it is so much a part of the very traditions that indigenous activists seek to preserve. Roman Catholicism is a part of indigenous traditions, and the influence of Catholicism is seen in all domains of modern indigenous culture, including narratives, shamanic chants, agricultural rites, festivals, near-death experiences, and rites of passage such as baptism and marriage.

This chapter began with a colonial description of the brutal punishment of an indigenous woman upon a priest's orders. I repeat here the first part of the testimony of Juan Paulino Carlosama because it is historically significant: "The Sunday of Casimodo, at the time of the public *doctrina*. . . ." The *doctrina* was the context for the transmission of Roman Catholicism to indigenous people within their local settings. Attempts to eradicate the old religion and convert all indigenous Latin Americans to Christianity were strong; they enacted public punishments and depicted formidable torments in the afterlife. Concepts of death, passage, and thresholds together with the ability to transcend death through baptism and communion, were reworked into indigenous understandings of community, ritual, and the sacred landscape. The narratives of near-death experiences and the performance of rituals that parallel the Catholic sacraments reveal the limits of hegemony. Catholicism is a fundamental part of indigenous life for many people, an inseparable basis of many traditions that people celebrate with pride. But local communities responded to indoctrination in different ways and created rituals that allowed them control over some of the transformative powers monopolized by priests.

Salasacan Catholicism is more than a superficial overlay of Christianity on indigenous religiosity. It is embedded in sacred places of the local landscape, and it is part of the traditional systems of life and death with which indigenous people identify in modern and millennial Ecuador. The rites on the sacred mountain are part of the collective memory of the past as well as individual practice in the present. The hegemony of the church failed to end the practice of mountain offerings. Indigenous peoples accommodated, appropriated, and subverted church powers in different ways.

It has been argued elsewhere that subaltern representations of "race" can be learned by paying attention to indigenous festivals, myths, and rituals (Whitten and Corr 1999, 2001). The same can be said for reading indigenous constructions of power, history, and worldview. Narratives and rituals are vehicles of expression through which people reflect on experiences, produce alternative discourses, and express their own representations of the sacred order. As "texts" (Geertz 1973), the rituals described here can be "read" on various levels. At one level, they are humorous and entertaining; at another, a necessary tradition that unites members of the community. They can also be read as containing a "hidden transcript" that challenges church authority, or at least as an assertion of indigenous control over the transformative powers of life and death. Everyone who watches the *mondongo miza* is aware that sacred Catholic symbols are being replaced by raw potatoes and maize beer. Rituals as text are, as Geertz (1973:448) states, a people's reading of their own experience. The experiences here include history, conversion, resistance, accommodation, worldview, humor, death, and life. By paying attention to local-level representations as expressed in narratives and rituals, we hear the voices that are not included in the dominant discourse of nation-state nationalism.

ACKNOWLEDGMENTS

I would like to thank the people of Salasaca for their patient and generous assistance during my research. In order to protect their identities, I have not included the names of real individuals in this chapter. I gratefully acknowledge the financial support for research in Ecuador provided by a Fulbright IIE grant from 1991 and 1992, grants from the Tinker Foundation and Beckman Institute in 1996, and a Fulbright-Hays Grant from 1998 and 1999. I also benefited from a Beslow Fellowship and a Dissertation Completion Fellowship at the University of Illinois at Urbana-Champaign. Support for research on historical church documents in 2002 was provided by a Research Initiation Award from Florida Atlantic University. I thank Patricio Caizabanda, Patricia Villalva Bermeo, and Miguel Vasquez for their help. I would like to thank Norman Whitten, Michelle Wibbelsman, and two anonymous reviewers for their helpful comments on earlier drafts of this chapter. Any shortcomings are my own responsibility.

NOTES

1. Moreno Yánez (1991:536) cites the testimony of Juan Paulino Carlosama: "que el día Domingo de Casimodo hallandose toda la gente India congregada en

el ciminterio . . . a tiempo de dotrina publica, sucedio que este parroco sin que aya precedido la correspondiente averiguacion del echo de la berdad . . . executo aquel biolento castigo hasiendo latase a mi muger in un arbol de nogal sujetandola al impulso de dos indios asiendole despojar el rropaje de la espalda mando descargar cien azotes y yo dolorido . . . de ber a mi muger en tan micerable estado . . . me llege a lo de ella y con mi manta la cubri; y solo por este echo mando dicho Cura, a sujetarme con dos indios, y me izo dar sinquenta y dos azotes." [Expediente de Juan Paulino Carlosama y Rosa Solano, indios del pueblo de Atuntaqui, contra el Dr. Dn. Miguel Michilena, cura del dicho pueblo, sobre agravios. Año 1792. (ANH/Q. Fondo Corte Suprema. Sec. Indígenas, 1792). Directly quoted from Moreno Yánez, nonstandard spelling because of 1742 date. File of Juan Paulino Carlosama and Rosa Solano, Indians of the town of Atuntaqui, against Dr. Dn. Miguel Michilena, priest of the said town, regarding offenses.]

2. Salasaca today is an independent parish, but until 1972 it was part of the parish of Pelileo. As part of the parish of Pelileo, Salasaca was incorporated into the system of Catholic indoctrination operating in the region. There was a special concern for bringing la doctrina to the Salasacans. Various priests undertook this task until 1945 when the Madres Lauritas, a mission of nuns based in Colombia, permanently established residence in the parish. Since that time, the Madres have been involved in religious instruction and the teaching of Catholic prayers to indigenous orators, called rezachicuna.

3. Major orders include deacons and priests. Minor orders include porters, lectors, exorcists, and acolytes.

4. The church, as a colonial power, represented colonial interests but often clashed with the political and economic interests of encomenderos over the treatment of indigenous and Black peoples (Albuja Mateus 1998). Individual priests also paternalistically defended indigenous peoples in colonial and postcolonial times. In a 1907 letter to the archbishop of Quito, a local priest wrote that the way to attend to the spiritual needs of the Salasacans was to send them a priest who truly loved them, one who would not treat them as they generally treat the "poor Indians . . . with whips and lashes, insults and harshness, but rather with softness, tenderness, and compassion" (Carlos María de la Torre, Legajos IV: 11, Diocese of Ambato).

5. All names have been changed.

6. Some Salasacans interpret this festival as preserving the memory of the 1895 Liberal Revolution, in which indigenous peoples and Black soldiers collaborated to protect Eloy Alfaro, the leader of the revolution (Whitten and Corr 1999; Corr 2000).

7. Salasacans distinguish their own ritual from the Catholic Mass in their pronunciation of the word for "mass." Miza refers to the indigenous funeral rite of Mondongo Miza. Misa is used to refer to the Catholic Mass said by an ordained priest.

REFERENCES

Abercrombie, Thomas

1998 *Pathways of Memory and Power*. Madison: University of Wisconsin Press.

Albuja Mateus, Augusto E.

1998 *Doctrinas y parroquias del obispado de Quito en la segunda mitad del siglo XVI*. Quito: Abya-Yala.

Athens, Olivia, et al.

1975 (editors) *Urdimal Tiempomunda. Proyecto Piloto de Educación Bilingüe*. Quito: Instituto Interandino de Desorollo.

Belote, Linda, and Jim Belote

1988 *Gender, Ethnicity and Modernization: Saraguro Women in a Changing World*. Multidisciplinary Studies in Andean Anthropology. V. J. Vitzthum, ed. Ann Arbor: Michigan Discussions in Anthropology, fall 1988, v.8: 101–117.

Brown, Michael, and Eduardo Fernández

1991 *War of Shadows: The Struggle for Utopia in the Peruvian Amazon*. Berkeley: University of California Press.

Bruner, Edward M.

1986 Experience and its Expressions. In *The Anthropology of Experience*. Victor W. Turner and Edward M. Bruner, eds. Pp. 3–29. Urbana: University of Illinois Press.

Carrasco, Eulalia

1982 *Salasaca: La organización social y el alcalde*. Quito: Mundo Andino.

Corr, Rachel

2000 Cosmology and Personal Experience: Representations of the Sacred Landscape in Salasaca, Ecuador. Ph.D. dissertation, Department of Anthropology, University of Illinois, Urbana-Champaign.

2002 Reciprocity, Communion, and Sacrifice: Food in Andean Ritual and Social Life. *Food and Foodways* 10(1–2):1–25.

Crain, Mary

1991 Poetics and Politics in the Ecuadorean Andes: Women's Narratives of Death and Devil Possession. *American Ethnologist* 18(1):67–89.

Douglas, Mary

1966 *Purity and Danger: An Analysis of the Concepts of Pollution and Taboo*. New York: Routledge.

Geertz, Clifford

1973 *The Interpretation of Culture*. New York: Basic Books.

Gillespie, Susan

1993 Power, Pathways, and Appropriations in Mesoamerican Art. In *Imagery and Creativity*. Dorothea S. Whitten and Norman E. Whitten, Jr., eds. Pp. 68–107. Tucson: University of Arizona Press.

Griffiths, Nicholas

1999   Introduction. In *Spiritual Encounters*. Nicholas Griffiths and Fernando
Cervantes, eds. Pp. 1–42. Lincoln: University of Nebraska Press.

Hartmann, Roswith

2001   El obispo de Quito Luis Francisco Romero y el catecismo Quichua del
1725. In *Historia de la Iglesia Católica en el Ecuador Tomo III La Iglesia de
Quito en el Siglo XVIII*. Jorge Salvador Lara, ed. Pp. 1439–72. Quito:
Abya-Yala.

Hill, Jonathan

1988   (editor) *Rethinking History and Myth: Indigenous South American
Perspectives on the Past*. Urbana: University of Illinois Press.

Hughes, Robert

1968   *Heaven and Hell in Western Art*. New York: Stein and Day Publishers.

Kohn, Eduardo O.

2002   Infidels, Virgins, and the Black-Robed Priest: A Backwoods History of
Ecuador's Montaña Region. *Ethnohistory* 49(3): 545–82.

Le Goff, Jacques

1981   *The Birth of Purgatory*. Arthur Goldhammer, trans. Chicago: University of
Chicago Press.

Lyons, Barry

1998   "Taita Chimborazo and Mama Tungurahua": A Quichua Song, a
Fieldwork Story. *Anthropology and Humanism* 24(1): 33–46.

MacCormack, Sabine

1991   *Religion in the Andes*. Princeton: Princeton University Press.

Marzal, Manuel

1993   Andean Religion at the Time of the Conquest. In *South and Meso-
American Native Spirituality*. Gary H. Gossen, ed. Pp. 86–115. New York:
Crossroad Publishing.

Moreno Yánez, Segundo

1991   Los Doctrineros "Wiracochas" Recreadores de Nuevas Formas Culturales.
In *Reproducción y Transformación de las Sociedades Andinas Siglos XVI–XX*.
Segundo Moreno Yánez and Frank Salomon, eds. Pp. 529–53. Quito:
Abya-Yala.

Parsons, Elsie Clews

1945   *Peguche: A Study of Andean Indians*. Chicago: Chicago University Press.

Peña Montenegro, Alonso de la

1995 [1668] *Itinerario para párrocos de Indios*. Madrid: Consejo Superior de
Investigaciones Científicas.

Phelan, John Leddy

1967   *The Kingdom of Quito in the Seventeenth Century*. Madison: University of
Wisconsin Press.

Rappaport, Joanne

1985   *The Politics of Memory: Native Historical Interpretation in the Colombian Andes*. Cambridge: Cambridge University Press.

Saignes, Thierry

1999   The Colonial Condition in the Quechua-Aymara Heartland (1570–1780). In *The Cambridge History of the Native Peoples of the Americas*, vol 3. Pp. 59–137. Cambridge: Cambridge University Press.

Salomon, Frank

1983   Shamanism and Politics in Late Colonial Ecuador. *American Ethnologist* 10(1):413–28.

1986   *Native Lords of Quito in the Age of the Incas*. New York: Cambridge University Press.

Silverblatt, Irene

1988   Political Memories and Colonizing Symbols: Santiago and the Mountain Gods of Colonial Peru. In *Rethinking History and Myth*. Jonathan Hill, ed. Pp. 174–94. Urbana: University of Illinois Press.

Starn, Orin

1991   Missing the Revolution: Anthropologists and the War in Peru. *Cultural Anthropology* 6(1):63–91.

Stoller, Paul

1995   *Embodying Colonial Memories: Spirit Possession, Power, and the Hauka in West Africa*. New York: Routledge.

Taussig, Michael

1987   *Shamanism, Colonialism, and the Wildman: A Study in Terror and Healing*. Chicago: University of Chicago Press.

1993   *Mimesis and Alterity*. New York: Routledge.

Taylor, Lawrence

1995   *Occasions of Faith: An Anthropology of Irish Catholics*. Philadelphia: University of Pennsylvania Press.

Trouillot, Michel-Rolph

1995   *Silencing the Past: Power and the Production of History*. Boston: Beacon Press.

Urton, Gary

1980   Celestial Crosses: The Cruciform in Quechua Astronomy. *Journal of Latin American Lore* 6(1):87–110.

Whitten, Dorothea S., and Norman E. Whitten, Jr.

1993   Introduction. Imagery and Creativity: Ethnoaesthetics and Art Worlds in the Americas. Pp. 3–44. Tucson: University of Arizona Press.

Whitten, Norman E., Jr., and Rachel Corr

1999   Imagery of "Blackness" in Indigenous Myth, Ritual, and Discourse in South America. In *Representations of Blackness and the Performance of*

Identities. Jean Muteba Rahier, ed. Pp. 213–33. Westport, Conn.: Bergin & Garvey.

Whitten, Norman E., Jr., and Rachel Corr

2001 Contesting Images of Oppression: Indigenous Views of Blackness in the Americas. In *NACLA Report on the Americas: The Social Origins of Race* (special issue) 34(6):24–28.

Wogan, Peter

1997 Nationalism, Historical Consciousness, and Literacy in Highland Ecuador. Ph.D. dissertation, Department of Anthropology, Brandeis University.

Wright, Robin

1998 *Cosmos, Self, and History in Baniwa Religion: For Those Unborn*. Austin: University of Texas Press.

CHAPTER 5

Purgatory, Protestantism, and Peonage

Napo Runa Evangelicals and the
Domestication of the Masculine Will

MICHAEL A. UZENDOSKI

There is considerable variation in the cultural dynamics and political processes in cases of native Amazonians incorporating Christian identities. Donald K. Pollock (1993:166, 191) has written that one main feature of the native Amazonian Christianity is its "rarity" and association by indigenous peoples as being "the problem, not the solution" (e.g., Muratorio 1984). Some native Amazonians use Christianity to "tear their traditions apart" and create a new order (Brown and Fernández 1991:212–14), while others use it more "conservatively," subordinating its theology to their own symbolic and mythical worlds (Wright 1998:7, 293–94). While more dialogue and research are needed to comprehend these larger "politics of religious synthesis" (Stewart and Shaw 1994; Barker 1998:434; see also Barker 1993; Hefner 1993; Kempf 1994; van de Veer 1996) in Amazonian contexts, my purpose here is to explore how transformations of value are central to such processes among lowland Quichua speakers of Napo Province.

I address three main questions about conversion to Evangelical Protestantism among indigenous Napo people, none of which has been addressed elsewhere. First, why would Napo Runa become "Evangelical" in the first place, and what does "conversion" mean in their terms? In other words, how are the components of Evangelical Protestantism "internally related" (see Ollman 1971) to other realities of indigenous socioculture (and to Catholicism as well)? Second, given the visibility of the new "explosions" of Protestantism in Latin America (see Stoll 1990), I seek to understand the principle issues surrounding a multigenerational Evangelical movement in Napo. Is it expanding or declining? I raise the questions of how religion is transmitted and how converts are reproduced and pursue the contradictions and/or transformations involved. Third, I ask the question of whether this case of Evangelical native Amazonian Christianity forces us to rethink the problematic nature of "conversion" itself (see Asad 1996; Comaroff and Comaroff 1991, 1997; van de Veer 1996) and to consider the local complexities of how people rework Christian forms to express their own social values and political concerns. These questions and issues are revisited in the conclusion.

The first difficulty in writing about Evangelicals is the need to define what *Evangelical* means. The meaning of *evangélico*, however, is complex and does not correspond to a simple English translation of *Evangelical* or its mutations (such as *fundamentalist*) as they are commonly employed in the United States (Brusco 1995; Stoll 1990). In Latin America, *evangélico* usually describes any non-Catholic Christian, including Mormons and Jehovah's Witnesses, as well as those more "liberal" Protestants with a less fervent view of proselytizing (Stoll 1990:4). Elizabeth Brusco (1995:15), for example, states that the Colombian Lutherans, Baptists, Presbyterians, and more theologically "radical" Assemblies of God all identify themselves as *evangélicos* and use the term to describe one another's denominations. I have also observed that most people prefer to use a general term, such as *creyente* (believer) or *evangélico*, rather than specific denominational labels (Brusco 1995:15).

Other ways of classifying *evangélico* movements in Latin America can be formulated by examining specific denominations and their "waves" of arrival (Stoll 1990:4–5). Generally, however, typologies of the *evangélico* scene in Latin America are misleading, especially when compared to the values and practices of their North American or European counterparts (Stoll 1990:5), a point around which I intend to build this chapter.[1] As I will show, Evangelical Protestantism cannot be divorced from the context of Amazonian Runa systems of ideas, social values, and practices from which it derives its meaning and expression.

I now introduce a summary and analysis of an Evangelical Runa oratory, which I witnessed in November 1997, that contextualizes Evangelical Protestantism in opposition to its Catholic past in Napo. The issue here is purgatory, and how Evangelicals should settle their debts with God on the Day of the Dead. This oratory occurred in the local Evangelical church in Pano, an indigenous community on the outskirts of Tena. I include this oratory because it highlights a set of relations between socioeconomic exploitation, racism, and the purgatory concept that are central to the composition of Evangelical identities.

Santiago, an elderly Runa pastor known throughout the Napo region, begins by performing *camachina* (preaching or advising), the Runa practice of giving the gift of truth to others. Santiago uses the Bible to talk about the negative traditions of the Catholic Church, which have continued from *rucu timpu* or "the old times." Santiago explicitly brings up memories of how priests used practices of the Day of the Dead to deceive and exploit the Runa people by controlling their beliefs about the next world. Santiago complains of purgatory as a fantastic place dreamed up by priests to imprison their deceased (but not the white people's deceased). "We now need to know," he says, "not to be stupid like before. What does the Bible say? There are only two places, only two: Heaven and Hell."

Santiago continues, "The Catholics would ask for money in order to get one leg into heaven, more to get the other leg in, then the arms, the hands, the head would come out first. . . . What do they do? Each mass would only get a part out."

Santiago focuses on subversive acts such as reneging on your promise to God (Ecclesiastes 5:1–7), Peter's denial of Jesus (Matthew 26:33–35), and giving the "impure" gift (Hebrews 9:1–14). The last reference — giving impure gifts — is the most relevant for our discussion.

In quoting Hebrews 9:1–14, Santiago creates a parody of the Evangelical-Catholic comparison regarding the Day of the Dead. Verses 1 through 10 mention the "Earthly Tabernacle" where the "high priest" was accustomed to make offerings of blood for the sins of his people. The passage talks about how these offerings could not clear the conscience of the worshipper because they lack real power. While highlighting verses 11 through 14, Santiago also emphasizes that the only *true* sacrifice was the blood of Jesus. Santiago figuratively associates the Catholic church with the false "high priests" of whom Jesus chose not to become. Santiago then quotes Hebrews 7:12–14, which he posits as a general "rule" of conversion to Evangelical Christianity — that a change in "priesthood" necessitates change in the "law." For Santiago, the Evangelical "law" represents an enlightenment of Christianity from the bondage of *rucu timpu*. The oratory ends with reference to Jeremiah 2:22 and the problem of "purification." Santiago says, "There are some things that do not wash away our sins, if we seek to be pure. The important thing is not to live far away from God, to live close to him in everything we do."

I have given a brief description of Santiago's Day of the Dead discourse in which a series of positive and negative value contrasts emerge (e.g., Munn 1986). Santiago characterizes Catholic practices as creating negative value for the community, in contrast to the social and spiritual benefit of the "new law" of Evangelical practice. The connection I make between socioeconomic exploitation and purgatory is not unique to Napo, as demonstrated by Norman Whitten's (1974:129) ethnography of African Hispanic culture in Ecuador and Colombia. Like the African Hispanic people in Whitten's descriptions, Santiago complains that the Catholic priests do not let "our" people reach heaven. To grasp why Santiago and many other people in Napo found it desirable and progressive to reinvent themselves as Evangelical Christians,

I first give a brief overview of the Evangelical religion and the historical context of the Evangelical missions in Napo.

Napo was originally a mission field of the Jesuits, a rich and involved historical topic itself (see Jouanan 1941; López Sanvicente 1894; Muratorio 1981, 1991; Oberem 1980). However, after the Jesuits were forced out of Ecuador in the late nineteenth century (approximately 1892), the Napo region was without a missionary presence until the entrance of the Italian Josephines in 1922 (Spiller 1974). It was only a few years later that the first Evangelical missionary entered the region. Ruben Larson, of the Christian and Missionary Alliance, first entered the region in 1925 and a few years later established an Evangelical mission on the outskirts of Tena in Dos Ríos. It was not until 1942, however, that Evangelicals were able to establish a school near the Pano River. With help from the people of Dos Ríos, a mission was begun that later grew into the community of Pano (*Boletín de Pano* 1981).

From the beginning, Evangelicals in Napo began as a minority among the large and institutionally powerful Catholic missions in Napo.[2] Despite being branded as *supai pagris* or "devil priests"[3] initially, Evangelical missionaries gained footholds in rural spaces such as Dos Ríos and Pano because these were not places attended regularly by Catholic clergy (Gianotti 1997). The strategy of the Evangelical missionaries was to use their economic power and their goodwill to act as agents of change and liberation from the exploitative structures of the past. In contrast to the Josephines, who identified with a conservative strand of Ecuadorian politics linked to the former Ecuadorian president García Moreno (see Spiller 1974), Evangelicals sought and gained support from Ecuadorian "liberals" and liberal politics (Bastien 1994; Spiller 1974:204).

Obtaining a land base was essential for Evangelical proselytizing, for this "new" faith rose up only in communities in which the Runa had interpersonal relations with the Evangelical missionaries. For example, the permanent native settlement Shandia was made possible by the assistance of a liberal landowner, Manuel María Rosales, who had been a rubber collector, institutional administrator, and "liberal" in Napo. The Josephine Catholics opposed him for his liberalism and association with the Protestants. In his history of the Josephine mission in Napo, Spiller brands Rosales as "old and obstinate, a liberal of a pure line of those that professed laicism with the fanaticism of a Muslim" (Spiller 1974:204). Such political-religious language between Catholics and Evangelicals used to be common and reflected a struggle for territory throughout Napo. Along the road from Tena to the Jatun Yacu River, for example, Evangelical and Catholic territories dot the landscape as confirmation of past religious battles. Pano, Shandia, and Santa Rosa are mainly

Evangelical territories, although Pano also has a small "counter-reformation" Catholic church competing with the larger Evangelical one. Tálag is the site of a large Catholic mission with a high school and a resident Runa priest. As Spiller (1974:204) indicates, the Catholic mission in Tálag was begun in direct competition with the Evangelical mission in Shandia.

The elder Evangelical generation of Pano has fond memories of the early missionaries. People also associate them with the times of missionaries as a golden age of Evangelical activity, as they received concrete benefits by constituting an Evangelical core area. Missionaries living in close association with the Runa made great (mostly successful) efforts to be seen as generous. Runa Evangelicals received gifts, funding, jobs, and infrastructure from the North American and European missionaries. They received referrals from missionaries to job opportunities with North American and European oil and fruit companies, as well as with the Summer Institute of Linguistics–Wycliffe Bible Translators. Evangelical Runa gained regional prestige from the attention and importance attached to their community by people associated with powerful, materially wealthy, and technologically advanced foreign institutions. These Runa had succeeded in opening up relationship with generous foreigners, becoming a new kind of global "hinge group" (Rogers 1995; Taylor 1988).

While in residence with the Runa, the Western–North American missionaries were perceived as more or less abiding by Runa social values and acting "lawful" in the Runa sense. I never heard anyone in Pano describe a missionary as *mitsa* (withholding or greedy). Many Pano Runa reported enthusiastically how missionaries had gotten them jobs, performed ritualistic roles in marriage ceremonies, cured them, educated them, and taught them various trades and to play musical instruments. I heard accounts of how many missionaries were fond of drinking manioc beer and eating Amazonian cuisine, a sharp distinction to the manioc beer prohibitions promoted by the missionary groups working with the Shuar and Achuar peoples (see Taylor 1981:663).

Runa cultural values and social forms influenced and delighted many Evangelical missionaries of the Tena region, although as missionaries they were not tolerant of the more esoteric aspects of Runa life (i.e., shamanism) or of the indigenous drunken fiestas. The missionary David Miller (April 3, 1997), who grew up in Pano, writes to me in a personal letter:

I had no trouble drinking *chicha*, eating monkeys, or grubs in people's homes. One time I didn't realize that the *chicha* was quite so fermented and paid the price with an incredible hangover the next day. But by and large we tried to enter into the people's customs as much as possible. There are scores of Quichua people there in the area that are my *ahijados* [godchildren].

The North American missionaries pulled out of the Evangelical missions in the Tena region in the early 1980s, at the same time that the Ecuadorian Government refused to renew the Summer Institute of Linguistics' contract to continue working in Napo and in the rest of Ecuador (see Stoll 1990:281–82). Some people, both missionaries and Runa, say that the North Americans left because they had trained enough local people to take over the movement; the missionary work was essentially finished. However, other people report that the North American missionaries left because strong anti-American sentiment (on the part of indigenous political organizations and Ecuadorian university personnel) did not make them feel welcome. Both accounts reflect the reality that Evangelical Protestantism had entered into a new epoch wherein Runa believers took control of the institutions of the mission and asserted their own self-determination in the Evangelical sphere.

In short, the Evangelical missions near the Tena region began as a movement that was considered progressive by liberal and Runa advocates. These missions contrasted in doctrine, politics, and practices with conservative Catholicism, which dominated the region and stereotyped Evangelicals as foreigners, devils, and fanatics. Rumors also circulated that the Evangelical missionaries stole children to grind them up and make sausages (Carol Conn, personal communication March 9, 1997).

Behind these labels stood the fact that Evangelical missionaries propagated a different kind of religious system that sought to transform not only religion but also everyday society in Napo. Before I look at how Evangelical missionaries worked to alter the socioeconomic landscape toward more "liberal" economic principles, I first discuss the debtor system of socioeconomic exploitation in Napo.

Through the 1940s and 1950s, the practice of debt-peonage kept indigenous peoples in a type of bondage to patrons and to many government officials. While a full treatment of Napo's history of debt practices is not possible here, a few points about debt and debt-peonage are crucial to my argument. As we saw in Santiago's discourse of purgatory, the message of Evangelical Protestantism for the Runa is one of liberation from the bondage of past structures. A more thorough account of the structures of labor control and debt-peonage in Napo is contained in the work of Blanca Muratorio (1991).

The social logic of exploitation in Upper Napo was defined by debt-peonage, a practice that provided for the labor needs of administrators, merchants, and missionaries. The system worked by creating debt, which then ensured more debt. The debt then "became" the person, who turned into a "living debt" (Taussig 1987:66). In Upper Napo, it is commonly understood that only Runa people became living debts in the sense that the ethnic label of *indio* placed them into the general pool of potential peons and exploitable labor. Ethnicity, as well as debt, was "fetishized" (e.g., Taussig 1987:70), an idea that I will further develop.

In the debt-peonage institution, patrons gave goods at outrageous "prices" to Runa people, who were obligated to receive them and then expected to pay with their labor (e.g., Gow 1991; Taussig 1987). Indigenous labor was devalued while goods were heavily overvalued. The logic of this system would be something like a modified commodity-commodity (C-C) exchange sphere transaction described by Marx (1976) in *Capital*. Like the form described by Marx, in Napo, labor power was exchanged directly for goods, but the goods were tremendously overvalued and labor undervalued by way of a mystical process (an "invisible hand") whereby the giver of goods fixed an outrageous "price." The system was one in which money did not change hands, only goods for labor; but in so doing, enormous "money" debts were built up on paper.

Evangelicals from North America and Europe are documented as saying that they found the debt-peonage system highly offensive and worked toward freeing the indigenous peoples from these and other coercive forms of social control. However, in the early days, under Ruben Larson (late 1920s), the Evangelicals adapted the peonage-patronage system in setting up their mission work. As Ruben Larson (n.d.) states in an informal interview about a "first encounter," people initially became affiliated with the mission in Dos Ríos by volunteering to be its "indigenous peons." Later, more indigenous peoples came from other places to join the mission, giving the mission its core group of people. People in town recognized these indigenous peoples as the "peons" of the Evangelical mission and so left them alone. The missionaries were thrilled to be able to "protect them" in this way (Larson n.d.; Páez 1992).

Although the Evangelicals drew upon the patronage system, they saw it as a foreign system of control that was exploitative. Here cultural factors were important. The strangeness of the debt system was at least partially due to the fact that Western and North American missionaries were accustomed to the softer and more modern forms of social control found in capitalist forms, such as the management of people by controlling the means of production. By contrast, the logic of debt-peonage, which continues to exist *culturally* in Napo even after the actual institution does not, is based upon the implicit racial hierarchy of racially mixed and culturally "whitened" people controlling the "money" sphere, and indigenous and Black people being subject to the "labor" sphere.

As the years went by, Evangelical missionaries did much to destabilize the legitimacy of the debt system, and practices of debt-peonage offered a unique historical opportunity for Evangelical missionaries to use capital in revolutionizing indigenous labor valuation. Missionaries "bought" many indigenous debts and gave indigenous people mission jobs so that they themselves could pay off their enormous balances to patrons. In the spirit of the times, the missionaries were "freeing" people. This buyout strategy was expensive, but it put money as well as Bibles in the hands of indigenous people.

This mode of social action undercut the most fundamental assumptions of the social hierarchy as the pseudo-money form of debt-peonage (the appearance of exchange) was replaced by a real money form (an actual "equivalent" form). This new social logic was something similar to what Marx (1976) describes in *Capital* as a transition to a "commodity-money-commodity" (C-M-C) sphere of exchange. Real money, not goods representing a "faked" abstraction of money, became the dominant factor in procuring labor power. Payment in money by the Evangelical missionaries sociologically freed indigenous peoples from the chains of debt-peonage, the purgatory of the economic sphere. New dependencies, however, would arise.

Within Evangelical mission spheres, Runa were free to buy what they wanted and were unfettered by well-known Catholic institutions of ideological and pragmatic control. In this sense, the Evangelical missionaries helped transform communities by offering a new, more "liberal" vision of the world and the social practices to go with it. Such actions were not foreign; they picked up on a liberal ethos of the times that spoke of liberating indigenous peoples throughout Latin America (Bastien 1994; Muratorio 1991; Padilla 1989).

Before these transformations, Catholicism focused on external, prescribed rituals for everyone, and a certain status was ascribed to indigenous ethnicity. This status was, and continues to be, concordant with the principles of exclusion and "backwardness" implicit within the dominant ideological tandem of *mestizaje* (racial mixing) and *blanqueamiento* (cultural whitening) present in Napo and elsewhere in Latin America (Guss 2000:60–63; Stutzman 1981:45–85; Whitten 1981:16). This ideological system was what made people in Napo potential and actual living debts (e.g., Taussig 1987). The social hierarchy kept nonwhitened people in the lower social spheres of both economic and religious life.

As Whitten (1981:16) has argued, the values of whiteness are becoming "more urban, more Christian, more civilized; less rural, less black, less Indian." David Guss (2000:60–61) maintains that while the all-inclusive language of *mestizaje* masks unequal social relations based on race, *blanqueamiento* operates as the implicit physical and cultural goal. The dominance of the ideology of racial mixing and whiteness continues to put the Runa (and blacks) in a double bind. The Runa are doubly excluded because they are perceived as being racially "pure" (not mixed) and as not sharing in the values of whiteness (e.g., Whitten 1981:15–16; Guss 2000:60–61). In practical terms, this ideology translates into various justifications for the mistreatment and exploitation of indigenous and Black people and transforms their cultural differences into negative values because they are not "whitened."

The dominance of mixing and whiteness has been observed not only in political-economic and religious spheres but also in education. The educational goals and policies of the Josephine and government schools have always prioritized the dominance of whiteness and the process of whitening the Runa (Muratorio 1991:163–64). Runa people expressed to me that in the "early days" of education they were afraid to send their children to schools or to let them pursue a trade career in town for fear of abuse and/or exploitation by the authorities. At that time, the Runa believed that their own forms of social praxis were only expressible and livable in the safe confines of interpersonal and family relations. There was a strict segregation between the "inside" and the "outside" worlds (Barker 1993:216; Whitten 1985:103).

By reworking Christianity as a form of Runa values writ large, Evangelical missionaries were able to draw the Runa into new ways of thinking about themselves and their social bodies in a changing "liberal" social order. There were structural conjunctures formed (Sahlins 1985). The key behind Evangelical missionary successes was their respect for Runa notions of generosity in social relationships, the "equivalent form." While the missionaries expected the Runa to accept the beliefs and practices of Evangelical Protestant life and become "equal" to them spiritually (in the eyes of God), the Runa expected the missionaries to accept the indigenous standards of giving and sharing with friends and kin.

The Runa gave much to the missionaries and essentially allowed their operation to function. They also were the main agents of conversion and proselytizing. In turn, the Runa obligated the missionaries more or less to respect Runa values and act generously with both goods and money. Many Runa told me that this pretense of spiritual equality with the missionaries created the expectation of material equality as well. From the point of view of Runa sociality, it makes sense to assume that new converts would be entitled to North American–European "global" wealth as well as faith. This sense of progress is what seemed to occur in the new liberal age. The closure of the North American missions in Dos Ríos and Pano in the 1980s, however, left the

Evangelical Runa, for the most part, outside the loop of international mission wealth.

The presence of World-Vision in many Evangelical communities is the only continuing link to global capital afforded by Evangelical identity. However, Evangelical Runa see World-Vision controversial and a poor substitute for real mission "wealth," and they find its accounting requirements socially awkward. In 1997, people of the church in Pano considered "canceling" World-Vision, but decided against it because of the high status it confers upon them among Evangelical communities. The consensus opinion was, "If it were not for the fact that the cancellation of World-Vision in Pano would 'sound ugly' (*irus uyarin*) [in the region], we would just let it go." I do not know how serious people were about actually following through with this idea, but it does show a primary concern for social "face" and status, not their "poor" economic condition.

Liberal ideas and practices fostered by the Evangelical missionaries helped to influence a new attitude among the Runa toward education. As more schools appeared in indigenous communities, people ceased to consider them a repressive mechanism of white control and began to see them as representing an opportunity for Runa betterment. Many Runa became teachers and others used their school education to become community leaders. Since colonial times, Runa leaders were those who could deal with outsiders and outside institutions while respecting and defending the values of the inside sphere of Runa life. Education became the latest tool in the continuing effort for self-determination. One could argue that Evangelical Runa were some of the first people in Napo to practice their own version of *autodeterminación indígena* (indigenous self-determination), which Whitten and Torres (1998:9) define as "the assertion that indigenous people . . . must speak to New World nation-states in modern, indigenous ways which they themselves will determine." Among many Evangelical Runa people, one can find various discourses with themes of *autodeterminación*, especially when people talk about the beginnings of educational institutions in Evangelical communities. I revisit the theme of *autodeterminación* in the conclusion. But before I can analyze what "development" or Evangelical self-determination might mean in Runa terms, I must examine their system of social values.

Amazonian Quichua kinship has been described as an "open-ended" and "polysemic" system that is manipulated by people (Whitten 1976:121). In daily life, the Runa conceptualize a distinction between two contradictory values in social and kin relationships. On the one hand, the Runa believe that people, especially males, should develop firm dispositions and become strong willed. The Runa begin this socializing process among young children through a series of practices designed to make them *sinzhi* (strong). This conceptual model of strengthening begins with fasting entailed in couvade practices. Later, children are strengthened by putting capsicum pepper in their eyes, making them drink the *puma yuyu* (jaguar plant), and bathing them in cold, early morning rivers (see Uzendoski 1999). All of these practices, the Runa say, contribute to the strengthening of the *shunguyachina* (will) and the *sinzhi tucuna* (becoming strong).

The Runa also say that people need to be sensitive to the needs and demands of others. People should listen (*uyana*) to their loved ones, help out whenever they are needed (*yanapana*), and reciprocate gifts and favors. The Runa stigmatize anyone who does not behave reciprocally and generously as *mitsa* (greedy). This sensitivity to the needs of others is held by the Runa as an implicit "law" that is sometimes glossed as "living with love" (*llaquisha causana*). One way of describing this value might be what Joanna Overing and Alan Passes (2000:14) term "conviviality," and this implicit value demands specific kinds of behavior in daily life. For example, one is expected to send gifts of food and meat to *auya* (affines) and *compadres* (ritual kin people) as well as offer manioc beer to those who visit. I see the Runa hold these two values — willfulness and lawfulness — in complementary opposition.

The will (*shungu*) manifests itself mainly in the problem of creating social arrangements. Among the Runa, the will as a social concept is a key ingredient in activating relationships of the *muntun*, or the extended-family residence unit. The paternal figure, which in past times (*ñaupa timpu*) was always an elder shaman, forms a node of social structure around which relationships congeal (MacDonald 1979; Whitten 1976, 1985). The nodal structure is characterized by an overall amorphousness and interconnectedness wherein almost everyone living in a region can be related to everybody else in some way. Networks of relationships span large geographical distances and are maintained through webs of reciprocal exchange.

The core relationships of the *muntun* expand and deepen as people mature. People grow up in a *muntun*, but as they mature they form their own. *Muntun* break up when their founders die (see Oberem 1980). Mature *muntun* are built up through relational links to other *muntun* through the high-value relations of siblingship (*wawqui, pani, turi, ñaña*), compadrazgo (*compadre, comadre*), and alliance (*auya*). These mature relationships all imply a status of full personhood based on the proposition that one is a successful life giver and producer of other people (i.e., children) through procreation, adoption, and/or co-parenthood (see Uzendoski 2000). Value is contained within these horizontal relationships among mature persons.

Although missionaries chose not to adopt social idioms of adoption and/or alliance in relating with the Runa, they did actively participate in the social forms of *compadrazgo* to become integrated into the Runa system of kinship. *Compadrazgo* among the Runa is not a white institution (as is commonly misunderstood), and it is fully woven into their system of kinship as a form of networking kindred groups within and between communities (Whitten 1976, 1985). *Compadrazgo*, like adoption, is a means by which people who may not be biogenetically related can become "substance" related kin (see Weismantel 1995). This kind of a metamorphosis goes on when people become *compadre* and *comadre* to each other. There is little that is "fictive" in such relations.

In daily life, it is the willfulness of certain persons that determines where people live and with whom they spend their time and resources. Willful people create nodal networks and viable social arrangements, which are a complex conglomeration of substance and alliance relationships. The substance relation between brothers, for example, is usually not enough to keep them together as a domestic unit without the presence of a strong paternal will. In addition, it is necessary to have a willful father (*yaya*) and godfather (*marca yaya*) to perform roles in courtship and wedding rituals. Willfulness is also expressed in alcoholic drinking bouts and fighting, and most young men regularly engage in such behavior.

Men do not engage in such drinking practices for pleasure but rather to demonstrate to one another and to the world that they are willful, dangerous, and powerful. At one drinking session, Jorge said to me, "Here we are Runa, drinking *aguardiente* [cane alcohol] because we are strong [*sinzhi*]." People also say that drunken states are good because one's innermost inhibitions come out and "one can see the real being underneath." Willfulness (or "hardness") is a core value of masculine personhood and drinking is one of its associated practices.

Drunkenness is perceived as a form of masculine knowledge. The term *machana*, which means "to be drunk," conveys both drunkenness caused by alcohol and an altered state of reality induced by shamanic hallucinogens (ayahuasca or *wanduj*); these altered states of reality are sometimes equated. Some men expressed the ability to "see" shamanic visions while being drunk and commented that the sinews of their bodies transformed into anaconda flesh. In terms of what it means to be a masculine person in Runa society, drunken states are a rite of passage and a form of attaining knowledge (see also Abercrombie 1998 : 317–67).

Although being willful and strong is mainly a masculine value, women are also *sinzhi*. In feminine terms, this means that women have the ability to nurture and maintain the home and the family sphere. Feminine powers are personal powers that derive from a cosmology of shamanism and are expressed through dreaming, ritual-healing practices called *paju*, and women's songs (see Harrison 1989; Muratorio 1991; Whitten 1976, 1985). In Runa life masculine/feminine are complementary aspects of the human condition, and all aspects of Runa social life revolve around the productive practices and concepts of the gender opposition (see also Whitten 1976, 1985).

It might be said that feminine willfulness facilitates masculine lawfulness and that femininity in Runa culture is associated with the collective value of lawfulness and social sensitivity. Women, however, perceive their feminine abilities as toughness, but simultaneously recognize that feminine strength and endurance are different from the masculine forms. While masculinity generally makes femininity appear "soft," life presents constant situations in which femininity covers up for the weaknesses of masculinity. For example, when a "strong" man sprains his ankle and needs a specialist to cure him, women are the ones who have the special powers (spiritual and physical) associated with massage. When men get tired (or drunk), women often do their work. Also, it is said that men do not really know how to grow food, cook, or prepare manioc beer "well." These are the true staples of life and social reproduction, and they are produced in feminine domains. Women enable men to live, a point that I revisit in the context of Evangelical redemption.

Drinking and the manifestations of traditional masculinity create specific problems for Evangelical men. In contrast to their Catholic neighbors, Runa Evangelicals maintain an active focus on personal sin and the conflict between the flesh and the spirit. Indeed, Evangelical law is almost synonymous with the individual avoidance of sin, an ideal that is described as becoming a *chuyaj Runa* (pure Runa). Practically, this means that Evangelical Runa must avoid drinking, dancing, smoking, and getting angry. However, because drinking, dancing, smoking, and fighting are physical manifestations of a strong will and quintessential of masculine will, Evangelical actors are constantly preoccupied with sin. All Evangelicals find it difficult to stay "pure," and many who attend Church occupy the category of *urmashca* (fallen).

Like other men, Evangelicals describe themselves as *sinzhi* and devoted Evangelicals describe themselves as *sinzhi ciricguna* (strong believers). However, Evangelicals have transformed the notion of a defining, masculine, and powerful will to a more passive state that they achieve through biblical reflection, prayer, and worship. To Catholic men, Evangelical men are feminized. Evangelicals see their masculinity in relation to a personal ability to avoid sin and to talk about such a state as having a "strong heart for God." Evangelicals are generally not concerned with any kind of aggressive action in this world, but rather see themselves as controlling otherworldly justice via, in their terms, "feminized" behavior.[4] Thus the inherent aggression of the male will has become more ascetic, disciplined, and domesticated.

Because the viability of Evangelical relationships depends upon their strict control of body practices, and members are constantly preoccupied with bodily control, the church paradoxically creates the "falling" of its members. This process presents new internal problems for relational symmetry and spiritual equality, for some members succeed while others fail, and even strong believers sometimes fall. Recognizing sin is a very delicate process.

It is the equality of potential and a shared similarity that is emphasized within relationships with the fallen, for every Evangelical family has them (usually more fallen members than faithful). The fallen are viewed as converts who either have not fully realized the conversion process or have briefly separated from it. Those who live within an Evangelical community or have knowledge of its "new law" are obligated to live within it, even if they are fallen. The faithful continue to treat their fallen loved ones well, yet family relations are stressed by the contradiction of altered status. This contradiction is felt most acutely by men. A father might have his moral authority questioned in the most inopportune of situations. A drunken son might bring shame upon his parents in his quest to display masculine willfulness. Despite the fact that an Evangelical has fallen, he or she cannot simply become Catholic. Evangelicals, like all Runa, are not only individuals; their identities are packed in the social relations that make up their person. They must live the contradictions.

Evangelical Protestantism also produces acute contradictions for feminine personhood, contradictions that adversely affect women's reputations in the church and the community. As Blanca Muratorio (1998:412) has argued, women must be generous and hardworking and worry intensely about having a good reputation in their in-laws' home based on the "sociality of their work." Like men, women must behave willfully in the appropriate and lawful manner. However, feminine personhood and the development of a willful and lawful self depends upon marriage and the severing of relationships from one's natal *muntun* (extended-family residence unit) for incorporation by her husband's *muntun* as a new daughter-in-law (*cachun*). It is in the social action of marriage and sexual cultural politics that Evangelical women's selves are most at risk. While men "fall" because of their need to be willful, women "fall" because of their need to marry (as marriage is the domain wherein women become "willful"). Just as the Evangelical Church paradoxically encourages the falling of men because of strict body practices, its equally strict regulation of feminine bodies in marriage and sexuality inhibits women from becoming full social persons as wives and mothers.

Evangelicals believe that one should marry by the literal instructions in the Bible and should marry a "pure" Evangelical person. Because many, if not most, Runa Evangelical men are fallen (or repeatedly fallen) in and out of the church, Evangelical women are hard pressed to find a man who fits the bill as a Runa man and a "pure" Evangelical. Evangelical women often choose marriage over their faith (marriage to a Runa rather than to God), which subsequently endangers their Evangelical reputations. Like men, women also fall. Even if women do not drink, smoke, dance, or get angry, they nonetheless are in danger of falling if they cannot keep their men pure. Any woman who makes pretenses to purity while her husband remains outside of Evangelical law (e.g., drinking) quickly is the object of gossip. Not only would a woman in such a position be seen as a hypocrite, but she also risks losing her femininity as well as her faith, since men are supposed to dominate the external aspect of the conjugal unit.

This dynamic between drinking and Evangelical reproduction is complex. In Runa society, celebratory practices that include alcoholic consumption (and dancing) are viewed as acts of social reproduction (e.g., Gow 1989) and a means to "making kin" (see Weismantel 1995). During drunken fiestas, of which ritual wedding ceremonies are the fiesta par excellence (*tapuna, pactachina, bura*), the relational barriers between people are transformed and new relationships are formed. During weddings, for example, collective drinking and dancing are the primary means of relational transformations that "make" a wife and mediate the opposition between the two families, termed the "man's side" (*cari parti*) and the "women's side" (*warmi parti*). The wedding fiesta process is what allows the asymmetry between "wife givers" and "wife takers" to be transformed into a sense of relational "equivalency." Drinking is part of a series of acts that transform the relationship between the two families from one of suspicion and hostility to one of intimacy and "love" (*llaquina*).

One way in which the groom's family achieves this transformation is through giving a lot of manioc beer as well as bottles of liquor to the bride's family to "show them a good time." These are gifts that are said to eventually obligate the bride's family to hand over the bride (see MacDonald 1979, 1999; Uzendoski 2000). The presentation of male and female dancing is also essential to the social transformation, as the lines of male/female dancing publicly "finish" the metamorphosis and represent the masculine/feminine complementarity. The two families are said to become "*shujllayachina*" (just one). Furthermore, wedding fiestas are the ideal time for young men and women to flirt; the ritual space of wedding celebrations provides an ideal context for initiating new sexual liaisons.

It is not surprising that weddings are difficult times for many Evangelical men and women, and many Evangelicals "fall" during weddings. One friend of mine was Evangelical up until his own wedding when he married a Catholic girl and was forced to drink with her father and brothers. Evangelical women who marry into non-Evangelical families also end up in the category of the fallen. Evangelicals try to emphasize the consumption of food over drink at weddings, but even weddings sponsored by Evangelical families must offer significant quantities of alcoholic drinks and manioc beer as gifts to others.[5] Evangelical practices have not transformed Runa society into a collection of individuals mainly because people emphasize a relational focus on creating and interacting with webs of kin. Practices of consumption are oriented toward creating relationships, not individuals, and are essential to achieving adult personhood. Like a weak magnet that creates a field that can draw but not hold an object as fixed, Evangelical Protestant ideals transform both male and female selves without being able to hold or fix the individual identities they create (e.g., Robbins 1994).

In the constant struggle against falling, women remain more steadfastly pure than men do, for they are under little pressure to consume strong alcohol and do not display the masculine behaviors that contradict Evangelical identity. However, because the Runa view the actions of husbands and wives as complementary, women cannot remain pure in the eyes of other Evangelicals if their husbands repeatedly fall. Complementarity is a complicated business. The flip side is that women often facilitate the redemption of their men (husbands, sons, and sons-in-law) by helping curb their drinking excesses and bringing them back into the activities of the local church. In life crises (accidents, sickness, death), Evangelicals are ready and willing to "bring people back to God," and women, as the main agents of crying, compassion, and nurturing, are the main facilitators in this process.

In the church it is the spiritual, visionary, and transformative powers of women that keep things going and are the basis of women's redemption of men. As the primary agents of song (see Harrison 1989), women also take on a leading role in this area in the Evangelical church. In Pano, for example, the women's group is mainly dedicated to song, and, when they sing, the women's voices always drown out clumsy masculine tones. It is said among the Runa that women make life *cushi* (happy) and feminine singing is a key application of this idea in the church context; without feminine voices, Evangelical life (and life in general) would be unbearable. It is my sense that the Runa see singing as an elevated and powerful form of prayer and worship, not as an "adjunct" to those worship practices led by men. I have often seen singers and other church members cry during Evangelical songs as well as seek comfort in singing and listening to them.

What do we learn about Christianity and religious synthesis from this brief study? From the material presented in this chapter, the macrocosmic aspect of Christianity incorporating people into socially expansive moral orders fits well as an explanatory paradigm (see Hefner 1993). For example, this essay has discussed how various Christian forms (Jesuits, Josephines, Evangelicals) were central to how Runa people related to authorities, colonists, and larger Ecuadorian society. My main argument in this respect is that Evangelical Protestantism represented a break with the past structures of conservative Catholicism in Napo, which kept the Runa in the lower spheres of the religious cosmos (purgatory) and in economic life (peonage). Evangelicals sought to produce new macroidentities and relations that articulated the values and ideas of Latin American liberalism. They preached and worked toward giving the Runa full personhood in both Christianity and the capitalist economy.

While macrocosmic, world building relations are a central aspect of Christianity in general, as shown clearly in Hefner's (1993:3–46) piece "World Building and the Rationality of Conversion," equally salient is the idea that Christian forms are highly adaptable when articulated with local social values and political culture in situations of change (see also Robbins 1998). In this respect, I examined how Runa people transformed the values and practices of the Evangelical message to reflect the realities of their social and cultural world; I gave examples of willful or strong Christians taking turns in leading their churches and preaching on Sundays — a mirror image of their social structure — and I offered and explored the hypothesis that the people understand many aspects of Christian theology through shamanic-cultural models of *samai* (breath) and power. I presented differences between masculine and feminine forms of strength and endurance (*sinzhi cari* and *sinzhi warmi*) and corresponding Evangelical forms of being a strong believer (*sinzhi ciric*). I also presented an analysis of the cultural factors and social processes that explain why Evangelical Runa are preoccupied with sin and bodily practices of not drinking, smoking, dancing, or displaying anger. This same cultural knowledge allows the Evangelical Runa to emphasize the practical healing power of Christianity and recognize the real presence of demons (or spirits), aspects of the Christian message that Walls (2000) argues most modern Euro-American Christians do not take seriously today.

These processes of transformation and active reworking of Evangelical Christianity in Runa culture are ongoing; they did not cease with the departure of the North American missionaries in the 1980s, and they will not cease in 2002 with the conclusions of this essay. On the contrary, the Runa continue to innovate their own and Christian forms and practices to reflect emerging cultural identities and concerns within Napo in relation to the nation-state and the larger world. One way to think about this problem is as an issue of scale — how the macrocosmic meets the local — and this concern is central to what Evangelicals think and do.

For example, the main talk in Upper Napo during summer of 2001 surrounded the events of a two-week-long uprising in Napo (and all of Ecuador) that occurred in February. Within the Tena-Archidona region, two people died during a military repression, and a good number were wounded in the violence that occurred.[6] Many of those protesting and the wounded were from Evangelical communities (including men and women), and some of those wounded are permanently disabled. The Federation of Evangelical Indigenous People of Ecuador (FEINE) works along with the flagship national federation, CONAIE, and FENOCIN to negotiate with the government indigenous demands surrounding a February 7 agreement that settled the uprising. Among the demands are compensation to the families of those killed and wounded by the military, and concerns with taxes, bus fares, and gas distribution.[7] These are important issues that have a critical impact on Runa life in the countryside of Napo.

In addition, indigenous Evangelical leaders in Napo have recently transformed their association (Association of Indigenous Evangelicals of Napo [AIEN]) into a full-fledged Evangelical federation. This federation also has its sister component run by women leaders who focus on projects for the betterment of women's lives. People told me that federation status allows them to negotiate and work directly with governmental, nongovernmental, international, secular, and religious organizations. Two areas in which leaders are interested in collaborations are in the areas of education and community-based ecotourism. Such Evangelical projects are run at the level of communities, so that all Evangelicals in a particular community benefit from their collectively oriented projects regardless of "pure" versus "fallen" members. The concept of an indigenous Evangelical federation is a complex and innovative move that reflects indigenous concerns with *autodeterminación* and the collective values of living in a *comunidad* (community) in a rapidly changing world (see Whitten 1976, 1985; Whitten and Torres 1998).

My endeavor in this section is to highlight a concrete example of *autodeterminación* as part of the action sphere of the indigenous Evangelical movement in Ecuador and specifically in Napo. As long as the Evangelical movement retains *autodeterminación* within the sphere of its operations, I believe it will remain a social force in Napo. Perhaps this situation echoes Sahlins' (1993:338) point that many cultures practice development from within their own cultural sense of value, "development from the perspective of the people concerned: their own culture on a bigger and better scale." It is clear that Runa people and Runa Evangelicals are concerned with development and value on their terms, their cultural practices on a different scale — the scale of an ever shrinking system of global relations. Santiago's oratory about purgatory was just that, an Evangelical statement of *autodeterminación* and *scale*, depicting how the Evangelical Runa should treat *their dead* on the day when all people are supposed to think about into which worlds the dead travel or will travel.

ACKNOWLEDGMENTS

This chapter was originally presented at the 1998 American Anthropological Association Meetings in Philadelphia. It is based on approximately twenty-six months of research carried out between January 1994 and July 2000. The fieldwork was supported by grants from the Fulbright Institute for International Education, Pew Charitable Trusts, the University of Virginia, and a teaching/research position with the Dirección Bilingüe Intercultural de Napo. I am grateful to all of these organizations. I thank Pastor Santiago Venancio Calapucha, who provides the inspiration for this essay.

I would also like to thank the following people for comments on earlier drafts of the chapter: Syed Ali, Rita Kipp, Mark Gruber, Katherine Wiegele, Joe Hellweg, Cynthia Hoehler-Fatton, Simon Bickler, Jean Jacques Decoster, Juliet Lee, Frederick Damon, George Mentore, Joel Robbins, Eduardo Kohn, Tod Swanson, and Rachel Corr. I also thank David and Henry Miller and Gerald and Carol Conn, missionaries who worked in Napo, for corresponding with me regarding the "early days," and Ramiro Páez for providing me with documents about Ruben Larson, the first Evangelical missionary to work in Napo. Excerpts from both Conn and Miller are presented here with their permission. I am also grateful to Carissa Neff for proofreading and insightful stylistic comments. I thank Norman Whitten for his careful reading and comments and the two external reviewers. I would like to thank numerous people of Napo Province, who have contributed in countless ways to my professional and personal development. Last, I thank my wife, Edith, who contributed to this article in countless ways. I must also mention that, though I have received much assistance along the way, I alone accept full responsibility for the chapter's shortcomings and offer my sincerest apologies to the many people I have forgotten to mention.

NOTES

1. It has been more than ten years since the publication of Stoll's (1990) study of Evangelical Protestantism in Latin America and more studies are badly needed on current transformations and political-cultural relations involved with Evangelical identities. For example, Stoll's (1991) study develops the position that Evangelicals (and Ecuadorian Evangelicals) have generally opposed Catholics and leftist positions associated with liberation theology. This essay suggests that the Ecuadorian reality is more complicated, as there are also highly conservative strands of Catholicism as well as emergent/historical forms of Evangelical liberation theology.

2. The late Maximiliano Spiller, Obispo Vicario Apostólico Emérito de Napo, in 1974 estimated that, in all, there were some 2,000 to 2,500 Evangelicals in Napo. In a more recent work, Spiller (1989) reports that "faithful Catholics" make up 71,330 of

the total population of 82,315 in Napo (this includes indigenous people, mestizos, and whites). Although these statistics are probably exaggerated, that would leave only 10,985 of the "not reached," "unfaithful," and Evangelical, or only about 14 percent of the total population. This is in a province where vast areas lack urban infrastructure, roads, and modern communications.

3. *Supai* has a double meaning in the Runa universe. It generally is used to describe any kind of supernatural being or spirit. These beings can be good, bad, or neutral depending on the specific context. For example, *supai* are agents of healing (or illness) in shamanic ritual (see e.g., Whitten 1976, 1985). Here, *supai* is translated as *devil* because this is the sense of the gloss I have cited.

4. Even Evangelicals themselves realize this. They will say that they are like "wives" to Jesus Christ, who is like their husband. "We must wait for Jesus, just as a wife waits for her husband."

5. Gerald and Carol Conn, missionaries who arrived in Pano in 1953, write in a personal letter (March 9, 1997): "We had no problem with the old style *bura* [wedding], again with the exemption of drinking. Colas began to be used or later on beer (which we did not favor). There was difficulty for the Christians [Evangelicals] if the family of the bride or groom demanded hard liquor. It was the custom of the family of the groom to have to give everything the parents of the bride demanded or the girl would not be given. . . . As for drinking *chicha* [manioc beer] . . . we never did forbid as did missionaries in the south jungle. But of course we did preach and teach against their old practice of preparing large amounts of *chicha* used for feasts or weddings when all would end up in a drunken stupor."

6. In interviews, people were not sure of the exact number of deaths but said between three and four and a number of wounded. News sources indicated that between one and four were killed. See "Police Kill Protestors" at http://www.americas.org/news, which cites as sources *La Hora* (Quito), February 7, 2001, from AFP. A boy from the El Dorado neighborhood in Tena was among those killed.

7. My source of negotiation data is a piece from the news Web site http://www.americas.org/news titled "Indigenous Dialogue Fails," which cites the following newspapers: *El Diario–La Prensa* (New York), July 18, 2001, from EFE; July 21, 2001, from AP; *La Hora* (Quito), July 17, 2001, and July 18, 2001; *El Telégrafo* (Guayaquil), July 18, 2001.

REFERENCES

Abercrombie, Thomas
   1998   *Pathways of Memory and Power*. Madison: University of Wisconsin Press.
Asad, Tal
   1996   Comments on Conversion. In *Conversion to Modernities: The Globalization of Christianity*. Peter van der Veer, ed. Pp. 263–72. New York: Routledge Press.

Barker, John

    1993   "We Are Ekelesia": Conversion in Uiaku, Papua New Guinea In *Conversion to Christianity: Historical and Anthropological Perspectives on a Great Transformation*. Robert Hefner, ed. Pp. 199–232. Berkeley: University of California Press.

    1998   Tangled Reconciliations: the Anglican Church and the Nisga'a of British Columbia. *American Ethnologist* 25(3):433–51.

Bastien, Jean-Pierre

    1994   *Protestantismos y Modernidad Latinoamericana: Fondo de Cultura Económica*. Mexico: Fondo de Cultura Económico.

Boletín de Pano, I. Panomandashimi

    1981   *Historía de la escuela "Guillermo Kadle."* Pano, Ecuador.

Bourdieu, Pierre

    1977   *Outline of a Theory of Practice*. Cambridge: Cambridge University Press.

Brown, Michael, and Eduardo Fernández

    1991   *War of Shadows: The Struggle for Utopia in the Peruvian Amazon*. Berkeley: University of California Press.

Brusco, Elizabeth E.

    1995   *The Reformation of Machismo. Evangelical Conversion and Gender in Colombia*. Austin: University of Texas Press.

Comaroff, Jean, and John Comaroff

    1991   *Christianity, Colonialism, and Consciousness in South Africa*, vol. 1 of *Of Revelation and Revolution*. Chicago: University of Chicago Press.

    1997   *The Dialectics of Modernity on a South African Frontier*, vol. 2 of *Of Revelation and Revolution*. Chicago: University of Chicago Press.

Gianotti, Emilio

    1997   *Viajes por el Napo: Cartas de un misionero, 1924–1930*. Quito: Abya-Yala.

Gow, Peter

    1989   *The Perverse Child: Desire in a Native Amazonian Subsistence Economy*. Man (n.s.)24:567–82.

    1991   *Of Mixed Blood: Kinship and History in Peruvian Amazonia*. Oxford: Oxford Press.

Guss, David M.

    2000   *The Festive State: Race, Ethnicity, and Nationalism As Cultural Performance*. Berkeley: University of California Press.

Harrison, Regina

    1989   *Signs, Songs, and Memory in the Andes: Translating Quechua Language and Culture*. Austin: University of Texas Press.

Hefner, Robert W.

    1993   World Building and the Rationality of Conversion. In *Conversion to Christianity: Historical and Anthropological Perspectives on a Great*

Transformation. Robert Hefner, ed. Pp. 3–46. Berkeley: University of California Press.

Jouanan, José

1941   *Historia de la Compañía de Jesús en la antigua provincia de Quito, 1570–1774*, 2 vols. Quito: Editorial Ecuatoriana.

Kempf, Wolfgang

1994   Ritual, Power and Colonial Domination: Male Initiation among the Ngaing of Papua New Guinea. In *Syncretism/Anti-Syncretism: The Politics of Religious Synthesis*. S. Charles and S. Rosalind, eds. Pp. 108–26. London: Routledge.

Larson, Ruben

n.d.   Informal interview with Dr. Rubén Larson in Dos Ríos. Archive of the Christian and Missionary Alliance, Tena-Napo, Ecuador.

López Sanvicente, Lorenzo

1894   *La misión del Napo 1894*. Quito: Imprenta de la Universidad Central.

MacDonald, Theodore

1979   Processes of Change in Amazonian Ecuador: Quijos Quichua Indians Become Cattlemen. Ph.D. dissertation, Department of Anthropology, University of Illinois at Urbana-Champaign.

1999   *Ethnicity and Culture amidst New "Neighbors": The Runa of Ecuador's Amazon Region*. Boston: Allyn and Bacon Press.

Marx, Karl

1976   *Capital*, vol. 1. Ben Fowkes trans. New York: Vintage Books.

Munn, Nancy

1986   *The Fame of Gawa: A Symbolic Study of Value Transformation in a Massim (Papua New Guinea) Society*. Durham: Duke University Press.

Muratorio, Blanca

1981   *Etnicidad, evangelización, y protesta en el Ecuador*. Quito: Ediciones CICSE.

1984   Evangelisation, Protest, and Ethnic Identity: Sixteenth-Century Missionaries and Indians in Northern Amazonian Ecuador. In *Religion and Rural Revolt*. J. Bak and G. Benecke, eds. Pp. 413–23. Manchester: Manchester University Press.

1991   *The Life and Times of Grandfather Alonso*. Piscataway, N.J.: Rutgers University Press.

1998   Indigenous Women's Identities and the Politics of Cultural Reproduction in the Ecuadorian Amazon. *American Anthropologist* 100(2):409–20.

Oberem, Udo

1980   *Los Quijos. Historia de la Transculturación de un grupo indígena en el oriente ecuatoriano*. Otavalo: Instituto Otavaleño de Antropología.

Ollman, Bertell

    1971   *Alienation: Marx's Conception of Man in Capitalist Society*. Cambridge: Cambridge University Press.

Overing, Joanna, and Alan Passes

    2000   Conviviality and the Opening up of Amazonian Anthropology. In *The Anthropology of Love and Anger*. J. Overing and A. Passes, eds. Pp. 1–30. London: Routledge.

Padilla, Washington

    1989   *La iglesia y los dioses modernos. Historia del protestantismo en el Ecuador*. Quito: Biblioteca de Ciencias Sociales 23.

Páez, Ramiro

    1992   Brief Biography of Dr. Ruben Larson, Renowned Missionary Who Planted the Seed of the Gospel of Jesus Christ in the Province of Napo. Unpublished ms in Archive of the Christian and Missionary Alliance, Tena-Napo, Ecuador.

Pollock, Donald

    1993   Conversion and "Community" in Amazonia. In *Conversion to Christianity: Historical and Anthropological Perspectives on a Great Transformation*. Robert Hefner, ed. Pp. 165–98. Berkeley: University of California Press.

Robbins, Joel

    1994   Equality As Value: Ideology in Dumont, Melanesia and the West. *Social Analysis* 36:21–70.

    1998   Becoming Sinners: Christianity and Desire among the Urapmin of Papua New Guinea. *Ethnology* 37(4):299–316.

Rogers, Mark

    1995   Images of Power and the Power of Images: Identity and Place in Ecuadorian Shamanism. Ph.D. dissertation, Department of Anthropology, University of Chicago.

Sahlins, Marshall

    1985   *Islands of History*. Chicago: University of Chicago Press.

    1993   Goodbye to Tristes Tropes: Ethnography in the Context of Modern World History. *The Journal of Modern History* 65(1):1–25.

Spiller, Maximiliano M.

    1974   *Historia de la Misión Josefina del Napo*. Quito: Artes Gráficas, Equinoccio Cia. Ltda.

Stewart, Charles, and Rosalind Shaw

    1994   (editors) *Syncretism/Anti-Syncretism: The Politics of Religious Synthesis*. London: Routledge.

Stoll, David

    1990   *Is Latin America Turning Protestant? The Politics of Evangelical Growth*. Berkeley: University of California Press.

Stutzman, Ronald

    1981   El Mestizaje: An All-Inclusive Ideology of Exclusion. In *Cultural Transformations and Ethnicity in Modern Ecuador*. Norman E. Whitten, Jr., ed. Pp. 45–94. Urbana: University of Illinois Press.

Taussig, Michael

    1987   *Shamanism, Colonialism, and the Wild Man: A Study in Terror and Healing*. Chicago: University of Chicago Press.

Taylor, Ann-Christine

    1981   God-Wealth: The Achuar and the Missions. In *Cultural Transformations and Ethnicity in Modern Ecuador*. Norman E. Whitten, Jr., ed. Pp. 647–76. Urbana: University of Illinois Press.

    1988   Las vertientes orientales de los andes septentrionales: de los bracamoros a los Quijos. In *Al oeste de los Andes*. FF. Renard-Casevitz, Th. Saignes, A.C. Taylor, eds. Pp. 13–61. Quito: Abya-Yala/IFEA.

Uzendoski, Michael

    1999   Twins and Becoming Jaguars: Verse Analysis of a Napo Quichua Myth Narrative. *Anthropological Linguistics* 41(4):431–61.

    2000   The Articulation of Value among the Napo Runa of the Upper Ecuadorian Amazon. Ph.D. dissertation, University of Virginia.

van de Veer, Peter

    1996   Introduction. In *Conversion to Modernities: The Globalization of Christianity*. V. Peter van der Veer, ed. Pp. 1–22. New York: Routledge Press.

Walls, Andrew

    2000   The Expansion of Christianity: An Interview with Andrew Walls. *The Christian Century* (117) 22:792–99.

Weismantel, Mary

    1995   Making Kin: Kinship Theory and Zumbagua Adoptions. *American Ethnologist* 22(4):685–709.

Whitten, Norman E., Jr.

    1974   *Black Frontiersmen: A South American Case*. New York: John Wiley and Sons.

    1976   (with Marcelo F. Naranjo, Marcelo Santi Simbaña, and Dorothea S. Whitten) *Sacha Runa: Ethnicity and Adaptation of Ecuadorian Jungle Quichua*. Urbana: University of Illinois Press.

    1981   (editor) *Cultural Transformations and Ethnicity in Modern Ecuador*. Urbana: University of Illinois Press.

    1985   *Sicuanga Runa: The Other Side of Development in Amazonian Ecuador*. Urbana: University of Illinois Press.

Whitten, Norman E., Jr., and Arlene Torres

    1998   To Forge the Future in the Fires of the Past: An Interpretive Essay on Racism, Domination, Resistance, and Liberation. In *Blackness in Latin America and the Caribbean*, vol. 1. Norman E. Whitten, Jr., and Arlene Torres, eds. Pp. 3–33. Bloomington: Indiana University Press.

Wright, Robin M.

    1998   *Cosmos, Self, and History in Baniwa Religion: For Those Unborn*. Austin: University of Texas Press.

CHAPTER 6

The Devil and Development in Esmeraldas
Cosmology as a System of Critical Thought

DIEGO QUIROGA

Western Christian cosmology is often portrayed as divided into a secular and sacred earth system, with hell below, heaven above, and, in some systems, purgatory as a mediating sector between the earth and heaven (e.g., Corr, this volume; Uzendoski, this volume). Afro-Esmeraldian people of northwest Ecuador have reworked this system to make one clear, but interpenetrating, division between what they call *lo divino* (the divine realm) and *lo humano* (the human realm). The latter includes the earth upon which humans live and work and the world controlled by the devil and his (or her) minions or associates, both human and spiritual. God, Jesus Christ, virgins, and saints come from the *divino*, but it is far away and hard to reach. Women, in particular, gain access to the *divino* through song and ritual performance. The *humano* is the sector of turmoil and toil, and whatever favors may be granted by the devil or other spirits, visions, ghouls, monsters, or creatures thereof come at a price. In this chapter, I first explore the realms of the divine and the human and then go on to explicate the character of open-ended, multivocalic, polarized (e.g., Turner 1973, 1974, 1986) symbols of the devil as tied to economy, society, and politics, not only in Muisne, which is the primary site of my ethnography, but elsewhere in Ecuador as well.

The *Divino* and the *Humano*

The Afro-Ecuadorians who live in the northern coastal province of Esmeraldas and in the Pacific lowlands of Colombia from Buenaventura south conceptualize the realm of the *divino* as comprehensible, ordered, and at least partially controllable by proper ritual and ceremony (Friedmann 1985; Rahier 1987). The realm of the *humano*, however, in which they live and work, is not entirely (or sometimes even partly) understandable. By contrast with the *divino*, the *humano* realm is alive with uncontrollable and threatening forces. One cannot understand either the *divino* or the *humano*, conceptualized as contrasting times-spaces, without reference to the other. Put simply, the realm of the *humano* with its unpredictability, uncontrollable qualities, susceptibilities to evil through sin, and interspersing of humans and bad spirits validates the domain of the *divino*.

The productive and social practices of people are related in a dialectic manner to the contrasting times-spaces. The province of Esmeraldas has experienced times of economic cycles of boom and bust (Whitten 1994). Cultural constructs that allegorically represent times-spaces of disorder and chaos, entropy and structure (Adams 1975) or order and control can be seen as characterizing both periods of growth and depression. During the economic cycles of wealth creation, the production of export goods such as *tagua* (*Epitelephas* sp.), banana (*Musa paradisaica*), shrimp (*Panaeus vanamei*), and timber are accelerated, but during periods of recession people concentrate on subsistence activities within the "traditional" economy. From a developmentalist perspective, economic expansion creates a certain type of order. Such expansion, as experienced by Afro-Esmeraldians, however, represents spaces and times of disorder and disruption (Fernández-Rasines 2001).

The most recent period of economic expansion was related to the production of shrimp in aquaculture ponds. As the business expanded in the late 1980s and early 1990s, work was created for local workers on the farms (Espinoza 1989), but, at the same time, the rapid expansion severely reduced or destroyed the mangrove forests where *concheras* (women who gather cockle bivalves, *Anadara* sp.) worked (Mera Orcés 1999). In 1998, when the white spot virus (WSV) resulted in an almost complete collapse of the shrimp industry, there was an economic recession in the entire coastal area. These cycles of production and recession and the contrast between the modern capital-producing and the traditional subsistence economy are allegorically understood using the powerful dichotomy of the *humano* and the *divino*.

Incongruous and mystical experiences, such as those described in the following paragraphs, are related to the expansion of the export economies and to transgressions of the moral code; as such, they provide the space of the *humano* with its dreadful affective forces. These incongruous experiences could result from the sense that people express when they say they are losing control over the local natural and human resources. People experience different types of uncontrollable forces when they interact with the modern sector, such as when they go to the large cities or work for agribusinesses. Furthermore, the racialized quality of whiteness itself and its relationship to Western development and developmentalism are directly associated in the domain of the *humano*. Other incongruous experiences that provide the affective basis for the domain of the *humano* are those related to death and decay, especially when relatives or friends die in a violent manner or when people engage in what is considered unethical or immoral behavior.

By strong contrast with the *humano*, within the traditional subsistence economy, behaviors that are considered ethical, normal, and fundamental to Afro-Ecuadorian identity systems are related to the domain of the *divino*. This domain comprises the spirits, virgins, and saints. The Virgen del Carmen, Santa Rosa, El Hermano Gregorio and San Antonio are among the figures who provide the space of the *divino* with its healing and ordering powers. These figures are celebrated in rituals called *arrullos*, which punctuate the year. Led by women, a male rhythmic ensemble composed of two large drums (*bombos*), two conga-like drums (*cununos*), accompanies female singers (*cantadoras*) who sing the *arrullos* (spirituals), shake maracas, dance, tell stories, and open a passageway to heaven. During these celebrations, the spirit of the saint or virgin is said to come to the world of the living (see Whitten 1994:127–38).

The people who live in the area conceptualize spiritual beings either as sources of miraculous power (the *divino*) or as evil power and wealth (the *humano*). In the case of the space of the *divino*, the beings provide local healers such as *curanderas*, *sobadores*, and *parteras* (midwives) with their blessed healing powers, so people can cope with the various problems and illnesses that afflict them, such as evil eye, evil air, broken bones, and giving birth. *Curanderas* know secret prayers that they use to deal with the causes of illness and to control the forces that make people sick. They consider that their main sources of healing power are the spirits of the *divino*, and that it is not so much what they know that makes them powerful, but that they believe in and worship the saints and virgins. During the *arrullos*, which are rituals to open portals to heaven, many *curanderas* and other healers tap the curing powers of the *divino* and acquire their force and healing potential. One of the most important of these saintly figures is Hermano Gregorio, a deceased Venezuelan physician, who condenses the spiritual power of Catholicism with the secular power of scientific medicine. As with other similar figures in Latin America (Margolies 1984; Low 1988a, 1988b), narratives about malign spiritual beings delimit the geographical and social space-time of the *humano* and constitute allegorical comment on chaotic and uncontrollable behaviors. Many of the figures of the *humano* provide people with wealth and material possessions that, within the local moral economy, are considered well beyond what people need to sustain their livelihood. Many of these narratives define others as an antithesis of self and thus externalize evil, placing it outside the moral community; and yet, paradoxically, accusations of magic and pacts with the devil internalize that very evil and provide a symbolic recognition that conflicts, fragmentations, and tensions are integral parts of daily communal life.

Conceptualizing Time and the Life Cycle in Spiritual Terms

The *humano* and the *divino* are conceptualized in spatial and temporal terms. The *arrullos* are times during which the positive forces of the saints and the virgins dominate the world. There are also periods during the annual cycle, as well as during the life cycle of individuals, when evil and disorder prevail. There are days of the year when the spirits of the *humano* wander among the living. Examples of such periods are *día de los muertos* (All Souls Day or Day of the Dead) and Semana Santa (Easter week). From the death of Christ until his resurrection, the forces of evil and disorder are ubiquitous, and devils and demons roam freely on earth. It is said that during this week *brujas*— women who have made pacts with Satan or who practice black magic — become mules or serpents. Moreover, there are days of the week, especially Tuesday and Friday, and hours during the day-night cycle, such as at midnight and dawn, that are said to be more propitious for black magic rituals. Rahier (1998) describes these periods as a liminal time of imminent danger.

Afro-Esmeraldians believe that a person's life cycle proceeds from being wild and precariously perched between evil and good before baptism, to good and sacred after baptism and before a child "sins," to finally fully human and morally ambiguous at puberty and into adult life. From the time a child is born and until he or she is baptized, the infant is called a *mora/o* (moor). *Moros* are related to evil in different manners. The devil steals children who remain *moros* for a long time (though the concept of long varies considerably). When an unbaptized *mora* dies, it is thought that her spirit stays on earth, where it wanders and cries. It is said that terrible things might happen to the parents if they become close to the lost spirit of their unbaptized child (Fernández-Rasines 2001).

People in the area take all necessary precautions so that spirits of unbaptized children do not remain on earth. When people hear the spirit of a *moro* crying at night, they sprinkle holy water in the place where the spirit is thought to reside. When a midwife discovers that an unborn child is dead, she throws holy water on the belly of the mother to make sure that the spirit will not bother the mother. In the case of a stillbirth or miscarriage, the midwife or another woman who is chosen to be the *madrina* (godmother) must bless the dead fetus. All the children who die unbaptized are to be given the *bautismo de oleos* (a baptism in holy oils).

Several baptisms introduce the *moro* into the Christian world. The first involves the cutting and eating of the hair and/or nails of the child by the *madrina*. As pointed out by Robert Hertz (1960) and Edmund Leach (1958), long hair and nails are associated with savagery and wildness. The implicit analogy is between the unbaptized child and a wild animal, because both lack the knowledge necessary to be members of the moral community. The ritual removal and/or shaping of these dead parts of the body introduces the child to the civilized world. Little children who are not properly baptized stay as *moros* and bother the living. They sometimes become cats, dogs, donkeys, or other animals. They can kill people when they become evil spirits.

After the ritual cutting of the hair and nails of the child, other rituals mark his or her complete integration to the Christian community. These rituals are necessary for the child to be transformed from a *moro* to an *angelita/o* (little [innocent] angel). There is some disagreement as to whether a living child can be an *angelito*, though many agree that only once a child dies does he or she become an *angelito(a)*. Others point out that children who have not sinned are also *angelitos*.

When completely baptized children die, they go directly to heaven as *angelitos*. Godparents wash the cadaver of the baby, wrap it in white clothes, and bury it inside a small white coffin, called a *cajita*. The wake for an *angelito*, called *arrullo* or *chigualo*, is different from that of an adult (*velorio* and *novenario*) (Whitten 1994:124–45). The *arrullo* or *chigualo* for an *angelito* is similar to the *arrullo* for a saint or virgin, as both have similar symbolic functions. Both connect the world of the living with that of the spiritual beings that belong to the *divino*. There are, however, some important differences. Whereas in the case of the *arrullo* for a saint or virgin, people summon the spirits from heaven, in the case of the *arrullo* for an *angelita* her soul is ritually directed from earth to heaven. In both cases, purgatory is avoided.

Adults are sinners and their souls can be either good or bad. People treat dead adults very differently from *angelitos*, and their wakes are somber occasions. After a person dies, relatives and friends wash the corpse and place it inside the house in a coffin. They put the coffin on a table in the center of the living room of the house, and place candles on each corner of a table. Close relatives of the deceased serve cane alcohol drinks to combat the cold bad air that emanates from the corpse and the spirit of the deceased. It is said that the spirit wanders, tracing back his or her final steps. Bad airs are especially dangerous to pregnant women and small children. The doors and windows of the house where the corpse lies are left open so that the spirit, which wanders around the house, is free to enter and leave. When adults have been sinners, their spirits wander around and they molest or disturb the living; the living must approach *angelito* spirits to find safety.

As time passes, if spirits of deceased humans remain on earth, they become increasingly impersonal and dangerous. After the *velorio*, the wake for an adult, other rituals must be performed to ensure that the spirit leaves the space of the living. Once they bury the corpse, people go to the house of the deceased to sit and stand around the table on which the coffin had been placed. They put the clothes of the deceased on top of the table. They may also put a cloth doll that represents the person (*el cuerpo ausente*) together with a cross and two or four candles. After burying the body, people hold a watch during nine subsequent nights. During these nights, relatives and friends of the deceased gather together and recite the rosary. Black people sing *alabados* (dirges or hymns of praise) celebrating the deceased. This period of mourning and of saying good-bye to the spirit is called the *novenario*. During the last day of the *novenario*, the *última noche*, relatives and friends arrive, some from distant towns, and form a group similar to that which gathered for the wake. That night, between midnight and dawn, people throw the clothes of the dead and the table on which the corpse had lain into the street. This ritual, called "the lifting of the table" (*levantar la mesa*) ritually directs the spirit to leave the house. Some claim to have actually seen the spirit leave during the lifting of the table. There are other rituals that reaffirm the externalization of death that occurs during the *novenario*. Many Afro-Ecuadorians celebrate the *cabo de año*, the one-year anniversary of a person's burial. They believe that only after this terminal celebration is performed does the soul leave the world of the living.

During *velorios, novenarios*, and rituals of the *cabos de años*, black people sing *alabados*. In both types of rituals described — the *arrullos* to the saints and virgins and the celebrations to the dead — a space of spiritual and living goodness and order is being generated. "The house in which an adult dies is precariously balanced between earth, Purgatory, and Hell" (Whitten 1994: 128). Whereas the *arrullos* call the spirits from the *divino*, the *velorios* expel the soul-spirit of the dead from the house and the community. *Velorios* transform this ambiguous space created by the presence of death by the ritual expulsion of the soul-spirit of the deceased, thereby externalizing death and decay from the community of the living.

After these rituals, a few souls — notably those of dead children and perhaps of good adults, such as virgin women — go directly to *el cielo* (heaven). Most souls, however, go to *purgatorio* (purgatory), but some go to *infierno* (hell) (Whitten 1994). From purgatory and hell, spirits return to the world of the living to demand the prayers and the masses that the living must give in their names and that they need to ascend to heaven. The spirits of adults who died in a sudden or violent way, those who were evil during their lives, or those who are not administered the proper rituals wander in pain on earth for an extended time. Eventually, it is thought that spirits in this condition make their way to purgatory. When one travels alone at night, there is always the possibility of encountering the spirit of either a dead friend or relative or an unknown person. Some say that they have also encountered helpful and harmful spirits in the towns and in the cities.

Spirits that remain on earth after the rituals or those that return from purgatory are not always dangerous. Many such spirits visit relatives and friends without hurting them. People talk with fondness and even humor about encounters with these friendly spirits. Rosa, a woman from Esmeraldas, for example, remembers that when she was young, a person called Finado Pesado wanted to touch her bottom, but she never let him do so. The man told her that he would fondle her even if that meant returning after his death. One afternoon while she was resting alone in her bed, Rosa felt someone touch her rear end; she immediately knew that Finado had died.

Some souls or spirits, called *ánimas*, that are associated with a particular person often help the living. Some tell living people important secrets. When an adult dies and the spirit leaves, the spirit makes a noisy last sigh (*un suspirismo*), but only other spirits or a person underneath the bed where the person is dying, can hear the final exhalation. A person who is brave enough to stay below the bed might be told by the spirit the secret of eternal life, which, some say, is found in a plant (see also Escobar 1990:45).

Spirits may help the living by teaching them about sorcery. Some *brujos* claim that they were taught how to cure by a spirit who visited them at night. Some say spirits of unknown people show the living where treasures were hidden. These treasures, according to some, are hidden by the owner of the spirit while alive, and the spirit must get rid of the wealth accumulated on earth to enter heaven. Others believe that indigenous people show the living where they left a treasure by illuminating the place during the night. These lighted places are called *minas* (mines), and people are afraid of getting close to them. There are places that are considered *pesados* (heavy places) where evil spirits can be found. These are places where unruly behaviors such as extramarital or premarital sexual intercourse take place or even places where there is garbage and filth. In these places, people might get *mal aire* (bad air). Other illnesses, such as *mal ojo* (evil eye), are in a sense the result of powers attributed to people who are on the side of chaos and disorder and have transgressed different social and cultural norms.

Spirits and spiritual forces that emanate from the *humano* and the illnesses they cause confront people with images of their mortality. These forces are frequently seen as dangerous, unfamiliar, uncontrollable, and as dwelling outside the space of Christian order. Some of them kill people by taking their souls from them. When several children died in Muisne, at about the same time, many believed the first to die took the others with her. Spirits may also threaten adults. In Muisne, it is said that the beautiful spirit of a dead woman, *la muerta*, walks around town luring men to the cemetery, where she kills them.

The danger that some spirits represent to the living derives from their association with death, uncontrollable forces, and, frequently, with evil. Spirits are tension-laden signifiers; as such, they condense fears of death and decay. They represent a threat to the sense of immortality associated with the *divino*. Rituals such as wakes, the *novenario*, and *cabo de año* externalize death and disorder and create a domestic space of Christian order. By so doing these rituals help people cope with the unsettling and threatening effects of spirits and *visiones*. As counterparts of the private healing rituals, celebrations for the dead deal with existential fears at the communal level. In these celebrations, a space of death and decay is ritually constituted as external to the moral community.

Conceptualizing Space in Spiritual Terms

In the same manner that spirits condense fears of death and decay, other signifiers condense feelings associated with wildness and the wilderness. Some of these wild areas, such as the forest, the mangrove swamp–forest, and the sea, are not only dangerous places, but also are the source of much wealth if properly exploited. People recognize the dangers they can encounter there, such as fierce, wild, and enormous animals (*fieras*) that blur the line between the fantastic and the real.

Nature is also menacing because of its tremendous uncontrollable and destructive potential. The threat of natural catastrophes is always present in the area of Muisne. Occasional tidal waves (*visitas*) have destroyed entire towns. Mompiche, a fishing village close to southern Esmeraldas, was destroyed in the beginning of the nineteenth century. Fearsome sea currents (*aguajes*) and storms that characterize an El Niño episode also destroy crops and take lives. The memory of these chaos-producing events is maintained, re-created, and passed down to new generations in the form of narratives, stories, and *décimas* (ten-line stanzas). Although these natural catastrophes produce great fear, they are not usually seen as the result of evil, since no human agency is responsible for causing them.

The primary and secondary tropical rain forest, *el monte*, can be domesticated and converted into a *finca* (farm). People gain control over the potential productivity of the forest by "cleaning" (*limpiando*) the forest or brush for cultivation. This domestication of space gives people a sense of control over some of the forces that exist in nature. Whereas the *finca* is associated with the domestic economy and God, land dedicated to pastures (*potreros*) is associated with the market. It is, then, in between nature and modernity that one finds *lo divino*.

Many people tell of dreadful encounters with *visiones* and other mythical beings that, in the area of Muisne, are now associated with the devil. Many of these encounters take place outside the civilized space of the town. *Visiones* are part of a mythical reality that contrasts with that of God, Christ, the saints, and the virgins. *Visiones* allegorically stand for uncontrollable forces and structure the conceptualization of space as they externalize evil. At night in the forest or brush, people gather in their houses to seek shelter from darkness, wild animals, and evil spirits. The house and the community are regarded as protected spaces. Outside of these spaces is a dangerous world where *visiones* and spirits wander.

Some *visiones* condense affects associated with wildness, evil, and death. One vision frequently seen by people in the estuaries at night is *el riviel*. This vision is associated not only with death, but also with the dangers present in nature, especially those in the sea and estuaries. *El riviel* appears only at night; when one sees him at a distance, all that is visible is the light of a torch (*churuco* or *pendil*) that travels very quickly over the water. Some who claim to have gotten close to the apparition report that they saw a bunch of bones inside a canoe.

Some believe that *el riviel* is the spirit of a deceased person who drowned and craves company. Others say that *el riviel* is the spirit of an unbaptized baby, while others argue that it is the spirit of an adult, and that when he finds a person traveling in a canoe at night, he attacks and drowns the person. The victim is said to become, like him, another wandering spirit. People believe that *el riviel* disorients sailors who get lost at sea. In the north, people say that *el riviel* is a particularly dangerous ghost of a person who once went to a cemetery and cooked and ate a corpse. He saved ashes from the corpse and drank them just before he died. In this way, he avoided being punished by God. He moves freely in the sea, in hell, and in the sky (Whitten 1994:100).

Women, *Visiones*, and *Brujas*

European cosmology historically has constructed female sexuality as chaotic (Hoch-Smith and Spring 1978) and attributed evil powers to women (Caro Baroja 1964; Ehrenreich and English 1973:48). This association of women with wildness and uncontrolled sexuality is not uncommon in other male-dominated societies. Hoch-Smith and Spring (1978:3) write about these associations in the West and about how the idea of female as evil is transformed into specific cultural expressions through the manifestation of that culture's ideological content in art and, one might add, in popular mythology. They consider that non-western cultures reflect a similar view of women. Matrifocality is a common feature among Afro-Esmeraldians, and, in some cases, households are dominated by grandmothers who assume the position of symbolic mothers; they are called mothers by their granddaughters as well as by their daughters. Despite the importance of women in the material reproduction of the family, men accumulate most of the social, symbolic, and political capital. Female sexuality is seen as a disruptive, chaotic force that must be controlled by men, periodically purified, and at times destroyed. Women are also often seen as the source of spells and witchcraft that affect men (Fernández-Racines 2001).

Rumors about women's intentions to control male sexuality are often motives for witchcraft and sorcery. To control their husbands or their lovers, it is said that women perform different ritual *ligaduras* (from *ligar*, which means "to tie") to make sure that he is not able to have sexual intercourse with other women. As conflicts among women create tensions and jealousies, rituals of magic serve to generate a sense of control, while also contributing to social chaos and disorder. The discourses and the practices of witchcraft mediate sexual conflicts and subvert the genderized order.

Female spiritual beings commonly seen in the area unite chaos, nature, and evil with femaleness and its attributed alluring powers. One such vision is the *brujas* (witches). As mythical beings, *brujas* are given supernatural powers and forms by the devil or diabolical spirits. Besides these supernatural beings, some real women are accused of being *brujas* and are attributed the power of divining and of causing and healing evil and witchcraft. These women are said to work with the devil. Some say *brujas* are offspring of the *tunda* apparition and the devil or a priest she seduced. As *visiones*, *brujas* become birds at night and go out searching for victims. They drink the blood of little children and eat dead bodies (e.g., Wachtel 1994:78).

La virtud (virtue) is a gift of capacity or power from the realm of the divine that God gives to some children. *La virtud* empowers the gifted to foretell the future and to help others. One can identify children who have *virtud* by a cross they have on their palates. *Brujas* are especially fond of children who have *virtud*, since they also need *virtud* to gain wisdom and power. *Brujas*, who are in an eternal fight with God, try to injure these children. They attack children mystically to render them "blind idiots," and in some cases, kill them. *Brujas* are afraid that such children will reveal the witch's true identity when they grow up. One can tell when a witch has attacked a child because she leaves his or her body covered with purple bruises where she sucked the child's blood.

Some people believe that there are methods to stop and even capture witches. To prevent a *bruja* from hurting a child who has the special powers of *virtud*, parents baptize such children as soon as possible and bless their clothes along with all their possessions. Other parents leave a pair of scissors in the form of a cross under the child's pillow. Some say the parents must put a plate with raw rice close to the bed where the baby sleeps. The witch will stop to count the grains of rice and then will not hurt the baby. A woman told me that a *bruja* can be killed by putting capsicum pepper on her skin, which she leaves behind when she goes out looking for children or dead bodies. When she returns and puts on her skin covered with pepper, she dies. To capture a *bruja*, parents must put a pair of pants underneath the bed in which their child sleeps. One of the legs of the pants must be inside out. Then they must make a line of one hundred uncooked lentils from the door of the house to the bed and set an alarm, by tying pots and other metallic objects with a rope, that wakes them up when the *bruja* comes. When the parents hear the noise made by the witch they must recite a secret prayer. If a *bruja* enters, she has to pick up all the lentils and reverse the pant legs, which should give the parents time to capture and kill her, or at least scare her away.

As in many patriarchal social systems, such as Muisne, the image of women has been polarized. A duality exists between the view of women, being associated with God on the one side and with the devil on the other side. *Curanderas* are female healers who use the powers of the *divino* to heal illnesses that are not the result of evil intentions and witchcraft. They are associated with all that is good and local. The opposite of *curanderas* are the *brujas* who are associated with marginality and evil. Muisneños associate *brujas* with the devil and claim that *brujas* gain their power from killing children instead of healing them as *curanderas* do. Witches are placed outside the local Christian community in contrast to *curanderas*, who are at its center.

La viuda (the widow) and *la muerta* (the dead woman) are other *visiones* that reinforce the association of women with evil and chaos. People say that the *viuda* is a well-dressed woman who comes from the sea in a big canoe. Although some people in Muisne claim to have seen her, this apparition is more common in the northern part of the province and in the highland provinces of Carchi and Imbabura. There, in the northern Sierra, she is said to have a luxurious umbrella, wear an expensive hat and use nice perfumes. When she finds a man, she kills and eats him (Whitten 1994; Escobar 1990). A similar *visión* is the *muerta*, a beautiful woman who lures men to follow her to the cemetery, where she kills them.

The *visión* that people report having seen most frequently is *la tunda*. The *tunda* is an important theme among Esmeraldian writers. Adalberto Ortiz (1975) has suggested that she has cognate spirits in Africa. In the area of Muisne, she usually takes the form of a relative of the person to whom she appears. One can nevertheless recognize her because one of her feet has the form of a *molinillo* (a wooden stick which is used to decorticate coffee beans). People know when the *tunda* has been around because of the characteristic footprints she leaves. The *tunda*, some say, was a woman who never had children and who did not want to do domestic chores — a moralizing figure in a male-dominated society. The *tunda* exists in the forest or in the mangroves, and she appears to men when they are hunting or to women when they are gathering cockles.

Some people tell stories about how they or their friends were called by a woman who looked like their mother or aunt but, in reality, was the *tunda*. Although the *tunda* attracts mostly young children, she also attracts older men and women. A few say that there is also a male *tundo* who attracts women.

Women gathering *conchas* in the mangroves or men and women gathering forest products are frequently victims of the *tunda*. While gathering, a person suddenly begins to find more and more of the products he or she is searching for. The person gets excited and careless and walks away from the group. Once alone, the person meets a woman who looks like a relative or friend. People told me that the *tunda* usually offers shrimp to her victim. She eats the shrimp raw and then defecates them cooked: "los caca por el rabo ya cocidos." Those who eat the "cooked" shrimp become confused ("*con eso los emboba*") and easy prey for the *tunda*. The person who is taken by the *tunda*, called *entundado/a*, behaves like a wild animal. He or she becomes a *jívara/o*, *salvaje*, or *alzado/a* (Amazonian head hunter, savage, or rebel). These people grow fangs and long hair and are unable to talk.

I was told that in order to rescue the *entundada/o* from this state of wildness, a long procession must be organized and led by the *padrino* (godfather) of the victim. Friends and relatives follow him singing *alabados* and playing the *bombo*. In this manner, the powers based on the *divino* penetrate the domain of wildness of the *humano*. The rescuers must take dogs with them and carry shotguns to scare the *tunda*, who will overpower them otherwise.

Those rescued are unable to talk; their mouths foam and they fight to stay in the forest. The *entundada/o* tries to bite his/her rescuers and must be bound in order to be taken back into town. It is said that the *entundado/a* can only hear the voice of his *padrinos*, who must throw holy water at him or her. Once back in town, a *curandera* must treat the person so he or she can behave normally again.

In the area of Muisne the *tunda* and other mythical beings create metonymical links among wildness, death, and the devil that contrast with the sacred associations that constitute the domain of the *divino*. Within such a cosmology, curing and baptism become liminal and transformative acts by which objects and people are moved from a space of disorder and wildness to that of Christian control and domestication. In other stories the *tunda* is said to be a white woman who is the daughter of the devil.

Different rituals serve to transport the person from the domain of wildness and/or evil to that of control and order. The use of sacred symbols in these rituals transform a *moro/a* into an *angelito/a* and the *entundado/a* into a *cristiano/a*. In both cases, long hair and nails mark the person as a savage and an outsider to the Christian ordered world. Hallpike (1979) suggests that the cutting of the hair is associated with entering society or living under a strict order of rules: cutting the hair equals social control. Similarly, during curing rituals, *curanderas* treat people who are ill by manipulating key sacred symbols. The analogy can even be extended to the cutting of the forest (*limpieza*), which is also perceived as the process of domesticating the land. Metaphoric and metonymic links unite the *entundado*, the *moro*, the *monte*, and the patient who suffers from *mal aire*, *mal ojo*, or *espanto* (magical fright).

Visions such as the *tunda* and the *brujas* draw on the negative connotations that associate femaleness with wildness, nature, evil, and chaos. Yet the devil as a polysemic and paradoxical figure is also associated with femininity. In some narratives, femininity is related to the virginal domestic economy and its resistance to the penetration of the external male capitalist system. This, again, is an image of *la tunda*. Men who succumb to her become *entundados*, they are rendered helpless, poor, wild, and in jeopardy of dying.

Polarities such as female/male, internal/external, and domestic/public are related to economic strategies that people have developed in contexts of increasing semiproletarianization. Carmen Diana Deere (1983) and others have pointed out that in areas characterized by disarticulated economic formations it is common for peasant women to do a large part of the agricultural work. Men, by contrast, are usually involved in producing for the capitalist sector, because they work in agribusinesses or migrate to cities. In Ecuador, in general, some 30 percent of agricultural work is performed by women. In the area of Zumbagua, in the central highlands of Cotopaxi, Mary Weismantel (1988) reports that a semiproletarianized economy drives women's orientation increasingly inward even as their men turn outward. Both sexes, in turn, differ from their parents, for whom language, knowledge, and wealth have never been polarized according to gender to the same degree (Weismantel 1988:5).

The devil, which is a multivocal and polarized symbol, mediates gender conflicts in complex ways. Although in some contexts the devil is associated with women (the *tunda*, the *brujas* and the *mula* [mule] are all female), probably reflecting the dominant viewpoint of a patriarchal society. In other contexts, the devil is associated with men, and women are considered his enemies, thus reflecting men's greater engagement in the capitalist economy.

Among Afro-Esmeraldians narratives about the devil are moral commentaries on the processes by which, in a boom and bust disarticulated economy, women — associated with use-value and subsistence production — rescue men from the fluctuations of the international markets. It is said that the devil appears to men when they are alone in fields and never appears when a woman is around. Reflecting on this common occurrence, Carmen told me that "el diablo con la mujer no quiere fiesta" (the devil does not want to party with a woman).

Accordingly, the devil, most say, never makes pacts with women, and women frequently help men get rid of the devil after they have made pacts. Carmen also told me the story of a man who had made a pact with the devil because he wanted cattle and other riches. The devil appeared to the man every day and asked him to guess Satan's age. Each time the man gave the wrong answer the devil hit him. The wife of the man was afraid that the devil would kill her husband. She took off all her clothes and waited naked in a crawling position. Since she was very hairy in both her front and her back, when the devil came and saw her, he confused her back and her front and introduced his finger into her anus thinking that it was her mouth. When he smelled his finger he screamed "in the sixty-eight years that I have been alive, I have never seen such a bad-smelling mouth." The woman told her husband the age of the devil and, in that way, she saved him from further beatings.

These extraordinary narratives question male authority, wealth, and development, which are based on the greater articulation of men with the modern sector. Capitalist development in Esmeraldas has meant new opportunities for some men who have accumulated money and power and have found jobs in the plantations, the lumber companies, and the shrimp farms. Most women, by contrast, have been deprived of a livelihood and a source of income as a result of the ecological changes and the biases brought by the recent political-economic transformations.

For a couple of months in 1999, people in Esmeraldas talked about a she-devil, called *la tacona* (the spirit with high heels) who appeared at night in the city of Esmeraldas and terrorized young men there. She was the spirit of a young beautiful woman who was gang raped and killed some years ago and was now seeking revenge. She appeared in the discotheques of Las Palmas, an upper-class neighborhood in the northern part of the city, and invited men to come with her. Those who went were later found dead on the street or on the beach with foam coming out of their mouths. I was told in Muisne that many young people in Esmeraldas were afraid to go out dancing at night and that the disco where *la tacona* first appeared was losing money.

The Devil in Ecuador and in Esmeraldas

In Ecuador, a country where Roman Catholic imagery mediates understandings in a variety of ways, the figure of the devil is part of a racist dominant discourse generated in the center of any social order and an antihegemonic response that emerges from the periphery of that same order.

Faustian stories about Satan can be heard in different areas of the country and in the most diverse contexts. In the schools of Ecuador, children read in their textbooks the legend of an indigenous man, named Cantuña, who was in charge of building the church of San Francisco, in downtown Quito, during the colonial period. As the deadline for completion approached, the man realized that he would not be able to complete his job. Afraid of the reprisal by the Spaniards, he made a pact with the devil, who offered to finish the construction for him in exchange for his soul. Dawn came, however, before Satan was able to set the last stone. Thanks to that last unplaced stone, the indigenous man saved his soul.

Stories about the devil and devil possession are constantly recreated in the large urban centers and by the popular media and the dominant institutions. Popular newspaper and magazines constantly remind people of the threat of devil attacks, the spread of devil worshiping, and pacts with the devil. An article in the popular magazine *Vistazo* (1991), entitled "Satanismo," points out that in the coast, particularly in Guayaquil, there is a worrisome increase in the cases of demonic possessions and black magic, and the article gives some dramatic examples to support its claim. In the same article, a bishop and two psychiatrists give their opinions and alternatively consider the phenomenon to be the result of the schizophrenic mind and actual demonic possession. Another article in the same magazine (July 5, 2001) called "En el nombre del Diablo" ("In the Name of the Devil"), discusses how rock concerts are related to beliefs in the devil, and thereby pose a threat to young people.

Highlanders frequently travel to the province of Esmeraldas, which they perceive as the land of *negros*. This tropical region is feared by the highlanders not only because of the physical strength of the black people who live there, but also because of the alleged knowledge of magic attributed to blackness. Most go to the coast for pleasure and for business, but some go there specifically in search of the famous *brujos colorados* (Tsáchila shamans), who are said to be good at healing sorcery. On the coast, then, in the eyes of many

Serranos, both indigenousness and blackness carry the powers of healing as well as those of mystical harm.

The Devil and Incest

From the perspective of the local community, entropic behaviors are not only those that result from the intrusion of "modern" values and practices, such as greed, but also from "traditional" moral transgressions, such as incest. Different anthropologists have pointed out that the aversion toward incest results from a recognition that such behavior represents a threat to society (e.g., Lévi-Strauss 1967) because it could undermine the sentiment on which the family depends for its existence.

For Afro-Esmeraldians, incestuous relations result not only from sexual intercourse between consanguineal relatives (father and daughter, mother and son, brother and sister), but also between fictive ones (*compadres* and *comadres, ahijado* [godchild] and *madrina* or *padrino*). The various baptisms — such as the ritual cutting of the umbilical cord, hair, and nails by the *madrina* and her sprinkling of holy water over those attending a sacred event — create several *compadrazgo* ties between the parents of the child and the different godparents. Even when an *angelito* dies, *compadrazgo* ties are created between the parents and the person who baptizes the dead baby or those who help prepare and enact the *chigualo* ritual of child death that sends the *angelito* directly to heaven (see Whitten 1965, 1994). These *compadrazgo* ties must be reaffirmed by visits and gifts. The lack of such reciprocities could dissolve the link and attenuate or obliterate mutual obligations.

People consider that social relations between *compadres* are "mucho respeto como si fuese una relación entre hermano y hermana" (requiring as much respect as the relationship between a brother and sister). Fighting or sexual intercourse between *compadres* and *comadres* is strictly forbidden. People tell stories about parents who, forced by circumstances, became godparents of their own child. These couples commit a serious sin as they are linked by *compadrazgo* ties first forged in marriage.

Those who have had sexual intercourse with a *comadre* or *compadre* are damned (*condenados*) and terrible punishments await them in hell. Manuel, a forty-year-old *larvero* (gatherer and seller of shrimp larvae), told me the story of his uncle who lived in a rural area with his daughter, with whom he had a son. Afraid that people would discover their forbidden relationship, they killed the child. Soon after, a son of the man and brother of the woman went to visit them and saw the body of the dead child. He forced his sister to confess and denounced them to the police. The incestuous couple was sent to jail. After they got out of jail, they disappeared. Manuel says that they were probably taken by the devil. After the incident, people claim to have seen a very big chicken and a pig that throws fire from his mouth wandering near the abandoned house.

Other stories tell of men who slept with their *comadres* until one day when they woke to find at their side, instead of their lover, a snake or a mule. Muisneños tell similar stories about incestuous relations between siblings or between parents and their children.

The Devil and the Discourse of Otherness

Ecuador is a country divided by ethnicity and race (Cervone and Rivera 1999), and popular imagery and fantasy speak of these divisions as they refer to religion, healing, and magic. In a process that is much older in Europe than the Spanish conquest of the Americas, healing power that rests on pacts with the devil is attributed to the oppressed and tortured Other. From the European conquest on, the attribution of curing powers to indigenous people and black people who live on the borders of civilization has been well documented by other authors for the area of northwestern South America (Whitten and Torres 1998). From the time of the European conquest, black people have been traditionally associated with magic and the devil. Adriana Maya Restrepo (1992:87) writes that "the black is not only stigmatized by his color and for his descent from Ham, but also as a figure always in pact with the Devil. From medieval times, this demonization of the African has dominated the European imaginary." Frank Salomon (1983) writes about the colonial times in Ecuador, when some of the most powerful *curacas* (indigenous leaders) in the Sierra used black shamans brought from Esmeraldas to gain magical protection from the whites who wanted to seize their land. The association of "savage Indians" or "evil blacks" with Satan and the tropical forest with hell is also amply documented in Taussig's book *Shamanism, Colonialism, and the Wild Man: A Study of Terror and Healing* (1986).

In order to be healed from curses placed on them by envious lovers and business competitors, some people from Quito and other cities of Ecuador often go to the areas where the "semiwild" black people and indigenous people live. Mestizos throughout the country share, with some local variations, a cognitive map or moral topography that attributes healing power to several interconnected magical nodes. Sites such as Esmeraldas, Santo Domingo, Manglar Alto, Ilumán, Archidona, the south coast of Colombia, and the north coast of Peru are some of the centers to which many Ecuadorians travel to find powerful indigenous or black *brujos*. Muisneños, too, travel frequently to some of these places to find magical relief from their sufferings. They go not only to nearby towns such as Tonchigüe or Atacames, but also to more distant centers of magical power. Ironically, some outsiders come to Muisne, where they believe powerful *brujos* live. James Boon (1982:19) discusses the process of "how cultures, perfectly commonsensical from within, nevertheless flirt with their own 'alternities,' gain critical self-distance, formulate complex (rather than simply reactionary) perspectives on others, embrace negativities, confront (even admire) what they themselves are *not*." The antithesis of the acceptable that forever garbs intracultural and intercultural discourse with the mantel of potential reversal must remain in all frameworks of cross-cultural understanding of patterned interaction.

Informal political discussions that question the dominant institutions occur during everyday conversations, such as those engaged in by women in the houses of local healers. This questioning also takes place in rituals such as the *arrullos* and in the telling of dreams and myths. By using the symbols of the *humano*, people generate even more radical critiques not only through the discourses generated by the centers of power, but also through the locally generated sense of order and community. By using these images, charged as they are with negativity, Muisneños do not create an alternative order, as in the case of the use of the imagery of the *divino*; rather, they generate nihilistic discourses and practices that posit absence and rupture of the very forces disrupting their lives.

Different scholars (Taussig 1986; Whitten 1976; Gudeman 1978; Salomon 1981; Scott 1985; Crain 1991) have reported the ability of people to unveil the illusion of order created by logocentric discourses such as *desarrollismo*, Catholicism, and *mestizaje*. Although indigenous and Black people have to some extent accepted, and in a few cases profited from, the dominant discourse that attributes to them the power to heal by making a pact with the devil, they also question and invert these associations. Through narratives about Satan, they recognize the entropic aspects that accompany the expansion of the white people's economic and political system. In these narratives, the metonymic associations linking God, order, whiteness, cities, and civilization are rejected.

Through different narratives, Muisneños describe the devil as a white, elegant, rich man; some say he is an *hacendado* (landowner) or an elegant gringo, but many add that if one looks carefully, one can see that he has horns underneath his hat and that the point of his tail comes out of his trousers. Symbolic associations of the wealthy "others" with the devil construct and validate a sense of mestizo identity that is neither *negro*, *indio*, nor *blanco*. Such definition accepts and rejects the hegemonic use of *mestizaje* and the ideology of *blanqueamiento* (whitening), which defines *blanco* as the desired Other.

The Devil, Globalization, and Modernity

The study of symbolic resistance has been one of anthropology's most cherished themes. In many areas, resistance has been seen as the response to change and the imposition of an external cultural system (Taussig 1980; Crain 1991). The use of rituals and symbols to create ruptures and openings in the established order has been an important element in much of the literature (Burton 1997).

In Ecuador, as *blanqueamiento*, developmentalism, nationalism, and Christianity are promoted syntagmatically by the central powers such as the church and the state, people reject these constructs using different analogical tactics. The tension between the desire for the novel and the fear of rapid and, at times, undesirable transformations, is allegorically commented on by the use of polysemic figures such as the devil. In Muisne, the devil and other *visiones* condense meanings associated with spaces outside the local community. These are areas where people have experienced uncontrollable forces thought to be caused by mystical (and mythical) beings such as those discussed previously. Narratives about these beings and the spaces in which they often appear act as powerful moral statements and mediate oppositions such as local/foreign, Christian/wild, domestic livelihood/capitalist economy, and female/male. In the area of Muisne, Satan is associated with untamed nature and syntagmatically related to the Tunda, Riviel, *brujas*, and other *visiones*, such as *la viuda* and *la muerta*.

Social, cultural, and ecological crises created to a large extent by the series of economic booms and busts that have characterized the effects of the globalized economy on the area generate a gap between the world as desired and the world as lived. Rapid socioeconomic transformations disrupt the dialogical process by which disposition, experience, and structure constantly shape one another. People allegorically express and exacerbate such disruptions in different images, stories, jokes, accusations, evocations of mythical beings, and performances of hidden rites that constitute the domain of the *humano*.

The devil, in some narratives, constitutes a moral critique of greed and economic predation on people and nature. A man from Manabí told me about a friend of his who went hunting in the woods. As he was seeking his game, he perceived a strong scent of sulfur. Without paying much attention to the odor, he kept hunting. During that day, he killed many agoutis, pacas, and *huacharacas* (a bird of prey). When returning home, he was stopped by Satan, who told him that if he wanted to continue with his good luck, he must sign a pact, a *contrato*. According to others, the man became the best hunter in the area because he had sold his soul to the devil.

The devil is associated with modernity and whiteness (Rahier 1998). The devil lives and owns large beautiful cities, where he takes those who have made pacts with him. I was told different versions of a story of a poor peasant who was walking alone in the forest when he suddenly encountered a tall white man with blue eyes, riding a horse, and wearing cowboy boots, golden spurs, and a nice hat. The white man — the devil himself (*el mismísimo*) — asked the peasant if he wanted to work for him. The man was hungry so he agreed to do so, and the devil took him to one of his beautiful cities. In the large city, the man worked building roads and houses. After a year of very hard labor, the man decided to go back to see his wife. The devil said that he would pay him for his work and took him to a large room full of charcoal and dry maize leaves. He told the man to grab as much as he wanted. The man, upset and tired, returned to his house with some charcoal and maize leaves and complained to his wife about how little the rich man gave him in payment for a year of very hard work. When he emptied the sack, to their great surprise, they found gold instead of charcoal and money bills instead of dry leaves.

In the southern coast of Ecuador, where much of the national wealth is generated through exports such as bananas and shrimp, there are many stories about the devil and his pacts. One famous and very wealthy person there is Manuel Encalada, a very prosperous cattle farmer, shrimp farmer, banana exporter, and owner of a large bank in Machala, the capital of El Oro. Many of his workers say that he has made pacts with the devil, which explain his large fortune. He is said to have offered one of his sons to the devil in return for large sums of money. Workers also say that when they receive their salaries their money disappears: it turns into powder. Many people do not want to work for him because they are afraid he will take them to hell. One person who used to work for him told me that he once went to Guayaquil to Encalada's office and saw many caves and tunnels there, that probably led to hell. He did not, however, go in to investigate out of fear of what he would find.

There are similar narratives in other parts of Ecuador and the Andes that allegorically relate the devil to wealthy *hacendados*. In Imbabura, an indigenous man told me the story of Taita Imbabura, the spirit-father of Mount Imbabura, who lives in his cities or in his hacienda inside the mountain. He asks people walking in the foothills of the mountain to come to work for him. After they work hard for a period of time, they are paid with leaves and charcoal. Weismantel has also described the way in which money, academic titles, whiteness, masculine sexuality, and evil are related in narratives and symbols. In Esmeraldas, Olaya told me of a friend who had made a pact with the devil by exchanging his soul in return for cattle. His friend always had plenty of cattle and even when he sold them in the market the next day, his corrals filled up again. Although the devil told him not to spend his money on friends and celebrations, the man did not obey. One night the *empautado* (a person who is "ruled" by another person or being) saw a car coming to his *finca*. He knew it was a *visión* because there were no roads to his property. The car stopped below the house and two tall young white women came out; they were the helpers of the devil. They looked around and left, saying nothing. The following night, the car returned and left again, but this time all the cattle that the devil had given the man left chasing the car. Olaya says that now, around his friend's house where there used to be different kinds of fruit trees and plantains there is only bare land where no fruits can be seen. One can still hear the cows lowing, however, at night during Easter week.

The shrimp-farming industry has been responsible for the rampant destruction of the mangrove ecosystem in the province of Esmeraldas. According to Fernández-Rasines (2001), the *tunda* is associated with the desire of men (not women) to overexploit the mangrove ecosystem. As mentioned previously, the *tunda* defecates cooked shrimp and gives them to the men she wants to attract. The attraction is fatal. As men make more money in the shrimp industry, prices rise and the subsistence base (use-value) is eroded. The result is sustained poverty in the midst of wealth. The problem with this specific interpretation of the *tunda* imagery is that these stories about the *tunda* had been circulating for generations prior to the expansion of the shrimp industry (Ortiz 1987; Whitten 1994).

In the new millennium, there is a clear relationship between the forces and the images of the *humano* and the processes of globalization and modernization. Nonetheless, care must be exercised. The spirits and apparitions that now seem to serve as devices of symbolic mediation have been around for a long time. In an effort to fit a paradigm based on the dichotomies of modernity and capitalism, subsistence and accumulation, man and woman, globalization and the local economy, some authors may ignore the social complexity and cultural reflexivity implicit in these multivocalic mythical figures. Devil beliefs and stories do not, in my opinion, represent an absolute rejection of the modern, the global, or the developmental, and they are not to be seen as sustained symbolic mediators. Instead, they shed light on that which is ambiguous and contradictory in quotidian life. Rather than form a dynamic mediation of oppositions, devil beliefs constitute ways by which people reflect, communicate, and reach an understanding of their own involvements in an uneasy new reality now called globalization (e.g., Wachtel 1994).

Pacts with the Devil and the Internalization of Evil

The discursive and ritual uses of the key symbols of the domain of the *divino* define a local moral community as a homogeneous space governed by an ideal of communitas, ignoring the ever increasing differences between rich and poor, "whites" and "blacks." Such differences result from the integration of the area into the national economy. This process has resulted in greater tensions across ethnic, class, and gender lines. These polarizations reflect and reaffirm, at least in part, the internalization by members of the community of the norms of accumulation and the "growth of money." Such norms contrast with more traditional ones that stress redistribution and sharing. These changes and transformations give rise to accusations of envy and social tensions (Bermudez and Suárez 1990; Brown 1970).

The peripheral discourses that associate dominant values and understandings with the devil constitute critiques of this "white" and urban paradigm. For Muisneños, like other people in similar communities throughout Ecuador, urban national and international reference to the paradigm of development constitutes an alluring and yet distant and marginalizing imaginary. The ethic of development and accumulation is, for many, based in the forging of moral principles on the anvil of communitas, but it is also the source of desired wealth, conformity, and status. Although the devil is said to provide many people with deeply desired commodities such as farms, cattle, houses, cars, and money, one must sell one's soul to the devil to succeed in the capitalist economy. The devil demands from the *empautados* whom he rules a very ascetic lifestyle reminiscent of that described by Max Weber (1964) concerning the early European Protestant capitalists. The *empautados* of the devil are not able to enjoy their wealth, and they cannot spend the money on luxuries and celebrations; nor can they enjoy life with friends. And, what for many is worst of all, their bodies disappear after death.

Some people tell stories about the devil that often depict him as a bank official, a big patron or a rich partner (*socio*). In these stories, the devil routinely inspects those accused of having signed a pact with him. He often appears riding his horse and visits those who sold their soul to him to control their businesses and behaviors. If they do not produce enough to satisfy him, or if they spend their money organizing parties and celebrations to give pleasure to their relatives, Satan strikes them and may take away their souls and/or their wealth and/or their health and even, at death, their bodies. The imagery of disembodiment at death corresponds to that of economic, social, and political disfranchisement in life.

Given this association of the devil with an ethic of asceticism and individualism, some Catholics accuse the Evangelists, many of whom lead a more ascetic lifestyle, of making pacts with the devil. The Evangelical churches have been gaining followers during the last few years. Catholics resent Evangelists in part because they tend to be wealthier. Many Catholics complain that *evangélicos* never spend their money in celebrations to the saints or drink *aguardiente*. Furthermore, Catholics also resent Evangelists because they ask those who are being converted to their faith to burn and destroy the images and the icons of saints and virgins. Some Catholics believe that *evangélicos* have made pacts with the devil. They say that Satan appears in their churches and that the Evangelists worship and chant to him.

These narratives question the dominant work ethic, the commodification of time and labor, and the intruding values that place the accumulation and display of wealth above social relations and people. Many people feel that these intruding values are now accepted by the majority of the people, both Catholic and Protestant, and, when asked if they have ever seen the devil or any of the *visiones*, many people told me that now everyone is the devil: "Ya no se ve al demonio ni a las visiones porque ahora el demonio somos nosotros mismos" (Now people do not see the devil or the *visiones* because the devil is us, ourselves). Accusations of pacts with the devil not only question the dominant developmentalist paradigm, but also reveal internal tensions that result from conflicting interests and desires. Accusations of pacts with the devil constitute allegorical substantiations of the entropic effects of the acceptance of the intruding capitalist values and sensibilities as well as a recognition of the ways by which local people cope with their problematic relationships with globalization and growth.

Probably the best-known local case of a person who made a pact with the devil is Gordo Ramón, "Fat Raymond," also known as El Gordo (fatso), who, until his death in 1987, was the wealthiest merchant in Muisne. He came from Manabí when he was a young man and made money buying export products such as bananas, cacao, *tagua*, and wood at low prices from the peasants. He then transported the products in his boats to Esmeraldas and Manta. On the same boats he brought contraband from Colombia and Panama. Public evidence of his wealth consisted of his large store, storage facilities, and a cement-buttressed harbor where he docked his two large boats.

Most people believe that his fortune came from a pact he made with Satan. Miguel, a man who used to work for him, told me that once, while he and other sailors were bringing contraband from Colombia to Muisne in one of El Gordo's boats, they saw a large city on the horizon in the middle of the sea. At first, they thought it was Bahía de Caráquez, but they knew that they were not that far south. As they got closer, they realized that the city was in flames and that those working in the city were eating hot coal. Among the people in the burning village, Miguel told me, they recognized some of the people who worked for El Gordo.

El Gordo died while I was in Muisne, shortly after the sudden death of his wife. Some claimed that their deaths were the result of sorcery by one of their many debtors after Ramón and his wife tried to forcefully collect the money the person owed them. Some say that during the funeral they could hear rocks rolling inside El Gordo's coffin. None of his three sons, who were in their early twenties, were able to run his business. Soon after his death, they were accused of dealing drugs and got into trouble with the law. The store and the other businesses were abandoned, and Ramón's wealth disappeared. Rumors circulated in town that the real reason for the disappearance of the large fortune was that his sons did not want to renew their father's pact with the devil.

Like the wealth generated in the extractive booms that disappear in the bust cycle after causing ecological and social devastation, the wealth created by the devil does not last long. In the middle of the city of Esmeraldas, there are a few abandoned plots of land. People claim that the plots belonged to a now-deceased man who once made a pact with the devil and that anything built there was, is, and will be consumed by fire.

The Devil Order and Disorder

The domain of the *humano*, which is that of the devil, is the antithesis of the domain of the *divino*. It questions and reaffirms the symbols and practices that generate the sense of a moral and ordered community. This process seems to be common in many religions that are built on antithesis and oppositions and in many cosmologies in which negation of a concept is necessary for the conceptualization of that concept. Freud (1959) understood the importance of reversal to thinking. He pointed out that with the help of symbols of negation, the thinking process frees itself from the limitation of repression and enriches itself with subject matter without which it could not work efficiently.

From a local point of view, the devil and *visiones* such as the *tunda* and *el riviel* are extraordinary and threatening figures that define spaces and times external and antithetical to the local moral community. These mythical beings belonging to the domain of the *humano* are expressions of incongruous experiences that often result from peoples' interactions with wilderness, wildness, and the capitalist economy. The basic opposition between the *humano* and the *divino* mediates and represents the dialogical relation between experiences in the world within which people interact.

Some Afro-Esmeraldian rituals such as *arrullos* and *chigualos* express and reaffirm the domain of the *divino* or act as bridges between domains (baptisms, wakes, and healing rituals). Rites such as those of magic and pacts with the devil question and challenge the hegemonic religious and secular discourses.

The multivocality and polarization of the image of Satan explains how it can be used by different sectors in different and, in some cases, contradictory ways to define Otherness. As part of the dominant discourse, it is associated with oppressed sectors of Andean societies such as indigenous people, black people, and women. Paradoxically, people attribute to these oppressed and marginalized sectors the power to cure the white person from *mal* and other types of evil magic caused by the tension, jealousy, and envy that are intensified by the intruding capitalist market economy.

The image of the devil within the domain of the *humano* gains affective force from dissonant experiences and constitutes an allegorical expression of ecological destruction and social tensions. Narratives about the *visiones* not only challenge and limit the dominant intentions of remaking the subjectivities of the Afro-Esmeraldians so that they regard the wage form as natural and wage work as a calling, but they are also figures that reflect the conflictive desires that modernization produces. The devil stands not only for the erosion of traditional norms that place value on redistribution, communal labor, and kinship ties, but also for the desires that modernity generates. Although narratives about the devil question the accumulation of wealth as a morally valid goal and equate wage work with spiritual impoverishment and increasing social tensions, greed, envy, jealousy, death, and internal chaos, narrow and closed interpretations of the devil must be avoided.

The devil constitutes an open-ended root metaphor of evil; people attach to this root metaphor, as adhesions, those beings that threaten and bring fear and terror to humans (e.g., *el riviel, la tunda, la viuda, la muerta*). Care must be taken so as not to fix people in modern and millennial times and events within the medieval imagery that they may deploy. To wrest a living in Esmeraldas in the new millennium in the face of devastation is no mean task, and the symbolic capital that comes to Afro-Esmeraldians must be appreciated in its contemporary creativity as well as its multiple historical ties to Europe, Africa, and the Americas.

The devil also refers in an allegorical manner to social and ethnic tensions. The Afro-Esmeraldian representation of Otherness, according to Rahier, inverts the discourse of race and Otherness. He writes:

[I]f Satan, as the ruler of Hell, is syntagmatically related to the various demons and *visiones* whom one might encounter while traveling in the forest, he is then related to the worst of all, the *Judíos*, who have put Jesus to death. This association made by Afro-Esmeraldians between Semana Santa and characters and demoniac forces, makes sense when considered within the liminal time of the celebrations: . . . Whites and white-mestizos are, from the perspective of Selva Alegre, urban Others with social, economic, and political power. (Rahier 1999:42)

Accusations of pacts with the devil to gain riches or to destroy lives and businesses unveil not only the illusion of order generated by the discourses of modernity, but also the local one, ritually generated in the centralized periphery. The reflexive narratives of the *visiones* and the devil are an implicit recognition that the threat of potential disorder is to be found not only outside, in the modern sector or in uncontrollable nature, but also inside, in the processes of community life itself. As a friend once told me, "en Esmeraldas ahora el Diablo está en nosotros mismos" (now the devil lies within ourselves). This erosion of the ever evasive and imaginary moral community may result from "traditional" moral breaches — such as incestuous relations, social transformations that generate greed, envy, and jealousy — and discourses about demonic rites such as pacts with the devil, witchcraft, and sorcery.

ACKNOWLEDGMENTS

First and foremost, I thank the people of Muisne for their patience and for offering me critical insights into their processes of analytical thought. Norman Whitten's assistance from my entry into graduate school at the University of Illinois at Urbana-Champaign through present collaborations is greatly appreciated. I am indebted to my wife, Tania Ledergerber, for her sustained support over many years and for her continuous collaboration in my current research. My parents, Manolo Quiroga and Amparo Ferri, have long provided me with necessary support.

REFERENCES

Adams, Richard N.
  1975 *Energy and Structure: A Theory of Social Power*. Austin: University of Texas Press.
Bermudez, Eduardo, and María Matilde Suárez
  1990 El papel de la envidia en una comunidad negra de Venezuela. *Caribbean Studies* 23(3–4):1–33.
Boon, James A.
  1982 *Other Tribes, Other Scribes: Symbolic Anthropology in the Comparative*

Study of Cultures, Histories, Religions, and Texts. Chicago: University of Chicago Press.

Brown, Peter

    1970   Sorcery and the Rise of Christianity. In *Witchcraft Accusations and Confessions*. Mary Douglas, ed. London, Tavistock: Association of Social Anthropologists Monograph No. 9.

Burton, Richard

    1997   *Afro-Creole: Power, Opposition, and Play in the Caribbean*. Ithaca: Cornell University Press.

Caro Baroja, Julio

    1964   *The World of the Witches*. London: Weidenfeld and Nicholson.

Cervone, Enma, and Fredy Rivera

    1999   (editors) *Ecuador racista: Imágenes e identidades*. Quito: FLACSO.

Crain, Mary

    1991   Poetics in the Ecuadorian Andes: Women's Narratives of Death and Devil Possession. *American Anthropologist* 18:67–89.

Deere, Carmen Diana

    1983   The Allocation of Familial Labor and the Formation of Peasant Household Income in the Peruvian Sierra. In *Women and Poverty in the Third World*. M. Lycette Buvinic and W. P. McGreevey, eds. Pp. 104–29. Baltimore: Johns Hopkins University Press.

Ehrenreich, Barbara, and Deirdre English

    1973   *Witches, Midwives, and Nurses: A History of Women Healers*. Old Westbury, New York: Feminist Press.

Escobar, Marta

    1990   *Frontera imprecisa*. Quito: Centro Cultural Afro-Ecuatoriano.

Espinoza, Fernando

    1989   *Situación actual de la maricultura del camarón en el Ecuador y estratégias para su desarrollo sostenido*. Quito: Instituto de Estratégias Agropecuarias. Fundación IDEA.

Fernández-Rasines, Paloma

    2001   *Afrodescendencia en el Ecuador: Raza y género desde los tiempos de la colonia*. Quito: Ediciones Abya-Yala.

Freud, Sigmund

    1959   The "Uncanny." vol. 4 in *Sigmund Freud: Collected Papers*. Pp. 368–401. New York: Basic Books.

Friedemann, Nina

    1985   *Carnaval en Barranquilla*. Bogotá: Editorial la Rosa.

Gudeman, Stephen

    1978   *The Demise of the Rural Economy: From Subsistence to Capitalism in a Latin American Village*. Boston: Routledge & K. Paul.

Gudeman, Stephen, and Alberto Riviera

  1990   *Conversations in Colombia: The Domestic Economy in Life and Text.*
         Cambridge: Cambridge University Press.

Hallpike, Cristopher Robert

  1979   *The Foundations of Primitive Thought.* New York: Oxford University Press.

Hertz, Robert

  1960   The Collective Representation of Death. In *Death and the Right Hand.*
         R. Needham and C. Needham, trans. New York: Free Press.

Hoch-Smith, Judith, and Anita Spring

  1978   *Women in Ritual and Symbolic Roles.* New York: Plenum Press.

Howard-Malverde, Rosaleen

  1981   Dioses y diablos: Tradición oral en Cañar, Ecuador. Serie Amerindia
         Número Especial 1. Paris: A.E.A.

Leach, Edmund

  1958   Magical Hair. *Journal of the Royal Anthropological Institute* 88(2) : 147– 64.

Lévi-Strauss, Claude

  1967   *The Savage Mind.* Chicago: University of Chicago Press.

Low, Setha

  1988a Dr. Moreno Cañas: A Symbolic Bridge to the Demedicalization of Healing.
         Social Science and Medicine 16(2) : 527–31.

  1988b The Medicalization of Healing Cults in Latin America. *American
         Ethnologist* 15(1) : 136–54.

Margolies, Luise

  1984   José Gregorio Hernández: The Historical Development of a Venezuelan
         Popular Saint. *Studies in Latin American Popular Culture* 3 : 28 – 46.

Mera Orcés, Verónica

  1999   *Género, manglar y subsistencia* Quito: Ediciones Abya-Yala.

Morgan, Lynn M.

  1997   Imagining the Unborn in the Ecuadorian Andes. *Feminist Studies* 23
         (summer) : 323–50.

Ortiz, Adalberto

  1975   La négritud en la cultura latinoamericana y ecuatoriana. *Revista de la
         Universidad Católica* 3 : 97–118.

  1976   *Juyungo.* Barcelona: Seix Berral.

  1987   *La entundada y otros cuentos.* Quito: Editorial Planeta.

Rahier, Jean

  1987   *La décima: Poesía oral negral del Ecuador.* Quito: Ediciones Abya-Yala.

  1998   Blackness, the "Racial"/Spatial Order, Migrations, and Miss Ecuador
         1995–1996. *American Anthropologist* 100(2) : 421–30.

  1999   Presence of Blackness and Representations of Jewishness in the Afro-
         Esmeraldian Celebrations of the Semana Santa (Ecuador). In

Representations of Blackness and the Performance of Identities. Jean
Muteba Rahier, ed. Pp. 19–47. Westport Conn.: Bergin and Garvey.

Restrepo, Adriana Maya

1992   Las brujas de Zaragoza: Resistencia y cimarronaje en las minas de
Antioquia, Colombia, 1619–1622. *América Negra*, 4 (December):
84–96.

Salomon, Frank

1983   Shamanism and Politics in Late-Colonial Ecuador. *American Ethnologist*
10(3):413–28.

1981   Killing the Yumbo: A Ritual Drama of Northern Quito. In *Cultural
Transformations and Ethnicity in Modern Ecuador*. Norman E. Whitten, Jr.,
ed. Urbana: University of Illinois Press.

Scott, James C.

1985   *Weapons of the Weak: Everyday Forms of Peasant Resistance*. New Haven:
Yale University Press.

Taussig, Michael

1980   *The Devil and Commodity Fetishism in South America*. Chapel Hill:
University of Northern Carolina Press.

1986   *Shamanism, Colonialism, and the Wild Man: A Study in Terror and Healing*.
Chicago: University of Chicago Press.

Turner, Victor

1967   *The Forest of Symbols: Aspects of Ndembu Ritual*. Ithaca: Cornell University
Press.

1973   *Simbolismo y ritual*. Lima, Peru: Departamento de Ciencias Sociales
Pontificia Universidad Católica.

1974   *Dramas, Fields, and Metaphors: Symbolic Action in Human Society*. Ithaca:
Cornell University Press.

1986   Dewey, Dilthey, and Drama: An Essay in the Anthropology of Experience.
In *The Anthropology of Experience*. Victor Turner and Edward Bruner, eds.
Pp. 33–42. Urbana: University of Illinois Press.

Vistazo

1991   La brujería en el Ecuador. 565 (March): 34–38.

1992   Sindicato de brujos colorados. 605 (November): 25–29.

2001   En el nombre del diablo. 813 (July): 43–47.

Wachtel, Nathan

1994   *Gods and Vampires: Return to Chipaya*. Carol Volk, trans. Chicago:
University of Chicago Press.

Weber, Max

1964 [1947] *The Theory of Social and Economic Organization*. Glencoe Ill.:
The Free Press.

Weismantel, Mary

    1988   *Food, Gender, and Poverty in the Ecuadorian Andes*. Philadelphia: University of Pennsylvania Press.

    1997   White Cannibals: Fantasies of Racial Violence in the Andes. *Identities* 4 (August): 9–43.

Whitten, Norman E., Jr.

    1965   *Class, Kinship, and Power in an Ecuadorian Town: The Negroes of San Lorenzo*. Stanford: Stanford University Press.

    1976   *Sacha Runa: Ethnicity and Adaptation of Ecuadorian Jungle Quichua*. Urbana: University of Illinois Press.

    1994 [1974]   *Black Frontiersmen: Afro-Hispanic Culture of Ecuador and Colombia*. Prospect Heights: Waveland Press.

Whitten, Norman E., Jr., and Arlene Torres

    1998   (editors) *Blackness in Latin America and the Caribbean: Social Dynamics and Cultural Transformations*. Bloomington: Indiana University Press.

CHAPTER 7

Return of the Yumbo

The *Caminata* from Amazonia to Andean Quito

NORMAN E. WHITTEN, JR., DOROTHEA SCOTT WHITTEN, AND ALFONSO CHANGO

"We are . . . in Quito; . . . all nations are here."

On April 24, 1992, the phone rang in the Whittens' home in Urbana, Illinois. "¿Causanguichu gumba?" (Are you living, *compadre*?), asked Marcelo Santi Simbaña, our longtime indigenous associate in Amazonian Ecuador. He went on to say, "We are here in Quito; we, the forest people, have arrived here. We walked here and we have arrived. We are many; all our brothers are here. All nations are here: Pastaza Runa, Salasaca Runa, Chimborazo Runa, Cotopaxi Runa; Yana Runa are also here, *compadre*; all nations have come to be within Quito." Marcelo, his wife, Faviola Vargas, and many of their relatives had just completed a peaceful protest march undertaken by indigenous people from their Amazonian homelands to Quito, the capital city of Ecuador. They had walked for thirteen days.

In this chapter, we draw attention to the unfolding dramatic structure of this event (the Caminata de Pastaza a Quito, later called the March for Land and Life) and to the symbolic processes of its enactment. By so doing, we contribute to an ethnology of practical activity and symbolic efficacy. We seek to portray, understand, and explicate aspects of the suasive cultural forces that created an aura of power that energized the pragmatic success of one of the most dramatic indigenous events in Ecuador's turbulent history.[1]

We begin by placing the *caminata* in the context of recent indigenous protest movements. We then present a chronicle of events as a composite description drawn from firsthand accounts by participants and other observers. These descriptions have been collected over several years from marchers themselves and from accounts in the national media. We then move to the symbolic affinity of this pragmatic march with a north Andean ritual festival, the *yumbada*. This festival enacts the story of a group of Amazonian people, collectively known as Yumbo, coming to Quito. Through the course of this chapter, the multivocality of the concept of the Yumbo as "shamanic healer from the forest" unfolds. The public narrative of the *yumbada*, as it was reported in the national media, was important because the marchers became increasingly aware of the mass audience reaction to their moving theater of power and because they commented specifically on the perceptions of their march by others after the *caminata* itself had ended. Finally, we discuss the political aftermath of the indigenous movement in Ecuador through June 1996.

"1492–1992" Recent Symbol and Protest in Ecuador

Ecuador contains a number of nationalities (*nacionalidades*) (CONAIE 1989), long called *naciones* in the vernacular of indigenous peoples. Since 1990, representatives of some of these nationalities have accomplished feats of political persuasion unprecedented in Ecuador's colonial, republican, or modern history. The public displays of force, unity, and peaceful tactics contradicted a number of assumptions and beliefs held by many Ecuadorian nonindigenous people and significantly affected the nationalist discourse about the structure of the nation-state itself.

The prevailing mood in Ecuador from about 1989 through mid 1992 was one of desire for radical change in the republic as a whole and for its nationalities in particular. For indigenous people in the Andes and Amazonia, the rallying cry was "¡Después de quinientos años de dominación, autodeterminación indígena en 1992!" (After five hundred years of domination, indigenous self-determination in 1992!). The year 1992 was chosen as the symbol of a cultural, political, and economic uprising, a choice made to highlight their opposition to the elitist rhetoric of the quincentennial celebration planned for the same year: the commemoration of the European "discovery" or "encounter," the conquest of ancient indigenous territory, and the eventual establishment of nation-state hegemony over indigenous people.

Indigenous efforts to gain self-determination occurred in various regions of the country at different times. In early May 1989, indigenous people and national representatives held a confrontational meeting in Amazonia, which produced the highly controversial Acuerdo de Sarayacu (Agreement of Sarayacu). This was followed by a sit-in and threats of a hunger strike by Andean people in the Santo Domingo "temple" in Quito in June 1990. The Levantamiento Indígena (indigenous uprising) of 1990 was, without question, the greatest mobilization of people in Ecuadorian history, and it publicly established an indigenous power source that could not be denied.

Over the course of 1990 and 1991, the symbol of 1992 and the Levantamiento Indígena conjoined imagery from the highest level of Ecuadorian society with the antipodes of Ecuadorian blackness and indigenousness. Much of the public rhetoric of the Levantamiento Indígena focused on making 1992 the year in which the Euro-American conquest would be publicly challenged and a new nation of indigenous peoples would regain its lost freedom and assert its cultural and political autonomy. In July 1990, a dramatic encounter between indigenous leaders of North and South America again emphasized the commonality of experience of five hundred years of external domination and the ideal of transforming societies and cultures of the Americas in 1992 to lands of indigenous autonomy (N. Whitten 1996).

As October 12, 1992, approached, a number of marches and other forms of indigenous protest took place throughout the Sierra. According to Lynn Meisch (1992), the climax of all "500 Years of Resistance" demonstrations was to be a huge, peaceful march and rally in the historic, colonial center of Quito on the anniversary of the day that Columbus had initiated his encounter with the people of the Americas. Thousands of indigenous people and supporters, including "Afro-Ecuadorians, white-mestizo students, campesinos, members of the clergy, and workers" (Meisch 1992:67) turned out for the rally, festive in mood but tightly controlled by military and police in full riot and combat gear. Many would-be participants, possibly thousands, were blocked by military and police at all points of entry to Quito and at strategic departure points from many provinces.

The Levantamiento Indígena of 1990 challenged nation-state control systems. There were clashes with police and military, and the military subsequently occupied large sectors of indigenous land in the Sierra. The *caminata* underscored and reaffirmed the challenge. Taken together, these two events emphasized the inner powers and externalized forces of politically conscious indigenous people on the move. *Doce de octubre* (October 12) demonstrations had the potential to expand the forces of the Levantamiento and the *caminata* but, just before and during the October 12 rally, nation-state officials moved decisively and with a massive show of armed force. The display of force against the indigenous and Afro-Ecuadorian liberation movements enacted the very core expressions of the 1992 symbol of ethnic oppression.

It is significant that both the military and the police actually facilitated the *caminata* once it was underway and that they refrained from actions leading to bloodshed in the Levantamiento after the initial clashes. From its beginning in Puyo to its arrival in Quito, the *caminata* was accompanied by the police; no marchers were officially impeded, although some individual conflicts and skirmishes took place. The minister of government, César Verduga Vélez, committed the government to helping the marchers maintain their integrity and make a case for their pragmatic goals. The president of the republic, Dr. Rodrigo Borja Cevallos, is often credited with issuing orders to the military and police leaders to protect these events from the violence of armed confrontation. "This is not against us, nor against our Government, it is against five hundred years of injustice," he is quoted as saying (Rangles Lara 1995:195). This stands in stark contrast to the tragic crushing of Asháninka people by military forces in Peru described by Brown and Fernández (1991).

The *caminata* began in Puyo on April 11, 1992, and ended there on May 14. Approximately two thousand indigenous people left Puyo in a driving tropical rainstorm; by the time they reached Salcedo, their number had grown to between five thousand and ten thousand. They spent two days in Salasaca, in an unprecedented festive and religious sharing of Andean and Amazonian symbolism. The marchers trekked for 180 miles and arrived in Quito thirteen days later. The campout in El Ejido Park in Quito and negotiations with the president's "social front" matched the drama of the Levantamiento and resulted in the promise of significant accessions of land from the nation-state to indigenous organizations of Pastaza Province.

The *caminata* was a powerful pragmatic and political event undertaken as a last resort after the participants had exhausted all other efforts to gain usufruct to their Amazonian territories. It was one of many such manifestations ranging from Mexico through Central America to Colombia, Ecuador, and Bolivia that preceded the quincentennial year 1992. In its general form, the *caminata* may be taken as a microcosm of similar international activities. To the best of our knowledge, the inner symbolism of an emergent movement and the pragmatic externalization of such symbolism has not been described in Latin American settings. This chapter deals with these two phenomena — inner symbolism and pragmatic externalization — as they are embedded in the discourse of those who marched and those who listened to the tales of the marchers.

The Sociopolitical Stage of the *Caminata* from Pastaza to Quito

Throughout the *caminata*, and subsequently, the polarized issue of indigenous leaders as bona fide representatives of indigenous movements on the one side and as coopted figureheads for national political powers and international NGOs on the other, was (and is) salient. No set of preconceived oppositions can help one to understand the pulling and tugging of political, economic, and ideological forces that themselves become intertwined in enduring paradoxes, contradictions, and antinomies (see N. Whitten 1985, 1988, 1996).

In late 1991 and early 1992, officers of OPIP held a series of meetings with representatives of affiliates to evaluate policy regarding territory and politics. The resultant decisions were to eschew national elections and instead support indigenous candidates for local offices; to march to Quito to negotiate territorial claims with the government; and to seek funds (specifically dollars) from the exterior.

The president of OPIP, Carlos Antonio Vargas Guatatuca (known generally in Ecuador as Antonio Vargas), left Ecuador under the sponsorship of the U.S.-based Rainforest Action Group to raise international funds to save indigenous people and their rain forest. Electronic mail networks carried messages urging supporters of the proposed march to send money in Vargas's name to a bank in Berkeley, California. Other accounts were allegedly set up in Seville and Brussels. After an apparently successful fund-raising drive, Vargas returned to Puyo, according to some accounts, with suitcases full of money.

Rumors about the success of the fund raising became coupled with confusion and misinterpretation of the initial OPIP goals. Some people thought, or hoped, that the march would also promote the indigenous candidates of the National Liberation (LN) Party for mayor of Puyo and prefect of Pastaza and raise money for their campaigns, while others said that the foreign money from the *caminata* fund was being usurped for party-based campaign expenses. This polarity of rhetoric resulted in intraindigenous charges of embezzlement and wider accusations that the march was being financed by or for a political party or a coalition of parties. This verbal jousting did not diminish the ultimate success of the march and indeed was completely muted among indigenous people until the *caminata* ended.

The four *planteamientos* (historical proposals) for the future resulting from the assessment and evaluation, and for which the *caminata* was initiated, were the establishment of permanent territorial rights for indigenous people; the derivation of rights to wealth from territorial commerce, including subsurface exploitation; the final resolution of 117 specific conflicts registered by indigenous people over land rights; and a national constitutional reform to make Ecuador a multicultural, multinational nation-state. The fundamental purpose of these history-making demands was (and is) to claim all indigenous territory legally controlled by the Ecuadorian nation-state through the agency of the Instituto Ecuatoriano de Reforma Agraria y Colonización (IERAC: Ecuadorian Institute of Agrarian Reform and Colonization) and to place the land occupied by indigenous people under the effective control of formal indigenous organizations.

Organizational plans for the march were drawn up during an OPIP meeting in early March 1992. At least eight commissions and a general coordinator were appointed, and the instructions to participants were issued. Among these were the following:

Each community should send as many delegates as it can — men, women, children, and elders — and should send powerful delegates, including holders of staffs (in communities where the Catholic church maintains this system); shamans; "strong ones" who can give orders; and elderly women with special knowledge.

Bring your own plate, gourd bowl, and spoon.

Bring your own wrapped chicha (manioc mash), dried rations, and dried meat. .

Bring your own blanket and warm clothes.

Bring musical instruments, including hand-coiled pottery cornets, drums, slit gongs, flutes, violins, and musical bows.

Bring lances, shoulder adornments, and headdresses, and come painted as warriors.

After Antonio Vargas returned to Puyo, he held a press conference on March 27 to announce the *caminata*. OPIP leaders called on indigenous people throughout Pastaza Province to undertake an arduous journey by river and land to assemble on April 10 at the headquarters of CONFENIAE. The organization's buildings are on a hill overlooking the indigenous community of Unión Base, the home of Antonio Vargas.

The appeal to the people was based on the clear message of the earlier (1991–92) pragmatic assessment and evaluation: "We either go to Quito now to present our proposals to the president of the republic, or we lose all our territory, and hence our livelihood." OPIP leaders specifically requested the Achuar Jivaroans (Descola 1994), the multicultural Shiwiar (Seymour-Smith 1988), and all Quichua-speaking people of Pastaza Province to unite with people from Canelos and the Comuna San Jacinto del Pindo and to march together from Puyo to Quito. According to *El Comercio* on April 23, 1992 (*Kipu* 1992b:79), representatives of 148 communities of indigenous people of Pastaza Province took part in the march.

On April 8, three days before the march was to begin, the Brigada de la Selva (Brigade of the Jungle) No. 17, based four miles from Puyo in Shell (named after the Royal Dutch Shell Petroleum Company), militarized Puyo-Napo and Puyo-Macas Roads and occupied Unión Base, including the bilingual school there. Troops guarded all gas stations and other way stations on the route of the *caminata*, in Amazonia and in the Andes.

On the rainy morning of April 11, roads were jammed with people walking from Unión Base into Puyo to join many others who swarmed into the central plaza. When nearly all were assembled, a pottery cornet was blown from somewhere in the crowd. People stood in the downpour to listen to leaders from provincial, regional, and national organizations give speeches.

The most moving of these was by Dr. Luis Macas, president of CONAIE. After they spoke, Macas, Valerio Grefa (president of CONFENIAE), and the other leaders joined the serpentine mass of people, which was colorful with the feather headdresses, bead and bone necklaces, and black and red face paints worn by marchers (*Kipu* 1992b:5). They crowded into the cathedral for a special mass celebrated by Monseñor Victor Corral, bishop of the Andean city of Riobamba and head of the indigenous ministry of the Catholic Church. The bishop blessed the march as a sacrifice "worthy of being justly examined by the Government and by the Ecuadorian people" (*Kipu* 1992b:5). The people reciprocated by presenting a feather headdress to the bishop.

On the other side of town, a countermarch organized by FEDECAP was underway to protest the right of OPIP to speak for the entire province. These protesters were accompanied by cars belonging to a bank and municipal, provincial, and national government agencies. As the *caminata* participants left the cathedral to begin their journey, Antonio Vargas addressed the largely colonist countermarchers, asking them not to see indigenous peoples as their enemies and assuring them that this fight would be for the good of all Pastaza habitants.

The town became quiet and empty: "Not one indigenous person was left in Puyo," wrote Alfonso Chango in 1992. Approximately two thousand Shiwiar, Achuar, and Canelos Quichua left the outskirts of Puyo that rainy afternoon, not knowing how long they would march, what dangers lay ahead, or when they would return. They were led by residents of the Comuna San Jacinto del Pindo, officers of OPIP, and representatives of independent communities loosely associated with OPIP. They marched under a rainbow-colored banner bearing an artist's rendition of the face of the Inca Atahualpa with the bold emblematic statement "¡Allpamanda, causaimanda, jatarishún!" (For land, for life, rise up!).

The march was composed of men, women, and children. Alfonso Chango's expanded kin participated. We have known many of the adults for thirty years. During our research in Puyo and its surrounding areas in 1992, 1993, and 1994, one of the most salient issues of discourse among women and men was their participation in the *caminata*. Our role was to listen to what they had to say, ask some questions for clarity, and record discussions on audio- and videotape for later transcription. Alfonso Chango took notes during the *caminata* itself and wrote them up in Quichua and Spanish in June and July 1992. Together with Luzmila Salazar, Alfonso's wife, we worked with all of the marchers who took an interest in the project. Alfonso Chango described the project as *cuintaushcata ricuchina quillcaushcata*, a "narrative written to explain." In Spanish, he clearly set forth the premise that *explicación* (explication) must precede *interpretación* (interpretation).

The *caminata* was undertaken to provide Ecuadorian leaders and the general Ecuadorian populace with a modern, radical alternative to nation-state power over frontier territories in Pastaza Province. Its spokesmen and spokeswomen suggested that, in lands where the nation-state had no colonists, control of such noncolonized regions be ceded to indigenous organizations representing people who knew how to wrest a living from their rainforest and riparian environment. To live productively in the rain forest is to live with the power systems generated by the forest itself and by the encompassing hydrosphere. The concept of "environment," they affirmed, is not something easily transformed into nation-state discourse and bureaucratic management. From their point of view, it would seem, ecology is cultural and the way to understand political-economic demands on the environment involves explication and interpretation (see, e.g., Chango 1984; Viteri 1993).

In their public dialogues, speakers made ceaseless mention of male shamanic power and female visionary power. The latter has been manifest in women's creation of songs and hand-coiled ceramics, which are both contemporary renditions of ancient traditions and knowledge (see Chango 1984; D. Whitten 1981; Whitten and Whitten 1988, 1993).

The Unfolding of a Ritual Drama of the *Caminata* from Pastaza to Quito

To the men, women, and children who participated in the *caminata*, the march was politically persuasive; it sought legal, ethnic-nationalist control over indigenous usufruct. It was also an aesthetically suasive manifestation of counterhegemonic power. Beauty and ethnic strength were seen to generate a fount of internal, indigenous power that complemented the ideological, political, and economic forces on display. Bolstered by this aesthetic force, people talked continually about their environment, which they hoped to bring once again under indigenous control through nationalist legal commitment, action, and compliance.

They talked of mythic time-space (*unai*) and its transformation (*tucuna*) into beginning times-places (*callarirucuguna*) and through times of destruction and ancestral times into the future (*caya*). The future was bound through these transformations to enduring indigenous history. People were clearly conscious of their role in making history, of taking the future into their own hands.

The march proceeded as a dynamic event and as a system of discourse of power on the move. A ritual drama unfolded, which involved the use of a large array of symbolically charged materials. These included foods from native gardens, forests, and rivers; special headdresses, necklaces, and armbands; carved palm-nut containers for spirit substances; plant dyes for body and face adornment; musical instruments; pottery items; and palm-wood lances. In 1992 and 1993, some people brought items they had worn or carried to show us the details of every one of these ritual symbols, and Chango made drawings with notes on the significance of each piece. Many people recalled the specific items that they had previously traded, given, or sold to the Whittens for further study or for use in exhibitions, underscoring the imaged efficacy of such signifiers. We see these ritual objects as constituting a cultural map of signifiers of specific markers of social and material indigenous endurance (e.g., Turner 1974:239).

Three ritual items — pottery cornets, face and body paints, and headdresses — illustrate the symbolic embeddedness of these objects in the drama of the *caminata*. Cornets, sounded at the beginning and then blown throughout the march, are made only by women, usually for special kinship festivals held in indigenous hamlets and geographically remote areas where the evidence of the Catholic church is typically reflected in the presence of a crude chapel. When the festival atmosphere escalates into chaos, a woman who made a cornet presents it, filled with *asua* (manioc brew), to an important man. He sits on a long bench that symbolizes the anaconda, drinks the *asua*, and then blows the cornet while other men beat drums, play flutes, and dance with women.

The cornet makes the haunting sound of the game bird Trumpeter who, in mythic time-space transforming into beginning times-places, comes as a forest warrior to rescue two beautiful women in distress. He fails. Other game birds as warriors arrive to liberate the two women and they also fail. Finally Toucan (*sicuanga runa*) arrives and frees them. The women then turn the warriors into the game birds of the forest and create the basic colors of red, yellow, black, and white to give beauty to the world (see Whitten and Whitten 1988 for more of these elaborations). Stories such as this one were told repeatedly, with much elaboration, by the marchers during 1992, 1993, and 1994.

Symbols of representation — face painting, feather headdresses, and special shoulder slings, necklaces and armbands — are ancient practices now mainly relegated to the ritual kinship festivals. The black and red paint (from *Genipa americana* and *Bixa orellana*, respectively) symbolize the beauty given to humans by the two mythic women (Widuj Warmi and Manduru Warmi) who transformed themselves into these trees. Men and women make special nut and gourd containers for their paints. The most treasured of these paints is *carawira*, made of *Bixa orellana*, red sap from one of several trees, and anaconda fat. The mixture itself is one of many substances called *simayuca*. Men and women paint a little of this along the edge of their eyelids before facing danger. By then looking directly at one's foe, one "sees" as the anaconda "sees." Foes are neutralized in that their vindictive will (*man-alli shungu*) is suppressed. In this aesthetic action, if the self in its mystic as well as human dimensions is correctly presented, the foe cannot injure the person so painted.

The headdresses worn by men constitute our third illustration of the ramifying and intersecting cultural map of signifiers. Each headdress must have a direct relationship to birds, reptiles, amphibians, and mammals that the maker or wearer (headdresses are often exchanged and traded) has encountered. Each man who makes a headdress must first encounter the being he is to kill in a dream and "know" in a transcendental way that this creature will be "his." Bird feathers, once woven into a headdress, represent the colors and sounds of the spirit world, because each feather exhibits flashes and streaks of color usually visible only to spirits. When a human being takes soul-vine brew, however, the colors and sounds of the spirit world may be revealed to the taker. Attached to the back of a headdress are pieces of cloth, bone, nut, or other tangible things. Each of these represents the transformation of a spirit with which the maker of the headdress is comfortable. Each spirit so represented has its distinct sound —*breep, breep, breep, breep*— and, when it moves, a distinct motion, usually in a directed spiral —*wshhh wshhh wshhh wshhh*. These sounds and motions can be heard and seen by spirits.

The moving performances of the *caminata* included dances and songs by women taking on the personae of powerful spirit-animals and birds (black jaguar woman, hawk woman, owl woman), of master spirits in feminine manifestation, and of other people of the rain forest (*llushtirunaguna*, unclothed forest people). Focal women were called *sinchi muscuyuj warmi* (strong visionary women, or women who "see").

Many men took on the personae of ancient warriors of mythology and history, including *sicuanga runa* (the liberator person) and *curaga* (ancient heads of different Quichua peoples) (see N. Whitten 1985). They called themselves *guerreros* (warriors) and *guardianes* (guardians). They were overseen by shamans called the *sinchi yachaj runa* (strong men who know) and motivated by the *sinchi muscuyuj warmi*. During the summers of 1992, 1993, and 1994, the Whittens worked closely with several *guerreros* and *guardianes* and with one of the *sinchi yachaj runa*, and also with several of the *sinchi muscuyuj warmi*. Several of Chango's relatives were among these special people; one of his brothers is a *sinchi yachaj*.

Spirits (*supai*) cannot be brought directly to a march; to do so would be to introduce a monster into the midst of the crowd (the Achuar and Shiwiar call such a being *iwianch*). The mystical work of spirits is recognized as the essences. It is the essences that constitute the signifieds. Quichua speakers think of these essences as a living force (*causai*) or breath (*samai*). They are said to have an inner proof and, on occasion, to manifest a special tangibility. These essences were brought into the march, where they were named and identified, and the forces they manifested were incorporated into what all described as a sustained emotional experience. The spirits included Amasanga, spirit master of the rain forest and indigenous territory; Hurihuri Supai, the dangerous underground spirit of other peoples' territories; Urcu Supai, the dangerous spirit of hills and their hidden caves; Waira Supai, the spirit of wind that brings torrential rains; and many others.

It was on April 12 that the ritual drama brought together the spirit forces of the rain-forest and riparian habitat of the native peoples of modern Pastaza Province. That night, in their camp at Río Verde on the Puyo-Baños road between Amazonia and the Andes, shamans gathered. The marchers were now in the veritable *montaña* (sometimes called the *yunga* by Andean Quichua speakers), the legendary topographical and ritual site of the Yumbo. By drinking soul-vine brews, the shamans sought mystical union with powerful legendary forces. As the shamans entered collective and individual trances, moving between the spirit world of the forests and the hills of this familiar environment, women sang and danced and the guardians and warriors prepared for whatever intrusion might occur.

On Monday, April 13, the two thousand marchers moved out before dawn toward their first Andean destination; from there they would begin their northward trek toward Quito across the immense Andes through the corridor of the volcanoes. They marched together rapidly and robustly, making loud noises — calling in falsettos, beating drums, playing flutes, blowing cornets, and shouting slogans. Past the hydroelectric plant and beyond Agoyán Falls, they moved through a long dark tunnel that eerily echoed their calls, songs, drumming, and cornet sounding. They forced their sounds to an even greater crescendo as they poured out into the sunlit Andean world and moved across the bridge over the huge dam near the headwaters of the Pastaza River.

Passing Baños late in the afternoon, they quieted as they veered off to the indigenous community of Quero (southwest of Pelileo), where they were met clandestinely by representatives from Salasaca. Thus the march entered the escalating drama of Andean theater on its third day, establishing what Victor Turner (1974) called a "charged field" wherein cultural paradigms emerge, are tested, and acquire a cultural life that transcends the dynamics of the social movement itself.

Passage into Liminality Phase 1

By the end of the day on Monday, a feeling of uncertainty shrouded the marchers. Many of them had injured their feet on gravel, cobblestones, and macadam. They were treated by shamans and by a physician using Western medicine. People wondered what would happen next and they decided to see what would transpire with anticipated new allies in enemy territory. Now the people were "betwixt and between" (Turner 1974 : 13) — out of their known environment and far from their destination.

The liminal period that began in Quero became transformed ceremonially into a remarkable series of events in Salasaca. Salasacans said that the Yumbo had arrived in the Andes and the marchers said that they took no offense with the use of the word in this context. At this point, everything changed; the shroud of uncertainty was removed. Salasacans came from all sectors of their territory in ceremonial dress associated with Corpus Christi, beating huge painted snare drums, playing flutes, and dancing as they do during the major festivals that punctuate the ritual year. Salasacans gave an abundance of food — corn, beans, potatoes, and fruit — to the marchers (whose own food, backpacked from Puyo, was by this stage depleted) and also loaned them warm clothes. As other men, women, and children from Amazonia and the Andes continued to arrive, the shamans of the lowlands drank soul-vine brew and received council from the Salasacan shamans about the mountain and weather spirits of the Andes.

Narrators later said that an integration had taken place, uniting contemporary worlds that had once been conjoined but had long been divided. Andean and Amazonian peoples united with Andean and Amazonian spirits. In trances, the lowland shamans "saw" that the frigid Andean winds would not blow, that rain, sleet, and hail would not fall as they crossed the *páramo* (high plateau) elevation of eleven thousand to sixteen thousand feet, and that Indi, the sun, would shine during the entire trek to Quito. They also foresaw that their powerful adversaries throughout the Amazonian and Andean regions would be overcome or circumvented as they marched forward, and that more and more compatriots would come to their aid. They saw victory in their immediate future (*cayamanda*).

The Salasacans spent that night and the next day partaking in festivities that had not been celebrated in many years. They were joined by even larger indigenous groups from various other parts of the Sierra, while still more indigenous people from the lowland rain forest arrived by bus and truck. The doubts the marchers had harbored on arrival in the Andes were now dispelled. Reinvigorated, they prepared to move out together on April 16.

"¡Puriáun!" (Trek on!). At dawn, spiritually, psychically, and physically fortified, they resumed their advance toward Quito, still far to the north. The marchers described their undulating procession as *amarun shina*, "like an anaconda."[2] During annual or semiannual kinship festivals that celebrate the oneness of a people, the Canelos Quichua walk in circles and dance to the pulse of many snare drums, creating a cultural force field (see N. Whitten 1985; Whitten and Whitten 1988; Whitten et al. 1976). Alfonso Chango and others saw the *caminata* as creating this same force, here in the form of movement evoking the powers of the spirit master Amasanga —*tan, tan, tan, tan, tan, tan* (blows on the head of the drum), *ween, ween, ween, ween, ween, ween* (buzzes of the snares)— and heading north toward the national capital.

Danger lay ahead, for the marchers had to circumvent the third largest city in Ecuador, Ambato — a treacherous urban zone known to be replete with residents who hated and feared indigenous people and their social movements. A hub between north and south Andean cities and towns, located between the coast and the Andes and between the Andes and the Amazonian region, Ambato had been virtually closed down for five days in 1990 by participants in the Levantamiento Indígena (see N. Whitten 1996).

Passage into Liminality Phase 2

As the *caminata* approached and passed through Ambato early on Thursday morning, hundreds of indigenous people joined it. Now heading due north toward Salcedo and the first night beyond Andean indigenous territory, three thousand to five thousand people were on the move — shouting, laughing, singing, beating snare drums, flourishing palm-wood (*chonta*) lances and knives, and calling out names to people watching from a respectable distance, "Hey you, monkey person; look here at us, the *indios*. We are on trek; be careful of us; we are the powerful ones."

North of Ambato, high above the Yambo Lagoon, marchers met with the parents of two "disappeared" youths, the Restrepo brothers, victims of alleged police atrocities (España Torres 1996). At an emotional end to the encounter, they collectively cast a palm-wood lance into the lake as a symbolic petition for justice for the Restrepo brothers. Following this ritual protest of injustice, the marchers took stock of where they might be in relation to their eventual destination. The longest period in ever higher and colder climes lay ahead. No one knew how many days the march would take. The sick were healed with medicines provided by the Red Cross, with "popular" medicines brought by Andean healers, and by shamanic performances and ministrations. Warriors, guardians, and shamans consulted with one another and all agreed that only the very ill might now turn back. The die was cast. The marchers would now press on to Quito.

The next day, Good Friday, the marchers departed by 6:00 A.M., resolutely heading toward Salcedo. More and more indigenous people from the provinces of Tungurahua, Chimborazo, and Cotopaxi joined, coming from feeder trails and roads onto the Pan-American highway, surging toward a route that would take them through the center of town. The *caminata* entered Salcedo around midday, and thousands more turned out to cheer on the marchers. To the surprise of many — indigenous and nonindigenous people alike — not a single negative comment or slur was heard as the marchers went through Salcedo. Everything was upbeat and positive. Firsthand reports indicate that the march was "like a celebratory parade"; people threw flowers from balconies and from the sides of streets and cheered "Long live the march!" and "Go to Quito and claim your rights as indigenous Ecuadorians!"

After camping overnight without further incident, the marchers pressed on to Latacunga and camped just outside this market-oriented city around midday. The ranks had swelled enormously with indigenous people from the *páramo* area of Zumbagua Parish to the west and from other settlements to the east of Latacunga. Here, for the first time, the indigenous people symbolically reversed the brutality of the colonial and republican rule over native Andean peoples. Nonindigenous people (some allegedly from the military) had infiltrated the march and were trying to elicit information to take to enemies of the *caminata*. As word passed among warriors, guardians, and shamans about the intruders, the guardians rounded them up, tied them to trees or stakes, stripped off their trousers, poured icy water on their buttocks and genitals — thereby supposedly cooling their machismo — and, in some instances, enacted what marchers called *la ley del indio* (law of the Indian) or *justicia indígena* (indigenous justice): practical or vigilante enactment of law. Some press releases called this practice *la ley de la selva* (law of the jungle). When the Whittens discussed this use of language, in Spanish, with people who had taken part in the *caminata*, some participants used the Spanish verb *castigar* (to punish) to describe such acts.

The importance of punishing spies was underscored by all marchers who chose to discuss the *caminata* with us. The guardians and warriors were entrusted with the obligation to arrest (*prender*), to punish (*castigar*), and to release (*soltar*) those found inside the *caminata* formation who had not been specifically invited by a marcher. We were repeatedly told by marchers, who spoke in earnest tones and made forceful and persuasive eye contact: "we also have laws" and "we also have rights."

This sequence of discovering, arresting, punishing, and releasing is itself a social drama within a larger social drama. It is an onstage reversal of the brutal practices of hacienda owners or overseers who tied indigenous serfs or sharecroppers to posts and publicly whipped them for refusing or failing to produce for the owners. Sometimes people died as a consequence of this punishment; moreover, they had no legal recourse. On the *caminata* (as in the Levantamiento of 1990) some marchers did take action against captured infiltrators but they released those they had whipped and, as they pointed out to reporters, their whips consisted of single strips of rawhide, unlike those used by the *hacendados*, which were made of multiple leather strips with steel tips on the ends, to lacerate, maim, and scar. Nor did indigenous marchers use their lances as spears. Their lances were only for defense, not for punishment. To spear someone with a lance would be a reversion to the cultural status of *auca* (savage).

Enactment of indigenous justice on the march was an onstage activity, one of many designed to communicate the sense of indigenous control to a regional and a national audience. Only those the marchers considered a threat were placed in the spotlight of punishment. Others, such as the Ecuadorian ethnographer Diego Quiroga, who met the *caminata* at Yambo Lagoon just beyond Ambato, were invited in, albeit clandestinely. Diego simply walked near the front line of the march until Marcelo Santi Simbaña saw him. Marcelo identified Diego to his brother, Bolívar Santi Simbaña, and together they motioned for him to enter their sector of the Comuna San Jacinto marchers and excitedly told him about what they were doing. This backstage activity — also open to selected representatives of the press and some politicians and social activists — carried numerous messages beyond that conveyed by the primary dramatic event. Such encounters always remained backstage and involved at most two or three designated spokespersons who chose their own times and places for formal interviews.

That Saturday afternoon and evening in Latacunga, a significant indigenous cultural exchange took place. Spokespersons for different indigenous organizations voiced mutual respect for one another and urged their followers to listen to and try to understand a range of indigenous perspectives. Leaders of various groupings gave formal speeches about their formations, strategies, and goals.

The next leg of the trek was the most arduous. The marchers walked one hundred kilometers through one of the coldest regions of Ecuador and camped at a frigid elevation of eleven thousand feet. Easter night was grim; one child, succumbing to cold and fever, died in her mother's arms.

Broken Barriers

The march from Latacunga across the *páramo* to the outskirts of Quito took three days. As they entered Machachi on the second day, people's spirits were buoyed by the knowledge that representatives of more organizations had joined them in solidarity (*Kipu* 1992b:63). Near the end of the third day, when Quito could be seen from the distance, cars and buses full of counter-demonstrators from FEDECAP blocked the way. These organized anti-*caminata* groups — which included some indigenous peoples — were armed with guns, axes, machetes, clubs, and other deadly implements. As they began to form a roadblock, small groups of guardians and warriors wielding lances as slicing clubs (*macana*) suddenly attacked them. The antagonists had expected a standoff during which the march would stop and the military and police would intervene. Instead they were attacked immediately. They retreated quickly with bleeding faces, cracked skulls, and bruised or broken limbs. The route of the march was successfully defended and the *caminata* proceeded along the Pan-American highway to the last camp before entering Quito: the old and once-indigenous community of Guamaní, now incorporated into expanding south Quito.

South Quito is a sector where the indigenous/nonindigenous polarity regularly dissolves and reemerges. Despite the potential for opposition here, the march was favorably received by thousands of residents of south Quito. No marcher reported any hostility. People arrived around 5:00 P.M. and rested in preparation for an early departure the next day. At least some residents of south Quito were familiar with the idea of forest people coming to the urban center; a ritual festival called the *yumbada* was performed in 1991 in Barrio La Magdalena, not far from the marchers' route. Roggiero's extended commentary of the south Quito *yumbada* urges readers of the popular newspaper *Hoy*, modeled on *USA Today*, to "comprehend and evaluate its profound significance" (Roggiero 1991).

Simón Espinosa (1992:159), wrote poetically about the politics unfolding as the *caminata* moved through south Quito.

And the Jungle Arrives in Quito
Before dawn on Thursday, the inhabitants of the south of the capital awoke frightened [as in a sudden surprise assault that terrifies]. The jungle had arrived in Quito. At four in the morning of the foretold day the march began its final assault. A dark and noisy army of *indígenas* advanced on the pavement miming monkeys and birds, howling [yelling, crying out], making falsetto calls, beating drums. The lights of the houses came on. The sleeping citizens got up and applauded. The great indigenous serpent encountered the factory workers entering their dawn shift. Two opposed worlds with one destiny crossed.

The marchers departed from Guamaní in the cold darkness well before dawn on April 23. They were now accompanied by indigenous delegations from Azuay, Cañar, Chimborazo, Tungurahua, Cotopaxi, Pichincha, and Imbabura — most of the provinces of the Sierra. Afro-Ecuadorian people who had come from Esmeraldas province on the north coast had also joined them. The march proceeded up the southern Pan-American highway through one urban barrio after another; residents came out just to look and often to cheer. One large elementary school released all its students and the teachers encouraged them to sing and shout and chant, "Welcome, indigenous brothers." The teachers waved Ecuadorian flags and white flags with "Equality," "Peace," "Love," and "Justice" printed on them (*Kipu* 1992b:110).

The march passed through the Santo Domingo Plaza, surged on to the San Blas Plaza and the Plaza de Independencia, and arrived at the Plaza San Francisco at 9:30 A.M. The stream of people, now between five thousand and ten thousand strong, moved through streets lined with police in full riot gear and curious onlookers standing ten to twenty deep. There were reports of minor confrontations with police. Shamans, warriors, and guardians wielding *chonta* lances countered the threats by police to strike marchers with rubber batons or the butts of their rifles. Conscious opposition, said those whose narration we follow, won out over the highly organized, repressive tactics of police.

The Plaza de Independencia and the Plaza de San Francisco are in the colonial center of Quito. The body of indigenous Amazonian and Andean people, now united with the heartland and headship of Ecuadorian nation-state power, provoked enormous social and political tensions that had significant ramifications for that very power.

As the Quichua, Achuar, and Shiwiar crowded into the Plaza de San Francisco, their indigenous leaders — Luis Macas, president of CONAIE; Valerio Grefa, president of CONFENIAE; and Antonio Vargas, president of OPIP; along with many others — accompanied by police, prepared to meet with the president of the republic, Dr. Rodrigo Borja Cevallos. On his way to the plaza to invite the leaders to Carondelet he hesitated before the multitude. Apacha Vargas, a master ceramist and daughter of Acevedo Vargas, once a great *curaga* of Puyo and its hinterland, took the president by the arm and, speaking in Spanish and Quichua, said, "Don't be afraid of us, we are all your *churis* and *ushis*" (sons and daughters). At the palace the president offered them their land, and Grefa and Vargas publicly thanked him gracefully in Spanish and in Quichua. Then the leaders returned to the Plaza de San Francisco and announced that usufruct would be ceded to indigenous people; the crowd cheered and shouted at the news.

The mayor of Quito, Rodrigo Paz (founder of the largest chain of money-exchange houses in Ecuador, and presidential candidate in 1996) offered the marchers space to set up camp in El Ejido Park. They readily accepted and the *caminata* proceeded northward out of the colonial sector and into the modern one, past the Central Bank of the Republic and to the park, which is surrounded by the House of Ecuadorian Culture, the Colón Intercontinental Hotel, several international banks, and other corporate and government buildings. Here, as thousands of marchers settled down, President Borja again spoke, sketching the details of the "gift" of Amazonian land to its indigenous inhabitants. The speech carried these chilling messages:

> The president could do nothing about changing the constitution to make Ecuador a multinational state; only the congress could do this.
> With regard to the request that government-owned land be transferred to indigenous people, the president promised that a "positive dialogue" would be opened between the two parties.
> The government would set up a fifteen-day period of "study" to be undertaken by a "social front" composed of representatives from the Ministry of Government, the Department of Defense, the Program for Welfare, and IERAC.

With this speech, the president made it clear — as it had not been hitherto — that the government would talk and delay. The marchers, however, had come for immediate results. To remain too long in Quito could be deadly for the Amazonian people. The conflict pitted indigenous against bureaucratic concerns.

The marchers were now out of liminality; they were no longer "betwixt and between" (Turner 1974:13). They had arrived at the antipode of their origins, the sacred center of the republic — urban, urbane, sophisticated, white, powerful, Catholic, stratified, and Iberian-oriented Quito.

During this period, supporters arrived from many parts of the Andean highlands, and another delegation of coastal black people from Esmeraldas Province also arrived. More people poured in from the south, heading for the park, and downtown Quito was heavily guarded by police outfitted in protective gear, including helmets with face protectors, shields, rubber batons, and canisters of tear gas. Few, however, carried firearms. Onlookers reported that it was exceedingly difficult to get through the police to speak to, or even see, the marchers. And if they did penetrate the police barriers, they were met by guardians and warriors wielding palm-wood lances that constituted the ultimate perimeter of defense of the march for life and land.

The Yumbo, many onlookers said, had returned. A new but ancient body of power was pulsating within the city. "Los selváticos nos interpelan" (The savages [forest dwellers] implore our [Quiteño] aid) announced the prominent headline of one editorial of the April 26 newspaper *Hoy*, written by the historian Galo Ramón Valarezo (*Kipu* 1992b:118–19):

Are We Interested in Their Visit?
[It is a] novel consequence that the Amazonian indians, those "yumbos of the jungle," address in the first instance the Quito Runa [*runa quiteños*] in a demand of solidarity. We remember the *yumbadas*, these famous festivals of Quito in which the indians from yumbos visit to celebrate this type of encounter. [It] appears interesting that they seek solidarity from numerous different groups to share the destiny of a subaltern sector [of people] of Ecuador [who are] ignored and segregated.

That Ecuadorian journalists and other writers turned to a north Ecuadorian Andean festival is significant. From the entry to south Quito onward, the collective consciousness of marchers and the massive Ecuadorian audience following the moving theater through radio, television, newspapers, and magazines increasingly focused on the symbolism — explicit and implicit — of this *yumbada*. For *caminata* participants, the space they now occupied represented centuries of cultural terror for native peoples; in the eyes of elite and other Quito residents, a reciprocal cultural terror might now, in turn, be imminent. Quito had become a living embodiment of what Michael Taussig (1986) calls "the space of death." Ironically, much like Taussig's description of such developments, out of this space of death came powers to heal.

We now turn to a north Ecuadorian ritual of reversal to ground such discourse in symbolic structures that emerge during a collective crisis involving encounters with Amazonian peoples.

Cultural Representation and Ritual Reversal

The symbolic evocations of the *caminata* bear dramatic resemblances to the Andean ceremony *yumbada* performed in north Ecuador during June and July, as a parallel to the Catholic festivals of Corpus Christi. Throughout the Ecuadorian Andes, Quito is described as the "head, heart, and soul" of the Ecuadorian social body. Members of the Quito elite and upper classes often use such lofty figures of speech. Although only a small percentage of the population of Ecuador lives in the Amazonian territories, Quiteños nonetheless think of Amazonia as inextricably bound to the past and future of its special society. More than half of this Amazonian body was severed from its Andean head in 1941 during a war with Peru, prompting the charged nationalist motto "Ecuador is, has been, and will be an Amazonian country!"

In north Quito, as in other areas of the Ecuadorian highlands, the *yumbada* is held by people who strongly identify themselves as Quiteños and indigenous. During the festival, the identifying emblem of Quito Runa (indigenous person of Quito) emerges. This figure reverses the hierarchical polarity of white over "indian" and white over black and negates *mestizaje* redemption. To be Quito Runa in the *yumbada* ceremony is also to evoke the power of the Yumbo people from the eastern tropical rain forest of Upper Amazonia (Whitten 1988).[3]

Yumbo is a multivocalic term that has its origin in the northwest rain-forest slopes of the western cordillera of the Ecuadorian Andes (Cabello de Balboa 1945; Fine 1991; Lippi 1986; Salomon 1981, 1986; Weismantel 1988). Some time after the Spanish conquest, the Catholic clergy and indigenous people of the Ecuadorian Andes and elsewhere began using the term to refer to powerful indigenous healers (including human healers and mystical, spirit healers) on either side of the Andes. Upper Amazonian rain-forest dwellers or inhabitants of the designated area of origin were particularly inclined to use the term (Oberem 1971; Salomon 1986). The term Yumbo is often used by indigenous Andean people as a synonym for *yachaj* (Quichua) or *sabio* (Spanish), both of which mean "one who knows" or "shaman." It is also a pejorative term in the Andes for Quichua-speaking people who come from Amazonia. Such people self-identify as Runa, by which they mean "fully human." Today, when used nonpejoratively in the Andes, Yumbo carries the connotations of spirit power, mystical founts of Amazonian knowledge, and shamanic gnosis.

In "Killing the Yumbo: A Ritual Drama from Northern Quito," Frank Salomon (1981) discusses the indigenous performance *yumbada*, which takes place during or near the time of Corpus Christi in urban (and urbane) north Quito. During this drama, Spanish-speaking native urbanites who also speak Quichua celebrate the coming of forest people to the capital city. In this context, the word Yumbo connotes "semicivilized" (Quichua) and "wild, free, and savage" (Auca), both with the specific designation of shaman. The Yumbos arrive in Quito; the world turns upside down; and a liminal space comes into being between urbanity and savagery, humanity and animality, city and forest, and head and body. Mediating this creation of reversal are the mountain mothers who stand in an intermediate position between Quito and the coastal rain forest, and between Quito and the Amazonian rain forest.

Salomon poignantly describes an event that occurs early in the ceremony, the transformation of a central participant, Segundo Salazar Imapanta, as he "looks both outward, toward the luminous snowcaps fencing the Andean *altiplano* [high plateau] off from the Amazonian and Pacific rain forest, and downward, toward the white skyline of the highland metropolis" (Salomon 1981:162–63). He is an urbane caretaker of the international airport, a true Andean Quiteño, with gray suit and trim mustache. Salomon then quotes Salazar Imapanta's feelings about the palm-wood lances that he keeps in his home to explain the difference between collectors' curios and the imagery of life forces that connect what other Quiteños take to be the antithetical extremes of city and forest, civilized and savage: "The mountain accompanies the lance, and the lance accompanies me; the lance and I are one single being when we are dancing" (Salomon 1981:162–63).

In July, 1979, Norman Whitten attended one Yumbo festival with Frank Salomon in North Quito. Whitten had returned from field research with Canelos Quichua, indigenous people of Pastaza Province, and it was soon clear to the festival participants that he was not only fascinated but also familiar with what they were doing and portraying. Parts of the *camari* feast, as well as the dancing of the *lanceros*, bore uncanny cultural resemblance to the *jista* with which he was familiar. Participants wanted him to know, though, that this was a festival, like a theater (*teatro shina*), and that they were miming or "playing with" (*pugllana*) the forces and images of the forest. They insisted that no real shamanic forces, such as those manifest in the spirits of rain forest or Andean mountains, were being summoned: the power to summon spirits belongs to those from or of the lowland forest.

We return now to the *caminata* of 1992. As symbolic activities coalesced and expanded amid intense scrutiny by the Ecuadorian populace and press, a transformation occurred wherein the spiritual realm acquired focal salience. Pragmatic activities were not diminished by merging with the spiritual; to the contrary, they were significantly enhanced. The *caminata* created a palpable rift in the social and political fabric of the Ecuadorian nation. Unlike the quasi-theatrical ceremonial drama of the *yumbada*, the passages into liminality of the march did establish powerful mystical links between the Andean and Amazonian shamans, Andean and Amazonian spirit forces, and Andean and Amazonian peoples. The marchers expanded their theatricality, but they were not "play-acting": they were *en*-acting.

The entry to Quito forced the nation to consider the reality of indigenous power, which embraced all people; events in El Ejido Park reaffirmed a reality of Quito Runa–Amazonian Runa solidarity that collapsed elite-sponsored polarities and oppositions, already weakened during the Levantamiento of 1990. The *caminata* was simultaneously pragmatic and theatrical. It both accomplished a political-economic goal and expanded the conjoined human and spirit spheres of power.

Life in El Ejido Park Alternative Modernities

Throughout Ecuador it was quite clear that the *caminata* was a quintessential political event. It was a dramatic and courageous act that called for radically alternative strategies of Amazonian development. It was also a quintessential ritual metaphor of the kind that is well known in modern and traditional pilgrimages: it created an affecting presence (Armstrong 1971, 1975) that transcended, while also undergirding, the political actions.

Those in the front section of the *caminata*, most of whom were residents of the Comuna San Jacinto del Pindo and Puyo proper, described their sense of elation that the event was "like a festival" (*jista shina*) but far more intense. During the *caminata*, Clara Santi Simbaña composed and sang this song:

> I am puma woman, I am black jaguar woman,
> walking through the mountains, walking through the rain.
> From my territory, I am just walking, walking to Quito.
> Puma woman,
> standing here in Quito, singing *¡hoo hoo, jijiji, meeoow!*
> Standing here before the palace, I am not afraid.

When she sang this in El Ejido Park, a number of people recorded it and asked her questions about her provenance and her life. One of her brothers, Marcelo Santi Simbaña, was asked to cure Quiteños of many afflictions, including magical fright (*susto*), evil eye (*mal ojo*), and evil or malignant air (*mal aire*). People from humble rural areas, sophisticated offices, and urbane homes alike came to the park and sought out shamans among the campers. Those who came to be cured were respectful; some remembered a trip to the Upper Amazon or a sojourn there in the military. Many other Quiteños stayed away and, when passing the park, looked away. For them, the Yumbo represented the embodiment of filth and contamination emanating from the distant forest to the enlightened civilization of Quito.

The combination of the female projection of song and the beauty that flows from it with the male projection of shamanic control and its own, complementary beauty provided the indigenous multitude in El Ejido Park with a nationally staged paradigm of indigenous culture. Multidimensional concepts of knowledge, vision, and power (see Salomon 1981; N. Whitten 1985; Whitten et al. 1976; Whitten and Whitten 1988, 1993) were now located in the capital city.

Clara, Apacha, Marcelo and more than two thousand other Amazonian residents of Ecuador had walked to Quito to claim, in an ethnic nationalist idiom, the territory that they said had belonged to their *mayores* (old ones, elders). The national press routinely translated *mayores* into *antepasados* (ancestors). The press often represented indigenous people as bumpkin relics from the past who did not know the Spanish language well enough to express themselves properly. Indigenous people were viewed by many Quiteños as *indios alzados* (unruly indians) and *indios fuera de su lugar* (indians out of place), and they were said to lack consciousness.

Indigenous marchers, however, clearly knew — and stated quite specifically — which of their elders had previously walked to Quito to request rights to their rain-forest territory. Indeed, the late Virgilio Santi (father of Clara and Marcelo) and his brother Camilo (who died in 1994 at over ninety years old), along with other brothers and indigenous leaders, made such a trek in the 1940s.[4] As a result, in 1947 they secured the Comuna San Jacinto del Pindo from the Ecuadorian *caudillo* (renowned leader) and president, the late Dr. José María Velasco lbarra (Whitten et al. 1976). Perhaps no onlookers realized that, years before, Velasco lbarra had been healed by a powerful Zaparoan–Canelos Quichua shaman, Eliseo Vargas, paternal grandfather of Antonio Vargas, in the small hamlet of Unión Base.

Clara composed her song while marching with a host of indigenous people numbering somewhere between two thousand and ten thousand. Clara, deliberately colorful in her two-piece jaguar-skin outfit and ocelot-skin hat, sunburned and with blisters on her feet, sang while accompanied by her husband, Abraham Chango, on a three-hole transverse flute (*Kipu* 1992b:69). She was widely recorded and photographed by Ecuadorians, Europeans, and North Americans.

Clara's theatricality in foreign territory showed that she was self-reflexive and that she knew that she and her kin were taking on the role of the ancient Yumbo who had traveled to Quito only to be killed and then resurrected by an Amazonian shaman (Salomon 1981; N. Whitten 1981, 1988). But, she later told us, she feared that the people who took her picture and recorded her songs and dances did not understand the underlying messages about the garden, the forest, domesticity, and the awesome danger of uncontrolled power — the very nature of indigenous concepts of territoriality. Nor did they know that she was an accomplished potter and gardener. She was a veritable *muscuj* (or *muscuyuj*) *warmi*— the feminine equivalent of a male shaman. For most Ecuadorians, epoch history in the making still excluded the specific history of women, let alone indigenous women.

¿Runa Wañungachu? — Will People Die?

In Canelos Quichua thought and cosmology, it is expected that people will, from time to time, leave their homes and travel to other territories. Their mythology revolves around two men, or two women, traveling in transforming times-spaces from one point to another. In real life, men and women trek to establish and maintain distant gardens, to fish, or to mine clay; men trek to hunt. People go to visit relatives or powerful ones in distant territories. These are exciting but normal events, and return is expected. Shamans in seance travel in and out of the spirit world, which is very dangerous; to stay in that world is to die in this one. Shamans, dreamers, and powerful image-makers may also travel to other times-places; if they do not return, they die (see N. Whitten 1985:106–63). When Marcelo Santi called the Whittens from Quito, he did not say anything about the possibility of being killed, although later, in June 1992, in Puyo, he told them that this could have happened.

On April 23, President Borja had requested a fifteen-day period to study the petition for adjudication of Amazonian lands. As days and nights turned into weeks and the deadline approached, tensions continued to mount among the campers. For most of them, serious reflection and a mood of growing trepidation replaced the excitement that had accompanied the intense activity of the *caminata*. It was reported that the cordoned-off encampment had expanded to cover about one-third of El Ejido Park. The city of Quito had set up portable latrines and provided water supplies. Food, medicines, blankets, and clothes were donated by private individuals and institutions and by numerous other indigenous communities. A reporter noticed that the lowland apparel of feathers and skins was being replaced by modern clothing and that some campers were selling Amazonian products, including pure snake oil and even a live boa constrictor for the equivalent of thirty-five dollars. People did not know how, when, or if they would return home. No one could have predicted the series of events that was to unfold as the campers awaited the results of Borja's response to their demands.

The government's efforts to resolve the land claim legally and equitably, without compromising subsoil rights or national sovereignty, became increasingly complicated because of an outpouring of opposition in the form of accusations, counterclaims, and demonstrations by the military, colonists, and sierran indigenous people. The military not only opposed the concept of plural nationality but, under the laws of national security, refused to sanction any decrease in the fifty-kilometer security zone along the border with Peru, where many indigenous peoples live.

As negotiations stalled, about seven hundred campers marched to the Ministry of Social Welfare on May 5 intending to occupy the building and thereby increase pressure on the government. The work of the national police security guards was slowed by indigenous guardians who surrounded the building, but after representatives of the demonstrators talked with the minister of state, all the marchers returned peacefully to the park. After this encounter, word spread that the government had reached a decision, which would be announced on May 6 on national television and radio networks. This advisory informed indigenous people throughout the republic that the administration would grant 1,115,574 hectares of land to all indigenous communities of Pastaza; that the security zone on the frontier would be reduced to forty kilometers; and that the territory of the Yasuní National Park would be extended but would remain under government control. Leaders of the march immediately expressed their dissatisfaction with the land offer, which amounted to a concession of about 65 percent of their initial request. They objected, also, to the refusal of their requests to reduce the security zone to two kilometers and to transfer the Yasuní reserve to indigenous control. Seven members of OPIP carried the protest slightly further the night of May 7 by occupying the IERAC building; they did not resist when they were removed several hours later by a detachment of three hundred police.

Back in Puyo, there was immediate reaction from the opposition organizations, some of whose members had jeered the departing marchers on April 11. In protest to the unilateral land accession to OPIP, they dynamited a section of the Puyo-Baños road, threatened to impede the return of the marchers from Quito, and declared a provincewide strike that would entail, among other acts, blocking all major roads in Pastaza Province.

There were parallel reactions and counterprotests on the coast, where Afro-Ecuadorians demanded the legalization of their land ownership and indemnification for centuries of unjust treatment and for the destruction of their forests and ecosystems. In several Andean provinces, indigenous people also stepped up their calls for an end to injustice and for legal rights to the land that they had occupied since time immemorial. The resounding fervor for fair adjudication of land disputes and for civil rights and social justice escalated, and cases that had been under "review by officials" for years were repeatedly cited by indigenous leaders. In Tungurahua Province, Salasacans closed major roads; in Cotopaxi and in Chimborazo Provinces, indigenous people invaded haciendas. Attacks on petroleum camps in Napo Province were also reported (*Kipu* 1992a:199).

The apparent escalation set off waves of nervous speculation that another Levantamiento was about to take place. The secretary-general of public administration, Dr. Gonzalo Ortiz Crespo, insisted that these were merely isolated events. As the nation approached the general elections scheduled for May 17, the president similarly assured the populace that peace and tranquility would be maintained, by force if necessary. Because citizens are required by law to vote where they are registered, many must travel large distances.

Ecuadorians now learned that disruption of major highways would not be tolerated.

The dialogue between Borja's representatives and the indigenous leaders nevertheless continued until the government announced that it would be ready to sign documents on May 14. This plan was postponed and then re-scheduled because the opposition organizations of Pastaza increased pressure on the government to grant them what they considered their fair share of provincial territory. The organizations reactivated their strike and renewed the threat to block the marchers' return to Puyo, using any kind of force available. The government was forced to send high-level representatives in haste to negotiate in Puyo's municipal colosseum. After further closed-door talks with officials of IERAC, a committee returned to Quito to talk with the president of the republic (*Kipu* 1992a:154).

Finally, on the night of May 13, President Borja, in three consecutive ceremonies, delivered titles of more than a million hectares of land to indigenous people. Each of three organizations received approximately one-third of the total allocation: FEDECAP, OPIP, and AIEPRA. The resale and subsurface exploration and exploitation of minerals and petroleum were prohibited, and the rights of colonists living on previously occupied or allocated land were protected.

The weary and partially satisfied leaders of the march returned from the two-hour ceremony to El Ejido Park for a brief celebration of music and speeches. Then they and approximately two thousand fellow campers boarded the forty to sixty buses, contracted by the government, that ringed the park. The honking of bus horns signaled the hour of departure and the long caravan began to retrace the route of the marchers. Protected all the way by national police, the caravan entered the streets of Puyo early the next morning and by 8:00 A.M. had discharged the last of the travelers into the central plaza whence they had departed thirty-four days previously. After a triumphant march through the main streets, the crowd reassembled in the plaza to hear brief speeches by Valerio Grefa and Antonio Vargas on the themes of peace, unity, and perseverance. Many returned to nearby homes, but for others the journey would continue for several days more.

Ethnic Multinationalism and Power

From beginning to end, the enactment of the *caminata* conveyed to the nation a message of two profound truths professed by the participants and by many others. First, the Quichua, Achuar, and Shiwiar are indigenous people, *gente indígena*, or Runa — fully cultured and capable and imbued with ideas, hopes, dreams, and realities of quintessential human beings. Second, as true indigenous peoples, they are also fully human residents of Pastaza Province of Amazonian Ecuador. Denied their rights to land, health, and prosperity, they are nonetheless full citizens, *ecuatorianos*. The message underscored the fundamental antinomy between an indigenous-based movement for ethnic multinationalism, in which "all our brothers" (Salomon 1981) are represented, and institutional nationalism, in which *mestizaje* ideology manipulated by whites excludes those classed as indigenous and black.

The symbolic power of the Ecuadorian indigenous movement gained strength that transformed it from a ritual drama to an active force for genuine change. This power, periodically unleashed through collective, pragmatic actions such as the Ecuadorian Levantamiento Indígena of 1990 and the *caminata* of 1992, was circumscribed by the state's nationalist war rhetoric in 1995, but became manifest again in the political movements of 1996.

In the early months of 1996, a strikingly flexible political alliance presented itself to the public as a social movement, *not as a party*. Officially termed Unidad Plurinacional Pachakutik–Nuevo País, it came to be called the Pachakutik–Nuevo País movement. For indigenous people, this was shortened to the Pachakutik movement; for others who did not identify themselves as indigenous or as supporters of the indigenous movement, it was often shortened to Nuevo País. The Pachakutik segment, organized by Dr. Luis Macas, Valerio Grefa, and other indigenous leaders sponsored several indigenous candidates throughout the provinces. The New Country segment was organized by its own presidential candidate, journalist Freddy Ehlers.

Overall, the new movement won about 20 percent of the votes in the elections of May 19, 1996. Although Ehlers lost his bid for the presidency, Valerio Grefa (from Napo Province) and other indigenous candidates were elected as provincial representatives to congress, and Dr. Macas was elected as a national representative — Ecuador's first indigenous people ever elected to congress. When he entered the legislative palace for President Abdalá Bucaram Ortíz's inauguration on August 10, 1996, Dr. Macas was accompanied by Rigoberta Menchú Tum, the Guatemalan winner of the Nobel Peace Prize.

The trajectory from the pragmatic march for life and land to the ritual drama of peaceful, mass protest and thence to organized, legitimate political action was — and is still — closely watched by national academic and popular writers in Ecuador. As Raúl Vallejo, the former secretary of education, put it:

Six Years Later Pachakutik
Six years after [the 1990 Levantamiento] the electoral victory . . . accomplished by Pachakutik-Nuevo País should be seen as a logical result of

a genuine organizational process and as an important step toward a democratic deepening (*profundización*) that permits recognition of the plurinational character of our country as a basis of wide political alliances. (1996)

On Local-Level Ritual Dramas and National-Level Political Transformations

The heart of the organizational process that led to Pachakutik and similar entities is embodied in social movements — paradigmatic cultural processes of organization that move people to action in which the accomplishment of pragmatic goals is often framed by ritual dramas. In the case presented here, the ritual symbolism of rain-forest imagery was emergent during the first camp out in Río Verde in the veritable *montaña* and was conjoined to imagery of mountain spirits and lowland forces that emerged in Salasaca. In Latacunga, the juro-political domain of appropriated and reversed justice became part of the ritual drama, and, as the *caminata* entered Quito, the force of north Ecuadorian *yumbada* ritual was evoked.

The power of ritual symbols in covert as well as overt discourses continues in local-level festivals throughout Ecuador. While the substance and contents of such festivals and ritual activities vary greatly, the ability of such dramatic activity to communicate to those at the social or ethnic antitheses of Ecuadorian life — nearly half the population of the nation-state — seems to be great. In these festivals, to see all one's relatives, all one's people — all one's *ushis* and *churis*, as Apacha Vargas expressed it to the president of the republic, or all the nationalities (*tucui naciones*), as Marcelo Santi Simbaña has expressed it to us on many occasions — is to understand the power and efficacy of symbols to overcome adversity. The power evidenced in the Levantamiento Indígena of 1990 and the *caminata* from Pastaza to Quito in 1992 synergized with other nationalist cultural forces in 1996 to effect a transformation of the ideological representation of the plural structure of Ecuador. The emergent structure of affirmation of indigenousness and public denial of the nation-state's efficacy in indigenous affairs creates a discourse of multifaceted dialogues, within which the nation-state is bound more and more closely to its representational antipodes of blackness and indigenousness.

ACKNOWLEDGMENTS

This chapter is a condensed and slightly revised version of an article published in the *American Ethnologist* 24(2) : 355–91. Copyright © American Anthropological Association. Published by permission of the publisher. The original article and this version could not have been written without the sustained collaboration of Diego Quiroga

(Quito) and Marcelo Santi Simbaña (Comuna San Jacinto del Pindo, Pastaza). Alfonso Chango thanks his wife, Luzmila Salazar, his mother, Clara Santi Simbaña, and his father, Abraham Chango, for clarifying and deepening his understanding of the world powers that can do harm, be deflected, or be used with discretion. Thanks also to Domingo Salazar, *sinchi yachaj*, whose insights, sought with care, revealed images not otherwise attainable. Funds for the Whittens' research leading to the original article were provided by a grant from the Wenner-Gren Foundation (No. 5232) in 1990 and by a National Endowment for the Humanities Summer Fellowship in 1992. Subsequent support was provided by the senior University Scholar fund for research awarded to N. Whitten by the University of Illinois, Urbana-Champaign, in 1992. The Sacha Runa Research Foundation in Urbana, Illinois, provided fellowship support to allow Alfonso Chango to undertake technical training at the Indigenous Writing School of the Centro Editorial en Lenguas Indígenas Latinamericanos, CELIL, in Oaxaca, Mexico.

NOTES

1. An extended note on methodology is given in the original *American Ethnologist* article, as are detailed notes on use of terminology and sources of information, including detailed ethnographic sources for inner symbolism and the externalization of such symbolism. The approach taken in this chapter is highlighted in the introduction, chapter 9, and the epilogue to this book, and in Whitten and Whitten 1988 and 1993.

2. The significance of the body of the anaconda moving toward the head is described and analyzed elsewhere (Whitten 1981, 1985, 1988). The rainbow-colored banner chosen as the emblem for the march is a visual manifestation of anaconda imagery, although the specific flag was appropriated from the 1991 indigenous Bolivian march from Bení to La Paz.

3. Other festival representations of the Yumbo also occur in Ecuador. For example, there are Yumbo dancers during Christmas festivities in Zumbagua Parish, Cotopaxi Province (Weismantel 1988). Painters from the dispersed community of Tigua in the same province portray Yumbos as a shaman from the Oriente (D. Whitten, this volume), or a Tsáchila from Santo Domingo de los Colorados in the western rain-forest *montaña*.

4. In the 1890s, a renowned *curaga* from Canelos, Pelate (Palate, Palati), is said to have trekked to Quito from Canelos. On the way to Quito, he meandered through the Sierra to gain indigenous support from one Quichua-speaking community after another. In Quito, he is said to have gained tremendous concessions of land from the liberal *caudillo* Eloy Alfaro Delgado. For a nationalist rendition of this history, see Ramón Valarezo 1992; for indigenous tales involving such treks, shamanism, and human-jaguar metamorphoses, see Whitten 1985:193, 221).

REFERENCES

Armstrong, Robert Plant

1971 *The Affecting Presence: An Essay in Humanistic Anthropology.* Urbana: University of Illinois Press.

1975 *Wellspring: On the Myth and Source of Culture.* Berkeley: University of California Press.

Brown, Michael F., and Michael Fernández

1991 *War of Shadows: The Struggle for Utopia in the Peruvian Amazon.* Berkeley: University of California Press.

Cabello de Balboa

1945 [1583] *Obras,* vol. 1. Quito: Editorial Ecuatoriana.

Chango, Alfonso

1984 *Yachaj Sami Yachachina.* Quito: Abya-Yala.

CONAIE

1989 *Las nacionalidades indígenas en el Ecuador: Nuestro proceso organizativo.* 2nd edition. Quito: TINCUI-CONAIE.

Descola, Philippe

1994 [1986] *In the Society of Nature: A Native Ecology in Amazonia.* New York: Cambridge University Press.

España Torres, Hugo Efraín

1996 *El Testigo: El caso Restrepo y otros delitos de estado.* Quito: Editorial El Conejo and Abya-Yala.

Espinosa, Simón

1992 Solidaridad en la Caminata. Marcha Indígena de Los Pueblos Amazónicos Puyo-Quito (Abril–Mayo). Suplemento Especial Kipu 18. Pp. 158–60. Quito: Abya-Yala.

Fine, Kathleen

1991 *Cotocollao: Ideología, historia, y acción en un barrio de Quito.* Quito: Abya-Yala.

Kipu

1992a El Mundo Indígena en la Prensa Ecuatoriana. 19 (January–June). Quito: Abya-Yala.

1992b Marcha Indígena de Los Pueblos Amazónicos Puyo-Quito (April–May). Suplemento Especial, 18. Quito: Abya-Yala.

Lippi, Ronald D.

1986 La arqueología de los Yumbos: Resultados de prospecciones en el Pichincha occidental. *Miscelanea Antropológica Ecuatoriana* 6:189–207.

Meisch, Lynn

1992 "We Will Not Dance on the Tomb of Our Grandparents:" 500 Years of Resistance in Ecuador. *Latin American Anthropology Review* 4: 55–57.

Oberem, Udo

    1971   *Los Quijos: Historia de la transculturación de un grupo indígena en el oriente ecuatoriano, 1538–1956*. 2 vols. Madrid: Facultad de Filosofía y Letras de la Universidad de Madrid.

Ramón Valarezo, Galo

    1992   Los selváticos nos interpelan. Marcha Indígena de Los Pueblos Amazónicos Puyo-Quito. Quito: Abya-Yala, Suplemento especial *Kipu* 18: 118–19. Original in *Hoy*, April 26, 1992.

Rangles Lara, Rodrigo

    1995   *Venturas y desventuras del poder*. Quito: Carvajal.

Roggiero, Roberto

    1991   Una "Yumbada" en la Magdalena. *Hoy*, May 5:3C.

Salomon, Frank

    1981   Killing the Yumbo: A Ritual Drama from North Quito. In *Cultural Transformations and Ethnicity in Modern Ecuador*. Norman E. Whitten, Jr., ed. Pp. 162–208. Urbana: University of Illinois Press.

    1986   *Native Lords of Quito in the Age of the Incas: The Political Economy of North Andean Chiefdoms*. New York: Cambridge University Press.

Seymour-Smith, Constance

    1988   *Shiwiar: Identidad étnica y cambio en el Río Corrientes*. Quito: Abya-Yala.

Taussig, Michael

    1986   *Shamanism, Colonialism, and the Wild Man: A Study in Terror and Healing*. Chicago: University of Chicago Press.

Turner, Victor

    1974   *Dramas, Fields, and Metaphors: Symbolic Action in Human Societies*. Ithaca: Cornell University Press.

Viteri, Carlos

    1993   Mythical Worlds: Runa. In *Amazon Worlds: Peoples and Cultures of Ecuador's Amazon Region*. Noemi Paymal and Catalina Sosa, eds. Pp. 148–50. Quito: Oxfam International and Sinchi Sacha Foundation.

Weismantel, Mary

    1988   *Food, Gender, and Poverty in the Ecuadorian Andes*. Philadelphia: University of Pennsylvania Press.

Whitten, Dorothea S.

    1981   Ancient Tradition in a Contemporary Context: Canelos Quichua Ceramics and Symbolism. In *Cultural Transformations and Ethnicity in Modern Ecuador*. Norman E. Whitten Jr., ed. Pp. 749–75. Urbana: University of Illinois Press.

Whitten, Dorothea S., and Norman E. Whitten, Jr.

    1988   *From Myth to Creation: Art from Amazonian Ecuador*. Urbana: University of Illinois Press.

1993 Creativity and Continuity: Communication and Clay. In *Imagery and Creativity: Ethnoaesthetics and Art Worlds in the Americas*. Pp. 309–56. Tucson: University of Arizona Press.

Whitten, Norman E., Jr.

1976 (with Marcelo F. Naranjo, Marcelo Santi Simbaña, and Dorothea S. Whitten) *Sacha Runa: Ethnicity and Adaptation of Ecuadorian Jungle Quichua*. Urbana: University of Illinois Press.

1985 *Sicuanga Runa: The Other Side of Development in Amazonian Ecuador*. Urbana: University of Illinois Press.

1988 Historical and Mythical Evocations of Chthonic Power in South America. In *Rethinking History and Myth: Indigenous South American Perspectives on the Past*. Jonathan Hill, ed. Pp. 282–307. Urbana: University of Illinois Press.

1996 The Ecuadorian Levantamiento Indígena of 1990 and the Epitomizing Symbol of 1992: Reflections on Nationalism, Ethnic-Bloc Formation, and Racialist Ideologies. In *Culture, Power, and History: Ethnogenesis in the Americas, 1492–1992*. Jonathan Hill, ed. Pp. 193–217. Iowa City: University of Iowa Press.

CHAPTER 8

Indigenous Destiny in Indigenous Hands

LUIS MACAS, LINDA BELOTE, AND JIM BELOTE

This chapter is based on the life and activities of Dr. Luis Alberto Macas Ambuludí, who became Ecuador's minister of agriculture on January 15, 2003. He was an early participant in the development of national literacy and bilingual education programs in Ecuador. He participated in the founding of CONAIE and served as its president between 1990 and 1996, a time when CONAIE organized or coordinated several important indigenous uprisings. In 1994, Macas was awarded the international Goldman Environmental Prize for his work on indigenous land claims in the Amazonian region of Ecuador. Macas was a leader in the Unidad Plurinacional Pachakutik–Nuevo Pais. As a member of that movement, he was the first indigenous person ever elected as *diputado nacional* (national congressional representative) to the legislature, where he served from 1996 to 1998. He was one of the founders of the Instituto Científico de Culturas Indígenas (ICCI) in 1986 and has served as its director since 1998. Finally, Luis Macas and like-minded colleagues founded the Universidad Intercultural de Nacionalidades y Pueblos Indígenas (UINPI Amautai Wasi) in 2000, and he serves currently as its president.

Macas was born about 1950 in De La Cuncha, a barrio of the community of Ilincho, in Saraguro Canton, Loja Province. By weaving together materials from his life as a member of a globalized world, as an Ecuadorian citizen, as a leader among the people of indigenous nationalities, and as an individual belonging to a community of indigenous people known as Saraguros, we may gain some understanding of the dynamics of indigenous movements in Ecuador.

Linda and Jim Belote became acquainted with Luis in the early 1960s when they were Peace Corps volunteers in Saraguro and he was a barefoot elementary school student. From that beginning, Luis Macas earned a degree in linguistics from Pontificia Universidad Católica Ecuatoriana (Quito), and a J.D. from Universidad Central (Quito). The three of us have maintained contact over the intervening years. To prepare to write this chapter Macas traveled to Duluth, Minnesota, in July 2001 where we spent one week of intensive discussion, all of which we recorded. These interviews and data collected by the Belotes in Saraguro, in the United States, and in Spain between 1962 and 2002, provide our primary source material. The italicized passages at the opening of several of the sections are direct quotations from the Macas interviews of 2001. His thoughts and contributions are also contained throughout the descriptive and analytical writing that follows.

Saraguro

Loja, the southernmost Andean province of Ecuador, is the traditional homeland of an estimated thirty thousand to forty thousand people who identify themselves as Saraguros, one of the Quichua nationalities. Many Saraguros now speak Spanish as their first language; bilingual programs have been developed to reestablish Quichua as a language to be used along with Spanish. In the middle of the twentieth century, the Saraguros were relatively land rich and self-sufficient. Most owned and controlled their own land and engaged primarily in agropastoralism. During the first part of the twentieth century, many Saraguros in search of more land began a process of colonization of Shuar territory (J. Belote 1998) in the Upper Amazon region of Zamora-Chinchipe.

Since the early 1970s, increased pressure on the land and greater openness in Ecuadorian society for indigenous peoples (especially in formal educational systems, including universities), have pushed and/or permitted many Saraguros, including Luis Macas, to pursue life courses other than, or in addition to, agropastoralism, both in their own and in other regions. Hundreds of Saraguros are now schoolteachers, others are shopkeepers, physicians, nurses, mechanics, politicians, veterinarians, construction workers, dentists or lawyers.

The economic crises of Ecuador at the turn of the millennium have made life much more difficult for all Saraguros — perhaps most of all for those pursuing new strategies that more immediately depend on national and global conditions than did the traditional Saraguro focus on agropastoralism. More than a thousand Saraguros, many of them teachers and professionals with postsecondary educations, are part of the swelling stream of Ecuadorians who seek economic opportunities in Spain.

Whatever their life strategies and wherever they are, most Saraguros maintain a strong, proud, self-identity as Saraguros. Important components of that identity include a shared history of struggles against ethnic- and class-based exploitation and exclusion, an elaborate fiesta system, and patterns of shared labor (*mingas*) at both the community and the family level. The visible markers of their mid-twentieth-century identity include wearing distinctive clothing — most of it dyed a very dark indigo blue-black — going barefoot, wearing hats, and wearing their hair in long single braids called *jimbas*.

All of these identity markers, except going barefoot, exist among Saraguros of the new millennium, especially during special events such as fiestas and weddings. However, less expensive factory-made clothing, finished in a variety of styles, has become commonly worn, especially by those living outside of the Saraguro area. A few people today, however, self-identify as Saraguros but do not exhibit any visible marker of that status. Most, both men and women, still wear their hair long and usually in a single braid (for more details on general features of Saraguro life, see L. Belote 2002; J. Belote 1998; Belote and Belote 2002; Chalan et al. 1994; Criollo 1995; King 2001; Sarango 1995; Volinsky 1998).

The *Jimba* As Metaphor

In the indigenous community school in Las Lagunas, Sra. Teresa would always stop any aggressive activity if someone treated another badly, but this was not the case at the 10 de Marzo boys elementary school in the town center of Saraguro. The kids there stepped on my feet because I was barefoot [while recounting this, Luis stomped on Linda's foot accidentally, resulting in a little pain, and a lot of laughter]. *Oh, we were treated so badly. The children pulled my* jimba. *The teachers there did not stop them; said nothing.*

I finished high school at Colegio Benigno Malo in Cuenca, the only indigenous student there. Some of the students pestered me, and pulled my hair, but not too much. And by this time I was wearing shoes. There is a citywide speech competition in Cuenca. I won the boys' competition representing Benigno Malo. ¡Que barbaridad! *With that, the Benigno Malo boys started to really like me.*

[At one point in his life Macas was in seminary in Loja, to begin studies for the priesthood.] *After one week, they wanted to cut my hair. I said, "No. I don't want that." "How are you going to be a priest then?" "Then I don't want to be a priest," I said. I collected my things and left, sneaking out. I went to my godmother's house in Loja. I told her they wanted to cut my hair: "Don't listen to them," she said.*

Hair worn in a long, single braid —*la jimba*— has long been an important visible marker of Saraguro ethnicity for both women and men. For most people, a braid conjures an image of three strands woven together. However, although Saraguros do wear three-stranded braids, the braid considered most elegant and traditional is many stranded. In its final form the braid has a dual or two-sided appearance. Hairstylists in the United States call this a herringbone or fish bone braid. One Web page describes it in this way: "It is the simplest braid on the planet to do, but one of the harder ones to make look good" (Berthke 2002). Saraguros can do the three-stranded braid for themselves, but to wear a herringbone braid, they need the help of someone else. To make the Saraguro version of the herringbone braid, the weaver starts with a careful combing and then parts the hair into two halves. About 15 to 20 percent of the hair is alternately taken in strands from the inside of each half and transferred to the inside of the other side without combining them with the original halves. When all the hair from the original halves has been transferred to the other side, the weaver then takes a strand from the outside of one half and that strand is placed on the inside of the other side. Then a strand is taken from the outside of the other half and placed on the inside of the first half. This pattern is repeated until the braid is completed.

Once a strand has been moved, it may lose some of its distinctive identity as a separate strand when individual hairs join with and separate from each other to form various combinations. Generally, however, strands tend to perpetuate themselves throughout the weaving process so that a particular strand is reworked after all the others are woven in.

We use the elegant herringbone braid as our metaphor (Davis 1998) to understand the ways by which indigenous people, particularly the Saraguros, in Ecuador have worked over the centuries to maintain their autonomy and identity through a process of ethnogenesis (Singer 1962; Whitten 1976:211–13) in which they combine and recombine their learning about life from family, community, nonindigenous people, and non-Ecuadorians. Elements of knowledge are combined into a strand of activity, then other elements enter into the strand and some strands are discarded. In politics, people may weave in and out of collaboration and conflict by incorporating or not incorporating such elements as groups with local, ethnically oriented interests on the one side, and elements dominated by nonindigenous interest groups such as teachers or workers or political parties on the other side. When they devise formal educational structures, they may weave together traditional learning, especially learning by doing, with ideas and forms emanating from national or international sources, and combine all these in new, creative ways. This multiple weaving together of educational, political, and other strands of life experiences is underlain by principles of community and collective effort, respect for the dignity of others, hard work and responsibility, and openness (transparency), consensus, equilibrium, and dialogue. It is based on life experiences of growing up in the community and through travel, study, and work in other parts of Ecuador and the world.

In this chapter, we examine how Luis Macas, the Saraguros, and the indigenous nationalities of Ecuador constantly weave an elegant, braided pattern that enables them to attain and maintain indigenous destiny in indigenous hands as together they confront and work within the conditions of early third-millennium Ecuador. We then apply our analysis to two particular cases: migration and education.

The Two Halves of the *Jimba*

We view the two sides of the *jimba* as representing autonomy and alliance constructed with six principle strands that run through the traditional life of the Saraguro people and have become important themes and issues at the national level in the political, educational, and civic lives of indigenous people. We now discuss these in turn.

AUTONOMY

Indigenous groups employed a variety of adaptations to survive colonialism. Religious ways, other ways. These adaptations constituted a people's wisdom. And this was the way of individuals, not just groups. For example, my father was very wise. "When the laichus *[Saraguro term for nonindigenous people] want to win, you have to just be quiet. It does not matter whether or not you are right; if you are going to lose, just be quiet. Why keep talking? I will not win in a fight with them, I will let them hit me if they want to." This keeps the people alive to defend the* pueblo.

For our people, it is better that state machinery does not reach into the community. Whatever happens, we live a tranquil life here. My father said, "It does not matter who wins an election. Will they help me plow? Plant? Weed the field? It will make no difference. You need to do what they ask when they ask. Politicians do not mess with the community internally." People said, "OK, we'll do what they ask." If we did not comply with them, they would have killed us, and we would not have survived. Compliance was a way by which to show resistance. There were a variety of such mechanisms and forms of resistance among our people. The mechanisms of resistance maintained the autonomy at the community level. People knew how to preserve their own culture, their own ways of doing things, their own institutions.

The subject of autonomy of indigenous groups in Ecuador is one of the most important to the indigenous peoples and one of the least understood by nonindigenous peoples. The passage above, as Macas readily acknowledges, was expressed in the context of the Saraguro experience, where the indigenous people performed *tambo* (rest stop, way station) service and provided lodging for government troops and mail carriers for centuries — until the 1940s — but retained ownership of their lands, successfully arguing that they would not be able to fulfill their responsibilities to the government in any other way.

Macas states that the participants in the indigenous movement rarely use the term *autonomy* because of the negative reaction this engenders. Even the terms *nacionalidades* (nationalities) and *pueblos* (peoples) have emerged only after lengthy discussion and argument among the members of CONAIE. (A substantial literature, much of it published on the Internet in *Boletín ICCI Rimay* [ICCI 2002a] discusses these terms; see also Ramón Valerezo and Gómez Barahona 1993). Macas also states that members of the indigenous movement fully recognize the Ecuadorian nation-state as their nation-state and at no time seek separation from it. The movement does not seek sovereignty, but rather plurinationalism or pluriculturalism (Macas 1993:111–133; Macas 2001; Selverston-Scher 2001; Andolina 1999; Pallares 1997).

They do, however, seek to acquire and maintain control of their own communities and regions and have worked diligently within the national system to achieve constitutional reforms that recognize their rights on a local and a regional level. The inclusion of bilingual education in the national constitution in 1980, and the 1998 inclusion of pluriculturalism and the rights to local-level administration of justice in the Constitution (Colloredo-Mansfeld 2002:173–95; Gutiérrez 2002), has given heart to indigenous peoples that their rights are being respected.

Many times, outsiders sympathetic to the indigenous movement have expressed puzzlement that they have not been told this or that fact about activities and ideas of movement leaders, since these outsiders see themselves as clearly supportive of the aims of the movement. This is not necessarily because of distrust, but rather can be interpreted as a means to reduce possible interference, whatever the source. The participants in the indigenous movement and their leaders have promised one another transparency and opportunity to discuss in depth all ideas and actions; they do not have this obligation to outsiders.

ALLIANCES

Although the need for autonomy prevails through all contexts of indigenous people's lives, alliances are more often short-term and specific to one or another topic or goal. Macas learned early that knowing "good" *laichus* was of benefit to him. His godmother, to whom he ran when told to cut his hair in Loja seminary; his first elementary schoolteacher, who taught within indigenous community values; the acquaintances and friendships with high school and university principals, chancellors, and instructors, who enabled him to acquire the education he sought, were all critical to his intellectual growth and development.

In the formative stages of CONAIE, there was a need to forge alliances among indigenous peoples and nationalities with very different cultures and perspectives. Macas's education during his teenage years at an Andean mission crafts school in Guano, Chimborazo, established by a United Nations agency, exposed him to some of these differences between indigenous populations. CONAIE worked from the beginning to form alliances with numerous nongovernmental organizations (NGOs) and United Nations organizations, as well as with indigenous organizations throughout the Americas. Some of these alliances have continued to be strong, while others eventually became weakened or defunct.

For ICCI and UINPI, one of the most important alliances formed has been with Seventh Generation Fund, a Native North American foundation and advocacy organization that raises and distributes funds to promote and maintain the uniqueness of native peoples and their nations (Seventh Generation 2000a). While vice president of CONAIE, Macas traveled to North America to explore the possibility of holding an international conference of indigenous peoples in Quito. During this three-month visit, he participated in ceremonies in the British Columbian mountains in the cold of winter and forged bonds with indigenous leaders and scholars at several Canadian universities. Later that same year, he was invited as an outside observer to the negotiations between the Mohawk Nation and the Canadian government. He observed the political negotiations, and he witnessed firsthand the importance of ceremony in this arena.

When the first Encuentro Intercontinental (Intercontinental Conference) was held in Quito in 1990, more than eight hundred invited guests attended from North, Central, and South America. Many of the persons who had hosted Macas in North America, including members of the Seventh Generation Fund, were among them. ICCI was subsequently invited to become a full member of Seventh Generation, the only non–North American entity so included. Macas has attended its annual meetings ever since. Seventh Generation has been one of the main financial contributors to ICCI and two Seventh Generation board members attended the inauguration of UINPI in 2000.

Other alliances were established with German and Spanish NGOs and universities in a visit to Europe in 1998. ICCI has also worked with international NGOs and United Nations organizations that have offices in Ecuador. These ties and alliances became even more important as the effort to create and establish an indigenous university intensified. A number of North American and European university friends sent letters of support, some offering long-term arrangements for exchanges of scholars and students. *El Comercio*, Quito's leading newspaper, reported that UINPI has many foreign *padrinos* (godparents) (*El Comercio* 2000a:A12).

The Weaving of the Strands

COMMUNITY AND COLLECTIVE EFFORT

I have been so lucky to have had the fortune of living in the half millennium before and the half millennium after. I said to my son Pacha, "I'm living in both centuries. But that is not what is important; what is important is that half of my life was in the community, plowing, working."

When the first organization of the Saraguros, Jatun Cabildo, was formed, I was the secretary and they pulled my ear and said I had to write the acta *and I said, "what's an* acta?" *I was a high school graduate but did not know this. Do you think they teach this in high school? My father said, "You went as a sheep and you returned home a sheep. What did you learn?" he asked. I didn't know how to get involved in the community. He was community president but he sent me as his substitute to the* minga *to clean the large drainage ditch down near Taita Joaquín's. I was president there for the day* [representing his father] *and I was in charge of the community leaders: Taita Joaquín Vacacela, Taita José María Guamán, Taita Manuel Antonio Quizhpe, Taita Lucho Vacacela, Taita Abel Sarango. What am I to do? I say, "Saca, saca, rápido. Dig, dig, fast!" They said, "Where do we dig?" I think it was a form of testing us. Can we or can't we perform? There were youths who did very well, even at a very young age. It was a way of measuring our worth. How one behaves in front of the community. They do not judge, but the community says how one should behave in the min-gas, meetings, and in daily life. My father dedicated fully 60 to 70 percent of his work time to community efforts.*

The *minga* has been widely used throughout Ecuador by indigenous peoples. In Saraguro, when Macas was young, it was the way trails were maintained, irrigation ditches dug, and homes constructed. Even plowing and harvesting were done with extended family *mingas*, working in one field, then another, until the work was completed. The *minga* is also important among other Quichua-speaking peoples as well as among other Ecuadorian nationalities. It became the model and the slogan for the Pachakutik campaign of 2000: *¡A la minga!* (Working together!) Community participation is also a fundamental requirement of UINPI students who are expected to fulfill community roles under the supervision and evaluation of community members.

While his father encouraged Luis to become an active community member, he cautioned him not to interfere in the private lives of the community members. Respect for the dignity and personal autonomy of others was important. As a teenager, Macas was a member of a Legion of Mary youth catechist group. The priest instructed members to make recommendations to the families they visited about hygiene, cleanliness, and domestic issues. His father told him he should not meddle in personal lives, but rather teach them about the Bible and teach them to pray; these are the areas of service on which he should concentrate. This was valuable advice for living together within a community.

Participation in the Saraguro fiesta cargo system (J. Belote and L. Belote 1977; L. Belote and J. Belote 1994; Volinsky 1998; Stiles 1996) was encouraged by both of his parents. Such participation was considered to be the route to establishing one's authority within the community. Macas entered the system as a *muñidor* (the lowest level in the fiesta hierarchy who served those in higher positions) and was impressed with the complexity and beauty of the organization. This involved a commitment for one year with weekly responsibilities to clean the local church, provide floral wheels for the altar, and commit many days to structured interaction with the other functionaries. For most fiestas there are two parallel groups, *mayor* and *menor* (major and minor), that cooperate to properly celebrate the feast day of the saint or member of the holy family.

Participation of the community members in decision making takes place at community council (*cabildo*) meetings. This means that community actions are governed by consent and discussion is held until consensus is reached. Decisions are made on *minga* activities, community regulations (which recently include control of traffic speed on community streets), and expenditure of community funds. This process is slow and difficult, but it provides a firm basis for collective action once it is achieved.

During Macas's term as congressional representative he was taken to task by *Vistazo*, a prominent Ecuadorian weekly magazine, for being "a paper tiger" because he told the interviewer that he would not reach a decision on issues until he had sounded out his constituency (Jijón 1994:20–22). The reaction to the article in the Saraguro area was mixed: most agreed with the principle he espoused, but some complained that he was not consulting with them, and therefore he was not living up to his own ideals.

The best examples of the full expression of collective effort are the various uprisings and marches of thousands of indigenous people in the 1990s. The first of these in the twentieth century was the Inti Raymi Levantamiento in 1990, which immobilized the entire country with strategically located *paros* (strikes, roadblocks). Strong resistance met police and military attempts to remove these roadblocks (Macas 1991; Almeida 1993:7–28; Pacari 1993: 169–86). In 1992, the massive march out of the Oriente was successful in gaining land titles for tropical forest indigenous peoples (Whitten, Whitten, and Chango 1997; Whitten, Whitten, and Chango, this volume; Sawyer 1997: 67–84). Later marches and *paros* have resulted in changes in the *ley agraria*

(agrarian law) in 1994, and, more recently, in 1998, in the constitutional inclusion of pluriculturalism and local-level administration of justice. Finally,
the coup of January 21, 2000, led to the removal from office of President
Jamil Mahuad Witt (Lucas 2000; Whitten introduction, this volume).

HARD WORK AND RESPONSIBILITY

Since our house was next door to our grandmother's, we spent a lot of time
with her, because our grandfather had died, and she wanted company; she was
all alone. We spent many of our days and our nights there. In my parents' house
was our other grandmother, my mother's mother. My parents went to the hills to
work. We went back and forth between the two houses. So the grandmothers
took care of us, told us stories, taught us how to take care of the things around
the house. We learned to pray, everything. And above all, they taught us to cook,
sweep the living room, the corridor. The child always has a chore. We were not
playing. In this time there weren't toys. We would go to harvest, not corn, but
achochas, or beans, and we had little baskets, and it seemed like play. But it
was directed and we learned responsibility from a very young age. We were very
happy. I was not enthused about going to high school where you have to sit and
write all day. When my father would say, "let's go to the minga," ah then I was
most happy. And when my father said, "go to colegio," whuh.

My father had more than twenty-five sheep, we had to take them to the hills,
pasture them, and bring them home in the afternoon. And our father taught us
that while we were herding the sheep we shouldn't walk with an empty body. We
had to gather grass for the guinea pigs or carry home firewood. We had to learn
to carry, because if not, the body learns to walk around doing nothing. So we did
this as we got bigger: carry firewood or grass; this was the job for those who were
around six years old. My oldest brother had to take care of the cattle, and when
I got old enough, I went to the cattle and my younger brother Pacho had to take
care of the sheep.

The responsibilities of family life, including the care of livestock, seem to
constitute favorite memories of many of the adult Saraguros who have since
entered non-agropastoral careers. As noted elsewhere, the self-esteem and
self-confidence of the young Saraguros is rarely in doubt. Those with a traditional family upbringing become skilled at useful tasks at a young age, and
they value this experience highly (Belote and Belote 1984:35–48). Adult
responsibilities include care of the family, participation in community life,
attention to religious life, and care of their animals and crops. Saraguros
whose living is based on agropastoralism always seem to be busy with a lot
of work to do. Even when visitors are present, the women spin or prepare a
meal; the men weave or repair tools. Their bodies are seldom "empty." The
lifestyles of the many Saraguros who have entered non-agropastoral em-

ployment as doctors, veterinarians, lawyers, teachers, office workers, and community development workers have undergone many changes, but most of them still try to participate in agricultural activities whenever they can, even if only family or neighborhood *mingas* are involved.

TRANSPARENCY AND CONSENSUS

It is not so easy to work with people. My father taught me this by pulling on my ears: that which you do with one hand, don't hide it from the other. If you try to hide it one time, the hand will get tired, and everyone will see. Everything will be known. You might be able to hide it for a moment, but not for a lifetime.

The average Ecuadorian's experience has been that the governments have been riddled with corruption, graft, and theft at the higher levels. This is the first explanation given by people for the economic chaos that caused the collapse of banks and businesses in the late 1990s. CONAIE, ICCI, UINPI, and the Pachakutik–Nuevo País movement have all committed themselves to avoiding the errors of their national government by requiring that all activities be openly viewed by all participants. Each group has established mechanisms by which open reporting is required of those chosen to lead them, and consensus is the model for decision making.

The phenomenon of political opposition is one of the better means of ensuring transparency. In Saraguro, there are two officially registered indigenous political groups: FIIS (Federación Interprovincial de Indígenas Saraguros [Interprovincial Federation of Indigenous Saraguro]), which is affiliated with the national organization FENOCIN, and CORPUKIS (Coordinadora de Organizaciones del Pueblo Kichua Saraguro [Coordinator of Saraguro Quichua Organizations]), which is affiliated with CONAIE (*El Comercio* 2000b; King 2001:52–56). They are often critical of, or even hostile to, each other, and often attempt to outdo one another to promote Saraguro interests.

A Dutch development worker in Saraguro once lamented "FIIS! CORPUKIS! They are so alike, why can't they get along?" Salvador Quishpe, a CONAIE officer who is a Saraguro himself, observed that this opposition is good, because it keeps everyone honest (personal communication December 22, 1996). They watch each other's expenditures of public funds very carefully. In addition, as long as it is reasonably balanced, this division fits into the ancient functioning of Andean tradition of dividing communities into *janan* and *urin*, upper and lower components, or in the Saraguro fiesta language of today, *mayor* and *menor*.

In fact, members of FIIS and CORPUKIS get along well enough when the need is great. During the national *paros* of 1990, 1992, and 1994, FIIS members blocked the entrance to one end of town and CORPUKIS members blocked the other. More recently, they have come together to agree on support of a slate of candidates for canton offices under the banner of Pachakutik–Nuevo País. They have also come together to agree on the placement of a branch campus of UINPI in the region.

BALANCE, HARMONY, AND EQUILIBRIUM

The principle that two halves of the traditional Saraguro *jimba* should be evenly the same size and proportion is expressed in other aspects of their lives. Bacacela writes of the need (as yet not achieved) for male and female equilibrium (Bacacela 2001a; Belote and Belote 1989:101–17) and Macas consistently reiterates this theme in discussions of a historical "horizontal" equilibrium between indigenous societies and colonial powers, of harmony between Catholics and Protestants, of balance between the groups representing ethnic issues and those focused on class, and of the aims of UINPI to achieve a balance between the traditional community life and modern science, utilizing the best from both.

He sees this as the principle of interculturality: organized as sectors, working together, but not mixed together. Each needs its own space to discuss particular issues, but each goes forward together with the other on the issues that are shared in common and each works with the other on projects that meet common goals.

DIALOGUE

I believe that one of the values of the indigenous peoples in Ecuador, independent of what they have achieved otherwise in relation with the government, has been the practice of dialogue. The indigenous people have made the presidents, Sixto Durán Ballén, Rodrigo Borja, and others, sit with us. We have said, "sit with us and let's talk." No other sector of society has done this. I think this is very important to do. Before this, the government only spoke with its own people. Finally, it is very important because on the one hand we reduce the tensions, and the other party who had believed himself so important realizes we mean business, and lowers his stance a little. And we who believe ourselves to be so small that we are afraid to speak, gain more confidence when we do it, and so the practice is not so difficult to do. We learn that we can live together.

[While president of CONAIE] *I was invited to Washington, D.C., to a meeting held in the International Development Bank facilities. I was surprised to see other Ecuadorians there: a high government official, a military officer, a church dignitary, and a business leader. Four gentlemen appeared who identified themselves as Harvard professors who teach classes in negotiation and conflict resolution. They said they wanted to reduce tensions in Ecuador, that it appeared we were headed for a serious fight, and they wanted to teach us how to dialogue. We were there for a week, simply talking, and each of us was allowed to talk and in-formally give our points of view. They gave us water and other beverages, and just let us talk. It was an effective method.*

Creating environments in which productive dialogue occurs has become a centerpiece of the ICCI and UINPI institutions. In addition to drawing on his community background, Macas has drawn from his experiences with Native North Americans when he served as an observer for the dispute between the Mohawk Nation and the Canadian government, and from the trip during his CONAIE presidency to Washington, D.C. ICCI regularly organizes "dialogues" in which scholars and practitioners from many fields meet and discuss topics of critical importance to indigenous people. UINPI also uses the dialogue method in its curriculum. Within CONAIE dialogue is an established institution. Sometimes the discussions become rancorous because there are many differences of opinion among the constituent members. But the dialogue brings these all out in the open, and eventually a consensus may be reached.

Tigramugrina, We Will Return

My father would travel to places outside of the Saraguro communities when there were fiestas, and exchange eggs and cheeses for panela [unrefined sugar] *and other things. My father taught me how to barter so I could go to Zaruma* [in the highlands of El Oro Province] *with him. The first time I went was when I was eight or nine. We took five mules of cheese — two hundred pounds per mule. We left at nine in the morning and spent the night in Gulac. It was raining; the trail was very muddy so it was slow going. When we got to Gulac, high in the* páramo, *my* papi *cut four poles, put some branches over, just for some shelter, even though it didn't keep out the rain. We always had to go with our rubber ponchos. It did not matter that it rained. We put branches on the ground topped with the horse blankets. The night passed, and it cleared off. The stars came out. At dawn we were already walking again. That's the first time I saw frost. The ground was cold, cold, cold. My father said we have to go fast, fast, fast, so our feet wouldn't freeze. We arrived about six in the evening. My father's friend there had pasture for the animals and he gave us a room and a bed. The next day my* papi *set up our things on a street and left me in charge, saying, "Be careful not to make a mistake," and reminded me of the value of the cheese. I enjoyed the trip a lot.*

My mother who had been very poor as a child and didn't even have an anacu *until she was sixteen went to the coast* [in the western lowlands of El Oro Province] *to work. She planted rice, yuca, sugarcane. Just for planting and harvest she went. So my mother was always crossing the mountains, starting when she was twelve. She knew the dangers because she had made the trip many times. So when I went she put special things in a little bag and tied it around my neck. To protect me. She met my father on one of these trips. She was very young and he was already old.*

For untold generations before the 1960s, Saraguros traveled outside of their highland community areas for trade (for example, trading cheese or eggs for raw sugar, rice, salt, and tropical fruits), for seasonal labor, to settle adjacent areas in the Upper Amazon (Zamora-Chinchipe Province), for pilgrimages, and to deal with legal or political issues. Before the 1940s, when a motor road linking Saraguro to Cuenca and Loja was completed, most travel was on foot or on horseback and within a radius of one hundred kilometers or so. After the arrival of the road, mode and distance of travel was extended for many Saraguros, although earlier patterns and purposes of travel were not all eliminated. By the time of Ecuador's oil boom of the early 1970s, many more Saraguros began to leave the area to pursue formal education and nonagricultural occupations in the cities of Ecuador. Others, facilitated by ever spreading road networks, extended agropastoral settlements further into Zamora-Chinchipe province. At the same time, Saraguros from the poorer, western part of their traditional homeland (the Selva Alegre region) established permanent settlements in the nonadjacent highland area of Vilcabamba (southern Loja Province), starting first as seasonal agricultural laborers, then becoming owners of their own plots of land. Although the Vilcabamba settlers (and especially the children born there) eventually lost most of their direct ties with the Saraguro region, they did retain the clothing, single braids, and some aspects of communal interaction patterns of Saraguro ethnic identity. Formal ties (including attempts to establish bilingual education) between the Vilcabamba Saraguros and Saraguro-area indigenous organizations were being initiated by the late 1990s (see Fischer 1999).

By the beginning of this millennium, with the combination of rapid population growth and national economic collapse, even more Saraguros had traveled even farther from their traditional homeland. Hundreds of Saraguros, among them laborers, domestic workers, university students, teachers, and other professionals, now live in Loja, Cuenca, and Quito; some of these are runaway youths who have left home without permission (Belote and Belote n.d.). Dozens have gone to other countries, including Austria, Belgium, Bolivia, Canada, Chile, China, Colombia, Cuba, Czech Republic, France, Germany, Honduras, Hungary, Italy, Mexico, Peru, the Philippines, Slovakia, Spain, Sweden, Russia, Thailand and the United States to work, to further their educations, to attend conferences or workshops, to seek medical attention, or to participate in cultural exchanges. More than one thousand Saraguros (including three of Macas's sisters) have emigrated to a coastal band of Spain stretching between Barcelona and Almería where most adult Saraguros — many of them trained as teachers — now serve primarily as agricultural laborers (Bacacela 2001b).

Saraguro emigration to Spain began in 1998 when two Saraguro men arrived in Vera (Andalucía) looking for work (Del Campo 2001:6). They quickly obtained agricultural jobs, earned considerably more than was possible in Ecuador, and sent word back to Saraguro that others should come. And they did. Many of the earliest emigrants (both women and men) went to Spain without other nuclear family members, including spouses. When both spouses went, they left their children in the care of grandparents. At one point in the late 1990s, one set of Saraguro grandparents living in Zamora-Chinchipe was caring for fourteen grandchildren left behind by emigrants to Spain. By the early years of the millennium, however, many Saraguro couples were taking their children to Spain with them. Younger children of the appropriate age were enrolled in school; most older children obtained at least part-time work. Although many Saraguros are content enough to be in Spain for now, it is hard to find an adult Saraguro who plans to stay in Spain for the rest of her or his life.

Employers of some of the early male emigrants to Spain requested that they cut off their long hair so that, it was said, they not be confused with Roma, a group that suffers considerable discrimination in Spain. But some Saraguro men refused to do so. Eventually, as Saraguros gained a regional reputation as reliable workers, wearing long hair in this foreign land became much less disadvantageous. In fact, for some Spanish employers, a braid became a kind of certificate of assurance that he or she was making a good hire. Nevertheless, summer heat, the nature of the work they do, and lingering issues with long-haired men (and boys) in Spain, have led some men to cut their braids, even when not asked to do so.

On the evening of December 31, 2001, nearly three hundred Ecuadorians, most of them Saraguros, along with several Spaniards and a couple of North Americans, converged at an old hacienda house outside of Vera to celebrate Año Viejo (New Year's Eve). Prominent individuals were "roasted" in humorous speeches, then their effigies were burned in great bonfires at midnight. Music, dancing, drinking and conversation lasted until dawn. This New Year's celebration is Ecuadorian in general, rather than specific to Saraguro. In this "foreign" environment it seemed to represent a kind of reaffirmation of both Ecuadorian identity and of Saraguro identity.

Another manifestation of Saraguro community building in Spain is the leading participation of Saraguro emigrants there in the formation of the

Fundación Jatari, an NGO whose overall goal is to "promote the process of integral community development, utilizing the human and natural potential of the area while respecting the environment and cultural diversity" for the Saraguro region (Fundación Jatari 2002). A current project is to assist in the building and equipping of a hospital in Tenta (a parish of the canton of Saraguro) in collaboration with UINPI.

Some Saraguros have discarded their indigenous identity to move more easily in the outside world (Belote and Belote 2000). But almost all who leave, whether students, seasonal laborers, year-round agricultural laborers, social-political leaders, teachers and other professionals, or runaways, have maintained their identity as Saraguros and intend to return to Saraguro. In the case of Vilcabamba and in some areas of the Oriente in which they have settled, Saraguros attempt to maintain their identity and to recreate Saraguro forms of community life such as fiestas and *mingas*. Those who return home bring back with them new experiences, new ideas, new sets of relationships with the outside world. All these are potential strands to be woven back into the changing nature of being Saraguros, and being *a* Saraguro.

Education

I was a Quichua speaker, and I suffered so much as one of two indigenous children in the 10 de Marzo elementary school for boys in Saraguro's town center. I started there in the third grade after attending the indigenous community school for two years; the only other indigenous boy was in the second grade. The other boys in my class learned quickly — geography, literature, math — and I didn't understand the language for the most part. It was a major struggle. I hated Spanish. When I had to use Spanish grammar, it made me very nervous to speak during the oral exams. Some teachers told me to leave if I could not speak correctly. These things made school very difficult for me, but it also made me study more.

Upon completing elementary school, Macas enrolled in Celina Vivar High School in Saraguro, which was a three-year institution at that time. He continued his high school education at the Dominican Military Academy in Cuenca on a scholarship provided by the principal, who had attended a musical program in which the Macas brothers Lucho and Pacho sang. When a new principal terminated the scholarship at that institution, Luis enrolled at Benigno Malo High School in Cuenca; he was the only indigenous pupil. Soon after graduation in 1972, Macas went to Quito to attend a conference on bilingual education; there he met Padre Hernán Malo, president of the Catholic University. Macas was offered a scholarship by Padre Malo and he earned an undergraduate degree in languages and linguistics in 1976. He was then appointed to a teaching position as a Quichua instructor at Catholic University.

In 1978, Catholic University created the Centro de Investigaciones de Educación Indígena, Center for Research for Indigenous Education (CIEI) and Macas and other indigenous scholars from the Sierra and the Oriente worked as researchers there. They conducted research throughout the indigenous regions of Ecuador, collecting ethnographic and linguistic data.

Their proposal to establish literacy education was accepted as a national program by President Jaime Roldós in 1980, and the phrase "that indigenous languages be used for language education where there is a major concentration of indigenous peoples in the country, and that Spanish serve as the language of intercultural relations" (Congreso Nacional del Ecuador 1996) was successfully added to the constitution. Almost six thousand literacy centers were established throughout Ecuador prior to Roldós's death in an airplane crash in Loja in 1981. His successor, Osvaldo Hurtado, was less supportive of the literacy effort, and the number of centers dropped to eight hundred, then disappeared entirely in 1984 with the presidency of León Febres Cordero. At the same time, a new president at the Catholic University dismantled CIEI in favor of research only in the traditional European languages. This divided the indigenous members of CIEI; some agreed to continue teaching Quichua at Catholic University, but others, including Macas, said, "Why does this have to depend on Catholic University? Why can't we form our own center?" And so they did. This became the Instituto Científico de Culturas Indígenas (Scientific Institute of Indigenous Cultures) (ICCI).

BILINGUAL EDUCATION

ICCI was formally recognized as an educational organization by the Ecuadorian Ministry of Education 1986, one month before the political organization CONAIE received its formal recognition from the Ecuadorian government. ICCI's purpose was academic, scientific, and reflective. Its mission was to provide training for indigenous teachers. All of its members were *indígenas*, and ICCI held teacher-training workshops throughout the country wherever there were concentrations of indigenous peoples. Meanwhile, CONAIE prepared a proposal for bilingual education that differed markedly from the defunct literacy program in that its new effort was to formally incorporate bilingual education into the public school system. This time CONAIE called for bilingual education for all Ecuadorians. In the early days of the presidency of Rodrigo Borja, in 1988, bilingual education — but only for indigenous children — was formally accepted by the government during a personal appearance of the president at the second CONAIE Congress, held in Cañar. CONAIE fulfilled the bilingual education leadership role as ICCI was almost dormant at this time.

Intense political opposition to the program's being administered exclusively by *indígenas* came particularly from socialists and members of the communist party who wanted to address issues solely on the basis of class. But CONAIE persisted, and its commitment to emphasize indigenous issues was firm. Slowly, CONAIE leaders began to understand that their primary purpose was not educational reform but political reform, and they could not do both. Thus, ICCI became more active in preparing pedagogical materials and developing teacher-training workshops for bilingual education for both elementary school and high school teachers.

But there were not enough native-language-speaking teachers to provide for all of the schools at which they were needed. Even when the principal of the school was indigenous, often the teachers were not. There was still much to be done. The only language being addressed was Quichua; the languages of the Shuar, the Chachi, the Siona, the Secoya, and other native peoples were being ignored. And there was very little money to do even the work in Quichua.

The University of Cuenca and the State University of Bolívar (in Guaranda) both began indigenous studies programs (with language and culture emphases) to prepare bilingual teachers, and both universities made efforts to enroll indigenous students in these areas. The Quito branch of the Politechnic University of Loja (which later became the Universidad Politécnica Salesiana [Salesian Politechnic University]) also offered a program that attracted small numbers of indigenous people. These programs made efforts to accommodate low-income indigenous students whose work needs hindered their ability to attend universities far from their home communities. They arranged week-long seminars in conjunction with voluminous reading assignments for the students to study at home while they wrote essays and papers to fulfill course requirements.

UINPI-AMAUTAI WASI

Macas, meanwhile, pursued a degree in law at the Central University of Quito by taking night courses, while he continued to teach Quichua at the Catholic University and work on the early meetings of indigenous peoples that ultimately resulted in the formation of CONAIE. He was elected vice president of CONAIE in 1988. Working with members of the other indigenous peoples and organizations in Ecuador gave him many insights into organizational structure and function. The need for transparency, collective effort, community participation, and dialogue became fundamental tenets for CONAIE and the value of these qualities were constantly reinforced during his tenure as vice president (1988–1990) and subsequently president of CONAIE (1990–96). This is the organizational structure that was adopted by ICCI, and later by UINPI Amautai Wasi (Macas 2000).

The idea for establishing an indigenous university began to form as the shortcomings of the Western model of educational systems became more apparent. In 1997, there were only sixty-eight Ecuadorian indigenous people pursuing higher education, more than half of them were from Saraguro. Even the universities with indigenous studies programs were sending their students to ICCI for educational materials. ICCI began publishing a journal and revived considerably with the return of Macas to its leadership. It did not, however, have much material available for scholars at the university level. Most of the literature available for study was written by outsiders and did not come from the perspective of indigenous peoples.

The first proposal for an indigenous university was written in 1997, but there was a lack of support for the bill on the part of the members of the national congress, and the proposal died. It was just as well, for when the ICCI team revisited the effort, the members realized that they, in fact, had tried to establish "just one more university," one like so many other current ones. If it was to be a genuine indigenous university, the designers needed something entirely different, with an entirely new curriculum. They adopted the model that had been so effective within CONAIE. They held a large workshop. Fifty people from the provinces of Ecuador came together to have a dialogue about the content of an indigenous university. They worked in groups and came to the consensus that the entire university should be dedicated to *Runa yachaicuna* (indigenous knowledge), *Shuctac yachaicuna* (universal sciences) and *Yachay Pura* (pure knowledge or scientific interculturality). Indigenous knowledge would include not just that of Ecuadorian nationalities but also that of North, Central, and South American nationalities, and perhaps that of other indigenous peoples from other continents. Learning was to be based on doing. Every student would have to become bilingual and produce work in Spanish and one indigenous language. The participants recognized the need to prepare students for a variety of careers, not just teaching, and identified six career paths: agroecological sciences; indigenous law; health and intercultural medicine; philosophy, languages, and education science; architecture and territorial planning; and economics and business administration (Macas and Lozano 2000; UINPI 2000).

Throughout the students' education, community participation would be mandatory. Not only the instructors, but also the members of the community in which the school was based would be asked to evaluate the students' performance. A major breakthrough was achieved when the founders and designers concluded that the university would be decentralized. It would be established in many regional centers, so that the students would not have to travel to an urban center to gain a higher education. The instructors would be the ones to circulate from campus to campus offering modules according to the wishes of the local populations. The modules were made available on the Internet (e.g., Sarango 2001) and the creation of a satellite telecommunication network accessible throughout Ecuador became a high priority.

On October 11 and 12, 2000, UINPI was formally inaugurated in the auditorium of CIESPAL (Centro Internacional de Estudios Superiores de Comunicación para América Latina) in Quito. ICCI and CONAIE jointly organized and sponsored the event. The first day's program included speeches by indigenous leaders and Ecuadorian dignitaries, including the *monseñor* of Cuenca, a former presidential chief of staff, a retired military general and former minister of defense who traced the roots of the contemporary indigenous movement and the Levantamientos from their differing perspectives. A panel of journalists presented their reflections on the indigenous movement, which was followed by a panel discussion by the leaders of indigenous organizations that have often been in conflict with one another over the direction of the indigenous movement: CONAIE, FENOCIN, FEINE, Peasant Social Security, and Ecuarunari. All of them spoke of their "common agenda" and the discussion became quite animated with questions and comments from the floor. In the evening, a panel of young indigenous leaders presented their visions of the future. The second day began with a ritual ceremony open to all who wished to participate, led by a Cayambe *yachac*, followed by the singing of the Ecuadorian national anthem in Quichua. The CIESPAL auditorium was packed with people from all sectors of Ecuadorian society as well as international visitors. Dignitaries who participated in this day's formal inauguration of UINPI and the installation of Macas as its president, included Gabriel Galarza, the president of the University of Bolívar and representative of CONESUP (Consejo Nacional de Educación Superior [National Council of Higher Education]); Antonio Vargas, the president of CONAIE; Leonel Cerruto from Bolivia representing TINKU, a network that links indigenous organizations and intercultural universities in the Amazonian-Andean regions of Bolivia, Peru, and Ecuador; Rosalie Little Thunder (Sicangu Lakota) board chair of the Seventh Generation Fund; Mikel Berraondo López from the Universidad de Deusto (Bilbao) Spain; Luis Maldonado of the Consejo de Desarollo de las Nacionalidades y Pueblos del Ecuador (CODENPE); and Luis Macas, the first president of UINPI. The program concluded with the launching of UINPI's first publication, a linguistics book entitled *El idioma del pueblo Puquina* by P. Federico Aguiló (L. Belote 2000).

In the events of these two days, the strands discussed in this chapter were actively incorporated — use of dialogue, respect for others' dignity, hard

work and responsibility, transparency, equilibrium, and community participation — to achieve the goal of establishing an indigenous university to meet
and serve the needs of indigenous peoples.

Conclusion

There is a saying in Saraguro: "Maquica ruracun, shimica rimacun" (The
hands make and the mouth talks). This means a number of things to people
from Saraguro. First, one should engage the world with the whole body, not
just one part. Second, the hands and the mouth should agree and should
say the same thing. Finally, if the hands make something, as when a person
weaves a beautiful *jimba*, the aesthetic should be reflected in the words the
person uses and the ideas the person expresses.

From the people of the communities of Saraguro to the members of ICCI
and the organizers of UINPI, and on through the members of Ecuadorian indigenous nationalities and peoples in indigenous movements, the ideas and
values practiced are offered to the rest of the world. The principle of interculturality, a weaving together of many strands that are nevertheless kept
separate can result in harmony if done with respect for the values and dignity
of others.

For now, for the Saraguros, braids are more than a metaphor of abstract
interpretation. The braid is a living metaphor for their identity, for who
they are in the world. This "real" metaphor, the braid itself, transmits its own
strands of meaning. For the other — the outsider — it can be woven into
strands of abuse and rejection, or strands of acceptance and good reputation,
or strands of exotic attraction. For other Saraguros, it can be woven into
strands of community identity and community bonding. It is not just a living
metaphor; it is a daily metaphor. Every day, when possible, it must be rewo-
ven. Every day, the living metaphor must be reconstructed, preferably with
the help of spouse, parent, child, or friend. Saraguro community life and
the life of people in other indigenous communities in Ecuador exist in a
global context and comprise human and cultural strands that are braided
together in ever changing ways, always with the potential of death or re-
newal. It is an idea and a reality that must be cleaned, nurtured, and reworked regularly.

The Belotes and a Saraguro friend, Aurelio Chalán, were standing in a
patch of land cleared out of the cloud forest above Saraguro, discussing the
future of the cloud forest and of the Saraguros. We admired a giant *mullón*
(an Andean conifer) that stood alone in the cleared space. It was no longer
healthy and showed signs of rot. Suddenly, tears came to Aurelio's eyes. "We
Saraguros are like the trees in the cloud forest," he said. "We are all different

individuals. In the cloud forest all the trees are distinct and different. But no matter how big they are, without each other they cannot stand."

ACKNOWLEDGMENTS

Luis Macas and Linda and Jim Belote gratefully acknowledge their debt to the people of Saraguro. Macas expresses gratitude for his upbringing in this community, which formed his thoughts and values through the teachings of the elders and the traditions of mingas and agriculture. These teachings are the basis of his understanding and the inspiration for his actions to do battle for the rights of indigenous peoples. The Belotes thank the Saraguros for friendship, shared wisdom, and instruction that now span a forty-year period of frequent association. Macas also acknowledges CONAIE, which has served him as an outstanding teacher and led to the fulfillment of his dreams to pursue the formation of a truly plural society for the generations to come. To ICCI, an organization that works tirelessly through paths of hope for both unity and diversity and which creates a space where communal conversation is celebrated, he owes his thanks. Linda Belote also wishes to acknowledge the support of the University of Minnesota Duluth for the Chancellor's Small Grant that provided funding for her attendance at the inauguration of the Universidad Intercultural de Nacionalidades y Pueblos Indígenas.

REFERENCES

Almeida, José
    1993   El levantamiento indígena como momento constitutivo nacional. In *Sismo étnico en el Ecuador: Varias Perspectivas*. Roberto Roggiero, comp. Pp. 7–28. Quito: CEDIME/Ediciones Abya-Yala.

Andolina, Robert James
    1999   Colonial Legacies and Plurinational Imaginaries: Indigenous Movement Politics in Ecuador and Bolivia. Ph.D. dissertation, University of Minnesota.

Andrade Macas, Manuel de Jesús
    2001   Gracias por acogernos y darnos trabajo. *La voz de Almería*, May 6 : 26.

Bacacela, Sisapacari
    2001a   La discriminación de la mujer indígena: Un peso histórico. Electronic document. http://www.ecoportal.net/articulos/discri.htm.
    2001b   La migración en los Saraguros: Aspectos positivos y negativos. Electronic document. http://www.ecoportal.net/articulos/saraguros.htm.

Belote, Jim
    1998   *Los Saraguros del sur del Ecuador*. Quito: Abya-Yala.

Belote, Jim, and Linda Belote
    1977   El sistema de cargos de fiestas en Saraguro. In *Temas sobre la continuidad y adaptación cultural ecuatoriana*. Marcelo Naranjo, José Pereira, and

Norman E. Whitten, Jr., eds. Pp. 47–73. Quito: Pontificia Universidad
Católica del Ecuador.

1984   Suffer the Little Children: Death, Autonomy, and Responsibility in a
Changing "Low Technology" Environment. *Science, Technology and
Human Values* 9(4):35–48.

n.d.   Teen Runaways in the Context of Saraguro Ethnicity and Migration.
Unpublished MS, Department of Sociology and Anthropology, University
of Minnesota.

Belote, Linda

2000   The Inauguration of la Universidad Intercultural de Nacionalidades y
Pueblos Indígenas del Ecuador, Amautai Wasi. Electronic document.
http://yachana.org/ecuatorianistas/bulletin/nov2000/nov2000.
html#belote.

2002   Relaciones Interétnicas en Saraguro 1962–1972. Quito: Editorial
Abya-Yala.

Belote, Linda, and Jim Belote

1989   Gender, Ethnicity, and Modernization: Saraguro Women in a Changing
World. In *Multidisciplinary Studies in Andean Anthropology*. Virginia J.
Vitzthum, ed. Pp. 101–17. Michigan Discussions in Anthropology, vol. 8.
Ann Arbor: University of Michigan.

1994   (editors) *Los Saraguros: Fiesta y Ritualidad*. Quito: Universidad
Politécnica Salesiana, Federación Interprovincial de Indígenas de
Saraguro, Editorial Abya-Yala.

2000   Fuga desde abajo: Cambios individuales de identidad étnica en el sur
del Ecuador. In *Etnicidades*. Andrés Guerrero, ed. Pp. 81–118. Quito:
FLACSO/ILDIS.

2002   Saraguro: Provincia de Loja, Ecuador. Electronic document. http://
www.saraguro.org.

Berthke, Mary

2002   Herringbone. Electronic document. http://dreamweaverbraiding.com/
braids/herringbone.htm.

Chalán Guamán, Luis Aurelio, et al.

1994   Introducción. In *Los Saraguros: Fiesta y Ritualidad*. Linda Belote and
Jim Belote, eds. Pp. 7–25. Quito: Universidad Politécnica Salesiana,
Federación Interprovincial de Indígenas de Saraguro, Editorial Abya-Yala.

Colloredo-Mansfeld, Rudi

2002   Autonomy and Interdependence in Native Movements: Towards a
Pragmatic Politics in the Ecuadorian Andes. *Identities: Global Studies in
Culture and Power* 9(2):173–95.

Congreso Nacional del Ecuador

1996   Constitución Política de la Rupública de Ecuador. Quito.

Criollo, Teresa

    1995   *Economía Campesina y Estrategias de Sobrevivencia en Zonas de Altura, caso: San Lucas–Loja*. Loja: Casa de la Cultura Ecuatoriana.

Davis, Natalie Zemon

    1998   Beyond Babel. *Occasional Papers of the Doreen B. Townsend Center* 10:15–28.

Del Campo, Eduardo

    2001   De cómo los Saraguros llegaron a Vera en busca del capital. *El Mundo* (Madrid), August 12:6.

El Comercio

    2000a La universidad indígena tiene padrinos. June 5:A12.

    2000b Los Saraguros son la fuerza en el Austro. June 6:A7.

Fischer, William

    1999   Saraguros in Vilcabamba. Electronic document. http://www.saraguro.org/vilcabamba.htm.

Fundación Jatari

    2002   Fundación Jatari. Electronic document. http://www.saraguro.org/jatari.htm.

Gutiérrez, Carlos Xavier

    2002   Justicia Indígena. *Vistazo* 834 (May): 40–44.

ICCI

    2002   Instituto Científico de Culturas Indígenas/Amawta Runakunapak Yachay. Electronic document. http://icci.nativeweb.org/.

Jijón, Carlos

    1994   Es Macas un tigre de papel? *Vistazo* 641 (May):20–22.

King, Kendall A.

    2001   Language Revitalization Processes and Prospects: Quichua in the Ecuadorian Andes. *Bilingual Education and Bilingualism*, 24. Clevedon, England: Multilingual Matters.

Lucas, Kintto

    2000   *We Will Not Dance on Our Grandparents' Tomb: Indigenous Uprisings in Ecuador*. London: Catholic Institute for International Relations (CIIR).

Macas, Luis (Lillian Granda, interview)

    1993   Tenemos alma desde 1637. In *Los indios y el estado-país: Pluriculturalidad y multietnicidad en el Ecuador*. Diego Cornejo Menacho, ed. Pp. 111–33. Quito: Ediciones Abya-Yala.

Macas, Luis

    1991   *El levantimiento indígena visto por sus protagonistas*. Quito: ICCI, Amauta Runacunapac Yachai.

    2000   Cómo se forjó la Universidad Intercultural? *Boletin ICCI-Rimay* 2(19):20–25.

2001　Foreword. In *Ethnopolitics in Ecuador: Indigenous Rights and the Strengthening of Democracy*. Melina Selverston-Scher. Pp. xi–xix. Miami: North-South Center Press.

Macas Ambuludí, Luis, and Alfredo Lozano Castro

2000　Reflexiones en torno al proceso colonizador y las características de la educación universitaria en el Ecuador. *Boletin ICCI-Rimay* 2(19) : 11–19.

Pacari, Nina

1993　Levantamiento indígena. In *Sismo étnico en el Ecuador: Varias perspectivas*. Roberto Roggiero, comp. Pp. 169–86. Quito: CEDIME/Ediciones Abya-Yala.

Pallares, Amalia Veronika

1997　From Peasant Struggles to Indian Resistance: Political Identity in Highland Ecuador: 1964–1992. Ph.D. dissertation, University of Texas at Austin.

Ramón Valerezo, Galo, and Elba Gómez Barahona

1993　Hay Nacionalidades Indias en el Ecuador? In *Sismo étnico en el Ecuador: Varias perspectivas*. Roberto Roggiero, comp. Pp. 187–205. Quito: CEDIME/Ediciones Abya-Yala.

Sarango Macas, Luis Fernando

1995　Los Saraguros. In *Identidades indias en el Ecuador*. José Almeida Venneza, comp. Pp. 339–69. Quito: Abya-Yala.

2001　Organización Política del Abya Yala. Electronic document. http://uinpi.nativeweb.org/modulos/sarango/sarango.pdf.

Sawyer, Suzana

1997　The 1992 Indian Mobilization in Lowland Ecuador. *Latin American Perspectives* 24(3) : 67–84.

Selverston-Scher, Melina

2001　*Ethnopolitics in Ecuador: Indigenous Rights and the Strengthening of Democracy*. Miami: North-South Center Press.

Seventh Generation Fund

2000a　Seventh Generation Fund. Electronic document. http://www.7genfund.org/.

2000b　Instituto Científico de Culturas Indígenas: Quito, Ecuador. Sovereignty Newsletter. Electronic document. http://www.7genfund.org/sovereignty_4.html#news.

Singer, Lester

1962　Ethnogenesis and Negro Americans Today. *Social Research* 29: 422–32.

Stiles, Thomas

1996　Almost Heaven: The Fiesta Cargo System among the Saraguro Quichuas in Ecuador and Implications for Contextualization in the Evangelical Church. Ph.D. dissertation, Trinity International University.

UINPI

    2000   Propuesta Técnica Académica para la Creación de la UINPI, vol. 1.
           Síntesis de la Propuesta. Quito: ICCI.

Volinsky, Nan Leigh

    1998   Violin Performance Practice and Ethnicity in Saraguro Ecuador. Ph.D.
           dissertation, Department of Anthropology, University of Illinois at
           Urbana-Champaign.

Whitten, Norman E., Jr.

    1976   *Sacha Runa: Ethnicity and Adaptation of Ecuadorian Jungle Quichua.*
           Urbana: University of Illinois Press.

Whitten, Norman E., Jr., Dorothea S. Whitten, and Alfonso Chango

    1997   Return of the Yumbo: The Indigenous Caminata from Amazonia to
           Andean Quito. *American Ethnologist* 24(2):355–91.

CHAPTER 9

Actors and Artists from Amazonia and the Andes

DOROTHEA SCOTT WHITTEN

While residing in Amazonian Ecuador during 1972 and 1973, Norman and Dorothea ("Sibby") Whitten were asked by the director of the Museums of the Central Bank of Ecuador, Hernán Crespo Toral, to make a large collection of indigenous-made artifacts for the museum in Quito. In return, we were given permission to take home a sizable research collection for further study and analysis. Both collections were primarily of decorated and smoke-blackened ceramics made by women, but the artifacts also included drums, flutes, blowguns and quivers, carved hardwood stools, large flat bowls and trays, and some ritual adornment such as feather headdresses and bead necklaces and headbands made by men. Pleased with the interest in their cultural artifacts and proud that these would belong to and eventually be exhibited in their national museums, many people contributed items, while others sold them for modest prices.

A few men and women of the Comuna San Jacinto del Pindo, near Puyo-Pastaza, made things specifically to educate the outside world through museum exhibitions. Marcelo Santi Simbaña, for example, carved a full-size canoe from a tree trunk, which he later saw in the Art Gallery of the Museum of the Central Bank of Ecuador. He also carved a huge *batea* from a single hardwood tree trunk. This type of bowl is used by his wife and other women to pound cooked manioc roots into a pulp. The late Soledad Vargas recreated a number of smoke-blackened vessels that her mother and grandmothers used to cook food and beverages, boil down salt brine, and serve food and hot pepper sauce. Juana Catalina Chango, who created a ceramic tapir almost as large as a real-life small calf, gave a lesson in tropical rain-forest ecology. Other people, especially Estela Dagua, formerly of Unión Base and now of Puyo, have repeated this didactic, intercultural practice from time to time as we have continued to collect.

Several pieces of pottery (here used interchangeably with ceramics) frame significant changes taking place in the lives of indigenous Pastaza and Napo residents during the early 1970s. The inner rim of a small, delicate drinking bowl, called a *mucawa* (maker unknown) is decorated with a symmetrical, stylized running border, a motif borrowed from an ancient sherd found in Napo Province. Beneath that is a meandering band of images copied from the school blackboard: 1, 2, 3, 4, then li, lu, la, le, followed by a newer construction "Mobil Especial." At the bottom of the bowl is the bold mark that represents the hallucinogenic plant datura (*Brugmansia suaveolens*) and symbolizes the inner world of shamanic vision.[1]

Under the auspices of the military government, petroleum exploration was in full swing and international consortia were recruiting and hiring indigenous men to cut paths through the rain forest, dig trenches, build camps, lug huge coils of dynamite wire, and cook for the workers. Social commentary on the impact of this intrusion is seen in three evocative figurines. One was made by Alegría Canelos, a master potter from Curaray, where she witnessed oil men constantly traveling in motorized canoes on the Curaray River. The round lower section of this figurine could have been the start of a small storage jar, but instead it turns into a canoe shape with a wide serving spout. The canoe is ridden by a caricature of a foreign oil boss, arm raised to his hard hat. The potter created this effigy for the purpose of serving *chicha* (*asua*) at a Catholic Easter service and to represent the *machin runa*, the monkey-person associated with Hurihuri, the forest spirit master of other people. She decorated the arms and body of the oil boss with spots of the dangerous anaconda, signaling domination and destruction, and around the base of the canoe she painted more anaconda symbols, a band of diamond shapes encapsulating small Christian crosses. The base is covered with the motif of the Amazonian water turtle, regarded as a spirit force and seat of power of Sungui, the first shaman and the ultimate source of all shamanic power.

Clara Santi Simbaña, then living in Comuna San Jacinto near Puyo-Pastaza, expressed the turbulence in her life during this period when her husband and several of her sons and brothers went off to work for exploration companies. A song she composed about the big monkey person and the two figurines she made reflect the dual meaning of *machin runa*, monkey/stranger person. One figurine is a straightforward representation of a woolly monkey, with his face blackened and his tail resting casually on his shoulder. A spout protrudes from his back, for this *machin* was designed to serve *asua* at a traditional kinship festival. The other figure has a round head placed on a body shaped like an edible gourd. One hand is raised to the baseball cap shoved back on his head, and the mouth is wide open. This monkey is the epitome of the *machin* as stranger. He is the oil boss shouting orders to his indigenous workers, orders that they must understand emotionally, if not literally. To Clara, the oil boss represented entrapment. She made the ceramic image to sell to tourists for much-needed money.

Clara and another master potter, Denise Curipallo ("Apacha") Vargas Canelos, along with their husbands and children, were active participants in the *caminata*, the March for Land and Life, of 1992. They were among many other people from the Puyo area who have shared their lives with the Whittens since 1968 and the early 1970s, and they were joined by the various nationalities representing an estimated 148 communities of indigenous people of Pastaza Province, especially the Canelos Quichua, Achuar, and Shiwiar (see Whitten, Whitten, and Chango, this volume). The peaceful march from Puyo to Quito was launched to petition the president of the republic, Dr. Rodrigo Borja Cevallos, for formal and recognized rights to their own land and hence the right to control their own livelihood. The march was propelled by Antonio Vargas Guatatuca and OPIP, of which Vargas was president. It was supported by CONFENIAE and CONAIE, with funding in part from the Rainforest Action Group. The OPIP office was in the center of Puyo; the headquarters of CONFENIAE were located south of Puyo, on a hill overlooking the hamlet of Unión Base, home of Antonio Vargas. CONAIE, the overarching national organization, was housed in Quito. The logistics of the march obviously demanded careful planning and coordination by the organizations; support groups provided food, blankets, medical care, and other necessities along the entire route.

As the marchers progressed into Andean territories, they gained national media attention, mostly favorable, and political and moral support from their highland compatriots when community after community of indigenous Quichua-speaking people joined the ranks. Men and women of the Tigua-Zumbagua area of Cotopaxi Province not only participated in the march but recorded it in their paintings. Julio Pello shows throngs of men and women heading down the narrow, winding road that links Tigua with the Pana (Pan-American Highway) at Latacunga. One group walks ahead of a truck packed with people; men sitting atop the cabin hold a sign that reads "Comuna Tigua Chimbacucho." A small group following the truck includes a drummer and two flute players, and still more people walk toward the truck from a side road. In the distance, buses and a truck are blocked by boulders that other indigenous people have rolled onto the middle of the Pana.

Just as the women potters of Pastaza incorporate references to their experiences and observations into their traditional ceramics, men and a few women Tigua artists portray ancient, historical, and contemporary themes in their relatively new art form. For untold years, some men from Tigua painted leather drum heads and carved and painted wooden masks to be used in their own festivals. Julio Toaquiza Tigase, generally credited as the first to paint in the new format, at one time sold old drums to antique dealers in Quito, but later switched to selling drums he made and painted himself. His version of how he began to paint on square or rectangular dried sheep hides stretched over wood frames is presented in Colloredo-Mansfeld (this volume; see also Colvin and Toaquiza 1994; Ribadeneira de Caseres 1990). According to the late Olga Fisch, a well-known collector and promoter of Ecuadorian arts and crafts, she suggested the change and provided him with the initial frames.[2] Her version, of course, does not negate Julio's memory of a shaman's vision and a subsequent dream that originally led him into the art world. His charming portrayals of indigenous life and festivals became popular among tourists and some nationals. Soon other men from Tigua were producing *cuadros*, as the paintings are known in Ecuador, as well as masks and drums for the tourist market.

From its birth in the early to mid 1970s, a highly popular and economically successful style of painting emerged from a relatively obscure native craft.[3] The new paintings rapidly transformed from an inwardly directed craft to an outwardly directed ethnic-arts market, in Nelson H. H. Graburn's (1976) terms. In aesthetic style and scope — scope here meaning the range of topics portrayed — paintings have moved from local to cosmopolitan orientations, in Robert Merton's (1957) terms. Merton examined the relation of mass communication to patterns of orientations of influential members of a small community. I have adapted his concepts as a means by which to review the range of orientations of paintings from local, circumscribed content toward cosmopolitan national or international content. The repertoire of subjects now includes examples of global political and economic events and their repercussions within the nation. The paintings themselves have become internationally recognized.

The first indigenous art cooperative was formed in 1989 by Julio Toaquiza and his sons; it was rebuilt in its present structure with Swiss aid following the earthquake of 1993. Paintings from the Toaquiza-based and other cooperatives (see Bielenberg 1996, 1997; Colloredo-Mansfeld, this volume; Colvin and Toaquiza 1994; Muratorio 2000) as well as those produced by a number of independent artists have been discovered and promoted by Ecuadorians, North Americans, and Europeans who have sponsored exhibitions in Ecuador, the United States, Canada, France, Brazil, England, and Germany.[4] There are at least two Web sites, one of which focuses on the first cooperative and a selection of some of its art. Two prestigious exhibitions of paintings by members of the Toaquiza family were held recently in Quito. One, presented in the presidential palace Carondelet in 2001, was the first such occasion organized by the national palace and was roundly endorsed by President Gustavo Noboa Bejarano. The Guayasamín Foundation opened a striking exhibition in its galleries in July, 2002.[5]

Drums used in the festivals of Corpus Christi were decorated with important Corpus characters, such as the *danzante* (ritual dancer), or motifs from the *danzante*'s costume, and these Corpus themes were transferred to many of the earliest *cuadros*. In 1979, Olga Fisch commissioned more than fifty paintings from Julio Toaquiza and exhibited them in Germany (Scheinman 1981:15). I suspect that some paintings from this batch were those included in her 1981 exhibition of Corpus Christi costumes at the Renwick Gallery of the Smithsonian Institution (Muratorio 1981a:32; 1981b:13; 1985:54–55). Early topics also portrayed the celebrations of Christmas, variously called *Christmas Night, Celebration of the Child*, and *The Three Kings*. Other *cuadros* depicted quotidian chores: planting and harvesting crops, spinning and weaving, or tending sheep and llamas. Some painters combined so many elements of pastoral, agricultural, and festival activities into one scene that I refer to them as "slice-of-life" paintings.

The largest, most expansive slice-of-life painting is a mural approximately eight feet by four feet by Juan Luis Cuyo Cuyo. It graces the wall of the entrance to La Bodega, a gallery in Quito, and contains scenes from every conceivable quotidian and ritual activity in the artist's experience and memory. Juan Luis carefully labeled and described each segment and periodically updates the mural in keeping with current national events, including the 1990 Levantamiento Indígena and the 1992 *caminata*.

In 1985, Mary Weismantel analyzed and described seventy paintings and drums; she noted fine details (such as earrings, lace on petticoats) and, in the earlier paintings, three levels or fields from top to bottom, with some integration or interchangeability between the middle and lower levels in later paintings (Weismantel 1985). She later referred to the levels as three distinct spatial zones (Weismantel 1998) that correspond to human activity in the foreground, the physical setting (houses, churches, fields) in the middle ground, and, in the upper level, the mountains and sky of the *páramo* that provide the cosmological and mythical settings for imaginative portrayals. The levels, or spatial zones, are still evident in many paintings in today's market, but they are diminished or absent in cases in which the painter concentrates on a full frame interior or on relating a particular scene or event, such as the Nativity taking place in a cave.

In the earliest paintings, festival characters were lined up against an Andean background that usually included a volcano, churches, and houses. Dancers, people in animal masks and costumes, and musicians, particularly drummers, were presented face on, staring at the viewer with Orphan Annie–like eyes. Over the years, painters developed their techniques and skills into styles that show greater depth perspective, much more sense of motion and action and greater refinement in details. One young artist, Rodrigo Ugsha Cuyo, has mastered techniques of rendering visual, dimensional perspectives and additionally employs the sequential perspective of a roving camera, changing location and adjusting focus. For example, in one pair of paintings he first shows bulls being rounded up by the famous *chagras* (cowboys) of Machachi, with the Pan-American highway and the Cotopaxi and Tungurahua volcanoes in the distant background. Looking closer, we see the *chagras* and their helpers loading cattle into a truck parked alongside the highway. In two views of one house, framed by cattle and sheep in nearby fields, the artist shows commercial activities — weaving, mask making — in front of the house and agricultural work behind it.

Along with this evolution came an expanded repertoire of themes ranging from the ones already mentioned to mythology, to reflections on the cosmos, to other Andean festivals such as La Mama Negra and the New Year's celebration of Año Nuevo, to the national sport of *futbol* (soccer). Portrayals offer commentary on modernization, ecotourism, and the social hierarchy of the world of the painters. They include Bible scenes, weddings, baptisms, funerals, and shamanic practices, including blessing llamas and sheep for luck. Current paintings are lessons in the multinationalism and multiculturalism characteristic of modern and millennial Ecuador. No longer purely local in orientation, the artists paint the nation as they see and experience it. Prominent people who visit an indigenous community are likely to be painted into history, as is the case with the ex-presidents Rodrigo Borja Cevallos, León Febres Cordero, Abdalá Bucaram Ortiz, and Jamil Mahuad Witt.

Bucaram's face adorns the back of a small chair owned by John and Jill Ortman of La Bodega, Quito. Mahuad's face appears on another small chair shown in Cuvi (1994:176).[6] Scenes of Borja visiting an indigenous artist's workshop and Febres Cordero attending a Christmas festival were painted by Juan Francisco Ugsha Llaquiche and reproduced in *Tigua: Arte primitivista ecuatoriano* (Ribadeneira de Caseres 1990:41, 53). In the first painting, Borja is accompanied by his red-headed advisor on indigenous affairs, Alfonso Calderón, author of *Reflexión en las culturas orales*, and first cousin of Borja. In regard to the artists of the Huanu Turupata sector of Tigua Chimbacucho, Ribadeneira de Caseres (1990:40) writes:

> At this time, there is a project to set up a modern village, with a church and everything, where all the painters from the Huanu Turupata community can move and lead a better life. The project is under the promotion of its author, Alfonso Calderón also an artist and architect.

In 1981, as a gift for her eightieth birthday, Julio Toaquiza painted Señora Olga into a Corpus Christi festival. She stands in the midst of the costumed dancers and people from several Andean locations and she holds a staff of authority and a *shigra* (fiber net bag). A tourist takes pictures of the dancers and the drummers. A birthday present to her in 1991, by and from Bernardo Toaquiza, places her beside the tourist site of Lake Quilotoa, about an hour and a half drive from Tigua. Ecotourism scenes may take viewers to the Galápagos Islands or to an Andean lake — which could be Quilotoa in Cotopaxi or Cui Cocha in Imbabura — where tourists are catered to by indigenous guides. A video produced by Burgos and Bielenberg (1998) traces a tourist trip from Quito to Quilotoa, where indigenous artists from this area try to sell their paintings to the bus load of foreigners busy filming and photographing the lake at the bottom of the volcanic crater.

Representations of myths of the condor, a national symbol, are ubiquitous. Most versions deal with a tale of courtship, abduction and spirit-beings who merge or cross human-avian boundaries. These paintings of the condor myth are based on a real courtship custom: a young man indicates his interest in a young woman by tossing pebbles at her as she sits guarding a flock of sheep. If she giggles demurely, the courtship is on. In the myth, a young woman is approached and charmed by a handsome young man wearing a black poncho, which he holds tightly across his chest. On his return visit, he opens the poncho to reveal his true condor presence and then flies her off to his huge nest or cave high in the mountains. Her angry parents manage to get her back home, but she refuses to eat or leave the house. One day she emerges, smiling and singing; condor-man arrives and she flies away astride his back. Both are now spirits who have merged and surpassed conventional human-avian boundaries. An elaborated and slightly different version is presented by Ribadeneira de Caseres (1990:46–48).

Market scenes are another favorite of some artists. Rodrigo Ugsha Cuyo offers accurate renditions of open-air markets crowded with indigenous shoppers buying produce, clothing, and housewares made of plastic, enamel, and aluminum. The goods are delivered by buses and trucks drawn in great detail and often named — Ford, Fiat, and Cotopaxi (a bus). In the left corner of one painting, a woman is cooking a big vat of food on a stove fueled by a tank of Dura Gas; people sit at a communal table eating bowls of an Andean stew or soup. In the opposite corner, a pizza is being delivered in a square wood box mounted on the back of a motorcycle driven by an indigenous man. The background includes Lake Quilotoa and the church spires of Zumbagua, landmarks that indicate the location is hours away from the nearest pizza parlor or delivery service.

Rodrigo Toaquiza placed his 1990 *Indigenous Market of Zumbagua* in the context of a paved plaza, concrete sidewalks and contemporary houses, all with red tile roofs, that multiply and expand into the surrounding hills, a scene very similar to another market scene he titled *Quito, Ecuador*. Other artists juxtapose vehicles, contemporary concrete houses, or urban streets with rural, mountainous backgrounds, testimonies to the spread of modernization into their homelands. Bernardo Toaquiza captured the prevailing philosophy of multiethnicity in Ecuador in 2001 in his rendition of Jesus ascending to the sky and blessing the apostles. Behind Jesus, a rainbow originates over a cluster of buildings and scatters sunbeams on the twelve Apostles, who are portrayed as representatives of all indigenous and Afro-Ecuadorian people of the nation.

The Art of Healing

The multinational, multicultural nature of Ecuador is clearly articulated in portrayals of shamanic healing. While these appear on the market frequently, with a great deal of repetition and copying, some stand out in their communication of patterns of interaction among healers, patients, and agents of illness and health. These layered connections exist across great social, topographical, and physical distances and extend from antiquity into modernity.

In the summer of 1996, we took several shaman scenes to Puyo to obtain lowland indigenous perspectives on the Andean paintings. We particularly sought the interpretations of our longtime collaborator, Alfonso Chango, who has traveled fairly extensively in the Ecuadorian Andes and lived for two years in Riobamba, the capital of Chimborazo Province (see Whitten, Whitten and Chango 1996, 1997). As he and his wife, Luzmila Salazar, studied the paintings, they realized that they needed the help of her father, Domingo Salazar, a well-known shaman who has treated numerous Andean patients in his home near Puyo and in their own locations in the highlands. His knowledge of the network of shamans and shamanic practice was a source of much of the following four interpretations.

In the first painting, Rodrigo Cuyo portrays the interior of the large house of *un curandero amazónico, sinchi yachaj*, a strong Amazonian healer who employs standard Canelos Quichua shamanic techniques. After drinking ayahuasca, he gains insights into the worlds of powerful spirits during a nighttime seance. Spirits guide his diagnosis of the cause of illness; once he "sees" the evil source, which resides in purple mucus inside the victim, he can suck it out and dispose of the harmful element while retaining the spirit force. The healer, his assistants, and family members are identifiable as Amazonian residents by their stereotypical feather headdresses and grass skirts. Through a window two more people, similarly dressed, search in a river for *carachamas*, a type of catfish found under rocks. Another feather-bedecked man poles a canoe bearing an Andean couple toward the big house. A cross-section of

Ecuadorians awaits treatment. An Otavalan husband and wife drink *trago* (cane alcohol), a Salasacan woman bundles up for a nap, and people from Cañar and Esmeraldas appear to be next in line to be cured.

The shaman is blowing on an Achuar woman to protect her from illness caused by mystical injections from two green spirit snakes coiled around overhead rafters. He also uses power stones and a staff made of *caña brava*, a special, strong riverbank cane that contains the force to defend against all sorcery or witchcraft. The patient's husband assists; he stands behind her, holding another *caña brava* staff and touching her with what appears to be a cutting of ayahuasca vine. Family members gather sacks of potatoes, corn, and peanuts brought to the shaman by his patients, while someone cooks for them. A large, round fish tank is guarded by an assistant holding a *caña brava* staff. Another green snake clings to the outer wall of the tank, which harbors a source of food (fish) as well as a source of illness, fish bones, which some people regard as evidence of magical darts blown by a shaman.

In contrast to the first painting, where the site was generalized, Domingo Salazar immediately pinpointed the location depicted by Francisco Vega Ugsha as Quindigua, also called Maca, high in the *páramo* near Guaranda, Bolívar Province. The shaman here learned his secrets in the nearby hills of Yanaurcu and Cariurcu. In this moonlit scene, an Andean shaman holds a power stone and blows *trago* breath and candle smoke on a woman standing in the icy fast-flowing stream, while his assistant also blows on her and cleanses her with an herb bundle. The three principle mechanisms of curing here are the use of spirit stones, sweeping-cleaning, and drinking *ayahuasca*. The woman's soul, stolen by evil-doers, has been hidden in a small crevice in Cariurcu. The shaman instructs the patient's husband to place a bright pink handkerchief in the crevice, which is portrayed by the artist as the mouth of a mountain spirit (*urcu mama* in the Andes, or *urcu supai* in Amazonia). The frigid water and the power of the shaman force the mountain spirit to "vomit" the woman's soul into the handkerchief, which the husband returns to the shaman who restores the soul to the patient, thereby curing her. As this curing takes place, some Andean people depart, more arrive, and others await treatment in nearby houses with both tile and thatch roofs.

In a third painting, according to the interpretation of Amazonian shaman Domingo Salazar, Francisco Vega Ugsha again creates a curing scene in a specific location: Tonchigüe, a coastal town halfway between Esmeraldas and Punta Galera. The raised bamboo and thatched-roof houses in the background are identified as those of Afro-Ecuadorians of Esmeraldas province. The central figure, a powerful shaman, is far from his home, for he is A'i (Cofán), from the Upper Aguarico area of the northern Oriente. He is identifiable by his collar of jaguar teeth and his green cotton kerchief. Part of his curing apparatus includes a *jatun rumi yacu tian*, a big stone (depicted as a human head) containing water. An unseen person is said to be cleaning, or sweeping, the big water-stone.

The Cofán shaman has traveled here to acquire two powerful material adornments: a collar of shells from the Pacific Ocean and a whale bone. He wears a characteristic headdress, but the feathers are from the coastal red parrot. He acquired his staff in Sua, en route to Tonchigüe. He blows *trago* breath and candle smoke to cure an Andean woman who is accompanied by a female relative or friend. Other people, husband and wife pairs from Cañar and Otavalo, have come to Tonchigüe with a variety of illnesses which the shaman, through his Coast-Sierra-Oriente mergers of powers, can cure. A couple wearing ponchos and round, white felt hats departs in a canoe that is paddled by a *costeño* with a wide-brimmed straw hat. According to Domingo Salazar, "The people in the canoe are from the Sierra, and are being taken down the Sua River to a wedding by a *montuvio de* Manabí, probably from Punta Galeras."

A fourth painting, by Jorge Toaquiza Ugsha, is set in the Sierra, again in Guaranda, in Bolívar Province. The shaman here is well known to Domingo Salazar; his nickname is "El Chino," or Juanito el Chino, and his permanent residence is in Riobamba (Chimborazo Province), on the Plaza de San Alfonso.[7] His Christian name is Victor Chambo. The curing here is being done in Pasa Grande, which is near Guaranda. Specifically, it is in San Fernando, across from Chirolliris. Parenthetically, this shaman also cures, in the Shuar language, on the Via Macas, south of the Pastaza River in Morona-Santiago Province. He is said to travel through all of the Andean, inter-Andean and Amazonian regions. The wife of the shaman cooks for the patient, who has not eaten in days. He lies on a straw mat and is covered by a blanket. He is accompanied by his wife and a friend who acts as a *suplicante* (supplicant) to formally request treatment by the shaman. His *mesa* (curing table) is set with paraphernalia that embody and mediate powerful forces: a human skull, *supai rumi* (spirit stones), candles, a mystical deer skull, a leaf bundle, a bowl of *huayusa* (*Ilex* species), a cup to drink this native tea, and another cup to drink *ayahuasca*.

Through a small opening in the wall of the house a huge green boa flickers its tongue as it stretches toward El Chino. This is the embodiment of the Tslamanga *supai*, or spirit, that inhabits an ice-cold lake contained in a large rock that exists somewhere within the extinct volcano of Cotacachi in Imbabura Province. The Tslamanga image is another representation of the big water-containing stone seen in the third painting.

The following paintings were not analyzed by Domingo Salazar, but are included here because of their vibrant presentations of the multicultural, multiethnic context and content of shamanic performance.

In 1988 and 1989, Julio Toaquiza T. produced contrasting scenes, one of a Tsáchila shaman curing in his house near Santo Domingo de los Colorados, the other of a Yumbo *yachaj* treating a woman from Zumbagua in a home in that area. Both healers have elaborate *mesas* replete with skulls, frogs, snakes, candles, stones, and other spirit devices. From a small drawer in each table, a little white demon emerges, while a large dark devil image appears hovering over and behind each shaman. The Tsáchila *curandero* holds a wood staff in his right hand and a devil's pitchfork in his left; a green boa is draped across his stomach and over his shoulder. The Oriente curer has a long staff of authority similar to the one held by the woman patient, who also wears a Christian cross around her neck. Both shamans blow tobacco smoke on their patients, as does the Tsáchila's assistant, who treats a man holding a pair of femurs. Two other patients in this scene undergo special herb steam baths in a side room. Andean and Afro-Ecuadorian people have traveled to both locations to seek treatments for a variety of afflictions.

Jorge Toaquiza carried out the devil theme in a starkly surrealistic setting that places tiny people in a huge room. Stars shine in the night sky seen through a window; inside, the room is lighted by a Coleman-like lantern hanging from a nail in the wall. Near the bed of a patient, a small dark devil figure raises a spear over its head. Perhaps it is directed across the room toward a Yumbo shaman who cleanses and treats an Andean patient. Looming large behind the *yachaj* is a second, much bigger devil. He holds his spear at his side. His tail rests over the handle of an enormous fire-blackened *paila* (cauldron). In the center of the room, a small, tan dog sits on a yellow chair painted with the same floral decorations seen on the bedposts and a trunk. The animal must represent a spirit mascot since it is highly unlikely that it would otherwise occupy the choice, and only, seat in the house.

María Ermelinda Cuyo, one of the first women artists known to us, painted two variations on a theme in 1991. The theme is that of an Oriente shaman curing in Andean locations in the midst of a full-blown festival that features masked, costumed characters, musicians playing flutes and *bocinas* (six-foot-long hide horns) and beating drums, and other participants in Andean dress. The shaman, wearing white pants, a blue shirt, and a feather headdress and necklace, sits on a simple log seat of power (*bancu*) and holds a long staff of authority. María Ermelinda identified him as "Domingo Salazar from the Oriente," the very same person who gave interpretations of the first four paintings described above. Not only did she transpose people and settings, as have other artists, but she collapsed historic and geographic time and space by placing several *conquistadores* on a hill overlooking the fiesta, while their sailing vessels are anchored in the ocean west of the Andes.

Julio Vega Llaquichi portrays the other, Western side of medical-care delivery: a clinic staffed by a nurse and an assistant who wear caps marked with red crosses and dispense medicines to Andean patients. This represents a type of medical care that coexists with traditional and alternative treatments but has, in recent years, been curtailed or discontinued altogether due to lack of government funds for the medicines, personnel, and facilities.

The failure of government agencies to provide adequate medical care is counterbalanced by the constitutional recognition and active encouragement of the rights of indigenous people to practice their traditional forms of curing and shamanism, and the promotion of shamanic endeavors as tourist destinations. Once considered illegal and practiced clandestinely at night, shamanism has come out of the closet and may be performed in broad daylight in public places open to all who choose to watch and partake. The city of Quito has organized bus tours to the famous archaeological site of Cochasquí, high in the mountains between Quito and Otavalo, where a veritable shamans' supermarket is held about the time of the summer solstice.[8] Tourist agencies and enterprising individuals advertise trips to various points in the Oriente where visitors can participate in shamanic sessions and even experiment with *ayahuasca*, which can be a dangerous experience for the uninitiated or for those who do not understand the language of shamanic guides.

At revitalized Inti Raymi–Corpus Christi festivals, ritual shamanic cleansing is featured along with typical foods, dance presentations, and fireworks. Associations of shamans are organized at provincial, regional, and national levels. According to the *El Comercio* Web site of November 6, 2001, the first national conference of shamans was held in Ambato during November, 2001, while an international meeting of shamans took place in Santo Domingo de los Colorados in July 2002 (*El Comercio*, July 20, 2002:D1). Traditional shamanism continues very much as it has for centuries, however, and exists along with a mixture of fakes, phonies, witchcraft, and alternative herbal medicines.[9]

In a multicultural country such as Ecuador, illnesses and the powers to cure them come from many different, distant sources. Power resides in the acquisition of distant knowledge, according to Mary Helms (1988:58–59):

In terms of the sacred or symbolic significance of geographical distance, the uncertainty or variability associated with distance, that is, the sense of "distance" as constituting some kind or degree of obstacle, may be as significant as the association of distance with concepts of the unknown or the "known about." . . . if distance is an obstacle, he who over comes, "controls," or "conquers" distance may evidence superior ability, power, wisdom, and worth.

Through their travels, both physical and virtual, shamans incorporate knowledge of broad networks of people and ideas, and control of that knowledge is a base of shamanic power. When people turn to shamans with problems of health, pending death, or even a run of bad luck, networks expand to include healers, patients, and the families of patients from many nationalities of Ecuador. A multicultural network centered on information about health, illness, and treatment forms one basis for cultural knowledge, respect, and identity shared by multiple *étnias*.

Victory through Indigenous Eyes

Commentary about the social hierarchy, past and present, is made by a few painters with apparently powerful insights. In *The House of the Patron*, by José Cuyo Toaquiza, a woman sits at a large table in the well-furnished living and dining room. She has a thick book, perhaps the Bible, open on her lap, and appears to be reading to family members who sit around the table eating bread and drinking coffee. In the adjoining bedroom and kitchen, indigenous maids clean and load clothes into a modern washing machine. Outside, indigenous cargo bearers with huge sacks on their backs head toward a truck parked next to the house.

Julio Toaquiza and his brother, José Alonso Toaquiza, well remember the time of the hacienda, emblematic of bondage and dominance, when people had to forfeit a considerable portion of their harvest to the patron whose land they worked.[10] Julio portrayed the oppression of that not-too-distant era in *Indigenous Life in the Time of the Haciendas* and *The Selection of Potatoes in the Hacienda*, both dated 1998. In the first, the overseer approaches the house on a horse being led by an indigenous woman; a barking, untethered Doberman follows the horse. The *patrona*, owner's wife, sitting on a chair in front of the house, holds a large tan dog by a chain while she watches one worker water the garden with a hose while another man with a fumigation tank on his back sprays plants. The second painting shows the *hacendado* seated on a bench in front of his house. He smokes a cigar and holds a Doberman by a substantial chain. Several indigenous men and women, a large tan dog at their heels, carry sacks of potatoes and pile them up for the *hacendado* to select the best of the crop. The presence of large, threatening dogs in the scenes reminds one of the cruel use of dogs to hunt and kill indigenous people during the Spanish conquest, as described by Varner and Varner (1983). Julio Toaquiza's art documents one of the reasons behind the protest movements that have swept the nation since 1990.

The recent political upheavals within Ecuador have been witnessed and recorded with the same detailed attention given to the natural eruptions of the Guagua Pichincha and Tungurahua volcanoes during 1999. Several other authors in this volume discuss the development of indigenous organizations and the actions of indigenous peoples throughout Ecuador as they have united in social movements and in public protests to change the course of participatory democracy and to enhance their roles within it. Indigenous involvement in major political events has been chronicled by observant artists.

Julio Pello, who painted the people of Tigua joining the 1992 March for Land and Life, also depicted supporters of CONAIE marching through an Andean town, perhaps Salcedo, to join the 1990 nationwide Levantamiento Indígena; they are burning tires and some women hassle police while another policeman trains his gun on the demonstrators. Juan Quindigalle presented two versions of the Levantamiento of 1994, the largely Sierran protest over land problems still unresolved since the agrarian land reform of 1964 and 1965. In both scenes, members of the indigenous organization of Cotopaxi march over a bridge and into a village, holding their defensive field staffs high as police try to stop them. Again, tires are burning in the street. In one scene, a policeman tugs at the poncho of one man while the leader shows a written petition to another officer.

Two paintings, quite similar in content and composition, portray different phases in the political career of Dr. Luis Macas. Both scenes are set on the Panecillo ("little bread loaf," a landmark hill that overlooks the colonial center of Quito), where Macas is surrounded by colleagues and supported by throngs of other Andean indigenous people. Before he took the oath of office in August, 1996, as national congressional representative — the first indigenous person so elected — he and other newly elected indigenous representatives were cleansed by shamans on the plaza atop the Panecillo.

Francisco Vega Ugsha shows the group assembled under a wide Pachakutik banner. They sit around a table where three shamans kneel and blow tobacco smoke toward them. The Guatemalan Nobel Prize winner Rigoberta Menchú Tum, who accompanied Macas during his investiture and the presidential inauguration, sits to the left of Macas and another newly elected congressional representative, Miguel Lluco. Music is provided by a drummer, several flautists, and one *bocina* player. A shadowy sky spirit blows its curative breath toward the gathering. The Virgin of Quito towers above the Pachakutik banner and Carondelet; the national flag and the statue of independence are in the left background.[11] Two gringo tourists with backpacks start to climb the steep, winding road. They are followed by groups of supporters carrying more rainbow banners that echo the real *arco iris* (rainbow) seen in the sky and identify the marchers as being indigenous people from Cotopaxi, Tungurahua, Imbabura, and Quito.

Another banner, adorned with the archaeological gold sun mask found in La Tolita (Esmeraldas) and adopted as the emblem of the Central Bank of Ecuador, hangs from a building from which people cheer on the marchers. At the base of the hill, more people, some with llamas, pour out of a small house and join elaborately garbed *danzantes* and other compatriots to begin the ascent to the congregation of indigenous power at the top. The volcano Cotopaxi looms in the right background, its spirit observing the rising sun and the huge rainbow that links a Tigua-Quilotoa setting to the political center of the nation.[12]

Julio Toaquiza places Luis Macas and other indigenous leaders (two men, three women) on a Panecillo-like hilltop. Behind them, a huge rainbow arches across the sky. Macas holds a large book of indigenous justice to be transformed into national law; in the distant clouds is a spirit book, the source of his traditional knowledge. Men and women, one carrying a rainbow banner stating "Movimiento Unidad Plurinacional Pachakutik Nuevo País" start to climb the hill. They are followed by two women bearing baskets of bread or cheese, and by a few men wearing fedoras and ponchos; a couple of them play flutes, one beats a drum, and another holds a bottle and a glass. They appear to be leading a multitude of people, most of them in red ponchos and all of them in white, round hats. Carondelet again is seen in the background, the national flag flying from the cupola. At the bottom of the hill, a nonindigenous man — identified as Abdalá Bucaram — runs away from the oncoming indigenous crowd, while looking back at it over his left shoulder. This painting, as the artist's son Alfredo Toaquiza explained, documents the strong role that Luis Macas played in uniting indigenous power with the voices of other segments of Ecuadorian society to force the ouster from the presidency of Abdalá Bucaram by vote of the national congress in 1997.

Along with the escalation of economic and political crises that occurred throughout Ecuador toward the end of the millennium came expanded indigenous representation and participation in national affairs. Their organizations, leaders, and spokespersons have become established voices of power in government policies and actions. Various protests of 2001 have been graphically recorded by artists who, more likely than not, were also active participants.

Rodrigo Toaquiza presents before and after perspectives of the demise of Jamil Mahuad. His first theme is the seizure of the government palace by indigenous people on February 5, ousting Jamil. Carondelet looms large against the background of purple, blue, green, and brown mountains. The national flag flies overhead and a number of Ecuadorians, most, but not all, wearing ponchos and white hats, wave red, blue, and yellow flags and hold a tricolor banner from the balcony of the palace where they stand. On the street below, two buses, one marked Congreso Nacional de Ecuador and the other Turismo, are blocked by three tree trunks and a camouflaged army truck. Between the logs and a barbed-wire fence, a group of soldiers faces an indigenous crowd. The military wear helmets and brown berets; they carry rifles with bayonets, and canisters of tear gas are attached to their belts. Antonio Vargas, the leader of the indigenous protesters, holds a written statement out to the soldiers. He is flanked by women and men from Otavalo and others from Chimborazo or Cotopaxi. Behind them are stereotypical Yumbos, bare-chested men wearing feather headdresses and body paint. People in this mixed crowd wave both tricolor and rainbow flags that symbolize, respectively, both the nation of Ecuador and the nationalities of its constituent members. They bear signs with clear messages: Long live indigenous unity. Long live the blockade. Down with corrupt politicians. Away with robber bankers. Jamil, we want justice for the people, enough fraud of the Ecuadorian people.

Rodrigo Toaquiza's second theme is the destitution of the ex-president of the Republic, Dr. Jamil Mahuad, the fifth of February, 2001, in which all of the indigenous people of the country participated in the indigenous uprising. Here the artist places Antonio Vargas in the middle of indigenous people on the balcony of Carondelet. They wave small Ecuadorian flags while the full-size flag flies over the palace. A bus and car are blocked by logs on the street. A crowd of indigenous men and women in white hats and colorful ponchos and shawls demonstrate with Pachakutik flags and signs that express opposition to corrupt politicians, naming Jamil, Noboa, the *diputados* and corrupt bankers, and affirm a resounding "no" to privatization. On a rural hillside setting that overlooks the protesters in central Quito, a couple from the Sierra is being cleansed and cured by two shamans, one a Yumbo, and the other an Andean woman. A third shaman, apparently from somewhere in the Sierra, blows his magical breath toward new indigenous leaders on the palace balcony. The underpinnings of shamanism mediate the contrast of rural-urban interests and places and of indigenous-governmental opposition.

José Eduardo Cayo Pilalumbo, who, with his brother Abelardo Cayo Pilalumbo, visited the Anthropology Museum, University of British Columbia in 1998 for an exhibition and sale (Muratorio 2000), painted and described the mood of Ecuador in 2001. Two finely detailed, seemingly similar paintings, show grim-faced indigenous people with round-brimmed hats — men in ponchos, barefoot women in pleated skirts and shawls — confronting uniformed soldiers who carry rifles and stand near their military truck labeled Fuerzas Armadas de Ecuador. The artist wrote his titles and descriptions on the back of each scene. The first title is *Indigenous Uprising*, the second is *The Military Detains the Indigenous People*. The artist accurately describes what is going on in each picture. The first scene shows the indigenous people of Cotopaxi Province arriving in the city of Latacunga, having been summoned by CONAIE to protest the government of Gustavo Noboa Bejarano because of the country's economic crisis. Here, "Soldiers with arms begin to confront indigenous people who defend themselves with poles." In the second scene, the army begins to detain indigenous people in different provinces of the country, and Cayo writes, "And for this reason the indigenous people unite more strongly to advance to the capital of the republic, Quito."

Through the lens of the painters, one can trace the history of indigenous protests that have occurred over the last twelve years, protests that are taking place more frequently, with an increasingly broader regionally based constituency. Protesters are also met with more governmental use of military and police control. The 1990 national indigenous uprising was settled with the help of church and government mediators. Local police actually escorted and protected marchers as they moved from one town or area to another during the 1992 *caminata*. Military in full riot and combat gear tightly controlled the 500 Years of Indigenous Resistance demonstration of October 12, 1992, and prevented many people from joining those who were already in Quito (Meisch 1992). One exception to the increasing use of force was seen in the 2000 ouster of President Mahuad. Portrayals by Tigua artists of recent, successful protests that have launched indigenous people into legitimate participation in national political life remind one of a phrase from the Ecuadorian National Anthem, written by Juan León Mera in 1865: "After the struggle, victory soared; liberty followed triumph."

Intercultural Knowledge and Power

Powers that derive from conquering geographic, psychological and social, hegemonic distances, as evidenced in paintings of shamanic and political performance, contributed to the success of the 1992 March for Land and Life. Its success was also due to several other factors: the insistence of the indigenous leaders on *peaceful* demonstration; the careful, though delayed, negotiations of representatives of President Borja; and the opportunity for residents of Quito to become acquainted with, and thereby support, fellow citizens from Pastaza. People from the Oriente tried to explain the nature of tropical rain-forest ecology and the meaning of their desire to protect their ancestral lands. Men taught Quiteños about their ancient shamanic beliefs and practices, while women gave demonstrations and explanations of their traditional pottery manufacture.

The strength and confidence to lead indigenous people into new realms of political participation appear in some cases to be associated with a close relationship with a shaman and a familiarity with shamanic knowledge. Eliseo Vargas, the paternal grandfather of Antonio Vargas, was a powerful shaman who spent his last years in Unión Base, near Puyo. We have been told by collaborators in Puyo that other leaders from Amazonia and the Sierra also are the sons or grandsons of shamans (see also Vickers, this volume). The feminine counterpart of the male shaman is a master potter who is grounded in the symbol system of shamanism and who clarifies and specifies the images that surround the male shaman. Such ceramists learn the imagery of the cosmos from their fathers, grandfathers, or husbands. Master potters also share the experiential knowledge and insights of powerful male relatives who are not shamans. *Sinchi yachaj* (powerful shaman), *sinchi curaga* (strong leader), and *sinchi muscuj* (strong visionary) are Quichua terms that link the spheres of shamanic knowledge, political leadership, and master potters.

Two *sinchi muscuj warmiguna* (strong visionary women), Clara Santi Simbaña and Denise "Apacha" Vargas played important roles during the 1992 march. Both are daughters of men who were among the early indigenous inhabitants of what was once the hamlet of Puyo and who later founded new indigenous *llactas* (kin-based territories) in the Comuna San Jacinto del Pindo after it was established in 1947 by President José María Velasco Ibarra.

Clara Santi spent her early years in the tiny village of Puyo and often accompanied her parents on periodic treks to dispersed settlements along the Conambo, Curaray, and Copataza Rivers. Her father, Virgilio Santi, originally from the Copataza River region, acquired shamanic powers that increased as he gleaned more knowledge of the worlds of other people through his own travels and from strangers who came to him seeking treatment. He became a widely known *sinchi yachaj* (a strong shaman), one who could "see" the cause of an illness and remove it from the patient's body. Clara learned by listening to his shamanic music and his telling of mythic and historic episodes. She incorporated this knowledge of distant worlds into her increasing familiarity with her rain-forest environment and her everyday experiences. From her mother, Antonia Simbaña; her grandmother; and the mother of her close sister-in-law, Soledad Vargas, she learned the art of pottery making and additionally, about the heritage of women's songs.

When Clara was about fifteen, Virgilio moved his family from Puyo to the newly established Comuna San Jacinto, and he also contracted her marriage to an Achuar youth, José Abraham Chango, better known as Paushi (curassow). The family settled in the Comuna San Jacinto and moved periodically from one location to another. Living among his wife's kindred in their territory, Paushi mastered the Quichua language while retaining his own native Achuar. Clara's knowledge grew as she learned more of her husband's language, customs, and myths from him and through visits with his relatives from Capahuari, a dispersed settlement midway between the headwaters and the mouth of the Capahuari River.

Clara's experiences bridge three cultures, those of the indigenous Quichua and Achuar peoples, and that of the nonindigenous colonists. The expansiveness of her knowledge and the depth of her observations over time inform her status as *sinchi muscuj warmi*. She has the rare ability to express her visions in ceramics and in songs. Over her lifetime, Clara has made innumerable pieces of pottery, ranging from very large storage jars to a tiny bowl from which her brother drank datura during a vision quest, to figurines such as the ones described earlier in this chapter.

Her repertoire of songs includes some she learned from older female relatives and some she composes herself. Many of them merge poetic descriptions of nature with ancient mythology and with her own personal experiences. In almost all of her songs, Clara reveals a multivocalic reflexivity through which she takes the role of actor while observing another's behavior, with references to herself and comments to other family members who may or may not be present.

As previously stated, Clara and Paushi participated in the *caminata* of 1992. Clara composed the following song that she sang in El Ejido Park:

> I am puma woman, I am black jaguar woman,
> walking through the mountains, walking through the rain.
> From my territory, I am just walking, walking to Quito.
> Puma woman, standing here in Quito, singing ¡*hoo hoo, jijiji, meeoow!*
> Standing here before the palace, I am not afraid.

Clara's father, Virgilio, was such a powerful shaman that he could transform himself into a jaguar and travel as one. According to Canelos Quichua cosmology, jaguars are corporeal representatives of Amasanga and sometimes are said to be the mascots of Sungui. Clara sings here as black jaguar woman, Amasanga warmi, the feminine counterpart of the master spirit of the rain forest, not afraid to confront the national government for her land and her life.

Another very well known master potter, Apacha Vargas, learned to make ceramics primarily from her mother, Andrea Canelos. Her father, Severo Vargas, was a strong *curaga*, a church-appointed leader who could rally his own people as well as mediate between church-state authority and indigenous dissidence. He was a legendary traveler throughout the Ecuadorian and Peruvian Oriente, and he acquired a vast knowledge of the flora, fauna, and indigenous peoples of the rain forest. He was a noted guide for other travelers, including the Swedish anthropologist Rafael Karsten and the German anthropologist Udo Oberem.[13] The knowledge Apacha gleaned from her father was amplified by her own experiences in the Amazonian rain forest, particularly in the Comuna San Jacinto del Pindo, where she and her husband, Dario Vargas, established their home and reared their many children.

As a witness to the transformation of Puyo, where her father had two houses, from an indigenous hamlet to a colonist settlement, Apacha experienced the pain of the newcomers' ridicule of her people as being dumb and illiterate. "Even the priest turned against us," she said, "while the colonists could all write and through writing got what they wanted from church and state."[14] These early impressions surfaced later in her ceramic expressions.

Her creative powers are grounded in her deep knowledge of history, mythology, and natural and supernatural beings, and in her existential experiences. She has made figurative representations of powerful forces of the cosmos, such as Amasanga, master spirit of the rain forest; and Sungui, the first shaman and master spirit of the water domain; and the soul of Sungui. Her ceramic images include every conceivable life force of the rain forest, from jaguars to rattlesnakes, from tapirs to turtles. During the 1970s, she made a series of insects — rhinoceros beetle, mole cricket, various larvae, and many others — that were so accurate they could be identified by an entomologist from the Smithsonian Institution who was doing research in the area. Her pottery statements about contemporary life are compelling: a worker's hard hat, decorated with the flower of a large rain-forest tree; two ticks, one thin, one fat from engorging the blood of cattle now pastured on land cleared of the forest; and Godzilla, Apacha's interpretation of the monster that arises from the Sea of Japan to combat the destructive forces of civilization.

Apacha's self-confidence as a powerful woman was apparent in a brief, significant event that occurred during the *caminata* of 1992. After reaching Quito, thousands of marchers assembled at the Plaza de San Francisco, in the colonial center, where President Borja was to meet them and invite their leaders to talk with him in the presidential palace. As a delegation of indigenous leaders and government officials escorted the president from the palace, he hesitated before the multitude. Apacha took him by the arm and, speaking in Spanish and Quichua, said, "Don't be afraid of us, we are all your *churis* and *ushis* [sons and daughters]." A photograph of this event was published on the front page of *Hoy* on April 24, 1992. By acting as a mediator between cultures, as her father had done before, she confirmed her identity as a bona fide indigenous person and a proud citizen of the Republic of Ecuador.

Several years before the *caminata*, a different sort of multiethnic, intercultural exchange took place, and it is remembered and discussed to this day. In 1987, we organized a bus trip to take about thirty-six people from Puyo to Quito to see ¡*Causáunchimi!* (We are living!), an exhibition of their creations in the art gallery of the National Museum of Ecuador (Museo del Banco Central). The dream of 1972, shared by the Whittens and many indigenous people, was now a reality. Most of the travelers were from the Comuna San Jacinto but four were not: the bus driver; a man who formerly taught school in the Comuna (and before that in Pacayacu) and who has several indigenous *compadres* and *comadres*; his wife, whose uncle was the bus driver; and the assistant driver who had gone to elementary school with passenger Severo Vargas, Apacha's brother, when they were boys growing up in Puyo.

We stopped in Salasaca for a buffet lunch provided by Rudi Masaquiza, a weaver and friend who has visited the United States a number of times. His wife was a university classmate and *comadre* of the wife of the Puyo schoolteacher. In Quito, the visitors were fed and housed in the headquarters of CONAIE. The artists examined and commented on every aspect of the exhibition, especially their own contributions. Pastora Guatatuca and Venancio Vargas lingered near the hardwood head of Atahualpa carved by their son, Alfredo, then studying in Russia. Estela Dagua delighted in renewing her friendship with a guide in the museum, a woman from Otavalo whom she had known years ago in Riobamba, when their fathers were consulting the same shaman. Several months later, the artists recreated their exhibition, with the collaboration of the Whittens and several townspeople, to celebrate the founding of Puyo. In honor of the event, a huge concrete replica of a *mucawa* was constructed in the center of town. The *mucawa*, now endowed by a fountain, pays tribute to the continuing, if diminished, importance of ceramics in Canelos Quichua culture.

A girl may learn to make pottery at her mother's knee or she may learn later from her mother-in-law or another close relative. Estela Dagua, for example, learned to make pottery from Apacha Vargas, her *comadre* and the aunt of her husband. Another of her early mentors was the late Pastora Guatatuca, master potter and mother of Antonio Vargas Guatatuca. Pastora's dominant motif was often the black anaconda, central symbol of the master spirit Sungui, the ultimate source of power. While working on her swidden garden in 1988, she was struck in the neck by a fer-de-lance (*Bothrops atrox*, a pit viper) and died before she could receive medical attention. She did not live to see her son rise to political prominence.

The actual production of pottery varies according to immediate circumstances, which change as a woman moves through her life cycle.[15] Creative ability is different for each woman and may fluctuate greatly during her lifetime. Until fairly recently, all women of Canelos Quichua culture were expected to make pottery for their families' needs, but this is no longer the case. Young women are extending their education beyond the mandatory six primary years and are going on to complete secondary school, technical and professional courses, and college and university programs that qualify them to work as nurses, secretaries, or teachers or to take active leadership roles in indigenous organizations. Others may spend a few years in domestic service for nonindigenous families, both locally and in the Andes, before returning home to marry and rear their own children. Pressures to migrate — economic, internal conflict within kin groups, and/or shamanic feuds, to mention only three — may place a woman far from a source of good pottery clay. This is an incomplete list of factors that have contributed to a gradual decline in basic pottery skills of some women. OPIP has attempted to remedy this perceived problem by hiring a few master potters to give courses in pottery making. How successful such courses were and are remains to be seen. If production of ceramics seemed to be disappearing in some places, it has been flourishing in Puyo and its immediate environs for about twenty years.

In addition to the household and ceremonial uses of pottery, I have mentioned several instances of women who want to communicate their cultural values to an outside world by making ceramics for museum display. There is also an important economic value involved. Potters and/or their husbands have long sold bowls, figurines, and even jars left over after a ceremony. Any number of women currently produce items to sell in the ethnic-art tourist market, either sporadically or regularly, to supplement the family income (Whitten and Whitten 1992). Quite a few women sell or trade their ceramics to obtain modern medical care for themselves and their families, especially for their children (Whitten and Whitten 1985; Whitten 1996). Their trust in contemporary Western medical care coexists with their belief in shamanic practice. Their exchange of beautiful ceramics for valued medical care follows an age-old pattern wherein patients bring gifts to a shaman in return for treatment.

Unfortunately, certain commercial pressures emanating from Quito are forcing standardized production of some pottery. In contrast to Galería Latina and La Bodega in Quito, which seek excellence in the art they sell, including Canelos Quichua ceramics, other retailers such as Camari and Fundación Sinchi Sacha lower the market by their insistence on standard, small-scale bowls, jars, and figurines that are "packable" by tourists. Under the guise of "helping people to help themselves," such organizations theorize that selling a volume of poor-quality bowls for about one dollar each is more profitable than selling one exquisite bowl for fifty or more dollars. Camari, which has two retail shops in Quito that sell low-end handicrafts and natural foods, is affiliated with the Italian-based Fondo Ecuatoriano Populorum Progresso (FEPP). This organization has its main office in Quito and concentrates on rural agricultural development. Fundación Sinchi Sacha is a Quito-based nongovernmental organization that runs a cavernous street-level craft store and café located in the Monastery of San Francisco, the oldest church in Quito. Sinchi Sacha also operates grassroots development projects in Pastaza and Napo Provinces.

Representatives from Camari make occasional trips to a new barrio of Puyo to solicit indigenous potters to make a given number of bowls, figurines, and/or jars of specified sizes. Sometimes they return to buy the pottery. Otherwise, they send word for the potters to deliver items to them in Quito. Sinchi Sacha, as the potters call the organization and its employees, usually asks women to deliver their pottery to Quito. The emphasis of both organizations is on standardization, not aesthetic quality, and potters take shortcuts to turn out pottery as quickly and cheaply as possible. These measures include using heavy grade, poor-quality clay, using insufficient wood to achieve optimum firing time and temperature, and glazing finished products with varnish instead of the traditional tree resin, *shinquillu* (or *shilquillu*). This results in crudely made items (widely available in Puyo and Baños) that sell for low prices and in economic exploitation of the potters who usually are not paid until their work is sold and who must pay for their own trips to Quito.

This sort of commercial meddling and manipulation is supported to some extent by foreign agencies such as the Inter-American Foundation, which has awarded grants to both Camari and Fundación Sinchi Sacha (see Inter-American Foundation Review 1995:27; 1999:25; 2001). According to Patrick Wilson (2001, in press), the latter has also received funding from the Fondo Ecuatoriano Canadiense de Desarrollo (The Canadian Fund for Ecuadorian Development [FECD]) for a three-pronged economic stimulus project in Napo Province that involved reestablishing pottery production, creating an ethnographic museum with gift shop, and building cabins to accommodate ecotourists. The undertaking was not only a dismal failure, but it also generated considerable tensions and even violence within the community (see Wilson 2001, in press).

Over the years, I have witnessed other efforts, usually well intentioned, to help potters by trying to refashion some aspect of their work, such as introducing commercial kilns, importing clays and paints, and adding ashtrays and coffee cups to their line of traditional products. These efforts failed because the innovators simply did not understand the depth of knowledge and creativity of the potters and because the potters themselves are confident of their knowledge and aesthetic creativity.

Sinchi muscuj warmiguna continue to reflect their visionary powers in the ceramics they produce and in the store of knowledge they pass on to new generations of potters and to interested outsiders. As noted in the beginning of this chapter, they blend contemporary themes into their traditional, symbolic designs. In the mid 1970s, when OPIP emerged from an earlier indigenous organization, Rebeca Gualinga collaborated with Amadora Aranda to make a small *tinaja* (storage jar) with three faces placed around the neck.[16] The wide-eyed faces, decorated for a fiesta, represent the national indigenous motto (now incorporated into the national constitution), adopted from the ancient Inca greeting, "ama shua, ama llulla, ama quilla!" (don't steal, don't lie, don't be lazy!). The coming together of thousands of indigenous people of Pastaza during the 1992 *caminata* inspired Filomena Santamaría to make a *tinaja* adorned with six faces that she painted to represent different *nacionalidades* and organizations. Following Abdalá Bucaram's bombastic campaign stop in Puyo in 1996, Estela Dagua produced a pair of figurines, one named "Abdalá" the other "Rosalía," even though Bucaram's running mate, Rosalía Artiaga, did not accompany him on this trip.

Later, Estela interpreted the meaning of the rainbow banner that represents the political force of Pachakutik and, by now, most indigenous organizations. She made two small *tinajas* in 1999, one with a bold face of *yacu supai* (water spirit) decorated with an undulating, three-tone band across the nose and cheeks. The neck of the second jar is filled with symmetrical motifs that symbolize the *charapa* (water turtle and seat of power of Sungui, first shaman); these, in turn, encapsulate bands of black diamond-shaped anaconda symbols. In the middle of the neck, the *charapa* designs are intercepted by a row of white anaconda spots that appear to float on a pink background. The shoulder of the jar is separated into sections by four rainbow arches painted pink, red, and black. The designs underneath and between the arches combine symmetrical and asymmetrical *charapa* motifs.

To achieve the soft pink color, Estela used a special *coral allpa*, coral-colored clay from Morete Cocha, north of her birthplace, Sarayacu. She explained that her *tinaja* represents *amarun cuichi* (rainbow anaconda), a very angry anaconda. Quichua dictionaries translate *cuichi* as *arco iris* (rainbow), but friends in Pastaza prefer to call a rainbow *amarun*, and they do not look at it as a thing of natural beauty. When an angry anaconda arises out of the water to span the sky, it unleashes powerful forces, just as Pachakutik and indigenous organizations have been doing since 1990.

Local, Cosmopolitan, Global

The Amazonian and Andean artists are actors in the political world and their political actions are seen in their arts. The actors as artists, artists as actors, continue to participate in an ever changing nation, and they are increasingly connected to global contexts through television, e-mail, their own travels and experiences with international collectors. Robert Layton's observations about the contemporary transformations of "traditional" creative expressions of Australian indigenous people seem applicable to the artists from these two vastly different regions of Ecuador:

> [T]hose who are competent in a cultural tradition use its intellectual resources to build outwards into the world. They construct metaphors, similes and other tropes that play on congruences between different orders of experience, and they construct causal hypotheses about how the world "works." . . . In a connected world, the social and natural environments promote or inhibit the effects of creativity but do not determine what the creative urge will produce. (Layton 2000:50)

Artists and political actors of Amazonia and the Andes are caught up in ongoing processes of democratization and modernization stimulated by global systems of communication. Antonio Vargas was seen repeatedly on CNN following the ouster of Mahuad. E-mail now brings happenings in once remote Puyo and Sarayacu into our Urbana home. As Smith, Burke, and Ward (2000:18–19) note, increasing involvement in a high-technological, global world does not negate local or regional ethnic identity and multiethnic affiliations.

Multiethnic interconnections encompassed by global events confronted us head-on when we returned to El Ejido Park on June 2, 2002, and greeted *comadre* Juana Cuyo and her son, Rodrigo Ugsha Cuyo. He had just put a painting, finished the night before, in the center of the family's sale booth. We were first attracted to his presentation of the basin of Quito, filled with white and blue buildings that expanded into the surrounding hills and mountains. Then his central focus hit us with breathtaking force. He had placed the Panecillo with the Virgin of Quito statue in the heart of modern Quito, and out of it rose the twin towers of the World Trade Center in New York City, black smoke billowing from the top floors. Behind them, to the right, are two smaller towers, both on fire. A jet plane, also belching smoke, is headed toward the ground. It is United Airlines flight 93. On a hillside overlooking the scene, people from various ethnic groups and a mestizo couple watch and talk about the unfolding tragedy. In the extreme right foreground, Rodrigo painted the Mitad del Mundo monument like a giant tombstone. On it he inscribed this message: "Twin Towers. In Quito?!"

ACKNOWLEDGMENTS

I wish to thank all of the Amazonian and Andean artists mentioned in this chapter for sharing their knowledge directly and indirectly. In addition, Marcelo Santi Simbaña, Faviola Vargas Aranda, Delicia Dagua, Alfonso Chango, Luzmila Salazar, Domingo Salazar, and Estela Dagua have given continuing insight into Canelos Quichua culture. Research has been facilitated in Puyo by Absalón Guevara, César Abad, and Felipe Balcázar R.; in Quito by María del Carmen Molestina and Diego Quiroga; and in Salasaca and Otavalo by Rudi Masaquiza and Julio Chicaiza. Rudi Colloredo-Mansfeld has shared his knowledge of the painters as well as a slide of an early painting. Pilar Cano, Gogo Anhalzer, María Fernanda Valdivieso, and especially Napo Albán provided history and hard evidence of the early paintings. I am indebted to the late Olga Fisch for her generosity and encouragement of our interest in Ecuadorian arts. My special thanks to Patrick Wilson for sharing his research findings from Napo Province with me. They filled a considerable gap in this chapter. As always, I am most grateful to Norman E. Whitten, Jr., for his store of knowledge, his advice and critical commentary, and his considerable editorial assistance.

The research on which this chapter is based has been an ongoing joint endeavor. Funds have been provided by the National Science Foundation (GS-2999), the Wenner-Gren Foundation for Anthropological Research (3287, 4405, and 5232) and the Graduate College, the Research Board, and the Center for Latin American and Caribbean Studies of the University of Illinois at Urbana-Champaign. Research in Ecuador has been conducted under the auspices of the Casa de la Cultura Ecuatoriana, the Instituto Nacional de Antropología e Historia, the Instituto Nacional del Patrimonio Cultural, the Museos del Banco Central del Ecuador, and the Universidad San Francisco de Quito.

NOTES

1. Information about shamanic performance, symbols, hallucinogenic use, visions, and power is given in Whitten (1976, 1985; Chango 1984).

2. Olga Fisch, personal communication (1979) and Fisch (1985). The influence of Olga Fisch is discussed by a number of writers, such as Cuvi (1994), Hunt (1982), Miller (1983), Rodman (1982), and Scheinman (1984).

3. Based on a letter from two indigenous painters, Ribadeneira de Caseres (1990) dates the first paintings to 1970, the year she claims Julio Toaquiza began to paint. Fisch (1985:100, 117) does not give a specific date but mentions that when she was preparing her Renwick exhibition she included five paintings of *danzantes* by Julio Toaquiza (see R. Muratorio 1981a, 1981b, 1985). Napoleón (Napo) Albán, a longtime

employee of Folklore Olga Fisch, dates some of the earliest paintings by Julio Toaquiza to at least 1980 and probably to 1979 (personal communication, July and August 1999).

4. See Colvin (1997, 2001), Colvin and Toaquiza (1994), B. Muratorio (2000), Espinosa Cordero (1999), anonymous (1980a, 1980b, 1998, 1999).

5. *Pintores de Tigua*, the catalog of the first-mentioned exhibition, is introduced by President Noboa's eloquent statement. The Guayasamín exhibition was organized around a series of large paintings by Alfonso Toaquiza, which illustrate his book, *Kundur kuyashcamanta* (2002).

6. Several years ago, artists began to sell painted wood items, including doll-sized and child-sized tables and chairs, small boxes, bowls, picture fames, spoons, and crosses. Their paintings on various carpenter-made things is usually as finely detailed and executed as their regular *cuadros*.

7. In July 2002, a local administrator tried to prohibit the showing of *Harry Potter and the Sorcerer's Stone* in a theater in Riobamba on the grounds that it promoted occultism. This sparked opposition, debate, and media coverage similar to reactions to the censorship proposed by conservative religious groups in the United States, Cyprus, and elsewhere. (*El Comercio*, July 13, 2002:B8; July 15, 2002:C11; *New York Times* January 17, 2003:A8.)

8. "Shaman's Supermarket" is the description given to this event by Diego Quiroga and Tania Ledergerber de Quiroga.

9. An article in *El Comercio* (June 17, 2002:C1) described efforts of Saraguros to rescue their traditional, alternative medical practices with governmental help, through the Provincial Department of Indigenous Health in Loja. The trained, certified medical team would include midwives, shamans, and specialists in natural, herbal medicines. The hope was to unify indigenous practices drawn from "a network of traditional medicine" with Western medical care. Two pages later (C3) this newspaper announced that six centers of natural medicine were closed in Salcedo (Cotopaxi Province) because the owners-curers lacked legal permission to work. Based on their findings of snakeskins, colored candles, and other questionable curative objects, the authorities suspected that these centers practiced witchcraft. Within weeks of the government's contradictory actions regarding alternative medical practice, physicians and public health workers throughout the nation went on indefinite strike because their salaries had not been paid for more than two months. About this time, ex-President León Febres Cordero returned to his doctors in Miami, a city favored by wealthy Ecuadorians for medical treatment, for an evaluation that led to his choosing not to enter the 2002 presidential campaign.

10. Tigua residents refer to a former large hacienda as that of "General Guillermo" (Rodriguez 1981:76). It was owned by General Guillermo Rodríguez Lara, who led the military coup of 1972 and headed the military government for four years before

being deposed by another military coup, whose junta remained in power until the restoration of democracy in 1979. For more information about the hacienda system in this region see Weismantel (1998 [1988]) and Umajinga (1995).

11. The huge statue of the Virgin of Quito is a modern rendition of the patroness of Quito and Ecuador, the Virgen de las Mercedes. The original winged sculpture, also known as La Inmaculada and the Virgen de Quito, was created by the eighteenth-century artist Bernardo de Legarda for the main altar of the colonial church San Francisco de Quito. Oettinger (1992:37) shows a painting by an unknown artist of the Virgin standing in the midst of patriotic banners and the national coat of arms. In the upper-left corner, she rides on top of a four-engine Ecuadorian Air Force bomber en route to battle the Peruvians in the "War of '41."

12. The widespread support by indigenous people of Macas and Pachakutik is reflected in the five signs carried by actors depicted by the artist as well as by his inscription on the back of his painting: "The Quichua people of Ecuador have transferred power to the elected indigenous congressman of Pachakutik. For the first time they have participated in the political arena." I wish to remind readers that native Quichua speakers may not speak or write perfect, grammatically correct Castilian Spanish. In a similar vein, their dating of important events in their paintings may be a fusion of different activities and therefore may not agree with reported dates such as the ouster of recent presidents. I have translated a number of their messages to English but have not changed their dates.

13. In preparation for his 1928 and 1929 expedition to the Aguaruna in Peru, Rafael Karsten (1935:72) paid Acevedo (Severo) Vargas one hundred U.S. dollars to obtain a canoe and crew and to guide him along the Pastaza to the Marañón through the territory of the hostile Muratos (Candoshi). See also Oberem (1974).

14. Translated from an interview about the early history of Puyo (Ruiz n.d.).

15. For more information about the techniques and symbolism of the ceramics, see Kelly and Orr (1976), N. Whitten (1976, 1985), D. Whitten (1981, 2003), Whitten and Whitten (1978, 1988, 1993a, 1993b).

16. An autobiographical statement by Rebeca Gualinga, as well as an inventory of her spirit myths and figurines, is presented in Paymal and Sosa (1993:153–57). A number of her figurines are illustrated in Whitten and Whitten (1988).

REFERENCES

Anonymous

    1980a *Arte y Marginalidad, Museo de Artesanías*. Quito: Banco Central del Ecuador and Dirección de Recursos Humanos y Empleo.

    1980b *Eucador: Hands, Light and Color — Ecuadorian Popular Art*. Eucador: Manos, Luz y Color — Arte Popular Ecuatoriano. Quito: Museo del Banco

Central del Ecuador. Washington, D.C.: Interamerican Development
Bank. March–September.

1998   *L'art Naïf de Tigua: Des peintres indigènes de L'Équatuer*. Nice: Galerie
Ecuador, 24 April–29 August.

1999   Pintores de Tigua en Bienal. *Hoy*, June 16: page 5B.

Bielenberg, Aaron

1996   Art from the Andean Heart Land. *Américas* 48(4): 5.

1997   Native Place: Art, Tourism and Community in the Ecuadorian Andes.
Honor's Thesis, Department of Anthropology, Brown University.

Burgos, Hugo, and Aaron Bielenberg

1998   *Painting Tourists: Indigenous Art and Tourism in the Ecuadorian Andes*.
Video shown at the American Anthropological Association ninety-eighth
annual meeting, Washington, D.C.

Chango, Alfonso

1984   *Yachaj Sami Yachachina*. Quito: Abya-Yala.

Colvin, Jean

1997   *Les Péintres de Tigua: L'art indigène de l'Equateur*. Paris: Exhibition at
UNESCO Headquarters, December.

2001   *Pintores del Tigua*. Quito: Ediciones del Banco Central del Ecuador.

Colvin, Jean, and Alfredo Toaquiza

1994   *Pintores de Tigua: Indigenous Artists of Ecuador*. Exhibition at the
Organization of American States, Washington, D.C.

Cuvi, Pablo

1994   *Crafts of Ecuador*. Quito: Dinediciones.

Espinosa Cordero, Simón

1999   *Hoy*, June 26, 9A.

Fisch, Olga

1985   *El folclor que yo viví / The Folklore through My Eyes: Memorias de Olga
Fisch / Memoirs of Olga Fisch*. Cuenca: Centro Interamericano de
Artesanías y Artes Populares.

Graburn, Nelson H. H.

1976   (editor) *Ethnic and Tourist Arts: Cultural Expressions from the Fourth
World*. Berkeley: University of California Press.

Helms, Mary W.

1988   *Ulysses' Sail: An Ethnographic Odyssey of Power, Knowledge,
and Geographic Distance*. Princeton: Princeton University
Press.

Hunt, Carla

1982   Olga Fisch: Gran dama de las artes. *Equinoccio* 3(3): 6–7.

Inter-American Foundation

1995   In Review. *Inter-American Foundation Review*. Pp. 27.

1999   In Review. Steps towards Sustainability. *Inter-American Foundation Review*. Pp. 25.

2002   Grants Given in 2001: http://.gov/grants/awards_year_en.asp?country_id=14&gr_year=2001

Karsten, Rafael

1935   *The Head-Hunters of Western Amazonas: The Life and Culture of the Jivaro Indians of Eastern Ecuador and Peru*. 2 vols. Helsinki: Societas Scientiarum Fennica. Commentationes Humanarum Litterarum.

Kelly, Patricia, and Carolyn Orr

1976   *Sarayacu Quichua Pottery*. Dallas: Summer Institute of Linguistics.

Layton, Robert

2000   From Clan Symbol to Ethnic Emblem: Indigenous Creativity in a Connected World. In *Indigenous Cultures in an Interconnected World*, Claire Smith and Graeme K. Ward, eds. Pp. 49–66. Vancouver: University of British Columbia Press.

Meisch, Lynn

1992   We Will Not Dance on the Tomb of our Grandparents: 500 Years of Resistance in Ecuador. *The Latin American Anthropology Review* 4(2):55–74.

Merton, Robert K.

1957   Patterns of Influence: Local and Cosmopolitan Influentials. In *Social Theory and Social Structure*. Robert K. Merton, ed. Rev. and enlarged ed. Pp. 387–420. Glencoe Ill.: The Free Press.

Miller, Tom

1983   Folk Arts Thrive in a Quito Shop. *New York Times*, 16 January:12, 16.

Muratorio, Blanca

2000   Etnografía e Historia Visual de una Etnicidad Emergente: El Caso de las Pinturas de Tigua. In *Desarrollo cultural y gestión en centros históricos*. Fernando Carrión, ed. Pp. 47–74. Quito: FLACSO. Empresa del Centro Histórico.

Muratorio, Ricardo

1981a   *A Feast of Color: Corpus Christi Dance Costumes of Ecuador (from the Olga Fisch Collection)*. Washington, D.C.: Smithsonian Institution Press.

1981b   Corpus Christi Dance Costumes of Ecuador. *American Craft* 41(1): 8–13.

1985   *Danzantes de Corpus Christi* (donación de Olga Fisch al Museo del Banco Central del Ecuador). Spanish version of the 1981 catalog, *A Feast of Color: Corpus Christi Dance Costumes of Ecuador*, corrected and expanded. Catalog by María Pilar Merlo de Cevallos. Quito: Museo del Banco Central del Ecuador.

Oberem, Udo

    1974   Trade and Trade Goods in the Ecuadorian Montaña. In *Native South Americans: Ethnology of the Least Known Continent*. Patricia J. Lyon, ed. Pp. 347–57. Boston: Little, Brown.

Oettinger, Marion, Jr.

    1992   *The Folk Art of Latin America: Visiones del Pueblo*. New York: Penguin Books.

Paymal, Noemi, and Catalina Sosa

    1993   (editors) *Amazon Worlds: Peoples and Cultures of Ecuador's Amazon Region*. Quito: Sinchi Sacha Foundation.

Ribadeneira de Caseres, Mayra

    1990   *Tigua: Arte primitivista ecuatoriano*. Quito: Centro de Arte Exedra.

Rodman, Selden

    1982   *Artists in Tune with Their World*. New York: Simon and Schuster.

Rodriguez, Luisa

    1981   Pintores campesinos: Sueños, recuerdos y premoniciones. *Nueva* 75:76–77.

Ruiz, Silvana et al.

    n.d.   *Pastaza: Manifestaciones culturales en la región de el Puyo 1984–1998*. Pastaza: Consejo Provincial.

Scheinman, Pamela

    1981   Olga Fisch, Collector. *American Craft* 41(1):14–15, 75.

Smith, Claire, Heather Burke, and Graeme K. Ward

    2000   Globalization and Indigenous Peoples: Threat or Empowerment. In *Indigenous Cultures in an Interconnected World*. Claire Smith and Graeme K. Ward, eds. Pp. 1–24. Vancouver: University of British Columbia Press.

Toaquiza, Alfonso

    2002   *Kuntur kuyashcamanta. El cóndor enamorado. The Condor Who Fell in Love*. Quito: Imprenta mariscal.

Umajinga, Baltazar

    1995   Zumbagua. In *Identidades indias en el Ecuador contemporaneo*. José Almeida Vinueza, ed. Pp. 247–71. Quito: Abya-Yala.

Varner, John Grier, and Jeannette Johnson Varner

    1983   *Dogs of the Conquest*. Norman: University of Oklahoma Press.

Weismantel, Mary J.

    1985   Descriptive Notes: Tigua Paintings and Drums. Unpublished manuscript commissioned by the Sacha Runa Research Foundation, Urbana, Illinois.

    1998 [1988]   *Food, Gender and Poverty in the Ecuadorian Andes*. Prospect Heights Ill.: Waveland Press.

Whitten, Dorothea S.

1981 Ancient Tradition in a Contemporary Context: Canelos Quichua Ceramics and Symbolism. In *Cultural Transformations and Ethnicity in Modern Ecuador*. Norman E., Whitten, Jr., ed. Pp. 749–75. Urbana: University of Illinois Press.

1996 License to Practice? A View from the Rain Forest. *Anthropological Quarterly* 69(3):115–19.

2003 Connections: Creative Expressions of Canelos Quichua Women. In *Crafting Gender: Women and Folk Art in Latin America and the Caribbean*, Eli Bartra, ed. Durham: Duke University Press.

Whitten, Dorothea S., and Norman E. Whitten, Jr.

1978 Ceramics of the Canelos Quichua. *Natural History* 87(8):91–99.

1985 *Art, Knowledge, and Health*. Cambridge: Cultural Survival; Urbana Ill.: Sacha Runa Research Foundation.

1988 *From Myth to Creation: Art from Amazonian Ecuador*. Urbana: University of Illinois Press.

1989 Potters of the Upper Amazon. *Ceramics Monthly* 37(10):53–56.

1992 Development and the Competitive Edge: Canelos Quichua Arts and Artisans in a Modern World. In *Redefining the Artisan: Traditional Technicians in Changing Societies*, Paul Greenough, ed. Pp. 149–68. Iowa City: Center for International and Comparative Studies, University of Iowa.

1993a Introduction. Dorothea S. Whitten and Norman E. Whitten, Jr., eds. In *Imagery and Creativity: Ethnoaesthetics and Art Worlds in the Americas*. Pp. 3–44. Tucson: University of Arizona Press.

1993b Creativity and Continuity, Communication and Clay. In *Imagery and Creativity: Ethnoaesthetics and Art Worlds in the Americas*, Dorothea S. Whitten and Norman E. Whitten, Jr., eds. Pp. 309–56. Tucson: University of Arizona Press.

Whitten, Norman E., Jr.

1976 *Sacha Runa: Ethnicity and Adaptation of Ecuadorian Jungle Quichua*. Urbana: University of Illinois Press.

1985 *Sicuanga Runa: The Other Side of Development in Amazonian Ecuador*. Urbana: University of Illinois Press.

Whitten, Norman E., Jr., Dorothea S. Whitten, and Alfonso Chango

1996 La paradigma de multinacionalidad y la red de salud en el Ecuador. Paper delivered at the Primer Congreso Ecuatoriano de Antropología in the Symposium Confluencia y Conflictos de Paradigmas Médicos en el Ecuador Contemporaneo. Quito: Pontificia Universidad Católica del Ecuador.

1997   Return of the Yumbo: The Indigenous Caminata from Amazonia to
        Andean Quito. *American Ethnologist* 24(2):355–91.
Wilson, Patrick C.
2001   Ethnographic Museums and Cultural Commodifications: Indigenous
        Organizations, NGOs, and Culture As a Resource in Amazonian Ecuador.
        Paper presented at the Twenty-third International Congress of the Latin
        American Studies Association, Washington, D.C.
in press Market Articulation and Poverty Eradication? Critical Reflection on
        Tourist-Oriented Craft Production in Amazonian Ecuador. In *Here to
        Help? NGOs Combating Poverty in Latin America*. Robyn Eversole, ed.
        New York: M. E. Sharpe, Inc.

CHAPTER 10

Tigua Migrant Communities and the Possibilities for Autonomy among Urban *Indígenas*

RUDI COLLOREDO-MANSFELD

Achieving political-territorial autonomy has become a foundational principle of indigenous movements in Ecuador, Colombia, Mexico, and elsewhere in Latin America. Fighting for the right to shape their economies, cultures, and politics according to their values within their own communities and towns, indigenous people claim space, both real and imagined, in a highly specific way. Economically, territorial autonomy suggests the enduring power of subsistence production, by which agriculture divides *indígenas* from industrialized mestizos (Nash 2001). Ethnically, it posits white-mestizo urban places faced off against a vulnerable native hinterland. Politically, it locates legitimacy in a decentralized landscape of bounded peasant sectors (for the Sierra), rather than sprawling urban shantytowns. Drawing on centuries of racial discourse, class subordination, and cultural resistance, the struggle for territorial autonomy tactically energizes the native movement. It even taps currents of neoliberal thinking about devolution of power from the state to private citizens to achieve backing from both the state and the World Bank.

Cities and urban careers of native peoples, however, challenge the premises of territorial autonomy. For decades, rural communities, especially those of Quichua-speaking Andean people on whom I focus here, have been emptying themselves into cities, large and small. While publications about indigenous people and their politics play up natural cosmologies, peasant organizations, and agriculture, native people themselves often live a composite of rural and urban lives. They work in cities, rent apartments, baptize children in urban congregations, shop in markets, and organize city-based economic and political associations. A political vision of autonomy anchored in bounded rural enclaves ignores this breadth of urban knowledge and experience.

If urban life has always fit poorly in countrified theories of native people, globalization raises still more concerns about the city as an empowering locale for indigenous society — or indeed for any ethnic or national identity that rests on the connections between people and places. Cities have been on the front lines of financial capitalist integration, pop culture trends, brand name consumerism, intercontinental migrant flows, and the creolization of everything from cuisine to music. As James Holston (1996:189) recently argued, the transnational flow of ideas, goods, images, and peoples "drives a deeper wedge between national space and urban centers." For native peoples who have tenuous claims on urbanity and citizenship, the accelerated, crime-ridden, globally connected millennial city can be especially problematic.

In this chapter, I challenge conventional understandings about autonomy and show how city lives can foster a connectivity that reinforces a Quichua community's push for self-determination. The space, mobility, and rhythm of urban autonomy break from the bounded vision of political-territorial autonomy discussed by most writers. Living in cities, indigenous people interact repeatedly within their communities and outside of them in fluid ways less tied to categorical divisions of place and people. Community stability and effectiveness, whether manifest in development projects or collective responses to crises, grows not through sovereignty over a place, but through interactions. Elsewhere, I write of this as "relational autonomy"— a potent, situational capacity to engage powerful others according to one's values (Colloredo-Mansfeld 2002). Here, I want to examine more thoroughly the place-making activities that pattern social and ethnic relations.

Particularly, I document where indigenous people tap the city's power for encounter and connection. When able, indigenous migrants develop such capacity by distributing their lives across places — by means of artisan production and sales, social spending, schooling, and formal and informal projects of mutual assistance — rather than by anchoring them within a primary location. In contrast to political-territorial assumptions about the importance of production, locales of exchange often orient creative effort and social contacts. At other times, though, migrants convene in the city's liminal spaces, such as sidewalks next to government offices, street corner miniparks, or parking areas of a tenement building. Here, in the urban interstices, the settings of action deliver few symbolic resources, thereby placing the burden of communication and coherence directly on the assembled people, for better or worse. In exploring how cities have empowered (and constrained) indigenous people, I focus on Tiguan migrants, members of a Quichua community with ties to Cotopaxi Province but who now live primarily in Quito. Hailing from about a half dozen peasant sectors of Guangaje Parish, colloquially known as Tigua for its river, the migrants number in the hundreds and live dispersed throughout Quito's southern neighborhoods and suburban fringe: Ecuatoriana, Guamaní, Gaupichu, and Santo Domingo de Cutalagua. I look, in particular, at three dynamics.

First, I trace urban institutions that Tiguans have developed to boost the economic and social clout of their art. While stereotyped as rural commerce that finds outlets in cities, native art as developed by Tiguans has often flowed in reverse. Throughout the 1980s, Tiguan artists shaped markets and development projects to channel urban artistic innovation and economic resources back into the countryside. Second, I briefly look at the preoccupations of adolescent boys, sons of the pioneering generation of migrants, and their restless mobility. Moving from the fixed points of family life, they develop their interests not by laying the foundations to settle down but by pushing the boundaries of their reach — their knowledge of markets, schools, and neighborhoods and their economic, social, and cultural capital to exploit the opportunities found there. Third, I consider the engagement of Tiguans with urban legal authorities. Coordinating with one another to cope with a capricious (or corrupt) legal system, migrants remind themselves of both their distance from the institutions of state power and of their mutual obligations to one another.

Following these processes, one direction leads to neoliberal structural reforms and the pressures of globalization. Ecuador's fitful efforts to solve its generation-long economic crisis with promarket policies have spurred a massive growth in the informal economy. Tiguans, for the most part, toil in this sector, cut off from subsistence safeguards, let alone possibilities for advancement. In neoliberal Ecuador, "informal" does not mean "alternative." Exclusion from the circuits of capital does not mean escape from daily competition, nor from the power of newly wealthy Quichua economic entrepreneurs, nor from the pressures of measuring up to an international level of consumerism.

Following the ethnographic lines in another direction, though, brings out the distinctive achievements of Tiguans. Their art counts here. By inventing a rich visual vocabulary, they have broadcast the energy of their fiestas, farming, curing rituals, and rural livelihoods to wide audiences. By so doing, Tiguans have also generated an economic vitality that restored, at least for a brief time, the partial autonomy and dignity once taken from them by backbreaking commercial farm work. A related dynamism thrives within their community associations. These indigenous organizations grow in Quito's cluttered swathes of market stalls, smoggy bus interchanges, vendor-colonized parks, and decaying modernist state offices. As both urban and Quichua collectivities, they are attuned to passing opportunities for community-oriented projects, even during an era of crisis.

The 1970s Laboring, Farming, Painting

The public face of Tigua radiates through bright enamel colors painted on sheepskin stretched over wooden frames. Simple, precise figures — men in red ponchos and white pants, women in dark skirts and cheerful shawls, costumed dancers at fiestas — take up the poses of country life against backdrops of green and yellow fields, held in place by brown, vertical planes of gully walls and cliff faces. In most paintings, the white-capped cone of the volcano Cotopaxi presides in the background. The rich colors, careful details, and decorated frames now offer such a coherent visual style that even when Tigua artists such as Juan Cuyo Cuyo copy the works of Frieda Kalho and Fernando Botero the result shines with an indigenous authenticity.

The thumbnail sketch of Tigua paintings given in catalog exhibitions, gallery materials, and Web sites emphasizes how this new expressive form emerged when Julio Toaquiza adapted a tradition of fiesta-based decorating for the ethnic arts trade. As Colvin and Toaquiza (2001) have put it on Tigua's Web site:

> Traditionally, the Quichua people of the highlands decorated drums and masks for festivals and fiestas. Painting on a flat surface is a relatively recent development. This art form began in the early 1970s when Julio Toaquiza, encouraged by a Quito art dealer, began painting pictures of daily life using sheephide stretched over a wood frame and a brush made from chicken feathers. Over the years, Julio has encouraged his children Alfredo, Gustavo, and Alfonso as well as many others in Tigua to paint.

While informative, this standard account skimps on economic suffering that initially induced men to attempt the art. When I interviewed Julio Toaquiza in June 1999 at his home in Tigua-Chimbacucho, I asked what he had done before he started painting. He pushed the story back, instructing me as much in the routes of Tigua peasant life in the 1960s as in its occupations. While his maternal uncles had moved over the ridge to the west and down into the center of Zumbagua Parish ("they sell gasoline; they have money"), his widowed mother remained in Chimbacucho to raise Julio and his brother alone.[1] Neither boy attended the school located on the hacienda a half hour's walk down the mountain from their home. Hemmed in within Tigua's social and economic world, Julio tried to move beyond it. At the age of eleven, he left for the commercial farms toward the coast near Quevedo, where he found work with a sugarcane mill making *raspadura* — a roughly processed sugar. After spending a year there and learning to speak Spanish, he returned to Tigua.

Over the next few years, Julio moved back and forth between jobs in

Guayaquil (including a year cleaning and cooking in a Chinese restaurant), stints of helping his mother in Tigua, and work in a lumberyard in Quevedo. "Then I fell in love," he told me. He and his sweetheart married and settled down in Tigua to try to live from the land. But in their third year together, their crop failed. Years of travel followed; sometimes venturing as a couple; sometimes Julio went alone. They opened a restaurant for migrants in Quevedo, gave it up, then tried to raise sheep in Tigua. Julio returned to work in the lumberyard, only to become gravely injured.

Despairing over years of fruitless effort and the physical toll it had taken, Julio visited a shaman who lived near Santo Domingo de los Colorados. Julio told me: "That lowland (*yumbo*) shaman (*chay yumbuca*) told me, 'you will have work. Before you suffered. You will now have your own work. You will not have to go around suffering like you have.'" The shaman informed Julio that a dream (*muscui*) would reveal his work and that he must not let go of that dream. Soon, a dream inspired him to paint a drum for a fiesta. Subsequently, a Quiteño folk art dealer and artist named Olga Fisch acquired the drum and promised to buy others that Julio could deliver. A second folk art dealer (remembered by Julio as Señora María Paula) urged him to paint *cuadros* (leather stretched over rectangular frames) rather than drums to facilitate production, sales, and display. Olga Fisch's commitment to buy all of Julio's output ensured that a small but dependable income would flow from his creative initiative. Here, finally, was Julio's "own work." It promised to hold their household's precarious economy together, when combined with cultivating crops, raising livestock, and picking up other odd jobs.

His art of the time suggests something of his life's newfound constancy. One painting from about 1978 photographed by Napoleón Albán of the Olga Fisch gallery shows two dimensional Corpus Christi dancers, frozen in profile, their arms raised exultantly against a flat, almost monotonous field of evenly and sparsely distributed plants. As I look at the slide now, I see the painting as a static celebration for tenuously stabilized lives.

Other pioneering painters similarly recounted tales of movement and fruitless labor. From a sector down the valley from Julio's community, César Ilaquiche went to Quevedo the year his father died, 1971, when he was fourteen. He packed fruit in crates for five years, "suffering, suffering." When he married in 1976, his father-in-law urged him to paint and offered to teach him. "Why do you go to Quevedo to suffer?" the older man asked. He believed that painting permitted escape from coastal work.

As it was first practiced by Julio Toaquiza, for César and a growing network of artists throughout the parish of Tigua, painting reawakened the possibility of a peasant-based autonomous livelihood. In the wake of land and labor reforms of the 1960s, peasants in Cotopaxi were often caught in an economic no-man's-land. Describing the changes that came to neighboring Zum-bagua Parish, Mary Weismantel (1988:74) writes, "The death of the haci-enda brought an end to many of the structures that had enabled hacienda pe-ons to satisfy their needs without cash. Yet they were also left without the wherewithal to enter the cash economy fully." Even where haciendas contin-ued as in Tigua, modernized labor practices (the replacement of workers with machinery) compelled the same transition. Without a stable income-earning activity, households wavered between unpredictable subsistence production and insufficient wages. The bind put people, mostly men, in mo-tion, although married couples also moved in search of secure livelihoods.

The economic independence offered by painting and selling drums and *cuadros* restored a limited viability to some peasant sectors. Drawing to-gether incomes from geographically dispersed places to sustain a commu-nity that physically sits in a remote location is an old social-spatial cultural habit in the Andes. John Murra's (1972) arguments about the ecological com-plementarity of Andean ethnic groups that attempt to control a maximum number of productive zones inspired many anthropologists to document both the diversity of vertically arranged productive niches and the kinship and community structures that manage them. But as Enrique Mayer (2002) points out, the idea of verticality is as political as it is ecological or economic. On the one hand, it focuses attention on the conflicts and innovations that arise from the communal management of a productive resource that indi-vidual households exploit. On the other hand, the model of complementar-ity underscores Andean village complexity that allowed different communi-ties and ethnicities to coexist and cooperate in the creation of production zones.

More than an economic mechanism, Andean schemes of complementar-ity culturally map the spiritual power of vertically organized places in rela-tion to one another. In the 1970s, for example, Quichua speakers in north Quito ritually enacted the conflict and intimate articulation of highland-civilized and lowland-savagery during *yumbo* dancing. Whitten, Whitten, and Chango (1997 this volume) demonstrate that the 1992 march of native people from the warm lowlands (the Caminata de Pastaza a Quito) enacted this symbolic complementarity to enhance both the spiritual and political power of their protest. The birth of Tigua art replays these connections on a personal level. Julio Toaquiza embraced the power of a *yumbo* shaman-healer to find a new direction for a highland life.

I proceed cautiously with this suggestion of complementarity, though. In the 1970s, Tiguans operated in an economic world that consisted of resource-starved peasant communities, commercial plantations on the coast, and a nascent market for artisan goods. Such contrasting and poorly articulated economic zones do not properly compare with the agricultural landscapes analyzed by Mayer and others. Nonetheless, I raise the matter of the economic and spiritual complementarity of places to make three points about transformations of spatial organization by Tiguans.

First, indigenous communities can adapt to, organize, and find power in space and place conceptualized in several ways. Although at the outset of this chapter I set up a contrast between two spatial modes — rural, political-territorial versus urban, interactive spatiality — they do not exhaust the ways by which people in communities coordinate places and channel power through them. Complementary organization of locales has long been a potent option for Andeans. Second, the exploitation of complementary productive zones shows how communities can be dispersed and their members mobile, but at the same time can firmly reproduce country life. In the 1970s, the advent of a new artisan trade in Tigua added yet one more migratory route for Tiguans, one that led into Quito's tourist economy. This new contact with the city, however, turned households back to a more productive agrarian existence.

Third, and finally, Mayer's analysis of the tensions that arise because of collective management of diverse production zones that are exploited by individual households foreshadows dilemmas facing Tiguans in the 1980s. Although removed from agronomic concerns, Tiguans' management of the patches of park space in which they sold their paintings sparked conflicts between collective efforts to ensure openness and inclusiveness in the trade and private efforts to expand sales and increase profits.

Urban Painters, Translocal Communities

From a few dozen practitioners in the late 1970s, Tiguan painting took off over the next two decades. By 1999, painters had formed ten different associations representing around three hundred members. This growth partly reflects the initiative of entrepreneurs who worked their way into established artisan markets, opened new ones, and diversified from paintings to other craft objects. The expansion of the trade also followed from Ecuador's deep financial crises of the 1980s, the uncontrolled growth of the informal economy, and the new international connections being made between peripheral artisan producers and well-heeled buyers in Europe, the United States, metropolitan Latin America, and Japan. This combination of factors displaced the creative initiative of the art from Tigua to migrant communities stretched from Latacunga north to Quito and on to Otavalo, the heart of Ecuador's ethnic artisan commerce.

The symbiosis between urban life and Tigua art started early and gained momentum through the efforts of José Vega. Reared in Quiloa, a remote sector even by Tigua standards, José, too, worked his teenage years on commercial fruit farms around Quevedo until his marriage to Mercedes Cuyo in 1969. The two stayed in Tigua for five years rearing their three young children. When frost killed their potatoes in 1974, though, he went to Quito to work on a construction job. Having learned to paint, José looked for opportunities to sell his art in his periodic trips to the city. In 1977, he scored a big break when he won second place in a national painting contest and earned a substantial cash prize that eventually enabled Mercedes and him to move their family to Quito in 1980.

More painters moved down from Tigua and other migrants in the city took up painting so that by 1983 they began to give a collective, institutional shape to their economic activity. In founding "The Association of Small Traders," José Vega intended foremost to give a legal voice to Tiguans who seek official recognition of their right to sell paintings in El Ejido Park in north-central Quito. The group deliberately chose to obtain legal jurisdiction in the province of Pichincha (Quito), not Cotopaxi, since they were told by a lawyer that if they organized in Cotopaxi, they "should go back to Cotopaxi."

As the first Tiguan artisan association solidified claims on Quito's park space, the ranks of urban painters swelled still more during Ecuador's hard times. The 10 percent fall in oil revenues in 1982 sparked a sharp rise in inflation and wide cuts in public spending. Things got worse. The first forceful neoliberal advocate, president León Febres Cordero, promised "Shelter, Food, and Work" in 1984. Instead, he opened Ecuador to imports, pushed domestic industry to the brink of collapse, and unleashed a massive rise in urban unemployment. Evidence drawn from twenty-six life history interviews I conducted in 1999 with painters from Tigua-Quiloa corroborates how these individuals turned to artisan work during these years of crisis. Only eight artists had learned their trade in the decade before the 1982 crisis, while sixteen learned it in the ten years thereafter. Although tourist demand, household demographics, and other factors influenced the profession's growth, the painters' own accounts emphasized that painting more or less afforded a steady income without too much hardship, relative to other work available at the time.

For the growing population of artists, El Ejido Park became the center of commerce, an exchange for ideas, and a social setting. Before establishing themselves there, individual painters traveled fitfully to north-central Quito, either briefly dropping in on Olga Fisch's store in the north or chancing it in the streets, hoping to sell to randomly encountered tourists. Now, with a steady weekly market, tourists, collectors, and dealers could come to them. As the painters regularly congregated, other urban Tiguans also showed up.

The new clarity in the economic geography of the migrants materialized in more creative art. Artists now spent time face to face, painting to painting. Looking back, Francisco Cuyo, president of Quiloa's main artist association in 1999, said, "we came to the park and tried to make a good presentation. There was a lot of improvement." Turning from the early motifs depicting uniform figures against stylized rural scenes, artists began to display a sophisticated cosmopolitanism. They composed scenes interweaving Catholic ritual with subtle Andean symbolism or else layering richly textured images of bullfights, dancers, and musicians in crowded snapshots of Cotopaxi culture. Some experimented with painting urban markets, capturing the world into which they were moving; others portrayed country life in a fresh way, by rendering interiors of peasant houses.

Paintings improved, but the accomplishment rested on the relocation and reorganization of household work as well as the newly stabilized market. When migration from neighboring Zumbagua broke down along gender lines, with men leaving and women assuming ever more responsibility for subsistence work, many Tiguan migrants followed Mercedes Cuyo's and José Vega's example and moved their entire young households to the city. Joining their men at the paint-splotched desks in tiny urban apartments, women took on themselves routine tasks of filling in background colors or completing repetitive details or decorating the frames. Their own compositions stayed small so that they could be multiplied and sold to tourists looking for inexpensive souvenirs. Filling this niche provided the household with small but steady earnings while men embellished more visible, larger, and expensive *cuadros*. Women also covered the commercial routes, which made still more time available for their husbands' painting. They left the house almost daily to tend market stalls or walk the streets in Quito's tourist districts looking for buyers. Creativity, then, does not inhere within a male individual, but was actually accomplished through women's new mobility and the *cusa-warmi* (husband-wife) division of labor that emerged in Quito in the 1980s. Men's reputations grew as painters, women's work intensified inside and outside the home, and households earned more.

In the midst of the rising urban fortunes, though, rural Tiguan communities still suffered. They lacked water and electricity, subsistence farming yields remained poor, and wage-work opportunities continued to deteriorate. To combat these troubles, Quito-based associations of artists became pathways connecting the economic clout of painting to the needs of Tigua. The Association of Small Traders and later others fostered traffic between Quito and Tigua.[2] To begin with, they protected and reproduced the identities of rural places by drawing members primarily from single sectors. They placed rural problems on their agendas and inserted urban painters into rural politics by physically alternating monthly meetings between Quito and those rural sectors. Cashing in on their artisan credibility, associations adeptly exploited decentralized development programs and the new emphasis on grassroots organizations. The Association of Small Traders, for example, persuaded a Spanish aid agency to construct forty adobe homes in three adjacent Tiguan sectors. Their contact with other funding agencies also secured a new communal house, a forestry initiative, and a soil-building project.

Associations, however, gradually dried up as conduits of money and expertise from Quito to Tigua. The groups secured fewer projects in the 1990s, so members lost interest in promoting or even maintaining the associations. Declining member participation, in turn, further weakened the efforts of leaders to attract the interest of foundations and aid organizations. Summing up the contrast between the 1980s and 1990s, José Vega told me in his abrupt way, "Well-organized, complete, that was good. People meeting, people listening in our sessions. People believed. Now nothing is happening. People do not believe." The current president of Asociación de Pintores y Artesanos Indígenas de Tigua-Quiloa (APAIT-Q), the second largest artists' association, complained that the members gave up regular interaction with Tigua-based members because people must work too hard for too little and do not have enough money for the bus fares to return to Tigua every other month.

The rise of wealthy Tiguan intermediaries over the same period further hampered the associations. Starting out as consignment sales of rural Tiguan art by their close relatives or *compadres* in Quito, the reselling of *cuadros* evolved into a more lucrative activity than painting itself. During the 1990s, people in fifteen to twenty households emerged as formidable resellers of Tiguan art, dominating the stalls in El Ejido, penetrating the Otavalo artisan market, and expanding international contacts for large orders. With kin-based networks of six to twenty-five regular painters supplying them, intermediaries made it difficult for young painters with little inventory to compete in the market. Meanwhile, the social and economic clout of the intermediaries competed with the influence of community organizations. When leaders of the associations periodically tried to end the practice of reselling they inevitably became mired in fruitless debates with both affluent indigenous middlemen and their dependents. The rise of rich resellers has thus led to an ironic reassertion of kin-based economic networks in the city, even as rural communities tend to orient social life toward more politicized peasant cooperatives and artisan associations.

In summary, during the 1980s, the growth of the migrant community overrode distinctions between a pristine "rural" domain and its opposite. The interconnections were hardly surprising. The urban critic Jane Jacobs

(1969:16) long ago challenged conceptual divisions between city and country when she wrote:

> both in the past and today, then, the separation commonly made, dividing city commerce and industry from rural agriculture, is artificial and imaginary. The two do not come down different lines of descent. Rural work — whether that work is manufacturing brassieres or growing food — is city work transplanted.

Through most of Tigua's modern history, the transplanting of urban work has been the purview of the white-mestizo oligarchy that devised property laws, haciendas, road systems, and civil regulations to fit the visions of modernity they pursued. Mass migration into the cities in the 1970s and 1980s, though, created new urbanites, including those whom I would call "organic professionals." People such as José Vega emerged who were articulate about community needs, well versed in nongovernmental organization (NGO) culture, and sufficiently effective in community politics to operate in an urban milieu. In essence, Tiguans broke the past monopoly on directing rural development by taking it on themselves to transplant a slice of Quito's multi-hued informal economy back to their parish.

This urban-based, artisan-led development embodied the new possibilities of neoliberal civil society: the promotion of local control, the collaborative approach of NGO-led development, and the social power of micro-enterprise. The trade's trajectory, however, also illustrated neoliberalism's persistent flaw. This autonomous space for economic and social development that stretched from El Ejido Park in Quito to the *páramo* in Tigua succumbed to the concentration of economic power. Shrinking from the countryside, urban Tiguans and their art became connected to and organized through the dozen or so newly wealthy households. The circumscribed economic power, however, has strengthened several extended, overlapping family networks, reinscribing kinship connections in the migrant community. For Tiguan children growing up in Quito, developing ties within these networks helps offset the centrifugal tendencies of urban life, including those of school and the "allure of the foreign," which includes everything from Colombian music to the possibility of international migration.

Schools, Culture, and Youth

Tiguan teenage boys whom I met in Quito seemed to tackle their tasks — whether enrolling in school, dressing for ceremonies, selecting music for a party, or picking out a guard dog — in the same way: by converting them into searches. This tendency seems to be part of a generic, global, consumerist youth culture. Eager to bring music to his class's end-of-the-year dance, for example, one youth rejected his collection of CDs, which featured the *música nacional* that no longer held his interest, and headed downtown. He cruised shops and sidewalk vendors, sampling collections of music from all over Latin America until he bought a bootleg recording of a DJ's performance at a Quito disco that featured Colombian dance music. Shops, however, were a less common destination for new things than were friends' houses. From my vantage point, living in a household of three boys, ages eleven, thirteen, and fifteen, traffic back and forth among homes dispersed in four different barrios was ceaseless. One day, the oldest boy in the house, Fabián, would head to a cousin's house to retrieve a dress shirt for a dance. The next day a young *compadre* showed up from a distant barrio to carry away furry, long-backed, short-legged puppies raised by the family's dog. The following day, the boys hit the road to see if a neighboring barrio had better volleyball matches. Between schools and these sojourns, the youths rarely came home before dark.

Fabián's fantasies could take him further afield than his daily travels. Failing to find a girlfriend among either Tiguans or classmates, he was stuck in a state of perpetual adolescent longing. He talked about his problems during one afternoon visit to me as he thumbed through a dozen photos I had of friends from an indigenous Otavaleño community until he came to a close-up of a sixteen-year-old girl in front of her neighbor's car. "This is the girl," he announced. He beseeched me to introduce him to her when he went up to Otavalo — a weekly destination for him as his parents have urged him to start selling paintings in that town's market. "In Otavalo, that's where the girls are," he declared, dreaming of life within the circuits of Otavalo's wealthiest merchant-artisan families.

Older peers dismissed Otavalo and Quito's offerings and pondered instead how to get a lead on work in Spain, Italy, or the United States. One of the most successful young painters spent two months obsessing about the recent return of his landlord's son from the United States, where he had worked without documents for five years. With his savings from restaurant jobs, this friend (a white-mestizo) had bought a Volvo bus and now worked the Quito-Latacunga route. The Tiguan would sometimes hang out at the gas station in Guamaní around 8:00 A.M. to watch the gleaming white bus pass by. Having quizzed the young bus-owner about how to get to New York, the painter computed how many paintings he would have to sell to afford the *coyote* (illegal guide for immigrants seeking to make it to the United States without their papers) and dreamed about what he would buy on his return.

Even schools, the one institution that would seem to offer youths some sense of grounding and place within Quito, have been turned into another cause for movement and exploration. When asked why they came to the city in the first place, Tiguans frequently cite the lack of good schools in their parish and their desire to find an educational system that will improve their children's lives. Once in Quito, parents stay committed to the dream of educational opportunity not only by getting their children enrolled in schools, but also by moving to other barrios if they hear of a better school for their children.

Tiguan youth, though, face school life with little practical support from their parents. This is a common situation for the offspring of migrants, according to Cliché and García (n.d.:70), who note, "parents work outside of the neighborhood and their presence in the school life of their children is almost imperceptible." In coping with school bureaucracies, youths begin to develop a rough and ready knowledge with which to deal with state authorities. These extracurricular skills of youths show up most when they must take responsibility for a younger sibling, as I learned in July 1999, when I spent time helping Fabián Cuyo at the age of fifteen enroll his brother Rodrigo in a *colegio* (high school). Fabián had a personal agenda for this task beyond his brother's academic career. He wanted to transfer to a more rigorous and prestigious school in the center of Quito, rather than the technical-vocational one at which he was studying accounting. As a first step, he had to get Rodrigo's teacher to hand over Rodrigo's school reports to him at the meeting of parents during the last week of classes.

The meeting began around 8:30 A.M. with about thirty parents present, who represented little more than half of the teacher's fifty-seven students. The teacher deferred administrative tasks to solicit a ten thousand sucre contribution per family (about eighty cents) for the end-of-the-year party and began to discuss what to buy. At this point, the silent mothers (only two of the adults present were male) stirred. Many wore their aprons or protective overcoats and looked as if they had just arrived from their market stalls. They debated quantities and prices, until they generally agreed on a sack of potatoes, forty chickens, lettuce, tomatoes, garlic, milk, and some desserts. The four indigenous women present who were dressed in hats and shawls seemed completely indifferent to the discussion, reserving their opinions to themselves. Fabián and two of his friends did chime in, although the women did not take them seriously. Even so, they were the only indigenous voices heard in the classroom that morning.

Finally, the teacher read his roll and handed out the grades. When Rodrigo's name was called, Fabián stepped up and took the report. Immediately, he went out and flagged down a bus to the city center to see whether he and Rodrigo could enroll in his preferred *colegio*. Returning later in the day, he complained that the school had already filled its enrollment (*no hay cupos*). For the moment, he signed up Rodrigo at his school. However, a month later he still had refused to give up his search for a better place, and went to visit a third *colegio* attended by his cousin.

In all the searches and yearnings, only Tigua seemed to be off the map. In 1999, none of the twenty or so young men and boys whom I knew made it back to their parish for the annual Corpus Christi celebrations, traditionally an important time for the return visits of migrants. Many have let years pass since their last visit. Nonetheless, their homeland can still command interest. Again, in 1999, for example, along with a Jean-Claude Van Damme movie, the most popular video that circulated among Fabián's cousins was footage of Tigua shot back in 1992 by two engineers involved in the Spanish-sponsored housing project. It documented the landscape, the house-building parties, and the celebration to inaugurate the homes. Fabián would sit on the edge of his parents bed, alone after his bored younger brothers had abandoned the room, watching llamas, mountain ridges, and adobe artisans flicker by, telling me with a wistful pride "My *papi* knows the names of all those places. I don't know them, but *papi* knows everything." Held rapt by a milieu too remote to be even considered a lost homeland, Fabián seemed to be cataloging its possibilities to learn what this place might offer up in relation to downtown's music, shoes, and shirts; Otavalo's girls; and El Ejido's tourists and volleyball games.

Tiguan youths, of course, share their interest in the offerings of other places and other people with Ecuadorian youth of all backgrounds. For that matter, they follow in the pathways of their fathers and grandfathers, who also set out from their home communities to gather the resources for adult life. However, the open-endedness of the Quiteño Tiguans' longings sets them apart from past generations. For their parents, coming of age meant marrying someone most likely from the parish and creating a home on inherited land. The generation of migrants to Quito in the 1970s and 1980s continued this practice, adding hearths to their parent's compounds of trim straw- or tin-roofed rectangular buildings back in Tigua, even though few had plans to reside in these houses.

Now, the parish has become transformed from a prime resource for living and a transcendent marker of identity to something more ephemeral for urban-reared Tiguans. In their city lives, places are more fleeting. Houses, tenement buildings, neighborhoods, markets, parks, and towns matter because of the goals they facilitate at a particular moment. Timing is crucial. Answering "where?" (to study, to work, to shop) means knowing "when"— if now is the time to go to Colegio Montufar for the best English courses, if Madrid still welcomes immigrants more readily than New York, or if Peruvian *chicha* rather than Colombian *tropical* can get everyone dancing at the next party. For a young, trend-conscious population, few locales hold exclusive dominion for long, and keeping up means staying informed and being prepared to move.

There is a rootlessness here. Years of occupying and deserting rented rooms according to concerns about education, crime, or proximity to fellow Tiguans, have attenuated geographic loyalties. But youths also have a practical knowledge and with it a willingness to experiment that I admire. Furthermore, their pursuit of the new operates more geographically than socially. Even young people have not forsaken families or artisan associations. In fact, in the first years of this new decade, despite their lackluster reputation, associations began to intervene again in community life and attract the involvement of young men. Now though, associations mobilize their members more in response to personal crises than to development opportunities. All too often, the problem at hand entails police, crime, and institutions of justice.

Law, Justice, and the Community

Rising delinquency and an ever deteriorating social order emerged in the 1990s as the most acute legacy of fiscal structural adjustment that cut state subsidies of transportation and other basic living expenses, aggravated unemployment, and weakened civil authority. Anxious about crime, Ecuadorians share their fears with residents of societies elsewhere in the Americas that similarly experience a polarization in incomes, an overburdened legal system, and a general decline in public services. Nash (2001:8) argues that global integration initiates these problems by depressing wages in favor of debt service, which produces hardship that "can be measured in rising crime rates, breakup of families, deteriorating quality of life, and the increasing gap between wealthy and impoverished sectors worldwide." Ecuador offers concrete proof of Nash's insights. From 1980 to 1992, after ten years of austerity measures, unemployment stood at 8 percent, underemployment at 46 percent, and monthly wages — in constant sucres — had declined by almost 70 percent.

Meanwhile, over the same period, violent crime had increased by 192 percent. The popular press obsessively reports such statistics. Crime frightened citizens all the more for the ineffectiveness of the legal system. The state had cut public sector services, allowed real wages of the police and court officials to fall, and let the conditions for bribery and other forms of corruption fester. In the face of state ineptness, people increasingly took the law into their own hands. Indeed, popular justice-making in Peru, Guatemala, and Ecuador has grown to become a key space in the production and reproduction of social order. Indirectly, coping with the criminal justice system — as a victim, potential victim, or an intimate of an accused criminal — increasingly shapes family obligations and community involvements in urban Ecuador.[3]

No exception to these patterns, Tiguans must adapt themselves to social demands of crime. Although an exceptional infraction, Humberto Vega's[4] arrest for drunk driving in 1999 illustrates how an urban extended family must organize to confront a legal crisis. Humberto was one of only two painters to leverage art profits to enter commercial trucking and become a role model for many young painters. In June 1999, he had been driving his truck up the Pan-American Highway, coming home to Quito from Ambato, when he was stopped at a routine police checkpoint in Cotopaxi, arrested for drunk driving, and incarcerated in the Latacunga jail. Although officials rarely held motorists for more than three days, the police planned to lock up Humberto for twenty-one days, the maximum term of imprisonment allowed by law. Married to a woman whose four sisters and their husbands comprise a pivotal node among those migrants in Quito from the western part of Tigua Parish, Humberto had an extensive kin network to call on in the face of such a crisis. A collective response was quick in coming.

Humberto's wife, Mercedes Cayo, worked closely with two of her brothers-in-law over the next five days. By the end of the week, they had hired a lawyer and arranged for two witnesses, both relatives, to come forward to offer testimony in the case. All this required considerable coordination since the four key protagonists — Mercedes, the two witnesses, and the lawyer — lived in four different cities. When trouble came it was not logistical but ethical; it involved learning to comply with the duplicitous procedures pursued by their lawyer. The man prepared a case that required the witnesses to swear to a story that was a pure fabrication. While drilling the witnesses in the testimony he had concocted and typed up in his office beforehand, the lawyer became exasperated with the witnesses's repeated deviations from the script to the truth: "Look," he pleaded. "These are all lies," he said, shaking the blue papers. "You are here for a lesson in lying. If you do not get this right, then the whole thing breaks, the whole thing is screwed." Suitably instructed, the witnesses marched down to traffic court on the day of Humberto's hearing and repeated their lines to the clerk. At the end, the judge's secretary asked the obligatory question, "Why have you come forward?" "Because we want the truth to be known," they said, following the lawyer's directions, and signed off on the forms. On returning to the lawyer's office, he praised everyone, saying that it went *super bien*.

The Tiguans had their doubts. I heard one of the witnesses talking it over with Humberto's brother-in-law and another friend. They rationalized the lies saying that there had not been an accident. No one had been hurt. Even so, all recognized this for what it was. "Do you have corruption like this in the U.S.?" one man asked me. I said vaguely that the U.S. court system works differently. "This is why Ecuador goes back, back, back," he went on. "The lawyers are corrupt, the judges are corrupt, the politicians are corrupt." In the end, the ploy achieved mixed results; Humberto served five more days after the hearing, eleven in all. Many of his relatives grumbled that hundreds of dollars spent on lawyer's fees went in vain.

Trouble with the law takes other forms for Tiguans. Later that summer, a Tiguan youth was found with a stolen stereo and television, arrested, and taken to Quito's main jail, the notorious Penal García Moreno. Inconsolable, his mother came in the company of her brother and a *compadre* to call on Juan Luis Cuyo Cuyo to ask for a loan to hire a lawyer. He did not hesitate in granting her request. Another young man was badly mugged — knocked out and robbed of his money, watch, pants, and shoes — only to be ignored when he went to the police. Amid the paranoia that now prevails in many barrios, the artistic occupation alone puts some migrants at risk of suspicions and accusations by their neighbors. Spending day after day indoors, they give others little clue as to how they earn their living. The *síndico* (lawyer) from one council barrio, for example, confronted a painter in 1999 and said that residents in the area believed he and his relatives were thieves, sleeping all day and leaving to rob at night. While the artist who told me this story laughed, I knew another painter who was falsely denounced as a thief and spent a harrowing week in jail.

A more troublesome case occurred in October 2001. In the barrio Chillogallo, two sons of an older Tiguan migrant named Segundo Millangalle[5] had joined a gang. Segundo himself represented the creative drive of the first generation of Quito migrants. He founded a Quito-based artisan association with migrants from the Tigua community of Chami in the mid 1980s, and also became a senior officer of a mostly white-mestizo artist organization in the late 1990s. In sad contrast, his sons suffered the mounting forms of exclusion their generation faced. Economically, they found it impossible to break into the artisan niche pioneered by their parents. Politically, their neighborhood had been run for decades by a tight clique of families that shut out newcomers such as the Tiguans. Violently making their own place in the city, the youths not only joined the local gang, but augmented its ferocity. Consequently, the neighborhood council enlisted thugs to go after the gang. In their vehemence, the hooligans beat up the father, not the sons, and then denounced the older man to the police who duly came and took Segundo to the *comisaría nacional* (national commissariat; police station). The day after the attack and arrest, Tiguans from both Segundo's family and association as well as associates from Quiloa's migrant community showed up at the *comisaría* to demand Segundo's release. In a savage and bizarre turn, Segundo's sons led an attack on the Tigua-Quiloan migrants right in front of the *comisaría*, injuring none other than Humberto Vega so severely that he had to be taken to a medical clinic.

The following day, approximately forty Tiguans gathered on the sidewalks in front of the *comisaría*. Going beyond Humberto's extended family, this conflict drew both present and past officers of APAIT-Q, the heir to the original artist association set up by Quiloa migrants. Some came from as far away as Pujilí. Suggestive of the complexity of the episode, the group lobbied first for Segundo's release from the police and his access to medical care. Second, they were going to hold him responsible for finding redress for Humberto and dealing with the gang. While angered by this episode, several past association officers were surprisingly positive as they shuttled among the dozens clustered on the sidewalks of Avenida 10 de Agosto. "I want to get more involved in the association again," a former officer who now resides in Pujilí told me. He saw this as a turning point for their group, a sign that it was getting back on its feet.

Confronting an ineffective judicial system, Tiguans turn to the spatial habits of the youths described previously — going in motion to solve problems, following up leads on potentially valuable allies, and selecting places for the utility they offer at a specific moment. Such mobilization, when it works, connects migrants with one another. It ties them into a moral practice predicated on an active community that looks inward for the resources needed to take on powerful others regardless of the setting. Self-determination relies on such efforts.

Conclusion

In her analysis of Chiapas Mayas and the Zapatista movement, June Nash (2001:120) traces the expanded definition for autonomy for Mayan people. She argues that it means not just self-determination, but "attaining dignity," encompassing "the generative basis of culture." For Ecuadorian indigenous peoples, decades of migration have contributed to this kind of dynamic autonomy. Indeed, for at least a generation now, direct, active links between country and city have invested households with cash incomes, social networks, procedural knowledge, contacts, market opportunities, and other resources to widen the base for reproducing distinctively Tiguan communities. And, conversely nowadays, men and women enact the values of indigenous autonomy in circumstances far beyond their parish boundaries. They negotiate with Quito's municipal authorities for special rights to sell in the parks, confront fellow Tiguans who have amassed enough wealth to threaten the viability of a community's occupation, secure due process in the courts, and deal with urban gangs.

In order to grant urban *indígenas* their political due, we must recognize the organizational possibilities that emerge as Quichua territory extends beyond peasant communities. Too often, even the most thoughtful writing about indigenous autonomy implicitly takes contiguous rural territory as the necessary condition, thereby linking transcendent indigenous politics to enclaves of subsistence production, as Nash herself does. Certainly, for the bulk of Sierran Quichua-speaking people, farming sustains household economies and carries paramount cultural meaning. Even for communities of smallholders, however, autonomy does not fit well within the confines of an Andean settlement. From the 1980s on, recession, NGO growth, and expanding tourist markets shuffled patterns of work and travel away from an undisputed cultural and economic homeland. Circular migration rooted in the *páramo* evolved into one-way movement tracing denser reference points in the city. Increasingly, it appears that, for migrant Quichua people, the community "is not a geographic location with clustered residency or neighborhoods, but rather it is fundamentally a widely scattered and frequently shifting network of relationships" (Lobo 1998:91), as has been noted for urban Native Americans in the United States.

This transitory place-making, often in the shadow of government buildings, packs an ambiguous power. A decade of mass indigenous protest — national, provincial, or communitarian — visibly concentrates a native presence in public to put observers and interlocutors on notice that there are collective, not just individual, stakes in the new ethnic encounters. Nonetheless, without a single fixed, urban locale of their own, Tiguans also must pay a pragmatic and symbolic price. Despite their efforts, communication does fail, interest flags, and a sense of common ground falters. Tiguan communities in Quito never wind up with a "homeland"— a place where their words and actions count for more, where the physical setting is not a neutral backdrop of action, but a place that comes to embody their history and values.

Many youths growing up in the city have known nothing but a widely scattered and frequently shifting life. It is too easy and misleading, though, to identify them by what they lack: intimate knowledge of their rural homeland or an undisputed identification as Quiteño. They have their own spatial sensibilities, including an intuitive feel for movement in the city. While oriented toward their own pleasures, the habits of moving, interacting, and seeking are a valuable political asset. The collective responses of migrant, indigenous communities depend on connecting across neighborhoods and congregating at the right place at the right time. Becoming more skilled at circulating among diverse locations, Quichua-speaking people shape a fluid Andean space — at once big city, small town, suburban, and rural — through which they attempt to develop their careers, protect their rights, and direct the affairs of their communities according to their own values. If not obviously exercising a form of territorial sovereignty, Tigua migrant communities still manifest their inclinations toward self-determination. In the context of a pluriethnic transformation in Ecuador, any and all new practices of autonomy deserve thoughtful attention.

ACKNOWLEDGMENTS

A CIFRE grant from the University of Iowa supported research in Quito and Tigua in 1999 and a University of Iowa Old Gold Fellowship underwrote research in 2000. Napoleón Albán offered helpful guidance on the history and marketing of paintings. I appreciate both his assistance and deep commitment to the art form. For the information on their lives and work, I thank the painters of Tigua, especially Alfredo Toaquiza, Julio Toaquiza, Juan Luis Cuyo, Maria Purificación Cuyo, and Francisco Cuyo Cuyo.

NOTES

1. I use first names because most of the Tiguans profiled here have the last name Toaquiza or Cuyo, making last names inappropriate for the task of differentiating among people.

2. Other Tigua artisan associations include Reunión Artesanal (primarily from Chami, although there are members from Quilotoa), Maki Rurai (explicitly identify as being Pichincha, although the leadership has historically drawn from Chami), Centro Artesanal y Artístico de la Cultura Indígena Andina (CENACIAT — founded in 1995 in Quito with members from Tigua-Chimbacucho, Quindicilli, and elsewhere), APAIT-Q (the heir to the Asociación de Comerciantes Pequeños and draws from Quiloa), Nivel Nacional (with membership from Tigua Yata Pungo, focused on non-painting trades, although most of the members paint), and the Asociación de Trabajadores de Cultura Indígena de Tigua Chimbacucho (the one group that explicitly shuns all connections to Quito).

3. Such preoccupations cut across all classes, although the justice-making strategies developed by the poor differ considerably from the walled communities and surveillance technologies employed by the rich.

4. A pseudonym, like all names used in this story.

5. A pseudonym.

REFERENCES

Cliché, Paul, and Fernando García

n.d.   *Escuela e indianidad en las urbes ecuatorianas*. Quito: EB/PRODEC.

Collier, George, with Elizabeth Lowery Quaratiello

1999   *Basta! Land and the Zapatista Rebellion in Chiapas*. Rev. edition. Oakland, Calif.: Food First Books, Institute for Food and Development Policy.

Colloredo-Mansfeld, Rudi

2002   Autonomy and Interdependence in Native Movements: Towards a Pragmatic Politics in the Ecuadorian Andes. *Identities: Global Studies in Culture and Power* 9(2):173–95.

Colvin, Jean, and Alfredo Toaquiza

2001   Pintores de Tigua: Indigenous Artists of Ecuador. *Electronic document.* http://tigua.org.

Holston, James

1996   Cities and Citizenship. *Public Culture* 8(2):187–204.

Jacobs, Jane

1969   *The Economy of Cities*. New York: Random House.

Lobo, Susan

1998   Is Urban a Person or a Place? Characteristics of Urban Indian Country. *American Indian Culture and Research Journal* 22(4):89–102.

Mayer, Enrique

2002   *The Articulated Peasant: Household Economies in the Andes*. Boulder: Westview Press.

Murra, John

1972   (editor) El "control vertical" de un máximo de pisos ecológicos en la economía de las sociedades andinas. In *Visita de la Provincia de Leon de Huanuco en 1562* (Inigo Ortiz de Zuniga, visitador). Pp. 427–76. Huanuco, Peru: Universidad Nacional Hermilio Valdizan.

Nash, June C.

2001   *Mayan Visions: The Quest for Autonomy in an Age of Globalization*. New York: Routledge.

Weismantel, Mary

1988   *Food, Gender, and Poverty in the Ecuadorian Andes*. Philadelphia: University of Pennsylvania Press.

Whitten, Norman E., Jr., Dorothea Scott Whitten, and Alfonso Chango

1997   Return of the Yumbo: The Indigenous Caminata from Amazonia to Andean Quito. *American Ethnologist* 24(2):355–91.

CHAPTER 11

Racist Stereotypes and the Embodiment of Blackness

Some Narratives of Female Sexuality in Quito

JEAN MUTEBA RAHIER

Negra, negra bullanguera,	Black woman, loud black woman,
Negra, juyunga, cuscunga,	Black woman, *juyunga*, dark woman,
Tu boca anoche me supo	Last night your mouth had the taste
A un mate de agua surumba.	Of a *surumba* herb tea.
Negra, negra bullanguera,	Black woman, loud black woman,
Negra, juyunga, cuscunga,	Black woman, *juyunga*, dark woman,
Hacé callá tu cadera,	Keep your hips quiet,
Dejá tranquila mi vida.	Allow me tranquillity.
Negra, negra bullanguera,	Black woman, loud black woman,
Negra, juyunga, cuscunga,	Black woman, *juyunga*, dark woman,
En la calle tu cadera	In the street your hips
Se cimbra como escalera.	Stick out like a stairway.
Negra, negra bullanguera,	Black woman, loud black woman,
Negra, juyunga, cuscunga,	Black woman, *juyunga*, dark woman,
De caderas de pantera,	With panther hips,
Te voy a hacé esta propuesta	I'm gonna make you this proposition
Por rebelde y altanera:	Because you're a rebel with pride:
Tengamos los dos un hijo	Let's you and I have a son,
Pa' que cuando yo me muera	So that when I die,
Sus puños color de brea	His dark fists
Conduzcan nuestra bandera.	Will hold our flag.

—Nelson Estupiñán Bass, "Canto Negro para la Luz"[1]

In this chapter, I focus on the way sexuality, a fundamental aspect of identities, has been negotiated and renegotiated by Afro-Ecuadorian women within what I call the Ecuadorian "racial-spatial order" from the perspective of the particular local context of Quito at the end of the 1990s. The premise is that identities are multiple, multifaceted, and nonessential; they are performed and performed anew within evolving socioeconomic and political situations, following personal or individual preferences and decisions. This requires us to view blackness in terms of personal, social, cultural, political, and economic processes embedded in particular time-space contexts, which are constituted within local, regional, national, and transnational dimensions.

My approach is twofold. First, I examine the reproduction of stereotypical representations of black females as hypersexualized beings in Ecuadorian society, or in what could be called the Ecuadorian common sense. Second, I analyze the narratives of sexual life history that four Afro-Ecuadorian women residing in Quito shared with me between 1997 and 2001, during long conversations held in a variety of locations. This examination provides not only the opportunity to appreciate the affects that these racist, stereotypical representations have had on the lives of these women, it also allows us to uncover the way these four women, as sociopolitical and sexual agents, have developed different strategies for pleasures and positive self-construction within a particular racist society. The focus is on the interface between the personal and the structural or societal, between self-presentation and interpellation. Indeed, the research reveals that different individuals or agents submitted to the same socioeconomic and political reality make different choices, which always express an original combination of both resistance and accommodation or adaptation to this reality (see Foucault 1975, 1978; Butler 1997).

This research follows the work of various scholars who consider the connections between power and sexuality important because the relation that we have with ourselves as sexual beings is a fundamental component of modern identity. Giddens (1992:15), for example, wrote, "Somehow . . . sexuality functions as a malleable feature of self, a prime connecting point between body, self-identity, and social norms." And before that, Foucault (1978:103) had already stated that "sexuality is not the most intractable element in power relations, but rather one of those endowed with the greatest instrumentality, useful for the greatest number of maneuvers and capable of serving as a point of support, as a linchpin, for the most varied strategies."

The work of Franz Fanon in *Black Skin, White Masks* (1967), although problematic because of its characteristic peripheral treatment of black women (Bergner 1995), has been conceptually fundamental to this research. For Fanon, sex and sexuality are not exclusively about personal or individual pleasures and desires. He approached sexual desires and sexual practices or performances as highly responsive to social and historical circumstances. Where other intellectuals such as Freud (e.g., Fuss 1995; Lévi-Strauss 1962; Merleau-Ponty 1962) had theorized about the body in such a way as to standardize the white male body into the norm with which all other bodies had to be evaluated and imagined, Fanon powerfully introduced the notion of the (nonwhite male) racialized body, the black body, which is, he asserts, in colonial and "postcolonial" (neocolonial) contexts, an ontological impossibility (see also Mohanram 1999). Although the former reproduced the Western tradition that includes "disembodying" the white male by standardizing his body, Fanon insisted on the opposite: the "embodiment of blackness," or the fact that blackness is nothing but body.

Stereotypes about Black Bodies and Black Sexuality

Stereotypes about blackness, black bodies, and black sexuality in particular abound in Ecuador. These stereotypes share many similarities with comparable representations of blackness in other national contexts or in the transnational scene.

The expansion of Europe into non-European spaces came along with the Otherization of non-European peoples and their transformation, from a Eurocentric perspective, into "inferior races." Indeed, since the beginning of the eighteenth century, European imperialist discourses of Otherization of non-European people very often used sexuality as a trope. In these discourses, sexuality is manipulated in two different ways, which are related to one another. References to sexuality serve to construct brown and black people as savagelike individuals whose character is denoted by "immoral," "abnormal," and "obsessive" sexual practices or, by contrast, sexuality appears as the very metaphor of the imperial enterprises by which white males conquer foreign and faraway lands that are symbolized by available brown and black female bodies waiting to be penetrated (Schick 1999). As Foucault (1978:32) wrote, "discourses on sex did not multiply apart from or against power, but in the very space and as the means of its exercise." Black and brown women's bodies and sexuality have been construed as directly opposed to the way in which white European women's bodies and sexuality were imagined or reported, idealized and standardized as norms for proper female bodily characteristics and behaviors. For instance, one can recall here the work of Sander Gilman (1985a, 1985b) on the tragedy of Sarah Baartman, the so-called Hottentot Venus, and the obsession of European medical doctors of the eighteenth and nineteenth centuries with her vagina lips — and especially with her so-called vaginal apron — and with her buttocks, which were compared to the same body parts of Italian prostitutes (abnormal or pathological white women), before reaching conclusions about the naturally enormous sexual appetite of black women in general.

Blackness and Ecuadorian National Identity

The previous statements briefly present known information about transnational, Eurocentric, racist, stereotypic representations of black women's bodies and sexuality. Although many of the representations under scrutiny here do share similarities with representations reproduced in other national contexts — at least in the Americas and in Europe — every national context does present a series of circumstantial particularities related to specific socioeconomic and political processes and histories that make of each one of them and its attendant racialized oppressions a singular story that needs to be approached with respect for its originalities (see Wade 1997:21; Hall 1992:12–13).

To comprehend the situation of Ecuador, one must keep in mind that black women's femininity and sexuality have been imagined and ideologically constructed in direct relation, if not definitive opposition, to the femininity and sexuality of two other categories of females: white females (including so-called white-mestizo females) and indigenous females. For the purpose of this discussion, I could limit the ideological landscape of Ecuadorian femininities to a simplified situation in which there are, without mentioning masculinities for now, three fundamental actors: white (and white-mestizo) females, indigenous females, and black or Afro-Ecuadorian females.

In Ecuador, as in other Latin American contexts, white and white-mestizo urban and national elites have imagined the national identity around the notion of *mestizaje* (race mixing). These elites have reproduced an Ecuadorian ideology of national identity that proclaims the mestizo (mixed-race person with both European [Spanish] and indigenous ancestry) as the prototype of modern Ecuadorian citizenship. This ideology is based on a belief in the indigenous population's inferiority, and on an unconditional, though sometimes contradictory, admiration and identification with occidental civilization (e.g., Whitten 1981; Stutzman 1981; Silva 1995).

Despite this hegemonic attempt at racial and ethnic homogenization, the Ecuadorian ideology of national identity results in a racist map of national territory: urban centers (mostly Quito, Guayaquil, and Cuenca) are associated with modernity, and rural areas are considered places of racial inferiority, violence, backwardness, savagery, and cultural deprivation. These areas, mostly inhabited by nonwhites or nonwhite-mestizos, have been viewed by the elites as representing major challenges to the full national development toward the ideals of modernity. For Ecuador, *mestizaje*, as Norman Whitten explains, does not mean that whites "indianize" themselves, but that, on the contrary, Indians whiten themselves "racially" and culturally: the official imagination of Ecuadorian national identity "[is] an ideology of *blanquea-miento* within the globalizing framework of *mestizaje*" (Whitten, personal communication; see also 2003).

In this official imagination of *ecuatorianidad* ("Ecuadorian-ness"), there is logically no place for blacks: they must remain peripheral. Afro-Ecuadorians, who represent between 5 percent and 10 percent of the national population, are the ultimate Other, some sort of a historical accident, a noise in the ideological system of nationality, a pollution in the Ecuadorian genetic pool. The best example of noncitizenship, "they are not part of *mestizaje*," unlike indigenous peoples (Muratorio 1994).[2] In the logic of the national racial-spatial order, the two traditional regions of blackness (both developed during the colonial period), the Province of Esmeraldas and the Chota-Mira Valley, are looked down on by whites and white-mestizos; this is what Peter Wade (1993) calls "cultural topography."

The ideological outsiderness of blacks in the biology of national identity is denoted in the discourse about black women's bodies and sexuality. Emma Cervone (2000) has written on the characteristic masculinity of the Ecuadorian elites' voice and imagination of *mestizaje*. The latter logically leads to the conception of (blond and blue-eyed) white and white-mestizo females and their sexuality as aesthetically and morally ideal. These ideals constitute more or less violent standards that every woman should try to attain at all costs. This standardization and its attendant construction of Other bodies have been encrypted in various aspects of the Ecuadorian landscape: everyday vocabulary and conversations, written and visual representations in the media, texts of songs and popular culture, and literature. Elsewhere, I have written on the place of blackness in national and other Ecuadorian beauty contests, in which black beauty queens altered the color of their eyes as well as the color and consistency of their hair to approximate these standards (Rahier 1998, 1999a).

In August 1999, on the plane from Miami to Quito, I met an Ecuadorian white-mestizo man, an acquaintance of mine whom I had not seen for years. He is an architect who was working at the time in the office of Quito's mayor. He explained that he had been traveling in the United States with some of his colleagues to look for funding for one of the mayor's construction projects. It was an evening flight, the plane was half empty, and we had been drinking wine with our dinner. After requesting some more wine from the flight attendant, he asked me why I was going to Ecuador this time. I responded that I was working on a new research project. He wanted more details and I began to explain that the project focused on black women's sexuality in Quito, as well as on the ways the racial order was, or was not, a major factor in the shaping of black people's, and in this specific case, black women's sexuality.

I wanted to go further in my explanation when he suddenly interrupted me to share his views on the matter. Making an abstraction of my own blackness, he went on to theorize that unlike white people and "Indians," he said, black people wherever they are found, fail to repress their sexuality; they had a much freer rapport with their bodies; their sexuality and their natural sensuality were important and normal parts of their daily lives. That is why they dance the way they dance, with lascivious body movements. "Even the way they walk," he said, "even the way they walk." From watching the facial expression he had at that precise moment, his wine glass in his hand, his eyes lost on the ceiling of the plane's cabin, I wondered if he was daydreaming about one of his phantasms. For him, this "sexual permissiveness," as he seemed to suggest, explained the particularity of many of black people's daily behaviors. His authoritative monologue was beginning to irritate me just when one of his colleagues asked him to join his group a few rows away. The relatively quiet violence of his "commonsensical comments" goes to the heart of what I try to accomplish in this chapter.

It is notable that just as it has been the case in other Latin American contexts, twentieth-century writers from regions associated with blackness have reproduced these stereotypes about black women's bodies and sexuality in their poems. That is the case of the Esmeraldian writer, Nelson Estupiñán Bass, in the epigraph of this chapter.[3]

From the perspective of modern, urban, Ecuadorian society, indigenous or "Indian" female bodies and sexuality have been construed as if they exist off to one side of the fundamental opposition described between white women and black women (see Rahier 1999a:108–10). If in many ways indigenous females do unequivocally enter in the category of "women" with the black females, unlike the latter, they do not appear in the same position when references to physical attractiveness and exotic sexuality are made. In fact, in the popular iconography, as well as in written texts, indigenous women very often appear as nonsexual beings who supposedly smell bad; who submissively work all the time to raise their children, work the fields, and sell in the markets; and who often beg at traffic lights with their most recently born child tied to their backs. Their bodies are usually represented as unattractively small and deprived of the curves that characterize black women's bodies in the popular imaginary. (An exception should be made here concerning indigenous women from Otavalo and their changing representations.)[4]

This relative "attractiveness" of black women when compared with the similar processes of imagination and cultural construction of indigenous females' femininity, bodies, and sexuality should not be simplistically interpreted as a positive feature within the racial order because, as Lola Young (1999:81) wrote,

> For the black women who have been deemed beautiful and objectified by a white masculinist gaze, their distance from the white feminine ideal has not produced unambiguous revulsion . . . : rather, it has been a substantial part of their appeal. However, this attraction, based on the exoticism of otherness, is just as problematic as the racism from which it has emerged.

Fragments of Four Narratives of Black Female Sexuality

Dominant stereotypical representations led the first woman, Salomé, who was born in Quito, to become obsessed with her virginity and to obtain and preserve respectability. Throughout the years, since her teens, she developed a phobia (her own term) for penetration that she had been unable to shed until very recently. Two of the other women, María and Yesenya, were born in rural areas and migrated to Quito, where they ended up becoming sexual workers.[5] Unlike Salomé, they have been, in a way, "capitalizing" on the popularity of stereotypes of black women's hypersexuality by selling their bodies to multiple penetrations by, mostly, white and white-mestizo men. The fourth woman, Saída, graduated from a university in Ibarra, the capital of Imbabura Province. She lives in Quito and self-identifies as a political activist engaged in the plight of Afro-Ecuadorians.

SALOMÉ

Salomé: I was an attractive adolescent. They called me *rompe corazones*, "heart breaker." I had quite a few white and white-mestizo boys chasing after me, because I was born and I grew up among white-mestizos, in Quito. Until adolescence I didn't really have black friends. The only black people around me were my relatives, but they lived far away, in the [Chota] Valley. When walking in unknown white-mestizo neighborhoods, I experienced racist aggression. If I crossed the street where some white-mestizo male kids were hanging out, they immediately shouted things like *negra rica*, "delicious black woman," "how attractive this black woman is," and things like that. Very often, they emphasized the curves of black women's legs and behind by saying: "That black woman has a nice butt!" I was able to understand that what they were saying was not complimentary but rather profoundly disrespectful. That is when I began feeling my condition as a black woman and as a sexual object. They have so many mottos about the fact that men can cure illnesses by having sex with black women, like to cure the kidneys. They say that black women have a lot of sexual energy. . . . I realized that what they were really after was my body, they just wanted to have sex with me. It would be quite strange, in fact, to see a white or white-mestizo Ecuadorian man wanting to be with a black woman as a partner for life. (fragment of a 1997 recorded conversation)

I met Salomé[6] for the first time in 1996, during a party organized in Quito by a friend we had in common. Thanks to the financial help of her older brother, who was then single and who was working as a government employee, Salomé graduated from a local university with the equivalent of a bachelor of arts degree. She now works for a foreign NGO. She was born in Quito to working-class parents who migrated from the Chota-Mira Valley. We progressively became good friends, and we meet on numerous occasions every time I visit the country. Puzzled by her insistence to claim a Quiteño background, I began the very first interview by asking her to share with me the way she conceived her black identity, how she identifies as a black Quiteña and what that means vis-à-vis the so-called traditional black communities, particularly the Chota-Mira Valley. I am used to spending time with Afro-Ecuadorians involved in political activism who often visit Afro-Esmeraldian and Afro-Choteño villages, who reproduce a discourse about black identity in which rural black communities appear as the source of "authentic blackness" and Afro-Ecuadorian traditions. I was, then, surprised by the negative tone Salomé adopted when referring to rural Ecuadorian blacks, who she sees as somehow inferior to her and to the other more educated, urban, young blacks in general.

Salomé: That's a fact, we are Afro-Ecuadorians. Our roots are in Africa. That's where our ancestors came from. . . . But, at the same time, there are two groups here in Ecuador that are located in a specific region: Esmeraldas and the Chota Valley. I do not identify with any of these two groups! Because I grew up in another space, I grew up in another environment, with other customs, with another worldview, and fundamentally with the objective of surpassing myself [superarme], with the desire of becoming better, with the commitment of showing to the world that black people can also be important. Unfortunately, there is a consensus out there that black people from Ecuador do not like to work. Many Ecuadorian blacks accept life with the little they have. They are not very ambitious.

JMR: It seems that you have a lot of negative feelings toward the people of the valley.

S: It's very simple. I wasn't born in that environment. Therefore, I cannot say that I identify with that group. Because there is a tradition out there that wants us, the black people, to always identify as a unified and homogenous group. It's a fact: I was born in another space, in another environment. . . . I do not feel as a part of that group. I do not identify with the people of the valley, or of Esmeraldas. I identify as an Ecuadorian! I feel Ecuadorian, and I like to be an Ecuadorian. It infuriates me that people do not believe . . . or accept that I am from Quito. Why is it that if you're black you automatically must be from Chota or from Esmeraldas?

Although she recognizes the existence of racism, which she says she has experienced since the age of ten or twelve, she nevertheless claims that most of the negative ideas about black people in Ecuador (see Rahier 1999b), and particularly the negative images of black women, are justified.

Salomé: It is very hard to feel racism, when young white and white-mestizo men denigrate you in the streets or segregate you just because you're black. It hurts. But I think that the people who act that way do so because they are ignorant, they don't know any better. But, I think that these racist things are also happening because of the people of my race. Because we have to acknowledge that what they say is true. Although we are a relatively small portion of the Ecuadorian population, the number of black men who are involved in delinquent acts is quite high. Black people have always been seen as violent and dangerous people. Even myself, as a black woman, I am sometimes afraid to get too close to them, particularly when I am alone. On the basis of my personal experience, I cannot say that it's a lie that black people are lazy, that they don't do a thing, and that they only think about leisure, that they are vulgar and disrespectful, that one has to be afraid of them. It is true because I have lived it. Unfortunately, because of the bad economic situation of the country, the majority of the sexual workers are indeed black women.

JMR: The majority?

S: Yes, I think that it's the majority. That's what I was able to observe in the streets of the city. Perhaps it's not the majority, but at least many of them are. Of course, there are many social and cultural reasons that have brought people to characterize black women as women who are preoccupied by sexual satisfaction. Unfortunately, they don't say this or that other woman. They simply say "black women!" And this is not true! And all of us, black women, we suffer from these images. Usually, when I wait for the bus in the street, it does not matter if I have a skirt that goes from the belt down to my shoes, white and white-mestizo men approach me and ask how much I charge for sexual services. They think that all black women are prostitutes or potential prostitutes who have children like rabbits, one after the other, from adolescence on.

Salomé has clearly been influenced profoundly by the racist, stereotypical representations of black people in Ecuadorian society to the point that she obviously contradicts herself. On the one hand, she accepts the stereotypical representations at face value and reaffirms their validity, while on the other hand, she wants to insist that not all black women fit the stereotype.

She explained how, for her, sexuality, and especially sexual penetration, has always been something very special that she wished to reserve for the man who would be her partner for life. She also explained that she had several boyfriends (mostly whites and white-mestizos) with whom she always refused to give the so-called *última prueba del amor* (the ultimate proof of love), that is to say vaginal penetration. She always kept in mind that she needed to educate herself, that she would not have children before finishing her education and before finding the right man with whom to found a family. She explained, referring to specific experiences she had, that she did not like either Afro-Ecuadorian men or Ecuadorian white and white-mestizo men because of their machista and their lack of respect for women in general, and particularly black women. She explained how she had grown up preferring European and North American men because, she said, they are more respectful of black women than are Ecuadorian men. She believes that they have more respect for blacks because in Europe and North America, it is normal to find respectable black women and men in a middle-class position, as professionals. She sees me as a good example of that. She stated that the depreciative comments of white and white-mestizo women concerning black females are hurtful.[7]

She also explained that she had reached her thirty-second birthday without losing her virginity thanks to the practice of masturbation. She had also developed, along with a clitoridean sexuality, a real phobia for penetration that seems to relate to her aspiration for respectability. As she puts it herself:

First, being a virgin, I always thought of sexual intercourse as something very special, healthy, as something that is not dirty. On the contrary, I think about it as something very special that one shares with somebody special. I think of [clitoridean] masturbation in the same way, as a search, an encounter with one's own body. Because if to scratch your nose when you have been bit by an insect gives you personal satisfaction, why not do it with the rest of your body? And all that crap about the fact that masturbation is a sin, I don't believe in it. I have masturbated since the beginning of my sexual awareness. Sometimes I masturbate a lot. I think that it is the most natural way to let off the steam of one's own sexual energy without needing the presence of a man.

I discovered that something was wrong with me, that each time I wanted to offer my body for penetration, I was invaded by a tremendous panic, like a trauma, a phobia of penetration. I was invaded by the sensation that I was going to be badly damaged. And sometimes, I even wished that it would be good in a way if one day someone would rape me, so that the fear that was in my head would go away.

Then she referred to specific occasions when she had tried to "give the ultimate proof of love" to a (European) boyfriend and was, at the very last moment, unable to let it happen. She emotionally explained how much that "phobia" had hurt her and made the possibility of a stable relationship with a man unreachable. She expressed her feelings of inadequacy about her womanhood. Through the years, Salomé developed a cyst around her uterus that progressively provoked unbearable pain to the point at which she decided to see a doctor. Two gynecologists who examined her diagnosed a psychosomatic ailment and expressed their surprise at a woman of her age who was still a virgin. For more than a year, she tried to avoid the cost of a surgical operation by visiting *curanderos* (healers) to no avail. Her cyst was surgically removed in 1999. A year after the operation, she forced herself to lose her virginity with the young European man with whom she was involved at the time, without telling him anything about her condition. To her great surprise, as she says, she did not feel anything: no pain, no pleasure! This feeling continued during the following penetrations she experienced with him and with one other lover. This lack of vaginal pleasure has been for her a great disillusion:

> For me, I had had orgasms at the level of the clitoris, but I've never had a similar or comparable explosion as the result of a penetration, and that has been quite frustrating. I know that we women are very different from one another. But I didn't expect to be a woman who is exclusively clitoridean, who doesn't get pleasure from vaginal penetration. I was left with a profound deception.

MARÍA

After listening to the story of Salomé, amazed by what I interpreted as the profound impact of the racial-spatial order, I decided to work on narratives of sexual history from Ecuadorian black women living in Quito. Salomé's obsession with respectability and her will to prove she does not fit the stereotypes of black women's sexuality, led me almost automatically to try to gather similar information from black women involved in sexual work, because I thought that their relationship to these stereotypes would provide good material for comparison. I expected them to be directly inverted to Salomé's relationship with the same stereotypes.

I met María through a friend, a white-mestizo woman who, as a social worker, had worked with the Association of Sexual Workers of the Province of Pichincha. She introduced me to the president of the association, who put me in contact with María, one of the association's black members.[8]

María was born in Quito to a black woman from the Chota-Mira Valley and a white-mestizo father who she never met. She believes that her father must be the last employer of her mother in Quito. Indeed, not long after María's birth, her mother moved from Quito to Ibarra to take on another job as a domestic employee. In 1999, her mother, who was sixty years old, was still a domestic employee in a white-mestizo home of Ibarra.

At the moment of our interactions in 1999, María was thirty-eight years old. She had not finished primary school and had married—both legally and ecclesiastically—a black man from the Chota-Mira Valley at a very young age. They lived in Ibarra and had six children. Her husband was abusive and often drank. He sometimes beat her. One day, because she refused to give him money she had earned herself, he burned all of her clothes. That is when she decided to leave him. She went to Quito with her children. Life in Quito was a struggle for her. Looking for a place to live, she found a big room (four brick walls with a zinc roof) that was to be used by the night guard (*guachimán*) of a garage. After negotiations, the owner of the garage allowed her to use the space free of charge in exchange for taking care of the place after hours; she just had to pay for the electricity and the water (she still lives there). She had different jobs as a domestic employee.

Yes, where I was working before, I experienced racism. Racism is strong in Quito. People say things like: "dirty nigger!" and "lazy nigger." When I worked in a family of rich people, they were sometimes saying *negra de mierda*, "shitty nigger," but not to my face, behind my back, and I was hearing it. But I was making out as if I hadn't heard it. But once I reacted and lost my job. This was when I was working in the house of [white-mestizo] people living in the González Suarez (an exclusive street with expensive high-rise apartment buildings in Quito).

One day, while on the bus on her way to work, she overheard a conversation between two other women (a black woman and a white-mestiza). One of them was explaining to the other that she had engaged in sexual work, that it was not so bad because the money came in every day in greater quantity than with any other job one could think of. The money to be made did not compare with the salary of a domestic employee. After hearing that conversation, María decided to become a sexual worker. She has been doing so in three different bar-brothels in the 24 de Mayo Avenue neighborhood since 1995.

When I began "working," the price of a sexual intercourse [*una ficha*] was seven thousand sucres [in 1995]. Then I went to another bar because I had problems with the owner of the first one. In that second bar, I was making between a hundred and two hundred thousand sucres a week. To get that, one had to make three, four or five *fichas* a day; it was the equivalent of twenty to thirty thousand sucres per day. This was not bad at all at the time. Today [1999], one *ficha* is twenty-five thousand sucres [one U.S. dollar] with one beer. The people who come to the clubs where I have been working are workers [*trabajadores*]; they are not executives. The people with more money go into the clubs of the north of the city.

María is proud that she has been working in the bar where I first met her, El Paraíso de Mujeres, the Paradise of Women, for more than three years. With Salomé's story in mind, I asked her what she thought of the stereotypes about black women's sexuality, if and how they had been hurtful to her. She enthusiastically responded, with a touch of pride:

They say that black women are hot, that they are hotter than white women, or white-mestizo women. They are hotter and they can satisfy men. They can have sex without getting tired of it; they have a good appetite. I'm like that, and my husband[9] became used to me and my sexual appetite; and he is white but he cannot get enough, we are the same, that is why we get along well in sex. We are good friends.

Talking about her condition as a black sexual worker working mostly among mestizo and white-mestizo colleagues and clients, she indicates that black sexual workers who work in the same bar usually stick together: There are always fights among women during which, whatever the initial problem was, "race" becomes very quickly the principal issue.

There are [mestizo and white-mestizo] clients who prefer to be with a black woman. In my case, I'm not in a rush, I'm not demanding them to go fast to finish, and they prefer me because I take my time and I do it well. I want them to talk well about me, so that they come back and make me a good reputation. I have my clients. I identify as a black woman. I have black blood and this will be like that until I die. I have had black clients, African clients. They are nice people. The only thing is that they don't like to talk a lot. They come to do what they want and that's it.

With Yesenya in mind (see the next interview), I asked María if she ever refused to have sex with black clients.

No, not at all. There are black men who prefer white women, there are other black men who prefer mulatto women, that's how it is. I have no problem with black men. Anyway, they are fewer than the mestizos and white-mestizos. There are some white-mestizo colleagues who do not like black men because they say that they have big penises and that they make love for too long, that it hurts, and so on. For me, all men are equals. I don't have this prejudice, but I know that black men have bigger penises, particularly African men. White men have penises of all sizes, many have it small, skinny, long and tiny, but others have a bigger one. But the majority are the same, an erected penis is an erected penis; it will get inside of you as deep as it can, that's all.

Many clients like to go with a black woman to have anal sex, because they say that black women have nice buttocks (*lindas nalgas*). Personally, I don't like anal sex, other women do, not me. To avoid it, I ask a prohibitive price that I know they will not be able to pay. Every woman does what she wants. One day, I'll leave that job. I can sew! I can cook!

YESENYA

Yesenya[10] was born in 1969 in Esmeraldas to Afro-Esmeraldian parents. Unlike María, she is very dark. I met her in the exclusive strip club and brothel in the north of Quito where she works. Seeking to interview a black woman involved in high-scale prostitution, I went to her club, El Rincón de Placeres, the Corner of Pleasures, with a white-mestizo male friend of mine. To approach her, I had to behave like any normal client would. I invited her to my table, offered her a drink, and engaged in a conversation. To be able to keep her at my table for an hour and a half, I had to pay her U.S. $50.00 (around 500,000 sucres in 1999). Although reticent to talk with me at first, she progressively felt at ease and accepted my invitation to meet outside of the club during the day. I visited her home several times and met her two "mulatto twins" (*mis gemelos mulatos*).

When she was two years old, her parents divorced and she went to live with her father in San Lorenzo, where he became a schoolteacher. She lived in San Lorenzo until she was twenty years old. After graduating as a *bachiller* (high school diploma) in accounting, she left San Lorenzo because of a conflict with her father's new wife. She worked for a while as a secretary in a law office in Santo Domingo de los Colorados, where she met the man who became her husband and the twins' father. Asked to talk about her youth and the stereotypes of black women's sexuality, she said:

When I was not a prostitute, before I got married, as a high school student, I had to go to the library. I wore short skirts and wherever I walked, cars would beep and people talked to me as if I were a prostitute. This has happened to me in various places in Ecuador. Ecuador is a backward country when you consider the issue of racism against blacks. They think that because one is black one has to be at the bottom, as if we were still in the colonial period, as if we were still slaves of white people. When I was younger, I was very attractive and a lot of men were interested in me. I had to go out without my mother knowing my whereabouts. She absolutely wanted me to finish my studies and not be distracted. I didn't make love with the men; we just kissed. We caressed one another but without doing anything more. When they asked for *la prueba del amor*, I rejected them saying that they were not serious.

She was a virgin when she met the man who was to become her husband. He took her virginity by raping her:

He was born in Ecuador, from Australian parents. He has the face of a gringo, and his eyes have a nice honey color, just like gringos. His hair is light brown and his skin very white. He was a traveling salesman of home appliances. He passed by Santo Domingo a lot. When I first made love, it was with him, although we were not married at the time. We went on a trip to Quito. We stayed in a hotel after dinner, in a room with two beds — one for me and one for him. At midnight, while I was sleeping, he came into my bed and, although he knew that I was a virgin, he penetrated me at once. I screamed because I was sleeping. It was horrible! I'm a very good sleeper, but my body was hurting so much. When I went to the bathroom, it was painful to walk, it was horrible. Ay! I don't want to remember this. He apologized. I slapped him several times. Then we went back to Santo Domingo. He said that he wanted to live with me, and that he loved me. I told him that if he really wanted to do that, we had to get married. He accepted and we got married. This marriage was more for my dignity and not so much for love. Then, we had the twins. I lived with him for eight years.

She explained about her life in Santo Domingo. He continued to travel for his business and returned as often as he could; he was very jealous. She did not have to work and even had a domestic employee for almost two years (a black woman from the Chota Valley). Her husband became increasingly jealous. He was twenty-four years older than she was. At one point, his jealousy got out of control and he began to lock her up in their house. She revolted and had a big fight with him. They later solved the conflict by moving to Quito, where she also was a housewife and received help from a domestic employee. Her husband was often drunk, sometimes for entire three-day periods. One night, two years after the birth of the twins, while drunk, he flew into a violent burst of jealousy and threatened her with a big kitchen knife;

"that's when I told him that I would never see him again, and until this day I haven't."

She left her house with her sister, who was living with them, and her twins. They went through tough times for a while. At first, they found refuge in the house of an Esmeraldian friend who was also living in Quito. The first job she found was as a cook in a restaurant.

When I got my first paycheck, it was only five hundred thousand sucres. I bought milk for my children and then I rented a room. Almost all of the money was gone. We all went there. We spent the first night on the floor covered with newspapers and towels. A friend of mine took my children. Her name is Alicia. She let the kids sleep in her bed while she slept on the floor. Alicia is from Ibarra. She is black as well.

Then she left the restaurant. She was ashamed to work in the restaurant as a cook, after having lived in many ways the life of a lady for years. She enlisted in an agency for temporary work, but they only wanted to give her jobs as a domestic employee.

Here, to be able to be an accountant, I had to show my documents. They did not recognize my diploma from San Lorenzo. They wanted me to take computing classes. In Ecuador, if you are black, they won't let you live like they let the whites live. All of that because you're black! That's why Ecuador is a mediocre country, because of racism. It will never get better!

She then worked as a domestic employee in the house of a white-mestizo medical doctor for a few weeks.

Everything was going fine until the doctor began to look at me as a woman and not as an employee. He was talking to me in the ear. He was taking me by the waist and saying things such as "Let me tell you, you are quite attractive!" When his wife wasn't there, he wanted to go to Ibarra with me. He was very much after me all the time. He was saying that I was suggesting sexuality just by being looked at. One day, he wanted me to work during the weekend and I went very well dressed. I also wanted to go well dressed because I very much liked a guy from the Galápagos who was living in Quito and I was hoping that he would see me. I wore a miniskirt. The doctor saw me dressed that way and told me that he would love to rent an apartment for me. That is when I decided to leave that job.

A few days later she was approached in the street by a middle-aged white-mestizo man who lured her into becoming, as he said, a masseuse in a spa for older people. He said that the beginning salary was very good (seven hundred thousand sucres monthly) and would increase according to her performance. She quickly found out that his expectations were not for her to be a masseuse; he wanted her to be a prostitute. At first, feeling cheated and disappointed, she thought of running away from the place, but the need for money made her stay. During the two years preceding our meeting, Yesenya had been a sexual worker in three different exclusive bar-brothels in the north of Quito. These bars are exclusive because of the high entrance fee as well as the high cost of their prostitutes. The clients who frequent them — Ecuadorian white and white-mestizo professionals and foreign businessmen — can easily spend the amount of the legal minimum salary (around one hundred and twenty thousand sucres in 1999) in one night. The women who work there are younger and generally have a "better" physical presentation than the women who work in the south of Quito. The bars are well kept and luxurious in comparison to the one like that where María works. During the course of a night of work, every woman must strip on stage several times. Clients choose the woman they like and either bring her to one of the equipped rooms on the second floor of the club or pay an extra fee and leave the club with her. Yesenya told me that on a good night, she goes home with almost two hundred U.S. dollars. When she works, she leaves the children in the care of an older white-mestiza neighbor, to whom she pays a monthly salary. Because of the relative financial affluence of the clients who go to her bar, Yesenya has had access to a kind of "relationship" unknown to María: Clients sometimes hire her to spend a few days with them on the beach or for the duration of a cruise in the Galápagos Islands or another vacation destination. When this occurs, a kind of romance may develop between the client and her, and the story always ends up with some financial gain. She says that she fell in love with her client on two of these occasions.

Parallel to Salomé's story, numerous sections of Yesenya's narrative denote a similar tortured relationship with blackness. For example, when talking about her first flirtations with men, before meeting her husband, she related an episode with a young black man from San Lorenzo.

One day, before meeting my husband, I went to San Lorenzo where I met an old love. One of these flirts that I was talking about earlier. He was black, very dark. He was beautiful, but then I said to myself: "I am black and I will marry a black man. Why would I do such a thing? We will get very dark kids, and I don't want to do that. I want to improve my race [*Quiero mejorar mi raza*]."

JMR: So you think that the black race is bad?

Yesenya: No, not bad, but I'm very dark. If I were marrying him, our kids would be very dark too, and this is ugly. I didn't marry him, but I loved him because he never asked me to have sexual intercourse. That's why I liked him. My color is beautiful, but just for me, not for my kids. My kids are beautiful, they are of your color [she points towards me] and they have good hair. I'm proud of being black but not for my kids. I don't take black kids in my arms. I don't like them. When my friend [a dark-skinned black woman] comes to visit, I don't let her touch the hair of my kids, because I don't want to take the risk that she could hurt [dañar] my kids' hair just by touching it. When they were little, my kids had straight hair and one day I made the mistake of cutting their hair very short. When the hair grew back, it became curlier, while it was entirely straight before. That is when I began thinking that I didn't want anybody with kinky hair to touch their hair. I don't want my kids to have such nappy hair. I'm very careful with the shampoo I choose.

I never had a sexual affair with a black man, never! As client, I had only one, a "black gringo" from Haiti. He was very dark. I didn't want to go to bed with him, but he offered me very good money and we had sex. He made love to me something like five or six times. At one point I told him that my vagina was beginning to hurt, that I wanted some peace now, that he had a big penis, that he should stop. He treated me as a prostitute and not like a woman. After that I decided that I would never again go to bed with a black man. My clients are always white, either Ecuadorians or gringos. I like to have white clients, particularly gringos, because they pay well. I also like white clients because they are not too demanding [fastidiosos] in bed. They do not have too much sexual appetite. There are also white men who have difficulties sustaining an erection. I also like the gringos because they like to go to fine places for dinner. They invite me to travel in the country.

The difference between a black client and a white one is this: white guys want to be with a black woman because they never penetrated one, and they want to have the experience. Also, the body of a black woman is very attractive. So, sometimes, they even say that they want to be well treated for their first time with a black woman. They say that black women have a particular flavor, that sex with them is better. They just say it. They say that white women are not passionate enough [son apagadas], that they go to bed just passively, waiting for the man to do everything. The black woman, on the contrary, is more active. They say that black women have a smaller and tighter vagina, and that their vagina is warmer, that their skin is soft, like the skin of a baby. White men like to caress the skin of black women in a way that black men don't, because black men also have this kind of skin. White men even fall asleep caressing one. I love to be celebrated, and white clients do that. The gringos, when they go to a club, look directly for a black woman, and if there are no black women, they go away. This is not all the gringos, of course, but most of them seem to like black women a lot; but the white and white-mestizo guys from here, the *longos* [pejorative word for *indio* and depreciative term for *mestizo*; see Whitten 2003], they like black women to discover them, to find out how they make love, to caress their curves, because we have nice bodies. Very few white women have nice bodies. They have flat behinds, not like black women who have nice, round behinds. Black women, we are hotter, we know how to make love in a more exciting way than white women.

SAÍDA

Saída[11] was born in Quito in 1970 to Afro-Choteño parents. Her mother was visiting relatives in Quito at the end of her pregnancy. Saída is the youngest of her mother's six children. Shortly after her birth, Saída and her mother moved back to the Chota Valley, where they lived until she became of age to attend primary school. She went to primary and secondary school as well as college in Ibarra, where she lived with her mother. They visited the valley almost every weekend and every holiday, particularly when it was harvest season. Although she spent a lot of time in Ibarra, she always kept in contact with the valley and grew up in Afro-Choteño environments. She obtained the equivalent of a bachelor's degree in education as a natural sciences teacher from Ibarra's Universidad del Norte. After graduating, she worked in a kindergarten in Ibarra. She has resided in Quito since 1997, after finding a job with a politician from Imbabura Province who was involved in national politics. She had met that politician in Ibarra a few years earlier. She worked for more than a year in the national congress and then found a job in a local university. In that university, she works as a staff member in a permanent workshop charged with seeking funds from national and international organizations to conduct development projects in rural black communities aimed at educating community leaders and helping young people enroll in high schools and colleges. When I asked her how she identifies as a black woman now that she lives in Quito, she responded:

> You're right, there are young black people who think that the black folks who live in the city constitute one group and that the black folks who live in the country constitute another. I think otherwise. It's obvious that we who live in the city have more opportunities. But that does not mean that black people who live in rural areas should be looked at as inferior, on the contrary. In the workshop in which I work, we always invite [black] rural community leaders. We look at them as important social actors. We try to make sure that they have good self-esteem. For me, there is no such thing as rural blacks separated from urban blacks. We are one black community.

You know, when women from the Chota Valley are selling their products at the market in Quito, they look away from me when I go there during my lunch hour, because I have a uniform. A uniform indicates that I've been to school and that I have a relatively good job in comparison to them. They look away and avoid acknowledging my presence as if they felt shame to still be selling their products in the market. So, I'm the one who calls their attention by saying "Hey, how are you doing? Why aren't you saying hi to me?" and so on, just to demonstrate to them that it's not because one has a title that one is different. We are all blacks and we are all brothers and sisters. And the ones among us who are higher up socially must help the others.

When people ask me where I'm from, I never say that I'm from Quito, although I was born in Quito; I always say that I'm from the valley. I say that because that is how I feel! I'm not from Quito!

Various sections of our conversations focused on Ecuadorian antiblack racism and particularly on racist stereotypical representations of black female bodies and sexuality. She explained that she mostly experienced racism while in Quito, much more so than when she was living in Ibarra, where racism was more underhanded, more hidden. In congress, she was the assistant to a very visible congressman. On more than one occasion during meetings she attended with him, other congressmen addressed her as if she were a servant, asking her, for example, to go find some coffee or bring some food. This was happening despite the fact that she was dressed professionally, like the other people in the room. Her response indicating that she was not there to serve coffee always provoked the biggest surprise. About the stereotypic representations of black females' bodies and sexuality, she said:

Obviously, and that is sad to say, we black women in Ecuador are looked at as sexual objects. At first they look at your figure, your body. Well, we must also say that in general, we black women have a voluptuous figure [una figura carnadita]: a small waist, long legs, and round buttocks. That is something that is true. Even the white-mestizo women, not only the white-mestizo men, are amazed by the body of black women. They even say "Wow, you have a beautiful body, I would love to be like that!" That's what some of them have told me. But when men look at you, you understand right away that they are undressing you and imagining you with them in bed.

White-mestizo men look at you differently than do black men. They look at you as if a black woman is valued only for sex. With black men, it's different. Even if they think you are pretty and attractive, they don't objectify you the same way. Because it's normal for a man to appreciate a woman who has a good body. But white-mestizos go directly to the sexual thing; they say things like: *Que buena es esta negra para los riñones* [this black woman is good for the kidneys]. I like to dress with tight clothes, but I don't do it often, because if I do I would be the target of vulgar comments in the street. When you get on the bus, as a black woman, you must be careful with the bus employees [*los oficiales*] who sell the tickets, because they will grab your behind shamelessly; they'll even feel under your skirt. I have no problem with people telling a black woman that she is pretty, but there are ways of saying it. Many just say it while looking insistently at her buttocks. That is when you feel like a sexual object.

On various occasions, Saída was approached in the street by white-mestizo men who addressed her as if she were a sexual worker. She explained how surprised and hurt she felt the first time it happened; she was so amazed by it that she didn't know how to respond. Now, when somebody wants to ask anything in the street, she just walks away without paying any attention.

Saída also told me about one of her white-mestiza coworkers who seems to be obsessed by her buttocks:

There is a white-mestiza at work to whom I have said a thousand times to stop touching my buttocks. One day I asked her if she liked women. And she responded no, that she is married, that my buttocks just amaze her. She must be around thirty-five years old; she is thin, and she has no butt whatsoever; she is flat as one can be. When I dress with pants, she comes and asks me if I put some cushions to augment the volume of my buttocks. Finally, I told her that if she wants to do so she can admire them, but from afar, without touching them. One day, she even told me that if she had a body like mine she would have a lot of men at her feet. I responded that a woman is much more than just a pair of buttocks. But then, she said that the first thing men look at is that, the body. And there, she's right.

Saída explained that she is a member of the Pichincha Province black women's association. One day, various members of the association organized a small rally in front of a large advertisement, a huge photograph of a nude, very dark, black woman with a voluptuous body and particularly voluptuous buttocks. It was an advertisement for a brand of rum called Ron Negrita. The face of the black woman was not visible. The most important body parts or the advertisers were obviously her back and her buttocks: she appeared bending over, from the back, as if offering herself to the public. The text of the poster read "El Placer Líquido con la Cola Negra," (The Liquid Pleasure [the rum] with the Black Tail [the advertised brand]). The sexual play of words consisting in suggesting that the "black behind" (*cola negra*) does provoke "liquid pleasure" (ejaculation). They went in a group to complain to the managers of the company that produces the rum and demanded the immediate removal of the poster because of its offensiveness to black women. The managers promised to do so, but the poster was not removed. One afternoon, at a time of the day when many people stood in front of the advertisement, they stained the poster. The police intervened without arresting anybody. The poster was removed two days later.

Here is some of what Saída had to say about her sexual life experience:

I didn't have a boyfriend until I was in the tenth grade. With him, almost three years into our relationship, I lost my virginity. It took a long time [three years] because we were often separated. He was studying in Quito and I was studying in Ibarra. He is from the village of El Chota. He is the father of my son. We met at a valley festival. When I was younger I did not like to hang out with men, and I don't know why. I didn't trust them. I met him at the wedding of one of my cousins. He was tall, handsome. I approached him; I was fourteen or fifteen years old. My body was already formed. That night, we almost didn't talk. Then I saw him another time, almost a year later, at a festival of *bomba* music,[12] in the valley. I approached him and told him that I liked him, and I hugged and kissed him. And that is how we became boyfriend and girlfriend. He was four years older than me. For him I also was his first girlfriend. He was studying medicine in Quito. At that time I wasn't that curious about sex. My curiosity began following conversations I had with white-mestizo classmates in high school. From experience, I can tell you that white-mestizas have much more sexual experience than black girls and black women. I think they begin doing things earlier than we do. They were my age but they already had had four or five boyfriends, some of them had two or three boyfriends at the same time; they had sexual intercourse with their boyfriends. They were the ones telling me: "Saída, you don't know what you are missing out on! You are wasting your time!" I was telling them that I was afraid, that I didn't want to be pregnant. They were telling me that sexual intercourse was so nice, that it was marvelous, that it was better than eating the dish you most prefer. These conversations awoke my curiosity about sex. I am the one who asked my boyfriend to have sexual intercourse. At first, he rejected my requests, saying that I was too young, that it would come in due time. He was such a nice guy. Finally, because of my insistence, he told me that we would make love after I graduated from high school. When graduation day came, I made him remember what he had said. And that is how we made love for the first time the day after my graduation. I basically discovered sexuality with him. We had a very nice relationship. Four years after having made love for the first time, I got pregnant. At that time he was living in Ibarra because he was an intern in a hospital there. But after my son was born, we had to separate because he began courting other women, and I didn't like that. He is very much involved in the education of our son.

After that I had another boyfriend; he was black. With him nothing really happened. It was a short relationship. The fact that the father of my son had betrayed me made me even more distrustful of men than I was before.

Then I had another boyfriend who was white-mestizo. That was when I was living in Quito. He was a guy from Ibarra. In fact, because his father was working in the sugar mill of Tababuela [located in the Chota Valley], he was living with his parents in the village of El Chota. He could dance very well. He asked me if I wanted to be his girlfriend and I agreed. But we didn't have sexual intercourse. He respected me very much. Our relationship lasted only three months. When people saw us in the street, hand in hand, particularly black men, they were always asking if there weren't enough black men out there for me to be with a white-mestizo, and things like that. That was a little difficult. He treated me in a very nice way, in a way that black men don't treat you. He held the door open for me, pulled the chair out for me to sit down, took my coat at restaurants. He made me feel like a queen. One day I went to his apartment in Quito and he cooked for me. At one point, we began kissing and caressing one another, and that is when he told me, for the first time: "Saída, your body drives me crazy!" I immediately got out of his embrace, stood up and asked him straightforwardly: "Why is my body driving you crazy?" He responded that it was because my body was beautiful and that since he was a healthy man, he was attracted by it.

For me, as soon as somebody talks to me, even in positive terms, about my body, I become distrustful. I don't know why. Perhaps it's because of what white and white-mestizo people always tell you in the streets, I don't know.

Our conversations ended with Saída explaining that she had had sexual intercourse only with one man: the father of her son; that since the end of their relationship she had some sort of a blockage with men; that even in the cases when she felt confident with a man and wanted to have sexual intercourse with him, because she loved him and was very much attracted to him, she was unable to let it happen. She became invaded by the fear of being used only for the attractiveness of her body and not loved for whom she was, above and beyond her body. She added that once, in the recent past, she met a U.S.-born African American student who was studying in Ecuador for a year, that they were very much attracted to one another, but that the relationship did not go anywhere because of her incapacity to relate to her sexual self without anxiety. They never made love and the relationship ended. She closed the last conversation we had by confiding in me that she will probably consult a therapist about this soon.

Conclusion

These narratives show that the stereotypical representations of black females as hypersexualized beings has had quite an impact in their respective lives, in their self-perceptions, and in the shaping of their sexuality.

Quito, as one of the centers of white and white-mestizo-ness within the Ecuadorian racial-spatial order, manifests virulent stereotypes and antiblack racism. Every narrative uncovers an individual's specific and original trajectory within the racial-spatial order; the greatest contrast appears between Salomé and Saída. While Salomé absolutely wants to identify with the white-mestizo Quito and disassociate herself from rural blacks, who she looks down upon, Saída embraces her membership in a translocal black community in which urban and rural blacks act side by side.

These narrative fragments indicate that other factors such as class, gender relations in Ecuadorian society, and religion have played a role in the way that each one of the four women has shaped and negotiated her identity and her sexuality. Undeniably, none of them would be able to escape from the dominant white and white-mestizo imagination of black bodies and black sexuality. The constitution of their subjectivities has not taken place in a vacuum, but within a societal context characterized by a white and white-mestizo hegemony that constructs blacks as Others in part through racist discourses about their sexuality and the alterity of their bodies. These discourses have been imposed on them more or less violently. As Foucault (1978) suggested, we must understand power as forming the subject, because power provides the condition of the subject's existence and the path followed by its desire. Judith Butler follows Foucault when she writes about the "psychic life of power":

As a form of power, subjection is paradoxical. To be dominated by a power external to oneself is a familiar and agonizing form power takes. To find, however, that what "one" is, one's very formation as a subject, is in some sense dependent upon that very power is quite another. . . . Power is not simply what we oppose but also, in a strong sense, what we depend on for our existence and what we harbor and preserve in the beings that we are. . . . Power that at first appears as external, pressed upon the subject, pressing the subject into subordination, assumes a psychic form that constitutes the subject's self-identity (Butler 1997:1–3).

Although on one hand Salomé, María, Yesenya, and Saída all oppose, in different ways, the racist stereotypes and the discursive construction of black women as sexual and moral Others, on the other hand, they reproduce some aspects of these stereotypes in a positive light, internalizing the perspective of the powerful in their self-constructions and self-presentations. To resist the "embodiment" of blackness denounced by Fanon (we are not just body; we are more than just a pair of buttocks; black women can be respectable and professionals; what do you mean when you say that I have an attractive body?), we can juxtapose the presentation of the black female body in terms of physical and even moral superiority (in Saída's narrative) vis-à-vis the white and white-mestizo female body and morality (black women have nicer and more attractive bodies; we have round buttocks and they are flat like a table; our skin is smooth and pleasant to touch; white and white-mestizo young females are more promiscuous than black young females). Statements about black women's bodily aesthetic superiority sometimes include the reproduction of racist stereotypes about black women's sexuality. That is what we can see in María's and Yesenya's narratives: "We, black women, we make love better, in a more exciting way, and longer than these *apagadas* [dull], white-mestizas."

These narratives also belittle the "manhood" of the powerful. Although they appear more gentlemanly than blacks, particularly if they are from North America or Europe, the white and white-mestizo sexual power is inferiorized (they have smaller penises and some of them have difficulties maintaining erections; they are not *fastidiosos*). The trace of power is found as well in Salomé's and Yesenya's problematic relationship to blackness, and the self-hatred that emanates from their narratives. Salomé ambiguously reproduces as valid the stereotypes that affirm the delinquency of black men and the hypersexuality of black women, without hiding her preference for white European men. Yesenya, by contrast, finds black children ugly and black men sexual brutes despite the fact that she was raped by a white Ecuadorian of Australian origin. She aspires to "improve her race."

Salomé's and Saída's narratives demonstrate how difficult it is for young black professional women, who do not follow the paths that lead to domesticity and sexual work, to negotiate a space for themselves in Quito.

A similar study conducted in another locality in another national context, in Salvador de Bahia in northeastern Brazil or in New York City, for instance, would surely provide data that contrast with those presented here. Antiblack racism in Quito and antiblack racism in Salvador or New York City, though they all participate in the same transnational general mechanisms and processes, have different local faces and affects.

The analysis of these narrative fragments of black female sexuality falls well within the scope of millennial Ecuador. The greater visibility of Afro-Ecuadorians in general, and of Ecuadorian black women in particular, in the urban centers of the country parallel recent developments that led to a strong indigenous movement and increased participation of Ecuadorian women in the debates about various aspects of the management of public life. For the first time, numerous women participated as candidates in the national elections of October 2002, and a recent article in *El Comercio*, entitled "Sexismo: un mal que persiste" (Sexism: An Illness that Persists), makes specific reference to the resistance of black women against the sexual manipulation of (black) women's bodies in the advertisement for Ron Negrita (*El Comercio*, August 19, 2002). Hopefully, this reference indicates a change toward a more inclusive Ecuadorian feminist movement. The latter had been mostly preoccupied by the plight of urban white and white-mestiza women. Afro-Ecuadorians still have a difficult and bumpy road in front of them to attain full respect for their civil rights. They will not be able to be successful without the greater participation of Afro-Ecuadorian women at all levels. It is in this context that the voices of Salomé, María, Yesenya, and Saída, as well as the voices of many others, appear to be important and fundamental to cultural transformations within Ecuador.

ACKNOWLEDGMENTS

Many thanks to the Afro-Ecuadorian women who confided in me and encouraged me to write this chapter. I am also thankful to James Sweet and Robin Sheriff, two friends and colleagues at Florida International University, for providing comments on an earlier version of this chapter. I am very grateful to Norman Whitten for his editing skills and for his mentorship.

NOTES

1. *Juyungo(a)* is a term used by the Chachi, indigenous people of the Province of Esmeraldas, to refer to Afro-Esmeraldians (see Barrett 1925; Estupiñan Bass 1983; Ortiz 1983). *Surumba* is a popular herb in Esmeraldas that is used in medicinal tea.

2. It is worth it noting that throughout the 1990s and beyond the Ecuadorian indigenous movement has been vigorously opposing the ideology of national identity that celebrates *mestizaje* (see Whitten 2003).

3. Very often, these writers have been either white or light-skinned "blacks" (to use a U.S.-based terminology).

4. About the emergence of an Otavaleño middle class, see de la Torre 1996; Colloredo-Mansfeld 1999.

5. One of the women refuses to use the politically correct term "sexual worker" to refer to herself.

6. Salomé is not her real name. Aware of my intention to publish this material, she asked me to call her Salomé, the name her mother would have loved to call her.

7. See my discussion of the racially informed concepts of *señora* (lady) and *mujer* (woman) in Rahier 1999a.

8. María is not her real name. I refer to her by this pseudonym to protect her identity. That is why I have also invented the name of her place of work, El Paraíso de Mujeres.

9. Her partner, a *mestizo* man, lives with her and her children. He works as a doorman at her workplace, which is where they met.

10. Yesenya is not her real name. I refer to her by this pseudonym to protect her identity. That is why I have also invented the name of her place of work, El Rincón de Placeres. Yesenya prefers to be called a "prostitute." She does not like to be called a "sexual worker" (*trabajadora sexual*), because this is the self-descriptive expression used by the (cheaper) women from the south of Quito, such as María. Women involved in sexual work in the north of Quito tend to look down on the women from the south.

11. Saída is not her real name. In order to protect her anonymity, I do not reveal her place of work in Quito.

12. *La bomba* is the traditional music of the Chota Valley.

REFERENCES

Anonymous
   2002   El Sexismo: Un Mal que Persiste. *El Comercio* Web site, August 19.
Barrett, Samuel A.
   1925   *The Cayapa Indians of Ecuador*. New York: Heye Foundation.
Bergner, Gwen
   1995   Who Is That Masked Woman? or, The Role of Gender in Fanon's Black
           Skin, White Masks. *Publication of the Modern Language Association of
           America* 110(1):75–88.
Butler, Judith
   1997   *The Psychic Life of Power*. Stanford: Stanford University Press.
Cervone, Emma
   2000   Machos, Mestizos, and Ecuadorians: The Ideology of Mestizaje and the
           Construction of Ecuadorian National Identity. Latin American Studies
           Association Meeting, Miami, Florida, March 17.
Colloredo-Mansfeld, Rudi
   1999   *The Native Leisure Class: Consumption and Cultural Creativity in the Andes*.
           Chicago: The University of Chicago Press.

de la Torre, Carlos
1996   *El racismo en Ecuador: Experiencias de los indios de la clase media*. Quito: Centro Andino de Acción Popular.

Estupiñán Bass, Nelson
1954   *Canto negro para la luz: Poemas para negros y blancos*. Esmeraldas: Casa de la Cultura.
1983   *Cuando los guayacanes florecían*. Quito: El Conejo.

Fanon, Franz
1967   *Black Skin, White Masks*. New York: Grove Press.

Foucault, Michel
1975   *Surveiller et punir: Naissance de la prison*. Paris: Gallimard.
1978   *The History of Sexuality*. New York: Pantheon Books.

Fuss, Diana
1995   *Identification Papers*. New York: Routledge.

Giddens, Anthony
1992   *The Transformation of Intimacy: Sexuality, Love, and Eroticism in Modern Societies*. Stanford: Stanford University Press.

Gilman, Sander
1985a Black Bodies, White Bodies: Toward an Iconography of Female Sexuality in Late-Nineteenth-Century Art, Medicine, and Literature. *Critical Inquiry* 12(1):204–42.
1985b *Difference and Pathology: Stereotypes of Sexuality, Race, and Madness*. Ithaca: Cornell University Press.

Hall, Stuart
1992   The Question of Cultural Identity. In *Modernity and its Futures*. Stuart Hall, David Held, and Tony McGrew, eds., London: Polity Press.

Lévi-Strauss, Claude
1962   *La Pensée Sauvage*. Paris: Plon.

Merleau-Ponty, Maurice
1962   *Phenomenology of Perception*. New York: Humanities Press.

Mohanram, Radikha
1999   *Black Body: Women, Colonialism, and Space*. Minneapolis: University of Minnesota Press.

Muratorio, Blanca
1994   Nación, identidad y etnicidad: Imágenes de los indios ecuatorianos y sus imagineros a fines del siglo XIX. In *Imágenes e imagineros: Representaciones de los indígenas ecuatorianos, siglos XIX y XX*. Blanca Muratorio, ed. Pp. 109–96. Quito: FLACSO.

Ortiz, Adalberto
1983   *Juyungo: Historia de un negro, una isla y otros negros*. Quito: Seix Barral.

Rahier, Jean Muteba

1998   Blackness, the "Racial"/Spatial Order, Migrations, and Miss Ecuador
         1995–1996. *American Anthropologist* 100(2):421–30.

1999a   Body Politics in Black and White: Señoras, Mujeres, Blanqueamiento, and
         Miss Esmeraldas 1997–1998, Ecuador. *Women and Performance: A Journal
         of Feminist Theory* 11(1) issue 21:103–19.

1999b   "Mami, qué será lo que quiere el negro?": Representaciones Racistas en
         la Revista Vistazo, 1957–1991. In *Ecuador racista: Imágenes e identidades*.
         Emma Cervone and Fredy Rivera, eds. Pp. 73–110. Quito: FLACSO.

Schick, Irvin

1999   *The Erotic Margin: Sexuality and Spatiality in Alteritist Discourse*. London:
         Verso.

Silva, Erika

1995   *Los mitos de la ecuatorianidad: Ensayo sobre la identidad nacional*. Quito:
         Abya-Yala.

Stutzman, Ronald

1981   El Mestizaje: An All-Inclusive Ideology of Exclusion. In *Cultural
         Transformations and Ethnicity in Modern Ecuador*. Norman Whitten, Jr.,
         ed. Pp. 45–94. Urbana: University of Illinois Press.

Wade, Peter

1997   *Race and Ethnicity in Latin America*. London: Pluto Press.

Whitten, Norman E., Jr.

1981   (editor) *Cultural Transformations and Ethnicity in Modern Ecuador*.
         Urbana: University of Illinois Press.

2003   Symbolic Inversion: The Topology of "El Mestizaje" and the Spaces of
         "Las Razas" in Ecuador. *Journal of Latin American Anthropology*
         8(1):14–47.

Young, Lola

1999   Racializing Femininity. In *Women's Bodies*. J. and J. G. Arthur, eds.
         Pp. 67–90. London: Cassell.

CHAPTER 12

Mothers of the *Patria*

La Chola Cuencana and La Mama Negra

MARY J. WEISMANTEL

Chola Cuencana, mi chola,	Chola Cuencana, my chola,
capullito de amancay,	Little branch of *amancay*,
en ti cantan y en ti ríen	In you sing and in you laugh
las aguas del Yanuncay.	The waters of Yanuncay.
Eres España que vive	You are Spain living
en Cuenca del Ecuador,	In Cuenca in Ecuador,
con reír de castañuelas	With the laugh of castanets
y llanto de rondador.	And the cry of the panpipes.
Con tu donaire y majeza	With your elegance and grace
evocas Andalucía;	You evoke Andalucía;
pero en todos tus sentires	But in all your senses
florece la cuencanía.	Cuenca's culture flowers.
Hay en tu cara morena	There is in your brown face
frescura de amanecer;	The freshness of the dawn;
y el sol quisiera en tus ojos	And the sun longs to set
cada día atardecer.	Each day in your eyes.
Guitarras y castañuelas,	Guitars and castanets,
concertina y rondador;	Concertina and panpipe;
alma de España que vive	The Soul of Spain that lives
en Cuenca del Ecuador.	In Cuenca in Ecuador.

Imagined Ecuadors

On Friday, May 30, 1997, a Listserv catering to expatriate Ecuadorian professionals received an enthusiastic e-mail from one of its members in the United States with the heading, "Desde Flushing, NY." Upon entering a park frequented by immigrants on a Sunday afternoon, Luis Franco had suddenly found himself immersed in familiar sights, sounds, and smells. "Come to New Jersey!" he exhorted his fellow exiles. "Here you will really feel at home."

Among the sensory impressions that made him feel he was back in Ecuador, the writer mentions hearing one particular tune: "La Chola Cuencana." And indeed, this song, the words to which every schoolchild knows by heart, is unmistakably and uniquely Ecuadorian even in its title. Cuencana refers to the colonial city of Cuenca in the southern highlands, and *chola*—a term also commonly heard among Chicanos and Mexicans — is used here in idiosyncratically Andean fashion.

To try to define the word *chola* is to confront the complexity of what it means to be Ecuadorian. The word opens up a cultural realm almost unfathomable to someone who did not grow up in South America.[1] The immediate referent is to folklore: a Chola Cuencana is a woman dressed in the traditional costume of the province of Azuay (of which Cuenca is the capital). This striking outfit includes layers of brilliant, deeply gathered skirts called *polleras*; a delicate shawl made of ikat-dyed cotton with long fringes knotted in complex macramé designs; a finely woven straw hat, tall and white; and hair worn in two long braids, tied together at the ends.

This image of a woman from bygone days seems lovely and innocuous; but in Latin America, the category of the folkloric is not so readily consigned to historical irrelevance (Caesar and Bueno 1998:6; Rowe and Schelling 1991:97). In the United States, "folklore" suggests something from the popular cultures of the vanishing past, already or soon to be replaced by the mass-cultural products of Madison Avenue and Hollywood. This temporal relationship is less absolute in South America, where despite the tremendous inroads made by mass culture, popular culture retains an exuberant vitality. The clothing associated with the *chola*, for example, is still seen on Cuenca's streets and on the country roads outside the city, even though most working-class and rural women today have abandoned the straw hat for a baseball cap, and the *pollera* for sweatpants.

Indeed, although Latin American artists, writers, and architects were among the inventors of the modern (*modernism* itself is a term coined in South America), modernity here, as George Yúdice (1992:23) memorably stated, feels less like an accomplished fact than "a series of unfinished projects." In this context, popular culture, perceived and defined by the bourgeoisie as antimodern, appears as an active threat rather than a harmless joke. In a country like Ecuador, which has a large nonwhite population with visibly distinct cultural practices, race intensifies this sense of menace. Ecuadorians today still invoke nineteenth-century racist doctrines, conflating progress with racial whiteness. Sarah Radcliffe and Sallie Westwood found that across Ecuador, people classed as "Indians" are uniformly "pic tured in a 'commonsense' way as backwards, uneducated and poor" (Radcliffe and Westwood 1996:109–12).[2] In this context, folkloric figures such as the *chola* provoke fearful visions of a nation dragged backward by its nonwhite citizens, who, by stubbornly refusing to adopt national culture, subvert the desires of a nation anxious to achieve and consolidate its modernity.[3]

But there is an odd twist to this relationship between modernity and nationhood: familiar folkloric characters such as the Chola Cuencana or the Appalachian hillbilly may claim premodern and popular roots, but their current incarnations are modern artifacts, promulgated by the bourgeoisie for their own ends. From the founding of the new American nations until at least the mid twentieth century, artists and writers contributed to the process of nation building by using popular imagery to construct appropriate national icons.[4] It was a contradictory undertaking, designed to contribute to the nation's progress even as the images themselves were presented as folkloric, and thus as aspects of traditional, even retrogressive, cultural practices.

The Chola Cuencana comes to us with just such a complicated past. Her costume is older than the nation itself, dating to at least the eighteenth century. It is the collective creation of the city's working-class women, who borrowed elements from peasant, Spanish and indigenous clothing and who have continually added new styles and elements as these appeared. The song about the *chola* is much more recent: the twentieth-century poet Ricardo Darquea Granda wrote the poem in 1947.[5] The verses he penned describe a beautiful woman with whom the narrator is enamored; the metaphors are of rivers, flowers, and music. It is not difficult to discern that the source of his inspiration is as much the city and the region as a flesh-and-blood woman, or that if such a woman exists, she excites his passion precisely because she so beautifully exemplifies the glories of Cuenca.

Beneath its romantic surface, the poem's metaphors make thinly veiled reference to some of the oldest and most intransigent social differences that bedevil the Americas: race and class.[6] A *chola* is, by definition, a member of the laboring, or popular, classes, and she is not white.[7] Darquea Granda, as is clear from his poem, is masculine, white, and educated; his beloved Cuenca, as he imagines her, is not. Like the Virgen de Guadalupe, the face of the woman in the song is *morena* (brown): she is thus, like Mexico's great icon, a local version of one of the most powerful political symbols of Latin America: *la mestiza*. In Ecuador, Venezuela, Peru, Bolivia, Mexico, and Brazil, artists and intellectuals created these figures by borrowing well-known images of racial and cultural admixture from the popular cultures of their respective regions and infusing them with elite notions of femininity.[8] Gendering race

ʾy to their success in forging enduring instruments of nation-
ʾse imaginary women were at once the sweetheart, the
ymbolic body of the modern Latin nation.

ʾnterparts elsewhere, the brown-skinned and alluring Chola
offers the promise of a nation and a citizenry beautiful in its ho-
ty, in which Indian and European mix harmoniously. In the twenti-
entury, such figures have been crucial vehicles by which Latin American
ates promulgated their vision of the nation as mestizo; as such, they have
been, and continue to be, contested territory. In Ecuador, the state ideology
of *mestizaje*, as Norman Whitten (and later his students and other scholars)
argue, does not, in fact, signify an embrace of the nation's nonwhite citizens,
but rather an assertion of *blanqueamiento* (racial and cultural assimilation).[9]
According to this ideology, to become a citizen, and so a member of the body
politic, nonwhites must assimilate to the dominant Hispanic culture. In the
neoconservative politics of the moment, this message is clearer than ever.

In the hands of elite artists and writers, representations of *mestizaje* likewise become whitened, as can be seen in the Chola Cuencana. A statue
erected in her honor in the city of Cuenca shows a slim woman with white facial features; but in popular usage throughout the Andes, a *chola* is a woman
who is not white. She is, rather, of mixed indigenous and white ancestry: not
just a *mestiza* but a woman "more Indian than white," or even "more Indian
than *mestiza*." Not surprisingly, given the racial stigma associated with *indios*, the word is often perceived as derogatory, and most people would hesitate to use it to someone's face.

Although Darquea calls his *chola* a *morena*, in other ways he paints her
very white; and it is in her whiteness that the poet finds much of her appeal.
Not only is she from the southern highlands, a region associated with racial
whiteness, but the structure of the song lyrics, which begin by lauding both
indigenous and Hispanic traits, but end with references only to the woman's
Spanish heritage, reinforces the superiority of European ancestry.

Although Spain is evoked through cultural products such as the guitar, her
Native American roots are found in nature: the flowering *amancay* and the
waters of the Yanuncay.[10] The Indianness of Darquea Granda's *chola*, then,
inheres within her physical body — and that of the nation itself — which appears fecund and flowering. This geographical theme has unpleasant political overtones when combined with the *chola*'s femaleness, for it evokes
longstanding metaphors of conquest, in which the feminine body of the
American continent becomes the trophy of the European male.[11] Chicana
and other feminist critics have expanded on the themes of violence contained within this imagined history, which then repeats itself across the generations through the actions of hacienda and plantation owners who raped

the land and enslaved their own children to enrich themselves (e.g., Alarcón 1989, 1983; Anzaldúa 1987; Smith 1996, 1997). According to this reading, the combination of female gender and racial admixture in the image of the *mestiza* nation is a repressive one, in which this supposedly democratic and inclusive icon instead becomes a sign of the repeated sexual conquest of non-white women by white men. The references to landscape gain further political sting in a country in which geography itself is heavily racialized. In the spatial imagination of Ecuadorians, cities — the centers of power and control — are white, while the rural highlands are "Indian" and backward, and the jungle is frighteningly savage: two landscapes in need of the firm hand of the white overseer (Whitten 1985; Radcliffe and Westwood 1996).

But if the idealized vision of the *mestiza* nation has come under attack from those who abhor its racial and gendered politics, it is being struck a far more lethal blow from those who simply find it irrelevant. For a country that has recently been wracked by "ruinous natural disasters, precipitous fluctuations in revenues from oil, collapse of the banking sector, a default on external loans, a coup and a 70 percent depreciation of the currency" (Tate 2001:46), flowery poems about women and landscape seem wholly inadequate. Twenty-first-century visions of the nation's future tend more toward the apocalyptic than the romantic. The modernist Latin American dream of a unified people inhabiting a single territory, sharing a political ideology and a national culture, seems to many Ecuadorians to lie in ruins, replaced by the nightmarish vision of a nation dismembered and fragmented racially, culturally, economically, politically, and even geographically. The image of the smiling Chola Cuencana pales before two other vivid images of contemporary Ecuador, both televised in full color before a shocked and amazed nation.

In the last decade of the twentieth century, a series of massive indigenous protest movements suddenly produced a radically new picture of Ecuador's political landscape.[12] Beginning in 1990 with a massive, tightly organized, and very effective uprising and strike, and culminating in 2000 with a brief takeover of the nation's government, the indigenous federation CONAIE and its allies produced unforgettable political drama. The sight of tens of thousands of indigenous people forcibly occupying the seats of national power, the Pan-American Highway, the central plazas of major cities, Quito's church of Santo Domingo, and finally the congress, the supreme court, and the presidential palace permanently changed Ecuador's understanding of itself, its past, and its future.

As the Ecuadorian social scientist Andrés Guerrero (2000) writes, the eruption of self-proclaimed *indígenas* into national political space appeared to white Ecuadorians as a double paradox, violating deeply held assumptions about the spatial and temporal order of things. Indians belonged in nature, and in the past: they were "pueblos y culturas que se desvanecían furtivamente por una puerta abierta" (peoples and cultures that were furtively disappearing through an open door). Long marginalized into social invisibility, they appeared to urban Ecuadorians to be literally vanishing from the earth. Beginning with my first trip to Ecuador in 1982, I had been repeatedly lectured by middle-class and wealthy Ecuadorians on the social Darwinist fate of *el indio*, who, already weakened and diminished, was doomed to a rapidly approaching extinction.

The "door" through which *indios* were supposed to disappear had been held open by several interrelated forces, all part of modernization: national integration, globalization, migratory movements, urbanization "y, sobre todo, el proceso de 'mestizaje'," (and, above all, the process of *mestizaje*; Guerrero 2000:10); now *mestizaje* had been dealt a fatal blow. Not only had the new protestors refused to either disappear or assimilate; they explicitly and vehemently rejected racial homogeneity as a goal, insisting instead that Ecuador the nation must embrace a pluricultural model of radical and permanent heterogeneity (Frank 1992). Ecuador thus entered the new millennium, in Lynn Meisch's (2000:14) pithy phrase, with "the strongest indigenous rights movement and the weakest economy in Latin America."

The weak economy has generated an even more profound threat to the nation, one contained within the very e-mail that celebrates the Chola Cuencana. Its author, despite his professed enjoyment of such typically Ecuadorian pastimes as eating roasted *cuy* (guinea pig), playing soccer, and listening to *pasacalles* and *sanjuanitos* on a Sunday afternoon, does these things not in Quito or in Cuenca, but in New Jersey. In contrast to the sudden, massive movement of tens of thousands of indigenous and other people who took over the nation's public spaces to voice their frustrations, hundreds of thousands of Ecuadorians of all races have simply abandoned the national territory altogether. Rather than seeking maximum visibility, these protests happen one by one, silently, invisibly, away from the scrutiny of the state. The demographic implications of this invisible, implacable leakage were momentarily brought to light in a single, horrifying picture: the smoldering wreckage of the World Trade Center towers.

The date September 11 is wrapped in the red, white, and blue of the American flag, but not all of those dead, missing, injured and miraculously saved that day were U.S. citizens. For listeners to National Public Radio, one of the most eloquent voices on the air describing all that had been lost was Ecuadorian: a floor manager at the restaurant Windows on the World, lamenting the death of individuals and the destruction of a workplace he eulogized as international, multiracial, and interfaith. On the Web page of the Ecuadorian consulate in New York are found the names of other Ecuadorians who were there that day, each listed along with two different homes: the South American cities where they were born—El Milagro, Riobamba, Ambato—and their last known addresses, in Brooklyn, Queens, or New Jersey.

It was inevitable that Ecuadorians would die in a disaster that took the lives of so many New Yorkers, for they constitute one of the city's fastest-growing immigrant groups, with populations rivaling that of older immigrant groups such as Puerto Ricans and Mexicans (Colloredo-Mansfeld 1999:11). The available statistics are unreliable, since most of this migration—perhaps 70 percent—is illegal, but even by conservative estimates, some four hundred thousand Ecuadorians now live in the United States. The rate of population flow out of Ecuador has been accelerating rapidly: two hundred thousand people left the country in the last three years alone (Jokisch and Pribilsky 2002; Jokisch 2001).[13] Even before 2000, as many as 10 percent of all Ecuadorians were living outside the national boundaries (Carpio 1992; Astudillo 1990:23; both cited in Miles 2001:11). As any Ecuadorian can tell you, New York, not Cuenca, is now Ecuador's third-largest city by population.

The *mestiza* nation, then, is simultaneously imploding and exploding: imploding as the rural indigenous population takes over the centers of white urbanity and exploding as Ecuadorians from all walks of life abandon the land of their birth for the United States. At the millennium, the myth of *la mestiza* seems to have taken on the form of more ancient myths, in which the mother goddess is killed by her children and from the limbs of her body grow a series of monsters intent on killing their father—*el país*, the Republican dream of the nation. But then, nationalist *mestizas* like the Chola Cuencana were never the seamless representations of a homogeneous nation they pretended to be: instead, popular and elite, white, indigenous, and black Ecuador all jostled uncomfortably together within one iconic body, which was always threatening to come apart at the seams. The contrast between the myth of racial mixture and the reality of racial tension may be no greater today than in previous periods of Ecuador's history.

In Ecuador, where region is as divisive as race, iconic images of nonwhite women vary tremendously, and so too do the tensions and conflicts that arise around them. Comparison between two such figures, Cuenca's famous *chola* and Latacunga's Mama Negra, reveal stark differences between the southern and the central highlands. It also, however, brings to light an underlying similarity: these images continue to act as lightning rods for class, racial, and gender conflicts within each region, as social actors strive to redefine them to meet their own needs. Rather than declaring these iconic mothers irrelevant, it seems appropriate to seize this moment to examine the source of their power. It is still possible — especially if we consider not only the rather pale figure of the Chola Cuencana, but also the uncompromising blackness of Latacunga's Mama Negra — that these metaphorical mothers may prove newly meaningful for the pluralistic nation trying to be born from the failures of the old.

Cuenca The Chola at a Distance

On a postcard sold in the municipal airport of Cuenca in 1998, a pair of barefoot women in full, brightly colored *pollera* skirts are shown sitting on the ground. One woman faces the camera while the other turns her back, revealing two long braids tied together at the ends, forming a thin black V. Their hands weave hats from fine straw; there are hats piled up beside them as well, and two more crown the women's heads, giving them an oddly masculine air that contrasts with the femininity of their frilly skirts. These hats are famous. Deceptively named "Panamas" in English, they are produced in southern Ecuador, where they once supported a flourishing export trade that provided stylish summer headgear for men throughout Europe and the Americas.

The setting for this lovely scene is apparently an outdoor marketplace in some tranquil countryside; but the postcard is sold as a representation of Cuenca, Ecuador's third-largest city and the major metropolis of the nation's southern highlands. Cuenca today is a city of contradictions, many of which find expression in the figure of its famous *cholas*. Unlike the nation's largest city, Guayaquil, conventionally described as a hot and dirty but bustling entrepreneurial and cosmopolitan port, this highland provincial capital projects the image of a quiet, proud aristocrat, nestled in a valley surrounded by placid agricultural towns, filled with archaeological and architectural treasures, and dedicated to the arts and intellectual pursuits. And yet, as Ann Miles notes, this image contrasts sharply with other aspects of the city and the region: its rapid recent growth, its own entrepreneurial history — exemplified by the international success of the "Panama hat"— and the fact that those surrounding towns are the origin point for most of the nation's emigrants. Ninety percent of all immigrants from Ecuador to the United States originate in either Azuay or neighboring Cañar (Pribilsky 2001a:254; Jokisch and Pribilsky 2002). The evidence can be seen in the list from the World Trade Center towers, where towns of the southern highlands — Sig Sig, Biblián, Azogues, and Paute — predominate among the victims' birthplaces.

In the past twelve years, Miles writes, "the city has grown from a population of approximately 180,000 to over 300,000 and its suburbs now extend deep into the surrounding countryside. . . . Transnational migrants, even

those who came from rural towns, are building new homes on the borderlands of rural and urban — creating a unique kind of Ecuadorian urban
sprawl where fancy two story homes bump up against one room adobe buildings" (Miles 2001:11). Remittances from overseas relatives, which Pribilsky
(2001a:255) estimated in the late 1990s as typically amounting to between
U.S. $150 and $400 a month, comprise a major part of the city's economy —
and the nation's.[14] Nor is Cuenca's immersion in the global economy a new
phenomenon. From its successful cinchona bark enterprises of the colonial
period to the twentieth-century production of Panama hats, which, in the
1940s, accounted for 22 percent of Ecuador's total export income, Cuenca
and its surrounding towns have always been oriented forward and outward,
even as it cherished its folkloric and historic past. Indeed, the buildings that
today constitute its cultural riches — Incaic fortresses, colonial churches,
and art deco mansions — are all the products of the region's long, intermit-
tently profitable economic and political engagement with the outside world
(Miles 2001:22–24).

It is no accident that the *chola* who became a national symbol was the
Chola Cuencana, for she is the whitest *chola* the country can produce. Race
in Latin America is always deeply connected to the complexities of regional
identity, and so too with Cuenca, a region that prides itself on a population
that is supposedly more European in heritage than is true elsewhere in the
highlands, even in rural areas and among the urban poor. This point of view
is firmly held by the city's traditional elites, the group known as *los nobles*,
who envision the rural residents of Azuay, like the aristocratic residents of
the city, as direct imports from Spain unblemished by racial admixture. According to this vision, the small towns and rural areas around the city were,
until recently, exact replicas of a long-vanished European pastoral, closely
connected in local imagination to the Spanish city of Cuenca for which the
Ecuadorian site was named.

When I arrived in Cuenca for a short period of research in 1997, I was
surprised by the degree to which Cuencanos of all walks of life upheld the
idea of the Chola Cuencana. Working-class and wealthy, educated and non-
professional residents of the city alike responded eagerly to my inquiries
about the city's famous icon, and everyone agreed that unlike other parts of
the Sierra, such as the central highlands around Latacunga where I have
done most of my fieldwork, in Cuenca the idea of a *chola* did not carry unpleasant racial overtones. But despite these averments, even before I arrived
in Cuenca, I had begun to discover that neither the city nor its famous *chola*
has entirely escaped the racial conflict and class prejudice endemic to the
continent. When I sent out e-mails to expatriate Listservs explaining my project, I received many friendly and helpful replies from ex-Cuencanos. One

anonymous correspondent in 1997 offered the following ironic commentary: "Everyone in Cuenca will tell you how proud they are of their Cholas Cuencanas. But just let their son bring a *cholita* home with him as the girl he wants to marry, and that little *morlaquito* [slang term for Cuencano] will find himself out in the cold. You won't hear anything about the lovely traditions of the *chola* then."

Indeed, many residents of the city, especially impoverished families of recent immigrants from the countryside, live with the everyday pain of racial stigma, which hurts its targets both objectively in terms of their lifelong economic and social opportunities and subjectively in their sense of self. Ann Miles (2001), in her sensitive portrait of one such family, documents some of the ways that racism operated poisonously both within and on the Chinchilima siblings.

Within the family, the darker-skinned children felt keenly their mother's open preference for her lighter children. Beto, sixteen, told Miles:

> Mami always treated Román better. . . . I think it was because of his color — because he is white. She's the same way with Jessica . . . and Billy too. But not Jenny, and not me. She's always saying that we are *morenos.* . . . It makes me feel so bad when she says these things to me [he starts to cry here]. (Miles 2001:127)

At the same time, all members of the family, light- and dark-skinned alike, suffered from the stigma of their surname, which denotes indigenous ancestry. In Beto's words,

> You tell everything by last name here. Vásquez, Suarez, Álvarez — these are the names of the rich people. They think that we are Indians. Their names are from Spain and they are smooth and easy to say — that's how they think. But I have this name and I have to carry it. (Miles 2001:128)

In Cuenca, then, as elsewhere in Ecuador, despite the rhetoric of *mestizaje*, it is always better to be white. Whiteness is a matter of culture as well as of skin: Beto's mother Rosario, despite her light pigment, was the target of constant abuse because she dressed in a *pollera*. In the first years of their acquaintance, Rosario recounted small daily injustices to Ann, such as being made to wait longer for service in offices, but she insisted that she would never put away her *pollera* for a white woman's skirt. However, her resistance was eventually worn down. The incident that finally broke her will was a humiliating meeting at her son's school, at which the priest singled her out for criticism as a bad mother, solely on the basis of her appearance. For him, a woman in a *pollera* exemplified someone backward and nonwhite, an unfit parent incapable of preparing her children for urban life (Miles 2001:62).

Idealized as a fiction, in fact the woman with a *morena* face or a *pollera* skirt must not show up as your son's fiancée or even as a parent in your classroom or a customer in your store. Even within the beloved fantasy itself, distances of both time and space are subtly inserted to hold such undesirable possibilities at bay. In the e-mail with which this essay opens, in which a man finds "home" in a figure so jarringly out of place as the Chola Cuencana in New Jersey, for instance, the *chola* is doubly elusive. The song that evokes this distant figure is itself dislocated: as the writer walks through the park, he cannot find the source of the music, or even be sure of what he is hearing. The tune comes to him "de repente, remotamente . . . los compases de una vieja melodia nuestra . . . Chola Cuencana?" (now and again, remotely . . . the verses of an old melody of ours . . . the "Chola Cuencana"?). Such displacements catch the attention of postmodernist geographers, who find them typical of newly hybrid and transnational cultures; but they are not really so new. Indeed, they are integral to the operation of modernist national folklore.

While foreigners and expatriates are happy to associate market women with Cuenca, a city they locate far away in the retrogressive world of Andean South America, the wealthy Cuencanos known locally as *los nobles* need to displace them still farther, away from the city into the countryside. When I gave a public lecture at the University of Cuenca, a small group of the city's elite attended, dressed in imported French fashion but very much there to represent traditional Cuenca. Afterward, they stood up to deliver a series of short impromptu speeches about the nature of the Chola Cuencana (some of which made the younger generation of Cuenca scholars who shared the platform with me wince in dismay). The audience of assembled students, many of them daughters or granddaughters of women who had worn the *pollera*, listened silently.

Dr. Lloret, the city's historian — the oldest and most distinguished of the four — spoke first. He thanked me graciously for my talk, but begged to correct a few errors, among them the notion that the Chola Cuencana was actually from Cuenca. Every woman wearing a *pollera* on the city streets was a country woman, he insisted, briefly come to town to sell some farm produce or to make a few purchases. For him, her rural origins were crucial to the *chola*'s folkloric charm — and, ironically, to her ability to represent the city. In Dr. Lloret's youth, Cuenca's export economy was expanding, buoyed by the international demand for Panama hats. The city's elites were justly proud to inhabit a truly modern city, home to beautiful new buildings that could rival those of Europe or the United States; at the same time, they also celebrated the existence of a rich and highly visible local culture. To Dr. Lloret, this dual identity had its own geography in which the fashionable districts in the heart of town were home to a sophisticated metropolitan life, while the rural hinterlands were the strongholds of Cuenca's regional traditions. The Chola Cuencana moved back and forth between the two, adorning and enriching the modern city with the fruits of the countryside: not only agricultural products, but her own rustic femininity as well.[15]

The two women who accompanied him, despite being of his generation, begged to differ with this masculine point of view. Many servant girls and market women, they reminded him, had lived in the city all their lives without ever dreaming of wearing anything but a *chola*'s hat and *pollera* skirts. The women reminisced with great pleasure about named houses in the center of town, inhabited by the wealthy *cholas* of a generation ago. In their memories, these "matriarchies" of mothers, sisters, and daughters had been renowned for their high-heeled shoes, ikat-dyed shawls, and silver filigree earrings — and for their commercial acumen as well.

When I spoke to the vendors in the city's produce markets, they too offered an interpretation sharply in contrast to Dr. Lloret's. Inside the Mercado 10 de Agosto, a municipal market in the center of town, every woman immediately and emphatically identified herself and her coworkers to me as Cuencanas: "We are from here, from the city, of course"; "I am a Cuencana, as you see me"; "Aquí nació la Chola Cuencana" (It is here [among the city's market women] that the Chola Cuencana was born). Most had inherited their professions, and sometimes even their stalls, from mothers, aunts, or grandmothers who were also born in the city. Rosa Loja, for example, who sells garlic, shallots, and rocoto peppers, has been a market vendor for forty-four years. Her mother was a *frutera*, a seller of fruit, in the now-defunct Mercado San Francisco.

She and the other *socias* (members) of the 10 de Agosto hold a contempt bordering on loathing for the women who come in from the outlying rural communities to sell. Without a booth or a license, these vendors are unwanted interlopers in the eyes of the Cuenca saleswomen — and this illegitimacy is unquestionably linked to their rural origins. While in-migrants from rural areas wear the *pollera*, so too do women proud of their deep roots in the city center. This working-class reality, however, does little to dislodge the idea of the *pollera* as an antiurban icon.

The *chola* is also pushed back into time: as with the nation's indigenous people, she is represented as a vanishing aspect of the city's colorful history. In Ecuadorian hotels that cater to tourists, the waitresses in the dining rooms wear bright polyester costumes that mimic those once worn by market women. In Cuenca, silver filigree earrings, embroidered blouses, woolen shawls, and *pollera* skirts lie on the shelves of expensive boutiques like flotsam washed up after a shipwreck, stained and tarnished by the dirt and sweat of the women who once wore them. The imagined *chola* who presides over these locales is an antique, a pleasant and harmless memory.

Bright *polleras* and tall white hats, however, do not always stay where the bourgeoisie want to see them. In the late 1990s, I saw women in *polleras* all over the city: riding in the back seats of passing taxis, perusing the shelves of the shiny new supermarkets, and waiting in line cheek by jowl with the tourists at the money exchange (see also Miles 1997). My last hour in Cuenca after a visit in December 1997 was spent in the airport restaurant, where middle-aged women dressed in elaborate *chola* finery waited expectantly for their Americanized daughters and sons, flying in from New York, Chicago, or Newark to visit home. Middle-class Cuencanos and foreign tourists alike find the presence of these old-fashioned figures in such settings incongruous, even laughable. In the minds of those who wish them to be merely folkloric, *cholas* should be neither modern nor mobile. For tourists, to travel to a distant land and see an exotic figure is rewarding; to find the same person at the airport imperils the very rationale for travel. White Ecuadorians, too, enjoy the image of the *chola* as rustic and antique far more than that of a *chola* wielding a video camera to film her son getting off the plane.[16]

The middle and upper classes, whether foreign or Andean, strive to contain the *chola* within a genre that Renato Rosaldo calls "imperialist nostalgia," in which white colonial societies of the recent past are imagined as "decorous and orderly," in implicit contrast to the conflict and chaos of our own times. These historical fantasies, he writes, invite the audience to enjoy "the elegance of manners [that once governed] relations of dominance and subordination between the races" (Rosaldo 1989:68). Such fantasies may be barely manageable in Cuenca — although I will have more to say subsequently about the fissures in the myth — but in the central highland city of Latacunga, city mythologies revolve around a far rowdier and more racially intransigent figure, the legendary Mama Negra.

Latacunga The Black Mother

I first saw the Mama Negra in September 1983, when I spent a few weeks in the city of Latacunga in Cotopaxi Province. I was just a student, on my way to begin field research in Zumbagua, an indigenous community in the mountains above the city. Although I did not know it at the time, a team of Ecuadorian anthropologists was in the city that week as well, recording the festival of the Mama Negra as part of a multivolume project to catalog all of the nation's rich folklore (Naranjo 1986). Latacunga, like Cuenca, is the capital of its province, and it too has an ancient and noteworthy past: its name can be found in the earliest Spanish documents, listed as the Inca settlement of La

Tacunga. Foreign visitors are attracted to the region by its "colorful Indian markets" and rugged Andean landscapes. But few tourists tarry long in the city. The archaeological sites boast few standing structures, and twentieth-century earthquakes demolished most of the city's colonial architecture. The climate is colder and gloomier than Cuenca's, too; its skies are dominated by the high mountain ranges on either side, capped by the towering hulk of Cotopaxi, one of the world's tallest active volcanoes. The surrounding province is rugged, poor, and indigenous, and the city itself is small, although it has a large and lively outdoor market. Ecuadorians know Latacunga primarily for a few local specialties, such as the hot biscuits called *allullas*, and for its famous annual festival, the Return of the Mama Negra, as colorful as the city's limestone buildings are gray.

I stumbled on the fiesta by accident, drawn out of my hotel by the loud noise of an enormous crowd. The normally quiet streets had been overtaken by long, raucous processions of costumed dancers; one figure towered above the others, riveting my attention. The notes that I scribbled begin abruptly: "It's the 'Mama Negra'— she is big."

The Mama Negra was indeed big, a huge woman on horseback who danced in her saddle and laughed uproariously as she sprayed the crowd with liquor from a baby bottle. Oddly, in this Andean city with a high indigenous population, where black people are a rarity, she was undeniably a *negra* — that is to say, the person playing her wore a shiny black mask with caricatural black features, a thick black wig, and huge gold earrings. Her sex was even more curious than her race. She was obviously a *mama*, surrounded by babies: a plastic doll that she held to her breast with one enormous hand, and two actual children, painted in blackface and wearing earrings, who sat behind her in saddlebags. But the person playing her was not a woman at all, but unmistakably a man. Her large, bouncing breasts and buttocks were not her own; they were made out of water balloons. Unlike better-known mixed-race female icons in Latin America, Latacunga's was a drag queen.[17]

This fantastic mother, who appears every September to lead a procession in honor of the Virgen de la Merced, is emblematic of a particular group of people, the women who sell fresh food and dry goods at El Salto, the largest market in the city. It is these market women, the city's *cholas*, who sponsor the fiesta of the Mama Negra; they hire the performers, the musicians, and the costumes, and the other residents of the city attend as their guests. The Mama Negra is their invention — although the roots of this peculiar cultural institution are now lost in the past.

In Latacunga, the racial meaning of the word *chola* is unmistakable, for racism in the central Sierra is virulent and unapologetic (see Weismantel 1988; Weismantel and Eisenman 1998). In Imbabura to the north, political activism and economic success have produced a local pride in being indigenous, irrevocably changing the city's racial hierarchy, even though Otavaleños still face prejudice at the hands of local whites;[18] in the south, as we have seen, an assumption of shared racial whiteness mitigates but does not eliminate racial prejudice. Here, in the central Sierra, a region of great poverty with a large indigenous majority, and a long, ugly racial history of indigenous people trapped for generations in involuntary servitude in colonial sweatshops and republican haciendas, the self-appointed protectors of Latacunga's public image cling grimly to a paper-thin veneer of bourgeois whiteness.

In local culture, *cholas* are simultaneously caricatured as physically unattractive compared to white women, eroticized as women whose racial degradation leaves them available for the taking, and assumed to be lazy, immoral, and depraved. Unsurprisingly, market women resent these vicious stereotypes and represent themselves instead as strong, hardworking, and respectable. Yet in their festival of La Mama Negra, the women of El Salto seem to have re-created the very image they detest of the nonwhite woman: dark-skinned in a nation that values whiteness and unfeminine according to bourgeois gender norms. On closer analysis, however, this grotesque figure offers a bold challenge to the evil mythology of race. As a big, black, masculine mother figure, the Mama Negra offers a working-class version of the *mestiza* nation, one that echoes many of the tropes found in other female icons, but with rather different political implications.

The Mama Negra both is and is not a sexualized mother figure like *la mestiza*, a meaning embodied in the *chola*'s fantasized breasts. Darquea Granda compared his Cuencana's breasts to rosebuds and to "trembling doves"; working-class men have more vulgar things to say. As a nationalist icon, these breasts are fetishized as both maternal and sexual. Lactating, they signify the mother of the nation, whose union with the white conqueror produced a new race; as the luscious objects of desire, they become the mixed-race fruit of this originary union, available for new sexual conquests by the Spaniards' descendants.

The Mama Negra, too, has big, bouncing breasts, heavy with meaning. Their plastic skins stretched taut over the liquid within, they contain ample liquid to feed the city — and the nation. Riding through the city, the Mama Negra squirts the crowd with her bottle, spraying "milk" onto all of Latacunga. According to the vendors, she feeds someone else as well. She is, they say, the Virgin's wet nurse, and the baby she holds to her breast is Jesus. For this Catholic nation, a symbolic mother must serve God and the Virgin as well as the nation. God himself, it would appear, needs the milk from the Mama's breasts.[19]

As a mother and a wet nurse, then, the Mama Negra is as generous as the elite could desire — but not so in her sex. For all her lascivious behavior, the large, masculine body of the Mama Negra is far too threatening for elite fantasies, in which the *chola* is passively available for the taking. In this, she resembles many actual market vendors. Muscular and powerful, dressed in work clothes, daubed with dirt or sweat — or, in the case of butchers, blood and bits of bone — they, too, look like women who can take care of themselves, financially and physically. In older depictions, the woman in a *pollera* carries a knife; today, vendors like to describe themselves as *machas* when they talk about their working lives.[20]

Like her masculinity, the blackness of the Mama Negra, too, offers a rebuff to certain sexual fantasies. The *mestiza* of fantasy is desirable because she is almost white and available because she is not. The Mama Negra destroys this tantalizing racial vacillation. Actual market women are diverse in appearance, and thus racially ambiguous as a group. The Mama Negra, by contrast, is clearly and uncompromisingly black — this in a part of the Andes where blackness exists almost solely as a fiction, the imaginary opposite of what is white. The powerful effect of her race on Latacungueños can be seen in the endless, almost obsessive debates about how and why a black woman could come to symbolize a city with few black residents, debates that dominate popular and scholarly treatments of the festival, eclipsing other aspects of its history and iconography.

If the Chola Cuencana of elite fantasy is a white and feminine figure, carefully held at a distance as an icon and only brought close in the sexual fantasies of predatory men, the Mama Negra is her antithesis. In making her big, black, and masculine, market vendors distance themselves from the unwanted image of the nonwhite women as the passive and degraded object of sexual predation. In their self-invention as the manly mother of Latacunga, the city's vendors represent themselves as generous enough to succor the entire city — and the baby Jesus to boot — but only on their own terms.

Mothers for the New Millennium

The new iconic Ecuadorians at the millennium are males. Indigenous political groups have resurrected an imaginary Inca king, a stern, manly figure who admonishes his subjects not to lie, cheat, or steal. In Cuenca, popular culture has generated other kinds of new Ecuadorian masculinities, less noble but more recognizable: the *cholo*-boys and the *ionys*. These images of the intrepid, streetwise migrant are based on the thousands of youths like Beto's older brother, who found no work and no future in Ecuador, and so departed for New York, where he works as a busboy.

In the popular imagination, both of these figures represent the failure of the mestizo nation. The Inca is clearly a rejection of Ecuador's Hispanic heritage; but in his popular incarnations, the migrant, too, is seen as a threat to the nation's culture and language. The older term, *cholo*-boy, was born in the 1990s; its hyphen names a hybrid, an Ecuadorian *cholo* whose speech is peppered with English. Only a "boy" in America, though, he still belongs to South America; not so the *iony*, whose name originates in the "I ♥ NY" bumper sticker he flaunts on his new car. Ecuadorian Spanish has vanished from his name, and so too has any perceptible ambivalence about the welcome he has received in his new country.

Neither of these figures is Ecuadorian mestizo, and neither represents the nation as a whole. In the United States, indigenous boys and Beto's white-skinned brother alike lose their Ecuadorian racial identities as they become U.S. Latinos. In Ecuador, the indigenous movement's fantasy pre-Columbian ancestor flaunts a racial purity no contemporary Ecuadorian can boast. This mirror-image of *blanqueamiento* has little appeal for the country's nonindigenous populations, despite the widespread appeal of the parties' economic platform.

The older figures of *mestizas*, then, may still fill a need in a country that remains hybrid and culturally multiple. The older attempts to use these symbols to impose racial homogeneity and paper over economic inequality are visibly bankrupt now; but the Chola Cuencana and the Mama Negra can also be seen as multivocal symbols, capable of expressing an image of an economically revitalized, ethnically plural, politically democratic Ecuador. Unfortunately, ongoing efforts by various constituencies across Ecuador and Latin America — the Latacunga city fathers, tourist agencies in Cuenca, or white intellectuals in Guatemala and Bolivia — to revitalize these figures have not focused on these elements, but instead seem mired in the white racial politics of the past.

Although the Mama Negra celebration is named for the big black mama, she is actually only one among a large group of performers and players. In addition to the man who plays the Mama Negra and others who serve as her attendants, the vendors of El Salto hire and invite many other participants as well. Market women from other cities and provinces come and march, as well as children and young adults from Cuenca, and indigenous performers come from the surrounding rural areas. From the countryside come the *curiquingues* — a highland bird of mythological significance, here portrayed by "happy dancers" dressed in paper plumes; *yumbos* or shamans from the rain-forest lowlands; and *huacos* (Andean shamans), men with white masks painted with stripes and spots, who carry deer skulls in their hands and make strange, inhuman noises. From town, there are schoolchildren dressed as angels who recite poems to the Virgin, and dance troupes of men and women dressed up as dancing *cholas*. (See Naranjo et al. 1986; Weismantel 2001). The only ones not pretending to be some fantastic alter ego are the market women themselves, who march stiffly and proudly, dressed in their finest *polleras*. The costumed figures dance along in no particular order, joined by any and all audience members who feel moved to participate. It is only because of the festival's name, and the attention paid by the crowd, that one knows that the Mama Negra is the focal point.

In the last few years, however, the market women's Mama Negra celebration, normally held on September 23, the feast day of the Virgen de la Merced, has been upstaged by a new event. In an innovation designed to attract more national and international attention, the city's *fiestas patrias*, or civic festival, held in November, has been made over into a new kind of Mama Negra procession. This event, unlike the market women's rowdy street party, is nationally televised, and its date is advertised in tourist guidebooks. The mayor and the historians of the city speak with pride of the way in which this new, secular festival, the creation of the city's most highly educated citizens, has "cleaned up" the market women's "disorderly" celebration. The choices that they have made in so doing are highly instructive: their Mama Negra celebration is not only more controlled and less spontaneous, but also far more hierarchical.

One of the organizers' first moves was to eliminate the heterogeneous, oddly costumed, and unpredictable rural performers — as well as the market women themselves — from the parade. In a videotaped interview with anthropology students from the Universidad de San Francisco, the city's mayor explained the reorganization as designed to focus the crowd's attention on the man portraying the Mama Negra. This, in his view, is a marked improvement on the chaotic market women's fiesta, in which groups representing different constituencies compete for the viewer's attention and interact with the crowd in unpredictable ways, sometimes teasing people, sometimes blessing them.[21] The new Mama Negra is still surrounded by troupes of dancers, but now the latter are identically dressed drill teams, whose similarity to one another emphasizes the singularity of the imposing central figure.

In this new configuration, the mayor and his political and business allies have imposed a new order on a fiesta that was originally not so much "chaotic," as they would have it, as "demotic": a people's party, suitable for a democratic city. Now, indigenous and rural residents have been relegated to the sidelines as mere spectators, while the parade has become a venue for white Latacunga to display its own, carefully orchestrated, vision of the region's celebrated modern folk culture. And while the central figure is still a cross-dressed man in blackface, the identity of the actor, and the gender and race of the troupes who surround him, have likewise been refashioned by the parade's organizers.

The new Mama Negra is surrounded by troops of white girls drawn from the wealthy neighborhoods of the city, dressed in matching *cholita* costumes, sexy and revealing versions of the market woman's traditional attire. In this retinue, the tranvestism of the Mama Negra and her company are reinterpreted in a fashion more in keeping with bourgeois sensibilities. The dancers' costume creates a temporary image of dark-skinned, exotic eroticism, but the viewers know that the body underneath remains safely white, bourgeois, and feminine.[22]

The ultimate remaking is of the *mama* herself. In the older religious festival, still held in September, the man who plays the Mama Negra is hired help, paid by the city's market women's associations to perform anonymously. In the new civic event, the Mama Negra is no longer an anonymous Everyman (or Everywoman); instead, a blue-ribbon commission selects a prominent politician or business leader to play the part. This alteration changes the significance of the performance. Now the black mask and false breasts of the Mama Negra mark a temporary inversion that solidifies rather than challenges the social order. When this wealthy and powerful man rides by on horseback, surrounded by scantily clad white women who pay him homage, his silly costume evokes nothing else so much as the degrading humor that so often targets nonwhite women. Far from playfully upending dominant ideologies of race and gender, the effect is a chilling reinforcement of the city's structures of power.

Not so long ago, Latacunga's politicians, business executives and even clergy were more interested in trying to suppress the Mama Negra celebrations than in incorporating them into the city's official *fiestas patrias*. These new efforts stem from a desire to emulate cities such as Cuenca, which have been far more successful at marketing their local folkloric customs to tourists. Type "Chola Cuencana" into a search engine and you will instantly be transported to a site managed by a Cuenca tourist agency (that will show you not an actual woman, but a photograph of an enormous statue to the Chola Cuencana erected at the city's main entrance, together with information about the sculptor). Approach the city by car, and billboards in the form of an enormous smiling Chola Cuencana greet you. The walls of every hotel, travel agency, and craft shop are adorned with photographs of market women in *polleras* and Panama hats, which reappear in miniature on postcards and brochures.

For the young entrepreneurs employed in this tourist industry, the ironies of the job are almost unbearable. English-speaking and cosmopolitan, they find themselves extolling those aspects of the city they consider most rustic and provincial. As tourism expands in otherwise contracting economies, such antiquated images as *la cholita* of the marketplace with her baskets of fruits and flowers become the only attractions capable of luring enough scarce foreign currency to shore up the faltering prosperity of the middle class. The tourist industry thus offers a Faustian bargain to its members, who hope that by selling romantic images of underdevelopment, they can make it go away.

Tourists are happy to find "the living past," but for Ecuadorians, the sight of a woman in a Panama hat can serve as a catalyst for disillusionment with the nation. On the Web sites, chat rooms, and Listservs that cater to the international diaspora of computer-literate Ecuadorians, one occasionally finds expressions of a nostalgic desire to sing songs about *cholas*, or to eat the traditional market foods now on sale in Ecuadorian neighborhoods in the United States, such as *cuy* (guinea pig), *mote pilo* (sugar cakes), *hornado* (roast pork), and *canelazos* (hot toddies made with cane alcohol). These are rare interludes, however, among an almost constant flow of critical analyses of the endemic political corruption, economic inefficiencies, and cultural blockages that prevent young professionals from returning home. For the highly educated, whose ambitions for themselves and their nations have been so long frustrated, the continual existence of open-air markets, and of women who dress as *cholas*, can seem like simply two more indicators of a collective inability to progress.

To the popular classes, the thick wool skirts, handmade hat, and silver jewelry of the twentieth-century market vendor have a very different significance. For them, rather than representing factors that drag the country back from modernity, this clothing symbolizes a vanished prosperity and self-respect once available to the city's hardworking, entrepreneurial residents, since destroyed by the short-sighted and self-serving policies of the political and financial elites. The Panama hat, which, though it was once worn in Cuenca by people of many classes and sexes, was nonetheless especially identified with the women in *polleras*, became the city's most successful export. Less evident to the city's bourgeoisie is that for ordinary working people in Cuenca, the *pollera* itself, as an expensive and beautiful object affordable by every *chola*, was the materialization of that economic success as experienced by the very people who, in their own eyes at least, made it happen. By the same token, it is today a bitter symbol of their economic and cultural losses.

A Cuencana selling masks for New Year's Eve, for example, was delighted to be asked about *cholas*. She evinced a great deal of pleasure in pointing out women dressed in *polleras* and Panamas, pinpointing specific neighborhoods around the city from which these women came and discussing the many positive associations that such clothing held for working-class Cuencanos. But when I asked her why she did not wear the *pollera* herself, a deep bitterness emerged. "I can't afford to," she said, and began to deluge me with figures. She knew exactly how much each item in a traditional *chola* outfit cost and contrasted these large sums angrily with her own earnings from seasonal items such as masks or the underwear she sells the rest of the year. Her grandmother had worn the *pollera* with pride all her life, but she would never be able to do so.

Many of the economic disasters that have befallen Latin America defy explanation; but there is some truth to the idea that disregard for Ecuador's human, cultural, and natural assets on the part of its elites is partly to blame for its current crisis. Despite recognizing the value of the woman in the *pollera* for the tourist industry, Cuenca's political and business classes, not unlike the Latacungueños, have long been determined to clean up the messy street performances of *chola*-ness and to replace them with photographs, statues, and museum displays. The city fathers seem intent on eliminating the *pollera* even from the places most associated with it: women who have licenses to sell in the city markets, and so come directly under municipal control, are forbidden to wear them while they are working.

Indeed, policies regarding the urban markets are an example of the way by which the deeply held racial prejudices of the professional classes distort political and economic policy in the Andes. Bourgeois beliefs about the women who work there are a force preventing development, or at least this is the conclusion reached by the authors of a USAID-sponsored policy study of Ecuador. They were baffled by the state's refusal to provide basic infrastructure and sanitation for the produce and meat markets that feed most of the country's residents. This policy, coupled with uniformly repressive management and legislation, prompted the authors to conclude that so perverse a strategy could only be explained by "a deeply ingrained bias" toward the markets and those who worked there (Tschirley and Riley 1990:193). In refusing to allow this lively economic sector to develop, neoliberal politicians violate the very free-market principles they claim to hold dear.

In Cuenca, a city desperate for tourist dollars, efforts to eliminate the clothing, the livelihood, and the very presence of the women who inspired the city's iconic image seem similarly self-defeating. Policies to encourage development would provide incentives for women in traditional retail occupations to dress as *cholas*, and would invest in making the markets clean and safe, not only for tourists, but also for the Ecuadorians who work and shop there. Such a plan would recognize the economic value of the produce markets, which employ many more people than the supermarket chains that are supplanting them. And it would also revitalize the once-prosperous small businesses, now slowly disappearing, that produce and sell *pollera* skirts, ikat-dyed shawls, heavy silver earrings, and starched white hats. But such a vision of local and regional development is unlikely as long as educated people remain convinced that the road to progress lies in imitation of the United States and Europe — in short, in *blanqueamiento*.

In New York, as the rubble of the twin towers was steadily cleared and debates heated up over the site's present and future use, the tale of a sudden and disastrous ending slowly turned into a story of becoming. Ecuadorians such as Darwin Maldonado, one of the hundreds of undocumented immigrants hired to clean dirtied and damaged shops and homes around the ruins of the World Trade Center, became part of the *blanqueamiento* process (*All Things Considered*, National Public Radio, January 15, 2002). The nation of Ecuador, too, has endured a collapse of its own, more gradual and less publicized than the events of September 11, 2001, but intensely traumatic nonetheless. It too must salvage what it can, make shrines to the dead, and begin anew. In both Cuenca and Latacunga, there are efforts afoot to revitalize local cultural symbols; but to the extent that these are still plagued by the politics of *blanqueamiento*, they can only recapitulate the errors of the past and so continue the nation's dissolution.

In Ecuador, people feel betrayed by modernity itself. Instead of bringing with it an inevitable and irreversible *mestizaje*, the processes unfolding at century's end energized and mobilized the nation's impoverished nonwhite members in ways not seen since the colonial period. Now the traditional political classes seem to many to be obsolete and exhausted, while the one group whom they never even bothered to consider a threat, indigenous people in alliance with others, seized the political initiative.

Indigenous intellectuals have exacerbated this sense of time out of joint by seizing on the powerful metaphors of the millennium and of the quincentenary. Slogans painted on walls and shouted in the streets announced that the era of white domination had ended, and a "new five hundred years" has begun. Nonindigenous Ecuadorians have learned a new concept from Quichua metaphysics, the Pachakutik or "earth-turn," in which a radically new order suddenly emerges to replace the old.

No one is actually suggesting a return to a premodern past. What is needed is a new definition of progress, of nationhood, and of Ecuador's place in the global political economy. The effort to impose a homogeneous whiteness on a richly diverse nation has had devastating effects, resulting in a populace alienated from their nation and their state. Little wonder that indigenous people have so vehemently rejected the pretense of *mestizaje* and forged instead an indigenous ideology that decenters whiteness once and for all. Nor is it surprising that a generation of Cuencanos known as the *hijos de la pollera* (the sons and daughters of the city's working women) feel little loyalty to the place of their birth. "We are forgetting the *pollera*," said a young woman who wore blue jeans to her job as a maid in the Hotel Crespo. "All everyone can think of is buying an airplane ticket to the United States. There is nothing here for us now" (see also Miles 1997:55, 2001).

The story is not over. Jason Pribilsky (2001a) suggests that rather than seeing the migrants from the southern highlands as having left for good, it is more accurate to see them as long-distance commuters, with wives and children as well as houses and investments in Ecuador. Neither the migrants of Cuenca nor the indigenous protestors have actually abandoned Ecuador; instead, both groups are determined to do whatever it takes to make the nation a place where they and their families can live and prosper, even if that means tearing down the nation-state altogether or re-creating the entire society bit by bit in New Jersey, New York, Miami, Chicago, and Los Angeles. This new, transnational Ecuador has already begun to produce some revitalized *cholas*, pressed into service as emblems of new economic relationships. In Cuenca, where financial institutions are trying to capture some of the flow of dollars between young migrants and their rural mothers, a television commercial shows a *chola* at work in her wooden kiosk in the Azogues market. Clad in a New York T-shirt peering out of her cardigan draped over her *pollera*, she looks into the camera, smiles, and proclaims: "Todo lo que me manda va directo al Pinchincha" (everything he [my son] sends to me goes straight to [the bank of] Pichincha) (Pribilsky 2001b).

In New York, in the meantime, on Roosevelt Avenue in Queens, a neighborhood with an enormous concentration of Ecuadorians,

> the chola shows her face in . . . the front windows of the immensely popular [appliance] store, Créditos Económicos . . . where migrants can go and shop for loved ones back home. They sell incredibly cheap gas stoves, fridges, and stereos (under $100) that are made and delivered in Ecuador. . . . The stoves are delivered in the rural communities and a photo is taken of the momentous occasion and sent back to Queens. Literally hundreds of photos of *pollera*-clad women are pasted to Créditos' front window — next to their new stoves and fridges. (Pribilsky e-mail 2002)

In the economic and social realm, then, the image of the woman in a *pollera*, like Ecuadorian culture itself, continues to find new spaces in which to thrive. What would it take, then, for the nation's political culture to undergo a similar revitalization, powerful enough to reverse the processes of implosion and explosion that threaten its integrity? Certainly it must begin by inviting the marginalized into the center and replacing *blanqueamiento* with a more pluralistic vision. Too, instead of a single icon, such a state will need a pantheon of figures; a few *cholas* could well find a place between the lofty Inca and the wisecracking *iony*. The Chola Cuencana could certainly find common ground with both these men. She is more than half *indígena* herself and full of street smarts, and, as Pribilsky states, she is already a familiar figure in Queens. But if these new *cholas* are to have any political clout with the disenchanted populace, they cannot be white girls playing *cholita* in a miniskirt and high heels or a leering businessman in blackface. What is needed is the kind of Mama Negra who invites everyone to her party, from Amazonian and Andean shamans to the baby Jesus himself, and then doesn't mind if all the attention isn't always turned on her. Along with the *chola morena*, she can remind the nation how it has really survived: through the generosity, hard work, clever innovation, and fierce combativeness of women and men nourished by the potent and intoxicating mother's milk of Ecuador's diverse peoples and vibrant cultures.

ACKNOWLEDGMENTS

My thanks to Norman Whitten for inviting me to contribute to this volume and for his own pathbreaking work on ethnicity and ethnogenesis in Ecuador. I also owe a great debt of gratitude to younger scholars such as Rudi Colloredo-Mansfeld and Amalia Pallares, but most especially to Ann Miles and Jason Pribilsky, both of whose work on Cuenca greatly informs this chapter. I am especially grateful to Jason, who commented on an earlier version of this chapter, and generously provided me with both published and unpublished material from his own research. I only wish that I could have incorporated more of them here, and I urge readers interested in Ecuador to look for his work, as well as that of the other authors mentioned above. I also wish to acknowledge the work of Elisabeth Enenbach, my research assistant (and someone who knows a *pasacalle* from a *sanjuanito*), who provided additional information about the history of the Chola Cuencana.

NOTES

1. For a much fuller discussion of the meanings of *chola* throught the Andes and a bibliography of works that discuss both *cholo* and *chola*, see Weismantel 2001. Especially important references include Seligmann 1989, 1993, 1998 and De la Cadena 1996 on Peru; Albro 2000, Rivera Cusicanqui 1996a, 1996b and Stephenson 1999 on Bolivia.

2. See also Orlove 1993; Whitten 1981.

3. For more on nineteenth-century Ecuador, see Clark 2001.

4. For a provocative discussion of this issue in Cuzco, see De la Cadena 2000.

5. The popular musical setting by Rafael Carpio Abad, best known today, is a *pasacalle;* it was originally published with a setting by Clodoveo Gonzalez. For more

information on the music, and to listen to the song, consult http://ingeb.org/songs/cholacue.html or www.cuencanos.com/cuenca/musica.html. (Elisabeth Enenbach, personnel communication, 2002). On the poetry of Ricardo Darquea Grande, see Lloret Bastidas 1982:271–77.

6. I will make only passing reference here to issues of gender; see Weismantel 2001 for a fuller discussion. See also Herrera 2001 for an overview of recent work on gender in Ecuador.

7. The term *popular class* (*clase popular*) is commonly used in Latin America.

8. For similar nationalist *mestizas* from other countries, see Abercrombie 1992; Albro 2000; De la Cadena 1996, 2000; Gillespie 1998.

9. See Whitten 1981. The most often quoted discussion of this topic is by Whitten's student Ron Stutzman (1981); other students of his who have discussed ethnicity, the state, and *mestizaje* include Marcelo Naranjo 1981, Weismantel in Weismantel and Eisenman 1998. More recently, other authors who quote Whitten's original discussion or Stutzman in developing their own argument include Cervone 2001, and Guss 2000.

10. Similarly, Mexico's *china poblana* has become increasingly European in her features (Gillespie 1998:36).

11. A longer discussion of this issue can be found in Weismantel 2001; see especially chapter 4.

12. Almeida et al. 1992; Frank 1992; Meisch 1992, 2000; Selmeski 2000; Whitten 1996; Whitten, Whitten, and Chango 1997.

13. This recent emigration is primarily to Europe rather than to the United States: by the year 2000, seven thousand migrants per month were arriving in Spain, the most popular destination (Jokisch and Pribilsky 2002).

14. See Jokisch and Pribilsky 2002 for a summary of the recent impact of remittances on Ecuador's economy.

15. For a discussion of comparable themes in Bolivia, see Albro 2000.

16. This image is thanks to Jason Pribilsky.

17. There is a widespread and lively tradition of male cross-dressing in women's clothes in indigenous fiestas, but this is rather different from the case at hand.

18. On Imbabura, see Colloredo-Mansfeld 1999; Meisch 1998. Indigenous attitudes are changing rapidly elsewhere in the country as well; see, for example, Pallares 1992 on Chimborazo Province.

19. Despite the inroads made by evangelical Protestantism, which has thousands of converts, Ecuador remains profoundly Catholic in its public and political culture, which, unlike Mexico's, never distanced itself from the Roman Catholic Church.

20. For a Peruvian example, see Seligmann 1995; for Bolivia, see Albro 2000.

21. My field notes reveal something of these interactions:

One pair danced separately . . . two men with white masks, painted with stripes and spots (later I saw more of them, six in a group). They had batons in one hand

and deer skulls with horns in the other, both of these also painted white, with colored bars and rows of spots. They wear pants made of crocheted lace from the knees down, and a woman's shawl tied neatly across the shoulders. . . . They had big backboards with all kinds of stuff sewn or fastened on, and lots of paper flowers attached on top of everything else. . . . They whistle and clack the deer head and baton together. They danced together in a circle, going up and down and waving the skulls and batons. Then, they got a nursing mother — in the act of nursing — with another babe clutching her skirts, out there, and started dancing in front of her, honoring/menacing her with baton and skull and chanting "A ha ha — A ha ha" as they thrust the baton and skull forward. Next they chose a small child. The child's father didn't want to, but the crowd said "let them *soplar* him" . . . the child crouched terrified, while his dad held him out towards the dancers, not letting him escape — but also providing comfort — while this whole thing of thrusting forward while chanting was repeated. Next, they did it to a market women's five-gallon container (I couldn't see contents) — she was delighted, smiling. Then the military band, just behind, decided to start playing again and the two went back to just dancing.

22. See Abercrombie 1992 for a fuller discussion of similar performances in a Bolivian context.

REFERENCES

Abercrombie, Thomas

1992 La fiesta del carnaval postcolonial en Oruro: Clase, etnicidad y nacionalismo en la danza folklórica. *Revista Andina* 10(2):279–352.

Alarcón, Norma

1989 Traddutora, Traditora: A Paradigmatic Figure of Chicana Feminism. *Cultural Critique* 13:57–8.

1983 Chicana's Feminist Literature: A Re-vision through Malantzin/or Malantzin: Putting Flesh Back on the Object. In *This Bridge Called My Back*. Cherrie Moraga and Gloria Anzaldúa, eds. Pp. 182–90. New York: Kitchen Table Press.

Albro, Robert

2000 The Populist Chola: Cultural Mediation and the Political Imagination in Quillacollo, Bolivia. *Journal of Latin American Anthropology* 5(2):30–88.

Almeida, Ileana, et al.

1992 *Indios: Una Reflexión Sobre el Levantamiento Indígena de 1990*. Quito: IDLIS/Abya Yala.

Anzaldúa, Gloria

1987 *Borderlands/La Frontera: The New Mestiza*. San Francisco: Aunt Lute Books.

Caesar, Terry, and Eva P. Bueno

1998   Introduction: The Politics of the Popular in Latin American Popular
        Culture. In *Imagination Beyond Nation: Latin American Popular Culture*.
        Terry Caesar and Eva P. Bueno, eds. Pp. 1–18. Pittsburgh: University of
        Pittsburgh Press.

Cervone, Emma

2001   Machos, Mestizos, and Ecuadorians: The Ideology of Mestizaje and the
        Construction of Ecuadorian National Identity. Unpublished ms.

Clark, Kim

2001   Género, Raza y Nación: La Protección a la Infancia en el Ecuador
        (1910–1945). In *Estudios de Género*. Gioconda Herrera, comp.
        Pp. 183–210. Quito: FLACSO/ILDIS.

Colloredo-Mansfeld, Rudi

1998   "Dirty Indians," Radical Indígenas, and the Political Economy of Social
        Difference in Modern Ecuador. *Bulletin of Latin American Research*
        17(2):185–206.

1999   *The Native Leisure Class: Consumption and Cultural Creativity in the Andes*.
        Chicago: The University of Chicago Press.

De la Cadena, Marisol

1996   The Political Tensions of Representations and Misrepresentations:
        Intellectuals and Mestizas in Cuzco, 1919–1990. *Journal of Latin American
        Anthropology* 2(1):112–47.

2000   *Indigenous Mestizos: The Politics of Race and Culture in Cuzco, Peru,
        1919–1991*. Durham: Duke University Press.

Frank, Edwin H.

1992   Movimiento Indígena, Identidad Étnica y el Levantamiento: Un Proyecto
        Político Alternativo. In *Indios: Una reflexión sobre el levantamiento
        indígena de 1990*. Ileana Almeida, et al., ed. Pp. 499–527. Quito:
        ILDIS/Ediciones Abya-Yala.

Gillespie, Jeanne L.

1998   Gender, Ethnicity, and Piety: The Case of the China Poblana. In
        Imagination Beyond Nation: Latin American Popular Culture. Terry Caesar
        and Eva P. Bueno, eds. Pp. 19–40. Pittsburgh: University of Pittsburgh
        Press.

Guerrero, Andrés

2000   Estudio Introductorio: El Proceso de Identificación: Sentido Común
        Ciudadano, Ventriloquía y Transescritura. In *Etnicidades*. Andrés
        Guerrero, ed. Pp. 9–60. Quito: ILDIS/FLACSO-Ecuador.

Guss, David M.

2000   *The Festive State: Race, Ethnicity, and Nationalism As Cultural Performance*.
        Los Angeles: University of California Press.

Herrera, Gioconda

    2001   Estudio introductorio: Los estudios de género en el Ecuador: Ester el conocimiento y el reconocimiento. In *Estudios de Género*. Gioconda Herrera, ed. Pp. 9–60. Quito: ILDIS/FLACSO-Ecuador.

Jokisch, Brad D.

    2001   Desde Nueva York a Madrid: Tendencias en la migración ecuatoriana. *Ecuador Debate* (December) 54:59–84.

Jokisch, Brad, and Jason Pribilsky

    2002   The Panic to Leave: Economic Crisis and the "New Emigration" from Ecuador. International Migration 40(4):75–102.

Lloret Bastideas, Antonio

    1982   *Antología de la poesía cuencana*. Cuenca: Consejo Provincial de Azuay.

Meisch, Lynn A.

    1992   "'We Will Not Dance on the Tomb of Our Grandparents': 500 Years of Resistance in Ecuador," *The Latin American Anthropology Review* 4(2):55–74.

    1998   The Reconquest of Otavalo, Ecuador: Indigenous Economic Gains and New Power Relations. *Research in Economic Anthropology* 19:11–30.

    2000   Crisis and Coup in Ecuador. *Against the Current* 15(3):14–16.

Miles, Ann

    1997   The High Cost of Leaving: Illegal Emigration from Cuenca, Ecuador, and Family Separation. In *Women and Economic Change: Andean Perspectives*. Ann Miles and Hans Buechler, eds. Pp. 55–74. Arlington, Va.: American Anthropological Association.

    2001   Like a River Rushing by: An Anthropological Story of Transnational Migration from Ecuador. Unpublished ms.

Naranjo, Marcelo V.

    1981   Political Dependency, Ethnicity, and Cultural Transformations in Manta. In *Cultural Transformations and Ethnicity in Modern Ecuador*. Norman E. Whitten, Jr., ed. Pp. 95–120. Urbana: University of Illinois Press.

Naranjo, Marcelo V., et al.

    1986   (compiler) La Cultura Popular en el Ecuador, vol. 2 *Cotopaxi*. Quito: CIDAAP (Centro Interamericano de Artesanías y Artes Populares).

NPR (National Public Radio)

    2002   *All Things Considered*. January 15.

Orlove, Ben

    1993   Putting Race in Its Place: Order in Colonial and Postcolonial Peruvian Geography. *Social Research* 60(2):301–36.

Pallares, Amalia

    2000   Bajo la sombra de Yaruquíes: Cacha se reinventa. In *Etnicidades*. Andrés Guerrero, ed. Pp. 267–314. Quito: FLACSO/ILDIS.

Poole, Deborah

    1997   *Vision, Race, and Modernity: A Visual Economy of the Andean Image World*.
           Princeton N.J.: Princeton University Press.

Pribilsky, Jason

    2001a Nervios and "Modern Childhood": Migration and Shifting Contexts of
           Child Life in the Ecuadorian Andes. *Childhood* 8(2):251–73.

    2001b From Sindrome del Dólar to Dolarización: Effects of Dollarization on
           Migrant Households of Southern Ecuador. Paper delivered at the Invited
           Session, "The Ecuadorian Crisis: Fostering Realms of Inclusion and
           Exclusion." Twenty-third International Congress of the Latin American
           Studies Association. Washington, D.C.

Radcliffe, Sarah, and Sallie Westwood

    1996   *Remaking the Nation: Place, Identity, and Politics in Latin America*. London:
           Routledge.

Rivera Cusicanqui, Silvia, et al.

    1996b Trabajo de mujeres: explotación capitalista y opresión colonial entre las
           migrantes aymaras de La Paz y El Alto, Bolivia. In *Ser mujer indígena,*
           chola o birlocha en la bolivia postcolonial de los años 90. Silvia Rivera
           Cusicanqui, ed. Pp. 163–300. La Paz: Ministerio de Desarollo Humana.

Rosaldo, Renato

    1989   *Culture and Truth: The Remaking of Social Analysis*. Boston: Beacon Press.

Rowe, William, and Vivian Schelling

    1991   *Memory and Modernity: Popular Culture in Latin America*. London: Verso.

Seligmann, Linda J.

    1989   To Be in Between: The Cholas as Market-women. *Comparative Studies in*
           Society and History 31(4):694–721.

    1993   Between Worlds of Exchange: Ethnicity among Peruvian Market Women.
           Cultural Anthropology 8(2):187–213.

    1998   Estar entre las cholas como comerciantes. *Revista Andina* 32(2):305–34.

Selmeski, Brian R.

    2000   *Imágenes impresionantes: El levantamiento indígena-militar ecuatoraino*.
           Video distributed by Latin American Video Archives.

Smith, Carol A.

    1996   Myths, Intellectuals, and Race/Class/Gender Distinctions in the
           Formation of Latin American Nations. *Journal of Latin American*
           Anthropology 2(1):148–69.

    1997   The Symbolics of Blood: Mestizaje in the Americas. *Identities*
           3(4):495–522.

Stephenson, Marcia

    1999   *Gender and Modernity in Andean Bolivia*. Austin: University of Texas
           Press.

Stutzman, Ronald

    1981   El Mestizaje: An All-Inclusive Ideology of Exclusion. In *Cultural Transformations and Ethnicity in Modern Ecuador*. Norman E. Whitten, Jr., ed. Pp. 45–94. Urbana: University of Illinois Press.

Tate, Winifred

    2001   Into the Andean Quagmire: Bush II Keeps up March to Militarization. *NACLA Report on the Americas* 35(3):45–54.

Tschirley, David, and Harold Riley

    1990   The Agricultural Marketing System. In *Agriculture and Economic Survival: The Role of Agriculture in Ecuador's Development*. Morris D. Whitaker and Dale Colyer, eds. Pp. 193–244. Boulder Colo.: Westview Press.

Weismantel, Mary

    1988   *Food, Gender, and Poverty in the Ecuadorian Andes*. Philadelphia: University of Pennsylvania Press.

    2001   *Cholas and Pishtacos: Stories of Race and Sex in the Andes*. Chicago: University of Chicago Press.

Weismantel, Mary, and Stephen F. Eisenman

    1998   Race in the Andes: Global Movements and Popular Ontologies. *Bulletin of Latin American Research* 17(2):121–42.

Whitten, Norman E., Jr.

    1981   Introduction. In *Cultural Transformations and Ethnicity in Modern Ecuador*. Norman E. Whitten, Jr., ed. Pp. 1–44. Urbana: University of Illinois Press.

    1985   *Amazonía ecuatoriana: La otra cara del progreso*. 2nd ed. Quito: Abya-Yala.

    1996   The Ecuadorian Levantamiento of 1990 and the Epitomizing Symbol of 1992: Reflections on Nationalism, Ethnic-Bloc Formation, and Racialist Ideologies. In *Culture, Power, and History: Ethnogenesis in the Americas, 1492–1992*. Jonathan D. Hill, ed. Pp. 193–217. Iowa City: University of Iowa Press.

Whitten, Norman E., Jr., Dorothea Scott Whitten, and Alfonso Chango

    1997   Return of the Yumbo: The Indigenous Caminata from Amazonia to Andean Quito. *American Ethnologist* 24(2):335–91.

Yúdice, George

    1992   Postmodernity and Transnational Capitalism. In *On Edge: The Crisis of Contemporary Latin American Culture*. George Yúdice, ed. Pp. 1–28. Minneapolis: University of Minnesota Press.

CHAPTER 13

Epilogue, 2003

NORMAN E. WHITTEN, JR.

I believe that one of the values of the indigenous peoples in Ecuador,
independent of what they have achieved otherwise in relation with
the government, has been the practice of dialogue. . . .
We learn that we can live together.— Luis Macas

The gala Ceremony of Hope to celebrate the inauguration of President Lucio Edwin Gutiérrez Borbúa began at 2:30 P.M. on Wednesday, January 15, 2003. Attending the inauguration itself, which began at 11:00 A.M. and ended at 1:00 P.M., were the presidents and their entourages from Cuba, Venezuela, Colombia, Peru, Bolivia, Chile, and Brazil, the prince of Spain and the president of the Organization of American States, among other lesser dignitaries. Forty-five thousand people, including delegations from all twenty-two provinces, attended the Ceremony of Hope, held in the Atahualpa Olympic Stadium in North Quito, while thousands of others remained outside. A column in *Hoy* (January 16, 2003) called the ceremony "political and symbolic," and described banners carried by well wishers as "one force only," "the people empowered," and "future of peace." The neologism *refundar,* to "refound" the country, was used to express the millenarianism of the event.

Musicians and singers from all over the country performed and a contingent of commandos parachuted into the stadium, one of them bearing Miss Ecuador (Isabel Ontaneda) as his "passenger," while a marimba band played Afro-Ecuadorian coastal music. The president and others arrived at 4:00 P.M. and the festivities continued. This ceremonial event and the quotidian, political, and ritual processes now underway bring this book to a close. The summary of ongoing day-to-day actions; executive, legislative, and judicial activity; new and old personalities, economic decisions, and social movements in the making are grist for new research. Here I critically review some salient dimensions that take us from January 21, 2000, to January 20, 2003.

On October 15, 2002, eleven candidates were running for the presidency of the republic. Two emerged as clearly ascendant: Lucio Gutiérrez, the decorated career military colonel (retired) presented in the opening paragraph of the introduction, and Álvaro Fernando Noboa Pontón, the richest man in

Ecuador and a member of one of the wealthier families of the world. Even with the vote split among the many candidates, Gutiérrez won more than 20 percent of the vote and Noboa more than 17 percent. Populist affirmation overwhelmed established party politics. In a not-so-distant third place was Socialist candidate León Roldós, brother of the late Jaime Roldós, the populist president elected in 1979. At the very bottom of the list were Osvaldo Hurtado, with a little more than 1 percent of the vote, and Antonio Vargas, with a little less than 1 percent. Only ten thousand votes separated the ex-president of the republic from the indigenous leader from Amazonia.

Gutiérrez constructed the party Sociedad Patriótica 21 de Enero (January 21st Patriotic Society) and modeled his campaign on the act of millennial rebellion of January 21, 2000. Often dressed in an army uniform, he stressed his background as that of a dedicated military citizen. He told of the need for the ouster of Jamil Mahuad and explained how his own career was truncated by the generals of the Ecuadorian military, even though the national congress voted unanimously to grant immunity to those leading the grassroots uprising. Noboa, an elite *guayaquileño* whose father made a fortune in the banana-plantation and export business, struck out against Gutiérrez, repeatedly calling him a "communist," and telling the electorate that he (Noboa) was a first-rate business man (*empresario*) who could run the country efficiently and solve its financial woes. His votes came mainly from sectors of coastal Manabí and Guayas and from north Andean Carchi. Wealthy businessman from the Coast versus self-made military careerman from the Oriente and Sierra provided the choice for the coming four years (2003–2007).

During the second phase of the runoff election campaign, Gutiérrez often dressed in stylized suits that represented a blend of civilian and military garb. He spoke constantly of democratization, the end of poverty, bringing the corrupt to justice, and ending the system of rule by the "political class." At the end of October, he traveled to and within the United States dressed in conservative blue suit with a white or light-blue shirt and a red tie to assure powerful figures from Wall Street to Capitol Hill that he would continue to pay the national debt, negotiate at once openly and honestly with the International Monetary Fund, avoid even the appearance of leftist politics, stay clear of Hugo Chávez, and honor the written contract with the United States for its military base in Manta. An extended interview with *Miami Herald* writer Andrés Oppenheimer opened his brief U.S. tour. In the published column, Oppenheimer (2002) questioned the use of the name 21 de Enero. This millennial date that so many Ecuadorians took (and take) as a symbol of liberation from corruption, political-economic elitism, and cronyism in government and business, could, perhaps, link the president-elect of Ecuador to Hugo Chávez and Fidel Castro. Oppenheimer's piece was reported in the

Ecuadorian press as painting Gutiérrez as a *golpista*, one who favors military or other coups, revolts, rebellions, or revolutions over democratic processes.

Golpista connects syntagmatically with "leftist" and "communist" in North American and Latin American unreflective and decontextualized imagery and signals a position of opposition to neoliberalism. Oppenheimer's column is, in many places, appropriately ambiguous, and ends with this message: "perhaps . . . the real problem of Ecuador is its lack of a democratic culture." After Gutiérrez's successful U.S. tour, the rating of Ecuadorian Brady bonds rose slightly, but the Ecuadorian reporting of Oppenheimer's column resuscitated Cold War ambience onto Latin American peoples and places.

On November 24, Ecuadorians again went to the polls and voted Lucio Gutiérrez into the office of the presidency, with an ample 17.5 percent margin over Noboa. Almost immediately, the president-elect began to link the nodes of modernity to his prior millennial agenda. Soon after his election, he went to Colombia to meet with president Álvaro Uribe Vélez to assure him that Ecuador would not involve itself in internal affairs in Colombia, but at the same time he indicated publicly his desire to meet with guerrilla leaders to work toward a peaceful settlement to the escalating conflict and reciprocities of violence. Back in Ecuador, he was not to be found when Fidel Castro and Hugo Chávez arrived in Quito to participate in the dedication of the Chapel of Mankind, but was reported by at least one major newspaper to have scheduled a meeting with Castro in Guayaquil after the ceremonies. No follow-up reporting on such a meeting occurred. Soon thereafter he was off to Europe to meet with heads of state and leaders of financial communities before returning to Ecuador for the Christmas holidays, spent in Tena and in Quito, to build his cabinet and prepare for the inauguration to take place on January 15, 2003.

The seemingly inconsistent alternation from a millennial to modern posture, from defiance of a system of global power to acquiescence to its Faustian hegemony, was not and is not lost on those involved in the indigenous movement and other social movements of Ecuador, or to others attracted to the possibility of alternative lifeways and social chances. We should not be surprised by pendulum swings — even rapid ones — between political economic poles, between the signs of radical change and those of institutional stability. As stated in the introduction:

> Modernity and millenarianism are inextricably intertwined. They constitute a mutualist dynamic that propels Ecuadorian cultural systems from one historical event to another. The conjuncture that they form is impelling and synergistic; it cannot be unbundled or its elements dissected. . . . No dichotomy or dialectic can help us understand the transformative dialogues, dramatic events, and charged political and cultural fields and par-

adigms that punctuate recent and distant history. Only an understanding of the changing significations and resignifications of diversity can lead us to an illumination of real people at local levels, the national affects of conjoined localities in motion, and the all-encompassing contradictory and complementary globalizations that constrain and release these affects. We seek to put human faces in the modern-millennial picture and to understand that real lives move into and through the conjunctures.

Inversions and Transformations

To understand Ecuador, and similar national systems undergoing modern transformations through millennial processes, it is necessary to return to the first epigraph of the introduction: "The world over, millenarian and revivalistic movements . . . originate in periods when societies are in liminal transition between major orderings of social structural relations."

The presidential inauguration in congress and the celebration in the Atahualpa Olympic Stadium together constituted a millennial event with built-in symbolic inversions of the structure of wealth, social prestige, and power. Symbolic inversion (Babcock 1978; Turner 1974) is especially salient in liminal periods of revelatory ideological transformation. Here processes of resignification emerge in multiple arenas such that hegemonic constructs become publicly recognized and contested. The indigenous uprising of 1990, the indigenous March for Land and Life of 1992, the subsequent uprisings and strikes mentioned by many authors in this book, the indigenous-military rebellion of January 21, 2000, and other moments of social movement (including the victory in the brief 1995 war with Peru), culminating in the election of Gutiérrez as president of the republic, all represent the phenomenon of symbolic inversion transformed into social action and consequent structural change. Symbolic inversions as manifest in such tropes as the "refounding" of the republic take place in liminal periods, which by definition come to an end. Symbolic inversions are powerful instruments of social change, and they often signal alteration in the fabric of society; but they are not themselves social reversals. Just because indigenous and other people use symbols, metaphors, and tropes of role and status inversion (e.g., Whitten 2003) does not mean that they have succeeded or will succeed in reversing the actual social role attributions and practices attached to positions of structural power.

The outcome in practical action at the end of the process of intense symbolic inversion may be a radical change, as in a revolution; or a restoration of the status quo, as in a ritual of rebellion (e.g., Gluckman 1958; Turner 1974); or something altered and at least partially inchoate and ambiguous, as in the present situation in Ecuador. Gutiérrez himself preferred to speak of a "rebellion," rather than a "coup," to refer to the 2000 ouster of Mahuad (Jijón 2001:34; Oppenheimer 2002). For a short time after the January 21 indigenous-popular-military *golpe* against the Mahuad government, radical change was signaled. But within three hours, more or less, it was clear that the government, soon to be under the presidential rule of then vice president Gustavo Noboa (no relation to Álvaro Noboa), was shaken but intact. Power was not held by the people in motion, but rather by the immense influence of the United States, which, through the agency of its State Department representative, Peter Romero, threatened total isolation of this small democratic republic if "order" were not restored.

Symbolic inversions and social reversals occur in complex interrelationships in local, regional, national, and global settings, and the actions and consequences of the people undertaking specific actions move, sometimes without their volition, from these various settings or levels of organization. The social and political — let alone economic — changes themselves may be minuscule, especially when compared to the critical symbolic structures revelatory of hegemonies to be contested and confronted and at least temporarily dissipated. By the time actual elections for the president and congress of Ecuador took place, the pendulum swings between structural power and contrastructural modes of power were inconsistent, and the new rhetoric of power reflected the former, even though the movement driven by the rhetoric began with the latter.[1]

Ephemeral though they may at times seem, the dynamics of symbolic inversion are, I argue, fundamental to the politics and poetics of local identity that contribute to transformed collective representations which, in turn, motivate social movements. *Dynamics* is a key word here; we are not seeking a baseline from which change takes place. Social dynamics in political-economic settings are always present, however small-scale they may be at any given time and place. Cultural systems constitute the motivating force of those dynamics, and symbolic action is at the core of these systems. Symbolic inversion involves mimetic equalization of power relationships that connect spiritual power to secular political power (Taussig 1997; Whitten, Whitten, and Chango 1997; Guss 2000; Whitten 2003). But the connections may attenuate as institutional order is at least temporarily restored. In Ecuador, social dynamics and symbolic action of a millennial character have moved through the social fabric like the weft across the warp of intricate abstract designs. The movement accelerates as this book goes to press.

These designs are evident in the presentations of the various chapters of this book, from the ghosts of colonialism to the medieval Catholic and ancient Andean imagery of millennial indigenous Salasaca; from purgatory and debt peonage of evangelical indigenousness in Tena to the modernist devil in Esmeraldas. Such a fabric was woven on the collective loom of indigenous movements as evidenced in the modern political transformations of indigenous Secoya people, the indigenous *caminata* from Puyo to Quito, and in the life-history lessons of Luis Macas; they are painted into history by the artists of Tigua. The highly diverse sexualities of Afro-Ecuadorian women conjoin in many ways with the exaggerated counterhegemonic images of the Chola Cuencana and the Mama Negra of Latacunga.

The tapestry of *la ecuatorianidad*— only facets of which are illustrated, explicated, and interpreted in this book — must be seen and at least partially understood by reference to the intersections of distinct significations and resignifications that ramify out from a colonial and modernist history, straining toward a millennial matrix to shape a desirable collective destiny expressed increasingly as a human phenomenon of interculturality. A populist rebellion, not a revolution, did occur in 2000 in Ecuador, and again in 2002; the consequences thereof are making themselves felt at all levels of human discourse and social action ramifying out of this important nation.

Social Ballast and Political-Economic Constraints

While Andrés Oppenheimer of the *Miami Herald* was interpreted in the Ecuadorian press as throwing metaphorical cold water on Gutiérrez by using the image of the Latin American political *golpista*, another bucket came from an Ecuadorian newspaper taking aim at his racial features. According to Simón Espinosa Cordero in his November 28 editorial in *Hoy*, the Guayaquil newspaper *El Telégrafo* carried the banner "un longo en la presidencia," to inform its readership of the "complexion" of the new chief of state. *Longo*, in Ecuador, is a pejorative word for *indio*. It is a *mala palabra*, a dirty word, street talk, bad graffiti denoting and connoting something or someone out of place. Dirt and delinquency come to mind in its connotations (Rahier 1999; Colloredo-Mansfeld 1999; Whitten 2003).

I will not dwell on this theme here, but we need to be reminded as this book comes to a close of the powerful representation of the "whitening" ideology attached to the macroconstruct of *el mestizaje* (blending), by which elite and other Ecuadorians characterize the body of the nation. Its unsubtle turn to skin complexion in pejorative dimensions was discussed in the introduction to this book and came up in one way or another in all of the ensuing chapters. Every time a specialist on Ecuador (or Venezuela, Colombia, Peru, or Bolivia) thinks she or he can avoid discussing the dimensions of *mestizaje*, the ugly side of pejorative labeling to diminish an accomplishment of some person by "darkening" that person's persona seems to emerge in one quarter or another (de la Torre Espinosa 2002; Robinson 2002). A president who is not of the *clase política* has been elected by a majority of *el pueblo*, and he speaks as an Ecuadorian to *el pueblo*. There are and will be those who resent this, irrespective of political tendency or economic standing. To such resentment must be added the matrix of global structural power and the racialized languages of control within which this small but highly significant nation exists.

Global and Regional Political Economy Simplified

The status of the person representing a foreign country to a host country during a time of power transition signals something of the position of that country toward the host. The presidents of Andean and other countries came to Ecuador for the inauguration of the new president, as did vice presidents and other luminaries. Fidel Castro, Hugo Chávez, Álvaro Uribe, Alejandro Toledo, Gonzalo Sánchez de Lozada, Ricardo Lagos, and Luiz Inácio "Lula" da Silva were all there, some with their spouses, in spite of pressing issues at home. Prince Philip represented Spain.

An official delegate of the United States to the Ecuadorian presidential investiture was Otto J. Reich, a self-avowed "anticommunist" Cuban exile whose nomination to the position of assistant secretary of state was blocked by Senate Democrats in 2001. According to the *New York Times* (January 10, 2003:A-6), Reich "botched relations with Venezuela and had taken too hard a line on Cuba." In view of opposition from senior Republican senators and lack of support from Secretary of State Colin L. Powell, President George W. Bush did not renominate Reich but instead appointed him to the National Security Council as "special envoy to Latin America," beyond the reach of congressional approval. Naming Reich as official delegate to Gutiérrez's investiture is certainly of political-symbolic significance.

César Gaviria, president of the Organization of American States, also attended and was reported by *Hoy* and the *New York Times* to be talking to Otto Reich of the United States on January 14. The subject of the discussion was the establishment of a Friends of Venezuela group to end the crisis in Venezuela, "whether President Hugo Chávez likes it or not" (*New York Times*, January 16, 2003:A-8). The day after the Ceremony of Hope in Quito, President Uribe announced in Bogotá that the narcotic-guerrilla situation in Colombia constituted a greater threat to the world than the problem of Iraq (*Hoy* online e-mail subscription list, January 16, 2003). Such a statement obviously carries very high political-symbolic significance and links by implication adjacent nations (*Hoy* January 15, online news) of Panama, Venezuela, Brazil, Ecuador, and Peru to a threat to world peace comparable to that of the Middle East and Asia.

In 2003, Ecuador's geopolitical position in world politics may be precarious. In his 2002 State of the Union address, Bush claimed an "axis of evil and its terrorist allies" existed in North Korea, Iraq, and Iran. On January 16, 2003, the president of Colombia asserted that his country was a greater threat than Iraq. As this epilogue draws to a close (January 20, 2003), the United States threatens an imminent war on Iraq and the rhetoric emanating out of North Korea and the United States is at best unnerving. Every morning I read the most recent world events online in *El Comercio* and *Hoy*; sometimes it takes a day or more before they are reported in the local newspaper or even in the national U.S. press. Bush seems to view North Korea as enemy number two, to be handled by diplomatic means. Reason and sense are hard to grasp and cartoonists and journalists in Ecuador, as in the United States and Europe, are having a field day. It has not been demonstrated that Iraq constitutes a nuclear threat and that country has opened its doors to United Nations inspectors to look for nuclear, biological, and chemical weapons. North Korea does constitute a nuclear threat and dismissed the UN inspectors in late December 2002. The United States targets Iraq and not North Korea. Iraq has the second-largest oil deposits in the world, and North Korea has none. Information on these subjects is on the front page of Ecuadorian newspapers, right alongside the latest activities of prominent indigenous people, the president, and his relationships with other powerful forces, and the most recent guerrilla, military, and paramilitary activities in Colombia.

The U.S. troops patrol and engage in relatively small-scale battles in the areas on the Afghanistan-Pakistan border, with U.S. air support. These military and pending military activities spread the military out to at least two distant fronts if war is launched and sustained in the Middle East and Asia, and if the war on terrorism continues it is spread even further. The debt-ridden military-industrial complex of the lone world superpower is stretched very thin and Bush tells the world that the United States will suffer economically by even the one war with Iraq. Estimates of the cost of this war range from $50 billion to $70 billion to $100 billion to $200 billion. Evidence of this situation is very familiar to all Ecuadorians through its excellent system of media reporting.

As the U.S. Congress votes modest increases for the Department of Education National Resource Area Centers and Fellowship Program (NRC-FLAS), most of the new funds go to instituting and/or implementing Middle East, North Africa, and South Asian cultural and language studies. This skewing shorts the very modest increases available for studies of Latin America and the Caribbean, the very regions that supply a rising tide of legal and illegal immigrant people with diverse and often poorly understood cultural systems. For urban Ecuadorians, the third most populous city after Guayaquil and Quito is not Cuenca, but New York.

As to the position of Ecuador as an Andean nation in the world systems of powers, Princeton historian Jeremy Adelman (2002:41) writes:

> The foundations of democratic states in the Andes are in serious trouble. Governments seldom complete their terms without armed insurrections, and economies have not grown in a generation. While citizens plead for basic justice from states bereft of functioning course, rulers grovel for loans in exchange for cutting public services.

Partially accurate though this is, phrases such as "armed insurrection" (entirely wrong in the case of Ecuador) attach metonymically to other condensed hegemonic images such as the pejorative "*longo*-as president," "indigenous uprising" (*indios alzados*), "military coup" "communism," "Bolivarianism," accusations and associations with revolutionary movements and drug trading in Colombia, the besiegement of the Chávez presidency in Venezuela, scandal upon scandal in Peru, and the ever present U.S. xenophobia projected onto Castro's Cuba. These metonymic and sometimes metaphoric attachments are all too often taken to be "real" in powerful places such as Washington and New York, where critical decisions are made on scant or absent local-level or regional information.

Facticity— that which is made up, unreal "facts" used to promote erroneous or misleading violent representations, violent epistemes, and violent action — seems to create a fictitious reality as 2003 opens and progresses. Some time ago Michael Taussig, writing of Colombia in a system of Western dependency, put the matter this way with regard to his own interests in the study of terror: "my subject is not the truth of being but the social being of truth, not whether facts are real but *what the politics of their interpretation and representation are*" (Taussig 1986: xiii; emphasis added). My concern is that the political weapon of facticity can be intensified with regard to Ecuador and other Latin American nation-states, especially given the current labeling of democratic processes in seemingly Cold War rhetoric. A highly salient illustration of what I am writing about is manifest in the New Year's message on this subject written by the distinguished columnist of the *Washington Post* Writers Group, George Will (2003). In an apocalyptical New Year's message Will wrote an editorial commenting on North Korea and the U.S. position on it. Before wishing his vast readership an ironic "Happy New Year," Will says that "the international left, and its American fellow travelers" are those who oppose effects of globalization and are consequently anti-

American. If this is not the dangerous, intolerant, xenophobic McCarthyist language of the Cold War or the 1950s, I do not know what is. This is representative of the language of structural power to which I have alluded.

It is certainly true that Ecuador has had seven presidents over the past decade, none of whom since Sixto Durán Ballén has served a four-year term. There have been indigenous uprisings independent of and/or conjoined with popular strikes, some of them resulting in territorial successes, increased esteem from nonindigenous people toward indigenous and other people, and expanded and expanding political spaces for intercultural encounters and negotiation in virtually every contested arena. But there have not been "armed insurrections." There is no serious communist movement in Ecuador, Bolivarianism is scarcely discussed there, and the blood-*less* ousters of corrupt presidents represent an unusual political phenomenon, one worthy of study in its own right with a careful focus on democracy beyond millennial capitalism.

There is something clearly Ecuadorian — and very human — in the great transformations that have racked the country, something that the authors in this book endeavor successfully to capture. The imagery of Ecuador is badly served by lumping it in with other nations confronting common pressures and powers in very different manners. Ecuador deserves to be understood in its own right, and its people, regions, and social dynamics need to be conceptualized in their diversity as well as in their oneness of a country in various processes of transformation.

Let us carry enduring and emergent political facticity further, using scholarly discourse as our base. Adelman's (2002) article, published in the *New Left Review*, carries a map of Panama, Venezuela, Ecuador, Peru, and Bolivia that very carefully identifies five regions of extreme danger to the stability of the hemisphere: Caquetá and Putumayo Departments in Colombia, and Esmeraldas, Carchi, and Sucumbíos Provinces in Ecuador. Maps, we are taught in school, are to be taken as "factual," what they name and demarcate is "real." No other specific departments or provinces (states) are so demarcated on Adelman's map for the entire rest of this vast Andean-Amazonian (and for all but Bolivia, coastal) region. It would appear that Ecuador has three of the five critically dangerous provinces in the entire Andean-Amazonian region.

The reasons for pinpointing Putumayo and Caquetá are sketched in the introduction to this work, as is the situation of the northern Ecuadorian provinces that abut Colombia. But the connotations here of map facticity are that the entire revolutionary-reactionary armed conflict and drug-producing system of southern Colombia is extant in northern Ecuador. And it is emphatically not. Odd, too, is the omission of the entire Pacific Lowlands area of Colombia (western sectors of the departments of Nariño, Cauca, Valle, and

Chocó) from the pinpointed hot spots, for here the AUC forces have added genocide of Afro-Colombians to their agenda (e.g., Pardo 2002). This system, too, is moving into Ecuador, creating a hazard to black people of Esmeraldas and Carchi far superseding the possible presence of coca-plant growing or paste production.

As the U.S. military-industrial complex accelerates its pace of production for possible war in the Middle East and Asia, and holds to its "War on Terrorism" expenditures and deployments, escalation of the expanding war machine under the banner of "homeland security" extends more and more to Colombia through the mechanism of Plan Colombia with its pivotal foci on the U.S. base in Manta, Ecuador, and Tres Esquinas (and other sites such as those at Mocoa and Florencia), Colombia. With this expansion, issues of political and economic interdependency and political-economic asymmetry not only receive scholarly attention in professional publications (e.g., *Cultural Survival* 2003), but also embed themselves in the system of knowledge of Latin American people, among others.

There is a culture of interdependence among political and economic power wielders in the United States. It behooves us to ask who stands to gain from the development of war apparatus to be deployed in another nation, in this case Colombia and elsewhere in the Andean-Amazonian countries. According to Adelman (2002:68) the top recipients of campaign funds from aerospace industries providing the UH-60 Blackhawk and Super-Huey UH-1 helicopters made by United Technologies and Textron for deployment in Colombia are Republican George W. Bush and Democrat Joseph Lieberman. Ecuadorians often wonder why the U.S. representatives in its country are so concerned with Latin American corruption in the face of its own cultural and social system of interlocking political and economic influences among powerful people in high places. We are reminded here that Republican Dwight D. Eisenhower, in his role of president of Columbia University after World War II, coined the trope "military-industrial complex" in 1961 to warn the U.S. citizenry about issues such as those sketched by Adelman, to whom we again turn:

> As the drums of war roll [George W. Bush] . . . is demanding a revision of the constitution [of the United States of America] to increase the powers of the Presidency. Washington, meanwhile, is expanding the scope of its "military aid" southwards under the so-called Andean Regional Initiative (ARI), stepping up its operations in Peru, Bolivia, *and Ecuador*. (Adelman 2002:70; emphasis added)

No wonder the new president-elect of Ecuador shed his hybrid uniform-suit that apparently garbed his image as populist leader imbued with military discipline, faith to *la patria*, and trustworthy honesty, in order to don a conservative red, white, and blue no-nonsense business suit for his visit to New York, Washington, and Miami. Money to Ecuador for the Andean Regional Initiative is the carrot, and the threat of isolation as the Cuba of the Andes is the stick. Geopolitics seem so simplistic compared to the intricacies of cultural life portrayed in this volume. All of the people in Ecuador, as elsewhere in the world, would seem to be caught up in, and endangered by, such simplicities of power, and many of them know it. Ecuador, along with Colombia and Venezuela, has one thing the U.S. economy requires and demands: oil. In the United States, a national news analyst on Friday evening, January 17, reminded viewers that when you go to war you need a dependable oil supply. The focus of the analyst was on Iraq (war) and Venezuela (oil). A huge oil reserve lies east of the Andes in the western Amazonas-Orinocan region of Venezuela, Colombia, Ecuador, and Brazil. This same region, half a world away from the threatened U.S. military action in Asia, is also a huge reservoir — one of the largest in the world — of fresh water, another commodity-to-come for U.S. interests, particularly in its western and southwestern states.

Within Ecuador itself the issue of the Free Trade Area of the Americas (FTAA) is highly contested. One of the issues is increased dependence on U.S. products subsidized by the U.S. government, especially in the framework of Ecuadorian dollarization. In October, 2002, Quito was the site of the seventh summit wherein ministers from thirty-four nations of the Americas gathered and were confronted by thousands of indigenous and nonindigenous protesters from many nations to be affected by U.S.-sponsored globalization and privatization (e.g., Becker 2002). Because petroleum, Ecuador's largest export, also threatens the environment, its means of exploitation are contested from various positions. On the one hand, the nation seeks to double its production, pumping twice as much crude as previously from the Amazonian region over numerous Andean fault lines down to the coast, and, on the other hand, people from all over the world join Ecuadorians in protesting the environmental destruction and pending disaster that may arise from such an ill-chosen route, which goes through some of the most biologically diverse and fragile ecosystems in the world.

As though staging its own protest (as one of many *urcu mamas* portrayed in Tigua art and in indigenous cosmology), in early November, 2002, the volcano El Reventador (the exploder) erupted in the northeastern *montaña* in the very route of the pipeline, sending sulfur gases and an inch of ash to blanket the northern Sierra from Quito to Ibarra. In Pastaza Province, site of the 1992 March from Amazonia to Quito, Canelos Quichua and Achuar indigenous people united in their opposition to petroleum exploration and exploitation in their territories, as did the Shuar in neighboring Morona-Santiago to the south. One hopes that the facticity of leftist political agitation does not come to adhere to the real people in action in Amazonian Ecuador or to their Sierran congeners who protest the danger of moving crude oil over innumerable fault lines in fragile ecosystems.

On Friday, January 3, twelve days before the presidential inauguration, the distinguished Quito newspaper *El Comercio* initiated a special section of interviews, milestones of transformation, special photographs of indigenous leaders, and a weird map of the indigenous areas of Ecuador. The title of the special section is *indios al poder* (Indians empowered). It is a strange and contradictory presentation, oscillating from negative stereotypes to justified transformation. The tertium quid that holds the contradictions presented in this special section together seems to be a chilling implication that suggests repeatedly that at the base of the indigenous and populist struggle is leftist politics. Serious research such as that by Amalia Pallares (2002:22) counters this pervasive idea.

These stereotypes and their underlying stigmata question the legitimacy of indigenous leadership. A question frequently raised is whether Ecuadorian people such as Luis Macas are prepared to assume major roles in the new government. In an interview for this section, Estuardo Remache, President of ECUARUNARI from 2000 through 2003, was questioned as to what qualifications indigenous people might *lack* and asked: "Are indigenous people prepared to govern the state?" Remache's answer was perfect: "We are not prepared to rob, to lie, to plunder," he answered in Spanish, echoing beautifully the forceful transformative rhetoric of the indigenous movement, *ama shua, ama llulla, ama quilla*. Then he went on to say what real people are prepared to do: "We are prepared for living, for working, and for supportive activities." Immediately thereafter, the interviewer raised the specter of leftist politics, citing Chile (presumably under Allende), Cuba, Nicaragua, Panama, Grenada and Venezuela. Remache's answer was that people did not want radical ruptures with the IMF or with other institutions that could help Ecuador in its development.

On January 5, the national legislature came to carnivalesque "order" and, through an alliance between the Social Christian Party (PSC) and the Democratic Left (ID), elected a member of the Democratic Left (which is not the dominant party) for the four-year parliamentary presidency. Except for this election, which at the time seemed to violate the constitution, chaos reigned in the congress. All of this was broadcast live on television and radio networks. Writers for national newspapers underscored the lack of national governability. As the congress continued its opposition to the president elect, he made plans to visit George W. Bush on February 11 and took a dramatic stand against the congressional leadership.

The struggle seems to endure and even escalate. The legislative, judicial, and executive powers of the nation-state of Ecuador are not on the same course. At the time of this writing the military leadership, altered by the new president, seems also to be perturbed by civil events. It remains to be seen how Ecuador fares in the new milieu with a president not of the *clase política*, with the legislative majority mostly outside of his range of influence, and with an indigenous movement increasingly suspicious in some quarters of the apparent posture toward acquiescence to global powers and the U.S. superpower. Of what worth, then, is this work? Can it be taken to be more than a collection of essays by a group of committed scholars talking about a small and atypical place in South America?

Millennial Ecuador in the Modern World

It is abundantly obvious, in Ecuador or elsewhere, that multiple local and regional cultural, ecological, social, aesthetic, and cosmological systems are articulated variously to so-called global systems. In a speculative and quite generalized (and consequently abstract) essay on the nature of capitalism, Fernando Coronil (2001:82) has this to say:

> Insofar as globalization works by reinscribing social hierarchies and standardizing cultures and habits, it is a particularly pernicious imperialist modality of domination. But insofar as it decenters the West, effaces differences between centers and margins, and postulates, at least in principle, the fundamental equality of all cultures, globalization promotes diversity and represents a form of universality that may prefigure its further realization.

If this polarization of the dynamics of globalization and cultural diversity is juxtaposed to a position taken by the British Latin American Bureau (Corkill and Cubitt 1988:1) some fifteen years ago, that "in some ways [Ecuador] is the most purely 'typical' Latin American republic," part of our answer emerges: *In Ecuador, we view dramatic processes that exist throughout the region and around the globe.* Our critical perspectives on cultural transformations and social dynamics for this small but highly significant country may carry considerable potential for the sharpening of analytical powers in a rapidly changing world. Analytical skill is required at every level of civil society, if understanding is to replace political labeling and facticity, and if people's systems of symbolic action and praxis, their specific experiences of socioeconomic change, and the cultural and human consequences thereof are to be adequately understood.

Affirming that Ecuador seldom makes international headlines (except when a president is deposed or a volcano erupts), the authors go on to say that "Ecuador tends time after time to emerge as the median case where we can find something of every other country. Looking at Ecuador . . . can tell us a lot about Latin America as a whole" (Corkill and Cubitt 1988:1). When these authors wrote they focused especially on Ecuador under the presidency of León Febres Cordero, a man whom Ronald Reagan called "a champion of free enterprise" (Corkill and Cubitt 1988:77) and whose presence gained considerable favor from the banking elite as manifest in World Bank policy-based loans. Gutiérrez would seem to be the antithesis of Febres Cordero as populist contrapowers are opposed to right-wing establishment power. During the presidential regime of Febres Cordero, his antithesis was Frank Vargas Pazzos, a charismatic air force general who once held the president hostage in the air force base of Taura, near Guayaquil, detaining him at gunpoint until he made him cry on national television. Vargas released Febres when Vargas was granted congressional amnesty for his act. This antithesis between populist and right-wing can be taken through the Cold War xenophobic mentality and political facticity that I have tried to sketch, to connote right-wing/left-wing polarity, which the new president clearly wishes to avoid.

I noted at the beginning and the end of *Cultural Transformations and Ethnicity in Modern Ecuador* (1981), that Ecuadorian people and cultural systems tend toward increasing centralization and diversity at the same time. I went on to say that no set of stultifying polarities so cherished in the social sciences of the West can help us understand what is unfolding there and, by implication, elsewhere in the world of humanity in action, and humanity threatened. I think my generalization still holds, though it has caused great consternation among many colleagues who have reviewed this position and *insist* that Ecuador's people are *either* homogenizing *or* they are diversifying. The stultifying polarities that frame so much of the social sciences and political decisions of the modern West continue to baffle me, perhaps because I choose to spend time in Ecuador with diverse people in motion who use international systems of communication and transportation, pay their way in dollars, and fall prey to corrupt systems of banking and government. These people represent the quintessence of cultural difference, and their knowledge of survival strategies and their imaginaries of community, history, and destiny never cease to intrigue me. Regardless of what is happening within the political economy emanating from on high, these very different people regard themselves as *ecuatorianos/as*, as well as fully human beings.

It is my hope that the critical essays in this book captivate the reader, just as systems of Ecuadorian interculture intrigue the authors. These chapters may lead us together to think through the specific, here represented by facets of local and regional Ecuadorian cultural life and national social action, to the more general, which is Latin America, and on, of course, to the most general of all, the global, the world of people straining to escape from the myriad crucibles of domination and hegemony of the few and to achieve recognition and respect in their sustained and expanding interculturality.[2]

On December 31, 2002, president-elect Lucio Gutiérrez made an important millennial move. He announced two pivotal cabinet positions: Luis Macas Ambuludí as the ministro de agricultura and Nina Pacari Vega Conejo as the canciller. An indigenous person is now the minister of agriculture, and another indigenous person, a woman at that, occupies the position of secretary of state, the first indigenous woman to do so in all of the Americas. Both of these Ecuadorians are superbly qualified for their appointments. In spite of its escalating urbanity, much of Ecuador is still a rural, agricultural-oriented country, and it is also very much a part of contradictory globalizing systems of money, power and influence. Now, for the first time ever, indigenous people of Ecuador — one from Saraguro, the other from Cotacachi — will be in key positions as the government faces inward to its diverse peoples who produce food for consumption and other products for commodification and export and outward toward the many forces that beset it. Let us hope that Macas's words are not only prophetic, but can be properly communicated worldwide: "We learn that we can live together."

ACKNOWLEDGMENTS

I am again indebted to the authors in this work who not only contributed these chapters, but of at least equal importance, engaged in a fairly steady conversation with me from their varied vantage points about the issues raised, discussed, and left partly unresolved. Brian Selmeski clarified some issues with regard to the campaign of Lucio Gutiérrez and offered insights into the role and imagery of the Ecuadorian military, for which I am grateful. I greatly appreciate the critical readings of drafts of this epilogue by Rachel Corr, Jean Rahier, Mike Uzendoski, and Michelle Wibbelsman and not only the several readings but also active collaboration on data retrieval and interpretation and final editing by Sibby Whitten. Linda Belote deserves very special thanks. She attended the entire buildup to the inauguration, the investiture itself, and the Ceremony of Hope in the stadium and corrected this epilogue accordingly. Without her firsthand account this work would have been weaker. As always, any and all shortcomings and failures to interpret effectively, explicate clearly, or communicate understandably, are mine alone.

1. In 1981, I used the trope "critical anthropology" (Whitten 1981:23) to characterize the kind of argument and discussion offered in parts of this epilogue, in the introduction, and elsewhere in this book, developing the concept further in other publications in the 1980s. By the 1990s, however, others used this phrase in very different ways. It took on more and more denotations and connotations of radical postmodernism, so I have dropped it. Nonetheless, the reader interested in historical continuities and discontinuities might wish to consult the orientation of an early predecessor work that led, eventually, through many twists and turns, to this book.

2. Authors in this book have discussed and mentioned some particular actors on the stage of Ecuadorian cultural transformations and social dynamics. No one, including the editor, has endeavored to mention everyone consistently involved in events that moved the nation from one critical moment to the next. From at least the early 1990s, and before, some very diligent people have contributed greatly to large-scale sociopolitical changes that those of high power, economic wherewithal, and self-ascribed prestige could not imagine. I list some of these people here who are mentioned only in passing, or not at all, in the text. Any one or any grouping of them could substitute for the names that we have brought forth in our chapters: José María Casabango, Oscar Chalá Cruz, Blanca Chancoso, Pedro de la Cruz, Juan García Salazar, Valerio Grefa, Leonidas Iza, Ampam Karankas, Ariruma Kowii, Miguel Lluco, José Manuel Quimbo, Salvador Quishpe, Estuardo Remache, Napoleón Santos, Cristobal Tapuy, Auki Tituaña, and Ricardo Ulcuango.

REFERENCES

Adelman, Jeremy
> 2002   Andean Impasses. *New Left Review*, n.s. 18 (November–December):
> 40–72.

Babcock, Barbara
> 1978   (editor) *The Reversible World: Symbolic Inversion in Art and Society*.
> Ithaca: Cornell University Press.

Becker, Marc
> 2002   Ecuador: Opposition to Wider Trade Pact Grows. *North American
> Congress of Latin America (NACLA)*, 36(3):1.

Colloredo-Mansfeld, Rudi
> 1999   *The Native Leisure Class: Consumption and Cultural Creativity in the Andes*.
> Chicago: University of Chicago Press.

Corkill, David, and David Cubitt
> 1988   *Ecuador: Fragile Democracy*. London: Latin American Bureau (Research
> and Action).

Coronil, Fernando

2001   Toward a Critique of Globalcentrism: Speculations on Capitalism's
        Nature. In *Millennial Capitalism and the Culture of Neoliberalism*. Jean and
        John Comaroff, eds. Pp. 64–87. Durham: Duke University Press.

Cultural Survival (multiple authors)

2003   Indigenous Responses to Plan Colombia. *Cultural Survival Quarterly*,
        26(4).

de la Torre Espinosa, Carlos

2002   *Afroquiteños: Ciudadanía y racismo*. Quito: Centro Andino de Acción
        Popular (CAAP).

El Comercio

2003   Indios al poder: Temas de interés. January 3 special section. Electronic
        document. http:/www.elcomercio.com/fotos/flash/indígenas/
        temas.html.

Gluckman, Max

1958   *Analysis of a Social Situation in Modern Zululand*. Rhodes-Livingstone
        paper No. 28. Manchester, England: Manchester University Press.

Guss, David M.

2000   *The Festive State: Race, Ethnicity, and Nationalism As Cultural Performance*.
        Berkeley: University of California Press.

Jijón, Carlos

2001   El coronel y sus laberintos. *Vistazo* 813 (July): 34–36.

Oppenheimer, Andrés

2002   Ecuadorean Candidate Vows to Pursue Harmony and Democracy. The
        Oppenheimer Report. *The Miami Herald* Web site, October 31.

Pallares, Amalia

2002   *From Peasant Struggles to Indian Resistance: The Ecuadorian Andes in the
        Late Twentieth Century*. Norman: University of Oklahoma Press.

Pardo, Mauricio

2002   Entre la autonomía y la institucionalización: Dilemas del movimiento
        negro colombiano. In *Black Identity and Social Movements in Latin
        America: The Colombian Pacific Region*. Peter Wade, ed. Special
        issue of the *Journal of Latin American Anthropology* 7(2):
        60–84.

Rahier, Jean Muteba

1999   ¿Mamí, que será lo que quiere el negro?: Representaciones racistas en la
        revista Vistazo, 1957–1991. In *Ecuador racista: Imágenes e identidades*.
        Emma Cervone and Fredy Rivera, eds. Pp. 73–110. Quito: Facultad
        Latinoamericana de Ciencias Sociales (FLACSO).

Robinson, Lori S.

2002   A New Day for Blacks in Ecuador. *The New Crisis*, 109(6): 32–35.

Taussig, Michael

 1986   *Shamanism, Colonialism, and the Wild Man: A Study of Terror and Healing*.
        Chicago: University of Chicago Press.

 1997   *The Magic of the State*. New York: Routledge.

Turner, Victor

 1974   *Dramas, Fields, and Metaphors: Symbolic Action in Human Society*. Ithaca:
        Cornell University Press.

Whitten, Norman E., Jr.

 1981   Introduction. In *Cultural Transformations and Ethnicity in Modern
        Ecuador*. Norman E. Whitten, Jr., ed. Pp. 1–41. Urbana: University of
        Illinois Press.

 2003   Symbolic Inversion, the Topology of "El mestizaje" and the Spaces of "Las
        razas" in Ecuador. *Journal of Latin American Anthropology* 8 (1):14–47.

Will, George

 2003   Worries Abound As We Contemplate a New Year. *The News-Gazette*
        (Champaign, Illinois). January 1:A-6.

General Information on Ecuador

MICHELLE WIBBELSMAN

The Nation

The Republic of Ecuador was one of three countries (with Colombia and Venezuela) to emerge from the collapse of Gran Colombia in 1830. Article 1 of the 1998 Ecuadorian constitution declares Ecuador a social, legal, sovereign, unitary, independent, democratic, pluricultural, and multiethnic state. Its government is republican, presidential, elective, representative, responsible, alternative, and participatory, and its administration is decentralized.

Location

Ecuador is located in northwestern South America, bordering the Pacific Ocean at the Equator, between Colombia and Peru. Longitude 77°30′ west and Latitude 3°28′ south.

Area

Ecuador's total area including the Galápagos Islands and 6,720 square kilometers of territorial sea is 283,560 square kilometers. Mainland area is 256,370 square kilometers. Total semiprotected area is approximately 2,769,030 hectares (27,690 square kilometers) in nine national parks, seven ecological reserves, and two faunal production reserves.

Geography

Ecuador is divided into four environmentally distinct regions: Coast, Sierra, and Oriente (Amazonian region) on the mainland and the Galápagos Islands in the Pacific Ocean. These regions, in turn, are divided administratively into twenty-two provinces, which are subdivided into cantons composed of parishes. Quito is the national capital and Guayaquil is the nation's largest city and principal commercial port. Elevations range from sea level at the Pacific Ocean to 6,267 meters (Chimborazo, Ecuador's highest peak). At 5,897 meters, snowcapped Cotopaxi is the highest active volcano in the world.

Biodiversity

Although Ecuador covers only 0.2 percent of the earth's surface, it contains some of the greatest biological diversity in the world. Ecuador's flora include twenty-five thousand plant species, most of them endogenous

375

to the region. Some areas feature the highest recorded concentration of plant diversity on Earth. Ecuador's fauna include more than 4,000 vertebrate species, 1,550 bird species, 1,250 fish species, 375 amphibian species, and 350 reptile species. The bulk of animal life in the country's unique and tremendously diverse environmental niches comprises insects and other arthropods.

Current Environmental Issues

Current issues include deforestation, soil erosion, desertification, water pollution, pollution from oil production wastes, toxic pesticides and herbicides, and mercury poisoning.

Population Dynamics

The population of Ecuador is 13,183,978 (July 2001 estimate). Population distribution is 65 percent urban (especially in Guayaquil, with approximately 3 million; Quito, with approximately 2 million; and Cuenca, with 272,708) and 35 percent rural. The annual population growth rate is estimated at 2.1 percent. According to CODENPE (Consejo de Desarrollo de las Nacionalidades y Pueblos del Ecuador), 30 percent to 40 percent of the population is indigenous, which means that one in every three Ecuadorians is indigenous. People often classed as mestizos comprise 55 percent of the population in this estimate; Afro-Ecuadorians 9 percent; and others, including blancos, 1 percent. These percentages range widely, however, with some estimates of the indigenous population as low as 10 percent, the Afro-Ecuadorian population at 5 percent, and the mestizo or blanco-mestizo population at 80 percent. Two recent phenomena raise important issues in assessing population size: mass emigration and increasing numbers of immigrant Colombians. More than half a million Ecuadorians have emigrated to other countries since 1998. When emigration is considered, New York City, not Cuenca, is the third-largest city of Ecuadorians. Since 1985, armed conflict in Colombia has displaced more than 2 million people, many of whom have crossed the border into Ecuador in search of safety. The northern Sierra province of Carchi is reported to have eleven thousand to thirteen thousand refugees and neighboring Imbabura to have 1,322. The NGOs monitoring the effects of Plan Colombia in Ecuador believe that the implementation of the plan will lead to the displacement of an additional fifteen thousand people, five thousand of whom are expected to seek refuge in Ecuador.

Distinct People and Languages

Spanish is the official language of Ecuador. In addition, multiple native languages are spoken among Ecuador's thirteen indigenous nationalities and other ethnic groups distributed in 1,334 communities in the Andes, 62 on the Coast, and 548 in the Oriente.

Sierra

Andean Quichua   language: Quichua   population: 3,000,000

Coast

Awá   language: Awapit   population: in Ecuador 900–1000

Chachi   language: Cha'palaa   population: 4,000

Tsháchila   language: Tsa'fiqui   population: 2,000

Epera   language: Siapedie   population: 250
  (Emberá in Colombia)

Oriente

Secoya   language: Secoya   population: in Ecuador 500

Siona: language: Paicoca   population: 250

Waorani   language: Wao terero   population: approximately 2,000

A'i-Cofán   language: A'ingae   population in Ecuador: 500

Záparo   language: Záparo,   population: 150
                      Quichua

Amazonian Quichua   language: Quichua   population: 70,000

Shuar   language: Shuar   population: 70,000

Achuar   language: Achuar   population: 3,000

Shiwiar   language: Shiwiar,   population: 600
                      Achuar, Shuar,
                      Quichua and
                      maybe Záparo

All Regions

Afro-Ecuadorians   language: Spanish   population: 500,000

The total indigenous population according to these calculations is 3,654,100 people, or 28 percent of the total population based on the July 2001 estimate.

Archaeological Record

Cultural and ethnic diversity in the past is as notable as the complex heterogeneity of contemporary Ecuador. The strikingly different topographical regions that make up Ecuador are geographically close to one another, permitting reasonably fluid contact and trade. Similarities in the archaeological record reflect trade networks among Coast, Sierra, and Oriente 4,500 years ago and coterminous pottery traditions 3,500 years ago, when long-distance trade extended for thousands of miles. Artistic and technological connectivity and specialization emerged in different cultural periods, but were overarchingly marked by interaction and exchange. The coastal Valdivia culture (5200 BP) marked a social revolution characterized by horticulture and sedentary lifestyle. Ceramics appeared in the archaeological record at this time. Machalilla culture shows continuity with Valdivia. Later, Chorrera brought formal and decorative innovations.

Sierra ceramics were more modest in artistic innovation and demonstrated a clear influence of coastal Machalilla and Chorrera. Subsequently (2500 BP to 1500 BP), local cultures developed in relative isolation from one another, including Jama-Coaque, Guangala, Chone, Bahía, and La Tolita. Highly diverse cultural manifestations and technologies adapted to local resources characterized this period, in which metalwork and semiprecious stone crafts appeared. Personal adornments gained importance, and specialized artisan and professional groups developed. Obsidian and Spondylus shell trade sparked increased long-distance commerce. From 1500 BP to 500 BP large-scale chiefdoms emerged: Manta, Milagro-Quevedo, Caranqui. This was a time of demographic expansion, diversification of technology, and specialization. Metalwork reached its apex. Coastal chiefdoms developed and sustained long-distance maritime trade with Peru to the south and with Mexico to the north. The archaeological record offers insight not only into the aesthetic sense of ancient Ecuadorian peoples, but also a glimpse into their complex and varied social organizations. Through all of these periods the region that is now Ecuador is often earliest in cultural and technological innovations compared with adjacent areas.

Religions

The population of Ecuador is predominantly Roman Catholic, with an increase in Evangelical Protestanism and other international religions. Indigenous cosmologies and folk Catholicism are also prevalent.

Literacy

According to U.S. government reports, 90.1 percent of the total population is literate in Spanish. Emphasis in education has turned increasingly toward bilingual and bicultural programs. Of the population, 66.8 percent completes primary school (six grades); 23.6 percent completes secondary school (six grades); 14 percent enrolls in college; and 6.4 percent receives a college degree. In 2000, Ecuador registered twenty thousand Internet users. This estimate seems very low given that Internet use and computer literacy among Ecuadorians is growing dramatically and exponentially.

Higher Education

In 1586, the arrival of the Jesuits inspired a commitment to higher education in Ecuador. The Colegio Magno Real y Seminario San Luis (founded in 1594) and the Universidad de San Fulgencio (founded in 1606), both in Quito and both Jesuit, were the first institutes of higher learning in the country and in Latin America. The rich culture of higher education and technical training that flourished through Ecuador's history continues today. There are now many major universities in Quito and Guayaquil, and lesser but highly respectable ones in other cities. Some are specialized, some general; together they offer an impressive array of liberal arts and sciences, medical, legal, engineering, and technical training. Funding comes from government aid, tuition, foreign aid, gifts, and private donations. There are at least three universities founded and developed by indigenous people that not only carry out a commitment to excellence in education, but also are dedicated to the exploration and application of creative pedagogical methods. Many Ecuadorians, from all classes and walks of life, go on to take M.A., Ph.D., M.D., and other advanced degrees in Latin America, the United States, and Europe.

Society

Class preoccupations permeate every facet of life in Ecuador. *Personalismo* (personal influence), *palanca* (leverage; the right contacts), and *compadrazgo* (relationship between parents and godparents, and between coparents) enable social connections and social status. Families and kindreds operate as networks to take advantage of shifting opportunities. Day-to-day hard work, entrepreneurship, and creative solutions to difficult economic circumstances define the existence of most Ecuadorians in the twenty-first century. The latter part of the twentieth century and the beginning of the twenty-first century have witnessed growing grassroots political movements to claim not only fair political representation, but also active participation in government administration and decisions that affect the country. The moral void left by corrupt governments in the 1990s is being filled with the indigenous principle of *ama quilla, ama llulla, ama shua* (don't be lazy, don't lie, don't steal). These indigenous admonishments are included in Quichua and in Spanish among the obligations and responsibilities of Ecuadorian citizenship in the 1998 constitution. The spirit of *ecuatorianidad* emphasizes family and the cultivation of social relations. Festival events punctuate and motivate social life through shared celebrations and community building. These festivals together with *futbol* (soccer), express Ecuadorians' regional pride and national euphoria. While Ecuadorians come together at times of celebration and national crisis, there also exists entrenched divisiveness. Colonial history traced deep ethnic and class lines that endure today in the form of social tensions and political injustices.

Literature and Art

Ecuador has a rich tradition of literary, musical, artistic, cinematographic, and theatrical production. Juan Montalvo, Juan León Mera, Alfredo Pareja Diezcanseco, Jorge Icaza, Benjamín Carrión, Jorge Enrique Adoum, Antonio Preciado, Alicia Yánez Cossio, Nelson Estupiñán Bass are only a few among many authors representative of Ecuadorian literature. Oswaldo Guayasamín, Eduardo Kingman, and Oswaldo Viteri are internationally renowned artists. Julio Jaramillo and Los Hermanos Miño Naranjo are the idols of national music. Camilo Luzuriaga (*La Tigra*) and Sebastián Cordero (*Ratas, ratones y rateros*) have drawn national and international acclaim to Ecuadorian cinema. The growing ranks of indigenous and Afro-Ecuadorian artists have made important and creative contributions to Ecuadorian culture in the twentieth and twenty-first centuries.

Politics

Until recently, elected presidents were sworn into office on August 10, the Ecuadorian national holiday that commemorates independence from Spain, which was achieved in 1809. Executive powers are balanced by legislative and judicial branches. *Caudillismo* (leadership by independent, strong, regional political figures) and personal charisma have defined politics in Ecuador. This is perhaps reflected in the numerous political parties and other special interest groups (between ten and twenty) that vie for control and influence in the national arena. Increasingly visible among these political contenders is the indigenous bloc. The trend in the twenty-first century is toward political and administrative decentralization.

Suffrage

Since 1978, suffrage has been universal and compulsory for all persons ages eighteen to sixty-five. Voting is optional for people over sixty-five.

Constitutional Presidents since the End of Military Rule in 1979

1979–1981	Jaime G. Roldós Aguilera, died in a plane crash in Loja on Ecuadorian Independence Day
1981–1984	Osvaldo Hurtado Larrea
1984–1988	León Febres Cordero Rivadeneira
1988–1992	Rodrigo Borja Cevallos
1992–1996	Sixto Durán Ballén
1996–1997	Abdalá Bucaram Ortiz, remembered as "el loco de la tarima" or "the madman of the stage," ousted by a popular uprising after six months in office
1997	Rosalía Artiaga, vice president to Bucaram, interim president for three days before congress voted in the chair of the senate, Fabián Alarcón; nevertheless, she draws full presidential retirement pay and benefits
1997–1998	Fabián Alarcón, interim president, elected by the members of the national congress
1998–2000	Jamil Mahuad Witt, ousted by an indigenous and grassroots uprising supported by a sector of the military
2000–2002	Gustavo Noboa Bejarano
2003	Lucio Ewin Gutiérrez Borbúa, military (retired), protagonist in ouster of Mahuad

Relatively Enduring Political Parties
(active at the end of the 20th century)

CFP — Concentración de Fuerzas Populares (Concentration of Popular Forces). Populist organization whose electoral strength declined after the death of Asaad Bucaram, its traditional and historical leader. Replaced in large part by PRE.

DP — Democracia Popular (Popular [Grassroots] Democracy). Came together as a party in the mid 1970s with intellectuals from the Christian Democrats as well as from radicalized sectors that promoted the social doctrine of the Roman Catholic Church.

FRA — Frente Radical Alfarista (Radical Alfarista Front). Maintains a decisive political influence, especially in the legislature. Fabián Alarcón was elected interim president in 2000.

ID — Izquierda Democrática (Democratic Left). Developed broad organization in the 1970s and 1980s that allowed it to carry one of its founders, Rodrigo Borja Cevallos, to the presidency in 1988. It is one of the most influential parties in the country.

MIN — Movimiento Independiente Nacional (Independent National Movement).

MPD — Movimiento Popular Democrático (Popular Democratic Movement). A Marxist organization with significant influence in different social sectors to maintain electoral presence in the last twenty years of the twentieth century.

PCE — Partido Conservador Ecuatoriano (Ecuadorian Conservative Party). Represents the most conservative sectors. Sixto Durán Ballén is the leader of this party, which developed out of a coalition between the PC, Partido Conservador (Conservative Party) and the PUR, Partido Unitario Republicano (United Republican Party), founded by Durán Ballén in 1992 when the PSC did not support his presidential nomination. This is a very influential party.

P-NP — Pachakutik–Nuevo País (Pachakutik–New Country). Founded by Valerio Grefa in the Oriente, Luis Macas in the Sierra, and Fredy Ehlers in Quito. Miguel Lluco is the national coordinator.

PRE — Partido Roldosista Ecuatoriano (Roldosist Ecuadorian Party). A populist party with an important number of congressional and local government representatives. In the 1996 elections, Abdalá Bucaram Ortíz, its leader, was elected president of the republic.

PSC — Partido Social Cristiano (Social Christian Party). Represents the economic and political interests of the Ecuadorian oligarchy. In the twentieth century, the party had significant representation in the national congress, which allowed it to heavily influence economic policies in the decades of 1980 and 1990. Its leaders are Jaime Nebot Saadi and León Febres Cordero. This is a very influential party.

In addition to these established parties, many new parties or movements have sprouted in anticipation of the national elections in October 2002.

Prominent Indigenous Organizations and Political Pressure Groups

CONAIE — Confederación de Nacionalidades Indígenas del Ecuador (Confederation of Indigenous Nationalities of Ecuador). Leonidas Iza, president in 2002. (Valerio Grefa, president, 1990; Luis Macas, president 1991–1996; José María Cabascango, president, 1997; Antonio Vargas, President 1998–2001).

ECUARUNARI — Ecuador Runacunapac Riccharimui (Ecuadorian Indigenous People Awaken — the Sierran Indigenous Federation). Estuardo Remache, president in 2002.

CONFENIAE — Confederación de Nacionalidades Indígenas de la Amazonía Ecuatoriana (Confederation of Indigenous Nationalities of Amazonian Ecuador). Adolfo Shacay, president in 2002.

COICE — Coordinadora de Organizaciones Indígenas de la Costa Ecuatoriana (Coordinator of Indigenous Organizations of the Ecuadorian Coast).

ASONE — Asociación de Negros Ecuatorianos (Asociation of Ecuadorian Blacks).

CMS — Coordinadora de Movimientos Sociales (Social Movements Coordinator). Napoleón Santos, national coordinator in 2002.

FP — Frente Popular (Popular Front). Luis Villacís, national coordinator in 2002.

Economy

Ecuador has substantial oil reserves and rich agricultural areas. Because the country's primary exports are products such as oil, bananas, and shrimp, fluctuations in world market prices have a substantial domestic impact. Ecuador joined the World Trade Organization in 1996, but has failed to comply with many of its accession commitments. In recent years, growth has been uneven due to ill-conceived fiscal stabilization measures. The aftermath of El Niño and a depressed oil market in 1997 and 1998 drove Ecuador's economy into a free fall in 1999. The beginning of 1999 saw the banking sector collapse, which helped precipitate an unprecedented default on external loans later that year. Continued economic instability drove a 70 percent depreciation of the currency over the course of 1999, which eventually forced a desperate government to opt to dollarize the national economy in 2000. The decision stabilized the currency, but did not stave off the ouster of President Jamil Mahuad Witt. The new president, Gustavo Noboa Bejarano has yet to complete negotiation for a long sought International Monetary Fund accord. Ecuador's regional systems generally can be described as a boom and bust economy, susceptible to the ebb and flow of international markets and prices because of the country's focus on the production of raw materials.

Corruption Index

Based on information from the Global Competitiveness Report of the World Economic Forum of 1999, 2000, and 2001, the World Business Environment Survey of the World Bank 2001, the Economist Intelligence Unit 2001, and the PricewaterhouseCoopers Opacity Index, the International Transparency Organization published a corruption index on ninety-one countries. In 2001, Ecuador received a score of 2.3 on a scale of 10 (10 points registers complete transparency) and ranked among the twelve most corrupt nations in the world. In 1999, Ecuador received 2.4 points and in 2000 it received 2.6 points on the same scale, indicating that the country has not assuaged international perception of rampant corruption.

Official Currency

U.S. dollar. Before 2000, the sucre.

Exchange Rates

Exchange rates in sucres per U.S. dollar fluctuated as follows: 25,000 (January 2001), 24,988.4 (2000), 11,786.8 (1999), 5,445.5 (1998), 3,988.3 (1997), and 3,189.5 (1996).

Gross Domestic Product

Ecuador's purchasing power parity is $37.2 billion (2000 est). The GDP is distributed by sector as follows: 14 percent agriculture, 36 percent industry, and 50 percent services. Labor force distribution in these same sectors is as follows: 30 percent agriculture, 25 percent industry, and 45 percent services. Industries include petroleum, food processing, textiles, metalwork, paper products, wood products, chemicals, plastics, fishing, and lumber. Primary agricultural products include bananas, coffee, cocoa, rice, potatoes, manioc, plantains, sugarcane, cattle, sheep, pigs, dairy products, balsa wood, fish, and shrimp. Earnings from international migrants totaled $1.2 billion in 2000, second only to petroleum in total national income.

Economic Growth Rate

The economic growth rate is estimated at 0.8 percent (2000 est). It is steadily climbing after a negative growth rate of −8 percent in 1999.

Allocation in Percentages of Gross Domestic Product

Of the GDP allocated to military expenditures ($720 million in 1998), 3.4 percent goes to support fifty-eight thousand security force personnel; 3.0 percent of the Gross Domestic Product is allocated to education (1995); and 2.2 percent to health care (1995).

Inflation

The inflation rate for the last few years is: 60.71 percent in 1999, 91.7 percent in 2000, 22.44 percent in 2001, and 12.99 percent projected for 2002.

Poverty

Poverty and subpoverty affects 56 percent of the total population. Six of every ten Ecuadorians fall into an at-risk category in their ability to meet basic necessities including housing, food, health services, and education. Among the 56 percent of the population considered poor, 21 percent fall into the category of extreme poverty or indigence. One of every five Ecuadorian households is unable to cover its basic food necessities. This percentage is up a dramatic 9 percent since 1995.

Distribution of Income and Consumption

Only 2.2 percent of total income and consumption falls to the 10 percent of the population at the lowest end of the economic scale, while the highest 10 percent of the population accounts for 33.8 percent of income and consumption. These figures point to the significant disparity in wealth distribution in the country.

Unemployment and Underemployment

The national unemployment rate calculated in 2000 was 13% (doubled since 1995). However, underemployment reaches as high as 49.3% (1999), a fairly uniform percentage throughout decade of the 1990s.

External Public Debt

Ecuador's external public debt totaled $15 billion in 1999.

Exports

Exports of petroleum totaled an estimated $5.6 billion in 2000, petroleum, bananas, shrimp, coffee, cocoa, cut flowers, and fish.

Export partners

United States, 37 percent; Colombia, 5 percent; Italy, 5 percent; Chile, 5 percent; Peru, 4 percent (1999).

Imports

Imports totaled an estimated $3.4 billion in 2000, machinery and equipment, raw materials, fuels, and consumer goods.

Import Partners

United States, 30 percent; Colombia, 13 percent; Venezuela, 6 percent; Japan, 5 percent; Venezuela, 6 percent; and Mexico, 3 percent (1998).

Foreign Economic Aid

In 1995, Ecuador was the recipient of $695.7 million in economic aid. The recent implementation of Plan Colombia channeled $1.3 billion in aid to the Andean area under the Clinton administration, the largest aid package ever granted to Latin America. Of this aid, $20 million was allocated to Ecuador for drug interdiction and alternative development programs. In 2002, China made a $40 million loan to Ecuador for development.

Crime

Nonviolent crimes range from pickpocketing, burglary of personal effects, and thefts from vehicles, to breaking and entering and car theft. Increasingly, aggressors are armed with guns, knives, and incapacitating drugs. Since 1998, the cities of Quito and Guayaquil have experienced a rise in crimes such as armed robberies, assaults, car jackings, kidnappings, assassinations, and gang violence. Kidnappings for ransom increased dramatically in the last five years, making Ecuador second to Colombia in this type of crime in South America.

Infrastructure

Of a total of 43,197 kilometers of highway, 8,165 kilometers are paved. Most transportation for industry and agriculture operates by road. Ecuador has two international airports in full-time use, one in Guayaquil and one in Quito. Latacunga is used when construction, repairs, or volcanic activity disrupt regularly scheduled flights at the Quito airport. The airport at the Manta Naval base, currently the U.S. Southern Command Base, operates as an international airport for noncommercial flights. Pipeline for crude oil spans 800 kilometers and pipeline for petroleum products spans another 1,358 kilometers. Several international companies were contracted in 2001 to build a northern route for the OCP (Oleoducto de Crudo Pesado, Crude Oil Pipeline). The controversial new pipeline is projected to run approximately 225 kilometers through some of the most environmentally sensitive and seismically unstable areas of the country and the world.

U.S. Military Presence and Influence

The United States used the Galápagos Islands in the nineteenth century for its commercial war against Britain in the Pacific. Again in the twentieth century, the United States used Baltra Island, just north of Santa Cruz Island, as a military base. In 1999, the United States established its Southern Command Base, a counterdrug FOL (Forward Operating Location) in Manta, Ecuador. Ecuador receives $61.3 million for the five-year lease of this base. According to the annual *Foreign Military Training Report*, the United States trained 681 Ecuadorian military and police personnel in 1999. In addition to this, the School of the Americas trains between ten and twenty-eight Ecuadorian military students each year; the Inter-American Air Forces Academy between thirty and seventy Ecuadorians each year; and the Center for Hemispheric Defense Studies, four to ten each year since 1998.

International Conflict

Border conflicts with Peru erupted in 1980 (Paquisha) and again in 1995 (Cenepa Valley Conflict, Tiwintza). A peace agreement was finally signed and the area in dispute was declared an international park in 1999. International tensions provoked by Colombian paramilitary and guerrilla groups (AUC, ELN, FARC) along the northern border have entangled Ecuador in transnational circuits of drug transit and trafficking, money laundering, and illicit networks of illegal commerce.

SOURCES

Acción Ecológica

2001   Ruta del OCP Trinchera por Trinchera. *Alerta Verde: Boletín de Acción Ecológica.* 112 (June): n.p.

Amnesty International

2001   Annual Report: Ecuador. Electronic document. http://www.web.amnesty .org/web/ar2001.nsf/webamrcountries/ECUADOR.

Central Intelligence Agency

2000   Country report. Electronic document. http://www.cia.gov/cia/ publications/factbook/geos/ec.html.

CONAIE

1989   *Las Nacionalidades Indígenas en el Ecuador: Nuestro Proceso Organizativo: 1992: 500 Años de Resistencia India.* Quito: Ediciones Tincui, Abya-Yala.

Corporación de Estudios y Publicaciones

2001   *Constitución Política de la República del Ecuador.* Quito: Talleres de la Corporación de Estudios y Publicaciones.

Ecuadorian Embassy in Washington, D.C.

2002   Ecuador: General Information. Electronic document. http://www .ecuador.org/geninfo.html.

Ember, Melvin, and Carol R. Ember

2001   (editors) *Countries and Their Cultures*, vol. 2. New York: Macmillan Reference USA.

Enciclopedia del Ecuador

2000   Barcelona: Océano Press.

Handelsman, Michael

2000   *Culture and Customs of Ecuador.* Culture and Customs of Latin America and the Caribbean. Westport, Conn.: Greenwood Press.

Kintto Lucas

2000   Population-Ecuador: Colombian Refugees Pour over Border. Electronic document. http://www.oneworld.org/ips2/oct00/20_15_074.html.

Marchán Vélez, Marcelo

1996   *Almanaque Ecuador Total 1996.* Guayaquil: Publimprent S.A.

Myers, Norman

    1984   *The Primary Source: Tropical Forests and Our Future*. New York:
            W. W. Norton.

Peregrine, Peter, and Melvin Ember

    2001   (editors) *Encyclopedia of Prehistory*, vol. 5. Middle America. New York:
            Kluwer Academic/Plenum Publishers.

Selverston-Scher, Melina

    2001   (editor) *Ethnopolitics in Ecuador: Indigenous Rights and the Strengthening
            of Democracy*. Coral Gables, Fla.: North-South Center Press.

SIISE

    2001   Sistema Integrado de Indicadores Sociales del Ecuador. Compact disc.
            Quito.

The World Bank

    1996   Country Report: Ecuador. Electronic document. http://www.worldbank
            .org/html/extdr/offrep/lac/ec2.htm.

    2001   Ecuador at a Glance. Electronic document. http://www.worldbank
            .org/data/.

U.S. Department of State

    2001   Ecuador — Consular information sheet. Electronic document.
            http://travel.state.gov/ecuador.html.

Vistazo

    2001   Corrupción sistémica. 815 (August): 90.

    2002   Año turbulento. Electronic document. http://www.vistazo.com/800/
            html/portada.htm.

    2002   Exodo sin anestesia. Electronic document. http://www.vistazo.com/
            805/html/portada.htm.

    2002   Migración: Oportunidad y dolor. Electronic document. http://www
            .vistazo.com/797/html/portada.htm.

Whitten, Dorothea Scott, and Norman E. Whitten, Jr.

    1988   *From Myth to Creation: Art from Amazonian Ecuador*. Urbana: University
            of Illinois Press.

afterology — Concept introduced by Marshall Sahlins to refer to all phenomena that are affixed by *post* as in postcolonial, postmodern, poststructural, and even postmemory and post 9–11.

AIEPRA — Asociación de Indígenas Evangélicos de Pastaza–Región Amazónica (Association of Evangelical Indigenous People of Pastaza–Amazonian Region).

al-Qaeda (al-Qaida) — "The base" in Arabic. A network of people allegedly dedicated to the overthrow of the United States and Israel by use of terrorist violence. The leader is Osama bin Laden. On September 11, 2001, four passenger jet liners were hijacked by this terrorist organization and flown into the World Trade Center in New York City (two) and into the Pentagon in Washington, D.C. (one); the fourth crashed in Pennsylvania.

ánima — Soul or spirit.

antipodal past — Concept of people from the furthest reaches and earliest periods of humanity on earth whose contemporary existence is taken as "relics," and they are considered "primitives" or "savages."

arrullo — In the Afro-Esmeraldian cultural system, songs sung by women to open portals to heaven.

ARUTAM — An organization composed of retired and active Shuar soldiers trained in guerrilla warfare.

arutam — In Jivaroan cosmology, *arutam* is the almost overwhelmingly powerful vision that a male youth encounters on a special quest to a site of rushing water.

asua (*aswa*) — Manioc brew in Oriente; corn beer in Sierra.

AUC — Autodefensas Unidas de Colombia (United Self Defense System of Colombia), a powerful Colombian paramilitary movement.

auca — "Savage" in Andean Quechua-Quichua and Spanish.

autonomía — Self-determination, attainment of collective dignity.

ayahuasca — *Banisteriopsis caapi* with plant additives; soul-vine brew.

blanco — Spanish for "white."

blanco-mestizo — Used in Ecuador to refer to the ethnic sector in which people are classed by elites as *mestizo* but usually self-identify as *blanco*. This sector is nonindigenous and non–Afro-Ecuadorian.

blanqueamiento — "Whitening" in both racial and cultural senses.

Bolivarian (*bolivariano*) — Used by some Marxists to conjoin guerrilla movements with movements of self-determination in the territory of the wars of liberation led by Simón Bolívar. Lumped together are Venezuela under Hugo Chávez, the FARC of Colombia, and indigenous movements of Ecuador. The term is sometimes extended to Cuba under Fidel Castro and the Zapatista movement of Mexico.

bruja—Witch.

brujo—Sorcerer, conjuror.

cabildo—community government council.

caminata—"March." Herein refers to the 1992 March for Land and Life from Puyo to Quito.

canton—gloss of *cantón*, similar to a county.

CAR—Comandante Amazónica Revolucionaria (Revolutionary Amazonian Command), a recent Marxist movement in the Ecuadorian Oriente.

Carondelet—Presidential palace, the national palace and seat of government in Quito.

caudillo—Powerful political figure in Latin American nations who is able to rally support from opposing parties and factions during a crisis.

Cenepa Valley conflict—1995 undeclared war between Ecuador and Peru on their mutual border in Amazonian Ecuador.

chigualo—In Afro-Esmeraldian cultural system, rituals to celebrate the death of a young child who goes directly to heaven.

chiliastic—Millennial.

chola—Market woman.

Chola Cuencana—Idealized and romanticized woman dressed in the "traditional" costume of the province of Azuay.

cholificación—Process of transformation from *indio* to mestizo. Used in Ecuador, Peru, and Bolivia as a vulgarization of *mestizaje*.

cholo—Pejorative synonym for *mestizo*. In some areas, it connotes special powers.

chronotope—Concept introduced by Mikhail Bakhtin to refer to time-space or space-time in literature as an integrated cultural construct.

CIEI—Centro de Investigaciones de Educación Indígena (Center for Research on Indigenous Education).

CODENPE—Consejo de Desarrollo de las Nacionalidades y Pueblos del Ecuador (Development Council of Nationalities and Peoples of Ecuador).

colonialism—Period of rule by the Spanish or Portuguese crown after the European conquest of Latin America. The ideology and processes of hegemonic domination of one society or people by another.

El Comercio—Daily Ecuadorian newspaper.

commodification—Transformation of labor, land, or debt to make a monetary profit.

commoditization—The making of something into a commodity.

compadrazgo—Extended relations tied to godparenthood.

CONAIE—Confederación de las Nacionalidades Indígenas del Ecuador

(Confederation of Indigenous Nationalities of Ecuador). Created in 1986; in 2002 comprised thirteen Ecuadorian indigenous nationalities.

condensing symbol — Symbol that draws many meanings together into one meaning.

CONFENAIE — Confederación de Nacionalidades Indígenas de la Amazonía Ecuatoriana (Confederation of Indigenous Nationalities of Amazonian Ecuador).

conjuncture — Economic, social, and cultural relationships that adhere through a span of time from ten to thirty years.

consanguineal relatives — People related by blood (contrasts with affinity).

contrastructural powers (contrapowers) — Concept adapted from usage of the late Victor Turner to refer to sociosymbolic forces that coalesce against dominant or structural power, such as the nation-state, military, police, or corporations.

cosmology — World view, cosmovision; the way people perceive of the world and the cosmos.

curandera — A woman well connected with the spirit world who has powers to heal.

curandero — A man well connected with the spirit world who has powers to heal.

debt peonage — Economic strategy of keeping people in perpetual debt to force them to continue working.

lo divino — Realm of the divine.

ELN — Ejército de Liberación Nacional (Army of National Liberation). A Colombian guerrilla movement.

Encabellado — Name given to Western Tucanoan peoples by Europeans because of their long hair.

epochalism — Concepts of the place of a country in its time and global situation. The political-economic chronotope.

essentialism — Concepts of the cultural essence of the people of a nation in a given time and global situation. The cultural attributes self-ascribed and represented by diverse people in epochal space-time. The symbolic, metaphoric, and cultural chronotope.

essentialist — Attribution of special, inner, cultural "essences" to a given people.

el Estado — The state.

el Estado-nación — The nation-state.

ethnicity — Identity of people vis-à-vis other people and representation of people vis-à-vis other people.

FARC — Fuerzas Armadas Revolucionarias de Colombia (Revolutionary Armed Forces of Colombia).

FARE-DP — Fuerzas Revolucionarias Armadas del Ecuador — Defensa del Pueblo (Revolutionary Armed Forces of Ecuador — Defense of the People).

FEDECAP — Federación de Desarrollo Campesino de Pastaza (Federation of Development for Small Farmers of Pastaza).

FEINE — Federación Indígena Evangélica (Federation of Evangelical Indigenous People).

FENOCIN — Federación Nacional de Organizaciones Campesinas, Indígenas, y Negras (National Federation of Peasant, Indigenous, and Black Organizations).

fetishism — The attribution of sentient powers to inanimate objects or to institutions, or to particular roles or statuses.

fictive kin — People related through ritual ties, such as *compadrazgo*.

FIIS — Federación Interprovincial de Indígenas de Saraguro (Interprovincial Federation of Indigenous People of Saraguro).

folklore, folkloric — Stories, sayings, songs, images, that supposedly exist in the present as relics of a nearly forgotten past.

folk-urban continuum — Schema of the late Robert Redfield that conceived of systematic change from sacred and religious to rational and secular as transformations of scale occur from rural to urban life.

Franciscans — In the Roman Catholic church, refers to the order of Saint Francis, founded in Italy in 1209 by Saint Francis of Assisi. Its members are also known as Minorities and Gray Friars.

gender complementarity — The undertaking of tasks by both men and women that contribute to the well-being of each opposite gender.

gente de bien, gente bien — Literally, good, proper, righteous people. People in the high or upper classes self-identify with this label, which is interchangeable with *la sociedad*, the society. Denotes old wealth, prestige, and power.

gente de bienes — Slang for "rich people." Ecuadorian newly established elite.

gente de categoría — Slang for "prominent people." Implies upward socioeconomic mobility as manifest in car, house, land holdings.

global economy — Manifestations of international capitalist economy associated with the most industrial of all the world's nations.

globalization — Meanings vary to the point of extreme vagueness. Often denotes false impression that "everything is becoming the same."

glyphosate — See ultra glyphosate.

el gobierno — The government.

golpe — Coup.

Gross National Product — The monetary value of everything produced in a nation-state in a given period of time.

Group of Paris — Informal group of official creditors whose role is to find sustainable solutions to the payment difficulties experienced by debtor nations. Created in 1956, the Group of Paris currently enlists nineteen permanent members and has negotiated 345 agreements concerning seventy-seven debtor countries for a total debt of $391 billion.

Guayacos — Slang for people from Guayaquil, or who identify with Guayaquil.

hacendado—Large land holder. Implies exploitation of those who work and/or live on the hacienda.

Harvard Boys—The technical experts who came to Ecuador to help President Jamil Mahuad and to whom he turned in the United States for advice.

hegemony—Domination by which the subalterns "accept" the ideology of the powerful vis-à-vis themselves.

historicity—What is taken in written or oral history to be salient in the past.

La Hora—Daily Ecuadorian national newspaper.

Hoy—Daily Ecuadorian national newspaper.

lo humano—Realm of the human, including the domain of the devil.

hypostasis—Belief so ingrained that it is taken to be fundamental fact.

ICCI—Instituto Científico de Culturas Indígenas (Scientific Institute of Indigenous Cultures). Founded in 1986. Luis Macas Ambuludí has been the director since 1998.

IERAC—Instituto Ecuatoriano de Reforma Agraria y Colonización (Ecuadorian Institute of Agrarian Reform and Colonization).

IMF—International Monetary Fund.

INCRAE—Instituto Nacional de Colonización de la Región Amazónica Ecuatoriana (National Institute of Colonization of the Ecuadorian Amazon Region).

indio/a—Indian. First used by Christopher Columbus to name all of the original people of the Americas. Pejorative when used by nonindigenous people, but sometimes used in political movements by indigenous people themselves.

indomestizaje—Indian-*mestizaje* (a mixture of indigenous and mestizo as a national image). Brought into Ecuadorian political ideology in 1981 by then Vice President Osvaldo Hurtado; seldom used.

INEFAN—Instituto Ecuatoriano Forestal de Areas Naturales y de Vida Silvestre (Ecuadorian Institute of Forestry for Natural Areas and Wildlife).

intipa'ikï—Literally "this one who lives." Designates a headman or shaman in Secoya culture.

Inti Raymi—Name of indigenous festival at summer solstice that is replacing other names.

ionys—Expression that originates in the "I ♥ NY" bumper stickers.

iwianch—Palpable and corporeal image of a spirit (demon) in Shuar, Achuar, and Shiwiar language.

IWIAS—Crack troop organization in Ecuadorian military stationed at the Batallón de la Selva, in Shell Ecuador; composed primarily of Canelos Quichua and Shuar soldiers.

iwias—Mythic Shuar and Achuar cannibal warrior, *iwianch*.

Jesuits (Jesuitas)—In the Roman Catholic Church, a religious order known as the Society of Jesus founded by Saint Ignatius Loyola in 1534. Expelled from South America in 1767.

jimba—Double-stranded single braid worn among the Saraguro.

Josephines (Josefinas)—Italian missionaries who entered the Napo region in 1922. They identified with the conservative strand of Ecuadorian politics linked to the former Ecuadorian president Gabriel García Moreno.

laichu—Saraguro term for nonindigenous people.

Levantamiento Indígena—Indigenous uprising. The first of the late twentieth century, subsequently called the Levantamiento del Inti Raymi, was in 1990.

liberation theology—Pedagogical trend within the Roman Catholic Church predicated on the notion of liberating people not only from illiteracy, but from social domination and economic exploitation.

liminal—A space and/or time of social significance between two quotidian periods of time, or two separate spaces, or both.

macrocosm—Setting, often global, that reflects the widest possible context within which local and regional events take place.

Manta U.S. Military Base—Site of the United States Southern Command. Established in Ecuador after the ceding of the Canal Zone to Panama in December 31, 1999.

Marxian—Use of theories or derivatives of theories of the late Karl Marx in any of his various published manifestations.

Marxist—Pertaining to praxis professed especially by Karl Marx and Friedrich Engels in *The Communist Manifesto*. May also be used as "Marxian."

matriarchy—Society in which women are the primary authority figures.

mestizaje—Ideology of "the blending," or mixing of race, ethnicity, and/or culture.

metatrope—A macro figure of speech or a macro image, such as "new millennium," "development," and "autonomy."

metonymic—A concept or image linked to other concepts or images by contiguity in discourse, such as Indians live in huts and whites live in houses; Christians have religion and others have cults.

microcosm—A setting in which events and activities reflect much larger issues and structures.

millenarian, millennial—Pertaining to the coming of the millennium (once every one thousand years), the second coming of Jesus Christ, or a transformation to a better or more desirable life out of the present one.

mimetic faculty—Ability to imitate others, especially those of other cultural orientations. Usually applied to groups or categories of people.

mimicry—Imitation in the sense of cultural copying.

minga—Communal or shared work force.

modern democracy—Associates constitutional government and competitive free elections with capitalist economy and the free marketplace.

modernity — Emerged in Iberia in the mid fifteenth century; bundles concepts of profit making, racial fixity, technology for profit, commodification of land and labor, and priority of print languages.

montuvio — Stereotypical depiction of rural person of Manabí Province, coastal Ecuador.

multiculturalism and multiculturality (*multiculturalidad*) — Carries the explicit text of respect for cultural diversity and the powers of unity across diversity; incorporated into the 1998 constitution of Ecuador.

multinationalism (*multinacionalidad*) — Carries the explicit text of respect for cultural diversity and the powers of unity across diversity; not incorporated into the 1998 constitution of Ecuador.

multivocalic — Multiple meanings of the same symbol.

muscuyuj warmi (*muscuj warmi*) — Visionary woman, the feminine equivalent of a male shaman.

la nación — The nation.

nacionalidades — Nationalities. Different people with different ethnicities of Ecuador.

nationalism — Applied to the nation-state, a national collectivity regards the state as its maximum reference category; applied to a social movement, an ethnic collectivity, or nationality, regards the people in the movement as its maximum reference category. Patriotism to one's nation and/or nationality and/or ethnic movement.

Négritud(e) — A celebration of blackness.

negro — "Black" or blackness in Spanish.

neocolonial — Systems after formal colonial rule that manifest the characteristics of colonial oppression.

neoliberal — Political-economic ideology that focuses on a decontextualized "free market" as a solution to national problems.

NGO — Nongovernmental organization.

novenario — Second wake for deceased nine days after death.

Nuevo País — See Unidad Plurinacional Pachakutik–Nuevo País.

OEPC — Occidental Exploration and Production Company.

OISE — Organización Indígena Secoya del Ecuador (Ecuadorian Secoya Indigenous Organization). Founded in 1983.

OISSE — Organización Indígena Secoya-Siona del Ecuador (Secoya-Siona Indigenous Organization of Ecuador).

ONISE — Organización de la Nacionalidad Indígena Siona del Ecuador (Siona Nationality Indigenous Organization of Ecuador).

OPIP — Organización de Pueblos Indígenas de Pastaza (Organization of Indigenous People of Pastaza).

OXY — Occidental Petroleum Corporation of Bakersfield, California.

Pachakutik — See Unidad Plurinacional Pachakutik–Nuevo País. Derives from Quichua *pachacutic*, which refers to a transformation of time-space to a better life.

el país — The country or fatherland.

parish (*parroquia*) — Administrative districts within cantons in Ecuador.

la patria — The motherland, or reverential country, or homeland.

patriarchy — A social system dominated by men.

patronage system — Institutionalized practice of granting protection, official positions, and other favors in exchange for political and personal loyalty.

peasant (*campesino*) — A person whose livelihood depends primarily on farming the land.

pendes — Shamans of the Quijos region of the northern Oriente who revolted against the Spanish in the sixteenth century. Celebrated today in an annual festival of *los pendoneros* in Otavalo.

Plan Colombia — $7.2 billion plan proposed by Colombian president Andrés Pastrana to fight guerrilla organizations and narcotics traffickers in Colombia.

polarizing symbol — Symbol that contains opposite meanings.

political-territorial autonomy — concept of self-determination in local and regional government.

polysemic system — Semantic system of multiple meanings.

polysemous — Multiple meanings attached to a word or trope.

postcolonial — A nation-state or social order in which people were once under colonial rule.

postmodernity — Concept that breaks with the canons of Euro-American modernity.

el pueblo — The dynamic collectivity of "the people."

Quichua — Northern dialects of Quechua, the language of the imperial Inca.

racial fixity — The belief that racial categories have a natural and enduring basis in sociobiological "fact."

reducciones — Mission settlements that combined noncontiguous communities in a single place.

Región Amazónica — The Oriente of Ecuador.

el riviel — An apparition associated with Esmeraldas Province and black people there.

root metaphor — An undergirding belief taken to be "natural" and "true."

runa — Indigenous person in the Quichua language, fully human.

runa shimi — The Quichua language; literally human speech.

Semana Santa — Easter.

shaman — A person with the ability to move back and forth, usually in séance, between this world and the world of the spirits. *Yachaj* (*yachac*), "one who knows," in Quichua; *sabio,* "one who knows," in Spanish; *uwishin* in Achuar, Shuar, and Shiwiar.

social praxis —The ways by which concepts become expressed during social and symbolic action.

social scale — Schema of the late Godfrey and Monica Wilson that conceived of systematic change from sacred and religious to rational and secular as transformations of scale occur from rural to urban life.

la sociedad—The society; refers to the old Elite sector who self-identify as *gente bien* or *gente de bien.*

structural power — Concept used by the late Eric R. Wolf to refer to dominant power of such entities as nations and corporations.

subaltern — In a system of patronage or oppression, a person in the victimized sector.

Summer Institute of Linguistics (SIL) — Also Wycliff Bible Translators (WBT); evangelical organization dedicated to translating the bible into all languages of the world.

supai—"Soul" in Amazonian Quichua; "devil" in Andean regions and sometimes in Amazonia.

symbolic capital — Nonmonetary resources that can help one achieve goals; can include family and friends and ritual coparents.

symbolic inversion — Discourses and tropes that reverse a system of social, ethnic, or cultural asymmetry.

syncretism, syncretic — Cultural constructions from two divergent sources that fuse into one system, such as "folk Catholicism," which blends African and/or indigenous religions with European.

syntagmatic structural or functional association — Ideological string of symbolic or metaphoric associations that can make different social movements — such as an indigenous movement for democratic participation — appear similar to a guerrilla movement to overthrow a government.

tambo—Rest stop or way station.

El Telégrafo— Daily national newspaper.

theocracy — Government with divine authority.

toponym — Geographic place-name.

transnationalism — Ideology that promulgates any system such as "international business" that crosses national boundaries on a regular and sustained basis.

transubstantiation — Roman Catholic doctrine of the literal transformation of Eucharist and wine into the Body and Blood of Christ during Holy Communion.

Tres Esquinas — Site in the department of Caquetá, Colombia, near the Ecuadorian border, where the United States maintains a surveillance base as part of Plan Colombia.

trope — Figure of speech.

la tunda — An apparition associated with Esmeraldas Province and black people there.

ultra glyphosate — Powerful herbicide used for systematic spraying of coca plantations. Made from a mix of Monsanto's "RoundUp" and "Cosmoflux," a herbicide manufactured in Colombia, not approved for use in the United States. Extremely toxic to subsistence crops, animals, fish, and humans.

Unidad Plurinacional Pachakutik–Nuevo País — The Plurinational Return to the Land–New Country Movement, established in 1996. Came to be called the Pachakutik–Nuevo País Movement, sometimes shortened to Pachakutik. A social movement that functions at times as a political party; often a political dimension of national indigenous organizations. Initiators were Valerio Grefa (Oriente), Luis Macas (Sierra) for Pachakutik and Freddy Ehlers (Quito) for Nuevo País.

UINPI Amautai Wasi — Universidad Intercultural de Nacionalidades y Pueblos Indígenas (Intercultural University of Indigenous Nationalities and Peoples). Founded in 2000. Luis Macas Ambuludí currently serves as president.

El Universo — Daily national newspaper.

velorio — Wake for deceased.

visión (pl. *visiones*) — Apparition(s).

yachaj (*yachac*) — Shaman, "one who knows."

yahé (*Yagé*) — *Banisteriopsis caapi* and leaf additives. Also known as *ayahuasca*.

yumbada — Festival that enacts the story of Amazonian people collectively known as Yumbo who come to Quito, are killed, and are resurrected.

yumbo — Shaman-healer from Amazonia or coast, from an Andean perspective.

CONTRIBUTORS

Jim Belote is adjunct professor of anthropology at the University of Minnesota Duluth, and has taught at the Universidad San Francisco de Quito in Ecuador. He began working in Saraguro, Ecuador, in the early 1960s. He is the author of *Los Saraguro*, published in Ecuador, and numerous articles on Saraguro peoples and culture. In 2001, he undertook research within the Ecuadorian diaspora in Spain.

Linda Belote is professor of anthropology and past associate vice chancellor at the University of Minnesota Duluth. She began working in Saraguro, Ecuador, in the 1960s. In 2000, she traveled to Quito and participated in the inauguration of the Intercultural University of Indigenous Nationalities and Peoples (UINPI), along with Native North American representatives, and in 2001 she undertook research with Ecuadorians in Spain.

Alfonso Chango is president of the Federation of the Quichua Nationality of Pastaza (FENAQUIPA) of Amazonian Ecuador. He is a native of Pastaza Province and has studied his own culture and the culture of other Amazonian peoples for two decades. He is the author of several publications, including a book on shamanic practice written in both Spanish and his native Quichua.

Rudi Colloredo-Mansfeld is assistant professor of anthropology at the University of Iowa. His recent book, *The Native Leisure Class: Consumption and Cultural Creativity in the Andes*, deals with economic transformations in Otavalo. He is now engaged in sustained research with Tiguan artists of Tigua, Quito, and Otavalo.

Rachel Corr is assistant professor of anthropology at Harriet L. Wilkes Honors College, Florida Atlantic University. She has undertaken field research in Salasaca, Cayambe, and other regions of Ecuador since 1990. Her research focuses on cosmological and historical dimensions of space, religious experience, and ethnic diversity. She has authored several articles on South American cultural systems.

Kris Lane is associate professor of history at the College of William and Mary. His most recent book is *Quito 1599: City and Colony in Transition*. Author of numerous articles on the colonial period in Ecuador and Colombia, Lane's core interests are ethnographic history and African diaspora studies. He is currently at work on a history of the conquest and transformation of the northwest Pacific coast of South America.

Luis Macas is the director of the Intercultural University of Indigenous Nationalities and Peoples (UINPI) in Quito, Ecuador. He is one of the founders of CONAIE, and served as its vice president during the first Levantamiento Indígena in 1990. He was among the first group of indigenous congressional representatives elected in the 1996 elections within the Pachakutik social movement, of which he is a founder. He holds a doctor of law degree from the Universidad Central in Quito, is internationally known for his speeches and analytical articles, and became minister of agriculture in 2003.

Diego Quiroga is professor of anthropology and dean of academic affairs at the Universidad San Francisco de Quito in Quito, Ecuador, and research associate in anthropology at the University of Illinois at Urbana-Champaign. His studies of Ecuadorian people began in the early 1980s, and he is the author of many works on systems of ecology, health, and cosmology of Ecuadorian systems, including those of the Galápagos Islands.

Jean Muteba Rahier is associate professor of anthropology, editor of the *Journal of Latin American Anthropology*, and past director of African–New World Studies at Florida International University. His research in Afro-Ecuadorian communities began in the 1980s. He has written and edited works of importance on Ecuadorian blackness and the representations of ethnicity in systems of performance.

Michael A. Uzendoski is assistant professor of anthropology at Florida State University. His research in the greater Tena area of Napo Province, Amazonian Ecuador, began in 1994. He has published on Upper Napo Quichua poetics and cosmology and is pursuing ethnohistorical research on Andean-Amazonian relations in this region.

William T. Vickers is professor of anthropology at Florida International University. His extensive field research in the Andes and Amazonia is especially salient in the Siona-Secoya cultural region of the north Oriente. He has an extensive list of published books and articles, and has been engaged in applied research in Amazonian Ecuador for a quarter of a century.

Mary J. Weismantel is professor of anthropology at Northwestern University, past editor of the *Journal of Latin American Anthropology*, and director of the Program for Latin American, Latino/a, and Afro-Latin American Studies. Her field research in Ecuador extends from the Central Andes of Cotopaxi to Cuenca in the southern sector. Her many publications include her recent book *Cholas and Pishtacos: Stories of Race and Sex in the Andes*.

Dorothea Scott Whitten is research associate at the Center for Latin American and Caribbean Studies and adjunct curator of the Spurlock Museum of World Cultures at the University of Illinois at Urbana-Champaign. She began research in Ecuador in 1968. She is the senior author of a book on Canelos Quichua aesthetics and senior editor of *Imagery and Creativity: Ethnoaesthetics and Art Worlds in the Americas*.

Norman E. Whitten, Jr., is professor of anthropology and Latin American studies, director of the Center for Latin American and Caribbean Studies, curator of the Spurlock Museum of World Cultures, affiliate of Afro-American studies, and Senior University Scholar at the University of Illinois at Urbana-Champaign. He has undertaken field research in coastal, Andean and Amazonian settings since 1961 and has published many books and articles on Ecuadorian cultural systems, ethnic systems, and social movements.

Michelle Wibbelsman is completing her doctoral dissertation on the subject of "Festive Rituals in Imbabura, Ecuador" in the Department of Anthropology at the University of Illinois at Urbana-Champaign. She undertook fourteen months of field research in Imbabura and Pichincha Provinces in 2000–2001 under the auspices of a Fulbright-Hays Doctoral Dissertation Research Grant.

INDEX

95–96; legacy of and Roman Catholicism, 121

colonos (homesteaders), 78–79

Colvin, Jean, 278

Comandante Amazónico Revolucionario (CAR), 19

Comaroff, Jean and John, 2

Comité de Paro, and Amazon shutdown, 68

compadrazgo, among Runa people, 140

complementarity, in Andean economy, 280–81

comunas (communes), 55–56

CONAIE, 58, 59; and alliances with other organizations, 222; indigenous values made a part of, 233–34; and opposition to FIIS, 226; and 2001 indigenous uprising, 146; and use of dialogue, 228

condor: myths of, 248; representations in Tiguan art, 248

CONFENIAE, 59; and indigenous claims to lost land, 5

Conrad, Joseph, 84

contrastructural powers, 14, 29, 30, 33; in spiritual/symbol systems, 25

cornets. *See* pottery

Coronil, Fernando, 368

Corr, Rachel, 13

corruption, 85–89; before and after independence, 86–89; as cause for economic crisis, 3, 226; as expected of politicians, 88–89; and *latifundismo*, 86, 88; in legal system, 290–91; rampant nature of, 22, 23; in the United States, 35n2, 365

Crain, Mary, 111

Crespo, Gonzalo Ortiz, and March for Land and Life, 208

crime, in Ecuador, 289–92

Cruz Pamba, 109–11; and purgatory, 114

cuadros, 245, 279. *See also* Tiguan art

Cuenca, 10, 332–37; emigration from, 332; and racial identity, 333

Cultural Transformations and Ethnicity in Modern Ecuador (N. Whitten, ed.), ix, x, xiii, 4, 34–35n1, 369

Cuyabeno community (Secoyan), 52

Cuyabeno Wildlife Reserve, 56

Cuyo, Ermelinda María, 252–53

Cuyo, Francisco, 283

Cuyo, Juana, 266

Cuyo, Mercedes, 283

Cuyo, Rodrigo, 249

Cuyo Cuyo, Juan Luis, 246, 278, 291

Cuyo Toaquiza, José, 254

Dagua, Estela, 242, 262, 265

Darquea Granda, Ricardo, 327, 328, 339

Day of the Dead, 130, 131, 157

Debt: foreign, 11–12; roots in the nineteenth century, 96

debt-peonage: compared with capitalist systems of social control, 135–36; and ethnicity, 135, 136; modern systems comparable to, 88; in Napo region, 134–35; and purgatory, 26; among Secoya, 52; used by Evangelicals, 135

Deere, Carmen Diana, 166

de las Casas, Bartolomé, 78

democracy, Ecuadorian, shaping by indigenous people, 25

Democratic Left Party, 5, 367

Department of Education National Resource Area Centers and Fellowship Program (NRC-FLAS), 362

devil: and capitalist economy, 175, 176; Christian imagery of in Salasacan cosmology, 109; and economic predation, 172–73; in Esmeraldas cosmology, 154–79; and globalization, 172, 174; images in Tiguan art, 252; and incest, 169–70; in modern Ecuador, 168–69; and modernity, 172–74, 178; pacts with, 175–77; and race, 168, 170–72, 173; and social tensions, 178; relation to wildness, 157–58, 165; relation to women, 166, 167; and wealth, 173–74, 177, 178

dialogue, as a value of indigenous people, 227–28

Dieterich, Heinz, 16

discourse, polarized, 6

disease, epidemic, brought by Europeans, 48, 51, 90

diversity: of Ecuadorian culture and people, 5, 12, 13, 14, 20, 29, 69, 369; and globalization, 368; ideology of and the military, 7

port of education for indigenous people, 232

FEDECAP, counterdemonstrations to March for Land and Life, 190, 199

Federación Interprovincial de Indígenas Saraguros (FIIS), 226

Federation of Evangelical Indigenous People of Ecuador (FEINE), 146

feminist movement, Ecuadorian, 321

FENOCIN, and 2001 indigenous uprising, 146

Ferdon, Edwin N., Jr., 24

Fernández, Michael, 187

festivals, indigenous adoption of Roman Catholic institution of, 116

fire, as symbol of punishment and purification, 113

Fisch, Olga, 246, 282; depicted in indigenous art, 247, 248; and origin of Tiguan hide painting, 245, 279

Flores, Juan José, 76, 87

Flores Jijón, Antonio, 78; and reestablishment of Roman Catholic church, 94

foods, indigenous ceremonial, 119

Forbes, Steve, 3

foreign aid, from United States, 19

foreign corporations, in Ecuadorian mining, 83–84, 85

foreign investment, recent increases in, 22

Foucault, Michel, 297, 298, 319

Franco, Luis, 325–26

Free Trade Area of the Americas (FTTA), 366

Freud, Sigmund, 177, 298

frontiers: and Amazonian indigenous people, 79; Ecuadorian, 76, 78–80

Fundación Sinchi Sacha, 264

funerals: among Afro-Esmeraldians, 158–59; infant vs. adult among Afro-Esmeraldians, 158; and ritual of Salasacan bread baby, 117; and rituals among Salasacans, 118–21

Galápagos Islands, 10

Garcia, Fernando, 287

Gaviria, César, 361

Geertz, Clifford, xi; on epochalism, 11

gender, and division of labor, 166

gender complementarity, 118

Giddens, Anthony, 297

Gilman, Sander, 298

global concepts: and competition for natural resources, 79–80; and racism, 92; and struggle for wealth and power, 85, 89

global economy, 2

globalization, 8, 28, 29; and the devil, 172–74; and diversity, 368; and economic crises, 289; and Ecuador in international view, 361–68; Ecuador as a unique system and microcosm of, 2, 28, 368, 369; and persistence of local-level practices, 104; and Tiguan artists, 266–67; as urban phenomenon, 275–76

gold: and folk miners, 82; and lost treasures in Ecuador, 80–81

golpista, 357

Graburn, Nelson H. H., 245

Grefa, Valerio: and March for Land and Life, 190, 200, 209; and Pachakutik movement, 210

Gregorio, Hermano, 156

Group of Paris, 2

Gualinga, Rebeca, 265

Guayaquil, 9, 332

Guayasamín Foundation, 245

Guerrero, Andrés, 329

guerrilla movements, 15, 16, 17, 357; and Bolivarianim (in Colombia), 14; Colombian, actions in Ecuador, 65–66; Colombian, as threat to world peace, 361, 362. See also FARC

Guss, David, 137

Gutiérrez, Lucio, 355, 356, 357, 359, 360, 369; and participation in coup of January 1, 1

Gutiérrez, Plaza, and dismantling of Roman Catholic church power, 94

Hacienda system: economic changes caused by end of, 280; creation of, 86; and class-ethnic differentiation, 7; theme of in Tiguan art, 254

Hallpike, Christopher, 166

Harvard Boys, 2

Hauka movement, 120
Hawkins, John, 91
headdresses, symbolism of, 193
healers: complementarity of shamans
    and Western medicine, 263; and
    Roman Catholic religion, 111; and
    source of power in the *divino*, 156
healing, themes and methods of por-
    trayed in Tiguan art, 249–54
healing powers: and the devil, 170, 171;
    magical nodes of in Ecuador, 170–71;
    and racism, 168–69, 170, 171
Hefner, Robert W., 145
hell: and four-handled cauldron, 110,
    111–12; geographic location of on
    landscape, 113
Helms, Mary, 253–54
herbicides, against coca: effects on
    agriculture, 66; environmental dam-
    age caused by, 18
Heritage of Humanity (UNESCO), 10
heroin drug trade, 18
Herzfeld, Michael, 30, 31
hierarchy, class-ethnic, 6
history, and cultural imagery of events,
    25
Hoch-Smith, Judith, 162
Holston, James, 276
homesteading, in lowland Ecuador,
    78–79
Horowitz, Nathan, 67
lo humano (the human realm), 26, 27;
    definition of, 154–55; as domain of
    the devil, 177; globalization and im-
    ages of, 172, 174; and opposition to
    divino, 177
Hurihuri Supai, 194
Hurtado, Osvaldo, 4, 23; as a *caudillo*,
    10; cultural and racial views, 5; and
    literacy education of indigenous
    people, 232; role in Mahuad ouster,
    3; in 2002 election, 356

Icaza, Jorge, 91
ICCI, 232–33; and alliance with Sev-
    enth Generation Fund, 222; founda-
    tion of, 232; and use of dialogue, 228
identity, 12, 23, 297; black, 303, 314–15;
    Ecuadorian, iconic images of, 340–
    41, 348; Ecuadorian national and

blackness, 299–302; of Ecuadorians,
    maintained after emigration, 230–
    31; maintenance through rituals, 105,
    116, 121; and mimesis, 121; rural vs.
    urban black, 314–15; and sexuality,
    296, 297, 319; and symbols, 30
Iglesia de Sucumbíos, 66
Ilaquiche, César, 279
Imbabura, Colombian refugees in, 66
incest, and the devil, 169–70
independence, drawbacks for indige-
    nous people and blacks, 91
indigenous movements, 184–211; and
    autonomy, 221, 275; and Bolivarian-
    ism, 14; contrast to Colombian guer-
    rillas and paramilitaries, 15–16, 17;
    helping people realize their power,
    184, 185, 186, 191, 204, 209–10; as in-
    tercultural movements, 31; and leftist
    politics, 367; and modernization of
    Ecuador, 329–30; and rise of federa-
    tions, 58, 70; and Secoya peoples, 69;
    and significance of the year 1992,
    185–87; and strength gained from
    March for Land and Life, 210; and
    terrorism, 16, 17. *See also* March for
    Land and Life
indigenous people, 10, 13; affected by
    international drug trade, 19–20; and
    alliances, 221–22; and autonomy and
    place, 293–94; in Ecuadorian poli-
    tics, 33–34; and Ecuador's hope for
    the future, 97; and education, 233–
    36; exclusion of from Roman Catho-
    lic clergy, 106; and importance of di-
    alogue, 227–28; and independence of
    Amazonia, 80; issues of self-identity,
    121–22; leaders of and shamanic
    power, 259; and leadership qualifi-
    cations, 367, 370; and legal system,
    282, 289–92; and methods of resis-
    tance, 220; nascent political organi-
    zations of, 4–5; not helped by Liberal
    Revolution, 88; obligated by law to
    organize communities, 55–56; per-
    sistence of native religious beliefs,
    103–04; and recognition of Ecuador-
    ian nation-state, 221; resistance of in
    colonial times, 77–78; and resistance
    to oil exploration, 366–67; as source

of revenue, 87, 90; and stereotypes of female sexuality, 301–02; and survival of indigenous religion, 122; and travel outside their communities, 228–31; as being urban as well as rural, 104

indigenous uprisings, 224–25; as examples of collective effort, 224–25; indigenous Evangelicals in, 146

indios, creation of the class by colonial Europeans, 89–90

Instituto Científico de Culturas Indígenas. *See* ICCI

Instituto Ecuatoriano de Reforma Agraria y Colonización (IERAC), 188

Instituto Nacional de Colonización de la Región Amazónica Ecuatoriana (INCRAE), 55

Inter-American Foundation, 264

interculturality, 236, 370; emergence in military, 7; and millennialism, 360; and social equilibrium, 227

international interaction, 11, 14–20. *See also* globalization

International Monetary Fund, 2, 3

Itinerario para párrocos de indios (Peña Montenegro), 103, 106

iwianch, 7

IWIAS, 7, 19

Jacobs, Jane, 284–85

January 21 (2000), coup of, 1, 7–8, 13, 24; as symbolic inversion, 358; and 2002 campaign of Lucio Gutiérrez, 356; U.S. demands after, 7–8

Jesuits: expulsion of, 51, 78, 93; return to Ecuador, 87; missions in Secoya territories, 49, 51; in Napo region, 132

jimba (Saraguro hairstyle), 218–20; as metaphor of Saraguro peoples, 219, 236; method of making, 218–19

Johnson, Orville and Mary, 52–53, 55

Junta of National Salvation, 1

Kalho, Frieda, 278

Kissinger, Henry A., xiii, 17

Lagarto Cocha, 59

Lago Agrio, and Colombian drug crisis, 63, 64, 65, 67

land: accessions promised as result of March for Land and Life, 6, 187, 200, 201, 208, 209; appropriation from indigenous communities, 86; and competition between Catholics and Protestants, 132–33; goals of indigenous people for reclamation of, 188; indigenous claims to lost, 5, 29; recovery of lost Secoya territory, 56; reform under military dictatorship of 1960s, 88

landscape: historical and religious meanings in, 108–09; and rural/urban dichotomy, 329; and sacred and historical imagery, 112; sacred, and journeys to afterlife, 110–11, 113, 114

Larson, Ruben, 132, 135

Latacunga, 337–40; racism in, 338–39

latifundismo, 86, 88

Latin American Association of Human Rights, 6

Layton, Robert, 266

legal system: corruption in, 290–91; and indigenous people, 289–92

León Mera, Juan, 258

Levantamiento Indígena: first, 5; of 1990, 185, 186, 210. *See also* indigenous uprisings; March for Land and Life

Levi, Mauricio, 52

Liberal Revolution: and changes to political and economic culture, 87–88; and dismantling of Roman Catholic church power, 94; ineffectiveness of, 95

liberation, 6, 7; wars of and millennial political movement, 14

literacy: indigenous views of, 115; as means of state and church control over indigenous people, 115, 116

llactacaru, 22

Lloret, Dr., 335, 336

Lucas, Kinnto, 15

Macas, Luis, 23, 31, 216–37, 355, 370; biography of, 216; depicted in Tiguan art, 255, 256; education of, 231–32, 233; and March for Land and Life, 190, 200; and Mohawk Nation/

monkey/stranger person, 243
Montalvo, Juan, 87
Moreno, García, 76, 91; and power of church, 94
Morga, Antonio de, 85, 86, 88
Mosquera-Pedemonte Treaty, 78
mountains: sacred, 203; spirits of, 173; worship of, 102–04, 116, 123
Muisne, 160, 161, 164, 165, 171, 172
multiculturalism, and treatment of illness, 254
multinationalism, 12, 210, 211
Muratorio, Blanca, 134, 142
Murra, John, 280

nacionalidades, 6, 24
ñakak (Andean bogey man), 3
Nambija, 82–83
Napo province, Runa people and Evangelical Protestantism, 129–47
Napo Runa people, 25, 26
narratives: and cultural representations of a community, 109, 115, 116; and expressions of indigenous sacred order, 103, 104, 108, 123
Nash, June, 289, 292, 293
nation-state: Ecuadorian, recognition of by indigenous people, 221; perpetuation of, 30
nationalism, Ecuadorian, 80; and racism, 30, 31
Nebot, Jaime, 10
neoliberalism, 3; vs. autonomy, 11; and concentration of economic power, 285; and Ecuador's economy, 2; and Mahuad, 2; and market economy, 12; and relaxation of laws limiting exploitation by foreign corporations, 83, 84
New Economy, 3
Noboa, Álvaro, and 2002 election, 355, 356
Noboa, Gustavo, 8, 359; endorsement of Tiguan art exhibition, 245

Occidental Petroleum Corporation (OXY), negotiation with Secoya, 46, 61–63
oil: and cultural survival of indigenous group, 62; and environmental de-
struction, 366, 367; images of the industry in indigenous art, 243; as impetus for development of remote areas, 55; reserves in Ecuador, 366; role in culture change, 10; spills in Amazonia, 60
OISE, 46, 70; history and organization of, 56, 57; issues confronted by, 59–63; and Occidental Petroleum negotiations, 62–63; and struggle to retain Secoya land, 56
ONISE, 62
OPIP: and call for indigenous zone, 19; and March for Land and Life, 208; and political goals of March for Land and Life, 187–88
Oppenheimer, Andrés, 2–3, 356–57, 360
Orellana province, and citizen protests against crisis in the northern Oriente, 67, 68
Organización Indígena de los Pueblos de Pastaza. See OPIP
Organización Indígena Secoya del Ecuador. See OISE
Organización Indígena Secoya-Siona del Ecuador (OISSE), history and organization of, 56, 57
Organization of American States, 361
Oriente: in colonial times, 78; crisis in, 63–69; description of, 10; as a frontier, 79; military organizations in, 19
Ortiz, Adalberto, 164
Otherization, of non-European peoples, 298
Otherness, 171, 178–79; and devil, 170–72; and race, 300; and race and sexuality, 319, 320

Pacari Vega, Nina Conejo, 370
Pachakutik–Nuevo País movement, 8, 58, 210; and consensus among indigenous organizations, 226, 227
paint, body, symbolism of, 192–93
Pallares, Amalia, 367
Panama hats, 332, 333, 335, 344
paramilitaries, 15, 16, 17
paro amazónico (Amazon shutdown), 67, 68

Quito: colonial, 77, 86, 87; and gold boom, 81; importance of in Ecuadorian identity, 202–03; lack of control over Amazonia in colonial times, 78; political-economic make-up, 9; Tiguan migrants in, 276–77; and *yumbada*, 184, 199, 203

race: and class, 90, 315, 320, 327–28, 334; and European colonization, 298; and gender, 327–28; and male/female relations, 318; and modernity, 326–27, 346; and regional identity, 333; and sexuality, 298, 301, 302–03
racial-spacial order, 297, 306
racism: black women's view of, 304, 307, 309–10; colonial to the present, 89–92; in colonial Roman Catholic church, 105–07; and economic opportunity, 311; and Ecuadorian identity, 341; effect on economy, 345–46; and Evangelical identities, 130; and female bodies, 301–02; as a global process, 92; and ideology of *mestizaje* and *blanqueamiento*, 136–37; as major "illness" of Ecuador, 23; Mama Negra and resistance to, 340; and national icon of Chola Cuencana, 326, 327, 328, 331, 333–35; and politics, 360; rebellion against in colonial times, 91; against Runa peoples, 137; and rural vs. urban blacks, 319; as unchanged after independence, 91
Radcliffe, Sarah, 326
Rahier, Jean, 32, 33, 157, 178–79
Rainforest Action Group, 188
Ramón, Gordo (El Gordo), 176–77
Ramón Valarezo, Galo, 202
Redfield, Robert, 27, 28, 29
Reflexión en las culturas orales (Alfonso Calderón), 5, 6
Reich, Otto J., 361, 362
Remache, Estuardo, 367
remittances, 10; high amount of, 21–22, 333
revolution, social, lack of in Ecuador, 95
Restrepo, Adriana Maya, 170
Restrepo brothers, 196

Ribadeneira de Caseres, Mayra, 247, 248
ritual, and access to the *divino*, 154, 156, 159, 178
Rodríguez Lara, Gonzalo, 5
Roldós, Jaime, 4, 5; on diversity, 13; and literacy education of indigenous people, 232
Roldós, León, 356
Roman Catholic church: and assistance of indigenous people in colonial times, 93, 124n4; as a colonial legacy, 92–95; and colonial wealth, 86, 87; and control of symbols and sacramental power, 105–07; conversion and political control, 112; and economic exploitation, 131; indigenous local and female interpretation of doctrine, 94; and persistence of indigenous ideologies and rituals, 103–04, 111, 112; and subversion of symbols and powers by indigenous people, 107–09; symbols and rituals of used by indigenous religions, 25–26, 107–09, 112, 116, 117–18, 119–21; and tensions with Evangelists, 175–76. *See also* sacraments
Ron Negrita rum, and female sexuality in advertisements, 316–17, 321
Rosales, Manuel María, 132
rubber, Amazon boom, 16, 78
Runa peoples: and Evangelical Protestantism, 129–47; and extended family, 139, 143, 144; and female/male complementarity, 141, 143; importance of drinking for men, 140, 141, 143; and social value of being sensitive to others, 139, 141; and social value of being willful, 138–39, 140, 141; traditional social values conflicting with Evangelical Protestantism, 142–44; weddings as difficult for, 143–44
rural areas, as hindering modernity, 299

sacraments, of Roman Catholic church: difficulty of administration in remote areas in colonial times, 105–06; in-

slavery, of indigenous people, 51, 89

Smith, Claire, 266

Social Christian Party (PSC), 367

social movements, of indigenous people, 7, 24; and symbolic inversion, 359. *See also* indigenous movements

social structure, Ecuadorian, changes in, 4

la sociedad (the society), 23

Society of January 21st, 8

Solórzano, Carlos, participation in coup of January 21, 1

Solstice Foundation, 56

Soltera Ñan, 108–09

songs, as expressions of visions, 260. *See also* singing

sorcery: as learned from spirits of the dead, 160; as source of illness and death, 51

South American Development Company (la SADCO), 84, 88

space: as evil in wild areas, 161–62, 172; domesticating, to control nature, 161–62

Spain, Saraguro emigration to, 230–31

Spanish colonization: economics of, 86–87; as a religious enterprise, 92–93

Spanish conquest, 14

Spiller, Maximiliano, 151

spirits: as danger to the living, 160–61; of deceased persons, 158–60; friendly and helpful, 160; invoked in March for Land and Life, 193–94, 196, 204; as teachers of sorcery, 160

Spring, Anita, 162

stereotypes: of black sexuality, 298–99, 301, 319; of black women as prostitutes, 304, 316; of black women as sexual, 304, 308, 309–10, 315, 320; racial (black), 296–322; seen in positive light, 320; sexual, 296–322

Stern, Steve, 75

Steward, Julian H., 47

structural power, 30, 364; global, and race, 361

Sucumbíos province: citizen protests against crisis, 67–68; political crisis in, 63, 64, 65–66

Summer Institute of Linguistics – Wycliffe Bible Translators: expulsion of, 4, 134; among Secoya, 52, 53, 55

Sungui, 243, 260, 261

symbolic inversion, 358–60

symbolism, Ecuadorian, 30–34; and modernity, 27–29

symbols, 29; empowering, 108; and identity, 30

Taita Imbabura, 173

Taqui Onquoy movement, 107

Taussig, Michael, 16, 29, 170, 202, 363; on mimesis, 120

terrorism, 15, 16, 18

Texaco, 24; lawsuit against, 46, 60–61

Texaco-Gulf oil consortium, 10

thresholds: relation to cross roads, 113; into spiritual worlds or afterlife, 109, 111, 113

Tiguan art, 27, 31, 32; and economic need as impetus for painting, 278–80; economic success of intermediaries, 284; and El Ejido Park, 282; growth of as industry, 281–82; history of sheepskin painting, 244–45, 278; international recognition of, 245, 281; and legal voice of artists, 282; refinement of techniques and skills, 246, 247, 283; showing political events and politicians, 244, 246, 247, 255–57, 265; showing shamans and scenes of healing, 249–54; themes of, 246, 247, 248, 249, 255, 265, 283; themes of indigenous protest movements, 254–58; and Tiguan migration to Quito, 281–82; women's role in, 283

Tiguan artist associations, 281, 282, 289, 292, 294n2; and assistance for rural Tiguans, 283, 284

Tiguan communities: and kin networks and the legal system, 290, 291; and kinship-based economic networks, 284, 285; in Quito, 276–77, 282–83, 285, 292–94; rural vs. urban, 275–77, 283–85, 292

Tiguan youths: and crime, 291–92; and education, 287–88; in modern cities,